RELEASE FROM IMPRISONMENT

The Law of Sentencing, Parole and Judicial Review

DAVID P. COLE
B.A., LL.B.

ALLAN MANSON
B.A., LL.B., LL.M.

CARSWELL
Toronto • Calgary • Vancouver
1990

Canadian Catologuing in Publication Data

Cole, David P., 1948-
  Release from imprisonment

Includes bibliographical references.
ISBN 0-459-34643-1

1. Parole — Canada.   2. Sentences (Criminal
procedure) — Canada.   3. Judicial review — Canada.
I. Manson, Allan.   II. Title.

KE9434.C64 1990   345.71'077   C90-095124-9
KF9750.C64 1990

1990 Carswell—A Division of Thomson Canada Limited.

For Ester, Mihael and Anat.

D.P.C.

For Jessamyn.

A.M.

Foreword

Parole was orginally the word of honour given by a prisoner of war of the officer class not to escape or commit an act of hostility to the forces of his captors. In return, he was allowed to live at large in a certain place, or even to visit his home, until he was exchanged or released on cessation of hostilities.

In more recent times the word was gradually adopted for a form of conditional release from incarceration of a convicted offender undergoing a sentence of imprisonment. In Canada, the term was first applied to discretionary release from periods of indeterminate imprisonment in provincial institutions in Ontario and British Columbia. Reduction of sentence as a reward for good behaviour, according to a prescribed scale of fixed terms of imprisonment served in federal penitentiaries, was introduced in 1868 under the designation of remission. Releases were not subject to any form of control. The terms of prisoners so released were treated as shortened, subject to re-imposition of the period of remission on conviction of an indictable offence during that period. Discretionary release under supervision from federal penitentiaries of inmates serving both life and fixed time sentences, on condition of good behaviour while at large, was authorized in 1899 under the title "ticket-of-leave". Unlike remission, release on ticket of leave did not shorten the sentence. This practice continued on a modest scale under what was called the Remission Service, without attracting much public attention, until 1958.

In 1956, a committee to study the Remission Service, chaired by former Chief Justice Fauteux, published a report recommending, among other reforms, extension of such discretionary release—now to be called parole—on a much larger scale. The recommendations included establishment of a National Parole Board to authorize parole and, if necessary, to revoke it, and to manage the supervision of parolees by members of a National Parole Service. These recommendations were carried out by the *Parole Act, 1958*, under which the new system came into effect in 1959. This was shortly after I joined the Faculty of Law at Queen's University, and throughout my academic career I have been an interested observer of the evolution of parole.

The new scheme was an expression of perhaps the high point of faith in Canada of the concept of the criminal law as an institution for the correction of offenders and of imprisonment as a form of correction. It was designed to focus attention on the experience of each penitentiary inmate with the object of determining when he or she had derived the maximum correctional benefit from imprisonment. At that time, the inmate was believed to be fit to be returned to society, ready to spend the remaining period of the sentence, and, it was hoped, of his or her life, as a law-abiding and useful member of society. This experience was to be facilitated by the kindly but firm supervision of a parole officer qualified and motivated to provide guidance through the difficulties of re-entry into the world outside the walls. This educational and tutorial process was considered to be greatly superior to a traumatic abandonment of the inmate in a perhaps hostile and certainly unhelpful society.

Although welcomed and praised by many correctional workers, including a number of penitentiary officers as well as after-case workers, and by many students of penology, the new system was far from receiving universal acclaim. It conflicted with and still conflicts with widely held beliefs in the punitive, retributional and deterrent purpose of criminal law and its sanctions. Legislators believe that their collective wisdom can determine the relative gravity of offences and the maximum (and in some cases the minimum) penalties that should be imposed on those who commit them. They place their greatest faith on imprisonment as a sanction, where the death penalty is not employed. Society is protected from the offender while he or she is in prison. With a few exceptions they allow judges wide latitude in imposing punishment on individual offenders.

A widespread article of judicial faith is that the sentencing court can fix the appropriate sanction for each offender and that the punishment so determined should be carried out without variation. Judges who hold that opinion resent the earlier release of an offender. Many police officers agree. Many members of the public share a sense of the appropriate degree of suffering that should be undergone by the offender for each reported offence, and resent any apparently unjustified leniency in imposition or execution of the penalty. In this they are encouraged by the public media, which highlight sensational offences, and what is seen as premature release from imprisonment of persons who commit offences while at large before expiration of their sentences. These attitudes have plagued the operation of the *Parole Act* ever since it came into effect.

Aware of the advisability of caution, the Parole Board began by careful selection of relatively few of the available candidates, those who appeared to offer the greatest hope of completing their paroles successfully. The policy apparently worked quite well for a short time. The Board was able during the early years of its operation to report a low incidence of parole failure. As time went on, the Board began to feel greater confidence in the reliability of its selection processes. Gradual increases in numbers released on parole during the early 1960's seemed to be equally successful.

However, during the later 1960's, a rash of parole failures, some marked by very serious offences, aroused the public media, Members of Parliament and considerable sections of the public. Investigation by a committee of the Senate and an appointed committee resulted in serious criticisms. Restrictions on the Board's power were introduced. Its new policy led to niggardly granting of parole for a number of years. From 1970 to the present time, the Board has exercised great caution in granting parole and considerable zeal in its revocation. Several sensational murders have been committed by parolees and day parolees, for which the Board has been severely criticized. On the whole, the Board has been more concerned to avoid parole failure than to carry out its original mandate. In fact, it is now expressly required to give first and greatest weight to protection of society in deciding whether to release each inmate. Parole officers follow a similar policy. Supervision of parolees now looks to surveillance and control rather than monitoring and counselling. The Board, in turn, is quick to revoke parole when breach of an important condition has occurred or is feared.

As an institution, parole suffers from several weaknesses. Its conceptual foundation is shaky. It is clear that criminal law and punishment, as at present administered, have little correctional impact on offenders. It is even clearer that the correctional value of existing systems of imprisonment has been grossly overestimated. Although valiant efforts have been made over many years by prison administrators to implement correctional programs within their institutions, and new and greater efforts are being made in Canadian prisons under the current Commissioner of Corrections, the system is simply incapable of producing consistently corrective results, or indeed such results on any scale adequate to justify detention of the majority of inmates. Canadian penitentiaries seldom inculcate penitence. Canadian reformatories seldom reform. Long-term detention of offenders serves only three possible purposes. It satisfies judges, police and the public that the offenders are suffering for their sins. It prevents offenders from committing offences outside the prisons while they are inside. It may help to deter some persons from committing offences.

Even though the theory of parole is flawed, the institution has value. It can release from custody those whose continued detention serves no useful purpose, except to satisfy the desire of some people to know that they are suffering, and who will not only not commit offences while at large but will have an opportunity to be self-supporting and to make a valuable contribution to society. Here, however, lies the second and more serious weakness. Fully reliable methods of predicting future behaviour have not yet been discovered. While not merely a lottery, such prediction involves so many variables and so many undiscoverable factors that a considerable element of error is inherent in the process. Two adverse consequences ensue. First, there is always a risk of releasing a dangerous person into the community. Second, fear of error based on past experience with others leads to refusal of release, on statistical grounds, of persons who would not commit offences while at large.

A weakness, not of parole itself, but of the Canadian scheme of combination of parole and remission, is that the two are not fully compatible. Although both are designed to shorten time of incarceration, they have different objects and are based on different principles. Remission is based on conduct within the institution. Prison administrators value it as furnishing an incentive to good behaviour, since the hope of early release is on the whole the strongest motivating factor in the behaviour of inmates. While such behaviour may incidentally assist in the decision whether to release on parole, it has little direct bearing on ability to predict behaviour of the inmate while at large. Parole, on the other hand, is based on such prediction. Inmates are encouraged to show repentence and to engage in programs and activities suggesting a willingness to conform to societal norms after release and designed as aids in preparation. Therefore, good conduct is interpreted as evidence of such willingness, even though it may be merely the expression of a choice to "do easy time."

At first, the prospect of early release without supervision on remission led some inmates to refuse to apply for release under supervision on parole, with the possibility of forfeiture and extended incarceration on failure. This factor, and the widespread belief that conditional release under supervision was better for all inmates than unsupervised release, led in 1970 to assimilation of remission to parole under the title of mandatory supervision. Combined operation of the two bases of early release has led to increasing complexities.

The three decades following the enactment of the *Parole Act* were marked by a gradually strengthening sense of disillusionment throughout North America with the correctional theory of criminal sanctions. The Canadian penal system did not escape the influence of this decline of faith. The theory that "nothing works" seemed to be supported in part by reports of several extensive and apparently reliable studies of success and failure on parole as compared with release from prison without supervision. That sense of disappointment was noticeable in statements, attitudes and policies of Canadian correctional administrators. In spite of it, the Parole Board, while continually subjected to and also voluntarily adopting new restrictions on release, has clung to its concept of the correctional value of parole. Within the past few years, the current Commissioner of Corrections, now responsible for both the penitentiary and the parole services, has strenuously sought to revive and strengthen throughout both systems the correctional goal of imprisonment and parole. He is having difficulty in wresting funds necessary for the required resources from a reluctant government, but has begun to gain some modest success in that direction.

The thirty-one years of functioning of the National Parole Board have been marked by gradual judicialization of its procedure. At the beginning, the Board operated with untrammelled discretion, bound by no rules. Decisions were based on written submissions by applicants, and secret reports and appraisals by officials. In most cases, each file was circulated among members, with an attached summary, appraisal and recommendation prepared by a staff officer. Each member could sign the sheet with a mark of approval and pass the file to the next or demand a meeting of the Board. Independence from judicial control was asserted. There was seldom, if ever, any personal contact between the inmate and the Board.

As time went on, inmates and their advocates, by pressure on the Board and skilful use of judicial review, have brought about revolutionary changes in the Board's behaviour. Progress was slow and difficult. The Board fought every step, and on occasion attempted regressive measures. The administrative law principles of fairness and due process slowly compelled piecemeal adoption of what is now a detailed code of procedure for each of the Board's function.

The pattern of penitentiary populations has been radically altered by the abolition in 1976 of the death penalty for criminal offences. There has been no resulting reduction of executions. None has occurred in Canada since 1962. The increase has been in the number of convictions for murder. Two factors have contributed. One has been an increase, not out of proportion to population, in the number of homicides. Another has been the conviction for non-capital or second-degree murder of a number of persons who would have been convicted of manslaughter if convicted murderers had faced execution. The price of abolition of the death penalty included ineligibility for parole of first-degree murderers for 25, rarely to be reduced to not less than 15 years, and for second-degree murderers, 10 to 25 years. The penitentiaries are being gradually overcrowded with convicted murderers who face life sentences and cannot hope for release until after very long periods of incarceration. The parole system is distorted by this phenomenon, coupled with the restrictive policies of the Board, self-adopted or imposed from above.

The authors of this book have explained carefully and lucidly the history and legal consequences of these developments. Their combined experiences make them uniquely competent to undertake that task. Each has devoted the main effort of his career to the struggle for human rights and particularly the rights of prison inmates, and those released from prison under supervision. David Cole's principal emphasis has been made through advocacy in litigation, supplemented by writing and teaching. Allan Manson has modified a similar career by adding professional teaching of law. Each has made a distinguished and perhaps unequalled contribution in all three ways to the cause he has undertaken. Between them they have done much personally to bring about the legal developments they describe.

The work places parole in the context of sentencing and imprisonment. At first glance, the chapters on remedies, independently and under the *Charter of Rights and Freedoms*, seem out of place. However, they are designed to make the following chapters more readily intelligible by furnishing a background to the detailed discussion of procedural problems arising at each step. These chapters reveal that the main battles on behalf of inmates and releases had been fought and won before the *Charter* came into effect. The latter chiefly enabled extension of gains previously made.

The chapter on legislation must be studied to enable the reader to follow the course of developments described in the following chapters by placing judicial decisions in their contemporary, statutory and regulatory contexts. The following chapters are self-explanatory. We must pause, however, to admire the analysis of the labyrinthine process of granting, or in some cases blocking, the various kinds of release and the mysteries of suspension, termination and revocation in each situation. The careful unravelling and exposition of the otherwise apparently chaotic consequences of parole failure on sentence calculation also deserve commendation. The chapter on Parole Board advocacy sums up the combined experience of two advocates of probably unparalleled careers in the field.

The work is written largely from the point of view of the inmate or releasee. It is marked, however, by impartial analysis and presentation. What criticism the authors allow themselves is restrained and to the point. The concluding plea for systemic integration and better understanding of punishment and of imprisonment as one of its agencies is coupled with a brief review of the recommendations of the recent Canadian Sentencing Commission. That Commission expresses the substantial rejection of the goal of correction and adoption of the myth of retribution as a basis for criminal law and punishment. That goal has no foundation or justification, but the authors carefully refrain from saying so.

H.R.S. Ryan
Professor Emeritus
Faculty of Law
Queen's University
Kingston, Ontario

Table of Contents

Table of Cases

Table of Statutes

CANADA

ONTARIO

PRINCE EDWARD ISLAND

QUEBEC

SASKATCHEWAN

YUKON TERRITORY

UNITED KINGDOM

UNITED STATES

Acknowledgements

When we became interested in the field of prison and parole law during the mid-1970's, very little guidance could be found in academic texts. Apart from occasional case comments, only two Canadian writers had attempted to synthesize legal theory, statutes, case law and policy in any consistent way. We are indebted to Professors Michael Jackson and Ronald R. Price for their example.

The Faculty of Law at Queens' University has provided an atmosphere conducive to research and writing, especially about issues of imprisonment. Professors Ron Delisle, David Mullan and Don Stuart have offered advice, dialogue and debate. Professor Stuart Ryan has been, and continues to be, a model of commitment, integrity and insight.

Although we have been sharply critical of many policies and procedures of Canadian penal and parole authorities, some employees of these agencies have been particularly generous with their time. Al Beaupre, John Currie, Sharon Hanna, Rick Hewton, Mary Leipciger, Doug Lewis, Marg Stanowski and Mac Stienburg offered helpful comments on portions of the text, as did government lawyers Maurice Charbonneau, Murray Chitra, Mario Dion, Claire McKinnon, Daniel Therrien and Lloyd Younger. Alison McPhail and her co-workers on the Corrections Law Review project have compelled us to sharpen our thinking about law reform.

Prisoners' lawyers and paralegals Bob Bigelow, John Conroy, Nicole Daignault, Judy Elliott, David Linetsky, Charlene Mandell, Phil McNeil, Renee Millette, Chip O'Connor, Sasha Pawliuk, Don Bailey and Arne Peltz deserve thanks, not only for keeping us abreast of case law across the country, but also for their commitment to penal and parole issues, causes in which too many of their colleagues remain uninterested. Thanks also to Trudy Hartley, Judith Honey, Allan Park and Sandra Tallen for word-processing the manuscript.

Finally, and perhaps most importantly, we wish to thank the many hundreds of prisoners and parolees whose experiences over the years provided the stimulus for us to embark upon and complete this work. When one realizes that those who challenge the system all too frequently suffer both subtle and obvious forms of discrimination, we can only applaud their courage and determination. We hope that this book repays their trust in some small way.

Davie Cole received financial assistance from the Laidlaw Foundation, the Law Foundation of Ontario, and the National Parole Board. Allan Manson received a research grant from the School of Graduate Studies and Research, Queen's University. Also, Dean John Whyte provided him with a partial research leave to permit the completion of this text. It goes without saying that the views expressed in this book are those of the authors, and should not be considered as the opinions of any other agencies.

This book attempts to summarize the state of law as of July 1, 1990.

D.P.C.
A.M.

Wherever Marius' thoughts led him, he always returned with a kind of horror to Jean Valjean. Whatever the extenuating circumstances might be, there could be no escaping the fact that the man was a felon, that is to say, rejected by society, below the lowest rung of the social ladder, the lowest and the least of all men. The law deprived men of his kind of all rights; and Marius, democrat though he was, was in this matter, implacable on the side of the law. He was not, let us say, wholly progressive, able to distinguish between what is law and what is right. He had not fully weighed these matters and was not repelled by the idea of revenge. He thought it natural that certain infractions of the law should be subject to lifelong punishment, and he accepted total ostracism as a normal social procedure. Until then, that was as far as he had gone, although it was certain that he would go further, being by nature well disposed and instinctively progressive. But in the present state of his thinking he was bound to find Jean Valjean repulsive. A felon! The very word was like the voice of judgment. His reaction was to turn away his head. 'Get thee behind me . . .'.

Victor Hugo
Les Miserables

1

Introduction

Despite the existence of numerous community-based alternatives to imprisonment—fines, probation, community service orders—Canadian judges continue to impose sentences of imprisonment at a rate considerably higher than that in most western countries.[1] The philosophy behind, and the day-to-day management of, our prisons and penitentiaries continues to be dominated by the same central element—the disciplinary regime—which characterized the infrastructure of our first penitentiary built in 1835. Parole and other related release mechanisms are attracting increasingly more criticism from the public, from participants in the criminal justice system, and from staff and prisoners involved in the penal process. In recent years several high profile trials and inquests involving homicides committed by conditionally-released prisoners have received extensive media attention.[2] Similarly, we have witnessed the beginning of aggressive advocacy by and on behalf of victims, arguing for harsher sentences and more restrictive release regimes.

Regrettably, it has been more than 20 years since a Canadian government body has been charged with examining all three elements of post-conviction dispositions—sentencing, imprisonment and release. It is surely more than coincidental that the *Ouimet Report*,[3] released in

---

[1] See J. Lynch "A Comparison of Prison Use in England, Canada, West Germany and the United States: A Limited Test of the Punitive Hypothesis" (1988), 79 Journal of Criminal Law and Criminology 180, where the author compares the extent of imprisonment for certain categories of offences after adjusting for differences in crime rates and the distinction between lengths of sentence and rate of imprisonment. While the Canadian data was not complete, Lynch concluded:

> For homicide and robbery, the United States had incarceration rates many times greater than those of England or the Federal Republic of Germany. The incarceration rate of Canada, however is not greatly different from that of the United States. The United States incarceration rate for burglary is 50% greater than that of England, but is quite similar to that of Canada. The incarceration rate for larceny/theft in the United States is about 65% greater than the rate in England. The rate in Canada is again, very similar to the United States incarceration rate. (pp. 193-194)

[2] For example, Inquest into the Death of Celia Ruygrok, Ottawa, April 4 to May 22, 1988; Inquest Into the Death of Tema Conter, Toronto, October 6 to December 15, 1988.

[3] Report of the Canadian Committee on Corrections, *Toward Unity: Criminal Justice and Corrections*, (Ottawa: Queen's Printer, 1969).

1969, was entitled "Toward Unity". While numerous academic studies and governmental reports have subsequently scrutinized various aspects of the three core elements of the sentencing process, none has been charged with the responsibility of attempting to construct an integrated framework of clearly articulated and mutually consistent alternatives.[4]

Following a series of riots and hostage-takings in maximum-security penitentiaries across the country in 1976-77, the "MacGuigan Sub-Committee"[5] (named for its Chair) was given a broad mandate to examine, *inter alia*, the adequacy of security arrangements, custodial facilities, and correctional programs, including the special problems faced by staff and management.[6] The Sub-Committee conducted extensive public and private hearings. While the Sub-Committee's *Report* contained some recommendations reflecting the need to improve pre-release programming and to expand community correction centres to serve as a "bridge" between close confinement and society, it could only recommend that a thorough review of the parole system be undertaken "with a view to lessening . . . the appearance of arbitrariness in parole."[7]

By contrast, the mandate of the Canadian Sentencing Commission did not permit an inquiry into the nature of imprisonment, thereby leaving unexamined the second major element of the system of post-conviction criminal justice. The Commission's *Report*[8] accepted that integration must be the dominant characteristic of our system of crimi-

---

[4] Numerous bodies and groups have and continue to be commissioned to examine specific sentencing, penal and release issues and problems. A partial list includes *Task Force on the Release of Inmates*, J.K. Hugessen, Chair (Ottawa, November 1972); Standing Senate Committee on Legal and Constitutional Affairs, *Parole in Canada*, C. Goldenberg, Chair (Ottawa, 1974); Law Reform Commission, *Imprisonment and Release*, (Ottawa: Supply & Services Canada, 1976); *Solicitor General's Study of Conditional Release*, Report of the Working Group (Ottawa: Supply & Services Canada, 1981); *Report of the Study Team; Seven Suicides in the Atlantic Region*, E.H. Botterell, Chair (Ottawa, April 30, 1984); *Report of the Study Group on Murders and Assaults in the Ontario Region*, J. Vantour, Chair (Ottawa, May 18, 1984); *Report on Allegations of Mistreatment of Inmates at Archambault Institution*, R. Stewart, Correctional Investigator (Ottawa, June 21, 1984); *Report on the Management of Correctional Institutions*, J. Carson, Chair (Ottawa, November 1984); Task Force on Program Review, *Justice System*, Study Team Report, E. Neilsen, Chair (Ottawa, November, 1985); *Reports of the Auditor General on the Correctional Service of Canada* (Ottawa, 1981, 1986).

[5] The Sub-Committee on the Penitentiary System in Canada, *Report to Parliament*, Standing Committee on Justice and Legal Affairs, Second Session, Thirtieth Parliament, 1976-77.

[6] Terms of the Reference, *Report, ibid.*, p. 2.

[7] *Report, ibid.*, Recommendation 64.

[8] Report of the Canadian Sentencing Commission, *Sentencing Reform: A Canadian Approach* (Ottawa: Supply & Services, Canada, 1987).

nal justice. Consistent with its goal of seeking better integration, the Commission paid some attention to the issue of conditional release. In looking at parole, it reiterated many of the defects which critics have pointed out over the years. Unpredictability, hidden decision-making and the opportunity for abuse of discretion are both legitimate bases for criticism and sources of grievance. Moreover, these inadequacies generate misunderstanding throughout the community, as well as frustration amongst the population of prisoners which they affect. Ultimately, the Sentencing Commission's response was to advocate the abolition of discretionary parole.[9]

After the Sentencing Commission Report, the "Daubney Committee" (named for its Chair) embarked on its inquiry with terms of reference sufficiently broad to permit it to examine all three major elements of the sentencing system.[10] The Committee, however, spent relatively little time examining the purposes and effects of incarceration upon offenders.[11] While noting that "[t]he correctional system must ensure that the necessary treatment and programs are available to the offender to facilitate reintegration into the community,"[12] the ambiguous phrasing of the recommendations dealing principally with incarceration (Recommendations 60-67)[13] stand in sharp contrast to the very specific proposals dealing with such areas as victim's rights, implementation of portions of the Report of the Sentencing Commission, and aspects of the functioning of the National Parole Board.

---

[9]   The scope of this book does not permit either a conceptual critique or an empirical evaluation of the Commission's Scheme of sentencing guidelines. In our concluding chapter we attempt to raise some questions which in our opinion require more sophisticated and detailed analysis than the Commission was prepared to devote to conditional release issues. While we agree in theory with much of the Commission's approach to sentencing, we do not support its corollary recommendation that discretionary parole be abolished.

[10]   It is noteworthy that this was not a Sub-Committee or Royal Commission which took its terms of reference from a higher body. The Daubney Committee was the Parliamentary Standing Committee on Justice and Solicitor General. Under the new parliamentary rules which had just been introduced, that Committee had considerable power to direct its own investigations, and was to a large extent self-governing. While the Committee charged itself, in its Terms of Reference, with "examin[ing] the efficacy, responsiveness and appropriateness of . . . sentencing, conditional release and related aspects of the correctional system" (p. 269), it chose not to examine the penitentiary system in any detail.

[11]   The Committee did make numerous comments and recommendations about the effects of incarceration on native and female offenders.

[12]   Report of the Standing Committee on Justice and Solicitor General, *Taking Responsibility* (Ottawa: Supply & Services Canada, August 1988), p. 243.

[13]   *Report*, p. 266.

Regrettably, our subject is only one core element of the sentencing structure, the law and process of conditional release from imprisonment in Canada. Our purpose, however, is twofold. First, by collecting, assimilating and analyzing the statutory components, the case law which interprets them, and the policy which implements them, we hope to assist prisoners and their representatives, penal and parole officials, release decision-makers, and judges, in their efforts to address particular problems and systemic issues. We begin with a brief description of the process by which people come to be incarcerated. After a discussion of pre- and post-*Charter*[14] remedy issues, we proceed through an historical account of the development of mechanisms of conditional release in Canada. As will be demonstrated, the recognition by the Supreme Court of Canada of a duty of fairness which controls all public and statutory decision-makers,[15] and the constitutional entrenchment of the protections of fundamental justice when liberty is in issue,[16] have provided the greatest stimuli for focussing litigious energies upon the prison and release systems.

The text then discusses in detail the legal and procedural elements of the current release system and offers a guide to preparation for and attendance at various types of hearings. These chapters are intended to assist both lawyers and workers within the system in their day-to-day dealings with cases. As well, we hope to provide observers, critics and students with a better understanding of the operation of the release system. Throughout, we shall see that the mechanisms for conditional release are complex; while various statutory and procedural aspects have been modified on several occasions since the proclamation of Canada's modern parole statute in 1959, many of these have been made in response to specific incidents,[17] with little concern for systemic coherence. Similarly, with each series of legislative and regulatory amendments, the body of law interpreting the elements and mechanisms of release has grown, either refining what has been said before or replacing it. Consequently, the reader is cautioned throughout that, in most instances, legislation, case law and policy and practice can only be properly understood in the context of their evolution.

---

[14] *Canadian Charter of Rights and Freedoms* (being Part I of the *Constitution Act, 1982* [enacted by the *Canada Act*, 1982 (U.K.), c. 11, s. 1]).

[15] See *Nicholson v. Haldimand-Norfolk Bd. of Police Cmmrs.*, [1979] 1 S.C.R. 311; *Martineau v. Matsqui Institution Disciplinary Bd.*, [1980] 1 S.C.R. 602.

[16] See Chapter 4.

[17] See, for example, the legislative response to *R. v. Moore; Oag v. R.* (1983), 33 C.R. (3d) 97, contained in S.C. 1986, c. 42 and c. 43, discussed in Chapter 7.

Explaining the law is but one of our purposes. Our second major aim is to demonstrate that the essential elements of the administration of criminal justice must be systemically integrated within a framework of clearly articulated and mutually consistent objectives. In this book, we attempt to offer a view of parole which presents the possibility of transcending the concerns which currently grate against the goals of an equitable and proportionate sentencing system. Equally important, however, is our view that, absent radical change in the nature of imprisonment, the existence of an effective release mechanism is an essential safeguard against the destructive capability of long sentences served within the penitentiary environment.

The book concludes with our thoughts for a proposal for an ideal release model. We concede that much of our analysis flows from a legal perspective; in both practical and academic terms, this has been the focus of our experience with the release system. However, we maintain that, at a fundamental level, the legal perspective is essential. Imprisonment is an instrument of law. Consequently, the validity of a release mechanism depends on its legality within the framework of its own structure, the rule of law and our Constitution. Regardless of different philosophical, political, or penological attitudes which generate different views of a release mechanism, its scope and operation are determined by the legal authority which facilitates it. Within the Canadian experience, although it has been the political process which has shaped the current release system, it has been the legal process which has controlled it.

Much of the current debate over sentencing, imprisonment and release from imprisonment is clouded by misperception and mistrust. Our main goal is to promote a better understanding of one element of this debate. Change is necessary, but fundamentally productive change can only result from informed and serious discussion of these complex issues. Our remand centres, prisons and penitentiaries are overcrowded and double-bunking occurs in too many institutions, especially within the medium security classification.[18] At the same time incidents of violence are all too commonplace; the environment is both brutal and brutalizing for all who live and work in it. The need for a comprehensive examination of our entire penal system is apparent if, as a society, we seriously desire to change a penal landscape characterized by a growing and more volatile prison population, a tendency towards increases in the length of prison sentences for many offences, and a growing sense of

---

[18]   See the legal challenges to this practice in *Piche v. Canada (Solicitor General)* (1989), 47 C.C.C. (3d) 495 (Fed. C.A.), affirming (1985), 17 C.C.C. (3d) 1 (Fed. T.D.).

concern about the integrity and rehabilitative utility of the internal prison environment and mechanisms of conditional release.[19]

---

[19] From a cross-culture perspective it is interesting to note that the *United States Sentencing Reform Act* of 1984 expressly rejects imprisonment as a means of promoting rehabilitation, 28 U.S.C. 994(k), and states that punishment should rather serve retributive, educational, deterrent, and incapacitative goals, 18 U.S.C. 3553 (a)(2). See *Mistretta v. United States*, 57 L.W. 4102.

2

Sentencing and Imprisonment

... [I]mprisonment was based on either religious objectives, the provision
of work and training, and, more recently, deterrence and rehabilitation. It is
... clear ... that imprisonment has failed to achieve any of those objectives
in any meaningful way and serves simply as a means of denouncing certain
aberrant behaviour and as an expression of latent vengeance.[1]

1. INTRODUCTION

While substantive criminal law defines the contours of guilt, the
adjudicative function of the criminal trial extends to the imposition of
sentence on those found guilty. Since imprisonment is so often employed as a response to criminality, in this sense it is an integral element
of the criminal process. Imprisonment can be viewed as applied criminal law, not separate from (or an adjunct to) the criminal process, but the
actual element which inflicts the community's response to criminality.
In *Gardiner*,[2] Dickson J. repeated Sir James Fitzjames Stephen's remark
that "the sentence is the gist of the proceeding. It is to the trial what the
bullet is to the powder."[3] It is the bluntest instrument of the criminal
law.

Within the Canadian system of imprisonment, a vast network of
penitentiaries, prisons and other facilities has evolved to implement
sentences of imprisonment. We also have vehicles designed to regulate
and oversee the process of release. Equally, these release mechanisms
are core elements of the criminal process which cannot be viewed in a
vacuum as autonomous exercises with distinct objectives.

In simplified form, it is safe to say that the constitutional structure
of Canada places criminal law within the federal domain.[4] The authority

---

[1] *R. v. McGinn* (1989), 49 C.C.C. (3d) 137 (Sask. C.A.), per Vancise J.A. (dissenting) at
    152.
[2] *R. v. Gardiner* (1982), 68 C.C.C. (2d) 477 (S.C.C.).
[3] *Ibid*, at 513.
[4] See *Constitution Act, 1867* (30 & 31 Vict.), c. 3, s. 91(27) which gives the federal
    Parliament exclusive legislative authority over the "Criminal Law, except the Consti-
    tution of Courts of Criminal Jurisdiction, but including the procedure in Criminal
    Matters." At the turn of the century, the Privy Council said that it is "the criminal law
    in its widest sense that is reserved" to the exclusive domain of Parliament: see *Ontario*

over imprisonment has been divided, however, such that penitentiaries are allotted to the federal government,[5] while other types of institutions—prisons, reformatories and local jails—are built and administered by the provinces.[6]

The *Criminal Code* determines whether a sentence of imprisonment will be served in a federal or provincial institution,[7] according to the somewhat arbitrary[8] historical division between sentences of imprisonment for 2 years or more. Section 731(1) of the *Criminal Code* provides:

> (1) Except where otherwise provided, a person who is sentenced to imprisonment for
> (*a*) life,
> (*b*) a term of two years or more, or
> (*c*) two or more terms of less than two years each that are to be served one after the other and that, in aggregate, amount to two years or more, shall be sentenced to imprisonment in a penitentiary.

(A.G.) v. Hamilton Street Railway Co., [1903] A.C. 524, at 529. It must be noted, however, that section 92(15) of the *Constitution Act, 1867*, empowers provincial legislatures to legislate the "Imposition of Punishment by Fine, Penalty, or Imprisonment for enforcing any Law of the Province made in relation to any Matter coming within any of the Classes of Subjects enumerated in this Section." The constitutional delineation of the scope of the criminal law power continues to be controversial: see, for example, *Canada (A.G.) v. C.N. Tpt. Ltd.; Canada (A.G.) v. C.P. Tpt. Co. Ltd.* (1983), 38 C.R. (3d) 97 (S.C.C.); *R. v. Westmore* (1983), 38 C.R. (3d) 161 (S.C.C.); and Professor John D. Whyte's comments in "The Administration of Criminal Justice and the Provinces" (1983), 38 C.R. (3d) 184. Also, see P. W. Hogg, *Constitutional Law of Canada*, 2d ed. (Toronto: Carswell, 1985), pp. 397-402.

5 See *Constitution Act, 1867*, s. 91(28) giving the federal Parliament authority over the "Establishment, Maintenance and Management of Penitentiaries." This power is now effected through the *Penitentiary Act*, R.S.C. 1985, c. P-5. See also Hogg, *supra*, note 4, at pp. 433-437.

6 See *Constitution Act, 1867*, s. 92(6) which provides provincial authority for the "Establishment, Maintenance and Management of Public and Reformatory Prisons in and for the Province."

7 It should be noted that it is not only a sentence of 2 or more years which must be served in a penitentiary, but also a term made up of shorter sentences if the aggregate is 2 years or more: see *Criminal Code*, R.S.C. 1985, c. C-46, s. 731(5).

8 The historical source of the 2-year dividing line appears to be lost somewhere in the 19th Century, although its utility has been the subject of much discussion since that time: see *Sentencing Reform: A Canadian Approach*. Report of the Canadian Sentencing Commission (Ottawa: Supply & Services Canada, 1987), at p. 28. As part of the criminal legislation passed after the union of Upper and Lower Canada in 1840, imprisonment in the penitentiary was for sentences of at least 7 years, while confinement in a "Common Gaol or House of Correction" was for periods "not exceeding two years": see Provincial Statutes of Canada, 1841 (4 & 5 Vict.) c. 24, s. 30, and c. 27, ss. 7, 10-13.

Sentences of less than 2 years are served "in a prison or other place of confinement within the province"[9] unless the law permits or prescribes a penitentiary[10] or the convicted person is already subject to an unexpired penitentiary sentence.[11]

Credits of remission, which operate to reduce a period of confinement after commitment for a criminal offence, are also determined by federal statutes—the *Penitentiary Act*[12] and the *Prisons and Reformatories Act*.[13] Modes of conditional release from imprisonment in respect of *Criminal Code* offences and offences against other federal statutes are prescribed by the *Parole Act*[14] which establishes the National Parole Board as the body empowered to grant conditional release from imprisonment in a penitentiary.[15] With respect to prisoners confined in provincial institutions, a province may, if it chooses, establish its own parole board with powers delegated to it by the federal *Parole Act*.[16] Thus, the structure of conditional release, in terms of eligibility, supervision and the consequences of failure, is generally consistent throughout Canada, even if effected by different bodies. All of these issues will be discussed in detail throughout this book.

The remainder of the legal framework of imprisonment—remission, the internal regime, classification, transfers, and other environmental issues—is prescribed by the various federal and provincial statutes enacted to regulate their respective institutions.[17]

---

9   *Code*, s. 731(3).
10   See for example, s. 149(1)(*b*)(ii) of the *Code*.
11   *Code*, s. 731(2); and *R. v. Dinardo* (1982), 67 C.C.C. (2d) 505 (Ont. C.A.).
12   R.S.C. 1985, c. P-5, ss. 25 and 26.
13   R.S.C. 1985, c. P-20, s. 6.
14   R.S.C. 1985, c. P-2.
15   *Ibid.*, ss. 3 and 13. The National Parole Board also retains certain powers over persons serving sentences in provincial institutions in provinces which have created their own Boards of Parole. To date those provinces are Quebec, Ontario and British Columbia.
16   *Ibid.*, s. 12.
17   Major Federal Legislation:
Parole Act, R.S.C. 1985, c. P-2 [am. R.S.C. 1985, c. 27 (1st Supp.), s. 201; R.S.C. 1985, c. 34 (2nd Supp.), ss. 1–9 and 12–14; R.S.C. 1985, c. 35 (2nd Supp.), ss. 1–14]; *Penitentiary Act*, R.S.C. 1985, c. P-5 [am. R.S.C. 1985, c. 24 (2nd Supp.), s. 48; R.S.C. 1985, c. 27 (1st Supp.), s. 203; R.S.C. 1985, c. 34 (2nd Supp.), ss. 10–12 and 14; R.S.C. 1985, c. 35 (2nd Supp.), ss. 15–28]; *Prisons and Reformatories Act*, R.S.C. 1985, c. P-20 [am. R.S.C. 1985, c. 24 (2nd Supp.), s. 49; R.S.C. 1985, c. 35 (2nd Supp.), ss. 29–33].
Major Provincial Legislation:
Corrections Act (Alberta), R.S.A. 1980, c. C-26 [am. S.A. 1984, c. Y-1, s. 36; S.A. 1985, c. 15, s. 7]; *Corrections Act* (British Columbia), R.S.B.C. 1979, c. 70 [am. S.B.C. 1980, c. 1; S.B.C. 1984, c. 30; S.B.C. 1987, c. 12, s. 43]; *Corrections Act* (Manitoba), S.M. 1988, c. C230; *Corrections Act* (New Brunswick), R.S.N.B. 1973, c. C-26 [am. S.N.B. 1979, c. 41; S.N.B. 1983, c. 21; S.N.B. 1985, c. 4; S.N.B. 1988, c. 59 (not yet proclaimed)]; *Prisons Act*

2. THE SCOPE OF THE CRIMINAL LAW

Defining the scope and aims of the criminal law has proven a difficult task for jurists and philosophers alike. The debate usually finds its focus either on morality or social utility. While it may be useful, and even desirable, for criminal law to have moral force, the ultimate questions are the extent to which moral validity is an essential requirement of criminal law and whether notions of morality can, by that reason alone, justify use of the criminal law. Moral legitimacy, both in terms of popular acceptance and internal coherence, are important features of an instrumental system like the criminal law. This is a far cry from attempting to infuse the justification for the criminal law with the force of a moral imperative. As Herbert L. Packer stated in *The Limits of the Criminal Sanction,*

> Our moral universe is polycentric. The State, especially when the most coercive sanction is at issue, should not seek to impose a spurious unity upon it.[18]

In the 19th Century, John Stuart Mill expounded the liberal view, often described as the "harm principle", that a State can only justify the exercise of a coercive power upon an individual to prevent harm to others.[19] He was challenged by Sir James Fitzjames Stephen, the source of Canada's first *Criminal Code,* who argued for an intrinsic inter-relationship between law acting as the prohibitory arm and morality as the guiding spirit.[20] In the current century, these antagonists were replaced by Patrick Devlin and Henry Hart. While accepting that a "function for the criminal law independent of morals must be found,"[21]

(Newfoundland), R.S.N. 1970, c. 305 [am. S.N. 1972, Nos. 11, 30, 52; S.N. 1975-76, No. 25; S.N. 1979, c. 35, Schedule A; S.N. 1986, c. 27; S.N. 1986, c. 42, Schedule B; S.N. 1987, c. 9]; *Corrections Act* (North West Territories); R.S.N.W.T. 1974, c. C-18 [am. S.N.W.T. 1975(1), c. 1; S.N.W.T. 1978(1), c. 2; S.N.W.T. 1978(2), c. 16; S.N.W.T. 1980(2), c. 10]; *Court and Penal Institutions Act* (Nova Scotia), R.S.N.S. 1967, c. 67 [am. S.N.S. 1970, cc. 35, 36; S.N.S. 1970-71, cc. 34, 35; S.N.S. 1977, c. 26; S.N.S. 1986, c. 6; S.N.S. 1988, c. 22]; *Reformatory Act* (Nova Scotia), R.S.N.S. 1967, c. 262; *Ministry of Correctional Services Act* (Ontario), R.S.O. 1980, c. 275 [am. S.O. 1984, c. 66]; *Jails Act* (Prince Edward Island), R.S.P.E.I. 1974, c. J-1 [am. S.P.E.I. 1983, c. 1; S.P.E.I. 1987, c. 6]; *An Act to Promote the Parole of Inmates* (Quebec), R.S.Q. 1977, c. L-1.1 [am. S.Q. 1988, c. 46]; *Corrections Act* (Saskatchewan), R.S.S. 1978, c. C-40 [am. SS. 1987, c. 39]; *Corrections Act* (Yukon), R.S.Y.T. 1986, c. 36 [am. S.Y. 1987, c. 22, s. 39].

18 H. Packer, *The Limits of the Criminal Sanction* (Stanford: Stanford University Press, 1968), p. 265.

19 J.S. Mill, *On Liberty* (Arlington Heights: Harlan Davidson Inc., 1947), pp. 75-76.

20 J.F. Stephen, *Liberty, Fraternity and Equality* (1873), reprinted in Blom-Cooper and Drewry, *Law and Morality* (London: Duckworth, 1976), pp. 13-17.

21 P. Devlin, *The Enforcement of Morals* (London: Oxford University Press, 1959), p. 7.

Devlin managed to extrapolate his views on the need for the protection of society into an attack on the Wolfenden Report, which recommended the de-criminalization of homosexuality between consenting adults in private.[22] His conclusion was premised not on morality as an intrinsic social value, as Stephen would have argued, but "on the ground that a shared morality is essential to society's existence."[23] Hart exposed the absurdity of Devlin's position by showing that it stood for the proposition that a society is identical to its morality, such that "a change in its morality is tantamount to the destruction of a society."[24]

This debate has also occupied the attention of the Law Reform Commission of Canada, which has accepted that "the enforcement of morality" is not the business of the criminal law.[25] However, in describing the societal role of the criminal law, the Commission said:

> In truth, the criminal law is fundamentally a moral system. It may be crude, it may have its faults, it may be rough and ready, but basically it is a system of applied morality and justice. It serves to underline those values necessary, or else important, to society.[26]

While this recognizes the undeniable normative function of the criminal law, the language is imprecise, incomplete and misleading. It fails to translate the identification of blameworthiness into terms of social context, and makes a facile leap from "morality and justice" to "those values necessary or else important to society." While a system of criminal law should be moral and just in its operation, the values it actually protects flow from a broader and more pragmatic base entrenched in the political and economic structure of the community.

A more helpful approach is to move from the realm of philosophy into the arena of social reality. In addressing the scope of the criminal law, Glanville Williams in his book, *Textbook of Criminal Law*, resorted to a more instrumental response by quoting from Lord Atkin in *Proprietary Articles Trade Assn. v. Attorney General of Canada (A.G.)*:

> The domain of criminal jurisprudence can only be ascertained by examining what acts at any particular period are declared by the State to be crimes, and the only common nature they will be found to possess is that they are prohibited by the State, and that those who commit them are punished."[27]

---

[22] *Ibid.*, pp. 22-23.
[23] This is Hart's paraphrase, from H.L.A. Hart "The Moderate and the Extreme Thesis" in *Law, Liberty and Morality* (Stanford: Stanford University Press, 1963), p. 50.
[24] *Ibid*, p. 51.
[25] Law Reform Commission of Canada, *Our Criminal Law* (Ottawa, 1976), p. 16.
[26] *Ibid.*
[27] G. Williams, *Textbook of Criminal Law*, 2d ed. (London: Stevens & Sons, 1983), p. 29 (quoting from *Proprietary Articles Trade Assn. v. Canada (A.G.)*, [1931] A.C. 310, at 324).

A similar, but more politically perceptive, view is offered by the author of *Russell on Crime*:

> In fact, criminal offences are basically the creation of the criminal policy adopted from time to time by those sections of the community who are powerful or astute enough to safeguard their own security and comfort by causing the sovereign power in the state to repress conduct which they feel may endanger their position.[28]

This represents a franker explanation of the variability of social utility. It emphasizes the impact of power and the self-interest of powerful segments of the community, and leads inevitably to the question of how a community should limit its use of the criminal law.

The Canadian Committee on Corrections (more commonly known as the Ouimet Committee) identified three criteria as properly delimiting the scope of criminal law:

1. No act should be criminally proscribed unless its incidence, actual or potential, is substantially damaging to society.
2. No act should be criminally prohibited where its incidence may adequately be controlled by social forces other than the criminal process. . . .
3. No law should give rise to social or personal damage greater than it was designed to prevent.[29]

The Committee agreed that the realm of private morality was not the business of the criminal law. More importantly, it concluded that punishment could be "justified only where manifest evil would result from failure to interfere."[30] The Committee's view reflected both the liberal harm principle as a threshold factor, and Jeremy Bentham's utilitarian notion of proportionality as a limit on punishment. Although "the protection of society" was offered as the "only justifiable purpose of the criminal process", the structure and elements of that social context remained unquestioned.

In the important work, *Struggle for Justice*,[31] the proper role of the criminal law was considered to be limited by the principle of restraint. The application of law and sanctions is acceptable only when:

1. There is a compelling social need to require compliance with a particular norm;
2. There is no feasible but less costly method of obtaining compliance;

---

[28] J.W.C. Turner, *Russell on Crime*, 12th ed. (London: Stevens & Sons, 1964), p. 18.

[29] Report of the Canadian Committee on Corrections, *Toward Unity: Criminal Justice and Corrections* (Ottawa: Queen's Printer, 1969), p. 12.

[30] *Ibid.*, p. 13.

[31] *Struggle for Justice: A Report on Crime and Punishment in America*, Prepared for the American Friends Service Committee (New York: Hill and Wang, 1971).

3. There is some substantial basis for assuming that the imposition of punishment will produce greater benefit for society than simply doing nothing.[32]

This principle of restraint has received growing acceptance.[33] The potential enormity of the criminal law power and the sanctions which it employs should be proof enough that the appropriate question is how to limit its use.

3. THE SUBSTANCE OF SENTENCING

Our inquiry is restricted to those kinds of confinement emanating from the criminal process. This is a significant starting point in that we recognize we are dealing with the state in its most forceful capacity as it responds to transgressions and harm to the order and values of the community. Our specific subject matter arises at the post-conviction stage. We do not address detention before trial or confinement that results from a finding of not guilty by reason of insanity.[34] As well, we have generally excluded other examples of detention or confinement that are premised on unique or special circumstances, such as detention pending trial, contempt, dispositions under the *Young Offenders Act*,[35] and imprisonment in default of payment of fines.[35A] The underlying rationale and the mechanisms for termination of these forms of imprisonment distinguish them from imprisonment as a direct sentencing response to a criminal conviction.

Part XXVI of the *Criminal Code* establishes the structure and the available responses of the sentencing process. Section 717(1) provides:

Where an enactment prescribes different degrees or kinds of punishment in respect of an offence, the punishment to be imposed is, subject to the limitations prescribed in the enactment, *in the discretion of the court* that convicts a person who commits the offence. [Emphasis added.]

With the exception of a small group of offences for which minimum custodial sentences are required by statute,[36] imprisonment, regardless

---

[32] *Ibid.*, pp. 149-50.
[33] See the discussion of the Report of the Canadian Sentencing Commission in Chapter 13.
[34] For a discussion of this process see *R. v. Swain* (1986), 50 C.R. (3d) 97 (Ont. C.A.), currently on reserve in the Supreme Court of Canada.
[35] R.S.C. 1985, c. Y-1, ss. 20 and 28-32.
[35A] See *R. v. Hebb* (1989), 47 C.C.C. (3d) 193 (N.S. S.C.); K.B. Jobsen, "Fines" (1970), 16 McGill L.J. 633; R.E. Kimball, "On the Imposition of Imprisonment in Default of Payment of a Fine (1976-77), 19 C.L.Q. 29; *R. v. Deeb; R. v. Wilson* (1987), 28 C.C.C. (3d) 257 (Ont. Prov. Ct.).
[36] See Report of the Canadian Sentencing Commission, *Sentencing Reform: A Canadian*

of the length of term, is within the discretion of the trial judge, subject to review by an appellate court.[37] The *Code* offers no guidance as to when imprisonment is an appropriate sentence, except to the extent that stipulated maxima provide both an upper limit to any imprisonment imposed and place the offence itself within a hierarchy of gravity as perceived by Parliament. Thus, the statutory structure of imprisonment as a sentencing response is skeletal and leaves this alternative, for the most part, to the judge's discretion.

Much has been written about the birth of the modern penitentiary. There are several theoretical, historical and legal justifications which shed some light on the rationale for imprisonment, both as a systemic tool and an individualized response. The reformers of the 18th and 19th Centuries—principally Baron de la Brède et de Montesquieu, Cesare Beccarea and Jeremy Bentham—advocated the amelioration of the excesses offered by the penal codes of the day. This led to an arduous transition from capital and spectacular punishments to imprisonment as the common response to crime. Underlying these reform efforts one finds a variety of policy and conceptual bases touching on the deterrent efficacy of excessive penalties, the legal respectability of a regime that condoned cruelty, respect for liberty and the need for proportionality, views spawned by the trends towards liberalism and utilitarianism. In Europe, the common theme that there should be equivalence or proportionality between the crime and the punishment was cast in humanitarian terms,[38] but was refined in economic terms by Bentham who argued that punishment cannot be justifed "when it produces more evil than good or when the same good can be obtained at the price of less suffering."[39] The efficacy of punishment was viewed both from the perspective of the individual and the observing community, and encompassed incapacitation, reformation and intimidation.

Approach (Ottawa: Supply & Services Canada, 1987), pp. 64-65. Also see the discussions of *Smith, Chief* and *Goltz* in Chapter 4, all of which are examples of a court ruling that a particular minimum punishment contravenes s. 12 of the *Canadian Charter of Rights and Freedoms* (being Part I of the *Constitution Act, 1982* [en. by the *Canada Act, 1982* (U.K.), c. 11, s. 1]).

[37] Sentences are subject to appeal both by the accused and the Crown: see *Code*, ss. 675(1)(*b*) and 676(1)(*d*), respectively, for indictable offences, and ss. 813(*a*)(ii) and 813(*b*)(ii) for summary conviction offences. However, see *R. v. Guida* (1990), 51 C.C.C. (3d) 305, where a majority of the Quebec Court of Appeal held that in appeals to the Court of Appeal from judgments of summary conviction appeals courts, quantum of sentence is not subject to appellate review, because the wording of section 839 of the *Code* speaks of appeals being limited to questions of law alone.

[38] See L. Radzinowicz, *A History of English Criminal Law, Volume I* (London: Stevens and Sons, 1948), pp. 268-300.

[39] Radzinowicz, *ibid.*, p. 383.

Modern social historians have been more astute in assessing the factors, both political and economic, which give rise to the penitentiary.[40] However, it is the ostensible rationale which generated the set of contemporary justifications and objectives for punishment which seem to dominate the process of sentencing that have been characterized by George Fletcher as either "retributivist" or "consequentialist".[41] Others have used the labels "moral" and "utilitarian"[42]—that is, the objective either flows directly from the offence itself or is geared to producing some practical effect on the offender or the community. Punishment and denunciation are retributivist goals, while incapacitation, specific deterrence, general deterrence and rehabilitation are consequentialist. With the social and political change throughout this century, these justifications have experienced a predictable movement in and out of fashion. In 1979, the vicissitudes of penology over this period were described by Gerhard Mueller:

> ... sentencing and corrections have gone through four distinct eras: from the era of retribution, which was marked by relatively fixed, severe, although not necessarily brutal, sentences there was a passage to the so-called era of utilitarianism. During this latter period there was a spirit of unbounded optimism which created the conviction that the crime rate could be controlled by manipulating sentencing and correctional schemes, whereby the behaviour of individual perpetrators or of whole potential offender groups could be redirected. There followed, well into the 1970s, an era of humanism which aimed at a more equitable and more liberal recognition of the human rights of those caught in the meshes of the criminal justice system. Sentencing and corrections then entered a fourth phase, preceded by pointed research which aimed at examining what does work and what does not, which concluded that nothing does work as expected, and thereby initiated the era of nihilism.[43]

Regardless of one's view as to the nature of the current era—nihilistic or dominated by incapacitation and punishment[44]—it is clear that the judiciary continues to resort to all available justifications, albeit in

---

[40] See M. Ignatieff, *A Just Measure of Pain, The Penitentiary in the Industrial Revolution, 1750-1850* (New York: Pantheon Books, 1978); M. Foucault, *Discipline and Punish* (New York: Pantheon Books, 1978); D. Rothman, *The Discovery of the Asylum* (Boston: Little Brown, 1971); D. Melossi and M. Pavarini, *The Prison and the Factory* (London: Macmillan, 1981). All of these authors seem to have benefitted from the perspective offered in G. Rusche and O. Kircheimer, *Punishment and Social Structure* (New York: Columbia University Press, 1939).

[41] G. Fletcher, *Rethinking Criminal Law* (Boston: Little, 1978).

[42] C. Ruby, *Sentencing*, 3d ed. (Toronto: Butterworths, 1987) p. 2.

[43] G.O.W. Mueller, "The Future of Sentencing: Back to Square One", in *New Directions in Sentencing* by B. Grosman, Ed. (Toronto: Butterworth's 1980), p. 13.

[44] J.W. Mohr, "New Directions in Sentencing", in *New Directions in Sentencing, ibid.*

inconsistent and often enigmatic ways, usually masked under the general objective of the protection of society.

4. THE METHODOLOGY OF SENTENCING

In *Wilmott*,[45] MacLennan J.A. stated:

> For the purpose of protecting society, prevention, deterrence and reformation should all be considered . . .
>
> . . . .
>
> In coming to a conclusion as to the comparative weight to be attached to the three main elements serving to protect society for the purpose of deciding upon an appropriate term of imprisonment, one fact to be considered is the nature and gravity of the crime because generally there should be what has been referred to as a "just proportion" between the crime and sentence.[46]

Justice MacLennan also remarked that while "express repudiation by the state of the particular unlawful conduct" is a necessity, retribution in the sense of vengeance should play little or no role.[47] Clayton Ruby, in his book, *Sentencing*, states:

> Sentencing in Canada, according to case law, combines a strange liaison of both the moral and utilitarian positions. Generally speaking, there is agreement that in determining any sentence, regard must be had to deterrence, reformation and retribution.[48]

The case law is rife with examples of this amalgam approach to sentencing. While this blending of penal objectives permeates the sentencing process and provides both systemic and individual justifications, it generates its own inevitable tension due to the inherent contradictory nature of some objectives. At the same time, it hides the uncomfortable observation that precision and consistency may be unattainable goals.

Added to this calculus we see judicial recognition of particular factors which highlight the influence of one or another of the principles of sentencing. Cases involving youthful offenders, mentally ill offenders or recidivists, and cases arising from violence against children, women or racial minorities have provoked judges to emphasize particular principles. Thus, notwithstanding the general acceptance of the amalgam approach, the existence of some distinctive features highlights the significance of protection of the public, rehabilitation, deterrence or denunciation in direct response to the category of case. Necessarily, this

---

[45]   *R. v. Wilmott*, [1967] 1 C.C.C. 171 (Ont. C.A.).
[46]   *Ibid.*, at 178-179.
[47]   *Ibid.*, at 178.
[48]   *Supra*, note 42, p. 4.

emphasis has consequential impact on whether confinement is appropriate and, if so, the length and place of confinement.

5. TARIFFS OR INDIVIDUALIZED SENTENCES

Once we begin talking about distinctive features and the notion of categories of offenders, we enter the controversy over whether the sentencing process should reflect an individualized response to the offender and the offence or whether, in fact or theory, a "tariff" approach is more appropriate. Commonly, an individualized sentence means one which gives primary effect to the principles of punishment, individual deterrence and rehabilitation without regard to symbolic impact on the community. Thus, the circumstances and conduct of the specific offender provide the essential framework for sentencing. In many cases, the offender's rehabilitative prospects will play a dominant role. In some cases, incapacitation to protect the community will receive the highest attention. A tariff, in its manifold guises, pushes the issue of rehabilitation into the background in order that a message of denunciatory or generally deterrent nature be broadcast to the community. A useful example of the "tariff" approach in its most rigid form is the mandatory life sentence required by the *Criminal Code* in cases of murder.[49] The stipulated response is a function of the intrinsic gravity and harm entailed by acts which satisfy the elements of the offence of murder. The impact on the offender, whether with reference to individual deterrence or rehabilitative prospects, is deemed irrelevant. Within the realm of judicial sentencing, the "tariff" approach suggests that some offences[50] necessarily are sufficiently grave and generate such harm or threat as to warrant a pre-articulated penal response. That is, intrinsic blameworthiness justifies a particular deterrent and denunciatory sentence in order to leave no doubt in the community's mind about the values which have been threatened and the extent to which the State will respond to that threat.

As an explanation of judicial sentencing, the notion of a tariff has been generated by David A. Thomas' analysis of sentencing and appellate review in England.[51] In his view, the tariff takes the form of a range within which sentences are considered fit. Another form of tariff might involve a norm or starting point to which aggravating or mitigating factors can be applied. Clearly, tariffs can be imposed explicitly or implicitly.

---

[49] See *Code*, s. 235.
[50] On subspecies of offences, see the discussion of *R. v. Sandercock, infra.*
[51] D.A. Thomas, *Principles of Sentencing*, 2d ed. (London: Heinemann, 1979).

The extent to which some form of tariff has crept into Canadian sentencing is debatable.[52] What is clear is that concern over disparity, or at least the perception of disparity, is a common feature in the current debate over sentencing.[53] As the *Code* provides no formulaic equation or methodology for producing a fit sentence, the resolution of what constitutes a fit sentence is ultimately determined by our provincial appellate courts.[54] In an effort to inject uniformity, at least within an individual province, some appellate courts have begun to consider new methods of structuring discretion including the idea of a judicially imposed tariff.

Until recently, it was generally accepted that sentencing proceeded on an individualized basis. Operating within the unstructured discretion created by the *Criminal Code*, the judge's own experience, preconceptions and biases have influenced sentencing.[55] Moreover, in any given jurisidiction experience over time with like cases builds and guidance is offered by appellate courts. Phrases like "usual range" or "appropriate range" are commonplace. Yet, the allegiance to individualization has continued. In a sentencing handbook prepared by the Canadian Association of Provincial Court Judges, the amalgam approach is repeated[56] and accompanied by a well-known quotation from *Willaert*:[57]

> ... the true function of criminal law in regard to punishment is in a wise blending of the deterrent and reformative, with retribution not entirely disregarded, and with a constant appreciation that the matter concerns not merely the Court and the offender but also the public and society as a going concern. Punishment is, therefore, an art—a very difficult art—essentially practical, and directly related to the existing needs of society.

---

[52] See the discussion in *R. v. Johnas* (1982), 32 C.R. (3d) 1 (Alta. C.A.) of the opposing views offered by Ruby and Nadin-Davis.

[53] See *Sentencing Reform: A Canadian Approach*, *supra*, note 36, pp. 71-77.

[54] The Supreme Court of Canada has decided that, as a matter of policy, it will not entertain sentence appeals which raise only a question of quantum or fitness as compared to a question of law in relation to the process of sentencing: see *R. v. Gardiner* (1982), 68 C.C.C. (2d) 477 (S.C.C.), per Dickson J., at 506. See also the dissent of Laskin C.J.C. at 492-493 where he questioned whether there is any jurisdiction to entertain sentence appeals even in respect of an issue like the burden of proof as raised in *Gardiner*. He concluded that the court ought not to accept jurisdiction.

[55] See generally, J. Hogarth, *Sentencing as a Human Process* (Toronto: University of Toronto Press, 1971); also see *St. George v. R.* (1968), 5 C.R.N.S. 371 (Que. C.A.) per Casey J.A.

[56] *Sentencing Handbook*, Canadian Association of Provincial Court Judges, 1982, pp. 23-27.

[57] *R. v. Willaert* (1953), 105 C.C.C. 172 (Ont. C.A.), at 176.

While "intuition" may have been more appropriate than "art", the quotation neatly reflects an individualized impression of the sentencing function.[58] However, on the very same page of the handbook, there is reference to the "usual" sentence in a "run-of-the-mill case" implying that experience creates standards. Individualization is a misnomer at best and perhaps even an illusion.

In his comprehensive examination of English sentencing practice, Thomas has suggested that courts, taking their guidance from the Court of Appeal, follow either a tariff or individualized approach depending on the nature of the case.[59] He suggests that a tariff should be imposed when the gravity of the offence needs to be emphasized to the community. While proportionality is an "overriding principle", the tariff invokes, often in the same case, notions of general deterrence, denunciation and occasionally "expiation". The tariff ignores or subordinates the concern for the future rehabilitation of the offender in favour of a punitive or denunciatory response required by the gravity of the offence or the status of the offender. The individualized approach on the other hand is predicated on the desire to influence the offender's future behaviour. Thomas views the sentencing function as commencing with the threshold question as to which approach is appropriate. Accordingly, experience has developed certain categories of offence which compel the application of the tariff and special classifications of offenders which attract an individualized sentence. The "tariff" will apply to such offences as "rape, robbery, wounding with intent to do grievous bodily harm, dealing with controlled drugs, perjury and related offences, arson and blackmail",[60] as well as offences involving a breach of trust or privilege. An individualized approach should be fashioned for such groups as youthful offenders, intermediate recidivists, inadequate recidivists and mentally ill offenders.[61] Of course, cases do not always fit neatly along these two avenues. In some instances, while an individualized approach would otherwise make sense in light of the offender's circumstances, unavailability of appropriate facilities or a history which suggests little chance for success may move the case back into the tariff stream. As well, many cases will not point presumptively in either direction:

---

[58] Shortly afterwards, at p. 26, the *Sentencing Handbook* states, "[that] there are no fixed formulas to pre-determine the outcome of blending or balancing the principles as individualized in a given case."

[59] The following comments capsualize Thomas' views discussed in *Principles of Sentencing*, 2d ed. *supra*, note 51, pp. 29-61.

[60] *Ibid.*, p. 15.

[61] *Ibid.*, pp. 17-25.

. . . where the nature of the offence is not such that a tariff sentence is clearly indicated without regard to the future of the individual, the Court will approach the primary decision without any presumption either way, endeavouring to balance the competing claims of each approach to sentencing in the context of the particular case.[62]

Canadian writers disagree about whether Thomas' account accurately reflects the English practice.[63] This controversy, somewhat pedantic, asks whether a formalized tariff is the intentional creation of English courts or merely Thomas' observation of systemic experience. More importantly, however, Canadian writers bring the same disagreement to questions about the existence and use of a tariff methodology in Canada.[64]

While much of the methodology and substance of sentencing in Canada has been clouded by unspecific judgments and a generalized embrace of the amalgam approach, an examination of practice reveals many of the features of Thomas' bifurcated system. Albeit without consistency, we find judicial recognition of certain offences which attract a tariff response and certain offenders who have been the subject of individualized sentences.[65] The real question is whether these pronouncements fit into anything that resembles even a notional systemic approach to sentencing.

The Alberta Court of Appeal has provided a frank statement of its view of the sentencing process as follows:

> The proper approach in sentencing, as we have said, is to calculate a fit starting point on the basis of sentencing guidelines expressed by or extracted from the decisions of this court. The specific sentence for the specific accused should then be adjusted on a balance of the compendium of aggravating and mitigating circumstances present in the case. The end of this process is not uniform sentences, for that is impossible. The end is a uniform approach to sentencing.[66]

While there is something refreshing in a court's willingness to explain its sentencing methodology,[67] the implications of the "starting point" ap-

---

[62]   *Ibid.*, p. 25.
[63]   See C. Ruby. *Sentencing*, 3d ed., *supra*, note 42, p. 389.
[64]   See P. Nadin-Davis, *Sentencing in Canada* (Toronto: Carswell, 1982) pp. 40-41.
[65]   Paul Nadin-Davis, who has argued that an operative tariff (albeit not a formal one) exists in Canada, has cited trafficking in hard drugs, rape and armed robbery as categories requiring tariff sentences; individualized sentences are usually imposed on youthful offenders and mentally ill offenders and the group described by Thomas as "intermediate recidivists": see Nadin-Davis, *Sentencing in Canada supra*, note 64. His examples, however, are consistent with a tariff in the sense of a range of usual sentence from which departure will only exceptionally be justified, as compared to the starting point approach discussed *infra*.
[66]   *R. v. Raber* (1983), 57 A.R. 360 (C.A.), at 360.
[67]   In *Raber, ibid.*, a case involving convictions for kidnapping for ransom, the court

proach cannot be ignored. In *Johnas,* the same court ruled that henceforth in Alberta there should be a 3-year "starting point" for unsophisticated armed robberies of "relatively small commercial establishments, open at night for service to and convenience of the public."[68] The court then considered six appeals, all involving adult "youthful offenders", by assessing relevant aggravating and mitigating factors in order to reach an appropriate sentence. Of the seven offenders, five received sentences ranging from 2½ to 4 years; only two received less than penitentiary time.[69] Thus, the articulated starting point of 3 years' imprisonment must have the effect of sentencing more youthful offenders to longer terms of incarceration and, more likely, to penitentiary terms.[70]

With the exception of sentencing for robbery by the Appeal Division of the Nova Scotia Supreme Court (which has recently been moving in the same direction as the Alberta Court of Appeal[71]), the sentenc-

---

dismissed Crown appeals against 12- and 14-year sentences for kidnapping, extended by consecutive 1- and 2-year sentences respectively for the use of firearms contrary to s. 83(1)(*a*) [now s. 85(1)(*c*)] of the *Code.* Interestingly, the court did not pinpoint a starting point but instead made passing reference to the normal range for kidnapping for ransom as being from 10 to 20 years' imprisonment; *cf., R. v. Gillen* (1979), 8 C.R. (3d) S-5 (B.C. C.A.) in which a life sentence was upheld in the case of a disturbed woman who snatched a baby in an effort to make it her own. She was arrested 2 days after the kidnapping. Emphasizing the pain suffered by the child's parents, the court accepted the trial judge's assertion of the need for "society's ultimate condemnation of most serious crimes as deterrence from repetition by others" (at S-9). In so doing, it rejected the argument that kidnapping for ransom was a more serious offence.

68   *R. v. Johnas, supra,* note 52, at. 6.

69   *Supra,* note 52, at 15-27. These two cases involved, respectively, a youthful offender with no previous experience of incarceration, and an incompetent offender who, while drunk, demanded only $20 from a cashier before passing out outside the store.

70   The sentences in *Johnas* should be contrasted with the substantially lower sentences imposed in similar cases in other provinces: See *R. v. Casey* (1977), 20 Crim. L.Q. 145 (Ont. C.A.); *R. v. Vandale* (1974), 21 C.C.C. (2d) 250 (Ont. C.A.); *R. v. Windsor* (Ont. C.A., December 30, 1986); *R. v. Demeter* (1976), 3 C.R. (3d) S-55 (Ont. C.A.); *R. v. Harrison,* [1978] 1 W.W.R. 162 (B.C. C.A.); *R. v. Sherwood* (1976), 13 N.B.R. (2d) 118 (C.A.); *R. v. Gonidis* (1980), 57 C.C.C. (2d) 90 (Ont. C.A.); *R. v. Thomas* (1984), 65 N.S.R. (2d) 338, 147 A.P.R. 338 (C.A.); *R. v. LeCoure* (1984), 57 N.B.R. (2d) 82, 148 A.P.R. 82 (C.A.); *R. v. Large* (1984), 5 O.A.C. 328 (C.A.); *cf. R. v. Wall* (1984), 65 N.S.R. (2d) 58, 147 A.P.R. 58 (C.A.) wherein a sentence of 3 years' imprisonment was upheld in respect of a 17-year-old first offender on the basis of the prevalence of the offence. It should be noted that the judgment in *Wall* was written by Macdonald J.A. who had earlier expressed the view that a sentence of 3 years "*must*" be imposed in the absence of "exceptional mitigating circumstances." See *R. v. Owen* (1982), 50 N.S.R. (2d) 696, 98 A.P.R. 696 (C.A.), at 698.

71   In *R. v. Boutilier* (1985), 66 N.S.R. (2d) 310, 152 A.P.R. 310 (C.A.) the court stated "that in the absence of special circumstances a sentence *as lenient as two years' imprisonment* should only be imposed for the crime of robbery where the accused is youthful or is a first offender" (at 311).

ing principles enunciated in *Johnas* stand in sharp distinction to numerous judicial statements about the paramountcy of rehabilitation when sentencing young offenders[72] and the discouragement of penitentiary sentences as a first custodial term.[73] In this context one cannot ignore the state of overcrowding and violence which currently exists in Canadian penitentiaries.

The Alberta Court of Appeal has continued its attempt to develop a tariff.[74] In *Hessam*,[75] it held that the starting point for the robbery of night-time deposits of cash should be 4 years' imprisonment. More recently, and more importantly, the court in *Sandercock*[76] re-affirmed and refined its starting-point approach. Commenting that its goal was to provide uniformity of approach, not result, the court explained the three steps of its new regime:

1. The definition of a category or archetypal offence.
2. The articulation of a sentencing starting point for that offence.
3. The consideration and application of mitigating and aggravating factors in a given case to produce the appropriate sentence.

The court focussed on what it called a major sexual assault, which it defined as a sexual assault involving the use of violence or threat of violence to force "an adult victim to submit to sexual activity of a sort or intensity . . . that a reasonable person would know beforehand that the victim likely would suffer lasting emotional or psychological injury, whether or not physical injury occurs."[77] A starting point of 3 years was offered in cases of a mature accused of previous good character where there was no evidence of planning or stalking.[78] Both deterrence and denunciation were relied upon as the principle considerations in sentencing for a major sexual assault. The justificatory rationale stressed the need to denounce the "contemptuous disregard for the feelings and personal integrity of the victim" as well as recognizing in real and human terms the harm, aside from physical injury, which is caused:

---

[72] See *Demeter, supra,* not 70, at S-57.
[73] See *R. v. Dunkely* (1976), 3 C.R. (3d) S-51 (Ont. C.A.); *R. v. Elliot* (1976), 19 Crim. L.Q. 25 (Ont. C.A.).
[74] See *R. v. Littletent* (1985), 17 C.C.C. (3d) 520 (Alta. C.A.), re: aggravated assault "on the street" requiring 3 to 4 years; see also *R. v. T.; R. v. S.* (1983), 46 A.R. 87 (C.A.), re: guidelines for different categories of incest offences.
[75] *R. v. Hessam* (1983), 43 A.R. 247 (C.A.).
[76] *R. v. Sandercock* (1986), 22 C.C.C. (3d) 79 (Alta. C.A.).
[77] *Ibid.,* at 84.
[78] *Ibid.,* at 85.

This harm includes not just the haunting fear of another attack, the painful struggle with a feeling that somehow the victim is to blame, and the sense of violation or outrage, but also a lingering sense of powerlessness.[79]

In *Sandercock*, the accused had previously been sentenced to a 1-year term for another sexual assault.[80] While there appeared to be no physical injury and the victim may have been imprudent, the only mitigating factor was a late guilty plea. The court increased the sentence from 3 years to 4½ years' imprisonment.

To place *Sandercock* in perspective, one must first note that, within Alberta's own hierarchy, the starting point of 3 years equates major sexual assault to the kind of robberies considered in *Johnas* and subordinates it to the night-time deposit category addressed in *Hessam*. In the latter two cases, prevalence was the major justification compared to the more significant "harm" rationale offered in *Sandercock*. Secondly, *Sandercock* will necessarily generate substantial disparity between sentences imposed in different provinces. In Alberta, the fact that an accused is a first offender with no previous record is subsumed into the typical case, while most other appellate courts across Canada continue to recognize the mitigating effect of this fact.[81] By ignoring rehabilitative prospects generally and emphasizing denunciation, the starting point approach should produce longer sentences, even in cases where the future protection of the community appears not to be in issue.[82]

The impact of *Sandercock* has been noteworthy. In *Naqitarvik*,[83] three judges of the Alberta Court of Appeal, sitting as the North West Territories Court of Appeal, applied their sentencing blueprint to a native offender convicted of sexual assault in Arctic Bay, an isolated community of some 400 people, mostly Inu. The trial judge had sentenced him to 90 days' intermittent, followed by 2 years' probation. This would have avoided a transfer to the territorial correctional facility and

---

[79] *Ibid.*, at 84 (quoting from *R. v. Fait* (1982), 68 C.C.C. (2d) 367, at 374) and 85.

[80] *Ibid.*, at 89. The judgment refers to the respondent as being "on mandatory supervision" at the time of the incident. This is clearly wrong, as the regime of mandatory supervision applies only to those sentenced to 2 years or more.

[81] See *R. v. McCormick* (1979), 9 C.R. (3d) 248 (Man. C.A.); *R. v. Vandale* (1974), 21 C.C.C. (2d) 250 (Ont. C.A.).

[82] Compare with *R. v. Ashbee* (1985), 8 O.A.C. 341 (C.A.) where a sentence of 90 days was increased to 1 year imprisonment followed by 1 year probation. While giving effect to the appellant's "successful efforts at rehabilitation", the court stated that general deterrence could not be ignored. See also *R. v. Alderton* (1985), 44 C.R. (3d) 254 (Ont. C.A.) in which a 4-year sentence for break, enter and sexual assault was reduced to 3½ years to take into account the appellant's youth, "his lack of prior conviction for any related crime, and his potential for rehabilitation" (at 262).

[83] *R. v. Naqitarvik* (1986), 26 C.C.C. (3d) 193 (N.W.T.C.A.). Leave to appeal to S.C.C. refused 26 C.C.C. (3d) 193n (S.C.C.).

would have compelled the accused to participate in a traditional indigenous counselling process involving, *inter alia*, confrontation by elders. Although this sentence was imposed after the trial judge had heard over 12 hours of *viva voce* testimony, much of which was devoted to an explanation of the counselling process, in the presence of half the citizens of this remote community, the majority of the court chose to apply *Sandercock* and its 3-year starting point.[84] In result, the Crown appeal was allowed and the sentence raised to 18 months.

In dissent, only Belzil J.A. recognized the experience of the trial judge and the special situation of a remote, isolated community which, through its own cultural imperatives, had remained relatively crime free.[85] For the majority, however, the sentencing regime imposed in response to an act of sexual violence late at night in Calgary was transplanted far north of the Arctic Circle because, in their view, the cultural context was not "markedly different."[86]

Naqitarvik highlights the inherent difficulty in attempting to apply a guideline scheme across a broad range of cases, offenders and circumstances. While still maintaining its generalized guideline approach to sentencing, it is noteworthy that the Alberta Court of Appeal has deliberately refrained from issuing a starting point in cases involving criminal negligence causing death[87] or manslaughter convictions which, prior to *Vaillancourt*,[88] could have been constructive murder.[89] With respect to manslaughter, the court concluded that it could not define an appropriate archetypical category because of the wide range of culpability encompassed by the offence.[90] Perhaps this conclusion reflects a recognition of the need to retain the option of an individualized sentence in some circumstances.[91]

By comparison, in Ontario, a tariff approach to sentencing has been explicitly rejected with respect to sexual assault,[92] drug offences[93] and

[84] *Ibid.*, at 197-198; Belzil J.A. dissenting at 198-207.
[85] *Ibid.*, at 206.
[86] *Ibid.*, at 195.
[87] *R. v. Konkolus* (1988), 6 M.V.R. (2d) 220 (Alta. C.A.).
[88] In *R. v. Vaillancourt*, [1987] 2 S.C.R. 636 the Supreme Court of Canada struck down the "constructive murder" provision, then s. 213(*d*) of the *Criminal Code* on *Charter* grounds.
[89] *R. v. Tallman* (1989), 68 C.R. (3d) 367 (Alta. C.A.).
[90] *Ibid.*, at 371-372.
[91] See, for example, *R. v. Henry* (1977), 39 C.R.N.S. 45 (Que. C.A.); *R. v. MacKay* (1980), 40 N.S.R. (2d) 616, 73 A.P.R. 616 (C.A.).
[92] *R. v. Glassford* (1988), 42 C.C.C. (3d) 259 (Ont. C.A.) where the court expressly rejected the *Sandercock* approach but raised a 90-day intermittent sentence to 2 years less 1 day.
[93] *R. v. Hiquita* (Ont. C.A., November 21, 1983).

assaulting a peace officer.[94] Similarly, the Appeal Division of the Prince Edward Island Supreme Court has questioned the use of guidelines in response to impaired driving if their application precludes "weighing and balancing the aggravating and mitigating factors".[95] While various courts have remarked about the intrinsic gravity of certain offences (such as sexual assaults and spousal assault[96]) so as to subordinate the issue of rehabilitation in favour of general deterrence and denunciation, this response produces far different results than the "starting point" approach.[97]

Although the application of the criminal law is federal in scope, we have attempted to show not only that some principles of sentencing are given greater significance in some provinces, but also that the methodology of sentencing differs and produces different results. For the purpose of release from imprisonment, these distinctions do more than create disparate penalties for similar offences. Cases involving the same length of sentence may be responding to different issues and speaking to different constituencies, depending on the methodology employed. A purely individualized sentence flows from characteristics of the offender and directs itself to consequences, whether they be rehabilitative or incapacitative in nature. The "starting point" methodology derives its calculus from the nature of the offence and speaks to the community in a deterrent and denunciatory voice. Logically, one could assume that the offender's progress through the sentence is irrelevant to the impact of the sentence's message as to how the community considers the offence and the penalties to which an offender may be subjected. Added to these examples, we see some acceptance of the "usual range" kind of tariff and a more nebulous amalgam approach whereby the circumstances of each case create their own matrix of preferences. Ultimately, it appears that a warrant reciting a sentence of "x" years' imprisonment carries little meaning as to the intent of the sentence without knowing more about the particular reasons and the practice in the jurisdiction from which it originated.[98]

---

[94] *R. v. Herbst* (1984), 39 C.R. (3d) 61 (Ont. Co. Ct.).
[95] *R. v. Stephens* (1990), 51 C.C.C. (3d) 557 (P.E.I. C.A.), at 561. For an important discussion of sentencing impaired drivers see the judgments in *R. v. Ashberry* (1989), 47 C.C.C. (3d) 138 (Ont. C.A.).
[96] *R. v. Inwood* (1989), 48 C.C.C. (3d) 173 (Ont. C.A.).
[97] See, for example, *Ashbee, supra,* note 82.
[98] It is only within the past 2 years that the Correctional Service of Canada and the National Parole Board have begun to make sustained efforts to obtain reasons for sentence in most cases.

6. THE POSSIBILITY OF CONDITIONAL RELEASE AS A FACTOR IN SENTENCING

Shortly before the enactment of the *Parole Act*,[99] the Ontario Court of Appeal in *Bezeau*[100] upheld a life sentence and commented on the unlikely prospect of rehabilitation. Schroeder J.A., in concurring reasons, argued that "the function of an Appellate Court on an appeal against sentence is to correct a failure of justice and not to exercise the Crown's prerogative of extending clemency to a prisoner, or the powers of a board of parole."[101] Subsequently, in *Bailey*, Brooke J.A. stated:

> ... I have put from my mind the fact that this man may be relieved from serving the full amount of the sentence as determined by the Court by reason of time off which he might earn or that may be conferred upon him by statute. To regard these things in determining the sentence and, accordingly, to lengthen the term, is obviously to be at cross-purposes with Parliament.[102]

In *Wilmott*,[103] one of the most often quoted and influential Canadian sentencing cases,[104] the accused appealed a 12-year sentence for rape. The trial judge, expressly distinguishing a number of contrary decisions of the British Columbia Court of Appeal,[105] remarked that an appropriate sentence would be in the range of 6 to 8 years, but imposed the longer sentence in light of the possibility of release on parole or as a result of accumulated remission. The judgment of MacLennan J.A. offered an integrative view of the respective functions of the courts and the paroling authorities:

> The function of a Court in imposing a sentence of imprisonment and of the Board in reviewing the case of a prisoner for the purpose of granting or refusing parole, in my opinion, cannot be isolated one from the other, but

---

[99] S.C. 1958, c. 38.

[100] *R. v. Bezeau* (1958), 122 C.C.C. 35 (Ont. C.A.).

[101] *Ibid.*, at 47. Laidlaw J.A., in dissent, was of the view that insufficient attention had been paid to possible rehabilitation and that the issue of rehabilitation had been improperly delegated to parole authorities.

[102] [1970] 4 C.C.C. 291 (Ont. C.A.) at 305; see also *R. v. Mabee*, [1965] 1 O.R. 429 (Ont. C.A.). While Brooke J.A. was clearly speaking of earned and statutory remission, his comments have equal force in respect of discretionary release by a paroling authority.

[103] *R. v. Wilmott*, [1967] 1 C.C.C. 171 (Ont. C.A.).

[104] The case is usually cited in respect of the manner in which McLennan J.A. asserted the interaction of "prevention, deterrence and reformation" as factors relevant to the "protection of society" (at 178).

[105] *R. v. Courtney* (1956), 115 C.C.C. 260 (B.C. C.A.); *R. v. Heck* (1963), 40 C.R. 142 (B.C. C.A.); *R. v. Holden* (1963), 29 C.R. 228 (B.C. C.A.).

the two functions are part of one process designed and intended by Parliament to be complimentary [sic] one to the other in the field of correction.[106]

While McLennan J.A. accurately recognized that a grant of parole does not diminish a sentence, but rather changes the manner and place in which it is served,[107] his judgment is unclear and sometimes contradictory in delineating the interrelationships between sentencing and parole. While asserting that the sentencing function cannot be delegated to a parole board, he also stated that in cases where rehabilitation or general deterrence are the principle considerations in sentencing, the availability of parole is relevant to ensure a fair response to the progress of the particular offender.[108] He went further by adding that "a longer sentence than otherwise warranted may be imposed for the purposes of rehabilitation" in order to permit the completion of an appropriate program.[109] This proposition does not accord with subsequent cases which have consistently held that it is not the proper role of the criminal courts to sentence to periods of confinement solely in order that the prisoner may be exposed to a treatment program.[110] More specifically, this notion has been consistently rejected by appellate courts in British Columbia,[111] Newfoundland[112] and Manitoba.[113]

This controversy[114] was highlighted by the different approaches of the majority and dissent in *Pearce*,[115] where the accused appealed a 6-year term for trafficking in a controlled drug. In upholding the sentence, Jessup J.A. (Estey J.A. concurring) stated that it was "proper to take into account that the appellant need only serve four years and one month of the sentence imposed and that he will be eligible for parole in

---

[106] *Supra*, note 103, at 182.
[107] *Supra*, note 103, at 181.
[108] *Supra*, note 103, at 186-187.
[109] *Supra*, note 103, at 187. This statement is more than simply a corollary to the view expressed in *Bailey, supra*, note 102, that a sentence should not be so daunting as to discourage a realistic prospect of rehabilitation.
[110] See *R. v. Luther* (1971), 5 C.C.C. (2d) 354 (Ont. C.A.), per Kelly J.A. at 355, and Brooke J.A. at 357. A more refined view was offered in the later case of *R. v. Phillip* (1978), 20 Crim. L.Q. 297 (Ont. C.A.), in which it was held that a term of imprisonment can be imposed to facilitate and promote treatment, so long as the term fits within the appropriate range for the offence and is not imposed solely for treatment purposes.
[111] See *Courtney, Heck* and *Holden, supra*, note 105.
[112] See *R. v. Coffey* (1965), 51 M.P.R. 7 (Nfld. C.A.).
[113] See *R. v. Richardson* (1963), 40 C.R. 179 (Man. C.A.).
[114] This controversy is by no means restricted to the judiciary. As the recent Report of the Canadian Sentencing Commission demonstrates, Canadians are very confused in their anticipations of what a sentence of imprisonment is expected to accomplish.
[115] *R. v. Pearce* (1974), 16 C.C.C. (2d) 369 (Ont. C.A.).

two years. . . ."[116] In dissent Dubin J.A. bluntly disagreed. Referring to *Wilmott* he said:

> Although there may be situations . . . where it is appropriate to consider the question of parole the Court also pointed that a longer sentence should not be imposed than warranted by the particular circumstances of the case and according to the well-established principles merely because of the existence of the Parole Board.[117]

He went on to add that the likelihood of rehabilitation, if apparent at trial, should be taken into account in assessing a fit sentence "leaving it to the Parole Board to deal with cases where the rehabilitation prospects of the accused improved during the term of imprisonment."[118]

The debate seems to flow, for the most part, from what we have called individualized sentences, whether by reason of rehabilitation or incapacitation. In practice, the majority view reflects a misunderstanding of the effect of remission and the function of a conditional release decision-maker. A major contradiction, as illustrated by MacLennan J.A.'s remarks in *Wilmott*, is the notion that an exemplary sentence, particularly one generated by a recognition of the prevalence of a particular crime, can properly be ameliorated by a parole board's response to the progress of the offender while incarcerated.[119] Surely, the same confidence in the accurate and responsible actions of a parole board should operate in cases of incapacitation such that there should be no fear of "unwarranted" early release.[120]

---

[116] *Ibid.*, at 370.

[117] *Ibid.*, at 372.

[118] *Ibid.*, at 374.

[119] An example of this approach may be found in the British Columbia Court of Appeal decision in *R. v. Dixon* [summarized 2 W.C.B. (2d) 421], where the accused appealed a sentence of 10 years for his part in a conspiracy to import heroin. Some co-accused, who had been found by the trial judge to have been higher up in the conspiracy than the appellant, had received sentences as high as 14 years. However, because Dixon had insisted on his right to apply for, and had been granted, a severance from his co-accused on one of the counts, he was not tried and found guilty until 2 years after his co-accused had been sentenced. He argued on appeal that the 10-year concurrent sentence in practice amounted to a 12-year term, which was not justified in all of the circumstances. The court disagreed, holding that the sentence was within the range. If there was any unfairness arising from the fact that one of the principals had already been paroled, then it "was to be remedied by the National Parole Board if at all . . . if adjustments are to be made then it is for the Parole Board to make those adjustments."

[120] Remission must be viewed somewhat differently, since (absent "gating") it results in a release from confinement by entitlement, rather than through the exercise of discretion. However, release subject to mandatory supervision does not reduce a sentence, but rather changes its locus. The rigours of the mandatory supervision regime are discussed in Chapters 6 and 7.

The issue of rehabilitation is more difficult. Where there is no question of gross mental illness, we must recognize, as stated in *Luther*,[121] that the criminal law is not essentially a prophylactic instrument. There can be no question of its use to facilitate treatment. Thus, the potential for "early" release should not be a factor in determining the appropriate length of sentence. With respect to mentally ill offenders, the question must be one of danger to the community. Accordingly, the nature and circumstances of the offence and the offender should determine whether incapacitation to protect society is warranted, regardless of mental illness and treatability. As with addiction, obsessive illness that, for example, generates offences such as shoplifting, cannot be the focus of a sentence premised on rehabilitation or incapacitation. Crimes of violence committed by mentally ill offenders warrant an incapacitating sentence because of the perceived danger that the offender presents.[122] Treatability, however, should not operate to extend a sentence but rather should be considered because, if successfully treated, the offender no longer constitutes a danger. Therefore, it may be true that in this limited situation parole eligibility is relevant to ensure that a discretionary release is possible if and when success is achieved. These questions, however, become blurred by what is often an illusion that an appropriate treatment program can and will be implemented.[123]

Mary Campbell and David Cole, in an article entitled, "Conditional Release Considerations in Sentencing" argue that taking conditional release eligibility into account at the time of initial sentencing can only be justified if one accepts three assumptions:

---

[121] See *Luther, supra*, note 110.

[122] See *R. v. Robinson* (1974), 19 C.C.C. (2d) 193 (Ont. C.A.) at 198-199.

[123] In *Robinson, ibid.*, and *R. v. Deans* (1978), 37 C.C.C. (2d) 221 (Ont. C.A.), the court recognized that the relevant psychiatric programs often are not available within the penitentiary system. The court pointed to section 19 [now s. 22] of the *Penitentiary Act* as the mechanism by which a transfer to a provincial mental health treatment facility could be offered. While the mechanism exists, it is not triggered by the court's recommendation, but requires the mutual consent and will of penitentiary (and sometimes parole) officials and that of the staff of the mental health facility. A dramatic example of failure is *R. v. Poore* (Ont. C.A., August 2, 1978) in which a life sentence for manslaughter was predicated on the danger presented by the accused and psychiatric evidence which suggested that his rare disorder was treatable, but which required extensive, long-term therapy which was available at a provincial mental health centre. Regrettably, after assessment, the provincial facility rejected the prisoner and returned him to the penitentiary system where only short-term, pre-release psychiatric programs were available. Due to the life sentence, these would not commence until he had served at least 8 years. While noting the tragedy of the appellant's plight, the court dismissed his appeal against sentence.

(1) the majority of prisoners are released prior to completion of their sentence;
(2) sentencing and conditional release granting involve similar principles and objectives; and
(3) conditional release is effectively a reduction of sentence, and of the objectives to be achieved by the sentence.[124]

Relying on both empirical and conceptual arguments, the authors rejected the validity of these assumptions,[125] reaching the conclusion that a proper understanding of the respective functions of the participants precludes taking eligibility for release into account. Since the prisoner's locus of confinement, the awarding of remission, the granting of temporary absences or parole, or the application of the detention provisions of the *Parole Act* are decisions taken by other statutorily mandated decision-makers, who apply criteria which judges neither know nor are trained to understand, they conclude that judges should restrict themselves to a consideration of the appropriate sentence, rather than speculating about what may happen in the future.

7. REVOCATION OF PREVIOUS CONDITIONAL RELEASE AS A FACTOR IN SENTENCING

Two closely related questions arise on this opposite side of the equation. Can or should a judge take into account that at the time of sentencing on a new charge the offender is likely to be (or already has been) subject to the revocation of a previous release, and is therefore obligated to return to prison to serve the "remanet"[126] of the original sentence? Is the fact that an offender was on some form of conditional release at the time of the commission of the new offence an aggravating factor on sentencing?

(a) The Mechanics of Revocation[127]

Prior to October 15, 1977, full parole and mandatory supervision were deemed to be automatically "forfeited" immediately upon conviction for an indictable offence punishable by 2 or more years' imprison-

---

124 M.E. Campbell and D.P. Cole "Conditional Release Considerations in Sentencing" (1985), 42 C.R. (3d) 191, at 199.
125 *Ibid.*, at 200-206. See also *R. v. Meehan* (1990), 53 C.C.C. (3d) 496, at 500, where the Quebec Court of Appeal suggested that if a sentencing judge were to consider the possibility of parole or the crediting of remission, he would "warp the system".
126 This phrase, which is used in the jargon of sentence calculation, comes from the federal *Parole Regulations*.
127 This subject is discussed in detail in Chapters 5, 8 and 10.

ment (regardless of the length of the sentence actually imposed). Further, the offender usually did not receive any credit for the time successfully served out of custody on conditional release on the previous sentence.

Revocation of conditional release is no longer automatic upon conviction for a new offence. In the federal system, an offender's release may now be suspended . . . "when a breach of a term or condition of parole occurs or the Board or person [designated] is satisfied that it is necessary or reasonable to do so in order to prevent a breach of any term or condition of parole or to protect society".[128] The suspended offender is kept in custody until the release decision-maker decides what to do with him (regardless of whether bail is granted by the court). This decision may be made before or after new charges are disposed of by the court.[129]

(b) The Relevance of Revocation: The Totality Principle

It is a well-established principle of sentencing that the court must consider both the appropriateness of each sentence imposed on an offender and the cumulative effect of all sentences imposed.[130] Further, the totality principle applies both to sentences imposed at the same time

---

[128] *Parole Act*, s. 22(1). Revocation still remains the norm, because being convicted of a new offence is, of course, a breach of the mandatory condition of the conditional release which prescribes that the offender obey the law.

[129] An accused who insists in disposing of new charges before knowing what the Board will do with him may do so at his own peril. In *R. v. McQueen* (March 2, 1978), the Ontario Court of Appeal held:

It is submitted that although the trial judge obviously could not have taken into account on November 28th what the Parole Board did on December 29th, nevertheless *we* should do so, because, it is said, the present result is that the appellant faces sentences of two years, and 11 months respectively, and that the totality is, accordingly, too great. We do not agree with this submission. In our view, the trial judge was quite right in considering, as he obviously did, that he had his task to perform, and the Parole Board had their's. . . . If the order of things had been reversed, and the Parole Board had already acted, and in the same way as they in fact did, it would have been appropriate for the trial judge to take into consideration, in connection with the totality of the sentence he was about to impose, the fact that the appellant was going to have to return to penitentiary to serve the balance of the sentence as required by the Parole Board.

Given the authority provided to the Court of Appeal by *Code* s. 687, the court's reasoning has been criticized by Ruby as being "at the very least, irrational" (2d. ed., 1980 at 329).

[130] See D.A. Thomas, *Principles of Sentencing*, 2d ed. (London: Heinemann, 1979), p. 57 *et seq.*; see also *R. v. Switzer* (1978), 8 C.R. (3d) S-17 (Ont. C.A.).

and sentences previously imposed.[131] On this basis it has been argued that a sentencing judge must take into account the remanet (if known) of any previous sentence that the offender must serve by reason of the revocation of his conditional release, and must consider the total effect of all sentences to which the offender is then subject.[132] As a matter of strict logic, if the possibility of conditional release is irrelevant at the time of imposing the original sentence, perhaps the effect of revocation should be equally irrelevant in dealing with a remanet and a new sentence. Yet, the totality principle is by definition somewhat illogical. While it is clear that the principle operates notwithstanding the fact that appropriate sentences may have been awarded for each individual offence, why should a judge then re-examine the totality for the benefit of the offender? Thomas suggests that this is done for one (or both) of two reasons: either it is an extension of the principle of proportionality between offence and sentence in that the totality should not exceed the normal tariff for the most serious of the offences involved, or it is an extension of the practice of mitigation in that the totality should not be crushing, given the offender's record and prospects.[133]

The first explanation is not satisfying as it derives its strength from the tariff system of sentencing, which, as we have seen, is not so common in Canada as to make it a persuasive rationale. With some refinement, the "mitigation approach" is an acceptable, indeed salutary, basis for the adoption of the totality principle, albeit for reasons of policy, not logic. While logic may be desirable in the legal system, another value at work in our criminal justice system should be the avoidance of unnecessary oppression to the individual. In similar fashion, the movement away from retribution reflects the concensus that nothing is gained simply by crushing the offender.

When an offender is sentenced for a crime, the judge and the releasing authorities have separate roles to perform with regard to punishment and conditional release. If both perform their roles properly, unnecessary oppression to the prisoner will be avoided. However, when the offender is sentenced for a number of crimes, or when he has a remanet from a previous sentence, there is no one but the last sentencing

---

Thomas, *ibid.*, p. 57. In *R. v. Caskenette* [summarized 9 W.C.B. (2d) 218], the British Columbia Court of Appeal stated that "the principle of totality [is] not available to increase or inflate any one individual sentence but rather work[s] in reverse by reducing sentences which if dealt with consecutively would work an undue hardship on the accused."

[132] M.E. Campbell and D.P. Cole "Sentencing and Conditional Release" (1985) 2 *Crown's Newsletter* (Ont.) 39.

[133] Thomas, *supra*, note 130, pp. 56-61.

judge to take a global look at the position of the offender. The releasing authorities have little power,[134] and are not generally the appropriate agency, to remedy a situation where the totality of all sentences is too great. The totality principle can be justified as the one mechanism for ensuring that a person in authority examines the total effect of the amount of time to be served.

(c) Case Law

The applicability of the totality principle in conditional release revocation cases was recognized as early as 1930 in *Robinson*.[135] While on release under the *Ticket of Leave Act*,[136] the offender was sentenced to 10 years following a conviction for subornation of perjury; due to the automatic forfeiture of his original release he was also required to serve a 4½ year remanet from the previous sentence. The Ontario Court of Appeal held that the 10-year sentence by itself was appropriate, but that the totality was excessive:

> We have, however, ascertained from the trial Judge that it was not brought to his attention when sentencing the accused, that after serving a sentence of 10 years he would be obliged to undergo the further imprisonment above mentioned. If it had he doubtless would have taken that circumstance into consideration when determining the appropriate sentence, which under the circumstances we think should be that of 10 years less so much time as is equal to the unexpired portion of the sentence in respect of which he was granted a licence to be at large.[137]

Conversely a group of more recent cases from the Appeal Division of the Nova Scotia Supreme Court illustrates the considerable divergence of opinion on this issue. The relevance of the totality principle was recognized by Macdonald J.A. in *Evans*,[138] where the appellant had been convicted of assault causing bodily harm, for which he was sentenced to 18 months' imprisonment. As a result of the conviction, under the legislation in force at that time, his parole was automatically forfeited and he was additionally required to serve a 433-day remanet from the previous sentence. On an appeal against the 18-month term, speaking for the majority, Macdonald J.A. reduced the sentence so as (in part) to take into account the time to be served as a result of the forfeiture.

---

[134] They can, for example, re-credit remission lost upon revocation of conditional release. See *Parole Act*, s. 25(3) and *Gregson v. National Parole Bd.* (1982), 1 C.C.C. (3d) 13 (Fed. T.D.).

[135] *R. v. Robinson* (1930), 53 C.C.C. 173 (Ont. C.A.).

[136] R.S.C. 1927, c. 197.

[137] *Supra*, note 135, at 174-175.

[138] *R. v. Evans* (1975), 24 C.C.C. (2d) 300 (N.S. C.A.).

However, Cooper J.A., in dissent, held that to reduce a sentence because of parole forfeiture is to "in effect, lessen the sentence which the appellant was serving, albeit in the community since January 14, 1974, for the previous offences."[139] Both Cooper and Macdonald JJ.A. were able to reconsider this issue in *Jackson*.[140] While dismissing the offender's sentence appeal on its merits, Macdonald J.A. reiterated his position in *Evans*. Cooper J.A. concurred with the reasons given by Coffin J.A., who dismissed the appeal without comment on the effect of the parole revocation.

Several months later a differently constituted panel again considered the issue in *Orman*.[141] In dismissing Marcotte's sentence appeal, MacKeigan C.J.N.S. (Macdonald J.A. concurring) noted that the trial judge had relied on the majority view in *Evans* and had taken the parole forfeiture into account. Coffin J.A. concurred in result, but noted in *obiter* that he agreed with the dissenting judgment of Cooper J.A. in *Evans*. The same panel again considered this issue in *Rushton*;[142] strangely, no reference was made to *Evans*, MacKeigan C.J.N.S. simply noting for a unanimous court that the appellant would have to serve the remanet of a previous sentence as a result of the parole forfeiture.

Coffin, Cooper and Macdonald JJ.A. considered this issue yet again in *Lapierre*.[143] Coffin J.A., with whom Cooper J.A. concurred, summarized the *Evans* line of cases, and concluded that "[i]n my respectful opinion, there is a difference in the attitudes of the various courts on the application of the *Evans* principle and it should not be extended".[144] Accordingly, he again declined to rely on it, and concurred in the result of the judgment of Macdonald J.A., stating that "[i]n any event, as I understand the reasons of my brother Macdonald, he is not basing his conclusions here on *Evans*".[145] This is puzzling since Macdonald J.A. expressly stated that he *was* following *Evans* and noted that the trial judge did take into account parole forfeiture in imposing the sentence.[146]

---

[139] *Ibid.*, at 303. Cooper J.A. has misstated the essence of the totality principle, which is not directed at a particular sentence, but rather to the total effect of all sentences. The result of the application of the principle may be that one sentence, looked at in isolation, may be too low, but if the totality is deemed to be too great, the principle cannot be effected in any other way.

[140] *R. v. Jackson* (1975), 23 C.C.C. (2d) 147 (N.S. C.A.).

[141] *R. v. Orman* (1975), 25 C.C.C. (2d) 337 (N.S. C.A.).

[142] *R. v. Rushton* (1975), 13 N.S.R. (2d) 628 (N.S. C.A.).

[143] *R. v. Lapierre* (1976), 17 N.S.R. (2d) 34 (N.S. C.A.).

[144] *Ibid.*, at 38.

[145] *Ibid.*

[146] *Ibid.*, at 44, 48-51.

One year later the same panel reconsidered the issue in *Hutton*.[147] The trial judge had taken parole revocation into account as a factor in sentencing. The Crown's appeal against sentence was allowed, Coffin J.A. stating: "In my view in all the circumstances of this case, what would otherwise be a proper sentence for him should not be reduced to one of seven days by reason of the forfeiture of parole".[148] Cooper J.A. stated that he adhered to his dissent in *Evans*; nevertheless, he felt that the sentence should be increased, even taking into account the *Evans* majority, since the sentence imposed at trial was so inadequate as to reflect an error in principle. Macdonald J.A. reiterated his position in the *Evans* majority judgment.[149]

Evans was reconsidered one more time in Nova Scotia in 1981 in *Myers*,[150] where the majority held that: "[t]accused's forfeiture of parole was an irrelevant factor to sentencing except in accordance with the totality principle".[151] Pace J.A. held that parole forfeiture was completely irrelevant.

In *Keeble*,[152] the Prince Edward Island Court of Appeal adopted the *Evans* minority position, while several decisions of the Ontario Court of Appeal have been consistent with the *Evans* majority.[153] The British Columbia Court of Appeal wrestled with this issue in *Bernard*,[154] where the accused's day parole had been suspended as a result of a new charge being laid against him. At a post-suspension hearing held before the charge was disposed of, the Board decided both to revoke the day parole and to refuse to recredit any remission. Upon being apprised of these facts, the sentencing judge considered that the accused had already been sufficiently punished, and elected to impose a concurrent sentence. Upon hearing an appeal in which the Crown sought a modest consecutive term, a majority of the Court of Appeal held that while it was

---

[147] *R. v. Hutton* (1977), 36 C.C.C. (2d) 411 (N.S. C.A.).

[148] *Ibid.*, at 416. Unfortunately, this did not make it clear whether Coffin J.A. still considered parole forfeiture to be irrelevant, or whether it was relevant, but that the totality principle did not require a reduction in the total sentence in the case at bar.

[149] This same panel courageously faced this issue again later that year in *R. v. Marshall* (1977), 20 Crim. L.Q. 146, but the report of the decision merely states that "the trial judge referred to the parole forfeiture during sentencing and made no error in principle" (p. 147).

[150] *R. v. Myers* [summarized (1981), 6 W.C.B. 117 (N.S. C.A.)].

[151] *Ibid.*

[152] *R. v. Keeble* (1977), 37 C.C.C. (2d) 386 (P.E.I. C.A.).

[153] *R. v. Black* (Ont. C.A., January 10, 1975); *Ex parte Kerswill* (1975), 28 C.C.C. (2d) 362 (Ont. C.A.); *R. v. Connors* (1977), 34 C.C.C. (2d) 175 (Ont. C.A.); *R. v. Cassidy* [summarized (1977), 1 W.C.B. 489 (Ont. C.A.)]; *R. v. Forst* [summarized (1980), 4 W.C.B. 504 (Ont. C.A.)]; *R. v. Maskery* (1980), 23 Crim. L.Q. 316 (Ont. C.A.).

[154] *R. v. Bernard* [summarized (1986), 16 W.C.B. 307 (B.C. C.A.)].

not an error in principle for the sentencing judge to take the revocation into account, "some recognition must be given to the fact that it is appropriate that for this offence some time in prison must be served,"[155] and directed that the sentence be varied to one of 3 months' consecutive. Seaton J.A. concurred in result, but found it unnecessary to decide "[w]hether it is proper to give consideration, and what weight ought to be given, to the intervention of the parole authorities."[156]

While it is entirely proper that some sentencing factors may vary according to regional differences, a parolee should be able to expect that recognition of a fundamental sentencing guide such as the totality principle will not be dependent upon geography. The principle is not that the total sentence will be reduced in every parolee's case, as may have been the concern in *Keeble*, but simply that the remanet must be *considered* in any case where an offender is subject to two or more sentences.

(d) Conditional Release as an Aggravating Factor in Sentencing

It seems curious that few of the cases cited above considered that the prisoners were on some form of conditional release at the time they committed new offences to be an aggravating factor in sentencing. As Clayton Ruby notes:

> A sentence will be increased where the offender has reoffended after having been released from prison for only a short time before the new offence is committed. So too, if the offence is committed while on parole.[157]

The Saskatchewan Court of Appeal has held: "The fact that these offences were committed while the appellant was on parole evidences a failure on his part to respond to the worthwhile efforts made for his rehabilitation and reformation."[158] Courts in the Northwest Territories, Newfoundland and British Columbia have emphasized the same principle.[159] One reported decision of the Ontario Court of Appeal has attempted to balance both totality and the aggravating effect of a breach of parole.[160] In *McColl*, the trial judge had not been informed that the accused was on parole at the time of the offences with only a few days left until his warrant expiry date. The Court of Appeal concluded that this

---

[155] *Ibid.*

[156] *Ibid.*

[157] C. Ruby, *Sentencing*, 3d ed. (Toronto: Butterworths, 1987), p. 161.

[158] *R. v. Kissick* (1969), 70 W.W.R. 365 (Sask. C.A.), at 366.

[159] *R. v. Giroux* (1980), 23 A.R. 327 (N.W.T. C.A.); *R. v. Cousins* (1981), 22 C.R. (3d) 298 (Nfld. C.A.); (Case Comment) *R. v. Benedek* (1973), 15 Crim. L.Q. 259 (B.C. Co. Ct.).

[160] *R. v. McColl* (1975), 18 Crim. L.Q. 20 (Ont. C.A.).

fact was relevant to the quantum of sentence, both in terms of totality and in aggravation.[161]

While it is arguable whether being on conditional release is always an aggravating factor,[162] the proper procedure is to impose sentence for the new offence after taking into account, *inter alia*, the aggravating factor that the accused committed the offence while on conditional release, and after considering the totality of all sentences to which the offender is subject. An example of this can be found in *Gorham*,[163] where the appellant had committed two serious armed robberies after having gone unlawfully at large from a penitentiary at a point where he had an 8-year remanet. The trial judge imposed sentences for the armed robberies which, when added to the remanet, totalled 26 years. The prisoner appealed, arguing that the totality of the sentence was too severe and crushing. The Court of Appeal agreed in part, reducing the totality by 3 years. However, the court commented:

> ... the principle of totality must have a substantially reduced effect ... where a part of the total term is based upon a remnant [sic]. Neither one who is unlawfully at large nor one who is at liberty on mandatory supervision should be entitled to benefit from the remnant [sic] which must be served if a new offence is committed.[164]

8. CONCLUSION

While there are some differences between various Courts of Appeal, and even disagreements among judges of the same court, it appears that there is broad agreement that a sentencing judge is not allowed to increase a sentence which is otherwise proper in order to compensate for potential intervention by a release decision-maker. At the same time, a judge contemplating the appropriate sentence to be imposed upon a person subject to revocation of a conditional release as a result of his criminal behaviour must give some allowance for that eventuality, on the basis of the application of the totality principle.

---

[161] *Ibid.*

[162] It can be argued that an offender who is out of custody on mandatory supervision as of right should be viewed differently than the offender who is released on the "privilege" of parole. Moreover, the nature of the new offence is pertinent in determining whether an aggravating link ought to be drawn.

[163] *R. v. Gorham* (1988), 22 O.A.C. 237 (C.A.).

[164] *Ibid.*, at 238. While being unlawfully at large is clearly an aggravating factor, it is curious that the court referred to being on mandatory supervision, but not to being on parole, as a factor which should operate to decrease the application of the totality principle.

Despite these rules, however, it has been said that "[it] sometimes seems futile to try to persuade judges to completely ignore the parole system and its operation."[165] Similarly, in the course of its research the Canadian Sentencing Commission noted "there is evidence that current sentences (in this country and elsewhere) are affected by judges' perceptions about the likelihood of an early release on parole."[166]

If it is true that sentencing judges will take into account what they perceive to be the possibilities of conditional release, regardless of what they are directed to do by their Courts of Appeal, it becomes incumbent to examine the accuracy of their perceptions. In the absence of formalized and on-going dialogue and information sharing between the bench, the penal authorities and release decision-makers, it is obvious that judicial perceptions will inevitably be anecdotal and misinformed. In the Chapters which follow, we hope to take some steps to remedy these deficiencies. In our concluding chapter, we offer a model for better integration of these various decision-making functions.

---

[165] Ruby, *supra*, note 157, p. 225.

[166] J.V. Roberts, *Empirical Research on Sentencing*, Research Reports of the Canadian Sentencing Commission (Ottawa: 1988), p. 48. See also *Views of Sentencing: A Survey of Judges in Canada*, Report by the Research Staff of the Canadian Sentencing Commission (Ottawa: 1988).

3

The Prisoner Before the Courts: The Issue of Remedies

1. INTRODUCTION

This chapter examines the status of the prisoner as litigant. While the central focus of this book is release, the consideration of remedies evolves from, and applies generally to, the entire sphere of prisoner litigation. As will be shown, traditionally the absence of appropriate judicial remedies has insulated many prison issues from external scrutiny. For generations of prisoners in Canada, grievances about transfers, discipline, and ultimate release were never addressed on their merits for want of an accessible remedy. In truth, prison law in Canada has only really developed during the past decade, when laws and rules about the internal prison environment and the various aspects of conditional release could be exposed to judicial consideration, comment and intervention. Thus, this chapter is not simply an account of the development of judicial remedies; rather, it is an account of why before 1979[1] the law of imprisonment and release from imprisonment was restricted to a small set of questions about statutory entitlement. Although many important cases were decided before 1979,[2] their impact was restricted by jurisdictional and remedial controversies.

Regardless of distinctions between questions relating to the internal prison environment and those dealing with release, both share a common fundamental feature: the litigant is serving a sentence within a tightly controlled statutory regime. Both federally and provincially, a series of interacting statutes[3] provides the framework which both em-

---

[1] *Martineau v. Matsqui Institution Disciplinary Bd.*, [1980] 1 S.C.R. 602; *Nicholson v. Haldimand-Norfolk Regional Bd. of Police Cmmrs.*, [1979] 1 S.C.R. 311.

[2] *Ex parte McCaud*, [1965] 1 C.C.C. 168 (S.C.C.); *R. v. Institutional Head of Beaver Creek Correctional Camp; Ex parte MacCaud*, [1969] 1 O.R. 373 (Ont. C.A.); *Marcotte v. Canada (Dep. A.G.)* (1975), 19 C.C.C. (2d) 257 (S.C.C.); *Howarth v. National Parole Board*, [1976] 1 S.C.R. 453; *Mitchell v. R.*, [1976] 2 S.C.R. 570; *Martineau v. Matsqui Institution Inmate Disciplinary Bd.*, [1978] 1 S.C.R. 118; *McCann v. R.*, [1976] F.C. 570 (T.D.).

[3] The principal statutes are listed in Chapter 2, note 17.

powers the regimes under which sentences are served and determines the powers of releasing authorities. Historically, control and broadly-cast discretion have been the main features of this statutory framework. Of course, to the extent that statutes provided a minimum entitlement or inherent limit, courts have always been available to enforce the statute.[4] But in Canada, prior to 1979, the decision-making authority of institutional administrators and releasing agencies was exercised in private spaces without the obligation to conform with external standards or satisfy external inspection. Now, as a result of the expanded scope of *certiorari*,[5] the recognition of the common-law duty to act fairly[6] and the entrenchment of the *Canadian Charter of Rights and Freedoms*,[7] the judiciary has assumed a more active role in mapping the contours of powers, rights and privileges which characterize imprisonment in Canada. This chapter is intended to explain the past impact of remedial obstacles on the development of prison law and to help chart the future directions of litigious strategies and judicial resolutions.

2. JUDICIAL REVIEW AND THE DEVELOPMENT OF THE DUTY TO ACT FAIRLY

As a term of art, judicial review describes the avenue by which courts supervise the exercise of powers delegated to statutory, subordinate decision-makers.[8] It is important to distinguish this form of review from an appellate vehicle where a court is, within limits, required to re-examine the merits of a previously made decision in order to confirm or reverse it.[9] Supervisory review is a tool to ensure that subordinate authorities have carried out the powers granted to them by legislation without over-stepping, with proper consideration of the relevant factors and according to the process contemplated by the enabling legislation. Its purpose is to preserve the jurisdictional integrity of tribunals and decision-makers invested with delegated authority.

The major concerns of judicial review have been jurisdiction and process. For the most part, its history has been married to the develop-

---

4   See, for example, *Marcotte, supra,* note 2.

5   See *Martineau v. Matsqui Institution Disciplinary Bd., supra,* note 1.

6   See *Nicholson v. Haldimand-Norfolk Regional Bd. of Police Cmmrs., supra,* note 1.

7   Being Part I of the *Constitution Act, 1982* [enacted by the *Canada Act, 1982* (U.K.), c. 11, s. 1].

8   See generally J.M. Evans, H.N. Janisch, D.J. Mullan and R.C.B. Risk, *Administrative Law: Cases, Text and Materials,* 3d ed. (Toronto: Emond Montgomery, 1989); J.M. Evans, *DeSmith's Judicial Review of Administrative Action,* 4th ed. (London: Stevens & Sons, 1980).

9   This distinction is often difficult for prisoners and prison personnel to grasp.

ment of the prerogative writs,[10] principally *certiorari* and prohibition. The prerogative writs will be discussed more thoroughly later in this chapter.[11] For now, it is sufficient to explain their functions in simplified terms. *Certiorari* commenced as the form of royal demand for information and later became the instrument for reviewing orders and convictions of inferior tribunals. Prohibition was available before a decision was made to prevent an inferior tribunal from acting in excess of its jurisdiction.

Traditionally, not all public authorities and decision-makers were amenable to *certiorari* and prohibition. These writs applied only with respect to decision-makers who were required, either by statute or common law, to act in a judicial or quasi-judicial manner. A clear expression of this limited application can be found in the judgment of Lord Atkin in the *Electricity Commissioners*[12] case:

> . . . the operation of the writs has extended to control the proceedings of bodies which do not claim to be, and would not be recognized as, Courts of Justice. Wherever any body of persons having legal authority to determine questions affecting the rights of subjects, and having the duty to act judicially, act in excess of their legal authority they are subject to the controlling jurisdiction of the King's Bench Division exercised in these writs.[13]

For many decades, this statement alone provided an obstacle to judicial review of many statutory and public decision-makers since it appeared to establish two pre-conditions: (1) was there a duty to act judicially?; and (2) did the decision-maker determine rights?[14] A process could be insulated from review simply by characterizing its function as not carrying a duty to act judicially or quasi-judicially, or by defining the subject matter as a privilege, licence, benefit or interest, rather than a right.

The real impact of a denial of judicial review based on categorization of function or definition of subject matter was the absence of an

---

10   The phrase "prerogative writ" refers to orders which now emanate from superior courts, but which, in their historical origin, were issued by the sovereign as instruments for superintending "the due course of justice and administration": see S.A. DeSmith, *The Prerogative Writs* (1951-1953), 11 Cambridge L.J. 40, reprinted as Appendix 1 to the 4th Edition of *DeSmith's Judicial Review of Administrative Action, supra*, note 8.

11   See *infra*, pp. 64-82.

12   *R. v. Electricity Cmmrs.; Ex parte London Electricity Joint Committee Co. (1920)*, [1924] 1 K.B. 171.

13   *Ibid.*, at 205.

14   Another issue flowing from this statement which, though less relevant in prison litigation, but a serious obstacle in other administrative law contexts, is whether the function exercised is actually determinative, as compared to one of investigation or recommendation.

outside supervising role to scrutinize the actions of decision-makers. This supervisory role, where it applied, existed to preserve jurisdictional integrity. An examination of the traditional grounds for judicial review reveals the breadth of this conception of jurisdiction.[15] First, the writs exist to ensure that the tribunal or authority in question does not exceed the power granted to it or decline to exercise it. Secondly, there are procedural grounds for review. These flow from the recognition that the inferior tribunals embraced by the writs, until recently, were restricted to those, like magistrates or justices of the peace, who carried out adjudicative functions invoking procedures of fact-finding, interpretation and judgment akin to those found in courts. Hence, the label of judicial or quasi-judicial was developed, carrying with it procedural obligations known compendiously as natural justice. In order to exercise its jurisdiction properly and legally, an inferior tribunal needed to make available and enforce the procedural elements known as natural justice. The most fundamental aspect of natural justice is described by the maxim *audi alteram partem* which, in its most basic form, requires giving a party notice of allegations against him and an opportunity to respond to them.

Historically, there have been other grounds of review which are conceptually related to the proper exercise of jurisdiction. Generally, these can be considered as examples of abuse of discretionary power, and would include such issues as bad faith, irrelevant or extraneous considerations, and unreasonableness. As well, review based on the ground of no evidence in support of the decision fits into the category of jurisdiction-related issues. Perhaps distinct is the ground known as error of law on the face of the record, which permitted judicial intervention in some cases to correct a legal error.[16] Later, we shall consider the grounds for review in greater detail and will explain the limited applicability of this ground, particularly in light of privative clauses designed to insulate a decision-maker from a re-examination of non-jurisdictional errors.[17]

---

[15] See generally J.M. Evans, *Administrative Law, supra*, note 8; *DeSmith's Judicial Review of Administrative Action, supra*, note 8. See also H.W. Wade, *Administrative Law*, 5th ed. (Oxford: Clarendon Press; New York: Oxford University Press, 1982).

[16] This review power allows that where an error of law is apparent on the face of the record *certiorari* will lie to quash the decision of a statutory tribunal. If the error is one of fact, however, this will only be the case where the error goes to the jurisdiction of the tribunal, although the distinction between law and fact is far from settled. Beyond the decision itself, with any reasons which are incorporated into the record, the question as to what documents constitute the formal record of the decision which a court may examine for an error of law is open to argument. See *DeSmith's Judicial Review of Administrative Action, supra*, note 8, pp. 88-89; 294-304; and Evans, *Administrative Law, supra*, note 8, pp. 440-447.

[17] Legislation may contain clauses which appear to protect the decisions of an admin-

For the most part, it is safe to say that the traditional scope of judicial review has been directed to inquiring into the processes of inferior tribunals to ensure that they have acted within the authority delegated to them and in a manner that accords with some conception of natural justice.

According to the system of classification attributed to the *Electricity Commissioners* case, a vast array of decision-makers operated beyond the reach of judicial review. These included bodies exercising executive, legislative, investigative and recommending functions. More importantly, for our purposes, it included individuals and bodies classified as administrative because they had been given authority to administer institutions or agencies with a broad discretion as to how the statutory mandate should be exercised. Anyone subject to a decision from an authority whose mandate did not conform with the notion of an adjudicative model and, hence, could not be characterized as judicial or quasi-judicial in nature, was precluded from seeking judicial intervention. It takes little imagination to appreciate the set of people left with no judicial avenue for their grievances: for example, applicants for licences, recipients of social assistance, hospital patients, dismissed public employees, members of professional or trade associations, and prisoners. Judicial review was limited by classification, and those grievors who fell outside the circle were left only with political and executive processes to rectify bad administration, unfair treatment and erroneous decisions.

For the prisoner, the denial of access to judicial review and the concomitant procedural protections of natural justice arose from the simple application of this classification of function. A leading example was the 1964 case of *Ex parte McCaud.*[18] A prisoner applied for a writ of *habeas corpus* to a single judge of the Supreme Court of Canada on the grounds that the failure to give reasons and afford an opportunity to be heard prior to revocation of parole was a denial of natural justice and contravened section 2(*e*) of the *Canadian Bill of Rights.*[19] Without any reasoning or authority, Spence J. described parole as an "administrative matter" and stated that the protections of the *Bill of Rights* did not apply

---

istrative agency by stating that such decisions shall be final and not challengeable in any legal proceedings whatsoever, whether by way of prohibition, *certiorari*, declaration or injunction. Courts have usually interpreted such clauses as excluding their jurisdiction to review an error of law on the face of the record, but not their power to set aside those decisions which are outside the jurisdiction of the tribunal in question; those decisions being null and void, they are merely "purported" decisions. See Evans, *Administrative Law, supra*, note 8, p. 441; *DeSmith's Judicial Review of Administrative Action, supra*, note 8, pp. 370-375.

18 *Supra*, note 2.

19 S.C. 1960, c. 44 [see R.S.C. 1985, Appendix III].

to revocation by the Parole Board.[20] An appeal from this decision was dismissed without reasons by a five person panel of the Supreme Court.[21] From then on, the mere assertion of an "administrative" function insulated the Board from judicial review.

Inside the prison, similar results occurred. Remission could be forfeited by an internal disciplinary process without the prisoner having heard the evidence against him;[22] he could be transferred to higher security, even to another part of the country, without reasons;[23] he could be subjected to long periods of dissociation solely on the basis of a warden's opinion that the "good order of the institution" required it;[24] and visiting privileges could be terminated at will.[25]

Regimes of imprisonment are rife with tensions, rumours, false allegations and a general mistrust between the kept and their keepers. It is easy to appreciate the levels of unresolved hostility generated by adverse decisions which affect the daily living environment, contact with family, the likelihood of release on parole, and even eventual release due to accumulated remission. Insulation from judicial review is more than simply the unavailability of legal recourse. Within the hidden processes of imprisonment, the absence of external scrutiny exacerbates inherent tensions and entrenches the dichotomy between the powerful and the powerless.

In England, in 1964, a different view of the traditional classification of function scheme was offered by Lord Reid in *Ridge v. Baldwin.*[26] He concluded that courts had misunderstood the dictum of Atkin L.J. in the *Electricity Commissioners* case. In his view, subsequent cases had misinterpreted Lord Atkin by requiring a body to have both the authority to affect rights and some "super-added quality" that could be described as the duty to act judicially before judicial review was available.[27] Looking at both the judgments of Atkin L.J. and Bankes L.J. in the *Electricity Commissioners* case, he concluded that they inferred "a judicial element from the nature of the power".[28] In rejecting the need for a "super-added" judicial quality found somewhere in the statutory structure, Lord Reid articulated a functional analysis which encouraged courts to infer a duty to act judicially from the nature of the power exercised and

---

20 *Ex parte McCaud, supra*, note 2, at 169.
21 *McCaud v. R.*, [1964] C.L.R. viii.
22 *Martineau v. Matsqui Institution Inmate Disciplinary Bd., supra*, note 2.
23 *Re Anaskan and R.* (1977), 34 C.C.C. (2d) 361 (Ont. C.A.).
24 *Kosobook v. Canada (Solicitor General)*, [1976] 1 F.C. 540 (T.D.).
25 *Culhane v. B.C. (A.G.)* (1980), 51 C.C.C. (2d) 213 (B.C.C.A.).
26 [1964] A.C. 40 (H.L.).
27 *Ibid.*, at 74-79.
28 *Ibid.*, at 76.

its impact on the rights of individuals.[29] On the merits of the case, he concluded that a local Watch Committee could not dismiss a chief constable unless they "have informed the constable of the grounds on which they propose to proceed and have given him a proper opportunity to present his case in defence."[30] Although permitting judicial review, *Ridge v. Baldwin* still retained the traditional classification scheme by which some processes attracted natural justice protections, while others carried on as administrative functions without procedural obligations. The case, however, focussed judicial interest on the internal processes of decision-makers. It diverted attention from structure to function and upgraded the importance of the issue at stake as a factor in determining the availability of judicial review.

After *Ridge v. Baldwin*, English judges began to question the anomalous results of the traditional classification scheme. Although it had always been agreed that decision-makers, even if not required to act judicially, were required to act in good faith, it was not until 1967 that that same measure of procedural content was added to the notion of good faith. In *Re H.K. (An Infant)*,[31] Lord Parker C.J. clutched at the remaining threads of the rigid classification scheme by concluding that an immigration officer was not required to act in judicial or quasi-judicial capacity when considering the admissibility of an immigrant to the United Kingdom. But this did not end the matter. He stated:

> Good administration and an honest or bona fide decision must, as it seems to me, require not merely impartiality, nor merely bringing one's mind to bear on the problem, but acting fairly; and to the limited extent that the circumstances of any particular case allow, and within the legislative framework under which the administrator is working only to that limited, extent do the so-called rules of natural justice apply, which in a case such as this is merely a duty to act fairly.[32]

Ultimately, he dismissed the application on the basis that the immigrant had been afforded a fair opportunity to explain his situation even though a formal hearing was not conducted.[33] In a subsequent case, *Schmidt v. Secretary of State For Home Affairs*,[34] Lord Denning expressly rejected the relevance of distinguishing between judicial and administrative functions and accepted the existence of a general duty to act fairly which imposed some procedural obligations on all decision-makers.[35]

---

[29] *Ibid.*, at 76.
[30] *Ibid.*, at 79.
[31] [1967] 2 Q.B. 617.
[32] *Ibid.*, at 630.
[33] *Ibid.*, at 631.
[34] [1969] 2 Ch. 149.
[35] *Ibid.*, at 170-171.

By 1975, Professor David Mullan had found 18 reported English decisions which he characterized as having "recognized in some form or other the theory of procedural fairness".[36] To this list one should add the judgment of Lord Morris sitting on the Judicial Committee of the Privy Council on a case from New Zealand[37] involving the suspension of a teacher. Lord Morris capsulized the fundamental principle as follows:

> Natural justice is but fairness writ large and juridically. It has been described as "fair play in action." Nor is it a leaven to be associated only with judicial or quasi-judicial occasions. But as was pointed out by Tucker L.J. in *Russell v. Duke of Norfolk* [1949] 1 All E.R. 109, 118, the requirements of natural justice must depend on the circumstances of each particular case and the subject matter under consideration.[38]

3. THE PRISONERS' STRUGGLE FOR JUDICIAL REVIEW IN CANADA

Following *Ridge v. Baldwin*, the Ontario Court of Appeal attempted to apply a functional analysis to the prison disciplinary context in *R. v. Beaver Creek Correctional Camp; Ex parte MacCaud*.[39] The case examined the role of an institutional head, or warden, and the kinds of interests affected by disciplinary decisions. Having been the subject of disciplinary action, the prisoner applied in person for review by *certiorari*, which application was dismissed. An appeal was launched to the Ontario Court of Appeal, raising the single issue as to whether the institutional head of a penitentiary acting in his disciplinary capacity was amenable to *certiorari*. The court ignored any notion of a disciplinary exception which would absolutely insulate decisions for *certiorari*.[40] Instead, it developed an ambitious (yet ultimately unrealistic) view of prisons, which divided issues into those which affected the prisoner *qua* citizen and those which related to the prisoner as prisoner.[41] The court concluded that a process which affected the prisoner in his capacity as citizen—the prisoner's civil rights—could be reviewed by *certiorari*. In so doing, the court expressly recognized the fundamental

---

36 D.J. Mullan, "Fairness: The New Natural Justice" (1975) 25 U.T.L.J. 251, at 305-306.

37 *Furnell v. Whangarei High Schools Bd.*, [1973] A.C. 660 (P.C.).

38 *Ibid.*, at 679.

39 [1969] 1 O.R. 373 (Ont. C.A.).

40 In cases involving organizations such as the army or police, courts have at times used the notion of contractual commitment to rules of internal discipline to support the argument for a disciplinary exception (see for example *R. v. White*, [1956] S.C.R. 154). The Supreme Court of Canada, however, expressly denied the validity of such reasoning in the prison setting in *Martineau v. Matsqui Disciplinary Bd.*, [1980] 1 S.C.R. 602, at 624-628.

41 *Supra*, note 39, at 378.

element of any concept of prisoner's rights, that being the retention of all civil rights of citizens except those removed expressly by law or as a necessary incident of confinement.[42]

While this new subspecies of classification based on rights appeared to have the potential of opening up a role for judicial review, the actual delineation of included categories diminished substantially the impact of this attempted functional analysis. Only the forfeiture of statutory remission—because its effect was to lengthen the period of confinement—was viewed as an issue of civil rights.[43] With the exception of statutory rights, all other internal issues relating to the place and matter of confinement remained insulated from judicial review and entirely within the discretion of institutional authorities without any obligation to provide procedural safeguards.[44]

As exemplified by *Beaver Creek*, Canadian courts continued to operate under the burden of classification as the obstacle to judicial review.[45] Some sensitivity to the anomaly of requiring protection when a decision-maker fell on one side of the classification line can be found in the judgment of Pennell J. in *Beauchamp*,[46] an application for *habeas corpus* where a parolee argued that he was entitled to know the reasons for suspension and entitled to a hearing before parole could be revoked. Feeling bound by the administrative classification of the parole process by the Supreme Court of Canada in *McCaud*, Pennell J. dismissed the application but stated his view "that the person designate and the Board must act fairly in accordance with the principles of proper justice."[47] Looking at the impact of the Parole Board decision, he stated:

> ... the fact remains that the revocation of parole is akin to a punitive measure which carries with it a duty to act fairly. There is always a reasonable chance that a consideration of the inmate's side of the story might alter the result.[48]

In recognizing that the state of the law of remedies precluded him from granting relief, Pennell J. seemed to suggest that another remedy must be available. But if not *habeas corpus*, and not *certiorari*, what forum was left for a prisoner to take his claim?

---

[42] *Supra*, note 39, at 378-379.

[43] *Supra*, note 39, at 379.

[44] *Supra*, note 39, at 381-382.

[45] See *Martineau v. Matsqui Institution Inmate Disciplinary Bd.*, [1978] 1 S.C.R. 118; *Re Anaskan and R., supra*, note 23; *Matsqui Institution Disciplinary Bd. v. Martineau*, [1978] 2 F.C. 637 (C.A.).

[46] *Ex parte Beauchamp*, [1970] 3 O.R. 607 (H.C.).

[47] *Ibid.*, at 611.

[48] *Ibid.*, at 612. It is perhaps noteworthy that before his appointment to the Bench, Pennell J. had for a time been Solicitor General of Canada.

In 1971, the creation of the Federal Court of Canada[49] established a new forum for litigation for prisoners in federal penitentiaries or those subject to the control of the National Parole Board. Administrative law reform in the federal sphere moved judicial review of federal decision-makers from the jurisdiction of the provincial superior courts to the Federal Court. "The Federal Court, Trial Division was given exclusive original jurisdiction" to issue the prerogative writs of *certiorari*, prohibition and *mandamus* as well as declaratory relief against any "federal board, commission or other tribunal".[50] Significantly absent from the list of remedies in the Trial Division's arsenal was the writ of *habeas corpus*, the historical vehicle for challenging illegal confinement, which remained within the sole jurisdiction of the superior courts.[51]

Although *certiorari* seemed to be foreclosed to prisoners as a result of the Supreme Court's retention of the classification scheme, section 28 of the *Federal Court Act* appeared to create a new administrative law remedy:

> (1) . . . the Court of Appeal has jurisdiction to hear and determine an application to review and set aside a decision or order, *other than a decision or order of an administrative nature not required by law to be made on a judicial or quasi-judicial basis.* [Emphasis added.]

Given the emerging common-law duty to act fairly in England, and the apparent scope for review reflected by the grounds contained in section 28, this new remedy presented a potential avenue for prisoners' grievances. Around the same time, the establishment of provincial legal aid schemes and, more importantly, the beginning of specialized legal services projects for prisoners provided access to counsel and legal expertise.[52] Further encouragement flowed north as the United States

---

49 For a descriptive account see W.R. Jackett, "The Federal Court of Appeal" (1973) 11 Osgoode Hall L.J. 233-73. For more critical analysis see D.J. Mullan, "The *Federal Court Act*: A Misguided Attempt at Administrative Law Reform" (1973) 23 U.T.L.J. 14-53; N.M. Fera, "The Federal Court of Canada: A Critical Look at its Jurisdiction" (1973) 6 Ottawa L. Rev.; Law Reform Commission of Canada, "Working Paper 18: Federal Court—Judicial Review", Ottawa, 1977.

50 *Federal Court Act*, R.S.C. 1970, c. 10 (2nd Supp.) [now R.S.C. 1985, c. F-7], ss. 18, 20.

51 *Cavanaugh v. Cmmr. of Penitentiaries*, [1974] 1 F.C. 515 (T.D.); *Noonan v. National Parole Bd.*, [1983] 2 F.C. 772 (C.A.).

52 In 1967, the Ontario Legal Aid Plan became the first provincial plan to pay lawyers to handle both civil and criminal cases, becoming the "flagship" of legal aid plans in Canada. Thereafter all 10 provinces reviewed their provision of subsidized legal services and have established plans to provide similar legal services. The federal government increased its commitment in 1972 by agreeing to share the cost of services in criminal matters. Increased awareness on all levels thus led to a rapid expansion of services during the 1970's. (See generally F.H. Zemans, "Legal Aid and Legal Advice in Canada" 16 Osgoode Hall L.J. 663; Report of the Commission on United Funding,

Supreme Court began to reject the "hands off" attitude towards prisoners by entertaining constitutionally-based due process claims in respect of parole revocations[53] and the forfeiture of remission through disciplinary offences.[54] The key, however, to the availability of the section 28 remedy lay in asking whether the decision in question was "*required by law to be made on a judicial or quasi-judicial basis.*"

This premature optimism quickly dissolved as the Federal Court of Canada became entangled in a series of cases which turned on jurisdictional and procedural issues arising from the specific wording and structure of the new Act. In *Howarth v. National Parole Board*,[55] a prisoner attempted to use section 28 to obtain an order setting aside a revocation of parole on the ground that the Board failed to observe the principles of natural justice. On the facts, it was clear that the prisoner had not been given any reasons for the revocation, nor was he given an opportunity to be heard.[56] The claim had been dismissed almost out of hand by the Federal Court of Appeal.[57]

On appeal, the case represented the Supreme Court of Canada's first opportunity to address the scope of the new section 28 remedy. It also provided the court with a chance to re-think the foreclosure of Parole Board decision-making from review in the light of post-*McCaud* amendments to the *Parole Act*[58] and the articulation of a general duty of fairness found in recent English decisions. Pigeon J., writing for the majority, concluded that there was no reason to reconsider the conclusion expressed in *McCaud* that a decision to revoke parole was "not in any way a judicial determination";[59] hence, section 28 review was not available.

In dissent, Dickson J. embarked on a functional analysis as suggested by *Ridge v. Baldwin*. He stated that the "seriousness of the consequence or deprivation for the individual affected by the decision

---

S.G.M. Grange, Commissioner.) At the same time specialized legal services projects developed to provide legal help to those whom the legal aid plans could not reach. The Parkdale Community Legal Services Project at Osgoode Hall Law School was the first of its type in Ontario and became the model for others, including legal clinics providing services to prisoners. While such clinics existed for a time in New Brunswick, Saskatchewan and Alberta, only the Queen's University Correctional Law Project, the British Columbia Prison Services Project, and Legal Aid Manitoba currently provide a range of services to prisoners through clinic models.

53 *Morrissey v. Brewer* (1972), 408 U.S. 471.
54 *Wolff v. McDonnell* (1974), 418 U.S. 539.
55 [1976] 1 S.C.R. 453.
56 *Ibid.*, at 457.
57 [1973] F.C. 1018 (C.A.).
58 R.S.C. 1970, c. P-2 [now R.S.C. 1985, c. P-2].
59 *Supra*, note 55, at 472-473.

of the board or tribunal exercising statutory powers is manifestly the principle factor in determining whether the board or other tribunal is required to act judicially or quasi-judicially."[60] Recognizing the loss of personal liberty which flowed necessarily from a revocation decision, and after considering the statutory process of suspension and revocation and the forfeiture of all statutory remission coincident upon revocation, he concluded that "one need not look far to find within the function of the National Parole Board, having regard to the nature of its duties and the disciplinary effect of its order, identifiable judicial features."[61]

The majority position was the subject of substantial criticism;[62] subsequent developments make it unnecessary to re-hash its deficiencies. As the first salvo in a dynamic juridical process that consumed over a decade of Canadian prison litigation, a number of useful observations can be made about *Howarth*. First, Pigeon J. made passing reference to "cases dealing with the duty of fairness lying upon all administrative agencies".[64] While considering them irrelevant to the availability of the statutory remedy in section 28, he concluded his judgment by expressly indicating that he was offering no view on the scope of other remedies which might be available in the Trial Division.[65] Second, it was curious that the majority would rely on *McCaud*, while its author, Spence J., recanted from his earlier view[66] and joined with Dickson J. and Laskin C.J.C. in inferring a quasi-judicial function. Moreover, while Dickson J.'s dissent appeared to replicate the traditional classification process in asking whether a judicial or quasi-judicial function could be inferred, he specifically related his inquiry to the statutory requirements of section 28.[67] Another precursor of future developments can be found in Beetz J.'s brief addendum to the majority view in which he rejected the argument that amendments to the *Parole Act* making the loss of statutory remission automatic upon revocation had changed the nature of the revocation process, a factor which had influenced Spence J. to change his position.[68] From Beetz J.'s perspective one could anticipate reluctance to accept the *Beaver Creek* view that the loss of liberty generally, and the loss of statutory remission in particular, compelled the recognition of a duty to act judicially.

---

[60] *Supra*, note 55, at 459-460.
[61] *Supra*, note 55, at 469.
[62] See R.R. Price, "Doing Justice to Corrections?" (1977) 3 Queen's L.J. 214-294; D.J. Mullan, "Fairness, The New Natural Justice" (1975) 25 U.T.L.J. 251.
No footnote 63.
[64] *Supra*, note 55, at 472.
[65] *Supra*, note 55, at 475.
[66] *Supra*, note 55, at 456.
[67] *Supra*, note 55, at 469-470.
[68] *Supra*, note 55, at 475-476.

After *Howarth*, the sense of cynicism about the evolution of an appropriate remedy for prisoners was compounded by the Supreme Court's dismissal of a similar claim brought by way of *habeas corpus* in the case of *Mitchell*.[69] The only sources of optimism were the dissenting judgments of Dickson J. and Laskin C.J.C. in *Howarth*[70] and *Mitchell*[71] respectively. Although Dickson J. did not advert specifically to a duty to act fairly, the progressive quality of his opinion was evident from the functional analysis he employed.[72] In *Mitchell*, Laskin C.J.C. attempted to set adrift the traditional classification scheme as the barrier to judicial review by stating:

> The *Howarth* case appears to me to have proceeded as much on a classification of the Board as not being a judicial or quasi-judicial tribunal as on it being involved in an exercise of administrative authority only. I do not think it follows that a denial of judicial or quasi-judicial status to a tribunal relieves it from observance of some at least of the requirements of natural justice .... Whether a hearing must be given, whether at least an opportunity must be given in some other way to meet an adverse decision or proposed decision, should not be determined merely by a classification of the tribunal so as to carry the result by the mere fact of classification.[73]

Of course, during the same period some lower court decisions made reference to fairness in prison cases, but, with rare exceptions,[74] these were offered without procedural content and cast simply in terms of a requirement that the tribunal operate in good faith—that is, without malice or caprice. Prison lawyers continued unsuccessfully in their efforts to open up internal prison and parole processes to review.[75] Ultimately, the successful protagonist in this struggle arrived in the unlikely uniform of a police officer.

Arthur Gwynne Nicholson was a probationary police officer who had been discharged after 15 months of service without any opportunity to make submissions in response. The Ontario *Police Act*[76] and its

---

[69] [1976] 2 S.C.R. 570. This case is discussed *infra* at p. 93.

[70] *Supra*, note 55, at 456.

[71] *Supra*, note 69, at 574.

[72] *Supra*, note 55, at 462 et seq.

[73] *Supra*, note 69, at 579-580.

[74] See *Ex parte Beauchamp*, [1970] 3 O.R. 607 (H.C.); *Ex parte McGrath* (1976), 23 C.C.C. (2d) 214 (B.C.S.C.).

[75] In retrospect, declaratory relief was probably available as an avenue for pursuing a claim of fairness, but was not sought for a variety of reasons, for the most part relating to the cost, procedure and delay involved in such an action. As well, a declaration that fairness was owed would be meaningless without giving content to fairness. This goal, it was felt, could only be achieved through an extension of the administrative law concept of natural justice. Thus, the focus of interest was the recognition of an administrative law remedy.

[76] R.S.O. 1970, c. 351.

regulations required notice and a hearing as pre-conditions for the dismissal of an officer with more than 18 months' service, but was silent with respect to probationary officers. Because of the *Judicial Review Procedure Act*[77] in Ontario, there was no question that the Divisional Court had jurisdiction to hear the application for judicial review. The issue, however, was whether a duty to act fairly required the Board of Commissioners of Police to extend fair procedures to Nicholson. While he succeeded in the Divisional Court,[78] this decision was reversed by the Ontario Court of Appeal, which concluded that "the Board may act as it was entitled to act at common law, *i.e.*, without the necessity of prior notice of allegations or of a hearing . . . ."[79] In a 5-4 decision, with the majority speaking through the Chief Justice, the Supreme Court accepted that the decision-maker was required to give the officer reasons for his discharge and provide an opportunity, orally or in writing, for him to respond.[80] Laskin C.J.C. stated:

> In short, I am of the opinion that although the appellant clearly cannot claim the procedural protections afforded to a constable with more than eighteen months' service, he cannot be denied any protection. He should be treated "fairly" not arbitrarily. I accept, therefore, for present purposes and as a common law principle what Megarry J. accepted in *Bates v. Lord Hailsham,* at p. 1378, "that in the sphere of the so-called quasi-judicial the rules of natural justice run, and that in the administrative or executive field there is a general duty of fairness".[81]

The acceptance by the Supreme Court of a duty of fairness was premised on

> . . . the realization that the classification of statutory functions as judicial, quasi-judicial or administrative is often very difficult, to say the least; and to endow some with procedural protection while denying others any at all would work injustice when the results of statutory decisions raise the same serious consequences for those adversely affected, regardless of the classification of the function in question . . . .[82]

---

[77] S.O. 1971, c. 48. The Act allows an applicant to seek judicial review of a decision made by a statutory tribunal in Ontario. Its form of remedy embraces relief in the nature of both *certiorari* and declaration, and in any case where a declaration was previously available the reviewing court is empowered to quash instead of merely declaring. Thus, the issue as to whether appropriate relief at common law was *certiorari* or a declaration did not arise.

[78] *Re Nicholson and Haldimand-Norfolk Regional Bd. of Police Commrs.* (1975), 9 O.R. (2d) 481 (Div. Ct.).

[79] (1976), 12 O.R. (2d) 337 (C.A.), at 346.

[80] [1979] 1 S.C.R. 311.

[81] *Ibid.*, at 324.

[82] *Ibid.*, at 325.

The judgment in *Nicholson* did not, by itself, immediately transform the prisoner into a welcomed litigant with a receptive forum. Although the *Judicial Review Procedure Act* in Ontario provided a statutory remedy within the provincial sphere, the Trial Division of the Federal Court was still faced with a decision of its Court of Appeal upholding the distinction that the common-law remedy of *certiorari* was only available in respect of decisions required to be made on a judicial or quasi-judicial basis.[83] Other impediments to relief included the argument that only decisions which affected rights were amenable to *certiorari* and the vague notion of a "disciplinary exception". The answer to whether the Supreme Court of Canada would recognize an effective avenue of relief for prisoners did not arrive until the end of 1979, after Thomas Martineau's second trip to Ottawa over a disciplinary conviction entered some 4 years earlier. As will be shown, the judgment in *Martineau (No. 2)*[84] truly represented the beginning of a new era in prison litigation in Canada.

4. MARTINEAU v. MATSQUI INSTITUTION DISCIPLINARY BOARD

In 1975, Thomas Martineau and Robert Butters, prisoners at Matsqui Institution, were charged with two disciplinary offences in the "flagrant or serious" category: being two prisoners in a cell and committing an indecent act. During the hearing, each prisoner was asked to leave the room while the other was giving evidence.[85] Ultimately, both were convicted of a lesser and somewhat unusual offence described as "being in an indecent position". They were sentenced to serve 15 days in punitive dissociation. The procedure for conducting a hearing was set out in "Commissioner's Directive 213" which, at the time, included such fundamental provisions as requiring that the prisoner receive written notice of the charge against him, that evidence be given in the presence of the prisoner and that the prisoner be given an opportunity to make full answer and defence to the charge.[86] For procedural reasons, two applications were commenced challenging the conviction, both by

---

[83] *Martineau v. Matsqui Institution Disciplinary Bd.* in the Federal Court of Appeal, [1978] 2 F.C. 637 (hereinafter referred to as *Martineau (No. 2)*), reversing the judgment of Mahoney J. [1978] 1 F.C. 312, which recognized jurisdiction in the Trial Division of the Federal Court. See discussion *infra* at 54.

[84] *Martineau v. Matsqui Institution Disciplinary Bd.*, [1980] 1 S.C.R. 602 (hereinafter referred to as *Martineau (No. 2)*).

[85] See *Martineau v. Matsqui Institution Inmate Disciplinary Bd.*, [1976] 2 F.C. 198 (C.A.), at 199-210.

[86] *Ibid.*, at 207.

way of section 28 of the *Federal Court Act* and also by seeking relief in the nature of *certiorari* in the Trial Division. Eventually, as we have seen, the section 28 application ended without a consideration of the merits when the Supreme Court ruled that the Federal Court of Appeal had no jurisdiction to hear the matter since the decision was not one required by law to be made on a judicial or quasi-judicial basis.[87] The majority decision was premised on the narrow conclusion that the Commissioner's Directives were not law and, hence, did not create any legal requirement to comply with the adjudicative model which they described.[88] This restrictive conception of the threshold to section 28 has been the subject of much academic criticism.[89] In his dissenting judgment, Laskin C.J.C. characterized it as being "much too nihilistic a view of law" for him to accept.[90]

Martineau, however, persevered and resurrected his application for relief pursuant to section 18 of the *Federal Court Act*, which had been held in abeyance pending the result of the section 28 application. Using Rule 474 of the *Federal Court Rules*, a preliminary question of law was set down posing the narrow issue of whether jurisdiction existed within the Trial Division to hear an application for relief in the nature of *certiorari* based on an obligation of procedural fairness.[91] In the first instance, Mahoney J. answered the jurisdictional question affirmatively. He concluded:

> . . . it is manifest that the law envisages some process by which an inmate is to be determined to have committed a disciplinary offence, prescribed by law, as a condition precedent to the imposition of a punishment, also prescribed by law.[92]

Forcefully, he commented that it would be repugnant to hold that a public body imposing punishment was not bound by a duty to act fairly.[93] Written 2 years before the Supreme Court's decision in *Nicholson*, Mahoney J. foreshadowed the acceptance of a general duty to act fairly with procedural obligations, an alleged breach of which could be challenged by *certiorari*. This view, however, was rejected by the Federal Court of Appeal in a brief judgment delivered by Jackett C.J.F.C.[94] The

---

[87]   *Martineau v. Matsqui Institution Inmate Disciplinary Bd.*, [1978] 1 S.C.R. 118.

[88]   *Ibid.*, at 129, per Pigeon J.

[89]   See D.J. Mullan, "*Martineau & Butters v. Matsqui Institution Inmate Disciplinary Board*," (1978) 24 McGill L.J. 92; R.R. Price, "Doing Justice to Corrections?", *supra*, note 62.

[90]   *Supra*, note 87, at 123.

[91]   [1978] 1 F.C. 312 (T.D.), referring to *Federal Court Rules*, C.R.C. 1978, c. 663.

[92]   *Ibid.*, at 317.

[93]   *Ibid.*, at 318-319.

[94]   *Martineau (No. 2)*, [1978] 2 F.C. 637 (C.A.).

court held that *certiorari* "continues to have application only where the decision attacked is either judicial in character or is required by law to be made on a judicial or quasi-judicial basis."[95] The court's untenable and desperate attempt to accommodate the emergence of the doctrine of fairness without expanding the set of aggrieved persons who could seek judicial relief was reflected in the somewhat extraordinary step of releasing an Appendix to the judgment. Jackett C.J.F.C. commented that, in contra-distinction to persons who could avail themselves of *certiorari* or the new section 28 remedy, where a person "has a grievance in respect of decisions that are required to be made on a fair or just basis . . . his remedy is political."[96]

On appeal to the Supreme Court of Canada, the issue was neatly and clearly posed: is *certiorari* available with respect to prison disciplinary decisions? Beyond the jurisdictional issues, the case presented a fertile opportunity to address the diverse questions generated by the recognition that *Nicholson* planted the seed for the modern era of administrative law in Canada. The court reversed the decision of the Federal Court of Appeal in two concurring judgments written by Pigeon J. and Dickson J.[97] In a succinct judgment, Pigeon J. accepted the availability of *certiorari* as a vehicle to challenge prison disciplinary decisions on procedural grounds.[98] However, with specific reference to the prison context and the need to "maintain discipline in prison by proper, swift and speedy decisions", Pigeon J. offered the caveat that "the remedy be granted only in cases of serious injustice and that proper care be taken to prevent such proceedings from being used to delay deserved punishment so long that it is made ineffective, if not altogether avoided."[99] The opinion did not address any of the subsidiary issues which beckoned for consideration. Moreover, it provided little assistance in describing the procedural obligations of a prison disciplinary Board, other than pointing out that the "requirements of judicial procedure are not to be brought in."[100] Perhaps more significantly, because the judgment did permit the narrow reading that it was restricted to allegations of procedural unfairness, it left some ambiguity as to the general role of *certiorari* as a vehicle for reviewing decisions on other grounds.

---

95   *Ibid.*, at 639.
96   *Ibid.*, at 641.
97   *Martineau (No. 2), supra*, note 84, at 605, per Dickson J.; at 631, per Pigeon J.
98   *Ibid.*, at 637.
99   *Ibid.*, at 636 and 637.
100 *Ibid.*

The judgment of Dickson J. represented a more ambitious and comprehensive attempt to deal with the important administrative law issues which the case presented. In his view, the case compelled the resolution of a number of issues: the jurisdictional debate over sections 18 and 28 of the *Federal Court Act*, a closer analysis of the duty to act fairly and a consideration of the scope of *certiorari* in Canada. Looking first at the broad jurisdictional question, Dickson J. recognized that previous cases had highlighted "a difference in perception" but that the issue really boiled down to how one characterized the operative scope of the new section 28 remedy compared to the scope of *certiorari*.[101] The majority judgments in *Howarth* and *Martineau* fashioned a narrow role for section 28, restricting its ambit to those decisions "required by law to be made on a judicial or quasi-judicial basis". The counterpoint offered by the minority in *Howarth* "indicated a desire to read the new section 28 application to review and set aside as a remedy at least as broad as, if not broader than, *certiorari* . . . ."[102] Hence, as Dickson J. carefully pointed out, a resolution in favour of the narrow role for section 28 said nothing about the jurisdiction of the Trial Division to grant *certiorari* in respect of federal tribunals and decision-makers.[103] He rejected the tautologous conclusion of the Federal Court of Appeal that an inability to come within the threshold requirements of section 28 also precluded a resort to *certiorari* pursuant to section 18. He stated:

> I simply cannot accept the view that Parliament intended to remove the old common law remedies, including *certiorari*, from the provincial superior courts, and vest them in the Trial Division of the Federal Court, only to have those remedies rendered barren through the interaction of ss. 18 and 28 of the Act.[104]

In addressing the central question, the jurisdiction of the Trial Division to grant *certiorari*, he began with a history of judicial review and observed:

> The dominant characteristic of recent developments in English administrative law has been expansion of judicial review—jurisdiction to supervise administrative action by public authorities. *Certiorari* . . . evolved as a flexible remedy, affording access to judicial supervision in new and changing situations. . . . Nor has perception of *certiorari* as an adaptable remedy been in any way modified.[105]

---

[101] *Ibid.*, at 610-611.
[102] *Ibid.*, at 611.
[103] *Ibid.*, at 612-613.
[104] *Ibid.*, at 615-616.
[105] *Ibid.*, at 616.

Having set the tenor for his analysis, Dickson J. moved to the elements of the *Electricity Commissioners* case and the confusion generated by the ambiguously formulaic statements of Lord Atkin. He concluded that the phrase "rights of subjects" should not be viewed narrowly in the sense of a right to which a legally enforceable duty can be attached.[106] If the purpose of judicial review is to supervise the manner in which public bodies exercise their jurisdiction, then the nature of the interest at stake, whether it be a right or a privilege or some other type of interest, should merely be "but one factor to be considered in resolving the broad policy question of the nature of review appropriate for the particular administrative body."[107] In addressing the requirement of a "duty to act judicially", Dickson J. echoed the rejection by Lord Reid in *Ridge v. Baldwin* of a notion of some "super-added" judicial characteristic to be found in the statutory framework.[108] Thus, the existence of procedural obligations would flow from the nature of the power exercised and not from the presence or absence of an express legislative exhortation to act judicially. The critical issue is whether the procedural obligation can be inferred rather than simply labelling the decision-maker's duty in respect of individuals who come before it. In his view, *certiorari* must be available to enforce procedural obligations whether they flow from a duty of fairness or a duty to act judicially.[109] Accordingly, Dickson J. offered the important conclusion that:

> ... *certiorari* avails as a remedy wherever a public body has to decide any matter affecting the rights, interests, property, privileges or liberties of any person.[110]

Finally, the traditional classification of function approach was jettisoned as a precondition to the availability of *certiorari*. However, if a duty to act judicially gave rise to natural justice obligations, and a duty to act fairly gave rise to fairness obligations, had not a new process of classification evolved? In response, Dickson J. remarked that "there is much to be said against such a differentiation between traditional natural justice and procedural fairness. . . ."[111] Pointedly, in his concluding notes he stated that it would be wrong "to regard natural justice and fairness as distinct and separate standards and to seek to define the procedural content of each."[112]

---

[106] *Ibid.*, at 619.
[107] *Ibid.*, at 619.
[108] *Ibid.*, at 620.
[109] *Ibid.*, at 621-622.
[110] *Ibid.*, at 622-623.
[111] *Ibid.*, at 623.
[112] *Ibid.*, at 630.

Dickson J. then explained what has since been described as the "spectrum analysis" of procedural obligations.[113] At the one end of the spectrum are purely ministerial decisions based on broad grounds of public policy which give rise to no procedural protection. The other end of the spectrum approaches the judicial function where substantial procedural safeguards will be imposed. The enormous array of decision-making processes which fall between the ends of the spectrum will give rise to various modes of process. The extent of procedural safeguards required in any particular process will depend on a functional analysis of the nature of the power exercised and the structure of the process.[114] Of primary significance will be the importance of the issue at stake.[115]

The decision in *Martineau (No. 2)* represented a substantial contribution to the evolution of administrative law generally and to prison law in particular. However, it left a number of issues unresolved, many of which have been addressed by subsequent cases.[116] Because the comprehensive concurring judgment of Dickson J. has been accepted as authoritative, *certiorari* is available in respect of all public-decision makers and the grounds for review have not been restricted to procedural fairness.[117] As well, *certiorari* should not be restricted only to bodies which make decisions ultimately determinative of rights,[118] and the duty to act fairly has been recognized in respect of bodies exercising investigative and recommending functions.[119] However, divergence between the views of Pigeon J. and Dickson J., in respect of the extent of

---

113   *Ibid.*, at 627-628.
114   *Ibid.*, at 628-629.
115   Some might criticize Dickson J.'s spectrum analysis on the grounds that it induces uncertainty and encourages *ad hoc* judgments about the procedures which a particular process should invoke: see D.J. Mullan, "Developments in Administrative Law: The 1979-80 Term" (1981), 2 Sup. Ct. L. Rev. 1.
116   See *Dubeau v. National Parole Bd.*, [1981] 2 F.C. 37 (T.D.); *Re Davidson and Disciplinary Bd. of Prison for Women* (1981), 61 C.C.C. (2d) 520 (Fed. T.D.); *Minott v. Stony Mountain Penitentiary (Inmate Disciplinary Ct.)*, [1982] 1 F.C. 322 (T.D.).
117   Pigeon J. was ambiguous on this issue, while the judgment of Dickson J. expressly approved the decision of Widgery C.J.C. in *R. v. Hillingdon London Borough Council; Ex parte Royco Homes Ltd.*, [1974] Q.B. 720, which accepted the availability of *certiorari* on the dual grounds of *ultra vires* and an excess of jurisdiction in consequence of an error of law.
118   Dickson J. did not assert this requirement when reviewing the *Electricity Commissioners* case. As well, he relied on *Selvarajan v. Race Relations Bd.*, [1976] 1 All E.R. 12 (C.A.), in which a duty of fairness was applied to a body exercising investigative powers.
119   See, for example, *Abel v. Advisory Review Bd.* (1980), 56 C.C.C. (2d) 153 (Ont. C.A.) dealing with the Board constituted to review the confinement of prisoners found not guilty by reason of insanity or unfit to stand trial and to make recommendations to the Lieutenant Governor.

procedural obligations which arise from the duty to act fairly and the discretionary nature of *certiorari*, have caused controversy.

As will be seen in Chapter 4 in our discussion of the *Charter* and fundamental justice, courts continue to debate the existence of different standards of procedural obligations. In the judgment of Pigeon J. was a quotation from the judgment of Megarry J. in *Bates v. Lord Hailsham* which might be read as suggesting a distinction between the procedural content of fairness and natural justice.[120] This inference, however, requires reading the quotation out of context. The reference was used to refute the position that *certiorari* was only available in respect of tribunals required to act judicially or quasi-judicially. Laskin C.J.C. used the same quotation in *Nicholson v. Haldimand-Norfolk Regional Board of Police Commissioners*[121] for the same purpose and then concurred with Dickson J. in *Martineau (No. 2)*, who clearly expressed the view that it would be unfortunate to distinguish between the concepts of fairness and natural justice. More significantly, Megarry J.'s statement that "in the sphere of the so-called quasi-judicial the rules of natural justice run, and that in the administrative or executive field there is a general duty of fairness" was not addressed to the issue of procedural content. It arose in the context of considering whether a decision concerning the solicitor's tariff of fees was the exercise of a legislative power.[122] As we argue later with respect to fundamental justice, it is preferable to accept Dickson J.'s view that procedural standards should not be distinguished and that procedural content in a particular case should be resolved by inquiring into the nature of the function, the structure of the process and the interests at stake.

The question of discretion to grant relief has been problematic. Pigeon J. offered the expedient view that "the remedy be granted only in cases of serious injustice. . . ."[123] While Dickson J. also expressed concern about the need for "on the spot" decisions within the prison

---

[120] *Supra*, note 97, at 634.
[121] [1979] 1 S.C.R. 311, at 324.
[122] *Bates v. Lord Hailsham*, [1972] 3 All E.R. 1019, at 1024. The court held that the function of a statutory committee under *Solicitors Act, 1957* (5 & 6 Eliz. 2), c. 27 was legislative and was not bound by the rules of natural justice or general duty of fairness to consult all interested parties; hence the plaintiffs claim that any decision made without full consultation would be *ultra vires* was dismissed.
[123] *Martineau (No. 2)*, [1980] 1 S.C.R. 602, at 637. Pigeon J.'s concerns about the exigencies of the prison context flowed from the remarks of Lord Denning and Roskill L.J. in *Fraser v. Mudge*, [1975] 3 All E.R. 78 (C.A.), an injunction case—not an application for a prerogative writ—in which prisoners asserted a right to counsel at disciplinary hearings. After ruling that no absolute right existed, the judges went to pains to explain their concern about delaying the disciplinary process.

context, he concluded that judicial intervention should be avoided in situations of "trivial or merely technical incidents."[124] The gulf between the trivial and the serious injustice is extremely wide. The serious injustice test bespeaks of a deferential tilt towards administrators which has been followed in some cases.[125] Given that the nature of the interest at stake is a significant factor in determining whether a specific procedural obligation should be imposed, it seems inherently wrong to require a judge, after making a finding of procedural inadequacy, to assess in the calm and distant arena of the courtroom whether it represents a serious injustice. In a case involving a refusal of visiting privileges, Lambert J.A. held that the onus of establishing that relief ought not to be granted should rest on the party "seeking to uphold the decision that was reached by an unfair process."[126] More recently, the Supreme Court has held that a procedural defect which amounts to a denial of a fair hearing should always result in the quashing of the decision regardless of the reviewing court's attitude on the merits.[127]

Another important feature of the Dickson judgment was the reference to the decision-maker's own rules and practices.[128] This resurrected the importance of Commissioner's Directives which, though without the force of law, describe the kinds of internal processes that the Correctional Service of Canada considers appropriate and reasonable. As a minimum, these are significant factors to be considered when assessing what fairness requires. Since *Martineau (No. 2)*, Directives have played determinative roles in respect of penitentiary discipline[129] and transfers.[130] Similarly, the National Parole Board's Policy Manual can be referred to as indicating the procedural standards which the Board considers fair.[131] On judicial review, these standards should serve as guideposts for courts in addressing allegations of procedural unfairness. While fairness may require more than an internal rule or policy permits, it should never require less.

---

124 *Martineau, ibid.*, at 630.
125 See, for example, *Kelly v. Canada* (1987), 12 F.T.R. 296.
126 *Culhane v. B.C. (A.G.)* (1980), 51 C.C.C. (2d) 213 (B.C.C.A.), at 236.
127 *Cardinal v. Kent Institution (Director)*, [1985] 2 S.C.R. 643, discussed *infra* at p. 69.
128 *Supra*, note 124, at 614.
129 See, for example, *Russell v. Radley*, [1984] 1 F.C. 543 (T.D.); *Lasalle v. Leclerc Disciplinary Tribunal* (1984), 37 C.R. (3d) 145 (Fed. T.D.).
130 See *Jamieson v. Cmmr. of Corrections* (1986), 51 C.R. (3d) 155 (Fed. T.D.); *Lasalle v. Leclerc Disciplinary Tribunal, ibid.*; *Morgan v. National Parole Bd.*, [1982] 2 F.C. 648 (C.A.); *Hay v. National Parole Bd.* (1985), 13 Admin. L.R. 17 (Fed. T.D.).
131 Although see *Re Henderson and R.* (1982), 69 C.C.C. (2d) 561 (B.C.S.C.), where Hinds J. described the procedures in the Manual as "laudable", but considered them not applicable since they carried no statutory authority.

5. JUDICIAL REVIEW IN THE POST-MARTINEAU ERA

At a minimum, a duty to act fairly means an obligation to provide notice of allegations and an opportunity to respond. A process can address these objectives in a number of ways. The issue becomes whether the mechanism employed achieved fairness and an appearance of fairness in the circumstances. The extent of procedures which a court will impose on a decision-making process will depend upon a consideration of the statutory structure, the importance of the interest at stake, the decision-makers' internal rules and historical practice, and the exigencies of the particular case.

Issues of notice and an opportunity to respond generate questions of adequacy, reasonableness and appropriateness. Notice of allegations must be sufficiently clear and precise to enable the prisoner to know the case he has to meet. In other words, the prisoner should know which issues of fact must be resolved in his favour in order to produce a favourable result. Linked with this notion of adequacy is the requirement that the notice be sufficiently timely so as to provide an adequate opportunity to make inquiries and formulate a response. Next, the vehicle for responding must be appropriate to the statutory structure and must reflect the importance of the issue at stake. It should represent an effective method of ensuring that decisions are made on an accurate factual basis. This necessarily includes ascertaining and appreciating the prisoner's position on matters in issue. One can conceive of a variety of techniques by which an opportunity to respond can be provided. The least sophisticated may involve a response in writing or an oral response to an official who reports to the decision-maker. No matter how skeletal, the essential question will always be, in light of the consequences, whether the prisoner has had an adequate opportunity to respond. As one progresses along the spectrum, some processes will require hearings perhaps even approximating the procedural trappings usually associated with the judicial model.

Some of the early cases after *Martineau (No. 2)* espoused acceptance of the fairness doctrine, but made no inquiry beyond asking whether the decision-maker acted with malice or caprice.[132] These attempts to emasculate the concept of fairness in the prison context proved unsuccessful. Courts soon began developing modes of analysis consistent with fairness and appropriate to prison decision-makers. Because the *Parole Act* and Regulations require a hearing after the suspension of parole or

---

[132] See, for example, *Cline v. Reynett* (Fed. T.D., Addy J., March 18, 1981); *Sauvageau v. R.* (Fed. T.D., Dube J., July 8, 1980); *Re Morin and Saskatchewan (Director of Corrections)* (1981), 6 Sask. R. 401 (Q.B.).

mandatory supervision,[133] and given the obvious loss of liberty, it is not surprising that many of the early fairness cases arose in respect of parole revocations. In *Morgan v. National Parole Board*, the Federal Court of Appeal considered the impact of inadequate notice on the dynamics of the hearing.[134] It concluded that a prisoner could not be said to have a fair hearing when he arrived with notice of allegation X and was told at the commencement of the hearing that Y and Z were also issues.

More difficult cases arose where there was no express hearing requirement. In *Swan v. Attorney General of British Columbia*,[135] McEachern C.J.S.C. was faced with a *habeas corpus* application alleging that a prisoner's parole had been revoked without affording the prisoner the opportunity of an *in personam* hearing. He proceeded to examine the statutory structure and concluded, albeit reluctantly, that he was bound by a previous decision[136] which held that the Board could resort to its general power of revocation without completing the suspension procedure which it had commenced. Accordingly, he concluded that the *Parole Act* and the Regulations did not specifically mandate a hearing in the circumstances of the case before him. However, he then went on to consider what procedural content was required to satisfy the principles of natural justice and fairness. He asked:

> . . . are inquiries or ex parte reviews or discretionary hearings enough, or must there be a hearing as of right at which the parolee is entitled to attend, to present his side of the case, and to challenge the case against him in the presence of the tribunal?[137]

In answering the question, he recognized that what was at stake was "not just the rights and privileges of citizens" but the liberty of the prisoner.[138] He then looked at the statutory framework and observed that in other cases a prisoner would be entitled to a post-suspension hearing and concluded that "if a prisoner is entitled as a [sic] right to a hearing with the usual natural justice safeguards upon suspension of his parole, then there is no reason to think that there should be less protection after a decision to revoke his parole."[139] In other words, the rules and procedures of the tribunal itself, applicable in similar situations, were significant in determining what obligations should be imposed in the case at bar. Ultimately, McEachern C.J.S.C. ruled that a proper hearing

---

133 See Chapter 8.
134 *Supra*, note 130.
135 (1983), 35 C.R. (3d) 135 (B.C.S.C.). This case is discussed in detail in Chapters 4 and 8.
136 *Ibid.*, at 141 (referring to *Roach v. Kent Institution (Director)* (1983), 34 C.R. (3d) 249 (B.C.C.A.)).
137 *Ibid.*, at 145.
138 *Ibid.*, at 147.
139 *Ibid.*, at 146.

should have been afforded to the prisoner, even after revocation, in order to "ensure that the procedure most likely to attain justice is followed."[140]

Swan is an instructive example of how relevant factors must be assessed to determine the procedural obligations which a court will impose. It also supports the view, applicable to a number of prison decisions, that when a factual determination is required urgently, procedural safeguards should be afforded as soon as is reasonably practicable in order to confirm any initial decision and ensure that adverse consequences do not flow from an erroneous factual assessment.[141]

Martineau (No. 2) opened the modern era of prison law in Canada and exposed internal parole and prison processes to judicial scrutiny. As a result, some procedures have been found wanting and decision-makers have been compelled to revise their processes to conform with the notion of fairness.[142] But the impact of *Martineau (No. 2)* transcends questions of procedure. The opportunity for judicial scrutiny now compels judges to begin to examine the dynamics of internal decision-making with due regard to the competing tensions of liberty, self-interest and administrative exigency. In the course of judicial review, judges have made observations about the manner and appropriate bases for decision-making.[143] Such expressions of approval and disapproval should affect the activities of decision-makers and the expectations of prisoners.

A related product of expanded judicial review flows from the ability to challenge decisions on non-procedural grounds. For example, an application raising excess of jurisdiction as the ground for review requires the court to consider the appropriate scope of decision-making, including questions of acceptable criteria and extraneous considerations. Thus, the new era of judicial scrutiny represents not only the

---

[140] *Ibid.*, at 147. In this regard, it must be noted that the concept of *functus officio* does not apply to a decision-maker like the Parole Board which is entitled to reverse its own decisions in the face of new information to prevent injustice. See *Re Carde and R.* (1977), 34 C.C.C. (2d) 559 (Ont. H.C.) and *Re McDonald and R.* (1980), 56 C.C.C. (2d) 1 (Ont. H.C.). See also *Bains*, discussed in Chapter 6, which holds that a re-thinking of a decision originally properly formulated is unacceptable.

[141] A similar approach was taken by Walsh J. in *Lasalle, supra*, note 130, a case involving a decision to transfer to higher security.

[142] See *Hay v. National Parole Bd., supra*, note 130; *Jamieson v. Cmmr. of Corrections, supra*, note 130; *DeMaria v. Regional Transfer Bd.* (1988), 62 C.R. (3d) 248 (Fed. C.A.) (transfer cases); *Re Chester* (1984), 40 C.R. (3d) 146 (Ont. H.C.); *H. v. R.* (1985), 17 Admin. L.R. 39 (Fed. T.D.); *Cadieux v. Mountain Institution (Director)*, [1985] 1 F.C. 378 (T.D.) (confidentiality cases).

[143] See *Lasalle v. Leclerc Disciplinary Tribunal, supra*, note 129; *Bryntwick v. National Parole Bd.* (1987), 55 C.R. (3d) 332 (Fed. T.D.); *Litwack v. National Parole Bd.* (1986), 51 C.R. (3d) 53 (Fed. T.D.).

development of fair procedures but has also enhanced the evolution of substantive prison and parole law.

6. THE PRACTICE OF JUDICIAL REVIEW

Through legislative reform and the entrenchment of the *Canadian Charter of Rights and Freedoms*,[144] the nature of judicial review has changed dramatically. Many jurisdictions have enacted new statutory vehicles to replace the traditional prerogative writs of *certiorari*, prohibition and *mandamus*.[145] These new judicial review vehicles are conceptually similar in nature to the prerogative remedies but have arisen as a result of dissatisfaction with the technicality of their historical counterparts.

As many prison and parole cases involve issues of liberty, it has become common to see claims for *Charter* relief[146] joined in judicial review applications. However, neither the *Charter* nor the new statutory remedial regimes have rendered irrelevant an understanding of the prerogative writs. The principal remedy provision of the *Charter* does not create any new jurisdiction for review; rather, relief must still be sought in the court which, prior to the *Charter*, had jurisdiction over the subject matter and parties, and the authority to grant the kind of relief sought.[147]

Some decisions and acts are not encompassed by the new remedies; a dissatisfied party must still resort to the prerogative writs. The most significant example is the prison and parole context in the federal sphere. The broad review power created by section 28 of the *Federal Court Act* does not apply to "a decision or order of an administrative nature not required by law to be made on a judicial or quasi-judicial basis". This has been interpreted as excluding internal prison decisions and decisions of the National Parole Board.[148] Accordingly, in the federal system a prison can only seek relief by applying to the Trial

---

144 Being Part I of the *Constitution Act, 1982* [en. by the *Canada Act, 1982* (U.K.), c. 11, s. 1].
145 For example, see the *Federal Court Act*, R.S.C. 1985, c. F-7, s. 28. In Ontario, see *Judicial Review Procedure Act*, R.S.O. 1980, c. 224. In British Columbia, see *Judicial Review Procedure Act*, R.S.B.C. 1979, c. 209.
146 The subject of remedies under the *Charter* is discussed in Chapter 4.
147 *Charter*, s. 24(1). See also *Mills v. R.*, [1986] 1 S.C.R. 863, at 903-904, per Lamer J.; at 953, per McIntyre J.
148 See the discussions of *Howarth, Martineau*, and *Martineau (No. 2), supra*. Even after amendments to the *Parole Act* entitling the prisoner to a post-suspension hearing, which might arguably have changed the nature of the Board's decision-making processes, the Federal Court of Appeal continued to take a very restrictive interpretation of section 28: see *Meldrum v. National Parole Bd.* (summarized (1981), 6 W.C.B. 169).

Division of the Federal Court for a prerogative remedy or "relief in the nature thereof" pursuant to section 18 of the *Federal Court Act*.[149]

(a) Certiorari and Prohibition

The difference between the two remedies is temporally related to the decision-making process in question. *Certiorari* is available to quash an impugned decision. If the decision has not yet been made, but grounds exist to argue that the continuation of the process will result in a reviewable decision, prohibition lies to stop the process at that stage. The two remedies are "flip sides" of the same record and similar grounds for review are available in both situations. Historically, they have been the primary public law instruments by which superior courts have supervised inferior tribunals and the exercise of statutory powers.[150]

The recognition of the common-law duty of fairness has made most statutory decision-makers subject to judicial review. Even the "ministerial" end of Dickson J.'s decision-making spectrum is no longer entirely insulated from review as a result of the entrenchment of the guarantee of fundamental justice in section 7 of the *Charter*.[151] Historic impediments to review based on distinctions between rights and privileges[152] or the need for finality[153] are no longer applicable. However, preliminary hurdles still exist which can preclude prerogative relief.

---

[149] This is subject to recent developments in the scope of *habeas corpus* in cases dealing with a distinct form of confinement: see *infra*, pp. 89-102.

[150] The origin of *certiorari* was its use as the instrument by which the sovereign demanded information. Between the 14th and 17th Centuries, *certiorari* was used primarily:
1. to supervise the proceedings of inferior courts of specialized jurisdiction;
2. to obtain information for administrative purposes;
3. to bring into the Chancery or before the common-law courts judicial records and other formal documents for diverse purposes; and
4. to remove coroners' inquisitions and indictments into the King's Bench.
Prohibition was originally used to limit the jurisdiction of the ecclesiastical courts: for a detailed historical account see J.M. Evans, *DeSmith's Judicial Review of Administrative Action*, 4th ed. (London: Stevens & Sons, 1980), pp. 588-589.

[151] *Operation Dismantle Inc. v. R.*, [1985] 1 S.C.R. 441; *R. v. Swain* (1986), 50 C.R. (3d) 97 (Ont. C.A.).

[152] See Dickson J.'s judgment in *Martineau (No. 2)* discussed, *supra*, at p. 55, in which judicial review is extended to "any public body with power to decide any matter affecting the rights, interests, property, privileges, or liberty of any person".

[153] In *Martineau (No. 2)*, Dickson J. used the word "decide" in his ground-breaking statement about expanded review. However, other cases have applied *certiorari* and prohibition to bodies which exercise a substantial recommending function: see *Re Abel and Advisory Review Bd.* (1979), 97 D.L.R. (3d) 304 (Ont. C.A.); *Quebec (A.G.) v. Canada (A.G.)*, [1979] 1 S.C.R. 218.

First, it is necessary that the decision-making function in issue be statutory in nature. This requirement has been ameliorated by use of modern phrases like "public body" or "public decision-maker". In the prison and parole context there can be little doubt that powers are both statutory and public.[154] One issue which can and frequently does arise, however, relates to the strata and sub-strata of officials who make recommendations and participate in decisions. Some of these individuals or bodies exercise powers specifically bestowed by statute or delegated by statutory authority. Some participants exercise powers pursuant to internal subordinate instruments such as Commissioner's Directives or the National Parole Board's Policy and Procedures Manual. Clearly, these instruments cannot have the force of law for the purpose of giving review jurisdiction to the Federal Court of Appeal.[155] Moreover, courts have held that procedures mandated by them do not satisfy the "prescribed by law" element is section 1 of the *Charter*.[156] Thus, it is doubtful whether these instruments can, by themselves, constitute sufficient authority for reviewability. It therefore becomes necessary to examine the statutory framework to determine which body or individual actually exercises, or is responsible for exercising, the power in question. If the governing statute or set of regulations includes or implies a power of delegation, the fact that the delegation is achieved through a directive or policy does not necessarily mean that the delegate is not exercising a statutory power.[157] However, in the absence of authorized delegation, the appropriate respondent is likely an official higher up the statutory chain of command.

With respect to parole issues, the proper respondent will usually be the National Parole Board acting in one of its many capacities under the *Parole Act* and Regulations. The decision-maker may, however, be a

---

[154] In the labour relations field, there is a continuing debate over distinctions between statutory and consensual arbitrators. See *Roberval Express Ltd. v. Transport Drivers, Warehousemen & General Workers Union, Local 106* (1982), 144 D.L.R. (3d) 673 (S.C.C.); *Shalansky v. Regina Pasqua Hospital (Bd. of Governors)* (1983), 22 Sask. R. 153 (S.C.C.); and generally, R.M. Brown, "Developments in Labour Law" (1984), 6 Sup. Ct. L. Rev. 237, at 272-278.

[155] See discussion of *Martineau, supra,* at pp. 53-54; and *Martineau (No. 2), supra,* at pp. 54-60.

[156] *Cadieux v. Mountain Institution (Director), supra,* note 142; *Latham v. Canada (Solicitor General)* (1984), 39 C.R. (3d) 78 (Fed. T.D.); *Ontario Film & Video Appreciation Society v. Ont. Bd. of Censors* (1983), 34 C.R. (3d) 73 (Ont. C.A.). Where a law is so vague and undefined as to be discretionary, it is likely to be considered unacceptable where it attempts to limit a constitutional freedom by the use of section 1 of the *Charter*. An attempt to make the law more definite by the use of non-binding guidelines is insufficient to bring the law within section 1 of the *Charter* as the limit sought to be upheld will not be prescribed by law.

[157] See J. Willis, "Delegatus Non Potest Delegare" (1943) 21 Can. Bar Rev. 257.

parole officer exercising statutory power under section 22(1) of the *Parole Act*. In these circumstances, the delegated person should be named as a party.[158] Determining the proper respondent also identifies the specific acts being impugned. For example, within the penitentiary hierarchy there are various officials and bodies exercising responsibilities ancillary or preliminary to decisions, the ultimate authority for which rests with higher officials. By paying careful attention to the decision-making structure and the locus of statutory authority, the real issue may involve the manner in which the statutory decision-maker supervised or directed subordinates, or the response to their findings.[159] While naming an extra party may not be a problem,[160] leaving out the essential party can be critical.[161]

The second preliminary hurdle is that there must be something in existence to review. In other words, there must be a decision or process to quash by *certiorari* or, alternatively, to stop by prohibition. This prerequisite often manifests itself in arguments phrased in terms of prematurity. A respondent may well argue that the exercise of the statutory power in question has not been completed, or has not proceeded to the point where an allegation of irreversible error can be made. This argument usually arises in prohibition cases where the basis of the application is an alleged procedural defect such that a respondent can argue that the process, if allowed to proceed, could cure the defect. A useful example of how an applicant can respond to concerns about prematurity is the case of *H. v. R.*[162] H. was made aware that his parole file contained an allegation that he was the principle suspect in an old investigation into a number of unsolved murders. Notwithstanding substantial efforts to improve his prospects as a candidate for day parole, the existence of this allegation proved to be a continuing impediment to release. Both H. and his lawyer had made a number of attempts

---

[158] For example, in penitentiary transfer cases it has become common practice to name the Regional Transfer Board. This is probably unnecessary. The appropriate parties are the Warden and the Regional Deputy Commissioner of the Correctional Service of Canada. Interestingly, the failure in one case to join the Regional Deputy Commissioner produced the anomaly that a transfer decision was quashed but no order could be made directing that the prisoner be returned to the original institution, since none of the parties had the statutory power to effect the return: see *DeMaria v. Regional Transfer Bd.* (1988), 62 C.R. (3d) 248 (Fed. T.D.).

[159] See *Cardinal v. Kent Institution (Director)*, [1985] 2 S.C.R. 643, where the lack of fairness involved the Warden's refusal to follow a favourable recommendation from the Institutional Segregation Review Board.

[160] For example, *MacAllister v. Centre de Reception (Director)* (1984), 40 C.R. (3d) 126 (Fed. T.D.).

[161] See note 158, *supra*, as an example.

[162] [1986] 2 F.C. 71 (Fed. T.D.). This case is discussed in more detail in Chapter 6.

through various routes to find out the particulars of the allegation. At
one point, the Board itself indicated that if it could not obtain fuller
particulars and a current update of the allegation that it would treat it as
a "dead letter". Subsequently, at a day parole hearing the Board stated,
after communications with the R.C.M.P., that it would make no disclosure of the information on the ground that it would impair an
ongoing investigation. The prisoner's lawyer asked that the hearing be
adjourned so that he could seek judicial review. Litigation was commenced seeking an order prohibiting the Board from taking into account
information which it failed to disclose or, alternatively, an order of
mandamus requiring the Board to disclose sufficient details of the
information so as to permit the prisoner a fair opportunity to respond.[163]
Counsel for the Board argued, *inter alia*, that the application was premature since the Board had not yet made any decision on the request for
day parole. Reed J. dismissed the prematurity argument saying:

> In the course of the board's hearing . . . applicant's counsel asked the board
> for further details concerning the information before it. When such infor-
> mation was not forthcoming, applicant's counsel sought and obtained from
> the board an adjournment to allow this Court to review that refusal. Accord-
> ingly, as counsel for the applicant argues, the decision challenged is that of
> the board not to disclose further information to the applicant; it is not a
> challenge to a decision respecting parole.[164]

After concluding that fairness required disclosure of a degree of detail
that would enable a full and fair response, and that exemptions found in
the federal *Privacy Act*[165] were of no utility to the Board, the court issued
an order prohibiting the Board from taking into account any information received from police authorities about the unsolved crimes and
their suspicions in regard to the applicant. To ensure that future decisions not be tainted by suspicion of hidden agendas, Reed J. ordered
that the applicant's day parole application should "be heard by a differently constituted panel of the National Parole Board who do not have
knowledge of the details of the allegation against the applicant which
have not been disclosed to the applicant".[166]

---

[163] *Ibid.*, at 73.
[164] *Ibid.*, at 79.
[165] S.C. 1980-81-82-83, c. 111.
[166] *Supra*, note 162, at 81. The case demonstrates the fundamental distinction between
issues of confidentiality in the administrative context compared to the adversarial
litigious context. In *H. v. National Parole Bd.*, the Board knew the challenged information. The question was whether it was obliged to make disclosure to the party affected
by it. See the further discussion in Chapter 6.

(b) Grounds for Review

The usual objects of judicial review are the many specialized tribunals created to develop decision-making expertise in discrete and often technical areas of regulated economic or social activity. Historically, grounds for judicial review had their genesis in an era when the principal function of review was the supervision of Justices of the Peace and Magistrates who exercised criminal and quasi-criminal authority. Accordingly, any discussion of grounds for judicial review is coloured by the tensions involved in re-tooling old instruments for new contexts. In this section, we do not intend to provide comprehensive insight, but simply to outline available grounds and highlight some recent developments which bear directly on the prison and parole contexts. This discussion focusses on common law. In some jurisdictions grounds for review have been stipulated by statute, thereby avoiding some of the controversies which plague this highly technical area of law.[167]

(i) *Fairness*

Earlier, we discussed the evolution and acceptance of the common-law duty to act fairly. The content of fairness varies with the context as one moves along the spectrum from administrative to judicial decision-makers. Greater procedural protections must be available in dealing with tribunals which, similar to their judicial counterparts, exercise substantial authority to make findings of fact and law. Traditionally, such tribunals have been characterized as exercising a judicial or quasi-judicial function and natural justice has served to impose procedural requirements on them. Now, the duty to act fairly extends procedural protections across the range of statutory and public decision-making, regardless of whether the function has been categorized as judicial or quasi-judicial.

At a minimum, fairness requires that a party know the allegation and is afforded an opportunity, in some manner, to respond to it. What mode of fair procedure will satisfy this requirement is determined in reference to the interest at stake, the structure of the decision-maker created by legislation, the practice and internal rules of the decision-maker and the circumstances of the particular case. In *Cardinal v. Director of Kent Institution*,[168] the Supreme Court of Canada considered

---

[167] An attempt to achieve this objective in the federal sphere can be observed in Bill C-38, *An Act to Amend the Federal Court Act*, which received Royal Assent on March 29, 1990, but has not yet been proclaimed in force: see S.C. 1990, c. 8.

[168] [1985] 2 S.C.R. 643.

the duty to act fairly as it applied to a warden of a penitentiary in deciding whether to continue administrative dissociation. It had been alleged that the prisoners, while imprisoned in another institution, had been involved in a hostage taking. They were transferred to Kent Institution, where they were immediately placed in administrative dissociation. A review by the internal Segregation Review Board recommended that the prisoners be released to the general prison population, but the warden refused to follow the recommendation pending the disposition of the outstanding criminal charges. In finding that the warden had not treated them fairly, LeDain J. held:

> They were entitled to know why the Director did not intend to act in accordance with the recommendation of the Board and to have an opportunity before him to state their case for release into the general population of the institution. I do not think the Director was required to make an independent inquiry into the alleged involvement of the appellants in the hostage-taking incident. He could rely on the information he had received. . . . At the same time, he had the duty to hear and consider what the appellants had to say concerning their alleged involvement in the incident, as well as anything else that could be relevant to the question whether their release from segregation might introduce an unsettling element into the general inmate population and thus have an adverse effect on the maintenance of good order and discipline in the institution.[169]

The statutory structure created no procedural obligations but, with regard to the special circumstances of a penitentiary, LeDain J. found that the prisoners had been denied a fair hearing, which he characterized as "an independent, unqualified right which finds its essential justification in the sense of procedural justice which any person affected by an administrative decision is entitled to have."[170] In the formal adversarial context, notice would include a statement of the issue in a form akin to pleading and some obligation to disclose particulars. The opportunity to respond, in its fullest sense, would involve an impartial hearing complete with the examination and cross-examination of witnesses, the assistance of counsel, the right to produce evidence and make submissions on evidence, and the right to make final argument. Fairness does not necessarily require these complete procedural incidents. LeDain J. was not using "hearing" in the full adversarial sense but, rather, in terms of informing the party of what had been said and providing a fair opportunity to respond to it. The essential question will always be whether, given the function and structure of the decision-maker and the circumstances of the particular situation, the party should have confidence that he has been treated fairly.

---

[169] *Ibid.*, at 659-660.
[170] *Ibid.*, at 661.

The most important source in determining what fairness requires will always be the statutory instrument which empowers the decision-maker. The legislation or regulation will indicate not only the scope of the powers entrusted to the decision-maker but also the extent of discretion and any preconditions or criteria necessary to its exercise. Procedurally, the statutory framework should also indicate the kind of procedural apparatus contemplated for the decision-maker and, often, will provide a procedural framework. In the parole context, there are a number of mandatory procedural requirements prescribed by the statutory framework:

1. In-person hearings for parole reviews.
2. In-person post-suspension hearings with prior notice of the alleged breach.
3. The right to an "assistant" at a hearing.
4. Limited entitlement to disclosure.

While the statutory framework clearly indicates that a prisoner should have some opportunity to present his case, the framework does not provide the details of how the Board will conduct a hearing. Many court rulings have been incorporated by the Board through its Policy and Procedures Manual. However, little attention has been paid to the actual conduct of a hearing. Most parole hearings are conducted on the basis of reports and information produced in documentary form rather than oral testimony. Depending on the individual circumstances of the case, one may be able to argue that a fair hearing requires oral testimony and perhaps even an opportunity to cross-examine informants. Situations which might generate this argument include information or adverse reports from someone who has shown antagonism, information from children, or evidence of unprosecuted offences.

Prior to the enactment of the regulation entitling a prisoner to an "assistant",[171] a number of cases examined the question of right to counsel in the parole context. It is helpful to consider the case of *Dubeau v. National Parole Board*,[172] an early post-*Martineau (No. 2)* decision, to understand how fairness in the circumstances of a particular case can produce an obligation to provide further procedural safeguards. In *Dubeau*, the prisoner was suspended as a result of a new criminal charge. At his post-suspension hearing he could expect to be asked questions about the new charge, including questions relating to a statement apparently given to the police. To appreciate his situation before the Board,

---

[171] See *Parole Regulations*, SOR/78-428, s. 20.1, and the discussion of the role of the assistant in Chapter 12.
[172] [1981] 2 F.C. 37 (T.D.).

we can conceptualize some of the issues which confronted him. Could he refuse to answer questions about the new charge and run the risk that the Board would characterize him as uncooperative and recalcitrant? Could any remarks made to the Board be used in a subsequent criminal trial against him? For the purpose of understanding the admissibility of statements, was the Board a "person in authority"? Would the notion of confidential communications as discussed in *Slavutych v. Baker*[173] insulate a Parole Board member from disclosure if he was subsequently served with a subpoena? The range of legal questions facing the prisoner persuaded the court that an adequate opportunity to respond to allegations could not be provided without the assistance of a lawyer.

A similar analysis can be seen in *Morgan v. National Parole Board*,[174] where the suspended prisoner was notified of a specific reason for suspension. When he attended for his post-suspension hearing, he was advised for the first time that there were other grounds which also generated the suspension. The Federal Court of Appeal reversed a decision denying *certiorari* by holding that fairness was not provided when a prisoner, prepared to respond to one specific allegation, was spontaneously faced with new ones. Both *Dubeau* and *Morgan* illustrate how the judiciary has applied Dickson J.'s capsulized notion that the ultimate question is whether, at the end of the day, the party can have confidence that the process has provided a fair opportunity to present his case and respond to allegations.

Because the duty to act fairly is a common-law obligation, the statutory framework of a process can specifically exclude a particular procedural incident such that the courts are unlikely to rely on fairness to impose it. As well, if the procedural framework can be characterized as a complete procedural code crafted by legislation, courts will not generally entertain an argument that the duty to act fairly requires a tribunal to do more.[175] In Chapter 4 we examine the relationship between the common-law duty of fairness and the constitutionally entrenched obligation of fundamental justice. We shall see that the statutory exclusion or the articulation of a complete procedural code cannot totally foreclose judicial scrutiny premised on the procedural aspects of fundamental justice as guaranteed by section 7 of the *Charter*.

---

[173] [1976] 1 S.C.R. 254.

[174] [1982] 2 F.C. 648 (C.A.).

[175] See, for example, *Furnell v. Whangarei High Schools Bd.*, [1973] A.C. 660 (P.C.), at 686; *Wiseman v. Borneman*, [1971] A.C. 297 (H.L.), at 308.

(ii) *Jurisdictional Grounds*[176]

Commonly, applications for judicial review include the often imprecise assertion of excess of jurisdiction as a ground for review. The applicant alleges that the decision-maker has acted or inquired in a manner not authorized by the legislation which created it. One also sees the converse ground—a failure to exercise jurisdiction—by which an applicant alleges that a decision-maker has not carried out an action or inquiry which it was required by legislation to do. In these administrative law contexts, jurisdiction is roughly synonymous to power or authority.

All statutory and public decision-makers exercise powers that are delegated to them by legislatures. Aside from powers granted expressly or necessarily by implication in the statutory instrument which creates or empowers the decision-maker, it has no inherent power, except to protect its own process. The scope of the powers which enables and requires the decision-maker to act is commonly known as jurisdiction. The concept of jurisdiction and the powers and responsibilities which it creates can be understood by envisaging a picture frame. The legislature creates the frame around a blank canvas and directs the decision-maker to cover the canvas in some way, in respect of some subject matter, with some medium. Essentially, the decision-maker, our mythical painter, is insulated from judicial review so long as he carries out the project and follows the directions—even if the result is not as pleasing as was anticipated. The painter's creativity is analogous to the decision-maker's right to be wrong, unless the scope of delegated power has been exceeded or some requisite authority not exercised. Within the picture frame, many decisions will be made; right or wrong, they will generally not be subject to review on their merits.

Using parole as an example, section 13 of the *Parole Act* gives the National Parole Board "exclusive jurisdiction and absolute discretion to grant or refuse to grant parole. . . ." This, however, does not determine the dimensions of that jurisdiction. Section 16(1)(*a*) attempts to give it more detailed definition by providing the matters which must be considered by the Board:

(i) . . . the inmate has derived the maximum benefit from imprisonment,
(ii) the reform and rehabilitation of the inmate will be aided by the grant of parole, and
(iii) the release of the inmate on parole would not constitute an undue risk to society. . . .

---

[176] For a detailed analysis, see D.J. Mullan, "The Supreme Court of Canada and Jurisdictional Error: Compromising New Brunswick Liquor?" (1987), 1 Can. J. of Admin. L. & Practice 71.

For parole granting, these considerations are the picture frame. While other provisions in the statutory framework address how the Board must proceed with its authority, nothing amplifies these vague and ambiguous considerations. It is easy to state that any inquiry beyond those factors relevant to these considerations would be an excess of jurisdiction. Conversely, a refusal to consider relevant factors could be characterized as a failure to exercise jurisdiction. The difficulty lies in determining the perimeter of relevance in light of such broadly cast authority. Given the breadth and exclusivity of the Board's parole granting discretion, there have been few cases argued on the basis of excess of jurisdiction.[177] A claim of excess of jurisdiction, or the closely-linked converse concept of failure to exercise jurisdiction, can relate to the obligation to inquire as compared to the subject matter of inquiry. In *Perron*,[178] the Board was influenced by a report from the Correctional Service of Canada which characterized the prisoner as a security risk. The prisoner argued that the Board was obliged to make its own inquiry, and that its failure to do so amounted to a failure to exercise its statutory obligation.[179] The court upheld the Board's denial of parole affirming the Board's power to consider reports without an independent investigation.

In *Perron*, counsel also raised the argument that the decision was substantively unfair in light of the information upon which it was based. The issue of whether the duty of fairness includes substantive review is controversial.[180] If we resort to the picture frame conception of jurisdiction, we see that the quality of the painting is beyond scrutiny, so long as the statutory directions have been followed. Equally, what an external observer thinks of the rightness or wrongness of a decision should not affect its validity, so long as it is within the decision-maker's jurisdic-

---

[177] A related example is *MacInnis v. Canada (A.G.)* (1986), 4 F.T.R. 211, involving a parole application by a dangerous offender. In those cases, the Board's jurisdiction is amplified by section 761(1) of the *Code* which empowers it to "review the condition, history and circumstances" of the prisoner. Hence, the court ruled that a denial of parole based on the view that release would deprecate the seriousness of the prisoner's offences was within the Board's jurisdiction.

[178] *Perron v. Cmmr. of Corrections* (Fed. T.D., Mahoneoy J., December 22, 1982).

[179] It is easy to see how this argument can be framed either as (a) a failure to exercise discretion by failing to make independent inquiries, or (b) as excess of jurisdiction by reaching a conclusion on the basis of an extraneous consideration, i.e. another person's opinion. In the context of the review of a Lieutenant Governor's Warrant, the argument has succeeded: see *Lingley v. Lieutenant-Governor's Advisory Review Bd. of N.B.* (1988), 63 C.R. (3d) 326 (Fed. T.D.), at 250.

[180] See D.J. Mullan, "Natural Justice and Fairness" (1982) 27 McGill L.J. 250; D.J. Mullan, "Substantive Fairness and Review: Heed the Amber Light" (1988) 18 V.U.W.L.R. 293; and discussion of fairness and fundamental justice in Chapter 4.

tion. This jurisdiction includes how the decision was reached and requires that the decision-maker act reasonably in response to relevant material.[181]

Reasonableness has long been an independent ground for review.[182] It was applied by the Federal Court in the parole context in *Litwack v. National Parole Board*, a case dealing with a decision refusing to remove a special condition.[183] The court held that a factual conclusion would be reviewable if it was patently unreasonable in the sense that the fact could not reasonably support the conclusion.[184] Looking at reasonableness as a ground of review in this way shows its conceptual link with "no evidence" as a ground of review. The latter category, a decision without a factual basis, is simply an extreme example of an unreasonable conclusion.[185]

The concept of jurisdiction provides an opportunity to consider the difficult and controversial question of errors made in the course of reaching a decision, whether errors of law or fact. For a time, it appeared that the Supreme Court of Canada was promoting a regime of curial deference in which judicial intervention was only warranted in respect of errors which could be described as patently unreasonable. In other words, a decision or ruling took on an extra-jurisdictional aspect if it was

---

[181] In *Associated Provincial Picture Houses v. Wednesbury Corp.*, [1948] 1 K.B. 223 (C.A.), Greene M.R. observed that the lawful exercise of delegated discretion involved taking into account those matters which the authorizing statute indicated were relevant, and disregarding factors which were not germane. He concluded with the classic statement of "unreasonableness" as a ground of review:
  if a decision on a competent matter is so unreasonable that no reasonable authority could ever come to it, the courts can interfere. (at 230)
  See also the remarks of Lord Diplock in *Council of Civil Service Unions v. Minister for the Civil Service*, [1985] A.C. 374 (H.L.), where he equated "unreasonableness" with "irrationality" in the sense of a "decision which is so outrageous in its defiance of logic or of accepted moral standards that no sensible person who had applied his mind to the question to be decided could have arrived at it (at 410).

[182] See the decision of Reed J. in *DeMaria v. Canada (Regional Transfer Bd.)*, [1988] 2 F.C. 480 (Fed. T.D.).

[183] (1986), 51 C.R. (3d) 53 (Fed. T.D.). Surprisingly, and in our view unnecessarily, the court looked to section 7 of the *Charter* to find a reasonableness obligation. See also *Scott v. National Parole Bd.*, [1988] 1 F.C. 473 (Fed. T.D.), where Strayer J. refused to find a Board decision based in part on a 10-minute psychiatric interview to be patently unreasonable.

[184] Relying on *Blanchard v. Control Data Can. Ltée*, [1984] 2 S.C.R. 476 (S.C.C.) in which Lamer J. stated that a tribunal commits a jurisdictional error if it makes either a decision of law or fact which is patently unreasonable. Although not articulated in this form, *Lasalle v. Leclerc Disciplinary Tribunal* (1984), 37 C.R. (3d) 145 (Fed. T.D.), represents a similar view that a transfer could not be justified by the stated facts.

[185] See *Belmont v. Millhaven Institution Disciplinary Ct.* (1984), 41 C.R. (3d) 91 (Fed. T.D.).

patently unreasonable and, hence, was open to judicial review. A conclusion which, although wrong in the eyes of the reviewing court, was not patently unreasonable was insulated from review. More recently, the court appears to have become more interventionist and has held that any decision in respect of a tribunal's jurisdiction—that is, that interprets the scope of its powers—must be correct and will be reviewable on the basis of incorrectness.[186] Infra-jurisdictional errors will only be reviewable if patently unreasonable. This dictum includes both errors of law and errors of fact.[187] The Supreme Court has cautioned that judges should not rush to brand a decision as jurisdictional and, hence, open to broader review.[188] However, the recent trend points to a change in direction from the deferential approach of *C.U.P.E., Local 963 v. New Brunswick Liquor Corporation*[189] and *S.E.I.U., Local 333 v. Nipawin District Staff Nurses Assn.*[190]

Amendments to the *Federal Court Act* currently awaiting proclamation will clarify the grounds for review in the federal sphere.[191] Relief will be available in response to any error of law,[192] or an "erroneous finding of fact" made "in a perverse or capricious manner" or without regard by the decision-maker for the material before it.[193]

(iii) *Bias*

Statutory and public decision-makers should be "disinterested and impartial".[194] It has long been recognized that a decision-maker must be disqualified from participating in a process if there is a direct or pecuniary interest in the subject matter or, if a pre-existing relationship with the party creates a likelihood of bias (or at least an appearance of partiality). In the prison and parole contexts, these grounds for disqualification are equally applicable. However, the more difficult issue is that of an apprehension of bias that arises from previously stated attitudes and previous interactions. Regrettably, the penal environment is

---

[186] See *Syndicat des employés de production du Québec et de l'Acadie v. Can. Labour Relations Bd.*, [1984] 2 S.C.R. 412; *National Bank of Can. v. Retail Clerks' Int. Union*, [1984] 1 S.C.R. 269; *Blanchard v. Control Data Can. Ltée, supra*, note 184. It should also be noted that any time a tribunal interprets a statute other than its own enabling legislation, it must be correct: *McLeod v. Egan*, [1975] 1 S.C.R. 517.

[187] See *Blanchard v. Control Data Can. Ltée, supra*, note 184.

[188] *C.U.P.E., Local 963 v. N.B. Liquor Corp.*, [1979] 2 S.C.R. 227, at 233, per Dickson J.

[189] *Ibid.*

[190] [1975] 1 S.C.R. 382.

[191] Bill C-38, *supra*, note 167.

[192] *Ibid.*, s. 5, creating a new s. 18.1(4)(c).

[193] *Ibid.*, s. 5, creating a new s. 18.1(4)(d).

[194] See J.M. Evans, *DeSmith's Judicial Review of Administrative Action*, 4th ed. (London: Stevens & Sons, 1980), pp. 248-251.

inevitably permeated by mistrust which generates claims of bias and prejudice. It is not uncommon to hear prisoners challenge the impartiality of a decision-maker. Absence of confidence in the impartiality and fairness of a decision-making process is often explained in terms of a record of previous negative decisions or an account of previous unfavourable interactions between the prisoner and a relatively stable group of decision-makers making a number of decisions about a prisoner's future—*e.g.*, remission crediting, fence clearance, transfer, discipline, temporary absence, case management, work board, and Parole Board. While cast in terms of bias or prejudice, these claims may speak more directly to issues of procedural fairness or bad faith in the exercise of discretion.

Basically, the common law has focussed on whether a decision-maker has an interest or prior relationship which would cause a reasonable person to question the impartiality of the decision-maker. The test is cast in terms of a reasonable apprehension of bias.[195] By the same token that the guarantee of fairness extends to the appearance of fairness,[196] the guarantee of impartiality should extend to the appearance of impartiality. The *Parole Regulations* specifically adopt the common law and also ensure that the issue of bias includes concerns generated by statements of a Board member which impair the appearance of impartiality. As of 1986, the Regulations provide:

> 22.1 (1): A member of the Board shall withdraw from voting in the case of an inmate where a reasonable apprehension of bias may result from the particular circumstances of the case, including
> (a) a monetary conflict of interest with the inmate;
> (b) personal, family, social, work or business-related connections with the inmate or the victim of an offence in respect of which the inmate was convicted;
> (c) prior public statements made or positions taken directly connected with the matter; and
> (d) indications of hostility, or favouritism toward the inmate."[197]

Subsection (d) encompasses both conduct prior to the hearing and any remarks made at the hearing.[198]

---

[195] *Kane v. U.B.C.*, [1980] 1 S.C.R. 1105.

[196] See *Committee for Justice & Liberty v. National Energy Bd.*, [1978] 1 S.C.R. 369, a case involving a claim that the Board Chair's prior role as President of the Canada Development Corporation created a reasonable apprehension of bias, since he had participated in the decision to bring the application to authorize a MacKenzie Valley pipeline, the issue then before the National Energy Board, over which he now presided.

[197] SOR/86-817. Prior to the enactment of this Regulation, the issue of bias had been dealt with as a matter of policy.

[198] Unreasonably aggressive conduct toward a party at a hearing is reviewable either because it creates an appearance of unfairness or partiality: see *Re Golomb and College of Physicians & Surgeons* (1976), 68 D.L.R. (3d) 25 (Ont. Div. Ct.).

(iv) *Derivative Grounds*

The concepts of jurisdiction and fairness give rise to related grounds which, while often described as independent, are essentially derivative.[199] One example is the concept of fettering discretion which developed to ensure that each applicant or party obtains a full and fair exercise of discretion in accordance with the delegated statutory mandate. Essentially, the argument is one of declining jurisdiction. The issue may arise when a decision-maker rejects a particular case by reliance on a general rule or policy. In 1919,[200] however, the concept only applied in cases where a decision-maker "passed a rule, or [came] to a determination not to hear any application of a particular character by whomsoever made."[201] In more recent times, there has been more incentive to develop policy and give consideration to previous rulings in an effort to establish mature expertise and to structure discretion.[202] Moreover, policy and precedent produce consistency and predictability — virtues of any system. Hence, courts have been required to take a more refined approach to the issue of fettering discretion. They have encouraged the adoption and articulation of policy, so long as a decision-maker does not thereby prohibit itself from hearing a case which its mandate requires it to hear. Lord Reid has said:

> I do not think there is any great difference between a policy and a rule. There may be cases where an officer or authority ought to listen to a substantial argument reasonably presented urging a change of policy. What the authority must not do is to refuse to listen at all. But a Ministry or large authority may have had to deal already with a multitude of similar applications and then they will almost certainly have evolved a policy so precise that it could well be called a rule. There can be no objection to that, provided the authority is always willing to listen to anyone with something new to say . . . .[203]

---

[199] One could probably argue that bias as a ground for review is an emanation of fairness and that fairness derives from jurisdiction. If there is any contemporary significance to the distinctions it relates only to remedial issues and the application of privative clauses. The discretionary nature of prerogative relief should not apply to a decision made without jurisdiction which must be treated as void *ab initio*.

[200] See *R. v. Port of London Authority; Ex parte Kynoch, Ltd.*, [1919] 1 K.B. 176, at 183, per Bankes L.J.

[201] *Ibid.*, at 184.

[202] In his classic study, *Discretionary Justice* (Baton Rouge: Louisiana State University Press, 1969), K.C. Davis wrote in respect of discretion: "The principal ways of controlling are structuring and checking. Structuring includes plans, policy statements, and rules as well as open findings, open rules, and open precedents. . . ." (p. 55). This reveals the conceptual link between the two derivative grounds discussed here: fettering discretion and the obligation to give reasons.

[203] *British Oxygen Co. v. Minister of Technology*, [1971] A.C. 610 (H.L.), at 625.

A similar position has been adopted by Canadian courts.[204] Previous rulings have been treated in the same way as previously articulated policy. The authors Evans *et al.* note:

> The law here is thus very similar to that respecting policy statements. It is "reasonable and wise", "inevitable and desirable" to use prior decisions to lay down principles for guidance, but this must not be at the expense of at least some residual willingness to consider the merits of the particular application measured against the statutory discretion unadorned by any administrative gloss.[205]

While there is a virtue in consistency, a tribunal cannot use this objective to preclude the performance of its mandate in a given case.

As well, reliance on prior policies or decisions are only legitimate as guides to the exercise of discretion when they are openly stated and readily accessible.[206] Lack of consistency may represent a legitimate ground of review; it is perhaps the only ground which can be characterized as a manifestation of unfairness in a substantive sense.[207] A claim of this kind can only be made if the party is aware of prior conflicting decisions. In the case of the National Parole Board, Board members may be unaware of recent decisions, given that the Board operates out of five distinct regions. Although this has been eased recently with the publication and circulation of the new "Appeal Division Reports,"[208] it is still difficult for Board members (particularly for temporary and community Board members) to know at any given time whether other regions are applying a consistent policy.

Another derivative ground, closely related to the issue of publishing decisions, is the obligation to provide reasons. Generally, the common law has not recognized a duty to issue reasons for a decision in the absence of an express statutory obligation.[209] However, the development of the duty to act fairly has produced the recognition of an implied duty to give reasons in cases where a party has further contact with the decision-maker and needs guidance in order to make appropriate choices.[210] While this has not been precisely litigated in the parole context, an analogous situation is that of a compulsorily confined patient in a psychiatric facility who has a right to apply for discharge. In *Ex*

---

[204] See, for example, *Capital Cities Communications Inc. v. Cdn. Radio-Television Cmmn.*, [1978] 2 S.C.R. 141.

[205] J.M. Evans, H.N. Janisch, D.J. Mullan and R.C.B. Risk, *Administrative Law: Cases, Text and Materials*, 3d ed. (Toronto: Emond Montgomery, 1989), p. 797.

[206] See *Re Hopedale Dev. Ltd. and Oakville (Town)* (1964), 47 D.L.R. (2d) 482 (Ont. C.A.).

[207] See D.J. Mullan, "Natural Justice and Fairness" (1982), 27 McGill L.J. 250.

[208] Discussed in Chapter 8.

[209] See *DeSmith's Judicial Review of Administrative Action, supra*, note 194, pp. 148-151.

[210] See *DeSmith's Judicial Review of Administrative Action, supra*, note 194, p. 149 and the examples cited therein.

parte Pickering, the English High Court ruled that the patient was entitled to adequate reasons for a refusal so that he would know how to structure his program and conduct in order to meet the Board's concerns in the future.[211]

Federally, a duty to provide reasons has been imposed on the National Parole Board in respect of granting,[212] revocation and termination decisions,[213] and decisions not to re-credit remission.[214] The Board must, in these situations, provide reasons in writing, usually within 15 days. The Regulations do not qualify the extent or adequacy of the reasons which must be provided. Relying on *Ex parte Pickering*, and the implications of the duty to provide a fair hearing in the future, the adequacy of reasons can be understood in functional terms. Reasons must be sufficient to permit a prisoner to know the concerns of the Board such that he understands the thresholds which must be crossed before a positive decision can be expected. Thus, adequate reasons should tell a prisoner the kind of institutional program and progress, and the kind of release plan, which must be successfully effected to satisfy the Board.

(c) Mandamus

Although in the past *mandamus* was used for a wide array of purposes,[215] its contemporary function is limited. Essentially, *mandamus* is available to compel a tribunal, body or officer which is subject to a public duty to perform that duty according to law. If the duty involves the exercise of discretion, then the remedy applies only to ensure that it is performed — not how it is performed. For example, the refusal of a Justice of the Peace to receive an information is subject to *mandamus*.[216] Similarly, a tribunal which declines to hear an application which it ought to entertain can be challenged by *mandamus*.[217] But neither the Justice of the Peace nor the tribunal can be compelled to exercise their discretion in a particular way.[218]

---

[211] *R. v. Mental Health Review Tribunal; Ex parte Pickering*, [1986] 1 All E.R. 99 at 104. See also *Bone v. Mental Health Review Tribunal*, [1985] 3 All E.R. 330; *R. v. Mental Health Review Tribunal; Ex parte Clatworthy*, [1985] 3 All E.R. 699.

[212] *Parole Regulations*, SOR/86-915, s. 19(2).

[213] *Parole Regulations*, SOR/86-817, s. 21(1) and (3).

[214] *Parole Regulations*, SOR/86-817, s. 21(2) and (3).

[215] See *DeSmith's Judicial Review Administrative Action, supra*, note 194, pp. 538-539.

[216] *R. v. Read; Ex parte McDonald* (1968), 1 D.L.R. (3d) 118 (Alta. C.A.), at 121.

[217] See, for example, *R. v. Criminal Injuries Compensation Board; Ex parte Clowes*, [1977] 1 W.L.R. 1353.

[218] See *DeSmith's Judicial Review of Administrative Action, supra*, note 194, pp. 87 and 543.

Like the other prerogative writs of *certiorari* and prohibition, *mandamus* has been considered a discretionary remedy which should not be granted when an alternative effective remedy is available.[219] Recently, Canadian courts seem to be requiring real parallelism of effect before a prerogative remedy will be refused on this basis.[220] However, given that *mandamus* only applies when there has been a failure to perform a duty, there is now serious doubt about whether relief can be denied on discretionary grounds if a claim has been properly brought and proven.[221]

The essence of a claim for *mandamus* is the existence of a duty and a refusal to perform it. The question of situating and establishing the duty is not as simple as it might seem. First, there is the question of the proper respondent, particularly since relief does not lie against the Crown.[222] Thus, one must examine the relevant statutory framework to find a duty imposed upon an officer or body. If the officer is a Minister of the Crown, it will be necessary to argue that the duty was imposed as *persona designata* before *mandamus* will lie.[223] As well, in the federal sphere, section 18 of the *Federal Court Act* provides the jurisdiction to grant *mandamus* in respect of "any federal board, commission or other tribunal." Accordingly, a physician working at a penitentiary was held not to be subject to *mandamus* in respect of his obligations to prisoners, because he did not meet the definition in section 2 of the *Federal Court Act*.[224] Secondly, there is the question of the duty itself. It must be "due

---

[219] In *Re Hall and Johnson* (1974), 52 D.L.R. (3d) 237 (N.S.C.A.), *mandamus* was described as an "extraordinary remedy" which should be available "only in the absence of any other legal remedy, equally convenient, beneficial and appropriate" (at 239).

[220] This trend in Canadian law seems to require more than simply the existence of another avenue, but rather an alternative which would give the party the same effect as the prerogative remedy: A. Manson, Case comment on *Dubois v. R.* (1986), 19 Admin. L.R. 318. Although the language in *Re Hall and Johnson, ibid.*, note 219, is consistent with the requirement of parallelism, it is interesting that relief was denied in that case because the court did not find a duty to disclose the information sought.

[221] See, for example, *R. v. Hounslow Local Borough Council; Ex parte Pizzey*, [1977] 1 W.L.R. 58, at 62, per Lord Widgery.

[222] Evans *et al., supra*, note 205, refer to the maintenance of this anachronistic proposition as "ridiculous" (pp. 882-883).

[223] The test seems to be whether the Minister is accountable to the Crown or to the person to whom the duty is owed: see *Re Central Can. Potash Co. and Saskatchewan (M.N.R.)* (1972), 32 D.L.R. (3d) 107 (Sask. C.A.). It is not easy to apply: see *Re McKay and Minister of Municipal Affairs* (1973), 35 D.L.R. (3d) 627 (B.C.S.C.).

[224] See *McNamara v. Caros*, [1978] 1 F.C. 451 (T.D.). Section 2 of the *Federal Court Act* provides that " 'federal board, commission or other tribunal' means any body or any person or persons having, exercising or purporting to exercise jurisdiction or powers

and incumbent".[225] It is important to find a statutory source,[226] prefera-
bly one which casts the duty in clear and express terms, and it is good
practice to deliver a precise demand as a precursor to an application for
mandamus.

The availability or appropriateness of *mandamus* becomes more
suspect when the duty in question involves the exercise of discretion. A
failure to embark on an inquiry or to pursue an inquiry to fruition is
certainly redressible by *mandamus,* but an error in the course of an
inquiry may not be.[227] The same limitations placed on the availability of
certiorari to respond to errors apply to *mandamus* even though notionally it can compel a tribunal to perform its duty according to law.[228]

7. HABEAS CORPUS

(a) History

Throughout the history of Anglo-Canadian law, *habeas corpus* has
been the most important remedy by which to challenge the legality of
confinement. In 1628, John Selden described it as "the highest remedy
in law for any man that is in prison"[229] and Blackstone has called it "the
great and efficacious writ, in all manner of illegal confinement."[230] Its
historical roots as an instrument for securing personal liberty are
unclear:

> Its beginnings are shrouded in the dim past, but that it was recognized and
> enforced at common law is unquestioned. It arose at a time when the
> individual was too often the victim of tyranny in public and private prisons
> and when the King as the supreme lord might well be concerned about the
> fate of lieges.[231]

---

conferred by or under an Act of Parliament, other than any such body constituted or
established by or under a law of a province or any such person or persons appointed
under or in accordance with a law of a province or under section 96 of the *Constitution
Act, 1867.*"
[225] See *Karavos v. Toronto (City),* [1948] 3 D.L.R. 294 (Ont. C.A.), at 297. DeSmith refers
to the demand requirement as a "general rule" but cites exceptions: J.M. Evans,
DeSmith's Judicial Review of Administrative Action, 4th ed. (London: Stevens & Sons,
1980), pp. 556-557.
[226] Evans *et al.* mention the possibility that there may be public duties not created by
statute or royal prerogative which are subject to *mandamus,* but these would certainly
be rare: *supra,* note 205, 877, referring to *Re Morris and Morris* (1973), 36 D.L.R. (3d)
447 (Man. Q.B.) as an example.
[227] See, generally, the discussion in *DeSmith's Judicial Review of Administrative Action,
supra,* note 225, pp. 543-547.
[228] *Ibid.*
[229] 3 State Trials 95. (1627), 3 Cobbett's State Trials.
[230] 3 Blackstone's Commentaries 131.
[231] *Re Storgoff,* [1945] S.C.R. 526, per Rand J. at 577-578.

Aside from the incomplete and inaccurate records of the early years of English law, the reason for the conflicting views of legal historians as to the origins of *habeas corpus* likely lies in the multiplicity of writs which existed at the time.[232] At the time of Rannulf Glanvill and Henry Bracton, three ancient writs were used to protect the liberty of the subject: *de homine replegiando, mainprize* and *de odio et atia.*[233] Furthermore, early evidence of the use of *habeas corpus* itself revealed that a number of varieties existed with different purposes. Most of the forms of *habeas corpus,* such as *respondendum, satisfaciendum, prosequendum, testificandum* and *deliberandum* were purely procedural. They were used to remove prisoners from one court to another in order to commence new litigation, execute a judgment, prosecute a charge, or hear testimony.[234] While writs in these forms applied to persons in prison, they had little to do with liberty.

It is *habeas corpus ad subjiciendum* which has become the remedy by which the legality of confinement is tested[235] and, at least from the time of the *Magna Carta,* it appears to have been available for that purpose.[236] Reference to the *Magna Carta* provides an easy focal point

---

[232] E. Jenks suggested that the origin of *habeas corpus* can be found in the Royal Ordinance Assize of Clarendon issued by Henry II in 1166: see E. Jenks, "The Prerogative Writs in English Law" (1923) 32 Yale L.J. 523, at 524. However, J.C. Fox has argued that Jenks mistook writs of *capias* for writs of *habeas corpus*: see J.C. Fox, "Process of Imprisonment at Common Law" (1923) 39 L.Q. Rev. 46, at 46-59.

[233] See 3 Blackstone's Commentaries, *supra,* note 230, at 128-130; and 9 Holdsworth's *History of the Law of England,* 3d ed. (London: Methuen & Co. Ltd., 1944), pp. 104-108.

[234] For an explanation of these various archaic forms, see Blackstone's Commentaries, *supra,* note 230, at 130-131. Most of them have ceased to exist or have any practical utility. For example, *testificandum* was used to bring a prisoner to court to give evidence. That function seems to have been replaced, in the criminal context, by section 527 of the *Criminal Code* (R.S.C. 1985, c. C-46) and, in the civil context, by rules of practice: in Ontario, see *Rules of Civil Procedure,* O. Reg. 560/84, Rule 53.06. Pursuant to this rule's predecessor, it has been held that a court only has authority to order the attendance of a prisoner in custody in Ontario: see *McGuire v. McGuire,* [1953] O.R. 328 (C.A.). There is no reason why the *Code* provision emanating from a federal statute of general applicability should be subject to a similar limitation and judges often make orders which are directed to gaolers in provinces. *Testificandum,* however, could not have extra-jurisdictional effect. See the further discussion of this subject in Chapter 9.

[235] As Blackstone has said, "This is a high prerogative writ . . . for the king is at all times entitled to have an account why the liberty of any of his subjects is restrained, wherever that restraint may be inflicted": see Blackstone's Commentaries, *supra,* note 230, at 131.

[236] Clause 39 of the *Magna Carta* provided that "No freeman shall be captured or imprisoned or disseised or outlawed or exiled or in any way destroyed . . . except by the lawful judgment of his peers or by the law of the land", but the document made no

both chronologically and conceptually for linking the remedy with illegal imprisonment.[237] Some authors, however, question whether its early use was motivated by high principle. Holdsworth has said that the "cause of this development must . . . be sought in the desire of the courts of common law to extend their jurisdiction at the expense of rival courts."[238]

Regardless of the debate over its origins, by the time of the constitutional controversies of the 17th Century, *habeas corpus ad subjiciendum* was the primary instrument for the protection of personal liberty.[239] Vaughan C.J. in 1670 stated that "it is now the most usual remedy by which a man is restored again to his liberty, if he have been against law deprived of it."[240] The utility of the common law writ was, however, blunted by the political conflicts of the time.[241] Imprisonment as a means of responding to dissent was commonplace.[242] The disputes between the sovereign and the parliamentary opposition resulted in the constitutional reforms of the *Petition of Right* in 1628 and the *Bill of Rights* in 1689. During the same period of reform, some of the inade-

---

mention of *habeas corpus*: see C. Stephenson and F. Marcham, Eds., *Sources of English Constitutional History: A Selection of Documents From A.D. 600 to the Present* (New York: Harper & Bros., 1937), p. 121. Thus, it is unclear "whether courts of justice framed the writ of *habeas corpus* in conformity to the spirit of this clause, or found it already in their register, it became from that era the right of every subject to demand": see Hallam, 2 History of the Middle Ages 342, quoted in R.C. Hurd, *On The Right of Personal Liberty and On The Writ of Habeas Corpus* (Albany, N.Y.: W.C. Little & Co., 1858), p. 79. Also, Kerwin J. in *In Re Storgoff, supra,* note 231, remarked that the *Magna Carta* "may be taken either as the source of the writ of *habeas corpus* or as an admission by the Sovereign of its existence" (at 557).

[237] A number of historians commence the relationship at a later date. Cohen places its beginning in the 14th Century: see M. Cohen, "Some Considerations on the Origins of Habeas Corpus" (1938) 16 Can. Bar Rev. 92 and M. Cohen, "Habeas Corpus Cum Causa—The Emergence of the Modern Writ" (1940) 18 Can. Bar Rev. 10 and 172. DeSmith also accepts that it "emerged" in the 14th century: see Appendix 2, Aspects of Habeas Corpus, in *DeSmith's Judicial Review of Administrative Action, supra,* note 225, at 596. Holdsworth does not find a clear link until the 15th Century: see 1 Holdsworth, 7th ed. (London: Methuen & Co., 1956), p. 227; and 9 Holdsworth, *supra,* note 233, pp. 108-109.

[238] See 9 Holdsworth 109. In individual cases the ultimate result was the release of the prisoner. Holdsworth, however, characterizes the remedy as an element in the contest between the courts of common law and the local and franchise courts, as well as the rival central courts of Chancery, the Council, the Admiralty, Star Chamber and High Commission between medieval times and the 16th Century: see also 1 Holdsworth 227.

[239] See *Searche's Case* (1588), 1 Leon 70; *Darnel's Case* (1627), 3 State Trials 1.

[240] *Bushell's Case* (1670), 2 Jon. 13, 124 E.R. 1007.

[241] See Hurd, *supra,* note 236, p. 92.

[242] See Hurd, *supra,* note 236, pp. 85-89; and 9 Holdsworth, *supra,* note 233, pp. 114-116.

quacies of the common law writ of *habeas corpus* were also addressed in the *Habeas Corpus Act* of 1679.[243]

The new Act attempted to revise and repair the process by which *habeas corpus* could be obtained, but it did not create or expand substantive rights:

> ... it was not to bestow an immunity from arbitrary imprisonment, which is abundantly provided in Magna Carta (if indeed it is not much more ancient), that the statute of Charles II was enacted; but to cut off the abuses by which government's lust of power, and the servile subtlety of crown lawyers, had impaired so fundamental a privilege.[244]

The statute contained a number of provisions directed to ensuring a speedy enquiry into the cause of confinement and a speedy trial for those lawfully remanded.[245] Holdsworth pointed out two major deficiencies in the 1679 statute.[246] First, it applied only to confinement arising from a criminal charge. Accordingly, the detention of infants, mental incompetents, debtors and others committed by civil process were not touched by the new Act. This gap was remedied by the 1816 *Habeas Corpus Act* which applied solely to those persons deprived of their liberty otherwise than by reason of a criminal charge.[247] Secondly, the statute did not empower judges to inquire into the truth of the return made by the gaoler. While no specific power existed, there is some evidence that a limited scrutiny of the question of jurisdiction evolved as a matter of judicial handiwork.[248] Later, we shall look more deeply into this issue.[249]

It has also been suggested that, because one of the principal objects of the 1679 Act was to ensure speedy trials, the Act applied only to

---

[243] (31 Cha. 2), c. 10. For an historical discussion of the abuse of the writ, see 9 Holdsworth, *supra*, note 233, pp. 116-119.

[244] Hurd, *supra*, note 236, pp. 95-96.

[245] The Act provided that the writ could issue, either in vacation or term time, that the production of the body and a return was required within a specified time not to exceed 20 days, and the jailer was required to deliver to the prisoner a true copy of the warrant of commitment. Also, the Act required that a prisoner indicted for treason or felony must be bailed or tried at the next sessions unless it was shown that the King's witnesses could not be available: see the *Habeas Corpus Act* of 1679 and, generally, the discussion in 9 Holdsworth, *supra*, note 233, pp. 118-119.

[246] See 9 Holdsworth, *supra*, note 233, pp. 119-120.

[247] (56 Geo. 3), c. 100. See the discussion in 9 Holdsworth, *supra*, note 233, pp. 121-122; and E. Koroway, "Habeas Corpus in Ontario" (1975) 13 Osgoode Hall L.J. 149, at 153-154.

[248] See *Re Allison* (1854), 10 Ex. 561, 156 E.R. 561, per Parke B., where he interjected that "[S]ince there is no other mode of bringing the conviction before the Court, it is sufficient to produce it verified by affidavit" (at 563); see also the references in Henry J.'s judgment in *Re Sproule* (1886), 12 S.C.R. 140, at 157-158; and in *Re Trepanier* (1885), 12 S.C.R. 111, at 119.

[249] See the discussion of the scope of *habeas corpus, infra*, at pp. 89-102.

persons awaiting trial.[250] History does not bear this out. A number of English judgments show that the same process was available to prisoners who had not yet been convicted and for those under execution of a sentence after conviction.[251]

The common law writ of *habeas corpus* and its accompanying procedures came to Canada along with the body of English substantive and procedural law and followed its development closely.[252] The earliest formal recognition appears to be the 1784 Proclamation of Haldimand which was subsequently confirmed and entrenched in the *Constitution Act* of 1791.[253] Pre-confederation statutes provided the framework for *habeas corpus* in Ontario, Quebec, Nova Scotia and New Brunswick.[254] These are of particular importance because they were continued in force by section 129 of the *Constitution Act, 1867.*[255] In the remaining provinces and territories the historical source of the law of *habeas corpus* starts with the introduction of English law which incorporated both the 1679 and 1816 *Habeas Corpus Act.*[256]

(b) The Nature of Habeas Corpus

While Blackstone described *habeas corpus* as applicable to "all manner of illegal confinement,"[257] the provisions of English statute law

---

[250] Ritchie C.J. in *Re Sproule, supra,* note 248.

[251] See, for example, the discussion in *Leonard Watson's Case* (the case of the Canadian Prisoners) (1839), 112 E.R. 1389. This case represents an interesting anecdote in Canadian history. The prisoners had been participants in the 1837 rebellion in Upper Canada and, subsequently, were charged with treason. Prior to trial, they were pardoned on the condition that they submit to transportation abroad. On their way, their ship stopped in England where they were imprisoned on board. The *habeas corpus* application questioned the sufficiency of the warrants by which they were held on various grounds including the argument that the documentation emanated from Upper Canada and did not provide for incarceration in England while in transit. The application failed.

[252] See C. Harvey, *The Law of Habeas Corpus in Canada* (Toronto: Butterworths, 1974), p. 2. Also see T. Cromwell "Habeas Corpus and Correctional Law" (1977) 3 Queen's L.J. 295, at 298-99.

[253] *Constitution Act, 1791* (31 Geo. 3), c. 31. See the discussion in *Lorenz v. Lorenz* (1905), Q.R. 28 S.C. 330 referred to in *Re Storgoff, supra,* note 231, at 537, per Rinfret C.J.

[254] For Ontario, see *An Act for More Effectually Securing the Liberty of the Subject* (29 & 30 Vict.), c. 45; for Quebec, see *An Act Respecting the Writ of Habeas Corpus, Bail and Other Provisions of Law for Securing the Liberty of the Subject,* C.S.L.C. 1861, c. 95; for New Brunswick, see *An Act for Better Securing the Liberty of the Subject* (19 & 20 Vict.), c. 42; for Nova Scotia, see *Of the Liberty of the Subject: For Removing Doubts,* R.S.N.S. 1864, c. 153.

[255] (30 & 31 Vict.), c. 3.

[256] See *Re Storgoff,* [1945] S.C.R. 526, note 230, at 557-558, per Kerwin J.

[257] 3 Blackstone's Commentaries 131.

distinguished between criminal and civil imprisonment. In England, this mode of differentiation represents different stages of historical development. In Canada, however, it raises other questions because of federal/provincial legislative competence and differences between provinces. Thus, the nature of *habeas corpus* in criminal/civil terms is not simply an academic issue.

In *Re Storgoff*, the Supreme Court of Canada was faced with the question of whether a 1920 amendment to the *British Columbia Court of Appeal Act* could provide a route of appeal in *habeas corpus* proceedings relating to the validity of a sentence imposed after a *Code* conviction.[258] After a prisoner had obtained an order for discharge on the return to a writ of *habeas corpus*, the Attorney General of British Columbia appealed to the Court of Appeal, which reversed and ordered the prisoner's re-arrest. At the time, the *Code* provided no avenue of appeal in *habeas corpus* proceedings.[259] The Crown argued that the provincial legislation was valid since the central focus of *habeas corpus* was personal liberty, and that civil rights were within provincial legislative competence. It offered the view that *habeas corpus* was an "independent proceeding, unconnected with the criminal cause for which the commitment was ordered".[260] The Supreme Court, with Rinfret C.J. dissenting, rejected this argument by distinguishing between legislation which "affected" civil rights and legislation "in relation to" civil rights. According to Rand J., *habeas corpus* "takes its character from the proceeding into which it is introduced or which becomes its subject matter."[261] Hence, in relation to a criminal proceeding or commitment, it was a step in the criminal process, but its nature could be civil if it arose in the context of a civil cause.[262] Consequently, it was not within the authority of the British Columbia legislature to give a right of appeal in criminal *habeas corpus* proceedings.

This is not to say that the process and scope of criminal *habeas corpus* is necessarily identical in all provinces because the subject matter is within federal legislative competence. As mentioned above, pre-Confederation *habeas corpus* statutes are still operative in Ontario, Quebec, Nova Scotia and New Brunswick.[263] The New Brunswick and

---

258 *Supra*, note 256 (*British Columbia Court of Appeal Act*, R.S.B.C. 1936, c. 57; *Criminal Code*, R.S.C. 1927, c. 36).
259 In Canada, the *Code* did not include an appeal for the respondent until 1965: see the discussion in *Re Law and R. (No. 2)*, (1981), 64 C.C.C. (2d) 181 (Ont. H.C.); subsequently affirmed (1982), 65 C.C.C. (2d) 512 (Ont. C.A.).
260 *Supra*, note 256, at 540.
261 *Supra*, note 256, at 582.
262 *Supra*, note 256 at 574-575, per Taschereau J.
263 *Supra*, note 254.

Nova Scotia statutes apply to "any person confined in a gaol or prison."[264] The Quebec Act has specific provisions applicable to criminal matters[265] and general sections which apply both to criminal and civil *habeas corpus* proceedings.[266]

The Ontario Act appears to be modelled closely after the 1816 English statute, which extended *habeas corpus* to most cases of civil confinement. In particular, the preambles to both statutes are virtually identical. However, the operative scope of each statute is described differently. The English Act limits its application to people confined "otherwise than for some criminal or supposed criminal matter" and also excepts people imprisoned by reason of debt or "by process in any civil suit."[267] The scope of the Ontario statute is phrased differently, excluding:

> persons imprisoned for debt, or by process in any civil suit, or by the judgment, conviction or decree of any Court of Record, Court of Oyer and Terminer or General Gaol Delivery, or Court of General Quarter Sessions of the Peace. . . .[268]

In *Re Trepanier*, Ritchie C.J. suggested that the Ontario statute was enacted for the same purpose as the 1816 English Act.[269] Subsequently, in *Ex parte Johnston*, the Ontario Court of Appeal discounted Ritchie C.J.'s characterization as obiter.[270] After examining the two statutes, the court concluded that the Ontario statute was not restricted to civil forms of confinement, and that it applied to *habeas corpus* "in both its criminal and civil aspects."[271] Significant aspects of these pre-Confederation statutes were the express provisions applicable in Nova Scotia, New Brunswick and Ontario for an inquiry into the sufficiency of the return.[272] Until very recently, this issue remained controversial in

---

[264] For New Brunswick, see s. 1 (19 & 20 Vict., c. 42), and for Nova Scotia, see s. 4 of R.S.N.S. 1864, c. 153.

[265] C.S.L.C. 1861, c. 95, ss. 1-19.

[266] *Ibid.*, ss. 27-29.

[267] (56 Geo. 3), c. 100, s. 1.

[268] (29 & 30 Vict.), c. 45, s. 1.

[269] *Supra*, note 248.

[270] [1959] O.R. 322 (C.A.).

[271] *Ibid.*, at 329, per Morden J.A.

[272] The Nova Scotia and New Brunswick statutes contain identical provisions empowering the judge upon receipt of the return to "proceed to examine into and decide upon the legality of the imprisonment, and make such order, require such verification, and direct such notices or further returns in respect thereof as may be deemed necessary or proper for the purposes of justice": see respectively R.S.N.S. 1864, c. 153, s. 6 and (19 & 20 Vict.), c. 42, s. 3. More expansive, however, is the Ontario Act which provides that "although the return to any writ of Habeas Corpus shall be good and sufficient in law, it

Canada.[273]

(c) The Scope of Habeas Corpus

It is unhelpful simply to consider *habeas corpus* as the instrument by which a prisoner can challenge the legality of his confinement. The concept of legality is broad and imprecise. The *Magna Carta* guaranteed that no person could be imprisoned except "by lawful judgment of his peers, or by the law of the land." Section 2(c)(iii) of the *Canadian Bill of Rights* speaks to "the remedy of *habeas corpus* for the determination of the validity of his detention". A similar reference has been constitutionally entrenched in section 10(c) of the *Canadian Charter of Rights and Freedoms* to ensure that "[e]veryone has the right on arrest or detention . . . to have the validity of the detention determined by way of *habeas corpus*". But what exactly do we mean by phrases like the legality of confinement or the validity of detention? Is there any limitation on the kinds of questions about confinement which can be raised by way of *habeas corpus* applications?

Historically, there existed three kinds of writs: a writ of grace, which issued entirely in the discretion of the sovereign; a writ of course, which issued automatically upon request; and a writ of right, which required some showing of entitlement. With respect to *habeas corpus*, Blackstone noted that "it cannot be had of course."[274] *Habeas corpus* applications were brought in two stages.[275] In the first stage, the prisoner had to show "a probable ground" that he was "in prison without just cause."[276] Then, in traditional terms, the writ would issue to the jailer, requiring the

---

shall be lawful for the Court or for any Judge before whom such writ may be returnable to proceed to examine into the truth of the facts set forth in such return, by affidavit or by affirmation . . . and to do therein as to justice shall appertain . . .": see (29 & 30 Vict.), c. 45, s. 3. The Quebec Act is silent in respect of how the judge should examine the return.

[273] In *Mitchell v. R.*, [1976] 2 S.C.R. 570, four judges of the Supreme Court dealing with a Manitoba *habeas corpus* application in respect of a parole revocation were of the view that the inquiry did not extend beyond the face of the warrant produced on the return: see the discussion, *infra*, at p. 93 and, in particular, the dissent of Laskin C.J.C. The availability of a full inquiry including affidavits or other extrinsic evidence was not confirmed until the Supreme Court of Canada ruling in *Re Miller and R.*, [1985] 2 S.C.R. 613: see the discussion, *infra*, at p. 95.

[274] *Supra*, note 257, at 132.

[275] In many jurisdictions the two-stage process still exists. In Ontario, for example, while the traditional process continues to exist, contemporary exigencies have persuaded the Supreme Court of Ontario to empower its judges to telescope the process into one hearing—a discharge hearing—if the parties consent: see Rule 13 of the *Rules Respecting Criminal Proceedings*, SI/73-49, and the discussion in *Olson v. R.* (1989), 47 C.C.C. (3d) 491 (S.C.C.).

[276] Blackstone, *supra*, note 257, at 132-133.

production of the body of the prisoner in court along with a return disclosing the justification for confinement. Thus, the scope for *habeas corpus* is essentially determined by asking what kinds of questions can constitute probable grounds for issuing the writ, what is a sufficient return and in what ways can the return be challenged?[277]

In *Re Sproule*,[278] before the era of criminal appeals in Canada,[279] a prisoner convicted of murder and sentenced to death in British Columbia sought to challenge the conviction by applying to a single judge of the Supreme Court of Canada for *habeas corpus*. Although this procedure is no longer available,[280] in 1886 it permitted the prisoner to move his case to Ottawa, far from the jurisdiction of Sir Matthew Begbie, Chief Justice of British Columbia, the judge who presided at his trial.[281] The prisoner had unsuccessfully sought a writ of error in British Columbia,[282] so an approach to the Supreme Court by way of *habeas corpus* was his last resort. Although Henry J. granted the application,[283] his colleagues subsequently reversed his order.[284] Ritchie C.J. stated:

> . . . when it appeared by the records of courts of competent criminal jurisdiction, courts having jurisdiction over the person and over the offence with which he was charged, that he had been tried, convicted and sentenced, and was held under such sentence, the learned judge should have refused to grant the writ.[285]

---

[277] Interestingly, this last question was addressed in detail in Ontario's pre-Confederation statute: note 268.

[278] (1886), 12 S.C.R. 140.

[279] The right to appeal a criminal conviction was enacted by the *Criminal Code, 1892*, S.C. 1892, c. 29, ss. 742-750.

[280] The concurrent jurisdiction of a judge of the Supreme Court of Canada to hear *habeas corpus* applications was removed by the repeal of section 57 of the *Supreme Court Act*, R.S.C. 1952, c. 258, effected by S.C. 1969-70, c. 44, s. 4].

[281] The grounds for challenge included the allegation that the trial judge had concocted an order changing the venue after the trial had been completed. Combined with the intransigence of the Sheriff before Henry J.'s original order for discharge was reversed, this allegation reflects the politically volatile nature of this case. In fact, after the ultimate Supreme Court judgment, the Prime Minister, Sir John A. Macdonald, called to task both Henry J. and Strong J., for seeking to intervene in British Columbia justice: see D. Williams, *Begbie, The Man for a New Country* (Sydney, B.C.: Grays Publishing Ltd., 1977), p. 261.

[282] This application was dismissed unanimously by the full court of British Columbia: see the discussion of Taschereau J., *supra*, note 278, at 246-247.

[283] *Supra*, note 278, at 146-171.

[284] On the appeal to the full court, five separate judgments were rendered. Ritchie C.J.C., Strong and Taschereau JJ. concluded that the order ought not to have been made while Henry and Fournier JJ. dissented.

[285] *Supra*, note 278, at 190-191.

Clearly, the judges were directing their attention to convictions of superior courts.[286] One judge observed that to permit the prisoner to raise his challenge in this manner would mean that a single judge in Ottawa could thwart the decisions of a number of judges in the home province who had already dismissed the same argument.[287] For the time, at least, the case confirmed that *habeas corpus* could not be used to challenge imprisonment resulting from a conviction of a court of superior jurisdiction, the record of which appeared to be incontrovertible.

A related issue came before the Supreme Court in 1960 in *Goldhar*,[288] where the prisoner had been convicted of conspiracy to traffic in heroin and sentenced to 12 years' imprisonment. He had exhausted all of his appeals in respect of the conviction[289] and brought an application for *habeas corpus* before a single judge of the Supreme Court, arguing that the conspiracy alleged in the indictment commenced before an amendment to the *Code* increased the maximum available sentence for a conspiracy from 7 years to that of the substantive offence (which in this case was 14 years).[290] Martland J. refused the application, indicating that the issue had not been considered by the Ontario Court of Appeal, which dealt only with the appeal as to conviction.[291] The prisoner then obtained late leave to appeal sentence, but that appeal was dismissed.[292] An attempt was made to appeal the quantum of sentence to the Supreme Court; this was unsuccessful, the court resorting to its traditional concern to exclude sentencing issues from its purview.[293] At that stage, the indefatigable appellant resurrected his appeal in respect of the refusal of *habeas corpus*.

---

[286] *Supra*, note 278, per Ritchie C.J.C. at 200-201; Strong J. at 204-205; Taschereau J. at 245.

[287] *Supra*, note 278 at 246-247, per Taschereau J., after remarking that "rightly or wrongly, there is no appeal in criminal cases", he also pointed out that since the jurisdiction of a Supreme Court judge to hear *habeas corpus* applications was concurrent, then a single judge in chambers in British Columbia could equally have released the prisoner as Henry J. had ordered even though the argument had been dismissed by a panel of judges on a writ of error. It should be noted that a writ of error was not an appeal due to the limited nature of review and the precondition that the Attorney General consent to the process.

[288] *Goldhar (2) v. R.*, [1960] S.C.R. 431.

[289] An appeal to the Ontario Court of Appeal had been dismissed and leave to appeal to the Supreme Court of Canada denied: see Kerwin C.J.C.'s review of the case history [1960] S.C.R. 431, at 434.

[290] *Opium and Narcotic Drug Act*, R.S.C. 1952, c. 201, s. 4(3)(*b*) [enacted by S.C. 1953-54, c. 38, s. 3 and assented to June 10, 1954].

[291] *Re Goldhar*, [1958] S.C.R. 692.

[292] *Ibid.*

[293] *Goldhar v. R.*, [1960] S.C.R. 60.

With the history of the case set out in this manner, it is not difficult to anticipate the court's response. Recognizing that the jurisdiction of a Supreme Court judge to hear a *habeas corpus* application was concurrent with that of the High Court judges of the province, Kerwin C.J.C. concluded that it would be "unthinkable that after the Court of Appeal for Ontario has decided a point against the accused on the latter's appeal as to sentence, any judge in that province would decide differently on an application for a writ of *habeas corpus*."[294] It is only within the context of this view, clearly correct, that the remarks of the other judges can be appreciated. Cartwright J. held that a subsisting sentence of a court of competent jurisdiction was sufficient legal justification for imprisonment after observing that *habeas corpus* was "not a writ of course and may be refused where an alternative remedy by which the validity of the detention can be determined is available".[295] In his view, the remedy was by way of appeal, a route already exhausted by the prisoner. Fauteux J., as he then was, reached a similar conclusion expressing concern that *habeas corpus* not usurp the function of an appeal.[296] Unfortunately, he continued his comments to add that the scope of the writ does "not extend beyond an inquiry into the jurisdiction of the Court by which process the subject is held in custody and into the validity of the process upon its face."[297]

For many years, the various judgments in *Sproule* and *Goldhar* were considered to limit the scope of inquiry to the face of warrants produced on the return. One commentator has argued that this restriction applied only to sentences emanating from superior courts and ought not to preclude a fuller examination of the processes of inferior tribunals which resulted in imprisonment.[298] Regardless, when these two leading cases are taken in context, it seems clear that they were not so much dealing with the scope of inquiry, but rather with the limited question of the appropriate remedial role of *habeas corpus* when alternative remedies existed and had been pursued unsuccessfully on the same ground. *Habeas corpus* is not available as a form of collateral attack on the validity of a conviction or sentence when other effective opportunities to review the issue exist and have been exhausted.[299]

---

294 *Supra*, note 288, at 438.

295 *Supra*, note 288, at 440-441.

296 *Supra*, note 288, at 439.

297 *Supra*, note 288, at 439.

298 See R. Sharpe, *The Law of Habeas Corpus* (Oxford: Clarendon Press, 1976), pp. 144-145.

299 The alternative remedy caveat must be subject to the same requirements as section 776 of the *Code* imposes on the availability of *certiorari*—that is, where an appeal was taken or might have been taken. For a controversial discussion of this provision, see *Sanders v. R.*, [1970] 2 C.C.C. 57 (S.C.C.).

The inadequacy of applying *Sproule* and *Goldhar* to limit the scope of inquiry was made dramatically patent in *Mitchell*,[300] in which a prisoner resorted unsuccessfully to *habeas corpus* to challenge a parole revocation on *Bill of Rights* grounds. *Inter alia*, the prisoner argued that he was given no notice of the reasons for the suspension of his parole and no opportunity to respond to any adverse allegations. The application sought *certiorari* in aid of *habeas corpus* and attempted to describe the background events by affidavit evidence. The issue of *certiorari* in aid clouded the case, since the *Federal Court Act* had removed the jurisdiction to grant *certiorari* in respect of federal bodies from the provincial superior courts and placed it in the Trial Division of the Federal Court.[301] Laskin C.J.C., speaking for the dissent, noted the distinction between *certiorari* to bring up a record and *certiorari* to quash. In rejecting the argument that *certiorari* in aid could not be used to go behind the warrant, he characterized the approach as an "exercise in scolasticism . . . without merit."[302] Accordingly, while jurisdiction to grant *certiorari* to quash had been vested in the Federal Court, he concluded that *certiorari* in aid of *habeas corpus* continued to be available in provincial superior courts, otherwise the remedy was rendered ineffectual.[303] On this point four judges disagreed.[304] In their view, the judge of first instance was confined to a consideration on the face of the warrants.[305] The remaining two judges who dismissed the appeal did not consider the *certiorari* issue but relied on the sufficiency of the warrant of committal.[306]

In the aftermath of *Mitchell*, the utility of *habeas corpus*, especially in respect of internal prison and parole decisions, was suspect. Only Chief Justice Laskin and Dickson J., as he then was, seemed concerned to preserve its efficacy as a remedial instrument in respect of confinement. In so doing, they returned to its role in testing the jurisdictional legitimacy of imprisonment but offered an expanded, modern view of jurisdiction:

> . . . I have no doubt that jurisdictional questions may be raised on *habeas corpus* as going to the authority of the tribunal through which detention of a

---

[300] *Mitchell v. R.*, [1976] 2 S.C.R. 570.

[301] See *Federal Court Act*, R.S.C. 1970, c. 10 (2nd Supp.), s. 18.

[302] *Supra*, note 300, at 578.

[303] *Supra*, note 300, at 578-579.

[304] Ritchie J., with Judson, Pigeon, and Beetz JJ. concurring.

[305] *Supra*, note 300, at 594.

[306] See the judgment of Martland J. with De Grandpré J. concurring. Almost perversely, Martland J. rejected the appellant's contention that he did not know the reasons for his incarceration by pointing out that he was aware that his parole had been suspended-- hardly an adequate response: *supra*, note 300, at 587.

person has been effected, and defects of natural justice may be within that class of question.[307]

This broad conception of jurisdiction as the focus of *habeas corpus* was neither novel nor heretical. English courts had accepted that a formal showing of authority for detention would be an insufficient answer to an allegation of "abuse of power."[308] As well, in *Re Storgoff* Rand J. had explained that the essential question on *habeas corpus* "goes to the sufficiency in law of the process."[309] In the same case, Estey J. stated that "the competency of the legislation and the compliance with all the requirements imposed" were proper areas of inquiry in determining the legality of detention, including issues of process.[310] Thus, Laskin C.J.C.'s remarks only required the acceptance of procedural standards imposed by the common law rather than by statute to be in tune with precedent. However, it would take another decade before the equation of jurisdiction and defects of natural justice would extend the utility of *habeas corpus* to the internal processes of prison administration and parole.

After *Martineau (No. 2)*[311] confirmed the existence of the duty to act fairly, a number of prisoners resorted to *habeas corpus* in the provincial superior courts to raise fairness arguments in respect of decision-making processes that resulted in specific forms of confinement. *Re Cardinal*,[312] in British Columbia, used *habeas corpus* to challenge a warden's decision to segregate the prisoners in "administrative dissociation" as a result of allegations that they were involved in a hostage-taking incident at another institution. Their segregation was reviewed monthly. The Segregation Review Board recommended release into the general population, but the warden chose to continue segregation without providing any explanation for rejecting the recommendation. At first instance, McEachern C.J.S.C. held that *habeas corpus* was an available remedy for a prisoner to challenge detention in a "prison within a prison" as described by Dickson J. in *Martineau*.[313] Examining the affidavits filed, and utilizing *certiorari* in aid, he ruled that the applicants' segregation

---

[307] *Supra*, note 300, per Laskin C.J.C., at 578-579.

[308] For example, in *R. v. Governor of Brixton Prison; Ex parte Sarno*, [1916] 2 K.B. 742, at 752, Low J. commented:

The arm of the law in this country would have grown very short, and the power of this Court very feeble, if it were subject to such a restriction in the exercise of its power to protect the liberty of the subject as that proposition involves.

[309] [1945] S.C.R. 526, at 579.

[310] *Ibid.*, at 597.

[311] *Martineau v. Matsqui Institution Disciplinary Bd.*, [1980] 1 S.C.R. 602.

[312] *Re Cardinal and R.* (1982), 67 C.C.C. (2d) 252 (B.C.C.A.).

[313] *Ibid.*, at 257.

was initially lawful, but became unlawful as a result of a denial of fairness when the warden superseded the conclusion of the Segregation Review Board without providing notice of his reasons and an opportunity to respond. Accordingly, he ordered their release into the general prison population. The Court of Appeal agreed that the Supreme Court of British Columbia could issue *certiorari* in aid of *habeas corpus* even though the essential decision-maker was a federal body.[314] It also held that even on *habeas corpus* alone affidavits could be used to show want of jurisdiction, and that *habeas corpus* was available to challenge confinement of a prisoner by means of administrative dissociation. On the merits, however, Nemetz C.J.B.C. and Macdonald J.A. concluded that the warden did not breach his duty of fairness in making his decision to continue segregation, while Anderson J.A. dissented.

The cases of *Re Morin and Yeomans*[315] in Quebec, and *Miller*[316] in Ontario, involved challenges to transfers to Special Handling Units (S.H.U.). The S.H.U. program was established by the Commissioner's Directive to house prisoners considered especially dangerous usually by reason of participation in acts of violence within a penitentiary. The units were located within maximum security penitentiaries, but were separated from the general population. Upon being transferred to an S.H.U., a prisoner was classified with an S-7 security rating, which deemed that he must pass through four phases before returning to maximum security and an S-6 classification. This process could take a number of years.[317] The internal S.H.U. regime has been characterized as a "significantly more restrictive" form of confinement.[318] In *Morin*, the prisoner had been acquitted of the murder charge which had been the basis for his transfer to the S.H.U. Notwithstanding the persuasive value of *Cardinal*, both the judge of first instance and the Quebec Court of Appeal held that *habeas corpus* was not available and that the only avenue for challenging internal penitentiary decisions was *certiorari* in the Federal Court.[319] *Miller* raised arguments that confinement of S.H.U. was not lawfully authorized by statute or regulation, and that the procedure resulting in the transfer was unfair, since the prisoner had no opportunity to respond to evidence that he was involved in a disturbance.

---

[314] *Ibid.*, at 256, per Nemetz C.J.B.C.; at 261, per MacDonald J.A.; and at 269, per Anderson J.A. (dissenting in the result).

[315] *Re Morin and Yeomans* (1982), 1 C.C.C. (3d) 438 (Que. C.A.).

[316] *Re Miller and R.* (1982), 29 C.R. (3d) 153 (Ont. C.A.).

[317] For a full description of the process, as it operated in 1982, see *Miller, ibid.*, at 156 and *Re Chester* (1984), 40 C.R. (3d) 146 (Ont. H.C.).

[318] See *Miller, supra*, note 316, at 156.

[319] *Supra*, note 315.

Steele J. of the Ontario Supreme Court, influenced by the exclusive jurisdiction to grant *certiorari* vested in the Federal Court and the opinion of Ritchie J. in *Mitchell*, dismissed the application.[320] This was reversed in a unanimous judgment of the Ontario Court of Appeal, in which Cory J.A. concluded that *habeas corpus* was available to test the validity of confinement in an S.H.U., that affidavits could be used to raise jurisdictional defects, and that the court could issue *certiorari* in aid against a federal body, notwithstanding section 18 of the *Federal Court Act*.[321]

The three cases—*Cardinal*,[322] *Morin*,[323] and *Miller*[324]—were argued together in the Supreme Court of Canada. The judgments of LeDain J., speaking for a unanimous court, marked the end of an era of undue formalism which had stultified the use of *habeas corpus* as a contemporary remedy. Within the penitentiary and parole contexts, there could no longer be any doubt about a superior court's ability on *habeas corpus* to look behind a warrant or order which, on its face, appeared to have been regularly made by a person with authority to make it. To LeDain J. the starting point for analysis and the essential question was the continued efficacy of *habeas corpus* as the vehicle by which deprivations of liberty could be exposed to judicial scrutiny. In *Miller*, he stated:

> The proper scope of the availability of *habeas corpus* must be considered first on its own merits, apart from possible problems arising from concurrent or overlapping jurisdiction. The general importance of this remedy as the traditional means of challenging deprivations of liberty is such that its proper development and adaptation to the modern realities of confinement in a prison setting should not be compromised by concerns about conflicting jurisdiction. . . . Confinement in a special handling unit, or in administrative segregation as in *Cardinal*, is a form of detention that is distinct and separate from that imposed on the general inmate population. It involves a significant reduction in the residual liberty of the inmate. It is in fact a new detention of the inmate, purporting to rest on its own foundation of legal authority. It is that particular form of detention or deprivation of liberty which is the object of the challenge by *habeas corpus*.[325]

All the prisoners were lawfully incarcerated in penitentiaries. While they were not seeking liberty in an absolute sense, the more restrictive modes of confinement to which they were subjected were sufficient deprivations of liberty to trigger the availability of *habeas corpus*. LeDain J.'s

---

[320] *Supra*, note 316, at 164-165.
[321] *Supra*, note 316, at 157, 159 and 165-166.
[322] *Cardinal v. Kent Institution (Director)*, [1985] 2 S.C.R. 643.
[323] *Morin v. National Special Handling Unit Review Committee*, [1985] 2 S.C.R. 662.
[324] *R. v. Miller*, [1985] 2 S.C.R. 613.
[325] *Ibid.*, at 641.

notion of a "significant reduction in the residual liberty of the inmate" extended *habeas corpus* to situations where more onerous forms of constraints are placed on prisoners even though they are lawfully confined.[326] LeDain J. cautioned, however, that *habeas corpus* should not apply to question "all conditions of confinement", but does lie in respect of any "distinct form of confinement or detention in which the actual physical constraint or deprivation of liberty . . . is more restrictive or severe than the normal one in an institution", something different from simply the loss of privileges.[327]

In respect of issues relating to the scope of inquiry on *habeas corpus*, LeDain J. carefully examined the historical and technical issues, with sensitivity both to the modern role of *habeas corpus* and the peculiar nature of the penitentiary environment. With respect to *certiorari* in aid, he accepted the distinction offered earlier by Laskin C.J.C., dissenting, in *Mitchell*, between *certiorari* to quash and *certiorari* to bring up the record of an inferior tribunal.[328] While the former, a primary remedy, rests exclusively with the Federal Court, *certiorari* in aid is an ancillary remedy which exists to make effective another primary remedy, *habeas corpus*, the jurisdiction for which has not been removed from the provincial superior courts. Because confinement was in issue, it was irrelevant that the same legal issue could be raised in the Federal Court.[329]

Dealing with the kind of material a court can consider on *habeas corpus*, with or without *certiorari* in aid, the judgment reflected the tension between the contemporary concept of procedural fairness as it relates to jurisdiction and historical notions of the sanctity of the record. LeDain J. recognized that earlier judgments of the Supreme Court, such as *Sproule* and *Goldhar*, involved the records of superior courts, not inferior tribunals placed in issue as part of an attempt to use *habeas corpus* as a vehicle of appeal. Hence, their current utility as bars to *habeas corpus* relief was limited.[330] More significantly, he observed that many alleged procedural defects would not appear on the face of an order or record and can only be adduced in evidence extrinsically. Thus, he resolved both technical issues in favour of a broadened inquiry on *habeas corpus* applications relating to confinement effected by inferior tribunals.[331]

---

[326] *Ibid.*, at 634-641. This acceptance of a multi-dimensional view of liberty may well have further implications with respect to the refinement of the liberty interest protected by section 7 of the *Charter*. See the discussion of "liberty" in Chapters 4 and 6.

[327] *Ibid.*, at 641.

[328] *Ibid.*, at 624.

[329] *Ibid.*, at 625.

[330] *Ibid.*, at 629-632.

[331] *Ibid.*, at 632-633.

The judgment in *Miller*, combined with section 24(1) of the *Charter*, provided the remedial platform for the claim raised in *Gamble*,[332] where the applicant had been convicted of first degree murder on December 3, 1976, in respect of an offence committed on March 12, 1976.[333] The case against her was that, pursuant to section 21 of the *Code*, she was a party to the killing of a police officer after a bank robbery. At the time of the offence, the punishment for being a party to capital murder, as distinguished from someone who caused or assisted in causing the death, was life imprisonment without parole eligibility for 10 years, subject to the trial judge's discretion to increase parole ineligibility to a maximum of 20 years.[334] As of July 27, 1976, the homicide laws were amended to effect the abolition of capital punishment. The amendments created the categories of first and second degree murder accompanied by revised punishments.[335] Gamble was wrongly indicted on a charge of first degree murder and subsequently convicted. The Appellate Division of the Alberta Supreme Court noted this error, which ordinarily would require a new trial since the responsibility criteria under the first degree murder provision were broader and less onerous than those that previously existed for parties to capital murder.[336] However, a transitional provision in the *Criminal Law Amendment Act (No. 2), 1976* required that any new trials ordered by appellate courts in respect of offences committed before July 26, 1976 must be conducted according to the new homicide laws.[337] The court reasoned that since the applicant had already been tried according to those criteria, albeit wrongly, there was no point in ordering a new trial according to the same criteria. Her appeal was dismissed; further, this issue was not raised on her unsuccessful leave application to the Supreme Court of Canada. Moreover, the sentence of life imprisonment with no eligibility for parole until 25 years had been served, as required by section 669(*a*) [now s. 742(*a*)], was not questioned at any level since section 603(1)(*b*) [now s. 675(1)(*b*)] of the *Code* prevented an appeal against a sentence "fixed by law". Accordingly, she remained subject to a life sentence with a parole eligibility date of 2001.

The enactment of the *Charter*, and in particular section 11(*i*),

---

332 *R. v. Gamble*, [1988] 2 S.C.R. 595.
333 The facts of the case are set out in the earlier judgment of the Appellate Division of the Alberta Supreme Court in *R. v. Gamble* (1978), 40 C.C.C. (2d) 415.
334 *Criminal Law Amendment (Capital Punishment) Act*, S.C. 1973-74, c. 38, ss. 2 and 3.
335 *Criminal Law Amendment Act (No. 2), 1976*, S.C. 1974-75-76, c. 105, ss. 4, 5 and 21.
336 *Supra*, note 333, at 431-432.
337 *Supra*, note 334, s. 27(2). It is certainly questionable whether Parliament envisaged a circumstance like this, a trial under the wrong law, when it enacted this transitional provision.

seemed to provide a basis for the claim that, in light of an increase in the severity of punishment after the commission of the offence, she was entitled to be punished according to the lesser punishment—that which applied at the time of the offence. While the 1976 transitional provision precluded this argument at the time of her trial, section 11(*i*) of the *Charter* guaranteed the right to the lesser punishment in these circumstances. Of course, all of the section 11 entitlements are triggered by the phrase "any person charged with an offence". By 1986, it was difficult to characterize Gamble as a person still in this category, given the legitimate concern about the retrospective application of the *Charter*. Ironically, two men were able to make a similar argument about entitlement to the lesser penalty in respect of the punishment for a murder committed prior to July 26, 1976, because they were re-tried after the enactment of the *Charter*.[338] Hence, they came to the Ontario Court of Appeal as part of the ordinary appellate process while Gamble had exhausted her appeals many years before.

In *Gamble*, application was brought for relief in the nature of *habeas corpus* and relief pursuant to section 24(1) of the *Charter*. Relying on the judgment of Lamer J. in *Reference Re B.C. Motor Vehicles Act*,[339] the claim was premised on section 7 of the *Charter*, arguing that the principles of fundamental justice include the protection that one cannot be punished according to a scale harsher than that extant at the time of the offence. Thus, having served more than 10 years in custody, the applicant's continuing ineligibility for parole violated her section 7 rights in a current and prospective way. At first instance, the application was dismissed on three grounds:

1. There was no jurisdiction in the Ontario courts to entertain a claim for habeas corpus in respect of an Alberta conviction;
2. The claim was beyond the scope of habeas corpus since it involved examining the record of a superior court; and
3. The claim represented a retrospective application of the *Charter*.[340]

An appeal to the Ontario Court of Appeal was dismissed; curiously, the court did not rule that the courts of Ontario had no jurisdiction, but rather that relief should more appropriately be sought in Alberta by applying for an extension of time to appeal the sentence.[341]

---

[338] See *R. v. Dunbar* (1986), 51 C.R. (3d) 326 (Ont. C.A.) in which the court entertained the argument notwithstanding section 603(1)(*b*) [now s. 675(1)(*b*)] and reduced the parole ineligibility to 20 years, the applicable maximum for non-capital murder.

[339] [1985] 2 S.C.R. 486.

[340] See the unreported judgment of Watt J., Ont. H.C., released September 8, 1986.

[341] Unreported judgment released April 30, 1987, Ont. C.A., per Houlden, Grange and Tarnopolsky, JJ.A. The court added that its decision should not be taken as an approval of the views expressed below that the claim was retrospective.

Finally, more than 12 years after having been tried, convicted and punished under the wrong law, Gamble found a favourable forum in the Supreme Court of Canada. Wilson J., writing for the majority,[342] confirmed the availability of *habeas corpus* relief in the province of confinement as the proper vehicle for challenging the legality of that confinement. In her view, this was consistent with precedent[343] and "good practical sense."[344] Coupled with the "flexible" remedial role given to superior courts by section 24(1) of the *Charter*, the availability of *habeas corpus* in the provincial courts was essential to avoid hindering the enforcement of rights.[345] Relying on earlier assertions by the Supreme Court that there must always be a court of competent jurisdiction,[346] Wilson J. rejected the contention that the dubious prospect of a late sentence appeal in Alberta was an adequate remedy. Although accepting that a court could decline jurisdiction if the ordinary trial or appellate process was better suited to adjudicating the claim, she cautioned that "prompt and effective enforcement" and "local accessibility" were significant considerations.[347]

Wilson J.'s analysis of the scope of *habeas corpus* review agreed with the rationale behind traditional limitations, but was offered in less absolutist terms:

> Watt J. concluded at trial that to entertain the appellant's claim "would be to transform the present proceedings by way of *habeas corpus* from a jurisdictional inquiry to an appeal on the merits" of both the conviction and the sentence. If this were indeed the case, the appellant would most likely be denied relief because of this Court's decisions not to allow *habeas corpus* to be used to circumvent the ordinary appeal procedures. . . .[348]

However, Wilson J. recognized that Gamble's claim did not challenge the conviction nor did it impugn the integrity of the appellate process which had been exhausted at a time when the sentence was insulated from review. In her view, the case focussed on present and future parole ineligibility as a continuing deprivation of liberty. From a methodological and remedial perspective, Wilson J. looked beyond the words of the *Charter* to the interests which they were intended to protect

---

342 *Supra*, note 332: Lamer and L'Heureux-Dubé JJ. concurring; Dickson C.J.C. and Beetz J. dissenting.

343 She relied upon *R. v. Riel* (1885), 2 Man. L.R. 302; *Ex parte Stather* (1886), 25 N.B.R. 374; *R. v. Holmes*, [1932] 3 W.W.R. 76; *Laflamme v. Renaud* (1945), 84 C.C.C. 153.

344 *Gamble v. R.* [1988] 2 S.C.R. 595, at 632.

345 *Ibid.*

346 *Ibid*, at 633, where Wilson J. relied on *Mills v. R.*, [1986] 1 S.C.R. 863 and *R. v. Rahey*, [1987] 1 S.C.R. 588.

347 *Ibid.*, at 634-635.

348 *Ibid.*, at 636.

in support of the statement that applicants for *Charter* relief were entitled to "a reasonable measure of flexibility in framing their claims for relief".[349]

Consistent with the need for some degree of flexibility, Wilson J. accepted the applicant's argument that she was not seeking a retrospective application of the *Charter*, but simply invoking its guarantees in respect of the current regime of detention. To this extent pre-*Charter* events were relevant, especially where there was "unlawful conduct on the part of the Crown" (as shown in this case by proceeding to prosecute under the wrong law).[350] This error was characterized as "the overwhelmingly significant fact."[351] Wilson J.'s approach to retrospectivity involved searching for the relevant act which invoked the protections of the *Charter*. She found that act not in the conviction or the life sentence, but in the further execution of the parole ineligibility provision. Thus, the majority ordered that Gamble be immediately considered eligible for parole.[352]

In dissent on the retrospectivity issue, the analysis of Dickson C.J.C. was directed to the original sentence and its validation by the transitional provision. Hence, any injustice could only be grounded on pre-*Charter* events. While he did not preclude resort to sections 9 or 12 of the *Charter* to challenge the execution of a sentence which emanated from a pre-*Charter* process, he concluded that Gamble's section 7 claim flowed entirely from pre-*Charter* events and hence, was retrospective.[353]

Looking to the future, the *Gamble* decision, combined with the Supreme Court's earlier judgments in the *Miller* trilogy, confirm the vitality of *habeas corpus* as the primary instrument for challenging the legality of confinement. It can be issued from a provincial superior court in the province where a prisoner is detained, regardless of the cause of detention. The record necessary to make a claim can be expanded to include whatever extrinsic evidence is necessary, so long as the application is not an attempt to usurp the function of the criminal appeal process. When detention results from a decision of a federal board or tribunal, the existence of concurrent review jurisdiction in the Federal Courts does not preclude resort to *habeas corpus*.[354] More importantly,

---

[349] *Ibid.*, at 638. For an interesting application of section 24(1) in the penal context, see *Parker v. Solicitor General* (Ont. H.C., Henry J., May 18, 1990).

[350] *Ibid.*, at 630.

[351] *Ibid.*

[352] Following its ordinary processes, the National Parole Board granted Gamble day parole 6 months after the release of the judgment.

[353] *Supra*, note 344, at 613.

[354] Recently, the Ontario Court of Appeal upheld a ruling denying the availability of *habeas corpus* to a person challenging detention pursuant to the *Immigration Act*,

habeas corpus is available to assert challenges based on section 9 or section 12 of the *Charter.*[355] Narrow conceptions of jurisdiction and the inviolability of the record of a superior court,[356] have been superseded by a modern understanding of illegality which includes *Charter* protections and fair hearing requirements. An applicant is not restricted to a claim of complete liberty but can seek *habeas corpus* relief to argue the illegality of confinement within a discrete regime. The court can, by declaring the illegality of continued confinement, order a transfer to a regime where confinement would be legal. Thus, *habeas corpus* is available in respect of involuntary transfers to higher security[357] or segregation within an institution.[358] It can also be used to challenge a failure to move a prisoner to a less restrictive regime so long as entitlement can be shown.[359] Or, as in Gamble's case, the impediment to legality can be declared inoperative. LeDain J.'s caveat that *habeas corpus* is not available to challenge any privilege or condition of confinement continues to be a limiting feature. However, some conditions of confinement are so central to the characterization of the confinement that they can be viewed as creating a discrete regime which "involves a significant reduction in the residual liberty of the inmate".[360]

8. DECLARATIONS AND INJUNCTIONS

Both of these remedies find their roots in equity, where they provided adaptable corrective tools to vindicate private rights or inter-

---

R.S.C. 1985, c. I-2, s. 19(2)(*d*): see *Peiroo v. Min. of Employment & Immigration* (1989), 34 O.A.C. 43 (C.A.). The court held that the detainee had an adequate alternative remedy since the statutory framework provided for judicial review of a first-stage finding and an appeal to the Federal Court of Appeal, with leave, from a second stage finding. There is no analogous adequate alternative available to a prisoner except in those cases where the criminal appeal process can entertain the issue and, hence, *Peiroo* should not preclude *habeas corpus* relief.

[355] Since the *Gamble* decision, *habeas corpus* has been successfully used to challenge the detention of a person designated as a criminal sexual psychopath in 1953 on the basis of section 12 of the *Charter*: see *Steele v. Mountain Institution (Warden)* (1989), 72 C.R. (3d) 58 (B.C. S.C.). Affirmed (1990), 54 C.C.C. (3d) 334 (B.C. C.A.). Leave to appeal to S.C.C. granted April 12, 1990.

[356] See Wilson J.'s discussion of this point, *Gamble, supra*, note 344, at 643, where she accepts that "if the time for an appeal of an illegal sentence has gone by 'the law should provide another remedy' ", relying on Professor Sharpe's argument.

[357] See, for example, *Balian v. Regional Transfer Bd.* (1988), 62 C.R. (3d) 258 (Ont. H.C.).

[358] See, for example, *Cardinal v. Kent Institution (Director)*, [1985] 2 S.C.R. 643.

[359] See *Dumas v. Leclerc Institute*, [1986] 2 S.C.R. 459 which, while a parole case, supports by analogy the argument that once an entitlement can be shown *habeas corpus* is available to facilitate the move that ought to be made.

[360] See *R. v. Miller*, [1985] 2 S.C.R. 613, at 641.

ests. Injunctions were issued to prohibit continued interference with a proven right or interest usually of a contractual or proprietary nature.[361] Declarations were simply judicial assertions of a proven right or interest which, by themselves, provided no sanction for interference but usually accompanied some other equitable remedy. With the fusion in England of the courts of law and equity in the late 19th Century came the recognition that a declaration could be sought in an action by itself without any claim for damages or other consequential relief.[362] Necessarily, both injunctions and declarations are flexible in the sense that each responds to a specific interference or a precisely captured entitlement. Their applicability to public law issues has, however, been recent and underdeveloped.[363] In *Dyson*,[364] the English Court of Appeal confirmed the availability of declaratory orders in respect of the Crown by an action against the Attorney General. The plaintiff wished to question the legality of a demand made upon him by the Commissioners of the Inland Revenue. The Attorney General argued that he was not a proper defendant and that declaratory relief could not be obtained against the Crown in this matter. It was suggested that the plaintiff's recourse was to

---

[361] Both in equity, and now at common law, most injunctions issue to stop an interference which has already commenced and is continuing. However, mandatory injunctions are available to restore a right which has been impeded, but such relief is granted sparingly and with caution: see *Morris v. Redland Bricks Ltd.*, [1970] A.C. 652 (H.L.), at 654, per Ld. Upjohn. There is also a *quia timet* injunction which may issue in respect of an act which has not yet occurred but is anticipated. The threshold of persuasion to obtain such an order is extremely high and requires a showing that (1) it is virtually inevitable that the feared interference will happen; and (2) it will cause substantial injury: see *Fletcher v. Bealy* (1885), 28 Ch.D. 688 and *Hooper v. Rogers*, [1975] Ch. 43 (C.A.).

[362] In equity, this was achieved through the *Court of Chancery Procedure Act* (15 & 16 Vict.), c. 86, s. 50. In 1873, the *Supreme Court of Judicature (Consolidated) Act* (36 & 37 Vict.), c. 66, authorized the making of rules which ultimately resulted in 1883 in a rule which provided that "no action or proceeding shall be open to objection, on the ground that a merely declaratory judgment or order is sought thereby, and the court may make binding declarations of right whether any consequential relief is or could be claimed, or not": see (1883), Order 25, Rule 5 and the discussion in J.M. Evans, *DeSmith's Judicial Review of Administrative Action*, 4th ed. (London: Stevens & Sons, 1980), pp. 478-479. Interestingly, many modern Judicature Acts replicate the same 19th Century language when providing for declaratory relief. For example, see the recent *Ontario Courts of Justice Act*, S.O. 1984, c. 11, s. 110 under the sub-heading "common law and equity". Less archaic language is used in the federal counterpart, section 18 of the *Federal Court Act*, which simply gives exclusive original jurisdiction to the Trial Division to "grant declaratory relief against any federal board, commission or other tribunal."

[363] See, generally, *DeSmith's Judicial Review of Administrative Action, ibid.*, pp. 429 and 473-474.

[364] *Dyson v. Attorney-General*, [1911] 1 K.B. 410 (C.A.).

refuse to comply and then to challenge the imposition of a penalty for his default. The Court of Appeal unanimously held that, in proper cases, jurisdiction existed to grant the relief sought. Farwell L.J. concluded that:

> ... it would be a blot on our system of law and procedure if there is no way by which a decision on the true limit of the power of inquisition vested in the Commissioners can be obtained by any member of the public aggrieved.[365]

It is surprising that declarations did not quickly replace prerogative remedies as the primary instrument for challenging official decisions and actions, particularly since *certiorari* and prohibition were, until recently, available only in respect of judicial or quasi-judicial decision-makers.[366] Commentators attribute its virtual disuse as an instrument for challenging decisions to various reasons including the time and expense involved in pursuing an action compared to an application.[367]

This was certainly the experience in the Canadian prison context in which, for many years, prerogative relief was unavailable, yet actions for declaratory relief were not considered as an alternative. As most prison and parole decisions have immediate impact—transfers, segregation, parole revocation—a remedy that could not produce results quickly was unattractive.[368] Delay was, and is, not the only concern. Actions are procedurally cumbersome and expensive, involving pleadings and discoveries. Conversely, applications for prerogative relief proceed from an originating notice and affidavit material. These are important considerations in a context where there are few lawyers interested in prison

---

[365] *Ibid.*, at 421. He also remarked in respect of the equitable concern about the balance of convenience that "if inconvenience is a legitimate consideration at all, the convenience in the public interest is all in favour of providing a speedy and easy access to the Courts for any of His Majesty's subjects who have any real cause of complaint against the exercise of statutory powers by Government departments and Government officials, having regard to their growing tendency to claim the right to act without regard to legal principles and without appeal to any Court" (at 423).

[366] See the discussion, *supra*, of the evolution of the duty to act fairly and the expansion of the availability of *certiorari* at pp. 69-72, culminating in the Supreme Court of Canada decision in *Martineau v. Matsqui Institution Disciplinary Bd.*, [1980] 1 S.C.R. 602.

[367] See J.M. Evans, H.N. Janisch, D.J. Mullan and R.C.B. Risk, *Administrative Law: Cases, Text and Materials*, 3rd ed. (Toronto: Edmond Montgomery, 1989), p. 893, and *DeSmith's Judicial Review of Administrative Action, supra*, note 362, pp. 519-523 where the authors speculate about the historical disfavour towards declarations. Other reasons offered include the concern that a declaration was not available in respect of non-jurisdictional errors and that there were more stringent standing requirements.

[368] In retrospect, this attitude seems hard to understand and was probably short-sighted on the part of the few prison lawyers in Canada, including the authors. Even a remedy delayed must be better than no remedy. However, the limited legal resources of the day were invested in pursuing *habeas corpus, certiorari* and section 28 remedies: see the discussion *supra*, at p. 46.

issues and usually relatively little in the way of resources to fund litigation.

The principal example of the use of declaratory relief in the prison context is the case of *McCann*[369] in which a group of prisoners used the *Canadian Bill of Rights* to challenge the legality of long-term confinement on the segregation range at the British Columbia Penitentiary.[370] The case involved extensive evidence, both factual and expert, in support of the claim that continued confinement was cruel and unusual punishment. Ultimately, Heald J. found in favour of the prisoners and issued a bald declaration to that effect.[371] Although the litigation was successful and focussed much attention on the British Columbia Penitentiary, contributing significantly to its closure a few years later, this one line declaration produced little substantive change in the day-to-day lives of the prisoners.[372] In the future, we can expect to see similar resort to declaratory relief in respect of *Charter* claims. Time will tell whether the remedial provisions of the *Charter* encourage more judicial involvement in responding to unconstitutional standards.[373]

An interesting, albeit rare, example of an attempt to use declaratory relief to challenge internal prison decisions and actions was *Magrath*,[374] a case presented by the prisoner litigant in person. The action raised various issues, including discipline, the transfer power, missing personal property and trust fund deductions. While acceding to some challenges and not others,[375] Collier J. agreed that disciplinary tribunals must act fairly and that, in some circumstances, involuntary transfers could be questioned on fairness grounds.[376] These conclusions came over 2 years before *Martineau (No. 2)*, when most Federal Court judges were denying any jurisdiction to review prison and parole decision-making. In finding that the plaintiff had been denied a fair disciplinary hearing, the court was faced with the issue of appropriate relief, given

---

[369] *McCann v. R.*, [1976] 1 F.C. 570 (T.D.).

[370] For an extraordinary account of this litigation, see M. Jackson, *Prisoners of Isolation* (Toronto: University of Toronto Press, 1983).

[371] The declaration read: "[T]he confinement of all of the plaintiffs herein ... in the Solitary Confinement Unit at the British Columbia Penitentiary amounted to the imposition of cruel and unusual treatment or punishment contrary to section 2(*b*) of the *Canadian Bill of Rights*" (at 614).

[372] See Jackson, *supra*, note 370, pp. 134-203.

[373] See the discussion in Chapter 4 at pp. 141-157.

[374] *Magrath v. R.* (1977), 38 C.C.C. (2d) 67 (Fed. T.D.).

[375] Collier J. accepted that the plaintiff had not been afforded a fair disciplinary hearing (*ibid.*, at 81) and that interest on monies in the plaintiff's trust account could not be transferred to the general Inmate Welfare Fund without consent (*ibid.*, at 89); the claims in respect of transfers and missing property were dismissed.

[376] *Ibid.*, at 78-81 and 86.

that punishment had long since been imposed and the general view in the case law was that a declaration ought not to be granted if it would be "devoid of legal effect".[377] Ultimately, Collier J. decided to grant a declaration in an effort to erase the disciplinary conviction from the plaintiff's institutional record on the premise that "expungement will have some practical effect."[378]

One way of responding to the problem of the length of time required to complete an action for declaratory relief is to join a claim for injunctive relief and move for an interlocutory injunction.[379] This strategy is not without shortcomings.[380] While an injunction may not issue against the Crown, it seems clear that injunctive relief is available against a particular servant of the Crown or Minister.[381] However, as a precondition, the plaintiff must show an act which exceeds lawful authority and violates a right.[382] Thus, in *Fraser*,[383] the English Court of Appeal accepted that a prison disciplinary hearing must be conducted fairly, but refused an injunction restraining the prison officials from inquiring into the charge until the prisoner had been afforded representation by a solicitor and counsel of his choice. While *certiorari* might lie to quash a decision made after a denial of counsel,[384] the issuance of an injunction prior to the hearing would require showing an entitlement to representation,[385] as compared to arguing the impact of the denial on the fairness of the hearing.

---

[377] *Ibid.*, at 81.

[378] *Ibid.*, relying on *Merricks v. Nott-Bower*, [1964] 1 All E.R. 717.

[379] This was the path chosen in respect of the legality of random skin searches before leaving and upon returning to the penitentiary: see *Gunn v. Yeomans* (1979), 48 C.C.C. (2d) 544 (Fed. T.D.). After the plaintiff had been convicted by the disciplinary tribunal for refusing to submit, an interlocutory injunction was granted, restraining further searches pending determination of the issue at trial. Subsequently, the trial judge agreed and granted declarations as to the illegality of the order requiring the search and the conviction for non-compliance: see *Gunn v. Yeomans (No. 2)* (1980), 55 C.C.C. (2d) 452 (Fed. T.D.) at 462. Within a few days, the empowering regulation was amended to authorize such searches without a specific suspicion about the prisoner to be searched: see *Penitentiary Service Regulations*, SOR/80-462, s. 41(2)(c).

[380] See, generally, R. Sharpe, *Injunctions and Specific Performance* (Toronto: Canada Law Book, 1983), pp. 158-179.

[381] *Ibid.*, pp. 168-171, relying on *Jaundoo v. Guyana (A.G.)*, [1971] A.C. 972 (P.C.).

[382] *Ibid.*, p. 169.

[383] *Fraser v. Mudge*, [1975] 1 W.L.R. 1132 (C.A.).

[384] See *Howard v. Inmate Disciplinary Court of Stony Mountain Institution* (1985), 45 C.R. (3d) 242 (Fed. C.A.). Leave to appeal to S.C.C. quashed (1988), 41 C.C.C. (3d) 287; A. Manson, "Counsel at Penitentiary Disciplinary Hearings" (1987), 60 C.R. (3d) 120; *cf. Engen v. Kingston Penitentiary (Disciplinary Bd.)* (1987), 60 C.R. (3d) 109 (Fed. T.D.).

[385] *Fraser v. Mudge, supra*, note 383, at 1133, per Denning M.R.

The important question in respect of prison and parole cases is what the prisoner has to show to obtain interlocutory relief. One element of the test relates to the merits of the claim itself. Traditionally, this translated into the question of whether the plaintiff could show a strong *prima facie* case.[386] Recently, however, the threshold seemed to be lowered when the House of Lords cast it in terms of whether there is a serious question to be tried in the *American Cyanamid* case.[387] If applicable, this revised test may suggest a reduced consideration of the strength of the merits of a claim to whether it is more than frivolous. Even if there is a functional distinction between the "serious question" and "strong *prima facie* case" tests (a tentative proposition[388]), the new test has been rejected in most public law contexts.

When a prisoner obtained an interlocutory injunction to preclude the application of the voting disqualification in the *Canada Elections Act*,[389] the Federal Court of Appeal set it aside, holding that more was required than simply showing a serious question to be tried.[390] The court expressed concern that it was inappropriate to grant interlocutory relief, notwithstanding a serious *Charter* question, if the result would be to treat the applicant as if the law had already been declared invalid.[391] Within a few days the Supreme Court affirmed the ruling of the Federal Court of Appeal.[392]

In the subsequent case of *Attorney General of Manitoba v. Metropolitan Stores (MTS) Ltd.*, the Supreme Court explained its position, stating that the "serious question" test is adequate in the context of constitutional challenges to legislation so long as "the public interest is taken into consideration in the balance of convenience."[393] Beetz J., for a unanimous bench, distinguished between suspension and exemption cases; the latter merely exempted the individual plaintiff from the operation of the law while the former category effectively suspended the application of the challenged law generally pending ultimate disposition. Observing that the line between the two can be amorphous, given

---

[386] See Sharpe, *supra*, note 380, pp. 64-66.
[387] *American Cyanamid Co. v. Ethicon Ltd.*, [1975] A.C. 396 (H.L.), at 407, per Lord Diplock.
[388] See Sharpe, *supra*, note 380, pp. 76-77.
[389] R.S.C. 1970, c. 14 (1st Supp.) [now R.S.C. 1985, c. E-2].
[390] *Canada (A.G.) v. Gould* (1984), 42 C.R. (3d) 88 (Fed. C.A.), per Mahoney J. (with Marceau J. concurring and Thurlow C.J. dissenting) reversing the decision of Reed J. (1984), 42 C.R. (3d) 78 (Fed. T.D.), which applied the *American Cyanamid* test.
[391] *Ibid.*, at 93.
[392] The Supreme Court dismissed an appeal on September 4, 1984, indicating only that it "generally" shared the views of Mahoney J.: see Editor's Note, 42 C.R. (3d) 89.
[393] [1987] 1 S.C.R. 110, at 128, per Beetz J.

that an exemption granted to one applicant may make continued application of the law to others difficult, he concluded that the public interest favoured compliance with the existing regime in suspension cases.[394] The principal reason for caution in respect of interlocutory relief is the difficulty in assessing merits at this early stage.[395] This can arise for many reasons: the timing of the hearing; the absence of comprehensive written submissions; or the insufficiency of the evidence, particularly in respect of possible justification under section 1 of the *Charter*.[396]

---

[394] *Ibid.*, at 140.

[395] *Ibid.*

[396] An interesting example in the prison context is *Horii v. Cmmr. of Corrections* (1987), 62 C.R. (3d) 240 (Fed. T.D.), in which the prisoner had obtained a temporary transfer from the Prison for Women in Kingston to be close to her ailing husband, who was serving sentence at Mission Institution in British Columbia. She then sought a declaration pursuant to section 15 of the *Charter* alleging discrimination in the absence of a federal penitentiary for women other than in Ontario, and applied for an interlocutory injunction to restrain penitentiary officials from returning her to Ontario. Reed J. refused the application for interlocutory relief citing, as the most significant factor, the nature of the *Charter* claim and the inadequacy of the evidence and argument upon which to assess it (at 246-247).

4

Remedies Under the Canadian Charter of Rights and Freedoms

The enactment of the *Canadian Charter of Rights and Freedoms* has overshadowed the profile of the common law duty of fairness. The guarantee of fundamental justice found in section 7, the legal rights entrenched in sections 8 to 14, and the equality rights provided by section 15, have become major instruments in prison litigation. The rights and freedoms guaranteed by the *Charter* are constitutionally entrenched as Part I of the *Constitution Act*, 1982.[1] The language of the document indicates that the drafters built on the constitutional and human rights experiences of other jurisdictions and international organizations. The structure, however, is uniquely Canadian; its most distinctive structural feature is section 1:

> 1. The *Canadian Charter of Rights and Freedoms* guarantees the rights and freedoms set out in it subject only to such reasonable limits prescribed by law as can be demonstrably justified in a free and democratic society.

The principal function of section 1 is to impress the constitutional fact that while the substantive provisions and the underlying social and political values which they protect are guaranteed, they can be subject to "reasonable limits prescribed by law as can be demonstrably justified in a free and democratic society." Later, we shall look briefly at the manner in which our courts have, so far, applied this limiting provision.

It is essential to recognize that the *Charter* does not simply offer ideals and values, either as absolute notions or abstract sources of community aspiration. Nor does it simply protect "atomistic interests".[2] Rather, it seeks to place underlying values within an evolving and interacting social and political context. The process of interpreting and applying the *Charter* has created a new judicial responsibility and a new judicial mandate, emanating from a tradition of legalism, but embracing a broader sensitivity to the essential needs of the Canadian community, its values and political ordering.

---

[1]   Enacted by the *Canada Act, 1982* (U.K.), 1982, c. 11, s. 1, on April 17, 1982.

[2]   This phrase is borrowed from A. Amsterdam, "Perspectives on the 4th Amendment" (1974) 58 Minn. L. Rev. 349.

1. INTERPRETING THE CHARTER

We are still only in the early stages of appreciating the substantive and remedial scope of the *Charter*. As more cases reach higher courts and arguments become more refined, it is clear that the interpretive process is, and perhaps always will be, an evolutionary one. Unlike the pre-existing *Canadian Bill of Rights*,[3] the *Constitution Act, 1982* contains, in sections 24 and 52, specific remedial provisions for governmental actions which unjustifiably violate guaranteed rights or freedoms. Before considering remedy and infringement, it is important to understand the nature and scope of the entrenched rights and freedoms. A number of interpretive principles and themes can be distilled from the early cases.

(a) A Purposive Approach

In its first major analysis of a *Charter* issue,[4] the Supreme Court of Canada characterized the document and the rights guaranteed by it as "purposive" in nature, intended . . .to guarantee and to protect, within the limits of reason, the enjoyment of the rights and freedoms it enshrines. . . . to constrain governmental action inconsistent with those rights and freedoms . . .[5] Accordingly, the basic mode of interpretation must equally be "purposive".

In *R v. Big M Drug Mart Ltd.*,[6] Dickson J. (as he then was) applied the "purposive" approach to the interpretation of the fundamental freedom of religion in section 2(*a*). He explained that the meaning of a right or freedom must be understood "in the light of the interest it was meant to protect" and that the necessary analysis requires:

> . . . reference to the character and the larger objects of the *Charter* itself, to the language chosen to articulate the specific right or freedom, to the historical origins of the concepts enshrined, and where applicable, to the meaning and purpose of the other specific rights and freedoms with which it is associated within the text of the *Charter*.[7]

A useful illustration of the application of this mode of analysis appeared in *Hunter v. Southam Inc.* in which the Supreme Court was faced with a challenge to a search procedure mandated by the *Combines Investigation Act.*[8] Applying a purposive analysis to the section 8 *Charter* guaran-

---

3   R.S.C. 1970, Appendix III.
4   *Hunter v. Southam Inc.*, [1984] 2 S.C.R. 145.
5   *Ibid.*, at 156, per Dickson J.
6   [1985] 1 S.C.R. 295.
7   *Ibid.*, at 344.
8   Hunter, *supra*, note 4, *Combines Investigation Act*, R.S.C. 1970, c. C-23.

tee against "unreasonable search and seizure", the court found the nature of the right in the historical concern to protect reasonable expectations of privacy.[9] Consequently, a search provision which permitted an investigative agency to authorize its own searches without external scrutiny and objective criteria was held to be unconstitutional.

(b) Sources of Interpretation

The interpretation of law can be a subtle and demanding exercise; interpreting a constitutional instrument is always more complex, more textured, more significant and more lasting. With the entrenchment of the *Charter*, the scope of constitutional adjudication has been expanded by placing the content of legislation under judicial scrutiny.[10] While the nature of the task may have been succinctly described by Dickson C.J.C. when he referred to the "larger objects of the *Charter*" and its language and historical origins, the dimensions of the interpretive exercise remain daunting. Sources, tools and interpretive methodologies are necessary to assist jurists in formulating conceptions of guaranteed rights and fundamental freedoms which can have meaning within the current context and, at the same time, present the potential for future development.

The language of the *Charter* is, in many respects, reminiscent of other documents: the *Canadian Bill of Rights*, the *American Bill of Rights*,[11] the *International Covenant on Civil and Political Rights*[12] and the *European Convention of the Protection of Human Rights and Fundamental Freedoms*.[13] These historical, foreign and international instruments can inform and assist the interpretive process, but the uniqueness of the structure, and the context and origins of the *Constitution Act, 1982*, cannot be forgotten.

The *Canadian Bill of Rights* is a federal statute that, since 1960, has provided interpretive caveats for federal legislation. While many issues were raised in the context of *Bill of Rights* provisions that are similar or identical to phrases contained in the *Charter*, these cases were decided within a regime of Parliamentary supremacy. The validity of legislative objects was the common focus of judicial inquiry.[14] Since 1982, a

---

9   *Supra*, note 4, at 157-160.
10   See the judgment of Lamer J. in *Ref. Re S. 94(2), B.C. Motor Vehicle Act*, [1985] 2 S.C.R. 486, at 496.
11   U.S. Constitution, Amendments I-X.
12   Adopted December 16, 1966, G.A. Res. 2200 (XXI), entered into force for Canada on August 19, 1976.
13   November 4, 1950, 213 U.N.T.S. 221, entered into force on September 3, 1953.
14   See Lamer J. in *R. v. Smith*, [1987] 1 S.C.R. 1045, at 1066-1067.

number of these same issues have come before the courts. Litigants who sought scrutiny afresh under the *Charter* were often met in response with *Bill of Rights* decisions. While these historical examples of judicial reasoning are instructive, the Supreme Court has firmly announced that they are not, and cannot be, determinative. In *Therens*, LeDain J. commented on the uncertain and ambivalent judicial response to the *Bill of Rights* by reason of its non-constitutional nature as compared to the constitutional mandate created by the *Charter*, as follows:

> In my opinion the premise that the framers of the *Charter* must be presumed to have intended that the words used by it should be given the meaning which had been given to them by judicial decisions at the time the *Charter* was enacted is not a reliable guide to its interpretation and application.[15]

The restrictive approach found in *Bill of Rights* cases has been displaced by the more expansive purpose and effect analysis of statutory legitimacy required by the *Charter*.[16]

A second potential source of interpretive guidance is American jurisprudence, which may sometimes be of assistance to expose modes of reasoning which have been applied to similar issues. However, different constitutional histories, the uniqueness of the Canadian constitutional structure, and the distinct manner in which institutional and social legislation has developed in Canada should make one wary of attempting a direct translation. As Lamer J. remarked in *Reference re Section 94(2), British Columbia Motor Vehicle Act*[17]

> We would, in my view, do our own Constitution a disservice to simply allow the American debate to define the issue for us, all the while ignoring the truly fundamental structural differences between the two constitutions.[18]

Specifically, he pointed to the existence of sections 1, 33, and 52 of the *Constitution Act*.

In the United States, the definition of the scope of constitutionally protected rights is still influenced by a quest to discern the intention of 18th and 19th Century drafters[19] and is characterized by a "balancing of interests" methodology. With the exception of guaranteed rights and freedoms that have internal modifiers like "unreasonable", the only role for balancing the interests of the individual against those of the state

---

15 *R. v. Therens*, [1985] 1 S.C.R. 613, at 638.
16 For example, see the interpretation of the guarantee against "cruel and unusual treatment or punishment" offered by Lamer J. in *Smith, supra*, note 14.
17 *Supra*, note 10.
18 *Supra*, note 10, at 498.
19 See P. Bobbitt, "Methods of Constitutional Argument" (1989) 23 U.B.C. L. Rev. 449, at 451.

arises, in the Canadian context, at the section 1 justificatory stage, not the definitional stage. In *Reference Re Public Service Employee Relations Act (Alberta)*,[20] Dickson, C.J.C. illustrated this important distinction in constitutional adjudicative methodologies when considering the right to strike and freedom of association in the United States:

> In my view, these decisions illustrate an internal balancing of the implied freedom of association with the public interest at the point of definition of the freedom itself. The cases in which a line was drawn to exclude strike activity from the scope of constitutionally protected associational activities are indicative of the strength of the countervailing concerns (i.e., the public interest) which would find recognition under the *Charter* in section 1 rather than in defining the scope of s. 2(*d*).[21]

International human rights instruments provide a more "fertile source of insight into the nature and scope"[22] of protected rights and freedoms. From a review of the minutes of the Special Joint Committee of the Senate and of the House of Commons (1980-81), it appears that our "international human rights obligations served as not only the necessary and pervasive context in which the Charter of Rights was introduced and adopted, but also as the direct inspiration for amendments designed to strengthen the human rights protection provided."[23] Since the adoption of the *Universal Declaration of Human Rights* by resolution, without dissent, of the U.N. General Assembly in 1948, Canada has participated in various capacities in the development of international human rights norms, and is bound by a number of treaties, especially the *International Covenant on Civil and Political Rights* and its *Optional Protocol.*[24] The manner in which international commissions have interpreted these instruments necessarily has bearing on how Canadian courts should interpret and apply *Charter* provisions promoting common values, often in very similar language. Even though it only has inter-regional application, the *European Convention of the Protection of Human Rights* is another significant instrument, principally "because of the similarity between the legal, political and social systems of Canada and the Western European States."[25] Binding 21 states, it has

---

[20] [1987] 1 S.C.R. 313, dissenting.

[21] *Ibid.*, at 347.

[22] See Dickson C.J.C., in *Ref. Re Public Service Employee Relations Act (Alberta), supra,* note 20 at 348.

[23] See J. Claydon, "International Human Rights Law and the Interpretation of the Canadian Charter of Rights and Freedoms" (1982) 4 Sup. Ct. L. Rev. 287, at 287-288.

[24] Canada became a signatory by filing a letter of accession on May 19, 1976. Canada is also a party to the Convention, the Racial Discrimination Convention, the Freedom of Association Convention and the International Convention on Economic, Social and Cultural Rights: see Claydon, *supra*, note 23, at 311.

[25] See Claydon, *supra*, note 23, at 290.

an elaborate two-tiered adjudicative structure permitting complaints by both individuals against states and by states against other states. Since 1953, a body of jurisprudence has been developed by its Human Rights Commission and European Court dealing with issues directly related to the subject matter of the *Charter*.

The importance of international human rights documents as "persuasive sources for interpretation" was recognized by Dickson C.J.C.'s judgment in *Reference Re Public Service Employee Relations Act (Alberta)*:

> Since the close of the Second World War, the protection of the fundamental rights and freedoms of groups and individuals has become a matter of international concern. A body of treaties (or conventions) and customary norms now constitutes an international law of human rights under which the nations of the world have undertaken to adhere to the standards and principles necessary for ensuring freedom, dignity and social justice for their citizens. The *Charter* conforms to the spirit of this contemporary international human rights movement, and it incorporates many of the policies and prescriptions of the various international documents pertaining to human rights. The various sources of international human rights law—declarations, covenants, conventions, judicial and quasi-judicial decisions of international tribunals, customary norms—must, in my opinion, be relevant and persuasive sources for interpretation of the *Charter*'s provisions.[26]

While a number of early *Charter* decisions followed the pre-*Charter* tradition of characterizing a document like the *International Covenant* as an unimplemented treaty available only as a domestic interpretive tool in cases of ambiguity,[27] Dickson C.J.C. has argued for a higher and more instrumental profile. In his view, the context of *Charter* protections should be presumed, at a minimum, to be at least as broad as that provided in international human rights documents which Canada has ratified.[28] Moreover, structural differences aside, it can never be forgot-

---

[26] *Supra*, note 20, at 348.

[27] See *Mitchell v. Canada (A.G.)* (1983), 35 C.R. (3d) 225 (Ont. H.C.), where Linden J., at 238-242, applied the ambiguity rule as in *Arrow River Tributaries Slide & Boom Co. v. Pigeon Timber Co.*, [1932] S.C.R. 495 and *Capital Cities Communications Inc. v. C.R.T.C.*, [1978] 2 S.C.R. 141.

[28] *Ref. Re Public Service Employee Relations Act (Alberta)*, *supra*, note 20, at 349. But see *R. v. Lyons*, [1987] 2 S.C.R. 309, at 328-330, where La Forest J. used the State's legitimate "penological objectives" to determine whether the dangerous offender provisions of the *Criminal Code* (R.S.C. 1970, c. C-34 [now R.S.C. 1985, c. C-46]) survived the enactment of section 7 of the *Charter*. As well, he followed, at 331-333, with a consideration of comparable English and American statutory regimes and cases. One would have thought that these sources should have been left for the section 1 analysis as to what infringements of rights can be demonstrably justified in a free and democratic society: see M. Manning, "Lyons: A One-Stage Approach to the Charter and Undue Constitutional Notice" (1988) 61 C.R. (3d) 72.

ten that the birth of the *Charter* in 1982 reflects a moment informed by the Canadian historical, political and social experience. The values encompassed by the *Charter* cannot be assessed without regard to our past, particularly the institutions and programs which we have woven into our social fabric.

2. THE CHARTER AND THE GUARANTEE OF FUNDAMENTAL JUSTICE

At the heart of all prison and parole issues is the recognition of the state's power to deprive an individual of liberty. This power may be exercised in various ways, in different contexts and over long periods of time, but it is not absolute or unchecked. Aside from statutory restraints and the impact of the common-law duty of fairness, as enforced by the prerogative remedies, the *Canadian Charter of Rights and Freedoms* has entrenched certain protections and minimum guarantees. Section 7 guarantees that the right to "life, liberty and security of the person" cannot be denied, "except in accordance with the principles of fundamental justice." Sections 8 to 14 are specific illustrations of fundamental justice concepts which have been accepted as basic to our legal system. They represent the hallmarks—the essential characteristics—of a fair and just legal system, and include protections against arbitrary imprisonment and the imposition of cruel and unusual punishment or treatment. The compendious concept of fundamental justice is dynamic, both as it relates to different processes and in an evolutionary sense. Its breadth reflects the capacity to embrace new refinements along the border between state power and the individual's unencumbered sphere of activity as a member of the community.

Since the enactment of the *Charter* in 1982, prisoners have invoked section 7, along with the standard of fairness, to challenge a number of prison and parole decisions.[28A] These developments are discussed in later chapters in the specific contexts of parole granting, suspension, .revocation, the setting of conditions and the release of confidential information. At the general level, four important questions have received both judicial and academic attention:

[28A] Section 11 has also been argued in respect of prison disciplinary prosecutions: see *Re Peltari and Lower Mainland Regional Correctional Centre (Director)* (1984), 15 C.C.C. (3d) 223 (B.C.S.C.); *Russel v. Radley*, [1984] 1 F.C. 543 (Fed. T.D.). Ultimately, however, a three-person majority of the Supreme Court rejected the application of section 11 to prison discipline on the ground that the process does not give rise to penal consequences: *R. v. Shubley* (1990), 74 C.R. (3d) 1 (S.C.C.). Also see the discussion of this judgment in A. Manson, "Solitary Confinement, Remission and Prison Discipline" (1990), 75 C.R. (3d) 356.

1. What is the liberty interest which triggers the guarantee of "funda-mental justice"?
2. What is protected by the right to "security of the person"?
3. Is fundamental justice different from fairness and natural justice?;
4. Does "fundamental justice" mean more than procedural safeguards?

(a) Defining the Liberty Interest

Before one can resort to the principles of fundamental justice, it is necessary to show that the prisoner's liberty interest is implicated by a decision-making process. In 1983, the "gating" cases dealing with the Parole Board's refusal to release prisoners on mandatory supervision provided the Supreme Court of Canada its first oral argument based on section 7 of the *Charter*.[29] While the cases were decided without refer-ence to the *Charter*, it is interesting to note that the government's written submissions began with the assertion that a convicted person serving a sentence of imprisonment had lost all rights to liberty, such that section 7 could not apply to prisoners. Fortunately, this argument has received short shrift. The suggestion that liberty is a one-dimensional concept and that constitutional protections stop at prison walls would be re-gressive in the extreme. As well as offending internationally accepted standards of human rights protection, it would essentially banish pris-oners into a netherworld where only what is bestowed through legis-lative largesse would be available. This contradicts the conception of prisoners' rights articulated earlier in terms of the civil rights enjoyed by citizens, save those specifically denied by statute or necessarily removed as an incident of incarceration.[30] In the *habeas corpus* trilogy,[31] the Supreme Court confirmed that prisoners, while denied their absolute liberty, retain a spectrum of residual liberties.

The question remains where to situate the constitutionally pro-tected liberty interest along the line between physical restraint and absolute freedom from any state intrusion on conduct. American cases appear at first consideration to have cast liberty in terms of "the full range of conduct which the individual is free to pursue".[32] This must be contrasted with the narrow interpretation of McNair J. in *O'Brien v.*

---

[29] *Re Moore and R.; Oag v. Edmonton Institution (Director)* (1983), 32 C.R. (3d) 97 (S.C.C.).
[30] See *Solosky v. R.* (1980), 50 C.C.C. (2d) 495 (S.C.C.).
[31] See *R. v. Miller*, [1985] 2 S.C.R. 613; *Cardinal v. Kent Institution (Director)*, [1985] 2 S.C.R. 643; and *Morin v. National Special Handling Unit Review Committee*, [1985] 2 S.C.R. 662. These cases are discussed in more detail in Chapter 3.
[32] See *Bolling v. Sharpe* (1954), 347 U.S. 497, at 499, per Warren C.J.

National Parole Board,[33] a day parole case where the liberty interest protected by section 7 was defined to mean no more than "freedom from arrest or detention". The liberty debate has encompassed issues as diverse as the testing of cruise missiles,[34] the temporary surrender of a driver's licence,[35] the ability to practise medicine[36] and the regulation of public carriers.[37] For parole purposes, the issue arises in two contexts: granting and suspension.

Issues of suspension and revocation, discussed in detail in Chapter 8, have not proven difficult for Canadian courts. Early in the era of *Charter* litigation, a number of cases involving conditional release were argued with reliance on section 7. Whether the issue involved the opportunity for an in person hearing, or the internal elements of a fair hearing, judges saw recommitment to custody as a clear loss of liberty which invoked the guarantee of fundamental justice.[38] Notwithstanding the conditional and controlled nature of parole and mandatory supervision, the process of suspension and revocation was sufficiently analogous to the imposition of physical restraint through arrest or detention that the application of section 7 was easily accepted.

The parole granting stage has been more problematic. While the *Parole Act*[39] has, for many years, required a form of hearing in full parole cases, it was silent with respect to applications for the other forms of conditional release.[40] It had been the Board's practice, however, to conduct hearings in day parole cases. In 1983, the decision in *Mason*,[41] a revocation case, invalidated the Board's practice of conducting hearings before two members, while permitting a third absentee participant to cast a deciding vote. This spawned a series of cases challenging the form of hearing employed to deal with applications for day parole and temporary absence. Relying on basic administrative law principles,[42] McNair J., in *O'Brien*, held that once a hearing had been commenced the Board was obliged to proceed fairly. However, he commented that there was no legal or constitutional obligation on the Board to offer a hearing in

---

33 [1984] 2 F.C. 314. This case is discussed in more detail in Chapter 3.

34 *Operation Dismantle Inc. v. R.*, [1985] 1 S.C.R. 441.

35 *R. v. Neale* (1986), 52 C.R. (3d) 376 (Alta. C.A.) and *R. v. Robson* (1985), 45 C.R. (3d) 68 (B.C.C.A.).

36 *Mia v. Medical Services Cmmn. of B.C.* (1985), 17 D.L.R. (4th) 385 (B.C.S.C.); *Wilson v. Medical Services Cmmn. of B.C.* (1988), 53 D.L.R. (4th) 171 (B.C.C.A.).

37 *Gershman Produce Co. v. Motor Transport Bd.*, [1985] 2 W.W.R. 63 (Man. Q.B.).

38 The case law is discussed in Chapters 6 and 8.

39 R.S.C. 1985, c. P-2 [formerly R.S.C. 1970, c. P-2].

40 These various forms of release are described and discussed in Chapter 6.

41 *Re Mason and R.* (1983), 7 C.C.C. (3d) 426 (Ont. H.C.).

42 *Furnell v. Whangarei High Schools Bd.*, [1973] A.C. 660 (P.C.).

respect of day parole.[43] In so doing, he restricted the prisoner's liberty interest to matters of restraint by reason of arrest or detention, such that the discretionary granting of conditional release, which would not restore absolute liberty, was not constitutionally protected by the principles of fundamental justice. A persuasive factor in this decision was the majority opinion of the U.S. Supreme Court in *Greenholtz v. Inmates of Nebraska Penal & Correctional Complex.*[44]

Of course, American jurisprudence may be helpful in appreciating the potential scope of the concept of liberty, but as we have already noted, differences in our constitutional structures and history compel caution in permitting the "American debate to define" the content of our constitutionally protected interests. In *Meyer v. Nebraska,*[45] the Supreme Court examined the impact of the 14th Amendment to the United States Constitution on a state law which prohibited the teaching in schools in any language other than English. While the so-called ancient or dead languages were exempt, modern languages such as German, French, Spanish or Italian fell within the prohibition. It was argued that both the vocational opportunities of modern language teachers and the ability of parents to make choices about their children's education were wrongly denied by the state's legislation.

The 14th Amendment is the vehicle by which due process protections are extended to state jurisdictions. It reads, in part: "No state . . . shall deprive any person of life, liberty, or property without due process of law." The court in *Meyer* demurred from attempting to offer any precise definition of liberty but stated:

> Without doubt, it denotes not merely freedom from bodily restraint but also the right of the individual to contract, to engage in any of the common occupations of life, to acquire useful knowledge, to marry, establish a home and bring up children, to worship God according to the dictates of his own conscience, and generally to enjoy those privileges long recognized at common law as essential to the orderly pursuit of happiness by free men.[46]

Decades later, the court was again required to inquire into the scope of liberty in *Bolling v. Sharpe.*[47] While the court had previously held that the "equal protection clause" of the 14th Amendment prohibited state maintenance of a racially segregated school system, *Bolling* involved the District of Columbia, to which the 14th Amendment does not apply.

---

43 The interim result of this decision was that the Board, rather than sending all decision-makers to conduct day parole hearings, simply stopped offering in person hearings. As discussed in Chapter 6, this practice was reversed by Regulation.

44 (1979), 99 S. Ct. 2100; 442 U.S. 1.

45 (1923), 262 U.S. 390.

46 *Ibid.,* at 399.

47 (1953), 347 U.S. 497.

The federal "due process" analogue, the 5th Amendment, does not contain an equal protection clause. Accordingly, to invoke a similar prohibition required finding a violation of a constitutionally protected interest within the meaning of liberty. The court commented:

> Although the Court has not assumed to define "liberty" with any great precision, that term is not confined to mere freedom from bodily restraint. Liberty under law extends to the full range of conduct which the individual is free to pursue, and it cannot be restricted except for a proper governmental objective.[48]

These decisions suggested the adoption of a broad conception of liberty subject only to a government's ability to show a compelling interest in restriction. However, appearances can be deceiving.

According to Lawrence Tribe and others, there can be no doubt that since the early 1970s the set of interests protected by due process in the United States has been narrowed significantly. Today, protections are afforded only to positive entitlements flowing from constitutional provisions or state or federal law.[49] Thus, the optimism engendered by the important prison cases of *Wolff v. McDonnell*[50] and *Morrissey v. Brewer*[51] quickly turned to disappointment when the U.S. Supreme Court denied the protection of a hearing to a prisoner transferred to less favourable conditions in *Meachum v. Fano*.[52] The court hinted at the conceptual source of its desire to limit protected interests when it refused to extend the liberty interest "absent a state law or practice conditioning such transfers on proof of serious misconduct or the occurrence of other events."[53] This "preference for an inquiry into grounded expectations"[54] surfaced again in *Hewitt v. Helms* when the court insulated a transfer to solitary confinement from judicial scrutiny on due process grounds because it was considered within the conditions of confinement contemplated by a sentence of imprisonment.[55] Specifi-

---

[48] *Ibid.*, at 499-500.

[49] See L. Tribe, *American Constitutional Law*, 2d ed. (Mineola, New York: Foundation Press, 1988) p. 677 where the author says: "To be procedurally protected an interest must be grounded in substantive legal relationships defined by explicit constitutional provisions or by specific state or federal rules of law." He describes these limitations as "a profoundly novel vision of procedural due process" (p. 696).

[50] (1974), 418 U.S. 539.

[51] (1972), 408 U.S. 471.

[52] (1976), 427 U.S. 215. See also *Olin v. Wakinekona* (1983), 461 U.S. 238 involving a transfer from Hawaii to California which operated to divorce the prisoner from family and friends.

[53] *Meachum v. Fano, ibid.*, at 216.

[54] *Ibid.*, at 228.

[55] (1983), 459 U.S. 460, at 468, although the court left open a challenge on other constitutional grounds which might, in a particular case, means a cruel and unusual punishment claim.

cally with respect to the granting of parole, the court in *Greenholtz* held that due process protections apply only when the statute establishing the release regime creates an entitlement to release so long as statutory preconditions are met.[56] Accordingly, the possibility of release or even an expectation of release[57] are insufficient to impose due process burdens on purely discretionary decision-makers.

Recently, in *Board of Pardons v. Allen*,[58] the court re-affirmed the *Greenholtz* analysis and applied due process protections to parole hearings in Montana because "the Montana statute, like the Nebraska statute, uses mandatory language ("shall") to 'create a presumption that parole release will be granted' when the designated findings are made."[59] Thus, the political will of a state legislature, as evidenced by the structure, language and criteria it employs, is the determinant of whether due process avails a prisoner caught in the release process.[60]

Tribe has explained this limited set of liberty interests by reference to the predominant view of due process which has evolved in the United States. He argues persuasively that the U.S. Supreme Court in the past two decades has chosen an instrumental rather than intrinsic conception of procedural due process. Its value and effect lies in the imposition of procedures to maximize accurate decision-making and minimize errors. By comparison, an intrinsic view of due process would accept the value of participation in significant decisions by the state about one's life because of what that participatory inclusion says about the relationship between citizens and the state. In Tribe's words, this

---

[56] *Supra*, note 44.

[57] See *Connecticut Bd. of Pardons v. Dumschat* (1981), 452 U.S. 458, at 465.

[58] (1987), 107 S. Ct. 2415.

[59] *Ibid.*, at 2420, relying expressly on *Greenholtz*. The dissent (Rehnquist C.J. and Justices O'Connor and Scalia) was not prepared to find an entitlement in the statute imposing a high threshold of scrutiny such that "an entitlement is created by statute only if 'particularized standards or criteria' constrain the relevant decision-makers" (per O'Connor, at 2423). The reliance on "shall" was characterized as "semantics" which "ignor[ed] altogether the sweeping discretion granted to the Board of Pardons by Montana law" (at 2422).

[60] *Scales v. Mississippi State Parole Bd.* (1987), 831 F. 2d. 565 (5th Circ.); *Dace v. Mickleson* (1987), 816 F. 2d. 1277 (8th Circ.); *Gale v. Moore* (1985), 763 F. 2d. 341 (8th Circ.). Other related issues have been addressed by Circuit Courts of Appeal. In *Winsett v. McGinness* (1980), 617 F. 2d. 996, the 3rd. Circuit held that a statute which creates substantive standards for release thereby creates a liberty interest. Conversely, it has been held that statutes which prohibit release in certain circumstances, but which do not specifically require it in others, do not create a liberty interest: see, *Huggins v. Isenbarger* (1986), 798 F. 2d. 203 (7th Circ.); *Patten v. North Dakota Parole Bd.* (1986), 783 F. 2d. 140 (8th Circ.); *cf. Scott v. Illinois Parole & Pardon Bd.* (1985), 669 F. 2d. 1185 (7th Circ.).

approach begins with the proposition that there is an *intrinsic* value in the due process right to be heard, since it grants to the individuals or groups against whom government decisions operate the chance to participate in the processes by which those decisions are made, an opportunity that expresses their dignity as persons."[61]

While the reference in *Meachum v. Fano*[62] to "proof of serious misconduct" may have suggested an instrumental choice, subsequent cases have confirmed it.[63] In *Mathews v. Eldridge*, the court's conception of due process safeguards was cast entirely in terms of contribution to accuracy,[64] including a purported calculus of "erroneous deprivation" for weighing what amount of process is due.[65] This adoption of an instrumental approach was apparent in *Greenholtz*, where the Court distinguished between predictions about the future, which might result in discretionary release, and findings about the past or present, which create an entitlement to release. Only the latter, because of the need for accuracy, triggered due process safeguards because, by definition, predictions are subjective and ephemeral.

Thus, in the United States the liberty cart has been placed before the due process horse. What constitutes a liberty interest is not determined by its nature or significance to the individual, but rather whether the state has treated it in a way that requires enhanced fact-finding by calling the interest an entitlement. Certainly, this has not been the Canadian approach. Even in the pre-*Charter* era, our courts recognized the need to extend procedural protections to issues beyond those which could be classed as entitlements.[66] The distinction is apparent in comparing two cases dealing with the discharge of a police officer. In *Bishop v. Wood*, an officer with 3½ years service was dismissed without a hearing.[67] The United States Supreme Court ruled against judicial review on the ground "that an enforceable expectation of continued public employment in that State can exist only if the employer, by statute or contract, has actually granted some form of guarantee."[68] Conversely, the Supreme Court of Canada in *Nicholson v. Haldimand-Norfolk Board of Police Commissioners* used the common law of fairness to impose procedural burdens when a probationary police officer was discharged

---

[61] L. Tribe, *supra*, note 49, p. 666.
[62] *Supra*, note 52.
[63] See L. Tribe, *supra*, note 49, pp. 674-677.
[64] (1976), 424 U.S. 319.
[65] *Ibid.*, at 335.
[66] See the discussion of *Martineau (No. 2)* in Chapter 3.
[67] (1976), 426 U.S. 341.
[68] *Ibid.*, at 345, which Brennan J. in dissent characterized as a "resurrection of the discredited rights-privileges distinction" (at 354, footnote 4).

without a hearing regardless of whether a right was at stake.[69] Subsequently, with respect to the granting of a U.T.A. (unescorted temporary absence), Reed J., in *Cadieux v. Director of Mountain Institution*, held that "the fact that one is dealing with the granting of a privilege does not, in this case, lessen the applicability of either the rules of fairness applied through common law *certiorari* or the guarantee of fundamental justice provided for by the Charter."[70]

More to the point is the purpose and structure of the *Charter* itself. Section 7 of the *Charter* expressly guarantees to everyone "the right to life, liberty and security of the person" followed by the prescription on the state not to deprive anyone of these rights "except in accordance with the principles of fundamental justice." By comparison, the 5th Amendment, the American counterpart, consists of a series of constraints, one of which is the prohibition that no person "be deprived of life, liberty, or property without due process of law."[71] The focus of the Canadian constitutional provision is principally on the interests to be guaranteed and protected, not on the state and the instrument of protection.

To date, the Supreme Court of Canada has dealt with this issue only tangentially. In *Morgentaler*,[72] only the judgment of Wilson J. included an independent consideration of "liberty". In an earlier decision,[73] she considered the right to liberty in terms of personhood and autonomy. She defined it as "the right to pursue one's goals free of governmental constraint",[74] while attempting to situate it within the correlative obligations of members of an organized community. This expansive conception of liberty was refined in *Morgentaler* by reference to liberal political values which Wilson J. found embedded in the theoretical underpinnings of the *Charter*.[75] In her view:

> . . . an aspect of the respect for human dignity on which the Charter is founded is the right to make fundamental personal decisions without interference from the state. This right is a critical component of the right to liberty . . . . this right, properly construed, grants the individual a degree of autonomy in making decisions of fundamental personal importance.[76]

---

69 [1979] 1 S.C.R. 311: discussed in Chapter 3 at pp. 51-53.

70 (1984), 41 C.R. (3d) 30 (Fed. T.D.), at 40.

71 This Amendment was passed in 1791. An identical due process protection was applied to state laws by the 14th Amendment, passed in 1868.

72 *Morgentaler v. R.* (1988), 37 C.C.C. (3d) 449 (S.C.C.), discussed more extensively, *infra*, at pp. 123-125, in respect of "security of the person".

73 Wilson J.'s views were foreshadowed by her earlier comments in *Singh v. Minister of Employment & Immigration*, [1985] 1 S.C.R. 177, and *Operation Dismantle Inc. v. R.*, [1985] 1 S.C.R. 441, at 34.

74 *Operation Dismantle Inc. v. R., ibid.*, at 458.

75 *Supra*, note 72, at 550.

76 *Supra*, note 72, at 550-551.

Recently, a five-judge panel of the Supreme Court of Canada denied leave to appeal in *Wilson v. British Columbia (Medical Services Commission)*, a case which turned entirely on the scope of the liberty protection.[77] At issue was the legitimacy of legislation which attempted to control the number and location of physicians in British Columbia by imposing a scheme which regulated the granting of practitioner numbers permitting a doctor to bill the provincial health insurance plan. In a unanimous decision which has been the subject of substantial criticism,[78] the British Columbia Court of Appeal struck down the legislation, concluding that, while property rights and pure economic rights are not protected by the *Charter*, section 7 does protect the ability to pursue one's calling. The court observed that liberty:

> ... may embrace individual freedom of movement, including the right to choose one's occupation and where to pursue it, subject to the right of the state to impose, in accordance with the principles of fundamental justice, legitimate and reasonable restrictions on the activities of individuals.[79]

Aside from pointing out the inherent elitism involved in characterizing a profession as something more than a pure economic interest, one commentator has argued that the decision "far overshoots" the purposes of section 7.[80] It is regrettable that the decision will not be considered by the Supreme Court of Canada. However, it is not necessary to adopt the expanding, fish-eye lens view of liberty expressed by the British Columbia Court of Appeal to appreciate the wrongness of the narrow, constricting, and regressive view offered by McNair J. in *O'Brien*.[81]

(b) Security of the Person

While most parole and prison issues should be considered as implicating the prisoner's liberty interest, it is clear that some issues do not.[82] By itself, this does not necessarily preclude section 7 review of

---

[77] On November 3, 1988, a panel consisting of Dickson C.J.C., Lamer, LaForest, L'Heureux-Dubé and Sopinka JJ. dismissed the application for leave from the judgment of the B.C.C.A., reported at 53 D.L.R. (4th) 171.

[78] See, for example, M.D. Lepofsky, "A Problematic Judicial Foray Into Legislative Policy Making: *Wilson v. B.C. Medical Services Commission*" (1989), 68 Can. Bar Rev. 615.

[79] *Supra*, note 77, at 187.

[80] See M.D. Lepofsky, *supra*, note 78, at 622.

[81] Discussed in Chapters 3 and 6.

[82] See Le Dain J.'s caveat in *R. v. Miller*, [1985] 2 S.C.R. 613 that not all issues are amenable to *habeas corpus* review because the residuum of a prisoner's liberty does not extend to all aspects of prison conditions.

internal decision-making. The fundamental justice protection applies equally to a denial of the right to security of the person which presents another dimension for constitutional protection.[83] In *Morgentaler*, Dickson C.J.C. chose not to attempt an "all-encompassing explication" of the scope of section 7 of the *Charter*,[84] but offered significant interpretive insights into the breadth of interests which may be included within the concept of "security of the person":

> The case-law leads me to the conclusion that state interference with bodily integrity and serious state-imposed psychological stress, at least in the criminal law context, constitute a breach of security of the person. It is not necessary in this case to determine whether the right extends further, to protect either interests central to personal autonomy, such as a right to privacy, or interests unrelated to criminal justice.[85]

In his analysis of the impact of the abortion provision, Dickson C.J.C. considered both physical and emotional effects as they relate to an individual's "own priorities and aspirations".[86] Beetz J. concluded that the protection of life or health is a sufficiently important interest to warrant constitutional protection under the right to security of the person.[87] The dissenting view, however, held that the simple existence of state-imposed stress, strain, or anxiety did not violate the right to security of the person unless, in addition, it "infringed another right, freedom or interest which was deserving of protection under the concept of security of the person".[88]

In this very controversial and extensively debated case the most interventionist view of section 7 was offered by Wilson J. who saw the appellant's claim as implicating both liberty and security of the person.[89] Beyond recognizing the significance of emotional stress and "unnecessary physical risk", she found the denial of reproductive choice to be a sufficient diminution of human dignity and self-respect to represent an infringement of the pregnant woman's right to security of the person.[90]

A review of all the Supreme Court judgments in *Morgentaler* discloses both controversy and a willingness to entertain new "security of the person" claims when the state acts to impose serious personal

---

[83]   Wilson J. recognized the distinct interests protected by the guarantees of "life, liberty and security of the person" in *Singh v. Minister of Employment & Immigration, supra,* note 73, at 204.

[84]   *Morgentaler v. R.* (1988), 37 C.C.C. (3d) 449 (S.C.C.), at 461 (Lamer J. concurring).

[85]   *Ibid.*, at 465.

[86]   *Ibid.*, at 466-471.

[87]   *Ibid.*, at 492 (Estey J. concurring).

[88]   *Ibid.*, at 536, per McIntyre J. (LaForest J. concurring).

[89]   *Ibid.*, at 548-557: see the discussion of "liberty", *supra*, at pp. 116-123.

[90]   *Ibid.*, at 556.

disadvantage. While liberty may prove to be a limited interest for prisoners, the scope of the "security of the person" right should be interpreted with due regard for an individual's personhood in the broadest sense. The deprivation of opportunities to maintain and build positive links with the world outside the walls can, in many situations, generate psychological stress and be related to questions of dignity and self-respect. This is especially true when one views the parole process as the temporal link between the day-to-day rigours of imprisonment and the prospect of a productive future in the community. A myriad of issues which touch on family, friendships, education, health care and other positive re-integrative steps may well be encompassed by the fundamental justice guarantee because of their relation to "security of the person".[91]

(c) Fundamental Justice and Fairness

In our discussion of *Martineau (No. 2)*[92] in Chapter 3, we noted that Dickson J. expressed concern that the concepts of fairness and natural justice not be distinguished or treated differently so as to create two classes of decision-makers operating according to two distinct standards of procedural accountability. He quoted with approval Lord Morris' dictum that "fairness is but natural justice writ large and juridically."[93] Both concepts remain fluid. They reflect the common purpose of ensuring that processes and decision-makers treat their respective participants fairly and openly by affording the degree of procedural protections appropriate to the nature and structure of the process and the interests at stake.

Prior to the enactment of the *Charter*, representatives of the Federal Department of Justice suggested that fundamental justice, as used in section 7, was merely a reference to the traditionally accepted concept of natural justice embodying notions of fairness and *audi alteram partem*.[94] Subsequent judicial consideration requires us to question this

---

[91] In *Piche v. Canada (Solicitor-General)* (1989), 47 C.C.C. (3d) 495 (Fed. C.A.), while rejecting the prisoner's claim that the imposition of double-bunking without consultation or notice infringed the fundamental justice guarantee, the court assumed, without deciding that section 7 encompassed "the right of basic privacy and personal dignity." MacGuigan J.A. considered this a "theoretically tenable position" (at 502).

[92] *Martineau v. Matsqui Institution Disciplinary Bd.*, [1980] 1 S.C.R. 602.

[93] From *Furnell v. Whangarei High Schools Bd.*, [1973] A.C. 660 (P.C.).

[94] See excerpts from the *Proceedings and Evidence of the Special Joint Committee of the Senate and House of Commons on the Constitution of Canada*, 32nd Parliament, 1st Session, 1980-81, quoted in *Ref. Re S. 94(2), B.C. Motor Vehicle Act*, [1985] 2 S.C.R. 486, at 504.

assertion.[95] In the next section, we will deal specifically with the issue of substantive review. Here, we are concerned with process.

Since 1982, a number of prison and parole cases have challenged decision-making processes on arguments based on fairness and fundamental justice. Clearly, fairness cannot supersede the intention of a legislature. If a statute or regulation either expressly precludes a procedural element or creates a comprehensive procedural framework which implicitly precludes the element in question, the duty of fairness cannot be relied upon to insert it into the process. Fundamental justice, however, can play a different role, since it is now a constitutional yardstick by which statutory procedures must be measured. If found wanting, the remedial powers of section 24(1) of the *Charter* or section 52 of the *Constitution Act, 1982* empower the judiciary to rectify the deficiency. This distinction between fairness and fundamental justice relates not to their respective content but to the manner in which they are capable of being enforced.

In *Cadeddu*, Potts J. held that a prisoner released on provincial parole was entitled to an in person hearing before a decision could be made to revoke the parole.[96] The enabling statute derived its authority from the federal *Parole Act*, which is accompanied by Regulations requiring, in most cases, a pre-revocation (or post-suspension, as it is commonly known) hearing. Neither the applicable Regulations nor the provincial statute provided for a post-suspension hearing. Curiously, the court rejected the prisoner's argument based on fairness but held that fundamental justice, as guaranteed by section 7 of the *Charter*, mandated a hearing. Since there was no need to resort to the *Charter* to supersede a statute, the decision in *Cadeddu* was perhaps wrongly reasoned on the fairness issue.[97] However, it has been relied upon without question as an authority for the applicability of the *Charter* to parole decision-making.[98] Its implicit premise that fundamental justice ranks in higher order to fairness cannot be accepted uncritically without further examination.

In *Swan v. Attorney General of British Columbia*[99] a prisoner had apparently breached a condition of release, since his parole officer was unable to locate him. Although a suspension warrant had been issued it could not be executed as the authorities did not know the prisoner's

95 See *Ref. Re S. 94(2), ibid.*
96 *R. v. Cadeddu; R. v. Nunery* (1983), 32 C.R. (3d) 355 (Ont. H.C.).
97 A. Manson, Annot. *R. v. Cadeddu; R. v. Nunery* (1983), 32 C.R. (3d) 355 (Ont. H.C.).
98 *Cadeddu* has been cited with approval in two Supreme Court of Canada decisions dealing with *habeas corpus* and liberty: *R. v. Miller, supra,* note 82, at 638 and *Gamble v. R.,* [1988] 2 S.C.R. 595, at 641.
99 (1983), 35 C.R. (3d) 135 (B.C.S.C.).

whereabouts. As the prisoner's sentence was about to expire, the Board revoked his release without resorting to the usual suspension and post-suspension process. The use of the residual revocation power in section 10(1)(*e*) [now s. 16(1)(*e*) and (*f*)] of the Act had been the subject of controversy for many years, since it deprived the prisoner of the procedural protections following a parole suspension, particularly the right to an in person hearing.[100] Relying on fairness and the guarantee of fundamental justice, Swan argued that he should equally be entitled to a hearing, regardless of the procedural route chosen for revocation. McEachern C.J.S.C. agreed. His reasoning revealed the impact that section 7 of the *Charter* would have on judicial review. His analysis commenced with the question:

> ... are inquiries or ex parte reviews or discretionary hearings enough, or must there be a hearing as of right at which the parolee is entitled to attend, to present his side of the case and, to challenge the case against him in the presence of the tribunal?[101]

Put in these terms, the issue appeared to be a classic example of a functional analysis of what fairness required in the circumstances. The statutory framework did not deny a hearing; it simply did not provide for one. Accordingly, the duty to act fairly was a sufficient tool to enable a judge to impose this obligation. However, bolstered by the recognition that liberty was now constitutionally protected by the guarantee of fundamental justice, McEachern C.J.S.C. was prepared to assert that the protection of a hearing available at the post-suspension stage should be equally available as of right upon direct revocation pursuant to section 10(1)(*e*) [now s. 16(1)(*e*) and (*f*)].[102]

While *Swan* confirmed the application of section 7 to the revocation process, it did not necessarily suggest that the content of fundamental justice was somehow different from that of fairness. Section 7 was not used to generate more procedural protection than what fairness might require but, rather, to alert the court to the importance of the issue at stake and to discourage simple deference to the established process as an appropriate mode of response. The same result could have been reached by relying on the duty to act fairly, but the invocation of section 7 changed the tone of the inquiry and the degree of judicial scrutiny because a constitutionally protected interest was in issue.

A leading example within the prison and parole context of the impact of section 7 has arisen with respect to the issue of counsel at prison disciplinary hearings. Until 1981, an internal Commissioner's

---

[100] See the discussion in Chapter 8.
[101] *Supra*, note 99, at 145.
[102] *Supra*, note 99, at 147-148.

Directive prohibited representation by counsel.[103] In two judgments released almost simultaneously, *Davidson*[104] and *Minott*,[105] the Federal Court held that the duty to act fairly required that a disciplinary tribunal at least consider a prisoner's request to be represented and, if a fair hearing could not be conducted without the aid of counsel, representation should be permitted. The Directive was considered to be *ultra vires*, and the tribunal's discretion to permit counsel was confirmed.[106] However, in *Davidson*, Cattanach J. went on to comment that most disciplinary cases raised only simple questions of fact, and fair hearings could likely be conducted without the need for counsel.[107] After *Davidson* and *Minott*, disciplinary tribunals routinely entertained and rejected requests for representation by counsel.[108]

In England, relying solely on the concept of fairness, courts began to characterize circumstances in which the assistance of counsel might be necessary to ensure a fair hearing.[109] In Canada, this development did not occur until the prisoner's argument was cast in terms of liberty, fundamental justice and section 7 of the *Charter*.

The 1985 case of *Re Howard and Presiding Officer of Inmate Disciplinary Court of Stony Mountain Penitentiary* resulted in two concurring opinions from the Federal Court of Appeal which granted *certiorari* to quash disciplinary convictions based on the argument that, in the circumstances, the tribunal's denial of counsel was a denial of fundamental justice.[110] Within the context of disciplinary hearings this decision generated substantial controversy, since one judgment was open to the narrow interpretation that the entitlement to counsel only arose because the fundamental justice guarantee was triggered by the possible penalty of forfeiture of earned remission.[111] For our purposes, *Howard* is

---

103 See *Davidson, infra*, note 104.
104 *Re Davidson and Disciplinary Bd. of Prison for Women* (1981), 61 C.C.C. (2d) 520 (Fed. T.D.).
105 *Re Minott and Inmate Disciplinary Ct., Stony Mountain Penitentiary (Presiding Officer)*, [1982] 1 F.C. 322 (T.D.).
106 *Davidson, supra*, note 104, at 536.
107 *Davidson, supra*, note 104, at 534-535.
108 M. Jackson, "The Right to Counsel in Prison Disciplinary Hearings" (1986), 20 U.B.C. L. Rev. 221, at 242.
109 In *R. v. Secretary of State; Ex parte Tarrant*, [1984] 2 W.L.R. 613, Kerr L.J. explained that a request for counsel "must always be granted" if required to give effect to a prisoner's right to a full opportunity to present his case (at 647).
110 (1985), 19 C.C.C. (3d) 195 (Fed. C.A.). Due to the fact that the prisoner had been released by the time the Crown appeal came on for hearing, the Supreme Court of Canada quashed the appeal (1988), 41 C.C.C. (3d) 287 (S.C.C.).
111 Immediately following the release of the judgment, the Correctional Service of Canada amended the disciplinary regulations to create a new category of "intermediary"

instructive in the way that section 7 of the *Charter* was employed. While the case could have been argued on fairness grounds alone, the judgments reveal that the prisoner's success depended on the application of the principles of fundamental justice to protect his liberty interest.[112] After finding that a liberty interest was in issue, the court looked to section 7 of the *Charter* for an avenue by which to assert an entitlement to counsel. MacGuigan J. stated:

> The *Canadian Charter of Rights and Freedoms* does, however, introduce a distinctly new perspective: where it does not create new rights, it may nevertheless *enhance* existing ones. [Emphasis added.][113]

Thurlow C.J. found that section 7 "*enhanced* the quality of the less than absolute right conferred by the *Penitentiary Act*."[114]

This notion of the enhancement of rights is a curious one. It does not suggest that fundamental justice, as it relates to a particular process, dictates different safeguards than fairness would demand. Instead, it directs tribunals and judges to the importance of the procedural aspect under consideration, given that a constitutionally protected liberty interest is at stake. Thus, the impact of section 7 bears heavily on judicial review. If counsel is necessary in the circumstances to provide a fair hearing, it must be viewed as a pre-condition, such that a denial requires the ultimate decision to be quashed, regardless of what the reviewing court may think about prejudice to the prisoner.[115] This is analogous to the Supreme Court's later edict in *Cardinal v. Director of Kent Institution*[116] that all denials of a fair hearing are jurisdictional and must be quashed, no matter how the reviewing court responds to the merits of the case delegated to the tribunal.

---

offence, for which forfeiture of remission was no longer an available penalty (*Penitentiary Service Regulations* [as am. SOR/86-963]). A careful examination of both judgments reveals the error in concluding that only the potential loss of remission is sufficient to implicate a prisoner's liberty interest. Nevertheless, many disciplinary tribunals continue to deny representation by counsel on this view of *Howard*.

112 Both opinions, and that of Thurlow C.J. in particular, were obscured by the need to answer the respondent's argument that a denial of counsel was not subject to review since it was entirely within the discretion of the tribunal. Clearly, the issue of counsel is not an infra-jurisdictional question but is a matter of procedure. At the preliminary stage, a request is made on certain grounds and the tribunal's denial pervades the entire ensuing process.

113 *Supra*, note 110, at 218 (Fed. C.A.).

114 *Supra*, note 110, at 208 (Fed. C.A.) [emphasis added].

115 The distinction between a precondition and an incident is explained in A. Manson, "Counsel at Penitentiary Disciplinary Hearings" (1988) 60 C.R. (3d) 122, at 125-127.

116 [1985] 2 S.C.R. 643.

The distinction between a precondition and an incident is closely related to Tribe's distinction between instrumental and intrinsic values in the due process context. At common law, both the traditional protections of natural justice and the more recent notion of fairness were purely instrumental in nature. Legislatures could expressly preclude any given procedural protection, or could do so implicitly by offering what a court might characterize as an exhaustive code of procedure. The content of fairness has always been fluid, to be determined as a function of the statutory structure and purpose of the decision-maker, viewed in the light of the actual interest at stake. The goal of the common law protections has principally been to enhance decision-making by minimizing the risk of error. Thus, we see greater protections afforded participants in those processes considered to involve more serious issues. The legitimacy of any challenge to a given process is determined by assessing the alleged deficiency as it affected the decision-making process. Conversely, it can be argued that the guarantee of fundamental justice in section 7 of the *Charter* includes intrinsic elements which extend to a generalized respect for individuals in their relations with the state and public officials. The recent recognition that section 7 provides more than simply procedural review supports this view. The opportunity for some degree of substantive scrutiny of legislation, discussed below, suggests that there are essential entrenched aspects of the interrelationship between individuals and the state which cannot be overlooked. Similarly, one can argue that there are essential elements of process which accrue to a participant whose liberty or security of the person is at risk and which cannot be overlooked. Accordingly, fundamental justice provides enhanced protections in the sense that it includes some preconditions which, if absent, require intervention without regard to their functional impact on the decision as assessed by the reviewing court. The intrinsic factor relates to what the denial of a procedural incident says about the participant as an object of governmental action.

Looking back to the recognition of the duty to act fairly, an important consideration in determining what fairness requires in respect of a particular process has always been the nature and the gravity of the issue at stake. Prior to the entrenchment of the *Charter*, many courts found themselves unable or unwilling to transcend the era of deference to internal decision-makers in order to give proper consideration to the relationship between fairness and liberty interests. The *Charter*, however, focusses the judicial mandate when liberty is in issue. It is not so much that the content of fundamental justice is different from fairness, but rather that constitutional entrenchment has impressed the need for careful scrutiny and non-deferential application when a liberty interest is involved. The guarantee of fundamental justice does not require a reviewing court to jump higher; but it may require it to jump sooner.

(d) The Substance of Fundamental Justice

Much of the early *Charter* litigation involving fundamental justice claims raised the question of whether the phrase, distinct from the traditional nomenclature of natural justice, suggested more than simply procedural protections. Most judicial decisions accepted the views expressed to the Special Joint Committee prior to entrenchment in 1982 that the phrase was not intended to go beyond the sphere of fair procedures.[117] In 1985, the Supreme Court of Canada surprised many observers and commentators by decisively striking down a provision in the British Columbia *Motor Vehicle Act* on the ground that it was fundamentally unjust to impose a sentence of imprisonment for an absolute liability offence.[118] The statutory provision in issue purported to make the offence of driving while suspended subject to a mandatory term of imprisonment on proof of the act without any opportunity to show lack of notice, mistake or due diligence. Lamer J., for the majority, reasoned that it was a basic tenet of our legal system that only the blameworthy be subjected to the punishment of imprisonment.[119] The court confirmed that the protections of section 7 extended beyond procedure and enabled judicial scrutiny of legislation according to a new yardstick, the principles of fundamental justice.[120] The judgments in this case, generating both a new judicial mandate and the potential for evolving constitutional standards, set the stage for new claims of substantive review.

The scope of substantive fundamental justice claims may appear limitless, but in practical terms this is not the case, since they must proceed from a source that can be characterized as basic or fundamental to our legal system. To date, successful claims have been few. In *Vaillancourt*,[121] the Supreme Court struck down a constructive murder provi-

---

[117] See, for example, the judgment of Strayer J. in *Latham v. Solicitor General* (1984), 39 C.R. (3d) 78 (Fed. T.D.).

[118] *Ref. Re S. 94(2), B.C. Motor Vehicle Act*, [1985] 2 S.C.R. 486.

[119] In his judgment, Lamer J. avoided the phrase "substantive review", perhaps because of his oft-expressed concern not to import American concepts and controversies into Canadian constitutional law. Wilson J. expressed "grave doubts that the dichotomy between substance and procedure ... be imported into s. 7 of the *Charter*" (*ibid.*, at 531).

[120] Wilson J. recognizing the apparently open-textured content of the principles of fundamental justice, described them as "the basic, bedrock principles that underpin a system" (*ibid.*, at 530).

[121] *R. v. Vaillancourt*, [1987] 2 S.C.R. 636.

sion on the ground that it authorized the imposition of the punishment and stigma of a murder conviction in the absence of at least objective foresight of death. The applicable principle of fundamental justice can, perhaps, be described as the requirement of proportionate blameworthiness.[122] Subsequently, in *Gamble*, a three-judge majority found that the appellant ought not to be subjected to the 25-year period of parole ineligibility which attached to a 1976 first degree murder conviction because it is a principle of fundamental justice that people not be punished more severely than the law at the time of the offence provided.[123]

The elusive nature of the substantive principles of fundamental justice can be discerned from the various judgments in *Morgentaler*.[124] Although Dickson C.J.C. based his rejection of the abortion provision on the fact that the exculpatory aspect was illusory for many women, it is unclear whether he considered this defect of fundamental justice to be one of substance or procedure.[125] As Wilson J. commented in an earlier case: "In many instances the line between substance and procedure is a very narrow one."[126] For example, at the evidentiary end of the fundamental justice spectrum, where process and substance sit closely together, it is unresolved whether the privilege against self-incrimination is constitutionally entrenched.[127] The Supreme Court has, however, held that the "right to confront unavailable witnesses at trial is neither an established nor a basic principle of fundamental justice".[128]

While the opportunity for substantive review has expanded the judicial mandate, we have been considering only the scope for judicial scrutiny of legislation. It is a different matter to suggest that the judgments in the *B.C. Motor Vehicle Act Reference* case have changed the nature of judicial review of decision-making discussed in the last chapter. This remains subject to limited jurisdictional and process considerations. The acceptance of substantive review does not mean that the substance of a delegated decision is entirely open to judicial considera-

---

[122] See R. Macnab, Case Comment on *R. v. Vaillancourt* (1988) 13 Queen's L.J. 208.

[123] *Gamble v. R.*, [1988] 2 S.C.R. 595. See the lengthy discussion of this case in Chapter 3 under the heading, "*Habeas Corpus*".

[124] (1988), 37 C.C.C. (3d) 449 (S.C.C.).

[125] While disavowing substantive review (*ibid.*, at 463 and 471), Dickson C.J.C. found the breach of fundamental justice in the basic principle that a defence cannot be illusory (*ibid.*, at 476).

[126] See *Ref. Re S. 94(2), B.C. Motor Vehicle Act, supra*, note 118, at 531.

[127] Although Lamer J. in *R. v. Collins*, [1987] 1 S.C.R. 265, at 284, described the right against self-incrimination as "one of the fundamental tenets of a fair trial", situating the protection within section 7 of the *Charter*, remains controversial; *cf. R. v. Woolley* (1988), 63 C.R. (3d) 333 (Ont. C.A.) and *R. v. Hicks* (1988), 64 C.R. (3d) 68 (Ont. C.A.).

[128] Per Wilson J. in *R. v. Potvin* (1989), 68 C.R. (3d) 193 (S.C.C.), at 229.

tion. While there are some examples of this approach,[129] judicial intervention to rectify an untenable conclusion of law or fact is justified by reference to accepted administrative law principles, not some new notion of substantive review of the merits of a decision. While the yardstick of fundamental justice is not restricted to elements of process, the expanded judicial mandate has not transformed judicial review into appellate review.

3. THE EQUALITY GUARANTEE

Section 15(1) of the *Charter*, proclaimed in force on April 17, 1985, provides:

> Every individual is equal before and under the law and has the right to the equal protection and equal benefit of the law without discrimination and, in particular, without discrimination based on race, national or ethnic origin, colour, religion, sex, age or mental or physical disability.

The following discussion is intended only to be introductory.[130]

Before the Supreme Court of Canada first addressed the purpose and scope of the provision, it generated diverse claims of different or unequal treatment. It is not hard to imagine the various ways in which prisoners, subjected to restrictive and confirming regimes, would perceive themselves as the objects of unequal treatment under the law. Early cases generated two methodological approaches to equality claims. First, the difference or inequality had to be the product of a discriminatory or pejorative classification.[131] Second, the protection of section 15(1) only provided relief in cases of unequal treatment if the claimant could show that he was "similarly situated" to someone treated differently.[132] While discrimination continues to be a *sine qua non* of equality relief, the "similarly situated" test has been rejected.[133]

---

[129] See, for example, *Litwack v. National Parole Bd.* (1986), 51 C.R. (3d) 53 (Fed. T.D.), where Walsh J. relied on both *Ref. Re S. 94(2), B.C. Motor Vehicle Act* and various administrative law decisions to impose a duty of reasonableness on the Board.

[130] For more extensive discussions of section 15, see W. Black and L. Smith, "The Equality Rights" in G.A. Beaudoin and E. Ratushny eds., *The Canadian Charter of Rights and Freedoms*, 2d ed. (Toronto: Carswell, 1989), pp. 557-651; A. Bayefsky and M. Eberts, Eds., *Equality Rights and the Canadian Charter of Rights and Freedoms* (Toronto: Carswell, 1985).

[131] See, for example, *Century 21 Ramos Realty Inc. v. R.* (1987), 56 C.R. (3d) 150 (Ont. C.A.), where the court held that section 15(1) does not prevent any distinction but just those which are "invidious, unreasonable or unjustifiable" (at 171-174), criteria which have subsequently been rejected: see *R. v. Turpin* (1989), 69 C.R. (3d) 97 (S.C.C.), at 123.

[132] See, for example, *R. v. Ertel* (1987), 58 C.R. (3d) 252 (Ont. C.A.), at 273.

[133] See *Andrews, infra*, note 134, at 11-13.

In *Andrews*,[134] the Supreme Court clarified that the ambit of section 15(1) was linked to a conception of equality which aspired to the "admittedly unattainable ideal" that a law should not produce a "more burdensome or less beneficial impact" on someone because of an irrelevant personal difference.[135] The case involved the validity of a citizenship requirement before a qualified permanent resident could enter the legal profession in British Columbia. While the judges disagreed on the ultimate resolution of the appeal,[136] all judges adopted the analysis of section 15 offered by McIntyre J.:

> It is clear that the purpose of s. 15 is to ensure equality in the formulation and application of the law. The promotion of equality entails the promotion of a society in which all are secure in the knowledge that they are recognized at law as human beings equally deserving of concern, respect and consideration.[137]

Recognizing that the trigger for involving equality relief lay in a finding of discrimination, he relied on earlier human rights cases to support the conclusion that discrimination is a function of effect and not just intention.[138] He defined discrimination as

> . . . a distinction, whether intentional or not but based on grounds relating to personal characteristics of the individual or group, which has the effect of imposing burdens, obligations, or disadvantages . . . not imposed upon others, or which withholds or limits access to opportunities, benefits and advantages available to other members of society.[139]

The source of discrimination may be one of the enumerated grounds set out in section 15(1), which encompasses the most common and societally entrenched bases of discrimination, but other analogous grounds may also generate an equality claim. In finding the legislative distinction based on citizenship to be discriminatory, McIntyre J. described the class of permanently resident non-citizens as "a good example of a 'discrete and insular minority' who come within the protection of section 15."[140]

---

[134] *Andrews v. B.C. Law Society* (1989), 56 D.L.R. (4th) 1 (S.C.C.).

[135] *Ibid.*, at 11, per McIntyre J.

[136] *Ibid.* In dissent, McIntyre J. (Lamer J. concurring) held that section 1 saved the *prima facie* violative provision. Wilson J. (Dickson C.J.C. and L'Heureux-Dubé concurring) held that the provision was not justified. The judgment of LaForest J. reached the same result.

[137] *Ibid.*, at 15.

[138] *Ibid.*, at 17-18; McIntyre J. relied on *Re Ont. Human Rights Cmmn. and Simpson-Sears Ltd.*, [1985] 2 S.C.R. 536, at 547, and *Action Travail des Femmes v. C.N.R. Co.*, [1987] 1 S.C.R. 1114, at 1138-1139.

[139] *Ibid.*, at 18.

[140] *Ibid.*, at 24.

Wilson J.'s majority judgment, concurring in analysis but disagreeing on the ability of section 1 to save the impugned provision, examined the class of non-citizens in political terms, commenting on their impotence and vulnerability. In concluding that they fell into an analogous category for the purpose of section 15(1), she directed her inquiry at the place which groups occupy in the entire social, political and legal fabric of our society.[141] She also pointed out that the set of "discrete and insular minorities" can change over time as the normative and political structure of the community changes, and that section 15 must be interpreted today with sufficient flexibility to accommodate the disadvantaged minorities of tomorrow.[142]

The equality analysis of *Andrews* was refined in the subsequent case of *Turpin*, involving the issue of geographical disparity within the criminal process.[143] While Wilson J., for a unanimous court, found that the denial to a person charged with murder in Ontario of an opportunity to choose trial by judge alone constituted a violation of the right to equality before the law, she denied relief because the appellants were not victims of discrimination:

> In determining whether there is discrimination on grounds relating to the personal characteristics of the individual or group, it is important to look not only at the impugned legislation which has created a distinction that violates the right to equality but also to the larger social, political and legal context."[144]

She concluded that persons charged with murder in Ontario did not constitute a "discrete and insular minority" which had suffered discrimination in terms of "stereotyping", historical disadvantage or vulnerability to political and social prejudice.[145] These adverse effects represent the usual hallmarks of discrimination, the remedy of which is the central purpose of the equality protection.[146]

As welcome as the Supreme Court's response to the equality guarantee has been for many segments of the Canadian community, what

---

[141] *Ibid.*, at 32.

[142] *Ibid.*, at 33. In *Turpin, supra*, note 131, Wilson J. wrote that section 15 must be interpreted flexibly "to provide a framework for the 'unremitting protection' of equality rights in the years to come" (at 121).

[143] *R. v. Turpin, supra*, note 131. At the time, the *Criminal Code* permitted persons charged with murder in Alberta to be tried by judge alone, but people like the appellants charged in Ontario, were tried by judge and jury. The *Code* has since been amended: see ss. 469 and 472.

[144] *Supra*, note 131, at 125.

[145] *Supra*, note 131, at 126-127.

[146] On the question of geographical disparity, Wilson J. added the enigmatic comment that province of residence might be a personal characteristic capable of supporting an inequality claim in different circumstances.

does it say to prisoners? Differential treatment by or under the law is only actionable if it constitutes discrimination by reason of a personal characteristic of the individual or group. It has yet to be argued that prisoners as a class represent a "discrete and insular minority". Certainly, one can find historical evidence of the indicia of disadvantage and stereotyping referred to in *Turpin*. An important question, however, will be whether the status of prisoner is different from other recognized personal characteristics in that it is acquired in response, arguably, to anti-social choices. The suggestion that only personal characteristics which are immutable can qualify as an analogous source of discrimination is suspect given that the distinction which was struck down in *Andrews* was based on citizenship, a clearly mutable characteristic. One should not be so quick to dismiss the potential for an inequality claim premised on a prisoner's status as prisoner. However, given the justificatory role of section 1, it is unlikely that any but the most flagrant examples of comparative disadvantage will meet with a receptive judicial audience.[147]

Equality issues may also arise as a result of differential treatment between prisoners. Again, however, the distinction must result from discrimination. Recently, it was held that the policy restricting conjugal visits to heterosexual relationships violated section 15 of the *Charter*.[148] Dubé J. concluded that sexual preference was an analogous ground within the meaning of section 15(1) of the *Charter* such that a prisoner could not be denied a visit with a homosexual partner. In reaching that conclusion, he remarked on the various provincial human rights statutes which include sexual orientation as a prohibited ground of discrimination. This approach reflects the degree of permeability which exists between the constitutionally entrenched norm of equality and legislated anti-discrimination provisions.

4. THE SECTION 1 JUSTIFICATION

As we have already commented, a unique and distinctive element of the *Charter* is the inclusion of section 1, which permits a court to save an otherwise offensive statutory provision or action if it constitutes a reasonable limit "prescribed by law as can be demonstrably justified in a free and democratic society." Thus, unlike American constitutional adjudicative methodology, the question of countervailing interests arises within the operation of section 1, not at the stage of defining the

---

[147] Issues like voting rights, the ability to marry, and access to health care represent the kinds of claims which might generate a successful section 15 argument.
[148] *Veysey v. Canada (Cmmr. of Correctional Service)* (1989), 29 F.T.R. 74.

constitutionally protected zone and determining whether it has been breached.[149] In early cases, judges struggled with the conceptual implications of section 1.[150] Issues relating to its potential interaction with other *Charter* provisions are still the subject of debate.[151] Our concern in this section is restricted to the mechanics of justification. While this aspect is not free from controversy, the leadership of the Supreme Court of Canada has resolved a number of contentious points.

It is now beyond question that the onus of justifying a limitation on any guaranteed right or freedom rests with the party seeking to uphold the infringement of what the *Charter* otherwise protects.[152] Usually, justification will require evidence, although there may be some points in the process which are sufficiently self-evident that they can be argued without formal proof.[153] The standard of persuasion is the civil standard, a preponderance of probability.[154] Given that the inquiry into justification arises only after a finding of *prima facie* violation of a constitutionally protected interest, a "very high degree of probability" is required to meet the "stringent standard of justification".[155]

Courts have consistently demanded "cogent and persuasive" evidence of purposes, effect and alternative measures before granting their approval to governmental action which diminishes the guarantees of the *Charter*.[156] The mode of analysis of justification was explained by Dickson C.J.C. in the oft-quoted case of *Oakes*,[157] where the court had found that a reverse onus provision in the *Narcotic Control Act* violated the right to be presumed innocent in section 11 (*d*) of the *Charter* by requiring an accused to prove that he was not guilty. The justificatory

---

149 Of course, there are some guaranteed rights, which have their own internal modifiers, like the section 8 protection against unreasonable search or seizure, thus requiring some balancing of interests of the definitional and finding stages: see *Hunter v. Southam Inc.*, [1984] 2 S.C.R. 145, at 160-161.

150 See, for example, the thoughtful discussion of McDonald J. in *Soenen v. Edmonton Remand Centre (Director)* (1983), 35 C.R. (3d) 206 (Alta. Q.B.).

151 Dickson J., raised this question in the context of searches in *Hunter v. Southam Inc.*, [1984] 2 S.C.R. 145. Academics have also considered whether the values of a "free and democratic society" infuse the context of other *Charter* protections: see L. Weinrib, "The Supreme Court of Canada and Section 1 of the Charter" (1988), 10 Sup. Ct. L. Rev. 469.

152 See *Hunter v. Southam, ibid.*, at 169.

153 *R. v. Oakes* (1986), 50 C.R. (3d) 1 (S.C.C.), at 29-30, per Dickson C.J.C.

154 *Ibid.*, at 29.

155 *Ibid.*, at 28-29.

156 *Oakes, ibid.*, at 30. Also see the comments of Estey J. on the inadequacy of the section 1 record in *Law Society of Upper Canada v. Skapinker*, [1984] 1 S.C.R. 357, at 384.

157 *Ibid.*, dealing with prosecutions for possession of a narcotic for the purpose of trafficking under section 8 of the *Narcotic Control Act*, R.S.C. 1970, c. N-1 [now R.S.C. 1985, c. N-1].

inquiry was divided into two aspects. First, the provision must have been enacted to achieve a legislative purpose "of sufficient importance to warrant overriding a constitutionally protected right or freedom".[158] In societal terms, the objective must relate to concerns which are "pressing and substantial" to satisfy this aspect:

> The standard must be high in order to ensure that objectives which are trivial or discordant with the principles integral to a free and democratic society do not gain s. 1 protection.[159]

The second aspect of the inquiry relates to the means chosen for achieving the objective and its effects. There are three basic elements to the proportionality test, intended to balance the rights of the individual with those of society in general:

1. The means chosen must be "rationally connected to the objective",[160]
2. The means should impair the right or freedom in question "as little as possible",[161] and
3. The effect of the impairment of the right or freedom must be proportionate to the objective sought to be achieved by the impugned provision.[162]

Subsequent cases have repeated Dickson C.J.C.'s warning that the nature of the proportionality test may vary with the circumstances of other cases and that the relevant criteria as set out in *Oakes* should not be transformed into "rigid and inflexible" standards.[163]

In *Edwards Books & Art Ltd.*,[164] a case involving prosecutions for breaches of Sunday observance legislation, the "minimum impairment" issue was translated into the lower threshold of whether the provision abridged the freedom of religion ". . . as little as is reasonably possible."[165] Thus, the question was framed:

---

[158] *Ibid.*, at 30.
[159] *Ibid.*
[160] *Ibid.* Dickson C.J.C. explained that the means chosen cannot be "arbitrary, unfair or based on irrational considerations".
[161] *Ibid.*
[162] *Ibid.*, at 31, where Dickson C.J.C. explained that the "more severe the deleterious effects of a measure the more important the objective must be if the measure is to be reasonable and demonstrably justified in a free and democratic society."
[163] While section 1 is often discussed solely in terms of the *Oakes* test, some observers have commented that subsequent modifications may have produced other tests to determine whether a limit is reasonable and justifiable; see Mr. Justice R. Kerans, "The Future of Section One of the *Charter*" (1989) 23 U.B.C. L. Rev. 567.
[164] *R. v. Edwards Books & Art Ltd.*, [1986] 2 S.C.R. 713.
[165] *Ibid.*, at 772-773.

What must be decided, however, is whether there is some reasonable alternative scheme which would allow the province to achieve its objective with fewer detrimental effects on religious freedom".[166]

This case, unlike *Oakes*, was multi-dimensional. It affected the interests not only of the state and the accused, but also segments of the working and consuming public with their respective religious and familial preferences. In the criminal and penal contexts, most issues involve only the interests of the state and the individual. Hence, in these cases the courts may be entitled to demand a more rigorous justificatory showing.[167]

When courts are dealing with the constitutional legitimacy of a legislative provision, the section 1 inquiry is focussed. The impugned provision has been found to authorize or cause some infringement of an otherwise protected constitutional interest, and its underlying societal objective must qualify as "pressing and substantial" before the more difficult assessment of proportionality takes place. The inquiry is often more subtle when the issue relates to action rather than legislation. This is particularly true with respect to a decision attacked on fundamental justice grounds, or confinement challenged by reason of arbitrary detention or cruel and unusual treatment or punishment. In arguing to justify its action or decision the state must offer a reasonable limit which is prescribed by law. Some provision of a statute or regulation, or even a set of provisions, must be isolated as the source of the limitation before an *Oakes* type of inquiry can commence. Criteria or directions found in subordinate instruments which do not have the force of law cannot satisfy the "prescribed by law" requirement.[168] Thus, neither the National Parole Board's Policy and Procedures Manual[169] nor Commissioner's Directives, which apply to the Correctional Service of Canada,[170] can justify decisions or actions which violate *Charter* guarantees.

Although the Supreme Court has emphasized the degree of persuasion, the mode of analysis and the kind of evidence necessary to authorize an intrusion into a constitutionally protected sphere, some lower courts have failed to heed this guidance. For example, in *Gallant v. Canada (Deputy Commissioner of Correctional Service)*, the Correc-

---

166 *Ibid.*, at 772-773.
167 For example, in *R. v. Therens*, [1985] 1 S.C.R. 613, the Supreme Court applied the element of clarity in its section 1 analysis. See also *R. v. Thomsen*, [1988] 1 S.C.R. 640.
168 See *Ont. Film & Video Appreciation Society v. Ont. Bd. of Censors* (1983), 34 C.R. (3d) 73 (Ont. Div. Ct.), at 83-84. Affirmed (1984), 38 C.R. (3d) 271 (Ont. C.A.). Leave to appeal to S.C.C. granted (1984), 3 O.A.C. 318 (S.C.C.).
169 *Cadieux v. Mountain Institution (Director)* (1984), 41 C.R. (3d) 30 (Fed. T.D.), at 54, per Reed J.
170 *Weatherall v. Canada (A.G.)* (1987), 59 C.R. (3d) 247 (Fed. T.D.), at 282, per Strayer J. Varied on other grounds (1988), 65 C.R. (3d) 27 (Fed. C.A.).

tional Service of Canada appealed from an order which quashed a decision to transfer the prisoner to higher security on the ground that the disclosure of allegations was insufficient to satisfy the requirements of fairness.[171] Pratte J.A. concluded that the prisoner's claim could not be premised on the duty to act fairly, but that the denial of "a real opportunity to answer the allegation made against him" constituted a breach of the principles of fundamental justice.[172] Moving to the justificatory stage and without isolating a particular provision, he observed that the *Penitentiary Act* gives the Commissioner or his delegate power broad discretion to transfer prisoners.[173] While it is true that a broad power exists, that power exists without structure, limitations or criteria in any statutory form. The transfer was only lawful in the first instance because it was authorized by the *Penitentiary Act.* The issue for the court, however, was whether this power had been exercised in accordance with the principles of fundamental justice, or, if not, whether the action could be justified as a reasonable limit. Pratte J.A. concluded:

> ... the answer to the question appears to me to be so obvious that I do not need any evidence or argument to conclude that in a free and democratic society it is reasonable, perhaps even necessary, to confer such a wide discretion on penitentiary authorities.[174]

The logical extension of this view is that penal authorities can, in the context of deciding to transfer a prisoner, ignore and violate any constitutionally protected interest, since the power to transfer is its own justification. This approach does not conform with the "stringent standard of justification" which ought to be applied whenever governmental action fails to meet constitutional standards. It ignores entirely the elements of proportionality as described by Dickson C.J.C.:

> ... the limiting measures must be carefully designed, or rationally connected, to the objective; they must impair the right as little as possible; and their effects must not so severely trench on individual or group rights that

---

[171] (1989), 68 C.R. (3d) 173 (Fed. C.A.) an appeal from the decision of Dubé J. (1988), 62 C.R. (3d) 267 (Fed. T.D.). Leave to appeal to S.C.C. refused (1989), 102 N.R. 399 (note) (S.C.C.).

[172] *Ibid.*, at 181-183. This conclusion flowed from the curious reasoning that the procedural rules of fundamental justice, like fairness or natural justice, are flexible and vary with circumstances, but that the "rules of substantial justice" are not "variable or flexible".

[173] The only reference in the *Penitentiary Act* to transfers is found in R.S.C. 1985, c. P-5, section 15(3) which simply empowers the Commissioner or his delegate to issue a warrant directing that a person "sentenced or committed to penitentiary ... be committed or transferred to any penitentiary in Canada ...."

[174] *Supra*, note 171, at 183. Marceau J.A. agreed in the result but based his conclusion on different reasoning. Desjardins J.A. dissented on the ground that the authorities had not made an adequate showing to support non-disclosure.

the legislative objective, albeit important, is nevertheless outweighed by the abridgement of rights.[175]

5. REMEDIES FOR CHARTER CLAIMS

(a) Constitution Act, Section 52(1)

From a purely constitutional perspective, the most significant remedial provision is section 52(1) of the *Constitution Act, 1982*, which reads:

> The Constitution of Canada is the supreme law of Canada, and any law that is inconsistent with the provisions of the Constitution is, to the extent of the inconsistency, of no force or effect.

The entrenchment of this section ensures the fundamental shift from an era of Parliamentary supremacy to one of constitutional supremacy.[176] Any law which does not conform with the provisions of the *Charter* is, subject to the saving provision in section 1, of no force and effect to the extent of the inconsistency.[177] The Supreme Court has rejected the argument that, when faced with a constitutionally based inconsistency, it ought to "read down" the legislative provision to make it fit the constitutional mold.[178] In *Hunter*, it warned that it "should not fall to the courts to fill in the details that will render legislative lacunae constitutional."[179] This statement, however, was made in the context of a search power which was considered to be unreasonable. Later, we will consider the scope of remedial responses and the opportunity for judicial creativity under both section 52(1) and section 24(1) of the *Charter*. It seems clear, however, that in response to an unconstitutional intrusive power the court's role is not to decide how agents of the state should be equipped to intrude upon privacy rights. The question of safeguards and where they ought to be located on the plane above minimum constitutional standards is a matter for the legislature. This is not to say that other issues will not require judicial intervention to rectify a process or regime which is unjust, arbitrary or cruel.[180]

---

[175] *Edwards Books & Art Ltd., supra,* note 164, at 768.

[176] This statement is, of course, subject to the "notwithstanding clause" found in section 33 of the *Charter.* See the discussion of this unusual provision in R. Tasse, "Application of the Canadian Charter of Rights and Freedoms (Sections 30-33 and 52)" in G.A. Beaudoin and E. Ratushny, eds., *supra,* note 130, pp. 102-107; B. Slattery, "A Theory of the Charter" (1987), 25 Osgoode Hall L.J. 701, at 737-745.

[177] Per Dickson C.J.C., in *Hunter v. Southam Inc.,* [1984] 2 S.C.R. 145, at 148.

[178] *Ibid.,* at 168-169. See also *R. v. Noble* (1984), 48 O.R. (2d) 643 (Ont. C.A.).

[179] *Ibid.,* at 169.

[180] For a discussion of this conceptual distinction between section 52(1) and section 24(1), see A. Manson, Annot. *R. v. Varga* (1985), 44 C.R. (3d) 377 (Ont. C.A.), a case involving jury selection procedures.

Part of the controversy over section 52(1) relates to constitutional adjudicative methodology. At one time it was accepted by some judges that a *Charter* challenge to a legislative provision could only be raised by a claimant whose own case represented the factual basis for the challenge.[181] Subsequently, the Supreme Court has confirmed that everyone is entitled to be prosecuted[182] and punished[183] only under a statutory structure which is constitutionally valid. Thus, a ruling of invalidity can be sought in any court where a person is being prosecuted[184] and the same rationale should apply to the application of law by a tribunal.[185]

Recognizing that statutory provisions are often multi-faceted and complex, it may be that only one aspect is found to be constitutionally impermissible. Should only the infringing aspect be ruled of no force or effect, leaving the remainder of the provision intact? Similarly, how should a court respond when the operation of a provision will only sometimes, in certain circumstances, violate constitutional rights? Some courts have interpreted section 52(1) as providing not just a power to strike down legislation but also the ability to declare a provision inoperative only as it relates to certain people or circumstances.[186]

---

[181] See, for example, *Re Moore and R.* (1984), 10 C.C.C. (3d) 306 (Ont. H.C.), at 312.

[182] See *R. v. Big M Drug Mart*, [1985] 1 S.C.R. 295, at 312-313.

[183] See *R. v. Smith*, [1987] 1 S.C.R. 1045, at 1113, per LeDain J.; also at 1078 where Lamer J. said that pursuant to section 52(1) "courts are duty bound to make that pronouncement. . . ."

[184] *R. v. Big M Drug Mart, supra,* note 182, at 312-314.

[185] See *Cuddy Chicks Ltd. v. Ont. Labour Relations Bd.* (1989), 70 O.R. (2d) 179 (Ont. C.A.).

[186] In *R. v. Rao* (1984), 46 O.R. (2d) 80, dealing with section 10(1)(*a*) of the *Narcotic Control Act*, R.S.C. 1970, c. N-1, the Ontario Court of Appeal held that a search provision in the *Narcotic Control Act* was "inoperative to the extent that it authorizes the search of a person's office without a warrant, in the absence of circumstances which make the obtaining of a warrant impracticable . . ." (at 110). In *Reynolds v. British Columbia (A.G.)* (1984), 40 C.R. (3d) 393 (B.C.C.A.), the court examined a challenge to a provision of the *Election Act*, R.S.B.C. 1979, c. 103, which precluded persons serving a sentence from voting. It concluded that the prohibition was of no force and effect in respect of persons serving probationary periods but valid for persons serving terms of imprisonment. More recently, in *R. v. Ladouceur* (1987), 57 C.R. (3d) 45 (Ont. C.A.) (leave to appeal to S.C.C. granted April 21, 1988), the Ontario Court of Appeal considered a random motor vehicle stop power under section 189a of the *Highway Traffic Act*, R.S.O. 1980, c. 198, and concluded that it should receive a limited interpretation such that it authorized only organized programs of stopping or stops based on "articulable cause". The court reasoned that although a random stop without articulable cause was offensive, the provision did not need to be struck down but simply should be declared operative only when "exercised in a manner that does not violate the Charter" (at 75). In the subsequent case of *R. v. Hufsky*, [1988] 1 S.C.R. 621, the Supreme Court of Canada held that the same provision violated the guarantee against arbitrary detention, but justified the power in its entirety under section 1

Pre-*Charter* remedial analysis, whether flowing from division of powers cases, the *Canadian Bill of Rights*, or civil litigation in general, cannot respond easily to the new dimensions of the judicial mandate entrenched in the *Constitution Act, 1982*. Yet, the questions of remedy have remained, for the most part, unexamined.[187] Methodologically, one would expect that the choice of remedy can only be addressed distinctly after a *prima facie* breach has been found and the court has ruled that the impugned provision cannot be saved under section 1. Any dispositional decision which saves some part of the offensive legislation must necessarily take into account the purpose and effects of the provision and the matrix of individual and collective interests within which it operates. Thus, the remedial issue is inextricably bound up with the other aspects of constitutional adjudication and must be answered in consistent terms.

One approach that has received some judicial support is the mechanism of excision or "reading out" the offensive portion.[188] This would leave a smaller, less-intrusive power which conforms with constitutional strictures. In *Holmes*,[189] Dickson C.J.C. and Lamer J. would have chosen this remedial response in respect of the *Code* provision in issue had their interpretation of the breadth of the section won the day.[190] By excising part of a provision, the role of section 52(1) essentially produces a limited declaration of invalidity. It recognizes and maintains the legitimacy of Parliamentary will to the limited extent that the remaining legislation conforms with standards of constitutionality. Ironically, this approach can only apply when a provision is structured in a form that renders the offensive aspect severable. Accepting the legitimacy of excision also provides support for the acceptance of an exempting declaration which achieves the same result in response to a

---

because of the dangers of impaired driving, the difficulty of detection and the need to increase effective deterrence (at 631-37, per LeDain J.).

[187] See J. Cameron, "Enforcing the Charter: Four Remedial Vignettes" (1988) 9 Advocate's Q. 257.

[188] This approach was suggested by the comments of Beetz J. in the *Manitoba (A.G.) v. Metropolitan Stores Ltd.* case, [1987] 1 S.C.R. at 110, where he discussed the difference between "reading down" and "reading in." It was also used by the Ontario Court of Appeal in *Cdn. Newspapers Co. v. Canada (A.G.)* (1985), 44 C.R. (3d) 97 in respect of the ban on publishing the identity of the complainant in a sexual assault case. An appeal to the Supreme Court of Canada was allowed on the basis that the prohibition was a justifiable limit on the freedom of the press: (1989), 65 C.R. (3d) 50 (S.C.C.).

[189] *R. v. Holmes* (1988), 64 C.R. (3d) 97 (S.C.C.).

[190] *Ibid.*, at 117. The majority interpreted section 309(1) [now s. 351(1)] of the *Code* as not amounting to a reverse onus clause which imposes a burden of proof on the accused. Dickson C.J.C. and Lamer J., in dissent, offered a broader interpretation of the provision such that it constituted an impermissible reverse onus. As a remedy, they would have removed the words "the proof of which lies upon him" from the section.

differently constructed provision. There is little difference between excising the offensive element "Z" from the provision "X, Y and Z" and declaring the provision "X and Y" valid except when its application encompasses "Z".

Charter litigation is less than a decade old. As lawyers, judges and academics begin to feel comfortable with their new responsibilities, they should not be handcuffed by short-sighted rules which restrict remedial creativity. Still, the judiciary is not the only governmental body required to act in conformity with constitutional dictates, and the decisions of legislatures, by reason of their representative capacity, are entitled to serious consideration. An examination of some recent cases discloses two aspects of remedial analysis which deserve consideration. The first relates to the often subtle distinction between an inherent defect and one which arises only idiosyncratically because of a personal characteristic or circumstance peculiar to the claimant or class of claimants. The second aspect raises the question of a judicial or administrative void: what remains if a provision is invalidated? That is, will an agency or process be significantly disempowered by a declaration of invalidity?

A recent example of this problem arose in *Chief,* a case from the Yukon involving a trapper convicted of assault and possession of a weapon for a purpose dangerous to the public peace.[191] The offences occurred in a domestic context. On sentencing, after imposing a 21-day period of imprisonment followed by probation, the trial judge ruled that the imposition of the mandatory 5-year firearm prohibition would be cruel and unusual punishment contrary to section 12 of the *Charter,* in light of the accused's need for a weapon to earn his living. Instead, he imposed a 5-year limited prohibition which was restricted to the accused's residence. On appeal by the Crown, the majority[192] agreed that the mandatory prohibition contravened section 12. McEachern C.J. held that it was grossly disproportionate and shocking to the conscience of a reasonable person that the accused be deprived of his, and his dependants', means of economic support. The difficult question, however, related to remedy, particularly since the limited prohibition imposed by the trial judge was seen as a "sensible and reasonable disposition".[193] The only source of statutory power for a 5-year prohibition was section 100 [formerly s. 98] of the *Code*—the provision which was found to be offensive in its application to the convicted man. The

---

[191] *R. v. Chief* (1990), 51 C.C.C. (3d) 265 (Y.T.C.A.).

[192] Locke J.A. dissented on the ground that many occupations involved carrying a firearm. Hence, the impact on the accused in *Chief* was not, in his view, grossly disproportionate.

[193] *Supra*, note 191, at 280, per Esson J.A.

majority considered the trial judge's improvised prohibition to be an impermissible "reading down" of section 100 such that the order had to be struck out. Resorting to section 24(1) of the *Charter*, the remedy which did "justice in the instant case without damaging the general good"[194] was a declaration that section 100 was inoperative with respect to Mr. Chief, combined with an added probation term prohibiting the storage of firearms in his residence for the maximum allowable probation term. Agreeing with this disposition, McEachern C.J. commented that it would not be appropriate or just to strike down the entire prohibition since it was a "reasonable provision decided upon by Parliament which works well and beneficially in most cases."[195] This imports an element of public interest beyond simply the self-interest of the person whose right has been violated.

The decision in *Chief* represents a form of constitutional exemption, suggesting that section 52 does not dictate an all or nothing imperative. As McEachern C.J. noted, some support for this approach can be found in Dickson C.J.C.'s remarks in *Edward Books & Art Ltd.*,[196] where he commented that, had he found the legislation offensive, he would have been faced with the question of whether to strike it down or rule that it be "ineffective or inapplicable with respect to a limited class of persons."[197] By accepting the legitimacy of constitutional exemption, courts have injected a degree of unpredictability into constitutional adjudication and, at the same time, increased the opportunity for deference to legislative enactments beyond the application of section 1.

In *Smith*, the Supreme Court of Canada ruled that the mandatory minimum sentence for importing or exporting narcotics produced a potentially unconstitutional result because it would be grossly disproportionate to the blameworthiness of some accused persons.[198] In *Vaillancourt*, the converse constitutional requirement of proportionate blameworthiness rendered the constructive murder provision in section 213(*d*) [now s. 230(*d*)] of the *Code* unconstitutional because someone could be subjected to the punishment for, and stigma of, murder without proof of even an objectively foreseeable risk of death.[199] The offensive provisions in both cases were struck down. Arguably, these two cases are essentially different from *Chief*. In *Smith* and *Vaillancourt*, the offensive result was inevitable because the broad net of conduct encompassed

---

194 *Supra*, note 191, at 281, per Esson J.A.
195 *Supra*, note 191, at 279, per McEachern C.J.
196 *R. v. Edwards Books & Art Ltd.*, [1986] 2 S.C.R. 713.
197 *Ibid.*, at 784.
198 *R. v. Smith, supra*, note 183.
199 *R. v. Vaillancourt*, [1987] 2 S.C.R. 636.

by the provisions necessarily included some people who, if punished in the way required by the statute, would suffer a violation of their constitutional rights. According to Lamer J. it was a certainty that the accompanying responsibility provision made acts punishable by a mandatory sentence which would be grossly disproportionate.[200] Just as it would be cruel and unusual to sentence someone to 7 years' imprisonment for possession of a small quantity of marijuana for personal use, it would also be fundamentally unjust to convict someone of murder without proving at least an objective foreseeability of death. In contrast, the claim of unconstitutionality in *Chief* did not flow from any act encompassed by the provision itself or any circumstance necessarily included in it. Rather, the issue arose because of uncommon and peculiar personal circumstances of the accused. The provision itself was not inherently defective.

Chief provides an example of how the remedial question injects another layer of proportionality analysis even after the court has concluded that the impugned provision was not a reasonable limit on the claimant's constitutional rights. While this appears to be the sole function of section 1, some cases suggest a residual remedial power to achieve a similar end. In *Schachter v. Canada*,[201] Strayer J. invoked section 24(1) in response to a provision in the *Unemployment Insurance Act*[202] which he found denied equal benefit of the law to a natural father by failing to provide what would be available to a natural mother or an adoptive father. He recognized that it would not be "appropriate and just" to strike down the legislation and thereby deprive everyone of the child care benefit. Accordingly, he left the provision intact but issued a declaration that natural fathers and mothers of newborn children be entitled to the same child care benefits as adoptive parents.[203] Thus, an interactive view of section 52(1) and section 24(1) preserved an existing benefit and extended its reach to conform with the guarantee of equality in section 15(1). Any other choice would be antithetical to the purposes of section 15.

Process cases present other dimensions which differ from those cases involving responsibility or punishment. Any delegation of power or discretion can produce an unauthorized, abusive or offensive response depending on how it is exercised. The test of inherent defect may have some utility but requires a refined appreciation of the nature of the

---

[200] *R. v. Smith, supra*, note 183.
[201] (1988), 52 D.L.R. (4th) 525 (Fed. T.D.). Affirmed on appeal (Docket no. A-1002-88, Fed. C.A., Heald, Mahoney, Stone JJ.A., February 15, 1990).
[202] S.C. 1970-71-72, c. 48.
[203] *Ibid.*, at 547.

right which is implicated. In *Hunter v. Southam Inc.*, a search power was ruled invalid because it did not meet the minimum constitutional standard of prior authorization by a neutral arbiter based on some objective, credibly-based standard.[204] Thus, its exercise would always be inadequate in terms of respecting a person's justifiable expectation of privacy. In *Hufsky*,[205] the accused was stopped at a random spot check organized to check licences, insurance, mechanical fitness and sobriety. The broad statutory power to stop any motor vehicle was found to generate arbitrary detention because it was exercised without any criteria for selection. Thus, it could also be said that the defect was inherent in the statutory provision since it provided no specific criteria or grounds for the detention.[206] Whether the exercise of power is for reasons ultimately considered good or bad, the detainee had no assurance of legitimate justification because the distinction between good and bad was left entirely to the police officer at the moment of detention. In both *Hunter* and *Hufsky*, a constitutional violation was inevitable because of the absence of adequate structure or criteria for decision-making. These structural deficiencies were inherent in the intrusive powers, and the only available avenue of redemption was section 1.

Issues relating to the fairness of an adjudicative process require an assessment of the dynamics of the process and the powers of the decision-maker. In *Seaboyer*, the Ontario Court of Appeal was faced with the question of whether the protections granted to a witness from an inquiry into past sexual conduct denied the accused fundamental justice by excluding evidence which would be potentially relevant to his de-

---

[204] [1984] 2 S.C.R. 145.

[205] *Supra*, note 186.

[206] Like the guarantee against unreasonable searches, the section 9 guarantee from arbitrary detention provides a constitutional assurance that intrusions will only be permitted if based on legitimate justifications. As LeDain J. said (*Hufsky, supra*, note 186, at 632): "A discretion is arbitrary if there are no criteria, express or implied, which govern its exercise." Interestingly, in *Hufsky*, the Supreme Court accepted the section 1 justification while the Ontario Court of Appeal in *Ladouceur, supra*, note 186, rejected it. The Court of Appeal rejected the section 1 claim on the basis that the evidence did not disclose "a serious problem concerning highway safety caused by unlicensed drivers . . ." (at 71). Accordingly, the proportionality aspect of the section 1 test was not met. Having rejected the section 1 argument, on what basis could the Ontario Court of Appeal save part of the statutory power by declaring it invalid only in the circumstances of a detention without articulable cause? Given the conclusion on section 1, and the further observation by Tarnopolsky J.A. that it would be "difficult to envisage all the purposes for which the police may have to stop cars" (at 76), the decision not to strike the legislation down, but to issue a declaration of limited invalidity, is questionable. Ultimately, the Supreme Court, by a 5-to-4 majority, accepted the section 1 justification and saved the entire provision: see *Ladouceur v. R.*, an as yet unreported decision of the Supreme Court of Canada released May 31, 1990.

fence on a charge of sexual assault.[207] The majority held that in some situations the operation of the statutory provisions would deny an accused his right to a fair trial[208] and ruled that such infringement could not be saved by section 1.[209] Grange J.A. concluded, however, that the provisions should not be declared invalid:

> In my view the evidentiary restriction contained in s. 246.6 is not on its face contrary to any provision of the Charter. As I have stated, there may be occasions—very difficult to define—where that effect might result. But those occasions will be rare and will depend upon the circumstances of the case. I see no reason why it cannot be held that in those circumstances the section will be inoperative. In the great majority of cases, however, the section will be "invalid and operative".[210]

This response represents a residual proportionality test which focusses on the idiosyncratic occurrence of the unconstitutional effect in a situation where the nature of the infringement and its impact on an individual accused render it unsalvageable through section 1. But if one were to ask whether the provision was inherently defective in terms of whether an infringement was inevitable, the answer would be affirmative. It is inevitable that the provision will infringe the constitutional right to a fair trial in any case not covered by the exceptions to the prohibition where previous sexual conduct is relevant. Thus, the remedy of a limited declaration of invalidity cannot be supported by the inevitability test. The choice, however, makes sense if one accepts the beneficial impact of the legislated prohibition in most cases compared to the small number of situations where a claim of unfairness to the accused may arise. Its justification lies in asking what will remain if the provision is struck down entirely. Parliament enacted the provision to protect witnesses from unnecessary and intimidating cross-examination and attempted to craft exemptions which recognized the accused's

---

[207] *R. v. Seaboyer* (1987), 58 C.R. (3d) 289 (Ont. C.A.); Brooke J.A. dissenting. Leave to appeal to S.C.C. granted May 16, 1988.

[208] *Ibid.*, at 305-306.

[209] *Ibid.*, at 308, where Grange J.A. said that it "would be a rare case indeed where a breach of s. 7 of the Charter could be justified under s. 1."

[210] *Ibid.*, at 309. In *R. v. Wald* (1989), 68 C.R. (3d) 289, the Alberta Court of Appeal chose not to follow Grange J.A.'s remedial choice. Instead, it declared section 276 [formerly s. 246.6] of the *Code* of no force and effect. The principal reason for rejecting a constitutional exemption was the burden that this would place on an accused person. Surely, this is an exaggeration. Following *Seaboyer*, an accused could circumvent the statutory protection only in circumstances where questions about previous sexual conduct were relevant to a live issue such that precluding the questions impaired the accused's opportunity to defend himself. Showing relevance is commonplace in criminal prosecutions. It requires only an explanation of how a factual question relates to a substantive issue.

right to make full answer and defence. Invalidating the provision would leave both witnesses and accused persons in the hands of unpredictable and variable assessments of relevance in relation to material issues and credibility.

The question of what will remain was raised in *Goltz*,[211] a case subsequent to *Chief*, in which the British Columbia Court of Appeal addressed the issue of a mandatory 7-day sentence for driving while suspended contrary to a provincial statute. After finding that the provision contravened section 12 of the *Charter* by reason of the "inevitably" concept applied by Lamer J. in *Smith*, the court also concluded that it could not be saved by section 1 since it did not impair "as little as possible" the right protected by section 12. On the remedial issue, Wood J.A. considered the exemption in *Chief* and commented:

> By use of the phrase "to the extent of the inconsistency", s. 52 of the *Constitution Act, 1982*, clearly calls for a measured response when devising a remedy for anyone affected by legislation found to be incompatible with the Charter. No doubt as time goes by the court will develop rules by which such responses can be consistently crafted. One undesirable consequence of the approach adopted by the majority in *Chief*, as noted by McEachern, C.J., is that it leaves the law in an uncertain state where constitutional issues must be determined on a case-by-case basis.[212]

He observed that a declaration of invalidity in *Chief* would have left a void in the sentencer's arsenal by removing any power to impose a 5-year firearm restriction, whereas, in the case before him, striking down the mandatory sentence would still leave a sentencing judge with the ability to impose a term of imprisonment if appropriate. Accordingly, as in *Smith*, the provision was ruled of no force and effect. From the remedial perspective, the case represents an application of the "inevitability" aspect expanded to include consideration of the impact of a declaration of invalidity in terms of any subsequent disempowerment.

This is a significant pragmatic extension of previous analyses which has particular relevance to prison issues, most of which relate to decision-making processes. Faced with a provision which denies to a prisoner fundamental justice in respect of an interest protected by section 7 of the *Charter*, a court should first ask whether the provision is inherently or idiosyncratically offensive. In other words, is it inevitable that the application of the provision will infringe someone's rights? As well, the court should consider whether a void or significant disempowerment will be created if the provision is invalidated. In the context of a decision-making process this will rarely be the case, given the decision-

---

[211] *R. v. Goltz* (1990), 74 C.R. (3d) 78 (B.C.C.A.).
[212] *Ibid.*, at 94.

maker's ability, within the confines of its delegated mandate, to control its own process. From a practical perspective, except in the voting rights cases,[213] this remedial issue has not yet arisen in the prison context. When a statutory provision has been raised to defend a less than satisfactory hearing, courts have looked to the obligations of fundamental justice and have resorted to section 24(1) to order a new, fuller hearing.[214]

These remedial questions involve many of the factors relevant to the section 1 analysis: the purpose of the provision and the extent to which its scheme impairs the rights of individuals. Thus, in some situations, the remedial choice may provide another level of proportionality analysis. Necessarily, the remedial issue must be resolved consistently with any findings made as part of the section 1 analysis including the issue of "collective goals".[215] If forms of constitutional exemption or limited declarations of invalidity are permissible, they should be used only exceptionally. The balance should usually tip towards striking down a provision and leaving questions of criteria, procedural safeguards and limitations for the legislature. Still, courts should consider the extent to which invalidation disempowers a legitimate process. Exemptions, declarations of limited invalidity and excision should be restricted to situations where the intrusive legislative provision is ordinarily, and in most circumstances, exercised in a constitutionally valid and beneficial manner. This approach gives effect both to the dictates of section 52(1) and the expanded mandate of section 24(1) by imposing the remedy which is "appropriate and just".

(b) Section 24(1)

Unlike section 52(1), which deals with legislative provisions which are inconsistent with constitutional guarantees, section 24(1) is the source of remedial power for any individual whose *Charter* rights or freedoms have been infringed by any governmental action. In its original draft form, a broad singular remedial provision was included in the *Charter*, but concern about its impact on questions of admissibility of evidence persuaded the drafters to split section 24 into two subsections.[216] Now, section 24(1) reads:

---

[213] See the discussion of *Canada (A.G.) v. Gould* (1984), 42 C.R. (3d) 88 (Fed. C.A.), in Chapter 3.

[214] See, for example, *H. v. R.* (1985), 17 Admin. L.R. 39 (Fed. T.D.).

[215] See *R. v. Oakes* (1986), 50 C.R. (3d) 1 (S.C.C.), at 28.

[216] For the details of this historical evolution, see D. Gibson, "Enforcement of the Canadian Charter of Rights and Freedoms (Section 24)" in W. Tarnopolsky and G.A. Beaudoin, Eds., *The Canadian Charter of Rights and Freedoms: Commentary* (Toronto: Carswell, 1982), pp. 492-493.

Anyone whose rights or freedoms, as guaranteed by this Charter, have been infringed or denied may apply to a court of competent jurisdiction to obtain such remedy as the court considers appropriate and just in the circumstances.

A "court of competent jurisdiction" is one which, absent the *Charter*, would have authority over the subject matter and the parties, and the power to grant the remedy sought.[217] Thus, for example, in the face of *Charter* violations a criminal court cannot award damages,[218] but is restricted to its usual limited range of remedies including a judicial stay,[219] or dismissal.[220] Exclusion of evidence, because it is dealt with specifically through the standard set out in section 24(2), is not an available remedy under section 24(1).[221] In criminal cases, if the ultimate remedy of a stay or dismissal is considered inappropriate,[222] the accused whose rights have been infringed is compelled to seek redress in a court with the authority to award damages, perhaps including a claim for punitive damages beyond simple compensation for actual loss.[223]

The challenge of section 24(1) lies in the potential remedial scope created by empowering a court to grant the remedy which is "appropriate and just" in the circumstances. In the pre-*Charter* era, judicial intervention in Canada was limited by the accepted limitations placed on the remedies of declaratory and injunctive relief.[224] Thus, even in respect of proven violations of the *Canadian Bill of Rights*, judges were reluctant to do more than declare that an infringement had taken place.[225] Concerns about the need for future supervision and more fundamental questions about the proper constitutional role of the judiciary have produced a traditional reluctance on the part of judges to play an active role in restructuring deficient institutions.[226] Surprisingly, the

---

[217] *R. v. Mills*, [1986] 1 S.C.R. 863.

[218] See generally, M. Pilkington, "Monetary Redress For Charter Infringement" in R. Sharpe ed., *Charter Litigation* (Toronto: Butterworth & Co., 1987), p. 322. Also see *Mills, ibid.*, at 866, per Lamer J., and at 971, per LaForest J.

[219] See *R. v. Jewitt*, [1985] 2 S.C.R. 128, at 147, per Dickson C.J.C.

[220] See, for example, *R. v. Beason* (1983), 7 C.C.C. (3d) 20 (Ont. C.A.), at 43. For a creative use of section 24(1) in a quasi-criminal context, see *Parker v. Solicitor General* (Ont. H.C., Henry J., May 18, 1990).

[221] See *R. v. Therens*, [1985] 1 S.C.R. 613, at 647-648.

[222] See, for example, *R. v. Germain* (1984), 53 A.R. 264 (Q.B.); and *Mills, supra*, note 217, at 977-978, per LaForest J.

[223] See *R. v. Crossman*, [1984] 1 F.C. 681 (T.D.); *cf. Vespoli v. R.*, [1983] 2 F.C. 806 (T.D.).

[224] See the discussion in R. Sharpe, "Injunctions and the Charter" (1984) 22 Osgoode Hall L.J. 473, at 473-475.

[225] See, for example, *McCann v. R.* (1976), 29 C.C.C. (2d) 337 (Fed. T.D.), dealing with long-term solitary confinement at the B.C. Penitentiary, discussed in Chapter 3.

[226] See R. Sharpe, *supra*, note 224, at 479-487.

flexibility of equity has responded to new remedial demands in commercial and intellectual property cases through the invention of "Mareva" injunctions[227] and "Anton Piller" orders.[228] But there is, to date, little evidence of similar creativity in *Charter* cases.

The language of "appropriate and just" seems to exhort a court which finds a *Charter* violation to "fashion" a commensurate remedy. While the Supreme Court has yet to deal specifically with the question of remedial scope, some judges have commented in encouraging terms on the need for flexibility and responses that correspond to modern demands and constitutional dimensions. Accepting that "the *Charter* was not enacted in a vacuum", Lamer J. in *Mills* recognized the "unique character of a constitutional remedy" and emphasized the importance of ensuring that the enforcement of constitutional rights not be stultified by procedural difficulties.[229] In *Gamble*, Wilson J. reiterated the view that *Charter* remedies be flexible, functional and purposive.[230] She concluded that the scope of the traditional remedy of *habeas corpus*, when invoked pursuant to section 24(1) of the *Charter*, should be adopted "flexibly and generously" in order to protect commensurately the liberty interest of the appellant.[231] McLachlin J., speaking in an extra-judicial capacity, has also commented on the need to fashion new remedies to ensure that individuals are not denied their constitutional rights.[232]

An examination of most section 24(1) cases, however, reveals a residue of judicial reluctance to intervene in a way that appears to step on legislative toes. In *Badger v. Attorney General of Manitoba*, the

---

227 The remedy is named for the case of *Mareva Compania Naviera S.A. v. International Bulkcarriers S.A.*, [1980] 1 All E.R. 213 (C.A.), although it first appeared in *Nippon Yusen Kaisha v. Karageoris*, [1975] 1 W.L.R. 1093 (C.A.). For its application in Canada see *Aetna Financial Services Ltd. v. Feigelman*, [1985] 1 S.C.R. 2. The remedy permits a party in a civil case to freeze assets when there is a genuine risk that they will be surreptitiously removed from the jurisdiction, leaving a judgment unenforceable.

228 The remedy is named for the case of *Anton Piller K.G. v. Manufacturing Processes Ltd.*, [1976] Ch. 55 (C.A.). Ormerod L.J. (at 61) described the order, which empowers a party in a civil case to search for, and seize, evidence as being "at the extremity of the courts' powers." For Canadian applications, see J. Berryman, "Anton Piller Orders: A Canadian Common Law Approach" (1984) 34 U.T.L.J. 1; J. Berryman, "Anton Piller Injunctions: An Update" (1986), 2 I.P.J. 49. Also see *Bardeau v. Crown Food Service Equipment Ltd.* (1982), 36 O.R. (2d) 355 (H.C.); *Culinar Foods Ltd. v. Mario's Food Products Ltée*, [1987] 2 F.C. 53; *Titan Sports Inc. v. Mansion House (Toronto) Ltd.* (1989), 28 C.P.R. (3d) 199 (Fed. T.D.).

229 *R. v. Mills, supra*, note 217, at 882 and 893.

230 *R. v. Gamble*, [1988] 2 S.C.R. 595, at 640-641.

231 *Ibid.*, at 642-646.

232 Honourable Madame Justice McLachlin, "The Charter of Rights and Freedoms: A Judicial Perspective" (1989) 23 N.B.C.L. Rev. 579, at 585.

Manitoba voting rights case, Scollin J. found that the disqualification in respect of prisoners contravened section 3 of the *Charter*.[233] However, he refused to order the applicants be added to the voting list on the ground that it would not be appropriate and just "that the votes of the qualified and registered electors should now be diluted" in the absence of a legislated effort to craft a limited disqualification that might pass constitutional muster.[234] Restricting relief to a simple declaration of invalidity was upheld on appeal[235] although O'Sullivan J.A. added:

> In a proper case it might be possible for the court under s. 24 of the Canadian Charter of Rights and Freedoms to establish voting machinery if a legislature were to show itself contumacious in denying rights . . . .[236]

By relying on *Hunter*, Scollin J. surely misconceived the caveat about the judiciary entering the legislative sphere, by failing to appreciate the difference between judicial intervention which authorizes state intrusion and a remedy which vindicates rights.

Particularly within the context of constitutional challenges to public institutions, the proper role of the judiciary has been the subject of much debate in the United States[237] since *Brown v. Board of Education*.[238] Although the United States Supreme Court proceeded with some degree of diffidence in *Brown*, the remedial assertiveness which the court ultimately applied to the issue of school desegregation spawned a new era of institutional litigation.

A number of American federal courts have entertained claims that an institution, usually a state prison[239] or place for the confinement of the mentally ill,[240] failed to meet constitutional standards. These cases are premised commonly on the guarantee against cruel and unusual punishment and the courts have adopted a "totality of conditions"

---

[233] (1986), 51 C.R. (3d) 163 (Man. Q.B.).

[234] *Ibid.*, at 173.

[235] (1986), 55 C.R. (3d) 364 (Man. C.A.).

[236] *Ibid.*, at 368.

[237] For insightful discussions, see A. Chayes, "The Role of the Judge in Public Law Litigation" (1976) 89 Harv. L.R. 1281; J.H. Ely, *Democracy and Distrust: A Theory of Judicial Review* (Boston: Harvard University Press, 1980). O. Fiss, "Forward: The Forms of Justice" (1979) 93 Harv. L.R. 1; O. Fiss, *The Civil Rights Injunction* (Bloomington: Indiana University Press, 1978); M. Perry, *The Constitution, The Courts and Human Rights* (New Haven: Yale University Press, 1982).

[238] (1954), 347 U.S. 483.

[239] See, for example, *Newman v. Alabama* (1979), 466 F. Supp. 628; *Pugh v. Locke* (1976), 406 F. Supp. 318; *Ruiz v. Estelle* (1980), 503 F. Supp. 1265. Affirmed (1982), 679 F. 2d 1115 (5th Circ.).

[240] *Wyott v. Stickney* (1972), 344 F. Supp. 373.

analysis.[241] Unlike the one line declaration of the Canadian Federal Court in *McCann*,[242] U.S. judges have issued complex declarations amounting to blueprints for long-term and system-wide reformation.[243] In response to the problems of implementation and the need for ongoing supervision, masters have been appointed to monitor the progress of reform.[244] Regrettably, this has not precluded renewed litigation and some cases have remained the subjects of ongoing judicial intervention for over a decade.[245]

Before considering this approach to institutional litigation, it should be noted that much of the protracted litigation in the United States over the implementation of court orders has arisen in contexts where plaintiffs have sought the intervention of the federal judiciary in response to intransigence, neglect and disinterest by state officials. Perhaps, in these circumstances, less than complete co-operation should be expected. Still, there are important questions about this expansion of remedial scope aside from its impact on judicial resources at the supervisory stage. It is legitimate to ask whether courts have the expertise to restructure an institution, even with the assistance of partisan submissions. Moreover, given the large expense of public funds, there is a political question about the legitimacy of judicial decisions controlling the process, priorities and extent of reform. Yet, to respond to institutional or systemic deficiencies with only a declaration of unconstitutionality, leaving the problem of meeting constitutional standards in the hands of those who have deliberately denied them, seems to break faith with the judiciary's basic mandate.

It is interesting to note the U.S. Supreme Court's response to the remedial problem in *Brown v. Board of Education*.[246] Recognizing the complexity of effecting desegregation in the states which had employed the "separate but equal" myth to prevent blacks from white public schools, the court adjourned to hear further argument on the appropriate form of relief. Upon resuming, the court learned of the progress of some states and diffidence of others.[247] It concluded that the issue of implementation should be remanded back to the courts of first instance

---

[241] See *Holt v. Sarver* (1970), 309 F. Supp. 362. Affirmed (1971), 442 F. 2d 304 (8th Circ.), which marked the beginning of this mode of analysis.

[242] *Supra*, note 225.

[243] See, for example, *Pugh v. Locke, supra*, note 239.

[244] See S. Brakel, "Mastering the Legal Access Rights of Prison Inmates" (1986) 12 New Eng. J. of Crim. & Civ. Confinement 1.

[245] See *Ruiz v. Estelle, supra*, note 239 discussed in F. Cohen, "The Texas Prison Conditions Case: *Ruiz v. Estelle*" (1981) 17 Crim. L.B. 252.

[246] *Supra*, note 238.

[247] *Supra*, note 238, at 495-496.

who would retain jurisdiction over implementation during the ensuing transitional period before achieving non-discriminatory school systems.[248] Chief Justice Warren wrote:

> In fashioning and effectuating the decrees the courts will be guided by equitable principles. Traditionally, equity has been characterized by a practical flexibility in shaping its remedies and by a facility for adjusting and reconciling public and private needs . . . . Courts of equity may properly take into account the public interest in the elimination of such obstacles in a systematic and effective manner. But it should go without saying that the vitality of these constitutional principles cannot be allowed to yield simply because of disagreement with them.[249]

Even though subsequent remedial developments have seen some courts become the architects of institutional reform, there is merit in the *Brown* approach whereby the court maintains control over the process of change rather than its substance. In Canada, precedents lie in recent language cases where jurisdiction was maintained over the issue, in conjunction with remedies like declaratory and injunctive relief to ensure enforcement and compliance.[250] In *Reference Re Manitoba Language Rights* the Supreme Court declared all acts of the Manitoba legislature invalid because they were not enacted, printed and published in both official languages.[251] Because of the obvious concern over creating a legislative void, the court allowed the enactments to remain valid for a period of time during which Manitoba could comply with its constitutional duty. Not being able at the time of judgment to determine an appropriate period, the court adjourned and, after further argument from the parties, subsequently issued a detailed order providing a schedule for translation and the opportunity to reapply for further orders or time to ensure that the ultimate objective of constitutionality was achieved.[252]

In *Lavoie v. Attorney General of Nova Scotia*,[253] recognizing the complexity of the problem of minority language education, the court, in the course of ordering that a reasonably accessible program be designed, directed that the parties could report back.[254] Given the nature of the

---

[248] *Ibid.*

[249] (1954), 349 U.S. 294 (commonly known as *Brown II*), at 300.

[250] See the excellent discussion of these cases in N. Gillespie, "Charter Remedies: The Structural Injunction" (1989) 11 Adv. Q. 190, at 201-211. Also see *La Société des Acadiens du Nouveau Brunswick Inc. v. Minority Language School Bd. No. 50* (1983), 48 N.B.R. (2d) 361 (Q.B.), which illustrates the relation between the judicial role and the defendant's willingness or unwillingness to cooperate.

[251] [1985] 1 S.C.R. 721.

[252] *Ref. Re Manitoba Language Rights (Order)*, [1985] 2 S.C.R. 347.

[253] (1988), 47 D.L.R. (4th) 586 (N.S.T.D.).

[254] *Ibid.*, at 594-595.

issue, it was inevitable that subsequent applications would be necessary.[255] Ultimately, the Court of Appeal backed away from an interventionist role by demurring that it "is not the role of the court to specify in exact detail how and where the instruction will be provided."[256] In contrast, two Ontario cases exemplify a more active and constructive judicial role,[257] while at the same time illustrating the demands on judicial creativity and resources.[258]

In the United States there has been considerable academic criticism of the constitutional propriety of a reformative interventionist judicial role. Certainly, there are real questions of legitimacy, expertise and scarce judicial resources which are equally appropriate in the Canadian context.[259] However, to dismiss a reformative role entirely is to relegate public institutions to their pre-*Charter* status when courts would observe and comment on illegalities, leaving their rectification in the hands of the authorities who created them.[260] Of course, the primary function of courts in respect of public institutions is supervisory, but passive declarations are inadequate in the face of ongoing, long-standing constitutional violations. At a baseball game, an umpire who finds that all available bats are illegal can feel confident that declaring their illegality is a sufficient response: the game ends; the players and spectators go home. Within public institutions, however, confinement and the denial of rights continues. Simple declarations without some mechan-

---

[255] See (1988), 50 D.L.R. (4th) 405 (N.S.T.D.); (1988), 90 N.S.R. (2d) 16 (N.S.T.D.), at 308.

[256] (1989), 58 D.L.R. (4th) 293 (N.S.C.A.).

[257] *Association Française des Conseils Scolaires de l'Ontario v. Ontario* (1988), 66 O.R. (2d) 599 (C.A.).

[258] *Marchand v. Simcoe County Bd. of Education* (1986), 55 O.R. (2d) 638 (H.C.) and the subsequent application for an implementation order (1987), 61 O.R. (2d) 651 (H.C.). See the discussion in N. Gillespie, "Charter Remedies", *supra*, note 250, at 204-207.

[259] There are clear differences in constitutional structure between Canada and the United States. The important question relates to judicial role. While the constitutional entrenchment of the *Charter* has expanded the judicial mandate, its governmental position relative to legislatures and the executive branches has not fundamentally changed, particularly with the inclusion of the section 33 override provision: see M. Mandel, *The Charter of Rights and the Legalization of Politics in Canada* (Toronto: Wall & Thompson, 1989) p. 75.

[260] See, for example, the result of *McCann v. R.* (1976), 29 C.C.C. (2d) 337 (Fed. T.D.), which Michael Jackson describes with disappointment in *Prisoners of Isolation*:

> A year after Mr. Justice Heald's decision, it was clear that the judgment . . . had not changed anything of substance. Behind the thin veneer of physical changes, solitary confinement in maximum security was still characterized by virtually the same inhumanity and gratuitous cruelty that had existed before the trial.

See M. Jackson, *Prisoners of Isolation* (Toronto: University of Toronto Press, 1983), p. 144.

ism for change are futile. They represent an abdication of the judicial mandate to enforce the "supreme law of Canada". The idea of maintaining jurisdiction during a period of rectification is the only response which preserves the integrity of the court's function without transforming its role into an executive one. Parties can be required to bring forward proposals and progress reports. Just like other issues for adjudication, these can be the subject of mediation, argument, or even commentary by expert witnesses. The ultimate judicial sanction lies in the power to close an institution in the face of persistent intransigence.

5

Canadian Parole Legislation and Practice: 1800-1977

A Penitentiary, as its name imports, should be a place to lead a man to repent his sins and amend his life . . . but it is quite enough for the purposes of the public if the punishment is so terrible that the dread of repetition of it deter him from crime, or his description of it, others. It should therefore be a place which by every means not cruel and not affecting the health of the offender shall be rendered so irksome and so terrible that during his after life he may dread nothing so much as a repetition of the punishment, and, if possible that he should prefer death to such a contingency.[1]

1. THE ORIGINS OF PAROLE IN CANADA

The power "to dispense with or modify punishments which the criminal or penal law require to be inflicted" would appear in Canadian legal history to stem from two sources.[2] First, in English law the Sovereign has long retained, through the exercise of the Royal Prerogative of Mercy, the power to pardon convicted persons either absolutely or upon satisfaction of certain conditions. From Elizabethan times, conditional pardons were granted upon the prisoner agreeing to be transported to British colonies.[3] The modern equivalent of this power has been retained in Canadian law under sections 749(1) and 751 of the *Criminal Code*.[4]

The second source arises from a 1597 English statute[5] which authorized the banishment of "rogues that be dangerous, or will not be reformed." Transportation of offenders began in 1607 when convicted

[1] Report of a Select Committee on the Expediency of Erecting a Penitentiary, Journal of the House of Assembly of Upper Canada, 1831, reproduced in J.M. Beattie, *Attitudes Towards Crime and Punishment in Upper Canada, 1830-1850: A Documentary Study* (Toronto: Centre of Criminology, 1977), p. 82.
[2] *Ex parte Armitage* (1902), 5 C.C.C. 345 (Que K.B.), at 350, per Wurtele J. A brief but thorough discussion of these issues may be found in *Tremeear's Annotated Criminal Code*, 6th ed. (Toronto: Carswell, 1964), pp. 1219-1221.
[3] A comprehensive history of transportation may be found in R. Hughes, *The Fatal Shore* (New York: Alfred A. Knopf, 1987).
[4] R.S.C. 1985, c. C-46.
[5] *An Act for Punishment of Rogues, Vagabonds and sturdy Beggars*, 1597 (39 Eliz. 1), c. 4.

persons considered fit for slave labour were shipped to Virginia. In cases where death sentences had been imposed, pardons were occasionally granted conditionally upon the prisoner being banished.[6] This system expanded dramatically such that by 1776 approximately one thousand criminals a year were being transported to various British colonies in America.

"Banishment" was originally used to differentiate between political offenders and common criminals who were subject to "transportation."[7] However, by the time of George III the legislative language used in the various statutes restricted banishment to a form of punishment forbidding a convicted person to return to a specified place for the period of sentence. Transportation, on the other hand, involved a continuing deprivation of liberty following arrival in the colonies. Thus, a prisoner who was transported was "transferred to the use of persons . . . [who] . . . shall have a property in the service of such offender for . . . [the] . . . term of years for which any such offender shall have been ordered to be transported."[8] In practice, upon arrival of the pardoned offender in the colonies, his services were auctioned off, the new master receiving from the shipmaster a "property-in-service" agreement upon payment of a negotiated fee. The legal status of the offender became that of an indentured servant rather than that of a criminal. However, if the offender evaded transportation or returned to England prior to the expiry of the term of years for which he had been ordered transported or banished, additional jail terms or a death sentence could be imposed.

Following the American revolutionary war, settlement of convicts began in Australia. However, rather than vesting "title" to transported prisoners in the captains of ships used for transportation, governors of penal colonies were given delegated authority to sell or assign "property-in-service" agreements to free settlers. As there was little demand for such services, governors of penal colonies requested further authority to grant pardons. In 1790, enabling legislation[9] was passed by the English Parliament empowering governors to remit sentences of transported prisoners. Initially such pardons were absolute; soon a new type of conditional pardon, the "ticket of leave", was instituted. This form of

---

6   *An Act for the effectual Transportation of Felons and other Offenders*, 1917 (4 Geo. 1), c. 11, s. 1 provided that minor offenders could be transported for 7 years instead of being flogged and branded, while prisoners serving capital commuted sentences might be sent for 14 years. See Hughes, *ibid.*, pp. 40-41.

7   *Blacks Law Dictionary*, Rev. 4th ed. (St. Paul, Minn.: West Publishing Co., 1968.)

8   *An Act for enabling His Majesty to authorize His Governor or Lieutenant Governor of such Places beyond the Seas, to which Felons or other Offenders may be transported, to remit the sentences of such Offenders* (24 Geo. 3 Sess. 2), c. 56, s. 1.

9   *Transportation Act*, 1790 (30 Geo. 3), c. 47, s. 1.

conditional release consisted of a declaration by penal officials that the prisoner, on condition that he support himself, was authorized to be at liberty to seek employment in a particular area. In 1815, this policy was further amended to require that transported prisoners serve specified periods of time prior to eligibility to receive tickets of leave.[10] By 1821, rules were enacted so that convicts sentenced to 7 years could be freed after 4 years; those sentenced to 14 years could be granted tickets of leave after 6 years; and those sentenced to life imprisonment could be released after serving 8 years at hard labour. As summarized by Richard Hughes:

> There were only three ways in which the law might release a man from bondage. The first, though the rarest, was an absolute pardon from the governor, which restored him to all rights including that of returning to England. The second was a conditional pardon, which gave the transported person citizenship within the colony but no right of return to England. The third was the ticket-of-leave. The convict who had been given a ticket-of-leave no longer had to work as an assigned man for a master. He was also free from the claims of forced government labor. He could spend the rest of his sentence working for himself, wherever he pleased, as long as he stayed within the colony.[11]

Captain Alexander Maconachie, the governor of the penal colony located on Norfolk Island during the 1830's, was influenced by the views of such prison reformers as John Howard and Elizabeth Fry.[12] Recognizing the possibility of using conditional release as an integral step in the rehabilitation of offenders, he developed the "mark" system, under which a prisoner could earn grades for good conduct and industrious labour. The object of this system was "to place each convict's fate and future in his own hands." Contingent upon good behaviour, the prisoner could expect to pass through several stages, commencing with solitary confinement, proceeding through work on government chain gangs, partial freedom on a farm or in a manufacturing setting, and finally to a ticket of leave. A similar system was instituted in Ireland in 1863 by Sir Walter Crofton, who "introduced a style of prison management consisting of four stages designed to induce 'moral reformation' in the prisoner. Hard labour and religious instruction were combined with a graduated

---

10   *Transportation Act*, 1815 (55 Geo. 3), c. 156; *Transportation Act*, 1824 (5 Geo. 4), c. 84, s. 26. Whether or not this system amounted to a form of slavery is discussed in Hughes, *supra*, note 3, pp. 283-287.

11   Hughes, *supra*, note 3, p. 307.

12   Much of the discussion which follows borrows heavily from the work of Sheila Lloyd, to whom the writers acknowledge their gratitude. See S. Lloyd, *The Federal System of Conditional Release in Canada: Past and Present* (unpublished, November 1982). See also K. Jobson and G. Ferguson, "Towards a Revised Sentencing Structure for Canada," (1987), 66 Can. Bar Rev. 1, at 8-9.

system in which supervision of the prisoner was gradually reduced. The fourth stage—ticket of leave—served as the final transition phase to normal life."[13]

The English *Penal Servitude Act* of 1853, enacted largely in response to growing English and Australian opposition to the practice of transportation, substituted imprisonment for transportation in all cases of persons serving sentences of less than 14 years. In cases involving longer sentences, judges were given discretion to decide whether or not to impose transportation as an alternative to incarceration. The Act authorized penal administrators to grant "licences" to be at liberty during the pendency of sentence "upon such conditions in all respects as to Her Majesty shall seem fit." A licence could be revoked, in which case the prisoner was returned to custody to be "remitted to his or her original sentence, and shall undergo the residue thereof as if no such licence had been granted."[14] Later legislation specified the periods of time which had to be served prior to eligibility for a "licence."[15] The Irish and English systems in turn influenced the American penal infrastructure. Michel Foucault offers the example of well-developed conditional release programs used at the Elmira Reformatory in New York State by 1876.[16] Before a prisoner could be considered for parole, he was required to demonstrate continued good behaviour while incarcerated for 12 months and to present reasonable release plans regarding residence and employment. While on parole, the parolee was required to report to a "guardian" who forwarded progress summaries to the prison superintendent.

Banishment was used as a form of punishment in Canada until 1902.[17] This power was conferred in a statute passed in 1800; it authorized banishment as an alternative to transportation, since the latter form

---

13 Lloyd, *ibid.*, p. 1; Hughes, *supra*, note 3, pp. 489-522. It is interesting that Maconachie proposed that sentences should be indefinite and that the number of "marks" which the prisoner would have to earn befor release would be equivalent to a fixed number of years (Hughes, pp. 499-500).

14 *Penal Servitude Act*, 1853 (16 & 17 Vict.), c. 99, ss. 9-11.

15 *Penal Servitude Act*, 1857 (20 & 21 Vict.), c. 3; *Penal Servitude Act*, 1864 (27 & 28 Vict.), c. 47.

16 See M. Foucault, *Discipline and Punish: The Birth of the Prison* (New York: Pantheon Books, 1977). The word parole appears to derive from the phrase "parole d'honneur", which, in the military context, was an undertaking given by a captured prisoner, if liberated, to return to custody under stated conditions. The first use of this term in American law appears to have been a Massachusetts statute of 1837. By 1880, three states had enacted parole legislation. This grew to twelve by 1889. By 1944, all states had established a parole system.

17 *Report of the Sub-Committee on the Penitentiary System in Canada*, (Standing Committee on Justice and Legal Affairs, 1977), paras. 44-46.

of punishment could not "be carried into execution without great and manifest inconvenience."[18] The banished person was required to depart within 8 days of the imposition of sentence. Returning "without some lawful cause" was considered an offence punishable by death. This was modified in 1841 to provide for a penalty of 4 years' imprisonment followed by transportation. A pardon could be granted to allow a return to Upper Canada prior to the expiry of the period of banishment.[19]

Alex Edmison[20] has noted that transportation was frequently used as early as 1826 as an alternative in capital cases and for deserters from British garrisons in Canada. Following the uprisings of 1837 and 1838, some 150 rebels "whose guilt and whose dangerous characters render it indispensable that they should be removed," were transported to New South Wales and Tasmania and were not pardoned until 1844.[21] The practice of transportation from Canada apparently ended in 1853. Transportation from England finally ended in 1868.

Apart from banishment and transportation, pre-Confederation penal statutes contained no reference to any power to suspend or modify the operation of the sentencing process. Similarly, while the *Constitution Act, 1867*[22] authorized Parliament to create offences and to establish courts to adjudge and sentence offenders, it was not until the *Penitentiary Act* of 1868[23] that the concept of remission was formally introduced into Canadian law. "In order to encourage convicts to good behaviour, diligence and industry" penitentiary directors were authorized to establish rules permitting prisoners to earn up to 5 days' remission (reduction of sentence) for each month served. With the exception of changes in nomenclature and the rates of remission which could be earned,[24] no

---

[18] *An Act to amend the Laws relative to the Transportation of Offenders* (39 & 40 Geo. 3), c. 1.

[19] R. Splane, *Social Welfare in Ontario 1791-1893: A Study of Public Welfare Administration* (Toronto: University of Toronto Press, 1965).

[20] J.A. Edmison, "Some Aspects of Nineteenth Century Prisons" in W.T. McGrath, ed., *Crime and Its Treatment in Canada*, 2d ed. (Toronto: MacMillan, 1976), pp. 347-369.

[21] Letter of Governor Colborne to Lord Glenely, 5 May 1839, Q. Series, Vol. 275, p. 29, Public Archives of Canada, quoted in F.M. Greenwood, ed., *Land of a Thousand Sorrows: The Australian Prison Journal, 1840-42 of the Exiled Canadian Patriot Francois-Maurice Lepailleur* (Vancouver: University of British Columbia Press, 1980); J. Monet, *The Last Cannon Shot: A Study of French-Canadian Nationalism 1837-50* (Toronto: University of Toronto Press, 1969). See also the case of *Leonard Watson*, 112 E.R. 1389.

[22] (30 & 31 Vict.), c. 3.

[23] (31 Vict.), c. 75.

[24] *Penitentiary Act*, 1883 (46 & 47 Vict.), c. 37; R.S.C. 1886, c. 12, s. 55(1); 1906 (6 Edw. 7), c. 38; R.S.C. 1906, c. 147, s. 64; R.S.C. 1927, c. 154, s. 64; S.C. 1939, c. 6, s. 69; R.S.C. 1952, c. 206, s. 69.

substantial changes in the concept of remission were enacted until the advent of the 1961 *Penitentiary Act*.[25] Prior to the enactment of mandatory supervision legislation in 1969,[26] release as a result of accumulated remission amounted to an absolute reduction of sentence.

2. THE TICKET OF LEAVE ACT 1899-1959

Prior to 1899, apart from release as a result of accumulated remission, discharge from close custody at an earlier stage in a sentence could only be effected by Order of the Governor General through the exercise of the Royal Prerogative of Mercy. Several writers[27] have noted that such releases were most frequently approved on the basis of humanitarian considerations.[28] By the late 19th Century, it was realized that a more structured system was required to assist prisoners to bridge the gap between confinement and release. Officials of the federal Ministry of Justice studied the English, Irish and American systems, following which the *Ticket of Leave Act* was presented to the House of Commons in 1899.[29] Several principles which continue to affect the contemporary philosophy of parole in Canada emerged from this first legislation.

First, the *Ticket of Leave Act*, like the English *Penal Servitude Act* contained no reference to the purpose of release on ticket of leave. According to Sheila Lloyd[30] various views were expressed during the parliamentary debate over the Bill, some members viewing conditional release as a pragmatic solution to the problem of penal overcrowding, some consider it as an extension of clemency to deserving offenders (particularly first offenders). The Minister of Justice was among those

---

[25] S.C. 1960-61, c. 53, ss. 22-25.
[26] S.C. 1968-69, c. 38, ss. 101, 108 [proclaimed in force August 1, 1970]. This topic is discussed in more detail in Chapter 7.
[27] F.P. Miller, "Parole" in *Crime and Its Treatment in Canada, supra*, note 20; R.M. Zubrycki, *The Establishment of Canada's Penitentiary System: Federal Correctional Policy 1867-1900* (Toronto: University of Toronto, Faculty of Social Work, 1980); M.K. Evans, *The Prerogative of Pardon in Canada: Its Development 1864-1894* (unpublished M.A. Thesis, Ottawa: Carleton University, 1971).
[28] In *Canada (A.G.) v. Ontario (A.G.)*, [1890] O.R. 222, 19 Ont. App. R. 31, the Ontario Courts of Chancery and Appeal held that provincial legislation conferring upon the Lieutenant Governor the power to pardon offenders for breaches of provincial legislation was *intra vires* the Province. This decision was upheld on appeal to the Supreme Court of Canada, [1894] 23 S.C.R. 458.
[29] *An Act to Provide for the Conditional Liberation of Convicts*, S.C. 1899, c. 49; R.S.C. 1906, c. 150; R.S.C. 1927, c. 197; R.S.C. 1952, c. 264.
[30] Lloyd, *supra*, note 12, p. 2.

who spoke of conditional release as an integral part of the rehabilitative process.[31]

The *Ticket of Leave Act* represented the first attempt to establish responsibility for release decision-making. Lloyd has noted that, although the original draft of the Bill authorized the Governor General to grant tickets of leave on the advice of the Cabinet as a whole, several parliamentarians objected to this on the grounds that political influence might all too easily affect the administration of conditional liberation. As an alternative, they proposed that the Minister of Justice alone advise the Governor General since "love of reputation and the high tradition of the Justice Department . . . would make it a safer medium for the issue of ticket of leave."[32] This was the first in a series of measures implemented over the years to guard against direct political interference in the granting of parole. By 1913, a specialized "Remission Service" was developed within the federal Ministry of Justice. The vast majority of the work of "Remissions Officers" was devoted to granting, arranging supervision for and revoking tickets of leave. The Remission Service also dealt with clemency matters, such as gathering material for the appropriate Minister in applications for the commutation of death sentences, relief from the penalty of corporal punishment or forfeitures of property, pardons, and suspension of orders prohibiting driving.

The third aspect of the *Ticket of Leave Act* relevant to contemporary parole legislation was the concept of supervision during conditional release and penalties for actual or perceived breaches of that release. Upon being granted a ticket of leave, the prisoner was released on conditions for the duration of the unexpired balance of the sentence. Typical conditions included monthly reporting to the local police, abstaining from violations of the law, prohibitions on association with "notoriously bad characters, such as reputed thieves and prostitutes," and "not lead[ing] an idle and dissolute life."[33]

---

[31] Despite occasional amendments over the next 60 years, it was not until enactment of the 1958 *Parole Act* (S.C. 1958, c. 38) that statutory criteria were enunciated to guide decision-makers as to the appropriate factors to be considered in deciding whether or not to grant parole.

[32] Lloyd, *supra*, note 12, p. 2.

[33] See "Conditions of Licence", *Ticket of Leave Act*, Schedule A, reproduced in *Ouimet Report, infra*, note 55, p. 367. A breach of condition of a licence was in itself an offence punishable upon summary conviction for up to 3 months in jail. Conviction for an indictable offence while at liberty under licence resulted in automatic "forfeiture" of the licence and a return to custody to serve all of the "remanet" which remained unexpired at the time the licence was granted, with no credit for time successfully served while at liberty. Conviction for a summary offence did not result in automatic forfeiture; however, the sentencing judge was required to forward a record of the

During the period from 1899 to 1929, release under the *Ticket of Leave Act* was administered by the Salvation Army, local police forces and the R.C.M.P. In the years immediately following the end of World War I both the prison population and the use of tickets of leave increased. However, according to Lloyd:

> The sudden increase in crime rates after World War I heightened the atmosphere of unrest and precipitated demands for greater severity in the criminal justice system. For the first time, the liberal use of parole came under attack. The main argument put forward was not that parolees were directly contributing to the crime wave but that the liberal use of the parole system may have robbed punitive law of its terrors for evil doers. The record of the Remission Service demonstrated that only 2.2 percent of prisoners granted ticket of leave between 1899 and 1922 had committed a subsequent offence while on parole but such figures did nothing to allay criticism of the parole system. By 1924, the Justice Department could no longer resist the pressure for tightening up of conditional release.[34]

Restrictive eligibility criteria were developed which significantly reduced the number of prisoners eligible for consideration for tickets of leave. Further, the object of conditional release shifted from rehabilitation to clemency. Such factors as health, impaired mentality, youth or great age, assistance given to the Crown, improbability of guilt, lack of criminal intent and extraordinary provocation were now considered the principle bases on which conditional release on ticket of leave could be granted.

Following a series of riots at Kingston Penitentiary during the early 1930's, demand grew for a full investigation into the penitentiary system. Spurred by the activism of Agnes McPhail, M.P., the Archambault Commission was established in 1936 "to enquire into and report on all aspects of the penal system in Canada."[35] While most of the recommen-

---

proceedings to the Remission Service in Ottawa, which could recommend to the Governor General that the licence be revoked. It is interesting to note that because the policy of the Remission Service was not to disclose reasons for revoking a licence, courts were prepared to insist on a very high standard of procedural regularity; see *Re Munavish* (1951), 121 C.C.C. 229 (B.C. S.C.) and *Re Fischer and Manitoba Penitentiary (Warden)* (1961), 131 C.C.C. 101 (Man. Q.B.). For a discussion of the history and case law relating to the power of provincial Boards of Parole in Ontario (1916) and British Columbia (1948) to grant parole to prisoners serving indeterminate terms of imprisonment as authorized by the *Prisons and Reformatories Act* (R.S.C. 1906, c. 148), see C.F. Dombek and G.W. Tranmer "The Indeterminate Sentence Under the Prisons and Reformatories Act" (1977), 3 Queen's L.J. 3:332; *McKend v. R.* (1977), 35 C.C.C. (2d) 286 (Fed. T.D.).

[34] Lloyd, *supra*, note 12, p. 4.

[35] *Report of the Royal Commission to Investigate the Penal System of Canada (Archambault Report)* (Ottawa: King's Printer, 1938). For a fascinating "inside" view of the tensions within Kingston Penitentiary during the early 1930's, see the autobiography of Tim Buck, *Yours in the Struggle* (Toronto: N.C. Press Ltd., 1977).

dations of the *Archambault Report* dealt with penal conditions, the Commission severely criticized the functioning of the Remission Service. As noted by Lloyd:

> The Report expressed alarm and concern over ... [the new] ... eligibility rules on the grounds that they effectively made parole a clemency measure rather than a rehabilitative mechanism. The Report also noted that the assessment for eligibility amounted virtually to a judicial review which was not the role of the Remission Service. A second area of concern was the quality of information on which decisions were based. The Remission Service relied on information gathered from prison officials, the sentencing judge or magistrate and representations made on behalf of inmates by friends or relatives. In the assessment of the Commission, these sources were not satisfactorily impartial nor did they adequately reveal the prisoner's rehabilitative progress. The Report recommended that a parole officer be appointed in each province to receive and process applications, interview inmates and prepare case histories which would then be sent to the central parole authority."[36]

Legislative consideration of the Commission's recommendations on conditional release was deferred until the post-war period. During World War II, the Remission Service authorized the release of many prisoners to join the armed forces or to work in industry under "special war purposes" tickets of leave.

3. THE FAUTEUX REPORT OF 1956

In the post-war period, the development of more active after-care agencies (such as the John Howard and Elizabeth Fry Societies) and increased public acceptance of the value of a supervised period of readjustment in the community led to a recognition that existing release mechanisms were in need of examination and overhaul. At the urging of senior officers of the Remission Service, such as Frank Miller (later one of the first members of the National Parole Board) and A.J. MacLeod (later Commissioner of Penitentiaries), the Fauteux Committee[37] was appointed by the Minister of Justice to examine, *inter alia*, the principles upon which the Royal Prerogative of Mercy was exercised and tickets of leave granted. The *Fauteux Report* of 1956 formed the basis for the first *Parole Act*.

The *Report* addressed in detail the issue of remission. It recommended that, given the existence of appellate remedies, it would be

---

[36] Lloyd, *supra*, note 12, p. 5.
[37] *Report of a Committee Appointed to Inquire into the Principles and Procedures Followed in the Remission Service of the Department of Justice (Fauteux Report)* (Ottawa: Queen's Printer, 1956).

generally inappropriate for the releasing authority to substitute its judgment for the view of the court. Thus, remission of sentence by a parole agency should be limited to extreme cases, such as compassionate release to permit a prisoner near the end of a sentence to attend a family funeral, or as a reward for outstanding service within the institution.[38] This has since been recognized in legislation and practice. While the Parole Board is empowered to grant humanitarian relief from incarceration, either temporary (through escorted or unescorted temporary absence passes) or permanent release (through the use of parole by exception), the exercise of the Royal Prerogative of Mercy is reserved either to the Sovereign[39] or to the Governor in Council.[40]

As a result of the *Fauteux Report*, the 1961 revisions to the *Penitentiary Act* divided good conduct remission into two categories.[41] Statutory remission, amounting to a reduction of one-quarter of sentence, was automatically credited upon entry into a penal institution. This form of remission could only be lost upon conviction in internal disciplinary court for breaches of institutional discipline,[42] or upon conviction in a criminal court for escape-related offences.[43] Earned remission was granted at the rate of 3 days per month for each month actually served in custody during which the prisoner was considered by the penal authorities to have been of good behaviour. Once earned, this form of remission was not subject to divestiture. Added together, these two forms of remission provided a potential reduction of sentence of approximately one-third. It is also noteworthy that although the *Report* urged that consideration be "given to the implementation of a system whereby time earned by way of statutory remission would be a statutory parole period,"[44] this recommendation was not implemented until 1970. Neither the *Ticket of Leave Act*, nor the 1958 version of the *Parole Act*, affected release on remission. If the prisoner did not apply for, or was not granted parole, he was released as a free person when earned and statutory remission (added together) equalled the unexpired portion of the original sentence.[45]

---

38   *Fauteux Report, ibid.*, pp. 35-36.

39   *Criminal Code*, ss. 749(1), 751.

40   *Criminal Code*, ss. 749(2)-(4), 750. The origins and development of the Royal Prerogative of Mercy are discussed in Chapter 11.

41   S.C. 1960-61, c. 53, ss. 22-23. Equivalent provisions were enacted in the *Prisons and Reformatories Act* for prisoners in provincial institutions.

42   See *Marcotte v. Canada (Dep. A.G.)*, [1976] 1 S.C.R. 108.

43   This provision was repealed by S.C. 1976-77, c. 53, s. 40(2).

44   *Fauteux Report, supra*, note 37, p. 61.

45   If the prisoner was granted parole, the period of parole terminated at the stage when the remanet of the sentence was equal to the number of days credited through statutory and earned remission. After 1961, this was altered to provide that the period of parole

4. THE 1958 PAROLE ACT

(a) Parole Eligibility and Parole Granting

Based on the recommendations of the *Fauteux Report*, legislation proclaimed in force on February 15, 1959 abolished the *Ticket of Leave Act* and replaced it with the *Parole Act*.[46] At the organizational level, the authority to grant conditional release and to suspend and revoke such release was transferred to a Board whose members were to be appointed by the Governor in Council.[47] Provincial Boards of Parole in Ontario and British Columbia retained jurisdiction to grant and revoke paroles for persons incarcerated following convictions under Acts of these provincial legislatures and for persons serving indeterminate or indefinite terms of imprisonment in provincial institutions in addition to definite terms.[48]

---

would include the period of statutory remission accruing to the prisoner at the time of release on parole. For persons sentenced after August 1, 1970, the *Parole Act* and the *Penitentiary Act* were further amended to provide that the parole period would include earned remission through the introduction of the regime of mandatory supervision (S.C. 1968-69, c. 38, s. 108; see *Ex parte Beaucage* (1977), 31 C.C.C. (2d) 219 (Ont. C.A.); *Beaucage v. Canada (A.G.)*, [1977] 2 S.C.R. 293). Although the choice between parole and remission has now been removed from federal prisoners since the introduction of this regime, it should be noted that that choice still exists for a prisoner serving sentence in a provicial institution. A prisoner serving sentences of less than 2 years can decide to serve two-thirds of his sentence in a custodial setting or apply for parole, which, if granted, requires him to be subject to limitations on his freedom for the last two-thirds of a sentence. With the increased use of release to halfway houses on temporary absence for employment purposes all across the country, it is not surprising that many prisoners serving shorter sentences do not apply for parole. See also *Fauteux Report, supra*, note 37, p. 65.

[46] *Parole Act*, S.C. 1958, c. 38, ss. 24(1), 25. Section 24 established transitional provisions transferring the duty of supervision of persons previously released on tickets of leave to the National Parole Board.

[47] In addition, by section 18 of the Act the National Parole Board was empowered to assume certain clemency functions which had previously fallen under the aegis of the Remission Service. The most important of these were the power to revoke or suspend an order made under the *Criminal Code* prohibiting a person from operating a motor vehicle, and the conducting of investigations in connection with any request made to the Minister of Justice for the exercise of the Royal Prerogative of Mercy (see Chapter 11).

[48] The Ontario Board of Parole was initially established by an Order in Council dated November 24, 1910. In 1916, the Dominion Parliament amended the *Prisons and Reformatories Act* (S.C. 1916, c. 21) to formalize the Order in Council. Complementary legislation was passed in 1917 by the Ontario Legislature—*Ontario Parole Act, 1917* (S.O. 1917; 7 Geo. 7, c. 63). Although the *Fauteux Report* (*supra*, note 37, p. 50) had recommended that the federal government assume responsibility for all sentences of

Sections 5 and 8(*a*) of the 1958 Act specified certain factors to be considered by the Board in evaluating applications for parole. It could grant parole if in its "absolute discretion . . . the Board consider[ed] that the inmate ha[d] derived the maximum benefit from imprisonment and that the reform and rehabilitation of the inmate [would] be aided by the grant of parole". As compared with later versions of the legislation, it is noteworthy that the Board was not explicitly directed by statute to consider whether release on parole might "constitute an undue risk to society."[49]

Section 6 of the 1958 Act required the Board to "review" the case of every prisoner serving a sentence of 2 years or more[50] at times prescribed by the Regulations, regardless of whether the prisoner had or had not applied for parole. Where the sentence or sentences totalled less than 2 years, no review would be conducted unless an application for parole by, or on behalf of, the prisoner had been received. Except for cases involving life sentences or sentences of preventive detention, the Board was required to conduct its initial review within 6 months of the prisoner's admission to custody following sentencing or dismissal of appeal. Where the sentence was less than 2 years, the Board was required to complete its review within 4 months of receiving a parole application.

---

more than 6 months, and consequently for parole granting and supervision in such cases, the provincial governments varied in their response. See H.G. Needham, "Historical Perspectives on the Federal-Provincial Split in Jurisdiction in Corrections" (1980), 22 Can. J. Crim. 298, at 302.

[49] *Parole Act*, s. 8 [as amended by the *Criminal Law Amendment Act, 1968-69*, S.C. 1968-69, c. 38, s. 100]. While in practice the five original Board members did place considerable emphasis on the risk factor, it would seem that the limiting of the statutory criteria to rehabilitative factors was reflective of a reaction in correctional philosophy against extensive warehousing of prisoners. As noted by the Board:

> The rehabilitation policy placed more emphasis on the individual's motivation and less on the community. This era witnessed the growing concern with treatment and deviance was seen as characteristic of individuals. The change strategy became one of identification and people were thought to change through manipulations of intrapersonal and interpersonal relationships. The individual personality and social interaction were the important factors as the offender was recognized as a person who possessed specific traits that had to be modified through treatment so he would adjust more aptly to life in the free community.

National Parole Board: Policy and Procedures Manual (1988, unpublished), p. 7. See also *Archambault Report, supra*; note 35 *Fauteux Report, supra*, note 37.

[50] Despite the wording of section 731 of the *Code* it is not automatic that prisoners serving penitentiary-length sentences are, in fact, housed in penitentiaries. For example, by federal-provincial agreement some female prisoners serve penitentiary-length terms in the province in which they were convicted and sentenced. Conversely, procedures exist to transfer "provincial" prisoners to federal penitentiaries. See *Re Anaskan and R.* (1977), 34 C.C.C. (2d) 361 (Ont. C.A.).

Although the periods of time which prisoners are required to serve in custody before parole may be granted have been, and continue to be, altered from time to time, section 2 of the original Regulations[51] set the pattern for eligibility by specifying minimum periods. The general rule was that the prisoner had to serve "one third of the term of imprisonment, or four years, whichever is the lesser, but in the case of a sentence of imprisonment of two years or more to a federal penal institution, at least one year."[52] Where the sentence was less than 2 years, no minimum time was prescribed beyond the one-third limitation. Finally, the Board was empowered to consider a prisoner for parole by exception at any stage during the sentence.[53]

The rationale for this cumbersome legislative framework appears to have been derived from the view of the Fauteux Committee that

> [t]he Board should not be required to grant to inmates an opportunity for a personal interview with Board members. . . . [I]nterviews between Board members and inmates do not serve a sufficiently useful function . . . to justify the expenditure of time and money.[54]

Thus, since there was to be no opportunity for the decision-maker and the prisoner to meet to discuss parole plans, it was anticipated that heavy emphasis would be placed on "study and analysis of written material carefully collected from various sources."[55] Since considerable time and effort would be required to obtain, peruse and analyze such documentation, the early "review" dates arising well in advance of eligibility for release would act as a stimulus for the collecting of the necessary materials. According to the *Ouimet Report*, which examined, *inter alia*, the functioning of the parole system between 1958-69, such information typically included:

(a) The pre-sentence report which the trial judge or magistrate took into consideration before imposing sentence;

---

[51] *Parole Regulations*, SOR/60-216, s. 3.

[52] *Ibid.*, s. 2(1)(a). The 1-year requirement was lowered to 9 months by P.C. 1964-1827, s. 1. The 4-year maximum was raised to 7 years by P.C. 1973-1432, s. 1. This was, in turn, modified by the introduction of the concept of "violent conduct offenders" by- SOR/79-88, ss. 5 and 8, and through the expanded use of day parole and temporary absence by SOR/79-88, ss. 9 and 12. There were and are different rules for parole eligibility following escape, revocation or forfeiture. These formal and informal rules are described in the following chapters.

[53] *Parole Regulations*, s. 2(2).

[54] *Fauteux Report, supra*, note 37, p. 82. Section 9 of the 1958 *Parole Act* stated that the Board was "not required to grant a personal interview to the inmate or to any person on his behalf."

[55] Report of the Canadian Committee on Corrections, *Toward Unity: Criminal Justice and Corrections (Ouimet Report)* (Ottawa: Queen's Printer, 1969), p. 341.

(b) The report of the investigating police force concerning the circumstances that surrounded the commission of the offence;

(c) The previous criminal record of the inmate, if any;

(d) The information collected by prison authorities upon admission to the institution (better known as "the newcomer's sheet") as well as the initial report of the classification officer;

(e) Progress reports of the inmate's adjustment and progress in the institution and any special medical, psychological and psychiatric reports;

(f) The inmate's plans for the future;

(g) An investigation of home conditions and the possible reaction of the community to his release;

(h) Special reports from after-care agencies dealing both with the inmate in the institution and his family conditions in the community."[56]

The Fauteux Committee had proposed that the Board be composed of not more than five full-time members. This was reflected in the 1958 Act.[57] Unlike the current legislation, neither the Act nor subsequent Regulations specified the number of members required to vote on a particular case. The statute spoke throughout of decisions being taken by "the Board."[58]

(b) Parole Supervision, Revocation and Forfeiture

The *Fauteux Report* considered that the "day-to-day supervision of parolees should . . . be provided wherever possible by a voluntary after-care agency or a provincial probation service."[59] The Committee concluded that it would be an unnecessary expense for the federal government to become involved in the training and employment of parole officers. Hence, in deciding whether or not to attach to a grant of parole "any terms or conditions it considers desirable,"[60] the National Parole Board was expected to liaise closely with parole supervisors. In addition to standard conditions applying to all parolees[61] — reporting to a parole supervisor at regular intervals, complying with reasonable instructions

---

[56] *Ibid.*, p. 340.

[57] *Parole Act*, S.C. 1958, c. 38, s. 3(1) and (4). See also *Ouimet Report, ibid.*, p. 341.

[58] While "a member of the Board" could suspend a parole, "the Board" was required to "review the case" prior to cancellation of a suspension or revocation of parole. In practice, one member would review the file and circulate it with recommendations; only if concurrence was not reached would a meeting be held. Voting results were not required by any statute or regulation to be disclosed.

[59] *Report of a Committee Appointed to Inquire into the Principles and Procedures Followed in the Remission Service of the Department of Justice (Fauteux Report)* (Ottawa: Queen's Printer, 1956), p. 83.

[60] *Parole Act*, S.C. 1958, c. 38, s. 8(*b*).

[61] Section 10 of the Act required the Board to deliver a copy of a parole certificate containing the conditions of release to the parolee and the parole supervisor.

of the supervisor, obtaining permission before changing occupation, residence, marital status, travelling outside a set radius, or assuming substantial indebtedness—the Board was authorized to attach special conditions in individual cases and to amend parole conditions after release.

Once parole was granted, the parolee was deemed by section 11(1) of the Act to be serving sentence, which meant that the prisoner was allowed to remain at large unless and until parole was suspended, forfeited or revoked. The laying of an information alleging an offence committed while on parole did not automatically cause parole to be suspended and the prisoner returned to close custody. Suspension could only occur whenever a Board member or person designated by the Board[62] was "satisfied that the arrest of the inmate [was] necessary or desirable to prevent a breach of any term or condition of the parole."[63] Thus, although it was usual that parole would be suspended following the laying of a charge, the Board was given a discretion not to suspend in an appropriate case. For example, a parolee arrested for an offence allegedly committed prior to initial incarceration would not have breached a term or condition of parole. Similarly, a minor breach of parole conditions, such as being arrested for a liquor offence, might not trigger a suspension.

At the same time, section 12(1) of the *Parole Act* did not limit the authorities to suspending parole only in circumstances where a charge had been laid. The section was deliberately prospective, permitting suspension in order "to prevent a breach." Where the parolee had not been charged with an offence but his behaviour was perceived to be deteriorating, suspension of parole could occur.[64] The 1958 Act did not require that the person suspending a parole justify that decision to any other person or tribunal. Indeed, while the *Fauteux Report* considered that the Parole Board "should be a quasi-judicial body rather than . . . a Minister of the Crown acting in an exclusively administrative capacity," the Committee felt that "[t]he Board should not be required to make public, at any time, the reasons for any decision that it had made in a particular case."[65] Thus, section 9 of the 1958 Act attempted to insulate

---

62 In order to ensure that persons in authority are continually available to issue warrants, it was and continues to be necessary that persons other than Board members be authorized to suspend parole. Such designations are usually made by publishing the names or positions of the designated persons in Part I of the *Canada Gazette*.

63 *Parole Act*, S.C. 1958, c. 38, s. 12(1).

64 For discussion of this issue in another context, see the differing views of the appellate judges in *Oag v. R.* (1983), 33 C.R. (3d) 111 (Alta. C.A.).

65 *Fauteux Report, supra*, note 59, pp. 80, 82.

designated officials from judicial review by providing that "an order, warrant or decision made or issued under this Act is not subject to appeal or review to or by any court or other authority."

Once a suspension warrant was issued and the parolee apprehended,[66] the prisoner was taken "as soon as conveniently" possible before a magistrate who was required to remand the prisoner in custody. Since this procedure had existed under the *Ticket of Leave Act*, perhaps it was considered necessary to ensure that the prisoner was not incarcerated without appearing before a judicial officer.[67] After the appearance before the magistrate, the Board was required by section 12(4) to "forthwith review the case"[68] and decide to "either cancel the suspension or revoke the parole." After so doing, the Board was not required by statute to disclose reasons for revocation or cancellation.[69]

---

[66] In the event the prisoner was not apprehended after the issuance of the suspension warrant, sections 14-15 of the Act authorized the Board to move directly to revoke parole and to issue a warrant authorizing arrest upon revocation upon arrest.

[67] Following some litigation on the powers of the magistrate to investigate the circumstances behind the suspension, several courts ruled that the magistrate's only function was to sign the remand warrant. In *Re McKinnon and R.* (1976), 24 C.C.C. (2d) 536 (N.B. C.A.), it was held that the magistrate's act of remanding the prisoner in custody was an administrative act not reviewable by *certiorari*. See also *Ex parte Thompson* (1976), 25 C.C.C. (2d) 228 (N.S. S.C.) and *Ex parte Hanna* (1976), 27 C.C.C. (2d) 192 (Ont. C.A.).

[68] The issue of the term "forthwith" was not the subject of litigation until 1984. This seems surprising in that delays of several months were, and are not, uncommon. In *Mitchell v. R.* (1976), 24 C.C.C. (2d) 241 (S.C.C.) at 246, Laskin C.J.C. (dissenting) speculated *in obiter* that a court might not be able to "hold the Board to a reasonable period". See *Lennox v. National Parole Bd.* (1985), 43 C.R. (3d) 356 (Fed. T.D.), where Walsh J. held (at 358-359) that "undue delay . . . is contrary not only to the terms of the regulations but also to natural justice."

[69] As discussed in Chapter 3, this lack of procedural protection was examined in *Ex parte McCaud*, [1965] 1 C.C.C. 168, the first significant "prisoner's rights" case to come before the Supreme Court of Canada. The prisoner launched an application for *habeas corpus* on two grounds: that his parole had been revoked without any opportunity for a hearing at which he could be present, and that he was never informed of the reasons for the revocation. He argued that this contravened section 2(*e*) of the *Canadian Bill of Rights* (S.C. 1960, c. 44) which provides that:

[N]o law of Canada shall be construed or applied so as to . . . deprive a person of the right to a fair hearing in accordance with the principles of fundamental justice for the determination of his rights and obligations . . . .

Spence J., whose judgment was subsequently affirmed by a five-man bench, [1965] 1 C.C.C. 170n, held in a brief judgment that the *Canadian Bill of Rights* did not apply to parole revocation decisions. Since a parolee was deemed by section 11 of the Act to be serving the original sentence at liberty, a decision to return the parolee to close custody "is altogether a decision within the discretion of the Parole Board as an administrative matter and is not in any way a judicial determination" (at 169). Spence J. also

Upon revocation of parole, the prisoner was again taken before a magistrate who was required to direct that the prisoner be returned to "the place of confinement to which he was originally committed," or to an equivalent institution if the revocation occurred in a different territorial division.[70] Similar to the provisions of the original *Ticket of Leave Act*, the revoked parolee received no credit for time successfully spent at large prior to suspension, although the prisoner received credit for time spent in custody between suspension and revocation.[71] Upon revocation, the parolee was returned to close custody to "serve the portion of his original term of imprisonment that remained unexpired at the time his parole was granted" (s. 16(2)).

While revocation was a discretionary act on the part of the Board, the concept of forfeiture of conditional release was also retained from the *Ticket of Leave Act*. Regardless of whether or not a direct breach of condition was deemed by the Board to have occurred, parole was automatically forfeited if the parolee was convicted of an indictable offence punishable by imprisonment for 2 years or more. This applied even if a custodial sentence was not imposed.[72] Indeed, even if parole expired prior to the conviction for such indictable offences, section 17(3) of the Act deemed parole to have been forfeited upon the day the offence was committed, so long as the conviction was registered prior to the warrant expiry date. Upon forfeiture, the prisoner was required to "undergo a term of imprisonment equal to the portion of the term to which he was originally sentenced that remained unexpired at the time his parole was granted."[73] The prisoner thus received no credit for time spent at liberty on parole; however, statutory remission credits were not affected by forfeiture in this intial version of the Act.

(c) The Evolution of Board Policy

As discussed above, the *Fauteux Report* envisaged that the Board would base parole granting decisions on extensive written materials received from a variety of sources including sentencing judges, prison personnel and the prisoner. While section 9 of the 1958 Act did not

---

considered significant the fact that by section 9 of the Act Parliament had specifically exempted any requirement that in granting or revoking parole the Board be obligated to grant a personal interview to the inmate or to any person on his behalf."

[70] *Parole Act*, S.C. 1958, c. 38, ss. 14 and 16.
[71] *Ibid.*, s. 12(4).
[72] *Ibid.*, s. 13. If the offence charged was one on which the Crown could and did elect to proceed summarily, the parole authorities would not apply the forfeiture provisions.
[73] As might be imagined, these provisions gave arise to some extremely complex sentence calculation problems.

obligate the Board to "interview" a prisoner as part of the parole granting process, the Board generally considered it useful to have the prisoner interviewed during the early stages of a sentence by a representative of the Board (usually a parole officer from the National Parole Service), to discuss proposed release plans. Following the completion of this process, a community assessment was conducted to determine the attitude of family, employer and the local police to the proposed release.[74] A comprehensive summary of all material was forwarded to the Board, which could then decide whether to interview the prisoner.[75]

The Board developed a number of parole decision-making policies, some of which were designed to modify the strictures of the formal rules contained in the *Parole Regulations*.[76] For example, since a denial of parole meant that the Board was precluded by the Regulations from considering the prisoner again for 2 full years from the date of the original denial, the Board developed a practice, in appropriate cases, of "deferring" or "reserving" a decision. Thus, an immediate grant of parole was refused, but a further review was scheduled at a future date less than 2 years ahead.[77] Similarly, as the Act contained no provisions for release other than on full parole, various programs were developed to allow for carefully structured releases where immediate full release was considered by the Board to be inappropriate. "Temporary" parole was granted during the serving of sentence to permit a prisoner to attend

---

[74] Much of this description is taken from *Annual Reports of the National Parole Board* (unpublished), the testimony of the Chairman of the National Parole Board in *Proceedings of the Standing Senate Committee on Legal and Constitutional Affairs* (December 17, 1971); and P. Carriere and S. Silverstone, *The Parole Process: A Study of the National Parole Board* (Ottawa: Law Reform Commission of Canada, 1977).

[75] There appear to have been two reasons why in-person hearings were not held in all cases. First, travel time and the volume of cases made it extremely difficult for the five original Board members to see all applicants (see *Annual Report of the Department of the Solicitor-General*, 1971-72, pp. 64-65). Second, the Board continued to believe that since it was exercising an "administrative" rather than a "judicial" function, in-person "hearings" or "interviews" were not particularly important aspects of parole decision-making (see R.R. Price, "Bringing the Rule of Law to Corrections" (1974), 16 Can. J. Crim. & Corr. 209, at 215).

[76] With the exception of occasional adjustments in the Regulations, the legislative framework for parole was not altered between 1958 and 1969. *Annual Reports* forwarded to the Minister of Justice by the Chairman of the National Parole Board revealed no concern that the legislative framework in any way impeded parole officials from carrying out their mandate. The broad powers conferred by statute enabled the National Parole Board (and its provincial counterparts) to modify practices in order to encompass most factual situations and to institute procedures to reflect new policy directions.

[77] Strictly speaking this practice was probably illegal as a refusal to exercise a statutory obligation. See *Gregson v. National Parole Bd.* (1982), 1 C.C.C. (3d) 13 (Fed. T.D.).

school, to seek or accept short-term employment (such as working on a farm at harvest time) or for other rehabilitative purposes. "Parole with gradual" consisted of permission granted to leave the institution, with or without escort, for short periods prior to full parole release. It afforded an opportunity for parole personnel to monitor the prisoner's response to gradually increasing degrees of freedom.

The concept of "minimum parole" was initiated in 1964. This program, which was the harbinger of mandatory supervision, started from the assumption that "it would be desirable to have all persons coming out of prison under control for a certain length of time."[78] A prisoner who lost no statutory remission and earned all possible earned remission, but who either did not apply for, or was not granted parole, was required to be released as a free person upon completion of approximately two-thirds of sentence. At times the Board would offer a prisoner the opportunity of being released on parole earlier than his "remission release date" by 1 month for every year of the original sentence up to a total of 6 months. For example, a prisoner serving a sentence of 2 years, who would normally be released unconditionally after serving 16 months, could be released on this form of parole at 14 months, but would then be under supervision for the remainder of the original term. Since the National Parole Service and voluntary agencies were too understaffed to offer full parole supervision, parole conditions under this form of release were designed as a "minimum"—the parolee would have to report to the police and be subject to forfeiture and revocation during the parole period.[79]

Once parole was granted and the prisoner released, the Board was empowered to modify the terms and conditions of release. In rare cases where lengthy periods had successfully been spent at liberty on parole, the prisoner could apply for "parole reduced", whereby all terms and conditions were removed except the obligation to notify the parole authorities of any change of address.[80] However, the prisoner still remained liable to forfeiture upon conviction for the commission of an indictable offence.

---

[78] *National Parole Board Annual Report*, 1964, p. 2.

[79] While subsequent *Annual Reports* referred enthusiastically to this form of parole, the *Ouimet Report* (*supra*, note 55) referred to a "failure rate . . . in the order of 50%" (p. 351).

[80] This procedure still exists in section 16(1)(c) of the Act. While it is primarily reserved for lifers who, by definition, are on parole for life, it can be applied to parolees at any stage of parole release. Current Board policy is that non-lifers must successfully complete a period of 3 years on full parole before parole reduced may be considered. Lifers must complete 5 years on full parole.

Finally, although the Board was loathe to interfere with the for-feiture provisions contained in sections 13 and 17 of the 1958 *Parole Act*, it recognized that in certain rare circumstances it would be appropriate to grant "parole reinstated" following automatic forfeiture. According to the 1966 *Annual Report* "a forfeited parole may be reinstated . . . when the offence is not serious and the court declined to sentence the parolee to prison for committing the offence which had caused the automatic forfeiture."[81]

5. THE OUIMET REPORT AND SUBSEQUENT DEVELOPMENTS 1969-1977

While the *McCaud* decision[82] foreclosed judicial review of parole decision-making for almost 15 years (see Chapter 3), other pressures to modernize the parole system began to surface during the 1960's. These culminated in 1965 with the establishment of the Ouimet Committee, whose mandate was "to study the broad field of corrections, in its widest sense . . . including . . . release, parole pardon, post release supervision and guidance and rehabilitation."[83] In its *Report*, issued in 1969, the Ouimet Committee made numerous recommendations for modifying federal and provincial parole legislation. Some of these were enacted into law over the next few years.

(a) Mandatory Supervision

The Ouimet Committee noted that only approximately 60 percent of eligible penitentiary prisoners applied for parole. A major reason for this was that prisoners "prefer to complete their sentence in the institu-tion rather than place their . . . remission period in jeopardy."[84] In other words, since the maximum period of remission which could be earned was approximately one-third of sentence, and since prisoners were released as free persons when the remission period equalled the balance of the unexpired term, many preferred to serve additional time in custody after parole eligibility rather than be subject to limitations imposed on their freedom by parole authorities. Further, the Ouimet Committee concluded that another reason prisoners did not apply for

---

81   *National Parole Board Annual Report*, 1966, p. 6.
82   *Supra*, note 69.
83   P.C. 1965-998.
84   Report of the Canadian Committee on Corrections, *Toward Unity: Criminal Justice and Corrections (Ouimet Report)* (Ottawa: Queen's Printer, 1969), pp. 348-351. The Committee considered that a term other than parole be used in order that there "be no confusion in success rates of parole and (those) of this new program" (p. 350).

parole was that upon forfeiture or revocation of parole a prisoner not only received no credit for "street time,"[85] but also lost the period of statutory remission which stood to his credit at the time of release on parole, which could amount to as much as 25 percent of the original sentence.[86]

The Ouimet Committee proposed that prisoners from both federal and provincial institutions released by virtue of remission should be subject to the same terms and conditions as parolees, so long as the period of remission exceeded 60 days. In making this recommendation the Committee noted that "the practice of paroling only the better risks meant that those inmates who were potentially the most dangerous to society were still, as a rule, being released directly into full freedom in the community without the intermediate step represented by parole."[87] Similarly, "inmates who constitute the greatest danger and are not paroled are under control for a shorter period than the good risks who are paroled, since the parolee is under supervision for the remission periods."[88] The Committee was of the opinion that, since all prisoners would be subject to "statutory conditional release", there would be more incentive on the part of difficult prisoners to apply for parole at earlier stages in their sentences.

Parliament elected not to follow all of the Ouimet Committee's recommendations. First, for reasons which are not entirely clear in the public record,[89] the regime of mandatory supervision was not made applicable to prisoners released as a result of accumulated remission from provincial institutions. Secondly, Parliament decided not to allow credit for time successfully spent on the street prior to revocation or forfeiture of mandatory supervision. With these changes amendments to the *Parole Act* and *Penitentiary Act* proclaimed in force on August 1, 1970 ushered in the era of mandatory supervision.[90] Henceforth, all

---

85   *Ibid.*, p. 349.
86   The Ouimet Committee recommended that parole legislation be amended to allow credit for time spent on parole prior to revocation or forfeiture (*ibid.*, p. 350), but this proposal was not instituted until 1977 by S.C. 1976-77, c. 53, s. 31.
87   *Ouimet Report, ibid.*, p. 348.
88   *Ibid.*, p. 349.
89   In *Dempsey v. R.* (1987), 32 C.C.C. (3d) 461 (Fed. T.D.), Muldoon J. wryly noted that the rationale behind the legislative framework "is lost in the mists of our country's short history" (at 466).
90   Section 11B of the *Parole Act* was added by *Criminal Law Amendment Act. 1968-69* S.C. 1968-69, c. 38, s. 101(1). Section 25 of the *Penitentiary Act* was repealed by S.C. 1968-69, c. 38, s. 108, and a new section 25 was enacted to provide that the sentence of a prisoner released on parole or mandatory supervision would include the periods of both statutory and earned remission standing to his or her credit at the time of release. However, by section 101(2) of the *Criminal Law Amendment Act, 1968-69*, mandatory

persons released from federal penitentiaries as a result of accrued statutory and earned remission, where the amount of remission exceeded 60 days, were made subject to the control of the parole authorities. Release on mandatory supervision, like release on parole, could be suspended pending further investigation by the National Parole Board which could, in its "absolute discretion", revoke that release and order the prisoner returned to penitentiary. The prisoner not only received no credit for time successfully spent at liberty, but also lost all statutory remission standing to his credit at the time of release on mandatory supervision.[91] In addition, such release was deemed to be automatically forfeited upon conviction for an indictable offence.

(b) The Structure and Function of the National Parole Board

The Ouimet Committee considered that personal interviews with parole applicants would improve the quality of parole decision-making.

---

supervision was not brought into force until August 1, 1970 (SOR/1970-339). A useful discussion of the legislative history of remission and mandatory supervision may be found in the judgment of Kelly J.A. in *Ex parte Beaucage*, (1977), 31 C.C.C. (2d) 219 (Ont. C.A.), at 221-224. In that case the prisoner argued that since he had entered penitentiary in 1969, even though he had committed an offence in 1971, he should not be subject to mandatory supervision. Although successful in the court of first instance (1976), 24 C.C.C. (2d) 126 (Ont. H.C.), this was reversed by the Ontario Court of Appeal and upheld by a majority of the Supreme Court of Canada (1977), 33 C.C.C. (2d) 129.

[91] It was not until the 1974 ruling by the Supreme Court of Canada in *Marcotte v. Canada (Dep. A.G.)*, [1976] 1 S.C.R. 108 that it was ultimately established that the combined effect of section 16(1) of the 1958 *Parole Act* and section 25 of the 1961 *Penitentiary Act* was that a person sentenced to penitentiary prior to August 25, 1969 whose parole was revoked or forfeited, did not lose statutory remission standing to his credit at the time parole was granted. Although section 25 of the *Penitentiary Act* deemed the period of parole to include statutory remission, Parliament had not clearly made revocation or forfeiture by itself a basis in law for the removal of statutory remission credits. Since Parliament had only expressly provided for loss of statutory remission in the circumstances disclosed in section 22 of the 1961 *Penitentiary Act* (conviction in disciplinary court for certain kinds of institutional offences or conviction in a criminal court for escape-related offences), the Supreme Court was not prepared to give judicial sanction to the elimination of statutory remission upon revocation or forfeiture of parole in the absence of express language in the statutes. As noted by Dickson J. in his majority judgment, the fact that various courts across the country had come to different conclusions on this issue was a clear indication that the legislation was ambiguous. Compare *Re Morin*, [1969] 2 C.C.C. 171 (Sask. C.A.), *Ex parte Howden* (1974), 15 C.C.C. (2d) 415 (B.C. S.C.), *Ex parte Hilson* (1973), 12 C.C.C. (2d) 343 (Ont. H.C.), *Re Abbot* (1970), 1 C.C.C. (2d) 147 (Ont. H.C.) and *Ex parte Marcotte* (1973), 13 C.C.C. (2d) 114 (Ont. C.A.), with *Ex parte Marcotte* (1972), 10 C.C.C. (2d) 441 (Ont. H.C.), *Ex parte Kolot* (1973), 13 C.C.C. (2d) 417 (B.C. S.C.), and *Ex parte Rae* (1973), 14 C.C.C. (2d) 5 (B.C. S.C.).

Thus, the Committee recommended that the size of the Board be increased "to provide for sittings of the National Parole Board in panels of not less than three members . . . and . . . that the parole applicant shall have the right to appear before such a panel and make representations in person."[92] Although the Committee viewed parole granting hearings as "quasi-judicial,"[93] it was not prepared to recommend the institution of procedures for judicial review of such decisions.

Section 3(1) of the 1958 *Parole Act* was amended to increase the number of Board members from five to nine.[94] The Chairman was authorized to establish divisions of the Board, each consisting of two or more members; in carrying out properly authorized "duties and functions," a division could "exercise all of the powers conferred on the Board."[95] However, section 11 of the 1958 Act, which stated that the Board was "not required to grant a personal interview", was retained. No regulations were enacted providing for in-person hearings at either parole granting or parole or mandatory supervision revocation stages.

One other change contained in the 1969 amendments deserves to be mentioned. Section 12 of the 1958 *Act* had provided that once a parole or mandatory supervision was suspended, "the Board" was required to review the case "forthwith". This section was repealed and a new section 12 was enacted providing that, once a suspended parolee[96] had appeared before a magistrate, a designated official was required "within fourteen days . . . [to] . . . either cancel the suspension . . . or refer the case to the Board."[97] This procedure, which flowed from a recommendation of the Ouimet Committee, was tied to an expansion of the grounds upon which a decision to suspend parole or mandatory supervision could be made. While the wording of the 1958 legislation providing that parole or mandatory supervision could be suspended "in order to prevent a breach of any term or condition of the parole" was retained, as well release could be suspended "for the rehabilitation of the inmate or the protection of society."

Senior regional officials of the National Parole Service were authorized by the new legislation to institute a suspension for a parolee or person released on mandatory supervision whose behaviour was not

---

92 *Ouimet Report, supra,* note 84, p. 342.
93 *Ouimet Report, supra,* note 84, p. 341.
94 S.C. 1968-69, c. 38, s. 95(1). By S.C. 1973, c. 48, sections 1 and 4.1 of the Act were added to expand the Board to include part-time members. By 1976, the Board was composed of ten Ottawa-based members and ten regional members.
95 *Ibid.,* s. 96.
96 Under section 11B(2) of the amended legislation, S.C. 1968-69, c. 38, s. 101, this was also made applicable to persons released under mandatory supervision.
97 S.C. 1968-69, c. 38 s. 101.

considered to be acceptable. Such suspensions were intended to act "as a warning that action will be taken if he does not make a more serious effort."[98]

6. PAROLE LITIGATION 1969-1977

Apart from suggesting that decisions be taken expeditiously following a referral of a case to the Board, the Ouimet Committee made no recommendations as to whether or not in-person hearings should be held as part of the review process following suspension. General Board practice during the late 1960's and early 1970's was to hold hearings at the parole granting stage, but section 11 of the *Parole Act* was interpreted by the Board in such a way as to preclude hearings following suspension of parole or mandatory supervision. While the severe ramifications of revocation—reincarceration and no credit for time successfully spent on the street—had stimulated the litigation in *McCaud*,[99] the range of penalties was in fact extended by Parliament in the 1969 amendments to provide that the prisoner also lost all statutory and earned remission that stood to his credit at the time parole was granted.[100] It was therefore not surprising that, despite the ruling in *McCaud*, the absence of procedural protections stimulated considerable litigation during the years following the enactment of this legislation.[101]

In *Ex parte Beauchamp*,[102] the prisoner complained by way of *habeas corpus* that failure to inform him of the reasons for suspension deprived him, as a person "arrested or detained", of "the right to be informed promptly of the reasons for his arrest or detention" as guaranteed under section 2(c) of the *Canadian Bill of Rights*. Although the parole suspension had been cancelled before reserved judgment was delivered, Pennell J. (who had been Solicitor General of Canada prior to his appointment to the Bench) chose to express his views in light of what he perceived to be "questions . . . of continuing interest and importance." While recognizing the binding importance of the earlier judgment in *McCaud* that parole revocation was entirely an administrative matter and was "not in any way a judicial determination", Pennell J.

---

98   *Ouimet Report, supra,* note 84, p. 346.

99   [1965] 1 C.C.C. 168.

100 S.C. 1968-69, c. 38, s. 102 [proclaimed in force August 25, 1969].

101 See, for example, *Re Rowling and R.* (1979), 45 C.C.C. (2d) 478 (Ont. H.C.); *Ex parte Gorog* (1975), 23 C.C.C. (2d) 225 (Man. C.A.), reversed (1977), 33 C.C.C. (2d) 207n (S.C.C.); *R. v. Elliot* (1976), 34 C.R.N.S. 117 (B.C. S.C.); *Ex parte Collins* (1976), 30 C.C.C. (2d) 460 (Ont. H.C.); *Re Grabina and R.* (1977), 34 C.C.C. (2d) 52 (Ont. H.C.). These cases are discussed in detail in Chapter 8.

102 [1970] 3 O.R. 607 (H.C.). This case is more fully discussed in Chapter 3.

suggested that the Board was nevertheless required to act "fairly in accordance with the principles of proper justice." Since a decision to revoke parole would be of "vital importance" to a prisoner, "fairness demands a consideration of the inmate's side of the story. . . . if only in writing."[103]

In *Howarth v. National Parole Board*,[104] it was argued that section 28 of the newly proclaimed *Federal Court Act*[105], conferring jurisdiction on the Federal Court of Appeal "to hear and determine an application to review and set aside a decision or order, other than a decision or order of an administrative nature not required by law to be made on a judicial or quasi-judicial basis," provided a broader basis for judicial review than had previously existed. At the time it was felt that there were several reasons why section 28 might provide increased access to the courts.[106] First, the enunciation of the "duty to act fairly" in English law and by the Federal Court in other areas provided some support for the notion that contemporary concepts of natural justice were expanding, particularly given the *obiter* comments in *Beauchamp*. Secondly, it was felt that the logic of the unanimous decision of the United States Supreme Court in *Morrissey v. Brewer*,[107] holding that the due process clause in the American constitution created a right of judicial review in parole cases, would be compelling. Finally, several commentators considered that the wording of section 28 imported an approach which required that the reviewing court examine the consequences of the decision taken rather than the nature of the tribunal conducting the decision.[108]

The facts in *Howarth* were simple. Parole was suspended because a charge of indecent assault had been laid against the parolee. The charge was withdrawn prior to the date set for the preliminary inquiry; nevertheless parole was revoked. The prisoner, who lost almost 2½ years credit for time spent successfully on parole, together with approximately 9 months of statutory remission, complained that he had been given no reasons for the revocation of his parole. The Board, relying on *McCaud*, argued that it was obliged neither to afford the prisoner an opportunity to be heard nor to provide any statement of reasons for revocation. The Federal Court of Appeal held that it had no jurisdiction to review and set aside the Board's decision.[109] Thurlow J. regarded himself as bound by

---

103   *Ibid.*, at 608, 611, 612.
104   [1973] F.C. 1018 (Fed. C.A.).
105   S.C. 1970-71-72, c. 1. [proclaimed in force on June 1, 1971, subsequent to the decision in *Beauchamp, supra*, note 102].
106   R.R. Price, "Doing Justice to Corrections" (1977), 3 Queen's L.J. 288-229.
107   (1972), 92 S. Ct. 2593.
108   Mullan, "Fairness: The New Natural Justice" (1975), 25 U.T.L.J. 281.
109   *Re Howarth and National Parole Bd.* (1974), 14 C.C.C. (2d) 145 (Fed. C.A.).

the distinction between judicial (or quasi-judicial) and administrative functions described by Spence J. in *McCaud*. Jackett C.J., delivering the majority judgment, based his decision on section 16 [now s. 22] of the *Parole Act*. He concluded that since section 16(4) did not require disclosure to a person of "the facts upon which action is contemplated, [or] . . . giving him a fair opportunity to answer those facts," a revocation decision was an administrative act not reviewable by the Federal Court of Appeal.[110] A further appeal to the Supreme Court of Canada was dismissed (5-3).[111] Speaking for four members of the court, Pigeon J. held that section 28 of the *Federal Court Act* did not effect a substantive change in the law; that section was only concerned with transferring jurisdiction over federal tribunals from provincial superior courts to the Federal Court, and with distributing jurisdictions between the Trial and Appeal Divisions of that court. Since the introduction of section 28 did not change the law, Pigeon J. held that "the point was settled by the decision of this Court . . . in *Ex parte McCaud*."[112] In separate concurring reasons, Beetz J. commented that the loss of remission credits and "street time" credit was "unfortunate . . . since parole may be suspended and, presumably, revoked for reasons which are not necessarily connected with a breach of the terms or conditions of the parole."[113] However, in His Lordship's view this did not change the nature of the decision-making process.

Writing for the minority, Dickson J. noted "[t]he gravity of the impact of revocation upon the rights of a parolee," and concluded that the Board was acting in a judicial capacity "because the order of the Board (1) has a conclusive effect (2) is adjudicative (3) has a serious adverse effect upon 'rights'."[114] Dickson J. distinguished *McCaud* both because it had been decided prior to the enactment of the *Federal Court Act*, and because of the addition of section 16(4) of the *Parole Act* in the 1969 amendments.

This tension among the justices of the Supreme Court of Canada became more manifest in *Mitchell*,[115] where parole had been suspended a few days before the warrant expiry date, and revoked almost 6 weeks after the sentence would otherwise have expired. Because no credit was given for time successfully spent at liberty on parole, upon revocation the prisoner had to serve approximately 2 years additional time in

---

110 *Ibid.*, at 150.
111 *Re Howarth and National Parole Bd.* (1974), 18 C.C.C. (2d) 385 (S.C.C.).
112 *Ibid.*, at 388.
113 *Ibid.*, at 401.
114 *Ibid.*, at 399 and 397.
115 *Mitchell v. R.* (1976), 24 C.C.C. (2d) 241 (S.C.C.).

custody. The revocation was challenged by way of an application for
habeas corpus on the basis of an alleged breach of subsection 2(*c*)(i) and
(*e*) of the *Canadian Bill of Rights*. In order to distinguish his case from
Howarth, the prisoner based his complaint on the fact that he had not
been informed of the reasons for suspension either at the time of initial
apprehension or while the "review" under section 16(3) of the Act was
being conducted. Both the Manitoba Court of Queen's Bench and the
Manitoba Court of Appeal disposed of this argument by stating that "the
decision to suspend and the review which must take place between
suspension and revocation cannot be placed on a higher plane than the
process and determination that finally disposes of the matter."[116] On
further appeal to the Supreme Court of Canada, Ritchie J. (Judson,
Pigeon and Beetz JJ. concurring) held, on the basis of *McCaud* and
Howarth, that the "very nature of the task ... make[s] it necessary that
such a Board be clothed with as wide a discretion as possible and that its
decision should not be open to question on appeal or otherwise be
subject to the same procedures as those which accompany the review of
decision of a judicial or quasi-judicial tribunal."[117] Martland J. (de
Grandpré J. concurring) took much the same position, holding that the
prisoner was not entitled to know the reasons for suspension and
revocation.

Laskin C.J.C. (Dickson J. concurring) commenced his analysis
from the perspective that the facts "tend to shock from their mere
narration." His Lordship went on to say that:

> The plain fact is that the Board claims a tyrannical authority that I
> believe is without precedent among administrative agencies empowered to
> deal with a person's liberty. It claims an unfettered power to deal with an
> inmate, almost as if he were a mere puppet on a string. What standards the
> statute indicates are, on the Board's contentions, for it to apply according to
> its appreciation and without accountability to the Courts. Its word must be
> taken that it is acting fairly, without it being obliged to give the slightest
> indication of why it was moved to suspend or revoke parole."[118]

He then considered that *Howarth* was distinguishable because that case
had not considered the *Canadian Bill of Rights*. If section 2(*c*)(i)of the
Canadian Bill of Rights was "to have more than an empty meaning", it
would not be sufficient for the prisoner simply to be informed that he
was being reincarcerated because of the suspension of his parole; reasons
for suspension ought to be provided. While a full-fledged adversarial
hearing was not essential, section 2(*e*) of the *Canadian Bill of Rights*

[116] Quoted in *Ex parte Gorog, supra,* note 101, at 227.
[117] *Mitchell, supra,* note 115, at 257.
[118] *Mitchell, supra,* note 115, at 245.

mandated the existence of "minimum procedural safeguards". Because of a failure to comply with subsections 2(*c*)(i) and (*e*), the Board had exceeded its jurisdiction.

The short dissenting judgment of Spence J. is particularly noteworthy. His Lordship distinguished his own judgment in *McCaud*, holding that whereas parole revocation at that time had not entailed loss of remission, the 1969 amendments to the *Parole Act* providing for loss of remission upon revocation meant that such a decision was no longer merely administrative, but one which could deprive a parolee "of very important personal rights." For Spence J. it was therefore obvious that the procedural protections contained in the *Canadian Bill of Rights* applied to parole revocation decision-making.

Following these judgments it appeared for some time that arguments based on the application of the principles of natural justice to parole board decision-making would be unsuccessful. However, questions arose as to whether a person whose mandatory supervision had been suspended could claim any greater right than a parolee to know of reasons for suspension or be afforded an opportunity to make oral submissions prior to revocation. Several cases were argued during the mid-1970's on the basis that release on mandatory supervision was a right and not a privilege;[119] hence, a decision which interfered with that right was required to be made judicially. This argument was unsuccessful. Various courts held that since under section 15 of the *Parole Act* the statutory framework was the same as for parolees the legal basis for revocation of mandatory supervision was the same as for parole.[120]

7. DAY PAROLE

Although the Ouimet Committee had approved the need for gradual and carefully supervised release for most prisoners serving penitentiary terms, the *Report* did not specifically address itself to the concept of day parole. The various legislative amendments authorizing release on day parole were contained in the *Criminal Law Amendment Act, 1968-69*.[121] These amendments established the authority of the Board to

---

[119] *R. v. Moore; Oag v. R.* (1983), 33 C.R. (3d) 97 (S.C.C.); citing with approval *Truscott v. Mountain Institution (Director)* (1983), 33 C.R. (3d) 121 (B.C. C.A.) and *R. v. Moore* (1983), 33 C.R. (3d) 99 (Ont. C.A.).

[120] *Lambert v. R.*, [1976] 2 F.C. 169 (Fed. T.D.); *Ex parte Lambert* (1975), 27 C.C.C. (2d) 568 (Ont. H.C.); *Re Nicholson and National Parole Bd.*, [1975] F.C. 478 (Fed. T.D.); *Ex parte Thompson* (1975), 25 C.C.C. (2d) 228 (N.S. T.D.); *Re McKinnon and R.* (1974), 24 C.C.C. (2d) 536 (N.B. C.A.); *R. v. Daughton* (1978), 4 C.R. (3d) 287 (Man. C.A.).

[121] S.C. 1968-69, c. 38, ss. 94, 100 and 101 [proclaimed in force on August 26, 1969].

grant "parole the terms and conditions of which require the inmate . . . to return to prison from time to time . . . or after a specified period." Since a prisoner on day parole was "deemed to be continuing to serve his term of imprisonment in the place of confinement from which he was released on such parole,"[122] the Board was not required to wait until the time periods for eligibility for full parole had been served. This was further recognized in the statutory criteria which the Board was required to address; section 8(*a*) of the amended *Parole Act*[123] provided that the Board could grant day parole even if, *inter alia*, the prisoner had not "derived the maximum benefit from imprisonment."[124]

Despite the fact that eligibility for day parole arose upon admission to penitentiary, general Board policy was to postpone consideration for this form of release until 1 year prior to eligibility for full parole.[125] Only if the full parole eligibility date arose within the first year of imprisonment would the Board consider that eligibility for day parole had occurred at an earlier time. As the Board considered that 4 months was the minimum time necessary to conduct adequate preparation of a case for parole review, day paroles were rarely granted until 6 months had been served.[126]

Section 8 of the *Parole Act* was further amended to permit the Board to "terminate" a day parole.[127] Since the purpose of day parole was to permit a prisoner to be at liberty from close custody for certain specified purposes and to return to penitentiary at an anticipated future time, it was necessary for the Board to provide a mechanism for the normal conclusion of such authority to be at large, short of revocation which involved the automatic loss of remission. Thus, termination was designed in order that there would neither be any extension of the custodial portion of a term of imprisonment nor would there be any consequences of a disciplinary nature. While it was clear that a person released on full

---

[122] *Ibid.*, s. 101 [This became section 11(1) of the amended *Parole Act*].

[123] *Ibid.*, s. 100(1).

[124] While one can appreciate that the Board should consider whether "reform and rehabilitation . . . will be aided by the grant of parole" and whether parole release "would not constitute an undue risk to society," it is difficult to understand how the Board is to assess whether a prisoner "has derived the maximum benefit from imprisonment" (s. 8(*a*)).

[125] P. Carriere and S. Silverstone, *The Parole Process: A Study of the National Parole Board* (Ottawa: Law Reform Commission of Canada, 1977), p. 86.

[126] This reality was confirmed by Regulation. By SOR/79-88, ss. 9-10 of the *Parole Regulations* were amended to reflect that for penitentiary prisoners, depending on length of sentence, the minimum term of imprisonment which must be served before day parole may be granted is 6 months.

[127] S.C. 1968-69, c. 38, s. 100(3).

parole "exchanged all statutory remission standing to his credit" on his sentence for the right to remain "at large" for the remainder of his sentence according to the terms and conditions of the parole and was, thereafter, "not liable to be imprisoned by reason of his sentence" except in accordance with the provisions of the Act relating to the revocation and forfeiture, difficulties soon arose in the interpretation and application of the revocation and forfeiture of the *Parole Act* to persons on day parole.[128] It was argued in several cases that, due to the greater limitations on a person released on day parole, Parliament could not have intended that day parole would be subject to revocation and forfeiture and the consequential loss of remission. Prior to the 1977 amendments to the *Parole Act*, which clarified this matter by explicitly empowering the Board to revoke a day parole,[129] it was held in a number of cases that a day parolee was not subject to loss of remission and "street time" pursuant to the revocation provisions applicable to a prisoner on full parole,[130] but that a prisoner who committed an indictable offence while on day parole was subject to the forfeiture provisions of the *Parole Act*.[131]

---

[128] R.R. Price, *supra*, note 106, at 254-255.

[129] See *Re Jackson and R.* (1979), 44 C.C.C. (2d) 65 (S.C.C.).

[130] *R. v. Hales* (1974), 18 C.C.C. (2d) 240 (Man. C.A.); *Ex parte Carlson* (1976), 26 C.C.C. (2d) 65 (Ont. C.A.); *Skitt v. Canada (Solicitor General)*, [1976] 1 F.C. 566 (Fed. T.D.).

[131] *Ex parte Davidson* (1974), 22 C.C.C. (2d) 122 (B.C.C.A.); *Ex parte Kerr* (1975), 24 C.C.C. (2d) 395 (Ont. C.A.); *Re Zong and Cmmnr. of Penitentiaries* (1975), 29 C.C.C. (2d) 114 (Fed. C.A.).

6

Parole Granting

"Son, have you rehabilitated yourself?"
"Officer, you've got a lot of damn gall to ask if I've rehabilitated myself."
— Arlo Guthrie, *Alice's Restaurant*

1. INTRODUCTION

Following a lengthy process of federal-provincial consultation, public debate and hearings before the House of Commons Standing Committee on Justice and Legal Affairs, the 1958 *Parole Act*[1] and related legislation were substantially revised through a series of amendments proclaimed in force in 1977 and 1978.[2] Some of the most criticized aspects of the 1958 Act—automatic forfeiture, no credit for street time, and lack of procedural protections in the parole granting and revocation process—were repealed. However, as shown in Chapter 3, it was not until the acceptance into Canadian law of the duty to act fairly by the Supreme Court of Canada in *Nicholson v. Haldimand-Norfolk Board of Police Commissioners*[3] and *Martineau v. Matsqui Institution Disciplinary Board*[4] that an extensive volume of parole litigation began to develop. More recently, the *Charter*[5] has had a considerable impact on the judiciary's willingness to defer to the discretion of release decision-makers. Finally, when Parliament was recalled in special session to pass "detention" legislation in the summer of 1986 (discussed in Chapter 7), several overdue "housekeeping" amendments were made to the *Parole* and *Penitentiary Acts*, and a new regulatory package was proclaimed in force over the next few months.

This chapter considers the 1977 and 1986 amendments and discusses the case law to July 1, 1990. Reference is also made to formal

---

[1] S.C. 1958, c. 38.
[2] *Criminal Law Amendment Act, 1977*, S.C. 1976-77, c. 53. Most of the amendments were proclaimed in force on October 15, 1977. Reference will be made in footnotes to those sections which were not proclaimed on that day.
[3] [1979] 1 S.C.R. 311.
[4] [1980] 1 S.C.R. 602 (also referred to as *Martineau (No. 2)*).
[5] *Canadian Charter of Rights and Freedoms* (being Part I of the *Constitution Act, 1982* [en. by the *Canada Act, 1982* (U.K.), c. 11, s. 1]).

Board policy, as contained in the Board's *Policy and Procedures Manual*[6] and related documents. To the extent that experience permits, informal rules and practices are also included. Although the principal focus is on the National Parole Board, procedures of provincial boards of parole are discussed where applicable. The reader is cautioned not only that policies are frequently modified, but also that local and regional variations in implementation are often significant. While one can readily appreciate that the diversity of Canadian geography and the uniqueness of individual cases can and should militate against the rigid application of principle and policy, all too often "the predilections of particular Board members"[7] lead to an appearance of arbitrariness in the decision-making process. As well, the dominance of bureaucratic imperatives has created an inertia which impedes change.

2. JURISDICTION TO GRANT CONDITIONAL RELEASE

(a) Temporary Absence

Prior to the *Criminal Law Amendment Act 1976*, the National Parole Board had no direct role in the granting of temporary absences, this function being solely exercised by penal officials. At the federal level a series of amendments to the *Parole* and *Penitentiary Acts* over the past 15 years has gradually transferred power over temporary absences to the Board. Parliamentarians and parole authorities considered that this transfer of jurisdiction would better enable the Board to authorize and supervise gradual reintegration into the community, rather than being restricted by statute to consideration only of parole release.

The first change was the enactment of section 674(2) [now s. 747(2)] of the *Criminal Code*[8] which specifies that in cases involving prisoners serving life minimum sentences the Board must approve all non-medical escorted temporary absences.[9] The next change, part of the 1977 amendments, amended section 6 of the *Parole Act*[10] to empower the Board "to grant or refuse to grant . . . temporary absence without escort".[11] Finally, as part of the "housekeeping" legislation contained in

---

6 This unpublished document is available for inspection upon request in the Board's regional offices. Additions and deletions are made several times a year.
7 R.R. Price, "Bringing the Rule of Law to Corrections" (1974), 16 (No. 3) *Can. J. Crim. & Corr.* 209, at 218.
8 R.S.C. 1970, c. C-34 [now R.S.C. 1985, c. C-46].
9 *Criminal Law Amendment Act (No. 2), 1976*, S.C. 1974-75-76, c. 105, s. 21 [proclaimed in force July 26, 1976].
10 R.S.C. 1970, c. P-2 [now R.S.C. 1985, c. P-2, s. 13].
11 *Criminal Law Amendment Act, 1977*, s. 23 [proclaimed in force March 1, 1978].

Bill C-68, the power to grant unescorted temporary absences was transferred from the *Penitentiary Act*[12] to the *Parole Act*, with a residual power in the Board, through section 21.1(2) [now s. 25.2(2)], to delegate back the power to grant such passes in certain circumstances to penal officials.[13]

Although section 8 of the *Prisons and Reformatories Act*[14] was amended in 1977 to permit provincial parole boards to assume jurisdiction over the granting of unescorted temporary absence passes,[15] Quebec, Ontario and British Columbia have, to date, left this function in the hands of provincial penal authorities, as has the National Parole Board in those provinces and territories where it exercises jurisdiction.

(b) Parole

Since 1978, section 5.1(1) [now s. 12(1)] of the *Parole Act*[16] has provided statutory authority for the creation of provincial parole boards "to exercise parole jurisdiction, in accordance with this Act and the regulations, in respect of [most] inmates detained in a provincial institution". Prior to this amendment, the Ontario and British Columbia Boards of Parole were authorized under the *Prisons and Reformatories Act* to exercise parole jurisdiction over persons serving sentences for breaches of provincial statutes and over persons serving indefinite or indeterminate periods of imprisonment in addition to definite terms. To date, Quebec, Ontario and British Columbia have established Boards of Parole. In the remaining seven provinces and territories the National Parole Board continues to exercise parole jurisdiction.

It should also be noted that Quebec and British Columbia have entered into exchange of services agreements with the federal government,[17] whereby prisoners serving penitentiary-length sentences either remain in, or are transferred to, a provincial institution. For example,

---

12 R.S.C. 1970, c. P-6 [now R.S.C. 1985, c. P-5].
13 *An Act to amend the Parole Act, the Pentitentiary Act, the Prisons and Reformatories Act and the Criminal Code*, S.C. 1986, c. 43, ss. 6(4) and 14. This subject is discussed in more detail in Chapter 9.
14 R.S.C. 1970, c. P-21 [now R.S.C. 1985, c. P-20, s. 7].
15 *Criminal Law Amendment Act, 1977*, s. 45 [proclaimed in force July 1, 1978].
16 As amended by S.C. 1976-77, c. 53, s. 22 [proclaimed in force September 1, 1978].
17 Most provinces have entered into agreements, as authorized by section 4 of the *Prisons and Reformatories Act*. However, Ontario has declined to enter into any formal agreement with the federal government, except to the extent of housing prisoners pending transfer to penitentiary. For special provisions relating to Newfoundland, see the *Penitentiary Act*, section 16 and *Re Bell and Springhill Medium Security Institution (Director)* (1977), 34 C.C.C. (2d) 303 (N.S. C.A.).

unilingual francophone women or women from Western Canada serving penitentiary-length sentences sometimes remain in their home provinces.[18] In such cases, the Quebec and British Columbia Boards of Parole assume parole jurisdiction through the combined operation of section 12 [formerly s. 5.1] of the *Parole Act* and section 2 and Part II of the *Parole Regulations*.[19] However, through the definition of a "federal inmate" in section 2 and section 3(1) of the Regulations, the National Parole Board retains parole jurisdiction over prisoners detained in provincial institutions who have been sentenced to life imprisonment as a minimum punishment, prisoners in respect of whom sentences of death have been commuted to life imprisonment, and prisoners sentenced to detention in a penitentiary for an indeterminate period.

Section 18 [formerly s. 15] of the *Penitentiary Act* authorizes transfers to penitentiary of persons serving sentences of less than 2 years upon agreement between the two levels of government.[20] All provinces except Ontario have entered into such agreements. Once the prisoner is transferred to a penitentiary, the National Parole Board has jurisdiction over parole granting through the definition of "federal inmate" in section 2 of the Regulations.[21] Sections 12(3) and (4) [formerly s. 5.1(3), (4)] of the *Parole Act* contain provisions designed to deal with situations in which a person granted parole by a provincial parole board moves to another province. In the case of *Torrie*,[22] it was established that this is limited to approved transfers of residence. In that case, the prisoner had been

---

18 In *Re B.C. (A.G.) and Astaforoff* (1983), 6 C.C.C. (3d) 498 (B.C. C.A.) a female prisoner serving a 3-year term remained in British Columbia provincial institution pursuant to an agreement between the two levels of government. The prisoner went on a hunger strike. The Attorney General of Canada applied for an order compelling the provincial authorities to force-feed her. On the particular facts of the case, both the Chambers Judge and the British Columbia Court of Appeal declined to make the order requested. The federal authorities repudiated the agreement, transferred the prisoner to a federal penitentiary and force-fed her. *The Globe and Mail* 15 July 1983, p. 3.

19 SOR/78-428 [see amendment at SOR/78-628].

20 The validity of this legislation was upheld in *Re Anaskan and R.* (1977), 34 C.C.C. (2d) 361 (Ont. C.A.). However, in considering whether or not to effect a non-consensual transfer from a reformatory to a penitentiary, penal authorities are subject to a duty of fairness, requiring them in non-emergency situations to notify the prisoner of an intention to tranfer and to provide an opportunity to respond. See *Re Morin and Dir. of Corrections* (1982), 70 C.C.C. (2d) 230 (Sask. C.A.).

21 Thus, a prisoner serving less than 2 years who is transferred to a penitentiary through the application of section 731 of the *Code* will be subject to the potential application of the detention provisions, or to mandatory supervision by virtue of section 21(6) of the *Parole Act*. However, a prisoner transferred to penitentiary under an Exchange of Services agreement with a province will not be considered to be a "federal inmate" within the meaning of the Regulations, and will not therefore be subject to mandatory supervision upon release.

22 *Re Torrie and R.* [summarized (1983), 10 W.C.B. 318 (Ont. H.C.)].

granted day parole by the National Parole Board in New Brunswick. He went unlawfully at large from the halfway house and was finally apprehended in Toronto. He was incarcerated in Toronto, where, having no roots in the community, he had no realistic opportunity to re-apply for parole, which had been revoked in his absence. Upon hearing alternative applications for *habeas corpus* and *mandamus* to transfer him back to New Brunswick, Ewaschuk J. held that the more general provision of section 659(3) [now s. 731(3)] of the *Criminal Code*, which provides that a person not serving a penitentiary sentence is to be sentenced to a prison or other place of confinement within the province in which he is convicted, must yield to the specific provision in section 20(1) [now s. 25(1)] of the *Parole Act*. That section states that upon revocation of parole a prisoner shall be recommitted to the place of confinement from which he was paroled, or to the corresponding place of confinement for the territorial division within which he was apprehended. Furthermore, section 25(1) of the *Parole Act* is not limited solely to the place where the inmate is to be provisionally detained on parole revocation; rather, the section can require that the inmate serve the entire remanet of his sentence in the province in which he is apprehended.

3. ESTABLISHING CONDITIONAL RELEASE ELIGIBILITY DATES

(a) Unescorted Temporary Absence

Eligibility for release on unescorted temporary absence for prisoners serving less than 2 years imprisonment in provincial institutions is not limited by statute, there being no equivalent provision to section 12 in Part II of the Regulations. In theory there would be nothing to prevent a prisoner sentenced to a maximum reformatory term from being released immediately after the imposition of sentence. In practice, penal authorities are likely to consider length of sentence as one of the factors to be taken into account in determining when a prisoner should be granted such a form of release. For example, the Ontario Ministry of Correctional Services takes the view that in the absence of very special circumstances a prisoner is unlikely to be granted an "immediate" temporary absence pass (T.A.P.) if the sentence exceeds 90 days.[23]

---

[23] In *R. v. Wortzman* (1983), 12 C.R. (3d) 115 (Ont. C.A.), the trial judge had regarded himself as bound by a suggestion by the Provincial Ministry of Correctional Services that because of overcrowding on weekends intermittent sentences should not be imposed; rather, a trial judge should impose "straight time" and recommend "imme-

Section 12 of the *Parole Regulations* prohibits a federal prisoner from being released on unescorted temporary absence (U.T.A.) from a penitentiary until a specified portion of the sentence has been served,[24] except in cases involving absences for emergency medical care. Depending on length of sentence, a minimum of 6 months must be served. A reading of this section in conjunction with section 9 of the Regulations indicates that in the vast majority of cases eligibility for release on unescorted temporary absence arises on the same date as eligibility for release on day parole.[25]

(b) Day Parole

As part of the 1977 legislation section 2 of the *Parole Act* was amended to provide that parole "includes day parole", which term is defined in the same section as "parole the terms and conditions of which require the inmate . . . to return to prison from time to time during the duration of such parole or to return to prison after a specified period". Thus, day parole is a more restrictive and temporary form of release which requires that the prisoner return to close custody during the pendency of or at the conclusion of, the day parole period.

Sections 9-11 of the Regulations are designed to complement this legislation. A reading of these sections indicates that eligibility for day parole for federal prisoners arises prior to eligiblity for release on full parole. While most of the 1986 amendments to the *Parole Act*, the *Penitentiary Act* and the *Regulations* were designed to legitimate the practice of "gating",[26] the amendments were also designed to speed the process of identifying and "cascading" good parole candidates early in their sentences. Sections 15, 27(1)(*a*) and (*c*) [formerly ss. 8, 9(1)(*a*) and (*c*)] of the *Parole Act*, read in conjunction with sections 14-15 of the Regulations, make it clear that in considering an application for day

---

diate T.A.P.". The Court of Appeal considered that this amounted to an improper fettering of the trial judge's discretion. The court concluded that if an intermittent sentence was called for in all the circumstances, the judge should impose it, regardless of the Ministry's preferences.

24 Section 13 of the Regulations requires the Board to notify penitentiary prisoners of their unescorted temporary absence, day parole and full parole eligibility dates within 6 months of admission to penitentiary.

25 The differences arise when the sentence is greater than 12 years. Regardless of the length of sentence, Board policy (as contained in section III of the *Policy and Procedures Manual*) is that U.T.A. reviews are to be conducted without hearing unless the prisoner is serving a sentence of more than 6 years, which sentence includes an offence listed on the schedule to the *Parole Act*, or in any other case where it is deemed appropriate by senior parole officials.

26 This subject is discussed in Chapter 7.

parole in the case of a prisoner serving a sentence of up to 3 years, the National Parole Board must, at the same time, consider the question of full parole to become effective on the full parole eligibility date. If the Board decides not to grant full parole at that time, it must hold a further review prior to the full parole eligibility date. Conversely, if the Board grants full parole in principle at the time of the day parole hearing, but receives further information or new facts which would cause it to reconsider its decision, it may do so, but is required to conduct that reconsideration by way of a new hearing. In cases involving prisoners serving more than 3 years, prisoners are entitled to separate day and full parole hearings on or near their eligibility dates; however, in reality, there are considerable institutional pressures to combine both hearings.[27]

There are also rules limiting eligibility for grants of day parole by provincial parole boards[28] and by the National Parole Board where the prisoner is serving a reformatory sentence in a province or territory where no provincial parole board has been established.[29] However, day parole from provincial institutions is comparatively rare, due to the extensive use of unescorted temporary absences by provincial penal officials. Indeed, section 31(2) of the Regulations confirms that provincial parole boards may opt out of considering day parole applications.

It should be noted also that section 747(2) of the *Criminal Code* provides that persons convicted of high treason or first and second degree murder are ineligible for day parole until 3 years prior to full parole eligibility date. However, by section 746, the calculation of the parole eligibility date for these persons includes all time spent in custody between arrest and conviction. Although eligibility for day parole of persons serving life maximum sentences is not limited by section 747, the combined effect of sections 742(*c*) and 746 is that their day parole eligibility date includes any time spent in custody between arrest and conviction.[30]

---

[27] Some of the strategy considerations involved in waiving hearings are discussed in Chapter 12.

[28] *Parole Regulations*, s. 31.

[29] *Parole Regulations*, s. 9(*e*).

[30] A curious anomaly arises in cases of persons serving sentences for murder where the period of parole ineligibility is set, either by statute or by the sentencing judge, at more than 15 years. In these cases section 745 of the *Code* allows the prisoner to apply to a court composed of a superior court judge and jury for consideration for reduction in the *full* parole ineligibility period. The section purports to prohibit a prisoner from applying until he "has served" at least 15 years. While there can be no doubt that section 745 clearly applies to eligibility for release on full parole, it was argued in *Frederick v. Canada (A.G.)* (1990), 52 C.C.C. (3d) 433 (Ont. H.C.), that since a

(c) Full Parole

Eligibility for full parole is currently determined by sections 5 to 7 of the *Parole Regulations*, with the exception of persons convicted of high treason or murder on or after July 26th, 1976,[31] and those subject to preventive detention under Part XXIV of the *Code*.[32] Full parole eligibility for persons convicted of murder prior to July 26, 1976 is subject to complex transitional provisions enacted by Parliament.[33]

The effect of changes in eligibility through amendments to the *Parole Regulations* is not entirely clear. In *Ford v. National Parole Board*,[34] the prisoner had been convicted and sentenced at a time when full parole eligibility was based on the lesser of one-third of the term of imprisonment or 4 years. While serving sentence the Regulations were amended to increase the ineligibility period to its current level of the lesser of one-third or 7 years. Upon hearing an application for *mandamus* to compel the Board to consider the prisoner for full parole at the earlier time, Walsh J. held that parole ineligibility cannot be extended by subsequent amendments to the Regulations, but is determined by the Regulations in force on the date of conviction.

While *Ford* was a relatively simple case of construing and applying a penal statute, the designation of "violent conduct" offenders potentially raises several issues. Section 8 of the Regulations purports to authorize the Board to increase the period of full parole ineligibility until the prisoner has served the lesser of *one-half* of the sentence or 7 years, as compared to the usual *one-third* rule. In language somewhat similar to the definitions of "serious personal injury offence" contained in section 752 of the *Criminal Code* and the definition of "serious harm" contained in section 21.2(1) [formerly s. 15.2(1)] of the *Parole Act*, a prisoner may be designated as a "violent conduct" offender if he is sentenced to a term of imprisonment of five years or more . . . for which he was liable to imprisonment for ten years or more and the offence involved conduct that . . . seriously endangered the life or safety of any person, . . . resulted

---

successful prisoner would be retroactively deemed to have been eligible for day parole after serving 12 years, he should be allowed to apply to a jury after having served 12 years. This argument was rejected by Henry J., who held that the opening words of section 745 were clear and unambiguous. It should also be noted that Henry J. went even further, ruling that section 747(2) afforded no "positive" authority for the Board to consider a prisoner for unescorted temporary absences or day parole prior to full parole eligibility date.

31 *Criminal Code*, ss. 742-747. See also *Parole Regulations*, s. 4.

32 *Criminal Code*, s. 761.

33 *Criminal Law Amendment Act (No. 2)*, ss. 25-28 [proclaimed in force July 26, 1976].

34 [1977] 1 F.C. 359 (T.D.). See also *Schwimmer v. Hammock*, 59 N.Y. 2d 636 (1983).

in serious bodily harm to any person, or . . . resulted in severe psychological damage to any person. Section 8(2) appears to limit the Board's power to impose this designation only to persons having two convictions resulting in sentences of at least 5 years within a 10-year period calculated from the end of the first sentence to the commencement of the subsequent sentence, the conviction for which must occur subsequent to the proclamation date of the Regulation.[35] However, the Board has, on occasion, purported to extend this designation even to persons convicted for the first time of two "serious" offences.[36] Despite criticisms of the concept and wording of the Regulation, it was not altered during the 1986 amendments.[37]

In our view, the Regulation does not conform with the degree of clarity and procedural fairness which one should expect of the criminal justice system. The criteria for determining whether conduct is violent are so broad and vague that they could include break and enter yet exclude assaults punishable by less than 10 years imprisonment. Moreover, the Regulation neither provides any process for determining whether conduct is violent, nor specifies who the decision-maker will be. Although section 13 of the Act confirms the discretionary context of parole granting, the question of a prisoner's eligibility for full parole

---

[35] SOR/78-428 [proclaimed in force July 1, 1978].

[36] While the current version of the *Policy and Procedures Manual* (s. II.A) adopts a literal interpretation of the wording of section 8(2), the Board has considered applying the violent conduct designation to a prisoner who has committed separate offences on different days, even though convictions for the offences were imposed simultaneously. In explaining the original scheme of this Regulation to the House of Commons Standing Committee on Justice and Legal Affairs, then Solicitor General Fox stated that the purpose of section 8 was to catch "recognized offenders guilty of certain violent crimes *with a history of violent criminal activity . . .*" (emphasis added). See Minutes of Proceedings and Evidence of the Standing Committee on Justice and Legal Affairs (May 31, 1977, Issue No. 17) p. 24. Further, in response to a query from the House of Commons Standing Committee on Regulations and Other Statutory Instruments, then Chairman of the National Parole Board Outerbridge wrote that because "(t)he three phrases in paragraphs 9(1)(*a*), (*b*) and (*c*) are not defined . . . (t)hey must, accordingly, be taken as having the ordinary meaning of those words, subject to any gloss that may have been put on them by judicial interpretation of the same or similar phrases appearing elsewhere in statutes or in regulations". See Minutes and Proceedings of the Standing Joint Committee on Regulations and Other Statutory Instruments (November 29, 1979) pp. 37-39. Judicial consideration of similar phrases has generally resulted in interpretations which would run converse to those being considered by the Board. See *R. v. Skolnick* (1982), 138 D.L.R. (3d) 193 (S.C.C.), per Laskin C.J.C., citing with approval *R. v. Cheetham* (1980), 53 C.C.C. (2d) 109 (Ont. C.A.).

[37] This may have been an oversight, as the power to make this Regulation contained in section 9(1)(*d*) of the Act was repealed by S.C. 1986, c. 43, s. 5(2). The regulation-making power is now contained in section 27 of the Act.

should not be a matter for the exercise of subjective judgment by unknown officials. The comparison between the skeletal framework of this discretion to extend the period of full parole ineligibility and the procedural safeguards which circumscribe the trial and sentencing process is dramatic. The violent conduct designation affects the liberty interest of prisoners in a manner which does not meet the requirements of fundamental justice in the era of the *Charter*.

(d) Parole By Exception

Prior to the 1977 amendments to the *Parole Act* applications could be made to the National Parole Board and its predecessor, the Remission Service of the Department of Justice, on an *ad hoc* basis for a grant of parole prior to normal eligibility for release. Guidelines for the granting of such a form of release were established informally. These included: clemency on compassionate grounds, employment or schooling, preservation of equity, interdepartmental cooperation (particularly with respect to immigration), special representations from law enforcement authorities or the judiciary, and situations where "maximum benefit had been derived from incarceration."[38] Due to some public criticism about the use of parole by exception, the revised Regulations proclaimed in force consequent upon the enactment of the 1977 legislation excluded the possibility of this form of release. However, members of the National Parole Board soon realized that it was essential that the Board retain the authority to grant early release in exceptional circumstances. Thus, at the request of the Chairman of the National Parole Board, section 11.1 of the *Parole Regulations* was proclaimed in force on January 18, 1979,[39] giving the National Parole Board the power to grant parole by exception in very limited circumstances.

Despite continued public criticism of parole by exception, the criteria under which applications can be considered were in fact expanded as part of the regulatory package accompanying the 1986 amendments. Section 11.1 now provides that parole by exception may be granted to an inmate:

---

[38] National Parole Board, Memorandum re Exception from Regular Time Rules Ordinarily Governing Parole Eligibility (File 62298, August 11, 1970). Referred to in P. Carriere and S. Silverstone, The Parole Process: A Study of the National Parole Board (Ottawa: 1977) Law Reform Commission of Canada, pp. 28-29.

[39] SOR/79-88. Federal prisoners whose parole eligibility is governed by sections 6 to 8, 9(*a*) and (*b*), 10 and 11 of the Regulations cannot be considered. Thus, dangerous offenders, dangerous sexual offenders, prisoners serving life as a minimum sentence, and those whose death sentences have been commuted to life imprisonment, are excluded.

(*a*) who is terminally ill;

(*b*) whose physical or mental health is likely to suffer serious damage if the inmate continues to be held in confinement;

(*c*) for whom the penalty constitutes an excessive hardship that was not reasonably foreseeable at the time the inmate was sentenced;

(*d*) who completed a program recommended by the sentencing court or has satisfied specific objectives of the sentence expressly stated by the sentencing court; or

(*e*) who is the subject of a deportation order under the *Immigration Act, 1976* or an order to be surrendered under the *Extradition Act* or the *Fugitive Offenders Act*, where the order requires that the inmate be detained until deported or surrendered, as the case may be.[40]

A formal application by or on behalf of a prisoner is required unless urgent circumstances demand flexibility in the process. Review for full parole by exception[41] is conducted by way of hearing before two members of the Board who are first required to determine whether one of the criteria is met. Simply because a prisoner falls into one of the enumerated categories does not mean that parole by exception will be favourably considered. The initial screening process is deliberately designed to discourage applications in all but the most unique factual situations. Even cases involving terminal illness are usually dealt with by way of a grant of temporary absence pass, rather than through parole by exception.[42] Similarly, it seems that virtually the only persons considered under section 11.1(*b*) are those suitable for certification under provincial mental health legislation. Finally, Board members have maintained on numerous occasions that parole by exception for persons subject to deportation orders (or seeking parole for voluntary departure to another country into which they have a right of access) is not to be used as a way of reducing expense to Canadian taxpayers, or of "benefitting"[43] non-Canadians. In the event that the Board members decide that one of the criteria has been met, the voting and other procedural requirements laid

---

[40] As amended by SOR/86-817, s. 3 [proclaimed in force September 1, 1986]. Criteria (*a*), (*c*), and (*e*), existed in the previous Regulations, though (*e*) referred only to the *Immigration Act*.

[41] A hearing is not required if the application is for day parole by exception, though Board policy is that one is likely to be held if the prisoner is serving more than 6 years for a violent offence.

[42] In Appeal Division Reports, Case No. "PROC 010," November 24, 1987, a case involving a prisoner suffering from a serious heart condition, the Appeal Division drew a distinction between physical health which "might" be endangered and a physical condition which "is likely to" result in permanent harm. Despite a recommendation by the sentencing judge that the Board "consider medical parole", the Appeal Division upheld panel members who had interpreted the words of the Regulation strictly.

[43] Whether permanent departure from Canada is a "benefit" is often debatable.

down in the *Parole Regulations* for regular applications for day or full parole are applied. No internal re-examination to the Board's Appeal Division is available.

Section 31.1(1) of the *Parole Regulations* now authorizes provincial Boards of Parole to consider certain designated classes of prisoners for parole by exception.[44] An application for parole by exception is treated like any other application for parole.

(e) Conditional Release Eligibility and International Prisoner Transfers

On March 2, 1977 Canada signed a treaty with the United States providing for the transfer of Canadian nationals to Canada to serve sentence; other treaties have and continue to be signed with other countries. Canadian implementing legislation, the *Transfer of Offenders Act*,[45] came into force on March 22, 1978.[46] While a detailed review of the provisions of this legislation and its efficacy is beyond the scope of this text,[47] the legislation and the various treaties essentially provide that the sending and receiving states and the prisoner must consent in writing before a transfer can occur. Once transferred, section 11(1)(*a*) of the Act provides a Canadian offender transferred to Canada "shall be credited with any time toward completion of his sentence that was credited to him at the date of his transfer by the foreign state". Despite the fact that most prisoners sentenced in Canada are ineligible to be credited for time spent in pre-trial custody, Canadian sentence administrators will give transferred prisoners pre-trial confinement credits, if such credits are provided by the law of the sending state.

Sections 8 to 10 of the *Transfer of Offenders Act* provide that conditional release eligibility dates arise as if the offender had been convicted and sentenced in Canada. This is consistent with the general philosophy of the Act which is that, upon being transferred, the completion of the sentence should be "carried out according to the laws of the

---

44 SOR/86-817, s. 12 [proclaimed in force September 1, 1986].

45 Now R.S.C. 1985, c. T-15. The Schedule to the legislation contains an ever-expanding list of countries with which transfer treaties have been signed.

46 S.C. 1977-78, c. 9.

47 For an assessment of the transfer system created by this Act, see T.M. Schaffer, " 'Justice with Mercy': The Treaties with Canada and Mexico for the Execution of Penal Judgments" (1977-78) 4 Brook. J. Int'l. Law 246; M.C. Bassiouni, "Perspectives on the Transfer of Prisoners Between the United States and Mexico and the United States and Canada" 11 Vand. J. Trans. L. 249; "A Practitioner's Perspective on Prisoner Transfers" (1978) 4 Nat. J. Crim. Def. 127; and A.J. Nazarevich, "The Transfer of Offenders Act and Related Treaties: An Analysis" (1978), 4 C.R. (3d) 212.

Receiving State."[48] Thus, for both Canadians considering repatriation and non-Canadians contemplating a return to their home country, attention should be paid to obtaining accurate information as to eligibility for, and practices surrounding, release.[49]

4. PAROLE REVIEWS AND HEARINGS

(a) Initiating a Parole Application

Section 15(1) of the *Parole Act* requires the Board to consider the case of every person "sentenced to imprisonment in or transferred to a penitentiary for two years or more" unless the prisoner "advises the Board in writing that he does not wish to be granted parole by the Board". Conversely, where the prisoner is serving a sentence of less than 2 years in those provinces and territories where the National Parole Board has jurisdiction, it is only obligated to consider a case upon receiving an application by, or on behalf of, the prisoner.[50] This distinction reflects the reality that many prisoners serving shorter sentences prefer not to apply, since a grant of parole means that they are subject to supervision as compared to awaiting remission-based release.

A similar legislative scheme exists for provincial parole boards. Section 1(*b*) of the Quebec parole statute[51] limits the term "inmate" to a person imprisoned "for a term of imprisonment of six months or more,"[52] but states, in section 22, that all "inmates" shall be considered for parole at or near eligibility date. Section 42 of the Ontario Regulations[53] casts a duty on the Ontario Board of Parole to consider every

---

[48] See, for example, *Canada/United States Treaty*, Article IV, s. 1.

[49] In *Korrol v. Canada (Dep. A.G.)* (1984), 14 C.C.C. (3d) 495 (Fed. T.D.) the prisoner sought to declare his transfer from the United States invalid on the basis that he had not given a valid consent since he was unaware of the different dates when he would be eligible for parole and the duration of such parole. On the facts it was held that the prisoner had knowingly waived his right to be fully informed.

[50] In order to allow adequate preparation time, the Board is not required to grant hearings in provincial cases where the application is received less than 4 months before sentence expiry (*Policy and Procedure Manual*, s. III.A).

[51] *An Act to promote the parole of inmates and to amend the Probation and Houses of Detention Act*, S.Q. 1978, c. 22.

[52] *Quaere* whether this is lawful. Since the powers of the Quebec Parole Commission derive from section 12(1) of the federal *Parole Act*, surely the Commission cannot refuse to consider the case of a prisoner serving any sentence of imprisonment for breaches of federal statutes. In matters of breaches of provincial statutes, however, the Quebec Parole Commission derives its power from sections 2 and 17 of the provincial statute and could lawfully opt out of parole decision-making in such cases.

[53] R.R.O. 1980, Reg. 649.

prisoner serving a term of imprisonment of 6 months or more "notwithstanding that the inmate has not applied", but places the onus on a
prisoner serving less than 6 months to initiate an application. British
Columbia appears to have no formal rules on this subject.

In light of the automatic review requirement imposed on the National Parole Board by section 15 of the *Parole Act*, an information-
gathering process should commence immediately following sentencing.
At the federal level, section 6 of the *Penitentiary Act*[54] directs that the
Commissioner of Corrections is responsible for the "preparation" of
parole applications. Much of the information obtained in this phase
consists of duplicates of reports collected or prepared during the initial
process of determining in which institution the prisoner is to be placed.
For example, information respecting the offence and the offender—
previous criminal record, degree of violence, evidence of alcohol or
drugs, accomplices, outstanding charges, notoriety of the crime—is (or
should be) collected by a representative of the local office of the parole
service. Since much of this material will be relevant to release decision-
making, copies of documents received should be placed on the prisoner's parole and institutional files. However, despite the automatic
review requirement, one cannot assume at the federal level that active
steps to process the material will take place when no formal parole
application has been completed by, or on behalf of, the prisoner. Typically, the application is a simple document which requests the prisoner
to provide an outline of his release plan, identify persons in the community who would be prepared to support him, and specify why he feels he
should be granted conditional release, in order that a further information-gathering process may be initiated. As internal Board guidelines
indicate that 4 to 6 months should be allowed for case preparation, an
application for any form of release should be completed as early as
possible in the sentence.

Once the prisoner is housed in a penitentiary,[55] he is assigned an
institutional case management officer (C.M.O.I.) and a parole officer
(C.M.O.C.) from the local office of the parole service.[56] In addition to
providing guidance and advice, these persons are also required to pre-

---

[54] S.C. 1976-77, c. 53, s. 37.
[55] Similar, but less formal, structures exist at the provincial level. Practical advice on
preparation of a parole application and attendance at a hearing is contained in Chapter
12.
[56] These are the formal terms in those institutions which operate on a "living unit"
system. Prisoners (and staff) seem to prefer the older titles "C.O." (Classification
Officer) and "P.O." (Parole Officer), which are still the formal names for these staff in
other federal institutions.

pare and supervise the collection of various materials for the Board. Further, case management officers are expected to collect three main types of information to assist the Board in its assessment of risk. The first consists of "case specific" information, including (but not limited to) "details of the offence and criminal history, role of alcohol/drugs, mental status as it affects the likelihood of future crime, previous breaches of supervision conditions, and issues surrounding relationships and employment as they relate to the risk of reoffending."[57] The second type of information which must be collected consists of current assessments by mental health professionals. Whether these are mandatory depends upon the category of the offence as classified by the Board according to its policies. Prisoners who have committed "Category 1" offences[58] for which sentences of 2 years or more have been imposed are required to undergo a psychological or psychiatric assessment[59] prior to their first parole review, regardless of views which may

---

[57] *Policy and Procedures Manual*, s. III F.2.1(b). The sources and quality of information typically collected are discussed both in the following section on "Confidentiality Issues", and in Chapter 12.

[58] The current list of Category 1 offences is as follows:

Criminal Code Section	Offence
81	Causing Injury with Intent
220	Causing Death by Criminal Negligence
221	Causing Bodily Harm by Criminal Negligence
235	Punishment for Murder
236	Punishment for Manslaughter
237	Punishment for Infanticide
238	Killing Unborn Child in Act of Birth
239	Attempt to Commit Murder
244	Causing Bodily Harm with Intent
245	Administering Noxious Thing
246	Overcoming Resistance to Commission of Offence
247	Traps Likely to Cause Bodily Harm
248	Interfering with Transportation Facilities
268	Aggravated Assault
269.1	Torture
271	Sexual Assault
272	Sexual Assault with a Weapon, Threats to a Third Party or Causing Bodily Harm
273	Aggravated Sexual Assault
279	Kidnapping
279.1	Hostage Taking

[59] While the Board will attempt to have assessments completed by both "inside" and "outside" psychologists and psychiatrists, the policy has been left fairly open, in recognition of both the need to be flexible in individual cases and the lack of equal access to mental health professionals across the country. Current regional and case specific policies should be obtained from the Board's regional offices.

be held by case management officers as to the need for such assessments. In cases involving other offences case management officers may recommend to the Board that mental health assessments are unnecessary, unless the prisoner has previously served a penitentiary sentence for a Category 1 offence. The final type of information which case management officers are expected to collect consists of:

- The level of security.
- The visits and correspondence (who, how frequent).
- The type of work.
- The educational and rehabilitation progress in which the inmate is involved, as well as the degree of his participation.
- The relationship with staff and inmates.
- His behaviour while on temporary absence, the use of his leisure time, the number, date and type of misconduct reports, if any, as well as the type of disposition, (*e.g.*, loss of remission).
- Information from preventive security, *etc.*
- An analysis of relevant behaviour during the term of incarceration.

(b) Confidentiality Issues

As demonstrated in Chapter 3, the pre-*Martineau (No. 2)* case law required the Board to provide very little reason for its actions. When the regulation-making powers of the Governor in Council were revised as part of the 1977 amendments to the *Parole Act*, section 9(1)(*h*) [now s. 27(1)(*h*)] was enacted, providing that regulations could be passed "prescribing the information, and the form thereof, to be supplied . . . to an inmate . . . before any hearing". As a result, section 17 of the Regulations was enacted, requiring the Board to provide the prisoner with all information in its possession, except for written material prepared before the proclamation of the Regulation and any information prohibited from disclosure pursuant to section 54(*a*) to (*g*) of the *Canadian Human Rights Act*.[60] Although the Regulation spoke only of disclosure by the Board when reviewing an application for full parole, policies were developed to provide some disclosure in all types of conditional release granting and post-suspension decisions.[61]

---

[60] Section 17(3) adopted the exemptions contained in section 54 of the *Canadian Human Rights Act*, S.C. 1976-77, c. 33. Section 54 was itself replaced by sections 18 to 28 of the *Privacy Act*, S.C. 1980-81-82-83, c. 111, Schedule II [proclaimed in force November 23, 1982] [now R.S.C. 1985, c. P-21].

[61] The Board's *Policy and Procedures Manual* as it existed prior to January, 1988 stated "[a]t all parole hearings, including at post-suspension hearings, the inmate will be advised of the substance of the information which the Board has in its files and which it

In *Staples v. National Parole Board*, the affidavit material filed disclosed that "the board did indeed consider materials, including police reports, a community assessment report, and comments from the superintendent of the Oskana Centre in Regina, which neither applicant nor his lawyer saw before the decision was taken."[62] In the absence of any claim of "privilege in respect of non-disclosure of these documents", Strayer J. held that " 'fundamental justice' . . . requires that the applicant for day parole be made aware of the substance of the materials adverse to his cause which the board will be considering, in order that he may respond to it with evidence or argument."[63] This case may be seen as confirming that *prima facie* the decision-maker is obliged to release all materials in its possession in order that the applicant can be given an opportunity to respond, and that if the decision-maker is in possession of information which it feels it cannot disclose, it must disclose that fact to the applicant.

Section 17 of the Regulations was revised as part of the 1986 amendments.[64] The relevant subsections, which confirm the principle established by *Staples*, now provide as follows:

17. (1) Subject to subsection (2), where, pursuant to the Act or these Regulations, the Board reviews a case, it shall, orally or in writing, provide an inmate whose case is to be reviewed, with the relevant information in its possession that is to be considered in the review of the case or a summary thereof.

. . . . .

(5) The Board is not required to supply information that, in its opinion, should not be disclosed on grounds of public interest, including information the disclosure of which
(*a*) could reasonably be expected to threaten the safety of individuals;
(*b*) could reasonably be expected to lead to the commission of a crime;
(*c*) could reasonably be expected to be injurious to the security of penal institutions;
(*d*) could reasonably be expected to be injurious to the physical or psychological health of the inmate; or

---

considers relevant to his case". The policy permitted exemptions where the information was considered to be confidential under section 17(3) of the Regulations. See also paragraph 8 of the affidavit of W. Outerbridge, Chairman of the National Parole Board, reproduced in *Wilson v. National Parole Bd.* (1985), 18 C.C.C. (3d) 541 at 545 (Fed. T.D.), and "Information Sharing—A Guide for Staff", Appendix "H" to the current *Policy and Procedures Manual.* At a practical level it should not be assumed that disclosure will be automatically provided, or that it will be made available in advance of the hearing date.
62 (1985), 47 C.R. (3d) 186 (Fed. T.D.), at 189-190.
63 *Ibid.*, at 190.
64 SOR/86-817, s. 4; subs. (6) re-enacted SOR/86-915, s. 3.

(*e*) could reasonably be expected to be injurious to the conduct of lawful investigations or the conduct of reviews pursuant to the Act or these Regulations, including any such information that would reveal the source of information obtained in confidence.

(6) An inmate may waive the right to be provided with the information referred to in subsection (1) or a summary thereof.

In addition to this Regulation, the Commisioner of Corrections and the Chairman of the National Parole Board have jointly prepared an extensive set of guidelines for staff, many of which deal with disclosure prior to and at Board hearings.[65] The general thrust of these guidelines is that it is only in limited circumstances that material can be withheld. Nevertheless, since the question of the circumstances in which the Board may act on undisclosed information, and to whom the Board must justify such a decision, has been the subject of considerable litigation, it will be useful to examine the leading cases to demonstrate the kinds of issues which frequently arise, and the response of the courts to them.

In *Couperthwaite v. National Parole Board*,[66] a pre-*Charter* case, a challenge was brought to the Board's practice at that time of permitting the parole officer and institutional personnel to meet privately with the attending Board members prior to the entry of the prisoner into the hearing room. The Chairman of the National Parole Board filed an affidavit in which he asserted that the Board's concern was that if the prisoner were present at all stages of the hearing, he might come into possession of information which was prohibited from disclosure under section 54 of the *Canadian Human Rights Act*. However, the Chairman conceded in cross-examination that in general only a maximum of 10 percent of the information collected might fall into section 54. Upon hearing an application for *mandamus* to continue the hearing in the presence of the prisoner, Smith D.J. analysed the statutory framework[67] and acknowledged the Board's concerns about disclosure. However, he concluded that since the Board was required by section 17 of the Regulations to supply information prior to the date of a parole granting hearing, "[i]t should not be difficult in these circumstances for the ... board members to have whatever consultation they deem necessary and de-

---

[65] "Information Sharing—A Guide for Staff", *supra*, note 61.

[66] (1982), 31 C.R. (3d) 50 (Fed. T.D.).

[67] Although section 54 on its face required that only "the appropriate Minister" had the power to decide that information be withheld Smith D.J. concluded that the National Parole Board, upon "satisfy[ing] itself that the information asked for falls within the description stated in one or more of those paragraphs", was not required to furnish a prisoner with such material. Similar views were expressed on this point in the post-*Charter* cases of *Latham v. Canada (Solicitor General)* (1984), 39 C.R. (3d) 78 (Fed. T.D.) and *Wilson v. National Parole Bd.*, *supra*, note 61.

cide whether to supply the information to the inmate or not."[68] Where unanticipated questions of disclosure of possibly confidential information arose immediately prior to or during the hearing, Smith D.J. considered that it would be appropriate for the Board members to adjourn briefly, consider in the absence of the prisoner whether or not the information should be disclosed, and then resume the hearing.[69]

After the enactment of the *Charter*, the applicability of the statutory exemptions from disclosure was considered in *Latham*,[70] where, in the context of a post-suspension hearing, the Board refused to allow the prisoner to be present at all stages of the hearing, apparently because "confidential police information" might be discussed. The court's attention was drawn to section 54(*c*)(ii) of the *Canadian Human Rights Act*,[71] which allowed a Minister to decline to release information which "would be likely to disclose information obtained . . . by any government . . . investigative body . . . in the course of investigations pertaining to the detection or suppression of crime". While noting that in some circumstances a statutory exemption could be a legitimate limitation on the common law duty of full disclosure, Strayer J. held that the possible revocation of parole involved a parolee's liberty. Hence, the protections contained in section 7 of the *Charter* were engaged. Fundamental justice "requires procedural fairness commensurate with the interest affected. . . . and fairness requires at least an outline being given to the person affected of the allegations being considered by a tribunal in deciding whether to deny that person his liberty."[72] To permit the Board to apply the Regulation mechanically would amount to an improper fettering of its discretion. Moreover, to prohibit disclosure through blanket adoption of another statute intended to "protect the privacy of individuals with respect to personal information about themselves held by a government institution and . . . provide individuals with a right of access to that information,"[73] rather than deny access to information, was not, on the record before the court, a "reasonable limitation" within the meaning of section 1 of the *Charter*.

---

[68] *Supra*, note 66, at 65.
[69] A similar conclusion was reached in *Martens v. B.C. (A.G.)* (1983), 35 C.R. (3d) 149 (B.C. S.C.), a case questioning the propriety of Board and C.S.C. policy providing that the C.M.O.I. and C.M.O.C. could remain in the hearing room in the absence of the prisoner, during the Board's private decision-making process.
[70] *Latham v. Canada (Solicitor General), supra*, note 67.
[71] Although the case was decided after section 54 had been replaced by the *Access to Information Act*, the facts arose at a time when it was still the governing legislation.
[72] *Latham, supra*, note 67, at 91.
[73] *Privacy Act*, s. 2.

Another aspect of confidentiality was considered a few months later in *Cadieux v. Director of Mountain Institution.*[74] An application for a series of unescorted temporary absence (U.T.A.) passes had been approved by the Board. Prior to the date of commencement of the first of these passes the prisoner was informed that the Board was in possession of confidential information which caused it to order that his U.T.A. program be cancelled.[75] In support of an application to quash the Board's decision it was argued that the Board's refusal to disclose the information and to give the prisoner an opportunity to respond amounted to a breach of section 7 of the *Charter*. While acknowledging that the "liberty" interest involved in a U.T.A. application is more limited than in the case of day or full parole, Reed J. held that the character of U.T.A. passes is similar to parole. Accordingly, the decision-making process respecting U.T.A. passes becomes "subject to the requirements of fundamental justice prescribed by s. 7 of the Charter."[76] More importantly, she held that, since the Supreme Court of Canada in *Martineau (No. 2)* had removed the distinction between "rights" and "privileges" as a pre-condition for judicial review, it did not matter that the prisoner's U.T.A. program had not commenced, nor that there was no inherent right to be granted a U.T.A. pass. However, regardless of whether the issue was regarded as "fairness" or "fundamental justice," Reed J. was prepared to hold that "there are circumstances in which an inmate may be denied knowledge of the reasons underlying the revocation of his U.T.A. program."[77] She reasoned that, since the liberty being sought by a convicted prisoner for U.T.A. or parole "is not the absolute liberty to which every citizen is entitled," the rules of fairness or natural justice applicable to a determination of whether a U.T.A. program is granted or revoked will not necessarily be the same as those which apply to the criminal trial process.[78]

According to Reed J. one circumstance in which it might be appropriate for the Board "to rely on and use information which comes to its knowledge even though it does not pass the gist of that information on to

---

[74]   (1984), 41 C.R. (3d) 30 (Fed. T.D.).

[75]   Although no regulations were enacted respecting disclosure of information in U.T.A. applications, the Board's *Policy and Procedures Manual* being used at that time provided that the prisoner was to be informed by the releasing authority of the reasons for cancellation of a U.T.A. pass "unless those reasons contain material for which the Solicitor General can claim exemption from disclosure under the *Canadian Human Rights Act*".

[76]   *Supra*, note 74, at 39.

[77]   *Supra*, note 74, at 42-43.

[78]   *Supra*, note 74, at 48.

the inmate"[79] is where the identity of the informant might be disclosed. After analysing English and Canadian case law on disclosure of the names of police and other informants, Reed J. concluded that "[i]t is trite law that the identity of informers is protected from disclosure."[80] A similar view was taken by Nitikman J. in the subsequent case of *Wilson v. National Parole Board*,[81] where the Chairman of the National Parole Board filed an affidavit in which he offered the hypothetical example of a prisoner applying for parole whose spouse "informs the correctional authorities that she does not wish to live with the inmate again because of his assaults and threats upon her in the past and her fear of future reprisals. It is essential that the Board know this and equally essential that the Board withhold such information from the inmate."[82] Nitikman J. was persuaded to order only that the Board disclose to an already paroled prisoner any information which would not "automatically lead to the disclosure of the identity of the informer."[83]

Although concerns about disclosure of the name of the informer are attractive, analogies to the police-informant privilege in the parole context are not apt. In the parole context, unlike adversarial proceedings, the information is already in the hands of the decision-maker, and the issue is whether or not it should be disclosed to the prisoner. Thus, even where a parole board decides that it will not consider the undisclosed information, the prisoner may well be left with the impression that decisions are being made on the basis of hidden agendas. As noted by Reed J. in her later decision in *H.*, "[w]hile many courts and tribunals hear evidence which they eventually declare to be irrelevant and which they consequently ignore, this is often in the context of public disclosure of that evidence and of the court or tribunal decision."[84] Another reason why the analogy to "informer" cases in other contexts is strained arises because none of the cases referred to in *Cadieux* and *Wilson* raised questions of liberty. Similarly, those cases did not deal with the refusal of a decision-maker to disclose the substance of adverse allegations.

At a more practical level experience with the Parole Board demonstrates that concerns about disclosure of the name of the informant can all too often be manipulated and over-inflated to qualify as appropriate justifications for non-disclosure. While difficult cases do arise from time to time, it often seems that Canada's privacy legislation—statutes de-

---

[79]   *Supra*, note 74, at 49.
[80]   *Supra*, note 74, at 49.
[81]   (1985), 18 C.C.C. (3d) 541 (Fed. T.D.).
[82]   *Ibid.*, at 546.
[83]   *Ibid.*, at 554.
[84]   *H. v. R.*, [1986] 2 F.C. 71 (T.D.), at 81.

signed to ensure swift and standardized access to information held by government agencies—has provided a convenient rationale for non-disclosure of even the simplest and most controversial information or any substantive details of allegations of inappropriate behaviour. While it is to be hoped that the new initiatives signalled by the amendment of section 17 of the Regulations and accompanying policy statements will be successful, some examples from the recent case law are instructive as to the poor quality of disclosure. In *Latham*, the allegation was "a Child Welfare matter involving Latham and his step-daughter."[85] Similarly, in *Richards v. National Parole Board*, the reasons for parole suspension given were "the uttering of threats . . . to members within the community."[86] In *Cadieux*, the prisoner was informed that "the Board is in receipt of confidential information which satisfies us that you are a risk to reoffend on any form of release at this time".[87] In *H.* the prisoner was advised in 1985 that he was "suspected of having committed crimes involving the deaths of two young girls and the disappearance of a third in British Columbia in 1978."[88]

The second possible rationale for non-disclosure envisaged by Reed J. arises where "disclosure would automatically lead to the revealing of information collection methods and thus substantially undermine the future functioning of the Board." In this context she acknowledged "the public interest ... in preserving the parole board's ability to function effectively." However, Reed J. not only cautioned that the circumstances under which a claim for non-disclosure would be maintained would be "rare," but also stressed that the party seeking to justify non-disclosure would have to demonstrate "an element of necessity; mere convenience for the functioning of the Board is not enough."[89] While Nitikman J. in *Wilson* limited his principal reasoning to discussion of "identity of the informer" issue, the court held, without further analysis that the statutory exemption from disclosure contained in section 54(c)(ii) of the *Canadian Human Rights Act*—"information obtained or prepared by any government institution . . . that is an investigative body . . . in the course of investigations pertaining to the detection or suppression of crime generally"—would not offend section 7 of the *Charter*. On the facts in *Wilson* there was no express assertion by the Board that there was any type of ongoing investigation presently being conducted, nor did the Board offer any specific justification for

---

85 *Ibid.*, at 77.
86 (1985), 45 C.R. (3d) 382 (Fed. T.D.), at 384.
87 *Supra*, note 74, at 36.
88 *Supra*, note 84, at 77.
89 *Supra*, note 74, at 49.

non-disclosure of information which had previously been obtained from any source. Indeed, the affidavit of the Chairman of the National Parole Board merely recited that he had generally "been told by senior officials of police forces and the Correctional authorities, that if the Board discloses certain information received in confidence, the sources of that information will simply dry up."[90]

This lack of precise analysis was perpetuated in *Rice v. National Parole Board*,[91] a case involving facts very similar to those in *Cadieux*. A previously granted release was cancelled prior to implementation on the basis of information which the Board maintained could not be disclosed. The trial judge found:

> ... that three members of the Board re-examined the possibility of providing the confidential information requested by the applicant and that they decided that this was impossible without the source of the information being revealed; they also concluded that the lives of those who had provided this confidential information would be endangered if the said information was disclosed; they stated, finally, that if the identity of the source was revealed and the information disclosed, the National Parole Board's ability to obtain confidential information would be impaired and the institutional order of the Correctional Service of Canada also endangered.[92]

For Pinard J. both of the justifications offered for non-disclosure would be sufficient to bring the case into "serious and exceptional situation.... All these grounds of public interest invoked by the Board ... take precedence."[93] The trial judge appears to have been particularly impressed with the fact that there was before him both an affidavit and *viva voce* testimony from a member of the Board's staff indicating the Board's concerns.

If Pinard J. intended to suggest that disclosure should not be ordered in the event that it might make the task of penal and parole authorities more difficult, this represents a misapplication of *Cadieux*. Further, while referring briefly to the seminal decision of the Supreme Court of Canada in *Singh v. Minister of Employment & Immigration*[94] in the course of his reasons, Pinard J. ignored that court's rejection of administrative convenience as a rationale for denying rights guaranteed under section 7 of the *Charter*. Similarly, the court does not appear to have considered the importance of Laskin C.J.C.'s dissent in *Mitchell*,[95] cited with approval in both *Cadieux* and *Singh*, which questioned

---

90 *Supra*, note 81, at 546.
91 (1985), 16 Admin. L.R. 157 (Fed. T.D.).
92 *Ibid.*, at 167.
93 *Ibid.*, at 167, 168.
94 [1985] 1 S.C.R. 177.
95 *Mitchell v. R.* (1975), 24 C.C.C. (2d) 241 (S.C.C.), at 245.

whether prisoners should be required to accept the Board's assertion that it was acting in good faith.

A much more careful analysis of this issue arose in *H.*, where police authorities had provided information to the Board that the prisoner "continues to remain a suspect in the deaths of 2 young girls and the disappearance of a 3rd young girl, in the Matsqui, B.C. area."[96] The prisoner had attempted, through counsel, to obtain further information from the police and had also made application under the *Privacy Act* for information on his files. Neither of these routes provided him with any factual details of the allegations against him. The prisoner was similarly frustrated in his attempts to seek disclosure directly from the Board, the Board taking the position that it was prohibited from providing further information because of the privacy legislation.

Reed J. accepted that "the degree of detail that is required to be disclosed must be assessed by reference to the purpose for which it is required" in order "to enable the individual to make a full and fair response to the adverse allegations against him.[97] The Board had not even provided the "gist" of the information.

> [B]eing told you are suspected of having committed crimes . . . in British Columbia in 1978 is not enough. . . . [A]t the very least, the applicant would be entitled to information concerning the dates of the alleged offences, the place, presumably some indication of time and the identity of the victims.[98]

Reed J. then dealt with the Board's argument that it was constrained from giving further disclosure by the privacy legislation. While various sections of the *Privacy Act*[99] might provide for exemptions from disclosure of requests for information made pursuant to that legislation, "[t]hey do not operate so as to limit access to information to which an individual might be entitled as a result of other legal rules or principles, as for example . . . in this case, to have the case one has to meet disclosed pursuant to the rules of natural justice."[100]

---

[96] *Supra*, note 84, at 74.
[97] *H. v. R., supra*, note 84, at 76. See *Rogers v. Secretary of State for Home Development*, [1972] 2 All E.R. 1057 (H.L.).
[98] *Supra*, note 84, at 77.
[99] As noted in footnote 69, *supra*, sections 18 to 28 of the *Privacy Act* have effectively replaced section 54 of the *Canadian Human Rights Act*. They provide, *inter alia*, for exemption from disclosure of "information . . . which could reasonably be expected to be injurious to the enforcement of . . . the conduct of lawful investigation, including . . . any such information (i) relating to the existence or nature of a particular investigation (ii) that would reveal the identity of a confidential source of information, and (iii) that was obtained or prepared in the course of an investigation."
[100] *H. v. R., supra*, note 84, at 78.

Immediately before the case came on for hearing the Board offered a second justification for non-disclosure. In a filed affidavit a Board member asserted that having ascertained that there was an ongoing police investigation into the prisoner's pre-incarceration behaviour, "the details of the crimes under investigation are simply irrelevant to the Board's decision making," and that the Board would not consider the undisclosed information any further. Reed J. found that this was unsatisifactory in that "the applicant is entitled to the appearance of fairness as well as fairness itself"; the ends of justice would not be met by permitting the Board to judge the parole application against the background of such undisclosed allegations. Thus, an order was issued directing that "the parole application shall be heard by a differently constituted panel of the National Parole Board who do not have knowledge of the details of the allegations against the applicant which have not been disclosed to the applicant".[101]

Regardless of whether the issues at stake in a parole granting or post-suspension hearing are characterized as fundamental justice or fairness, any mechanism for assessing the validity of claims for non-disclosure can only be evaluated on the basis of the potential for harm. Harm to an informant or third party can sometimes justify non-disclosure. It occasionally transpires that real detriment to a significant investigation — such as premature disclosure of the existence or content of a wiretap — can also provide a decision-maker with a reason not to disclose. When a parole board receives information which it believes is important and which it feels it cannot disclose before taking a decision, the following steps are essential to a conclusion that disclosure cannot be made:

1. It must take all available steps to confirm the accuracy of the information.
2. It must consider the effect of disclosure on the source or a third party or, in a proper case, an ongoing investigation.
3. It must consider the impact of non-disclosure on the applicant's opportunity to respond to the matters at issue.
4. It must conclude that disclosure of the information will place the prisoner, the source or a third party in danger or will seriously impede a significant investigation.

---

[101] *Supra*, note 84, at 79 and 81. The solicitor, acting for the prisoner, filed an affidavit summarizing his conversation with the police officer in charge of the investigation, in which the officer stated that police did not have enough evidence to lay charges and that it was unlikely charges would be laid.

5.   It must consider techniques for disclosing the gist of the information and conclude that no satisfactory disclosure can be made without endangering the source or a third party or causing real detriment to an ongoing investigation.

Since the consequences to a conditional release applicant of a decision being made on the basis of undisclosed information are so potentially grave, if, after undertaking these steps, a Parole Board still maintains that it cannot disclose even the gist, the Board should be prepared to justify that decision to a court.

This possibility was discussed by Reed J. in *Cadieux*. Upon reviewing the affidavits filed by Board personnel in support of non-disclosure, Reed J. concluded that their "overall tone and content . . . is one of claiming a blanket class exception." That material was not sufficient to justify "refusing diclosure of even the *gist* of the case against Mr. Cadieux" (emphasis in original). She suggested that if it continued to resist disclosure "on some second application . . . the Board should be prepared to produce for the court the documents in question . . . (a procedure similar to that developed at common law in privilege cases and similar to that existing under section 36.1 . . . of the Canada Evidence Act . . .)."[102]

The opportunity for non-disclosure may be completely precluded in cases where there is a qualified right to release. This would apply in post-suspension and detention hearings. This is the position adopted by two British Columbia decisions, both of which deal with situations where the Board refused to disclose even the gist of the adverse allega-

---

[102]   *Cadieux v. Mountain Institution (Director)* (1984), 41 C.R. (3d) 30 (Fed. T.D.), at 53. If such a procedure is developed, one difficulty which may arise is whether, upon the hearing of an application to determine whether the Board can continue to act on the basis of undisclosed information, the prisoner or counsel may examine the material in order to present argument. In the Australian case of *Alister v. R.* (1984), 58 A.J.L.R. 97 (Aust. H.C.), the appellants had been convicted of serious offences. They sought disclosure of a number of police files to which objection was taken on the basis of prejudice to national security. The files were produced for the court, whereupon counsel for the applicant submitted that he should be permitted to see the contents to make argument as to their relevance and materiality. Though the Federal Attorney General indicated that he was content that counsel for the applicant could examine the materials the court refused to permit this. In *Re Abel and Advisory Review Bd.* (1981), 56 C.C.C. (2d) 153 (Ont. C.A.), a case involving disclosure of information to patients applying for reviews of their status under Lieutenant Governor's warrants, Arnup J.A. suggested *in obiter* that a resolution to the problem of disclosure might be to permit counsel to examine the patient's file upon giving an undertaking that the contents not be disclosed without the permission of the Chairperson of the Review Board. Of course this placed counsel in an undesirable position. It is difficult to obtain information and instructions on matters which one has undertaken not to disclose.

tions, on the basis that that disclosure would inevitably lead to identification of the informant. In *Tatham v. National Parole Board*, a detention case, MacDonell J. concluded:

> One would have thought that it could not be more fundamental to justice that a person know the case he has to meet. If he does not know the case he has to meet and is kept in custody because of [it], he is deprived of his liberty contrary to the principles of fundamental justice.[103]

In reaching that conclusion MacDonell J. adopted the concept of a "qualified" right to liberty as developed by the British Columbia Court of Appeal in *Re Ross and Warden of Kent Institution*,[104] one of the first cases interpreting the detention provisions. In such cases, section 7 of the *Charter* prevents the Board from acting if it refuses to provide a summary or gist of the adverse allegations. Since a denial of liberty not in accordance with the principles of fundamental justice can only be justified by satisfying the stringent standards of section 1, the judgments in *Ross* and *Tatham* support the proposal that non-disclosure should require judicial authorization.

(c) The Right to an In-Person Hearing

The issue of the right to an in-person hearing as part of the decision-making process has been the subject of considerable litigation. At the federal level, section 17 of the *Parole Act* states that "[s]ubject to such regulations as the Governor in Council may make in that behalf, the Board is not required ... to personally interview the inmate or any person on behalf of the inmate." Prior to the 1986 amendments, Regulation 15 specified that, with certain minor exceptions, the only form of review which was required to be conducted by way of an in-person hearing was a review for full parole. Though reviews of applications for initial release on unescorted temporary absence or day parole were not required to be dealt with by way of a hearing, until December 31, 1984, the Board developed a practice of conducting a hearing in virtually all cases.

Despite this laudable initiative, due to manpower shortages the full complement of Board members required by the Regulations in force at that time to vote on a particular application often did not attend. This was challenged in *O'Brien v. National Parole Board*[105] where a prisoner serving a life minimum sentence had applied for unescorted temporary

---

103 (Vancouver Registry #CC900534, B.C.S.C., MacDonell J., April 18, 1990).
104 (1987), 34 C.C.C. (3d) 452 (B.C.C.A.).
105 (1985), 43 C.R. (3d) 10 (Fed. T.D.). This case is also discussed in Chapters 3 and 4.

absence passes. Pursuant to section 23(2)(*a*) of the Regulations in force at that time, seven Board members were required to vote on his application. Only three Board members attended at his hearing; those members voted in favour of his application but were overruled by the negative votes given *in absentia* by four other Board members.

A motion for *certiorari* to quash the decision was launched on two alternative bases: that the procedure adopted breached section of the *Charter*, or that the duty of fairness required that the applicant be personally interviewed by all voting members. McNair J. held that the denial of the prisoner's application for unescorted temporary absence "did not constitute the deprivation of any constitutionally-enshrined right to liberty under section 7 of the *Charter*."[106] He distinguished a line of cases which had emerged in the post-suspension hearing context[107] on the basis that there was a difference between "a denial affecting the expectation of enjoyment of some anticipated privilege of liberty and the deprivation of some right of liberty, presently existing and enjoyed".[108] McNair J. then considered whether the duty to act fairly created a right to an in-person hearing, and held that since "[t]he procedure envisaged was that of review or investigation rather than that of a full-scale hearing with all the usual panoply of safeguards",[109] and since "the subject matter under consideration was the granting of a request for a temporary sort of liberty and not the revocation or curtailment of an existent liberty", the prisoner could not, in the absence of an "express statutory requirement", claim a right to an in-person hearing by all voting Board members.[110] However, because the Board had voluntarily "extended the latitude of fair review procedure and embarked on a hearing," McNair J. traced a line of authority "to the effect that once an administrative authority elects to embark upon a hearing ... then it automatically follows that such hearing must be conducted in accordance with the rudiments of natural justice." Applying this principle to the case, McNair J. found that the "determinative" decision of those Board members who voted "without having heard the applicant in

---

[106] *Ibid.*, at 23.
[107] See *Re Cadeddu and R.* (1982), 32 C.R. (3d) 355 (Ont. H.C.); *Re Mason and R.* (1983), 35 C.R. (3d) 393 (Ont. H.C.), discussed in Chapters 3, 4 and 8.
[108] *Supra*, note 105, at 22.
[109] *Supra*, note 105, at 23. Although not referred to in the judgment, this distinction was also noted by Pierre Carriere and Sam Silverstone, who wrote "in our experience, most parole hearings were not 'hearings' in the ordinary formal sense of the word. They were more like informal interviews and discussions among those participating . . . ." *The Parole Process: A Study of the National Parole Board* (Ottawa: Law Reform Commission of Canada, 1977), p. 82.
[110] *Supra*, note 105, at 23.

person, must be deemed to be ignorance sufficient to preclude the exercise of any fair judgment upon the merits of the application."[111]

Following the judgment in *O'Brien* and two related cases,[112] the Regulations dealing with voting structures were substantially modified,[113] the most important changes being that the number of members required to vote on a particular application was reduced, and that each voting member was required to be present whenever a hearing was held. However, until 1986 neither the Act nor the Regulations provided that a prisoner was entitled to an in-person hearing as part of the process of deciding upon any form of conditional release other than full parole. Indeed, from the release of the *O'Brien* judgment until the 1986 amendments, the National Parole Board maintained its policy of not holding hearings in "provincial" parole granting cases, and ceased holding in-person hearings when considering applications for day parole. Several cases considered whether this was constitutionally permissible. While in light of the 1986 amendments it might be argued that these cases are now only of historical interest, it should be kept in mind that section 11 of the Act still has not been amended, and that Regulations can be repealed without parliamentary approval. Before discussing the correctness of the various decisions challenging the Board's refusal to hold hearings, it is necessary to review the seminal decision of the Supreme Court of Canada in *Singh v. Minister of Employment & Immigration.*[114]

Singh involved a challenge to procedures established under the *Immigration Act*[115] for the determination of claims to refugee status. The legislative scheme involved the claimant being examined under oath by a senior immigration official. The transcript of this examination and supporting documentation were then forwarded to the Minister responsible, who in turn forwarded these materials to the Refugee Status Advisory Committee (R.S.A.C.) for "advice". Although the legislation did not prohibit the R.S.A.C. holding a formal hearing, the Supreme Court was advised that this was not the general practice. Further, as noted by Wilson J. the R.S.A.C. "acts as a decision-making body isolated from the persons whose status it is adjudicating and . . . applies

---

[111] *Supra*, note 105, at 23-24, 25.
[112] *Browning v. National Parole Bd.* (1985), 43 C.R. (3d) 31 (Fed. T.D.); *Ford v. National Parole Bd.* (1985), 43 C.R. (3d) 26. In *Ford*, apparently forgetting that three negative votes were required before day parole could be denied under section 23(3)(*a*) of the Regulations in force at that time, the prisoner's application for release had been denied on the basis of two negative votes. McNair J. held that this "amounted to no decision at all," quashed the denial and ordered a new hearing.
[113] SOR/1984-1123 [proclaimed in force March 7, 1985].
[114] *Supra*, note 94.
[115] S.C. 1976-77, c. 52 [now R.S.C. 1985, c. I-2].

policies and makes use of information to which the refugee claimants themselves have no access."[116] Once the Committee had made its recommendation, there was no right to a hearing before the Minister. Where a refugee claim was refused, the claimant could apply for a redetermination hearing (which would be a proceeding to which full natural justice safeguards would apply) only if the Committee was "of the opinion that there are reasonable grounds to believe that a claim could, upon the hearing of the application be established."[117] This phrase had previously been interpreted by the Supreme Court of Canada as being limited to cases in which the Board could conclude that "it [was] more likely than not" that the applicant could establish his claim.

Two judgments were issued by the Supreme Court.[118] Beetz J. (Estey and McIntyre JJ. concurring) specified that he was basing his judgment on section 2(e) of the *Canadian Bill of Rights*. He considered that "the process of determining and redetermining appellants' refugee claims involves the determination of rights and obligations for which the appellants have, under section 2(e) of the *Canadian Bill of Rights*, the right to a fair hearing in accordance with the principles of fundamental justice." He concluded that since the appellants' claims had "been finally denied without their having been afforded a full oral hearing at a single stage of the proceedings before any of the bodies or officials empowered to adjudicate upon their claim on the merits", section 2(e) had been breached. While an oral hearing before the decision-maker would not necessarily be required in all cases involving the determination of rights, "the nature of the legal rights at issue and the severity of the consequences to the individuals concerned" would be determinative. Since "life or liberty may depend on findings of facts and credibility . . . the opportunity to make written submissions . . . would be insufficient."[119]

Wilson J. (Dickson C.J.C. and Lamer J. concurring) preferred to base her reasoning on section 7 of the *Charter*. She sketched a very broad view of the ambit of section 7. Faced with the theory that the words "life," "liberty" and "security of the person" should be construed "as different aspects of a single concept rather than as separate concepts each of which must be construed independently", Wilson J. considered

---

[116] *Supra*, note 94, at 197, per Wilson J.

[117] *Immigration Act*, s. 71.

[118] Although oral argument had proceeded only on section 7 of the *Charter*, the Registrar of the court later wrote to all counsel indicating that the Justices wished to receive written submissions as to the applicability of the *Canadian Bill of Rights*.

[119] *Singh v. Minister of Employment & Immigration* [1985], 1 S.C.R. 177, at 228, 229 and 231.

that "it is incumbent upon the Court to give meaning to each of the elements, life, liberty and security of the person, which make up the 'right' contained in section 7."[120] At the very least, the threat of physical punishment following removal from Canada would give rise to a section 7 claim against deprivation of "security of the person."

Wilson J. stressed that her greatest concern with the procedural scheme envisaged in the *Immigration Act* "is not . . . with the absence of an oral hearing in and of itself, but with the inadequacy of the opportunity the scheme provides for a refugee claimant to state his case and know the case he has to meet." Some of the information which the Minister of Employment and Immigration might consider could properly be the subject of a valid claim for Crown privilege. However, Her Ladyship specified that lack of detailed knowledge of the Minister's case "is [the] aspect of the procedures set out in the *Act* which I find impossible to reconcile with the requirements of 'fundamental justice' as set out in section 7 of the *Charter*."[121]

While the factual context of *Singh* was obviously different from the parole granting context, it is also noteworthy that Wilson J. explicitly disagreed with the view taken by Pigeon J. in *Mitchell*,[122] whose restrictive view of the applicability of the *Canadian Bill of Rights* to the parole revocation context had limited access by prisoners and parolees to the courts. In Her Ladyship's view, "the recent adoption of the *Charter* by Parliament . . . has sent a clear message to the courts that the restrictive attitude which at times characterized their approach to the *Canadian Bill of Rights* ought to be re-examined."[123] Thus, Wilson J. suggested that the dissenting view of Laskin C.J.C. in *Mitchell* was "to be preferred . . . as we examine the question whether the Charter has any application to the adjudication of rights granted to an individual statute."[124]

In *Macdonald v. National Parole Board*,[125] the prisoner sought to quash a Board decision denying day parole, on the basis that he had not been offered the opportunity for an in-person hearing. Muldoon J. carefully reviewed the two judgments in *Singh* and noted that both Wilson J. and Beetz J. had agreed that the principles of fundamental justice do not necessarily mandate an oral hearing in all cases. According to Muldoon J., what the court found offensive in *Singh* was the fact that "there were . . . accuser(s) and . . . material or other information kept

---

[120] *Ibid.*, at 205.
[121] *Ibid.*, at 214 and 215.
[122] *Mitchell v. R.* (1975), 24 C.C.C. (2d) 241 (S.C.C.). For further discussion see Chapter 4.
[123] *Singh, supra*, note 119, at 209.
[124] *Singh, ibid.*
[125] [1986] 3 F.C. 157 (T.D.).

from the applicant's ken." Thus, where the day parole applicant was "fully informed" of the content of the materials which the Board would be considering, "there was no accuser (known or unknown) in any sense of the word to be faced by the applicant." In such circumstances he was not entitled to an in-person hearing, because "[t]his case ... fits not within the rule formulated in the *Singh* case, but rather within the exceptions expressed by both factions of the Supreme Court."[126]

In evaluating the correctness of this reasoning, it is important to note that *MacDonald* proceeded under Rule 324 of the *Federal Court Rules*, which permits a party to seek judgment "without personal appearance of that party or an attorney or solicitor on his behalf".[127] Thus, the case was decided solely on the basis of affidavit materials and written argument. On the record before Muldoon J. there were affidavits from a Board member and a Board official stating that "the only material which was considered on the applicant's request for day parole were the applicant's own written request and the two reports of progress summary with those favourable recommendations submitted by the case management team, in the preparation of which the applicant was fully informed of content and is said to have actually participated."[128] Were this to be the norm in parole decision-making, the reasoning in the case would be more persuasive. Unfortunately, as will be demonstrated below, the facts in *MacDonald* do not provide a complete picture of the kinds of materials which are usually considered by provincial Boards of Parole or the National Parole Board. A considerable amount of written information considered by the Parole Board is either deliberately withheld or is not disclosed because of the exigencies of time and expense.

A second reason why it is unfortunate that *MacDonald* and a similar judgment in *Eklund v. National Parole Board*[129] were decided without oral argument is that Muldoon J. approved the view of the scope of section 7 of the *Charter* enunciated in *O'Brien v. National Parole Board*[130] without reference to the differing reasoning of Strayer J. in *Staples v. National Parole Board*.[131] In that case, the Board had adjudicated on an application for day parole without affording the applicant an opportunity for an in-person hearing. Strayer J. noted that prior to the advent of the *Charter* it had been held in *Beaumier v. National Parole Board* that "any common law requirement of fairness

---

126 *Ibid.*, at 173.
127 C.R.C. 1978, c. 663.
128 *Supra*, note 125, at 173.
129 [Summarized (1986), 16 W.C.B. 302 (Fed. T.D.)].
130 (1985), 43 C.R. (3d) 10 (Fed. T.D.).
131 (1985), 47 C.R. (3d) 186 (Fed. T.D.).

as to holding a hearing on applications for day parole has been eliminated by s. 11 of the Parole Act."[132] While leaving open the question of whether section 7 of the *Charter* mandated a hearing with respect to an application for day parole, since that issue was not raised by the prisoner, it is significant that Strayer J. expressly disagreed with the characterization of the "liberty interest" postulated in *O'Brien*. He held that he was unable to make a distinction between "a decision to grant or refuse day parole . . . and one as to the revocation of parole. In both cases the decision will mean that an individual will or will not be at liberty." Without expressly referring to *Singh*, Strayer J. held that "[i]f there are distinctions to be drawn between such categories of decisions, they should result in differences in the requirements of fundamental justice or in the kinds of limitations permitted by s. 1 of the Charter".[133]

As discussed in Chapter 4, the premise that an application for limited release is "simply a request" which raises no question of "any constitutionally-enshrined right of liberty, conditional or otherwise,"[134] represents a regressive response to the liberty interest protected by section 7 of the *Charter*. The suggestion that this involves merely a concept of freedom from arbitrary arrest and detention ignores sections 9 to 11 of the *Charter*, which are explicitly intended to ensure protection from those same injustices. It cannot be seriously argued that section 7 was designed to apply generally and restrictively to the same matters. In the United States, it has long been accepted that the concept of liberty encompasses more than physical restraint.[135]

A further difficulty with the view of day parole taken by the court in *O'Brien* and *MacDonald* is that the judgments do not appear to appreciate the concept of staged release enunciated in the 1977 amendments to the *Parole* and *Penitentiary Acts*. Parliament has envisaged that the initial decision to grant unescorted temporary absences represents the Board's first assumption of its statutory obligation to determine whether the prisoner can begin to be released into the community; as such, an application for such form of release is no more a "simple request" than the later application for full parole release. This failure to appreciate the significance of the release "continuum" is revealed in

---

[132] *Ibid.*, at 188. *Beaumier v. National Parole Bd.*, [1981] 1 F.C. 454 (T.D.).

[133] *Supra*, note 131, at 190.

[134] *O'Brien, supra*, note 130, at 22, per McNair J.

[135] *Meyer v. Nebraska* (1923), 262 U.S. 390, 67 L.Ed. 1042, 43 S.Ct. 625, 29 A.L.R. 1446; *Bolling v. Sharpe* (1959), 347 U.S. 497, 98 L.Ed. 884, 74 S.Ct. 693; *Stanley v. Illinois* 405 U.S. 645; *Bd. of Regents of State Colleges v. Roth* (1972), 408 U.S. 564, at 572, per Stewart J. In the Canadian context see the post-*O'Brien* judgment of Lamer J. in *Re Mia and B.C. Medical Services Comm.* (1985), 17 D.L.R. (4th) 385 (S.C.C.), at 411-412. Also see the discussion of "liberty" in Chapter 4.

McNair J.'s judgment in *Browning v. National Parole Board*,[136] a case argued at the same time as *O'Brien*. In that case the prisoner had applied for both unescorted temporary absence and day parole. He asserted in his uncontradicted affidavit that the attending Board members had informed him "that they were favourably disposed to granting five unescorted temporary absences per month on a program of preparation for day parole subject to obtaining the required approval votes of other members".[137] A few weeks later he received a letter indicating that day parole had been denied, but no reference was made to release on unescorted temporary absence.

Under section 23(3)(*a*) of the Regulations in force at that time, if the first three members cast negative votes, there was no obligation to submit the case to other Board members. McNair J. concluded that:

> The evidence . . . viewed in totality, is to point unwaveringly to the irresistible inference that the three board members who personally interviewed the applicant . . . must have voted unanimously to deny his application for day parole. . . . Unescorted temporary absence may have been discussed . . . but I am satisfied, . . . that the raison d'être of the hearing and the decision made in respect thereof were concerned only with an application for day parole, and nothing more.[138]

While the three attending members may have unanimously decided not to grant day parole, this scarcely satisfies the prisoner's complaint that those same Board members told him that they would vote in favour of unescorted temporary absences leading eventually to day parole, which was later denied, apparently on the basis of the votes of absent members. Thus, with respect to the U.T.A. decision, the same result as *O'Brien* should have occurred.

In *MacDonald*, Muldoon J. attempted to draw a disctinction between applications for conditional release and parole revocation proceedings, suggesting that in the former case "the inmate is the actor who, in effect, places his own progress and behaviour before the Parole Board in order to persuade it to grant the request. . . . This may be contrasted with revocation proceedings in which the Board is the actor in calling upon the parolee, in effect, to explain his reported misbehaviour, failing justification for which he may be returned to prison."[139] While this view is superficially attractive, it simply fails to take into account the realities of parole decision-making. Even assuming full disclosure, it is always the prisoner who must justify his position. Furthermore, the analysis

---

[136] (1985), 43 C.R. (3d) 31 (Fed. T.D.).
[137] *Ibid.*, at 33.
[138] *Ibid.*, at 38.
[139] *Supra*, note 125, at 175.

fails to make any logical distinction between day and full parole granting. Muldoon J. appears to have been considerably influenced by the
fact that "Parliament has ordained, by section 11 of the *Parole Act*, that
the inmate seeking day parole is not entitled to be personally interviewed" and that "[t]his Court ought not unnecessarily to tack on to
those principles any extra procedures which conflict with the scheme of
the legislation."[140] While this is factually correct, it ignores the responsibility placed by section 1 of the *Charter* on the party seeking to deprive
a party of his rights to justify that decision. Beyond saying that "[a]fter
the judgments in *O'Brien* and *Ford*, the Board had to change the policy"
(of granting an in-person hearing at first day parole review) the material
before Muldoon J. did not disclose why a distinction could or should be
drawn between applicants for day and full parole.[141]

In sum, three compelling arguments can be raised in support of in-
person hearings in all cases. First, as discussed above, the narrow view of
"liberty" articulated by McNair J. in *O'Brien* cannot be sustained.
Secondly, until the release of the judgment in *O'Brien*, Board practice
for many years had been to hold in-person hearings in cases involving
applications for unescorted temporary absence and day parole by penitentiary prisoners. By so doing, the Board itself had recognized both the
importance of the issues at stake and the interest of fair and accurate
decision-making.[142] Finally, a full appreciation of the issue at stake in
day parole decision-making supports the view that a hearing must be
held as such applications involve issues of gravity and importance to the
individual; as such, day parole applications fit the rule formulated in
Singh.[143]

---

[140] *Supra*, note 125, at 174 and 176.

[141] Although the process of case preparation formally encompasses only day and full
parole applications, it is usual that recommendations concerning unescorted temporary absence are forwarded to the Board at the same time, since, in most cases,
eligibility for this form of release arises at the same time as first eligibility for release on
day parole.

[142] In this context reference might be made to the judgment of Dickson J. in *Martineau
(No. 2), supra*, note 138, where he held that a reviewing court might well look to the
historical practices of the decision-maker. This is akin to the concept of reasonable
expectation discussed in *Council of Civil Service Unions v. Minister for the Civil
Service*, [1985] A.C. 374.

[143] *Singh v. Minister of Employment & Immigration* [1985], 1 S.C.R. 177. Similar arguments could be developed in relation to in-person hearings before the Ontario Board of
Parole, as section 41(2) of the Ontario Regulations purports to empower the Board to
dispense with an in-person hearing where the prisoner is serving a sentence of less than
6 months. This situation would be unlikely to arise in Quebec, because section 32 of
the enabling legislation (S.Q. 1978, c. 22) provides that the prisoner is entitled, as a
matter of right, to a hearing before the Parole Commission.

Although section 17 of the Act was not amended in 1986, sections 14.2(3) and 15(1) of the Regulations were enacted to provide, with certain minor exemptions, that day and full parole reviews are to be conducted by way of hearing.[144] While no right to a hearing is given to provincial prisoners in those provinces where the National Parole Board has jurisdiction, Board policy is that hearings are held in considering applications for full parole, so long as the application is received more than four months before the expiry of the term.

(d) The Decision-Making Process[145]

(i) *Timing*

Once the various materials described above have been collected, the C.M.O.I. and the P.O. are required to prepare for the Board an overall assessment containing summaries of the materials together with their recommendations. Regulations 14.1 and 14.2(3) provide that the Board is required to conduct its review of applications for day or full parole on or before the prisoner's day or full parole eligibility dates.[146] While the Board makes every effort to complete the review process approximately 1 month before the eligibility date (so that necessary release formalities may be completed in good time if conditional release is granted following the review), it often transpires that information considered necessary by the Board in its determination is not available at the time the review takes place.[147] In this context, it is important to

---

[144] SOR/86-915, s. 2. It is noteworthy that in detention cases, section 21.4(2)(*b*) of the Act details that such cases are to be conducted by way of hearing.

[145] The following subjects are also discussed in Chapters 8 and 12.

[146] There are several exceptions to this rule contained in the Regulations and the *Policy and Procedures Manual*. Where the prisoner is serving a sentence of less than 2 years, the Board is not required to conduct a review for full parole if the application is received earlier than 4 months before a prisoner's full parole eligibility date, or if the application is received later than 4 months before expiry of the term of imprisonment. Where the sentence is 2 years or more, or where a prisoner has been transferred to a penitentiary pursuant to a federal/provincial transfer agreement, the Board is not required to conduct a review for full parole (a) if the prisoner signifies in writing that he does wish it to be considered, (b) if the prisoner signifies that he wishes his review to be conducted without hearing, (c) where the prisoner is a federal inmate confined in a provincial institution, or (d) when the prisoner is unlawfully at large on the full parole eligibility date.

[147] This has been a recurrent problem for many years. In their book, *The Parole Process: A Study of the National Parole Board* (Ottawa: Law Reform Commission of Canada, 1977), pp. 78-79, Carriere and Silverstone, noted:

Our discussions with Parole and Penitentiary Service Officers, and with Board

note the exact wording of the Regulations, which provides that the full parole review "shall be by way of hearing". It would therefore appear that where, at the conclusion of the in-person hearing, the Board wishes to defer decision pending the obtaining or verification of further information, the Board would be obligated to reconvene the hearing (should the prisoner insist) before taking a final decision. Although this precise issue does not appear to have been directly litigated, the case of *Calvin v. National Parole Board (No. 1)*[148] provides some support for this position. In that case the prisoner had applied for full parole and sought, in advance of the hearing, "all relevant information in the possession of the Board" pursuant to [then] section 17(1) of the Regulations. While [then] section 17(2) provided that, if the Board elected to supply that information in writing, it was required to do so at least 15 days prior to the date fixed for hearing, the Regulation did not make provision for disclosure in advance where the Board elected to provide the information orally. The evidence established that the Board had adopted a practice of advising prisoners only at the commencement of the hearing. Complaining that this gave him no opportunity to study the material and to prepare his response, the prisoner launched an action for *mandamus*. Collier J. agreed and ordered that, having elected to furnish information orally rather than in writing, all relevant information must be provided at least 36 hours before the hearing. Thus, if the Board is required to provide advance notice of information in its possession, it would appear that, unless the prisoner is prepared and in a position to provide an informed waiver, the Board would be under an obligation to reconvene the hearing where further information is required.[149]

(ii) *Board Members*

As previously discussed, the judgment in *O'Brien* and the subsequent changes in the Regulations indicate that upon a review for full

members and our observations at hearings indicated that Board members were occasionally reluctant to rely on case preparation as documented in the inmate's file. The frequency of inadequate, inconsistent and late preparation was a cause for this reluctance ... The parole hearing became in some cases the only opportunity for Board members to acquire information and opinion, to test them through questioning, to request further work.

[148] (Fed. T.D., Collier J., June 30, 1980).
[149] Section 17(3) of the Regulations details that where the Board elects to provide information in writing to parole granting cases, it shall do so at least 15 days prior to the hearing date, unless information comes to the Board's attention after that date, in which case it is to be disclosed "as soon as practicable" (s. 17(4)). In practice, the Case Management Team delivers copies of the materials they consider appropriate to release to the prisoner. It should not be assumed that these materials are identical with those in the Board's possession.

parole by the National Parole Board, all voting Board members must be present. Similarly, if the Board elects to hold a hearing where it is not obligated by the Regulations to do so, all voting Board members must be in attendance.

It should also be noted that section 8(1) of the Act authorizes the Solicitor General to appoint "regional community board members" to consider applications for conditional release made by, or on behalf of, prisoners serving life minimum or indeterminate sentences or sentences of death commuted to life imprisonment. Where such members have been appointed, at least two must participate in each sitting, in which case each regional community board member has the same powers as the other Board members at the hearing for which he was selected. Board policy is that such members are not generally involved in decisions to modify previously granted terms and conditions, except where day parole is to be expanded or extended.

At the provincial level, section 36 of the Regulations[150] directs that at least two Board members must vote on an application for parole. In our experience three Board members usually attend parole granting hearings.

(iii) *Parole Officers and Institutional Personnel*

Current Board and Correctional Service of Canada (C.S.C.) policy is that, whenever possible, all members of the prisoner's case management team are to be present at the parole hearing. These persons are usually asked for their input during the course of the hearing.

As mentioned during the discussion of confidentiality issues, above, prior to the decisions in *Couperthwaite*[151] and *Latham*,[152] Board policy was to permit members of the case management team to meet privately with the attending Board members both prior to the entry of the prisoner into the hearing room and subsequently while the Board was considering its decision. As a result of these decisions the Board has now ceased this practice, except when delicate issues of disclosure of confidential information are raised.[153]

---

[150] SOR/86-915, s. 8.

[151] *Couperthwaite v. National Parole Bd.* (1982), 31 C.R. (3d) 50 (Fed. T.D.).

[152] *Latham v. Canada (Solicitor General)* (1984), 39 C.R. (3d) 78 (Fed. T.D.).

[153] An interesting variation of this is reported in *Appeal Division Reports*, Case No. "PROC 017," where the prisoner wished to share some confidential information with the Board in the absence of his case management team. The Appeal Division ruled as follows:

> If an inmate wishes to address the Board in private, he may request to do so. Once the inmate's Case Management Officers have left, the Board will listen to the

(iv) *Assistants*

Section 27(1)(*i*) of the *Parole Act* authorizes the Governor in Council to establish regulations respecting the circumstances in which prisoners are entitled to assistance at hearings and the nature of such assistance. Although not proclaimed at the same time as most of the other regulatory changes necessitated by the 1977 legislation,[154] section 20.1 of the Regulations now provides that the prisoner has a right to the presence of an assistant at all parole reviews conducted by way of hearing. No equivalent regulations have been enacted under the *Penitentiary Act* to provide for assistance upon consideration of applications for unescorted temporary absences in the discretion of an institutional director. However, it is rare that any formal hearing is convened to consider such applications; it is our experience that institutional personnel will receive and consider written or oral submissions. Even when the prisoner attends with a lawyer, the Board maintains the pretense of referring to the lawyer as an assistant rather than counsel. Clearly, there is no magic in the nomenclature and no greater or lesser entitlements attach depending on what the Board calls someone.

Section 3(1) of the Regulations excludes the application of Part I of the Regulations to provincial parole boards. Consequently, nothing in the federal legislation requires a provincial parole board to allow assistants at hearings. Section 32 of the Quebec parole statute explicitly entitles a prisoner hearing before the Quebec Parole Commission to be represented by a person "other than another inmate imprisoned in another house of detention". The Ontario and British Columbia statutes are silent on this subject; however, these authorities will permit assistants to attend, subject to obtaining a security clearance from the institution.

There appears to be no statutory entitlement for an assistant to appear at hearings before a provincial temporary absence board. The

---

reasons for the request. If it does not consider the request to be well-founded, the Case Management Officers may be recalled, and the hearing is to proceed in their presence. The Case Management Officers will then be told the reasons for the inmate's request. If the Board decides that the request is well-founded, then the inmate is allowed to make his representations without the Officers in attendance. When the inmate has finished, the Case Management Officers are recalled and the hearing will continue as usual. It should be noted that the Board may disclose all or part of the information received in confidence with the Case Management Team if it feels there is no valid reason not to do so.

[154] Most of these Regulations were proclaimed in force on August 9, 1978 by SOR/78-628. Section 20.1 was proclaimed in force on April 9, 1981, by SOR/81-318. The wording was altered by SOR/86-817, s. 7.

Quebec statute providing for representation is limited to parole applications. The Ontario and British Columbia statutes contain no reference to this subject. In our experience applications to have an assistant present will be rejected in all but the rarest cases,[155] although written submissions and supporting documentation will be received and considered.

Section 20.1(2) of the Regulations states that the prisoner is to make arrangements for the assistant to attend. Well in advance of the hearing, the prisoner must indicate in writing to his case management team that he wishes to have an assistant present in order that a security clearance may be obtained. This form should be forwarded to the relevant custodial authorities and to the Regional Office of the Board no later than 14 working days before the scheduled hearing. Hearing dates and times will generally not be adjusted to suit the convenience of the assistant.[156]

It remains to be determined whether there is an absolute right to counsel at a conditional release hearing, and whether there may be a correlative obligation on the part of provincially-funded legal aid plans to provide funding. While this issue is likely to be more acute for a prisoner facing a post-suspension hearing as a result of a new criminal charge, it should be noted that in *Latham*, Strayer J. cautioned that the absence of counsel in a matter of this gravity will be an important factor in assuring the fairness of the process "if the board . . . is not able to demonstrate that it took some initiatives to give the parolee every reasonable opportunity to retain counsel, the integrity of its processes will in my view be vulnerable to attack on the ground of denial of fairness".[157]

(v) *Factors Considered*

The *Parole Act* provides little guidance as to the criteria which the Board should address in considering an application for conditional release. In deciding on an application for unescorted temporary absence the only relevant reference is in section 13, which merely provides that

---

[155] R.R.O. 1980, Reg. 649, s. 37(4) appears to authorize the Superintendent of an institution to permit "any other person" to attend. In practice, this is limited to interpreters.
[156] In *R. v. Roberts* Weekly Court File no. 2632/84, Ont. H.C., October 24, 1984, the prisoner had received no prior notice of the date of her post-suspension hearing before the Ontario Board of Parole. The Board denied a request for a brief adjournment to permit a social worker to be present as her "assistant". Boland J. quashed the revocation decision on the basis of unfairness and ordered a new hearing. A similar result was reached by Gray J. in *R. v. Smith* [summarized (1988), 6 W.C.B. (2d) 157 (Ont. H.C.)].
[157] *Supra*, note 152, at 92.

the Board has (subject to unescorted absences granted by other officials) "absolute discretion to grant or refuse to grant . . . a temporary absence without escort".

Section 16 of the Act provides that day parole may be granted if the Board considers that "the reform and rehabilitation of the inmate will be aided by the grant of [day] parole" and that "the release of the inmate on [day] parole would not constitute an undue risk to society". Where a grant of full parole is being considered, section 16(1)(*a*)(i) of the Act additionally directs the Board to consider whether the prisoner "has derived the maximum benefit from imprisonment". While the vagueness of these statutory criteria was sharply critized by Pierre Carriere and Sam Silverstone,[158] section 16 has not been substantially amended in either the 1977 or the 1986 revisions. This is particularly curious when it is recalled that, when the detention provisions were enacted as part of the 1986 amendments, section 15.4(4.1) [now s. 21.4(5)] of the Act detailed a list of factors which the Board is to take into account in deciding to exercise its powers under that section.

Severe public criticism was levelled at the Board following several homicides committed by persons on various forms of conditional release in 1987 and 1988. As a result, Board policies have become more explicitly oriented towards the assessment of risk. In addition to the case specific materials which the Board requires case managers to obtain, and reports from mental health professionals, the Board also examines general statistical data on recidivism. However, recognizing that over-reliance on such information would not only tend to remove the human element from decision-making, but might also leave the Board open to a charge that it would be improperly fettering its discretion, the policy is that such data is to be used only as one of a number of factors in the decision-making process. Other factors usually considered are:

— the criminal record, kinds of offences and their pattern, and length of crime-free periods between convictions;
— the nature of the current offence and how serious it was;
— what understanding the inmate appears to have of the situation that brought him to prison, and what he has done about it;
— what the inmate has done while in prison including training, educational and employment upgrading activities;
— institutional behaviour, offences;
— if there were any prior releases on temporary absences or day parole, how well had the inmate conducted himself;
— whether the inmate has any previous parole violations;
— what the relationship with family and friends is like;

---

158 *Supra*, note 147, pp. 121-143.

—what plans the inmate has for employment or training and how definite they are;
—what plans the inmate has for release including:
—where he would live;
—who, outside, could and would help him;
—how he feels his plans will keep him out of trouble;
—the possible effect on the community, if he were to return to a life of criminal activity;
—his personality, particularly his presence or absence of potential for physical harm to a member of the community"[159]

It should not be assumed that these are the only factors which are likely to be considered. For example, Carriere and Silverstone point out that "pre-decision contacts . . . defined as contributions to a parole file that take the form of a recommendation, evaluation or summary regarding the readiness for parole of an inmate . . . greatly influence the consideration of a case by Board members."[160] Similarly, personal knowledge of a prisoner, from perusal of a file or from previous conditional release hearings, often influence subsequent consideration of a case by Board members.[161]

A not infrequent occurrence is that an appeal against conviction or sentence may still be outstanding at the time the prisoner becomes eligible for conditional release. As part of the general process of case preparation, the prisoner's C.M.O.I. is expected to advise the Board as to the status of such matters.[162] If charges or Crown appeals are still outstanding at the time of an application for unescorted temporary absence, power to grant this form of release is always retained by the Board and is not delegated to the institutional director, regardless of the length of sentence.[163] Where any form of discretionary release is sought at a point where charges or Crown appeals are still outstanding, usual Board policy is to reserve decision for up to 4 months while further enquiries are made.[164] This policy arises in part because a successful Crown appeal against sentence or a further conviction and sentence may

---

[159] National Parole Board, A Guide to Conditional Release for Penitentiary Inmates (Ottawa: Supply & Services Canada, 1982).

[160] *Supra*, note 147, p. 141.

[161] In a series of decisions (*Appeal Division Reports*, Case Nos. "LEGAL 001-003," October 28 and December 1, 1987) the Appeal Division of the National Parole Board has decided that "general deterrence" is *not* a factor to be considered as part of conditional release decision-making, "since the Court deals with the general deterrence factor . . . in setting sentence." Further, "[i]ndividual deterrence is only relevant insofar as it is related to the risk of reoffending."

[162] C.S.C. *Case Management Policy and Procedures Manual*, s. 11.3.10, unpublished.

[163] National Parole Board, *Policy and Procedures Manual*, s. VIII C.2.2.3.2(b).

[164] See 3 Criminal Lawyers Association Newsletter (No. 10) July 1979, p. 6.

result in the prisoner no longer being eligible for parole. An example of this arose in *Rondeau v. Commission québécoise des libérations conditionelles*[165] where a prisoner serving a term of 6 months was granted and released on parole. Following his release a Crown appeal against sentence was allowed, and the sentence was increased to 2 years. Since the prisoner was not yet eligible for parole on the new sentence, the Quebec parole commission purported to revoke his parole on the basis that he was not yet eligible for release. The prisoner launched *habeas corpus* proceedings, arguing that he had not breached any conditions of his release. The court held that the propriety of the revocation was not in issue since the original parole had been "rendered inoperative" by the imposition of the higher sentence. For this reason, the Board's general policy of reserving decision pending the outcome of a Crown appeal against acquittal or sentence is tenable.

A related difficulty arises where the prisoner has outstanding arrest warrants or charges outstanding at the time he has a pending application for conditional release. Although there is no formal Board policy on point, the Board will sometimes insist that such matters be disposed of before a final decision is taken, at least if the warrants are "Canada wide". If the prisoner knows of the existence of the warrants or charges for indictable offences, and is prepared to enter a plea of guilty, he can take advantage of the appropriate sections of the *Code*[166] and "waive in" the charges. However, despite the fact that the prisoner's C.M.O.I. is obliged to attempt to confirm the existence of such matters as part of the process of case preparation, it sometimes transpires that, either unwittingly or by design, institutional authorities are not made aware of outstanding warrants or charges. The Fauteux Committee noted that it was a deliberate policy on the part of some police forces to "hold" an arrest warrant until the prisoner was scheduled to be released. Prior to the enactment of the *Charter*, Canadian courts joined with the Fauteux Committee in condemning such practices. For example, in *Burke*, the prisoner was about to be released at the conclusion of a custodial sentence, when "he was arrested and charged with the same type of offence allegedly committed four days prior to the date of the commission of the offence upon which he was previously convicted."[167] Hartt J. concluded that "[t]he procedure followed here, to use as neutral a word as possible, was most unfortunate"[168] and reduced the sentence to one of time served. A similar view was expressed by the British Columbia

---

[165] (Que. Sup. Ct., November 13, 1979).
[166] Ss. 478(3), 479.
[167] *R. v. Burke*, [1968] 2 C.C.C. 124 (Ont. C.A.), at 126.
[168] *Ibid.*

Court of Appeal in *Parisien*,[169] where, in reducing an otherwise fit sentence, Branca J.A. indicated that in order to take advantage of the *Code* provisions, an accused needs to know what warrants have been issued against him and that to withhold this information is unfair.

Since the enactment of the *Charter*, the courts have, through sections 7 and 11(*b*), greater power to control their own processes and have begun to impose stays of proceedings more frequently. The leading case to date in this area is *Young*,[170] where the Ontario Court of Appeal considered a fact situation in which various law enforcement authorities had been aware of possible charges of fraud and swearing a false affidavit since 1977, but no charges were laid until April, 1983. The trial judge had directed a stay of proceedings on the basis of section 11(*b*) of the *Charter*. The court held that this ruling was erroneous because in general section 11(*b*) "cannot be invoked if there is no delay between the time of the charge and the time of trial."[171] However, the court took an expansive view of section 7 of the *Charter*, holding that the section was not limited to the right to a fair hearing in accordance with the principles of natural justice. Section 7 could be used "where compelling an accused to stand trial would violate those fundamental principles of justice which underlie the community's sense of fair play and decency and to prevent the abuse of a court's process through oppressive or vexatious proceedings."[172] Despite this broad power the court noted that the power to enter a stay should be sparingly exercised by a trial judge. Extending its previous ruling in *Antoine*,[173] the court held that "absent any finding that the delay in the institution of the proceedings was for an ulterior purpose of depriving the accused of the opportunity of making full answer and defence, delay in itself . . . is not a basis for a stay of process." Nevertheless, where "executive action leading to the institution of proceedings is offensive to the principles upon which the administration of justice is conducted by the courts," it would be appropriate to direct a stay of proceedings.[174] Thus, where the police deliberately or by inadvertence "hold" a warrant, or where Crown counsel unreasonably refuses to consent to waive in a charge,[175] it might be possible to argue that a stay of proceedings should be ordered by the trial judge.

An example of this in the parole context arose in *Cardinal*,[176] where a charge of possession of stolen property was outstanding in a suburb of

---

[169] *R. v. Parisien* (1971), 3 C.C.C. (2d) 433 (B.C. C.A.).
[170] *R. v. Young* (1984), 13 C.C.C. (3d) 1 (Ont. C.A.).
[171] *Ibid.*, at 4.
[172] *Ibid.*, at 31.
[173] *R. v. Antoine* (1983), 5 C.C.C. (3d) 97 (Ont. C.A.).
[174] *Supra*, note 170, at 31 and 32.
[175] See *Foley v. Court of Sessions of the Peace* (1989), 66 C.R. (3d) 91 (Que. S.C.).
[176] *R. v. Cardinal* (1985), 21 C.C.C. (3d) 254 (Alta. C.A.).

Calgary. Upon learning that the accused was serving a sentence for another offence in British Columbia, the police officer in charge "decided to spare the public the expense of bringing him . . . to Calgary . . . under escort." When the authorities realized that the accused had applied for parole to Calgary, the officer in charge "figured when he got released we'd pick him up there . . . [Calgary]",[177] and took no further steps either to have the warrant validated outside the geographical jurisdiction of the signing justice under section 461 [now s. 528] of the *Code*, or to have the prisoner brought back. In considering a Crown appeal from an order quashing a committal for trial on the basis of unreasonable delay, Kerans J.A. noted that the behaviour of the authorities placed the accused in a "Hobson's choice" — he could either remain in jail in British Columbia by not accepting the parole condition that he return to Calgary upon release, or he could go to Calgary to be arrested on the outstanding charge."[178] It is significant that the court carefully tied its reasons for dismissing the Crown appeal to the rehabilitative purposes of parole. Since conditional release "is supposed to be carefully planned and conscientiously executed. . . . [a]rrest upon arrival would be totally disruptive of that plan. Failure to take this into account is unacceptable." Had the warrant been executed promptly, and had a consecutive sentence been imposed, this might have delayed parole eligibility. However "[t]hat sentence would have permitted a structured and organized plan of rehabilitation: it would not have totally disrupted such a plan. . . . parole would have been meaningful and [the prisoner's] life might have changed."[179]

A further extension of the application of section 7 to a delay issue arose in *Parker v. Canada (Solicitor General)*,[180] where the prisoner launched an action to clarify the date when he might apply for a "15 — year review" of his ineligibility for parole, pursuant to section 745 of the *Code*. An information charging the accused with murder was sworn in Ontario on November 12, 1975. At that time the officer who swore the information knew that the accused was in custody in Alberta awaiting trial on another matter. No steps were taken to arrest the accused either pursuant to section 528 of the *Code*, or by bringing the accused before the court in Ontario. The Alberta trial concluded in January 1976, but the police did not take any steps to arrest the prisoner until he was transferred to an Ontario penitentiary by the Correctional Service of Canada in May 1976. Due to the wording of section 746(*a*) of the *Code*,

---

177 *Ibid.*, at 256.
178 *Ibid.*, at 258.
179 *Ibid.*, at 256 and 258.
180 *Parker v. Canada (Solicitor General)* (Ont. H.C., Henry J., May 18, 1990).

which provides that in calculating time served for purposes of section 745 time spent in custody following arrest "in respect of the offence for which he was sentenced to imprisonment for life", the penal authorities took the position that the prisoner would not be eligible to seek a review of his status until 15 years had elapsed from the actual date of his arrest in May 1976.

After acknowledging that *Gamble*[181] was "instructive" to the extent that it recognized that a particular period of parole ineligibility deprived a prisoner of a constitutionally-protected liberty interest, Henry J. noted that while the Supreme Court had acknowledged that "there was a discretion in the court to require [Gamble] to rely on the ordinary appeal procedures" that court had "adopted a flexible and purposive approach to the enforcement of her *Charter* rights"[182] and had fashioned an appropriate *Charter* remedy by declaring her to be eligible for parole immediately. In the case at bar the unfairness in not executing the warrant for 6 months offended "one of the basic tenets of our legal system. ... fair treatment in the administration of justice",[183] and thereby contravened section 7. Nor did it matter that, on the facts, no one (the police, Crown or defence counsel, or even the sentencing judge) had appreciated the potential problem:

> The impairment of the applicant's fundamental rights under s. 7 need not be deliberate or malicious, or for an ulterior motive to attract the protection of s. 7; the fact of that impairment, even if unthinking or inadvertent, is sufficient.[184]

Because there had been an "abuse of the executive power of prosecution" Henry J. found that there had been a breach of the principles of fundamental justice of sufficient gravity such that to allow section 746(*a*) to be applied mechanically would offend "the community's sense of fair play and decency".[185] In result, Henry J. allowed the application and issued an order that the prisoner "be at liberty to serve, file and pursue an application for judicial review ... on or after November 12, 1990."[186]

Where this leaves the prisoner vis-a-vis the Board is not, in law, entirely clear. In practice, our experience is that Board members are

---

[181] *Gamble v. R.* (1988), 66 C.R. (3d) 193 (S.C.C.).

[182] *Supra*, note 183, at 8.

[183] Quoting *Re Lawrence and R.* (1989), 47 C.C.C. (3d) 462 (Nfld. S.C.), at 473.

[184] *Supra*, note 180, at 14.

[185] Quoting *R. v. Keyowski* (1988), 40 C.C.C. (3d) 481 (S.C.C.), at 482.

[186] *Supra*, note 180, at 29. The court noted that "the rememdy creates the fiction that, for the narrow purpose here required, the thing that ought to have been done is deemed to have been done."

suspicious of the continued existence of warrants or charges which have not been disposed of despite the prisoner's efforts to do so.[187] Unless the charges are particularly serious, the Board will often grant parole, and leave it to the parole supervisor to monitor their progress through the courts. However, in *Pizzuro v. National Parole Board*[188] the Board declined to grant parole because of the existence of outstanding charges similar to the offences for which the prisoner was serving sentence. It was argued that this decision violated the presumption of innocence. Jerome A.C.J. held in a brief judgment that the Board's power to exercise its "absolute discretion" was indicative of Parliamentary intention that the Board could consider outstanding charges. This difficult issue is discussed in more detail in Chapter 8.

(e) Types of Decisions

After the Board has retired to consider its decision, the parties are invited into the hearing room to hear the result and a summary of the Board's reasons, pursuant to section 19 of the Regulations. Where the Board elects to defer decision pending confirmation of facts related to the information discussed at the hearing, no new hearing need be held, although the final decision must be taken by the same Board members who attended at the hearing.[189] Where the decision is to deny or defer conditional release the Board is required by section 19(2) to provide, within 15 days, written reasons for the decision taken. In 2 or 4 votes cases where the Board members "split", the case will be put over for a new hearing with a panel comprised of different members. Immediately following the hearing the Board members write up their comments for the file, which form the basis of these reasons.

---

[187] Conversely, in criminal court a stay of proceedings is unlikely to be ordered if there is evidence that the prisoner knew of outstanding charges and did nothing to dispose of them. See *R. v. Brackenbury* [summarized (1988), 4 W.C.B. (2d) 128 and 333 (Alta. C.A.)] and *R. v. Bojkovic* [summarized (1988), 5 W.C.B. (2d) 408 (Ont. H.C.)].

[188] (Docket no. T-2035-85, Fed. T.D., October 18, 1985).

[189] In the view of the Appeal Division these procedures must be strictly followed. In *Appeal Division Reports*, Case No. "PROC 008," September 23, 1987, the Appeal Division decided that a final decision conducted on paper on the basis of a new psychiatric report requested by the panel members was improper, both because such a report "involves a subjective analysis of its content by Board members," and because "one of the voting members was not present at the hearing." Similarly, even where a panel hearing need not be reconvened, the prisoner must be advised of the confirmed (or new) factual information and be given at least 15 days to respond (*Appeal Division Reports*, Case No. "PROC 011," September 17, 1987).

(i) Denials

Where an application for full parole on the part of a prisoner serving a sentence of 3 years or less is denied at day parole eligibility date, section 15(3) of the Regulations directs that the Board shall conduct another full parole review in the 6 months preceding the full parole eligibility date. However, section 15(4) indicates that where less than 6 months have elapsed since the day parole review, the Board is not obligated to conduct the review by way of hearing. Further, unless there is significant new information, the time constraints imposed by the Board's policy of insisting on a fresh or updated community assessment upon each application tends to reduce the number of such applications. Where the sentence is more than 3 years, the Board is obligated by section 15(5) of the Regulations to hold a full parole hearing in the 6 months preceding the full parole eligibility date. If the Board denies full parole at full parole eligibility date, section 15(6) directs that the prisoner is not eligible for a new hearing until 2 years later.[190] However, nothing in the Regulations precludes the Board from setting a review date sooner than 2 years from the date of the negative decision. This might arise where the Board decides at the time of the initial hearing to refuse full parole, but to grant unescorted temporary absences or day parole. A new full parole review date will often be set to coincide with the expiry of the day parole period.

An unsuccessful applicant may appeal a denial or a deferral to the Appeal Division of the Board. This subject is discussed in Chapter 8.

(ii) Parole for Voluntary Departure or Deportation

A prisoner serving sentence in a federal or provincial institution may apply to the appropriate parole authority for full parole release in order to be deported or removed under the *Immigration Act*, to be surrendered under the *Extradition Act*[191] or the *Fugitive Offenders Act*,[192] or to leave voluntarily for another country upon release.[193] The

---

[190] If the prisoner is again denied full parole at that time, s. 15(6) provides that he is entitled to a review at 2-year intervals.

[191] R.S.C. 1985, c. E-23.

[192] R.S.C. 1985, c. F-32.

[193] Applications may also be made pursuant to sections 11.1(c) or 31.1(e) of the *Parole Regulations* for parole by exception for the purpose of deportation. Such applications are rarely granted prior to full parole eligibility date, unless the release is for surrender under the *Extradition Act* or the *Fugitive Offenders Act*. Reference should be made also to section 24 of the *Extradition Act*. Although that section refers to a person serving sentence in Canada not being "surrendered until after he has been discharged . . . by

latter form of release applies to persons who, in addition to Canadian citizenship or some other right of entry into Canada (who are therefore not deportable) hold citizenship or a right of entry into another country. In such cases, parole can be granted by a parole board upon condition that the parolee not return to Canada prior to the termination of the sentence imposed. In the event that the prisoner returns to Canada without prior permission before warrant expiry date, a warrant suspending parole is usually issued and the case is referred to the appropriate parole board for a decision as to whether or not to revoke the release.

Section 54(1) of the *Immigration Act*[194] provides that any person under an order of deportation or order of removal may be permitted to leave Canada voluntarily. Thus, if the immigration authorities elect not to execute a deportation order,[195] full parole may be granted by a parole board to facilitate a voluntary departure. One of the factors which may influence immigration and parole authorities in making a decision whether or not to execute a deportation order is cost; in the event of voluntary departure C.S.C. is responsible for the cost of escort to the point of departure and for ensuring that the prisoner pays for travel outside Canada. If a deportation order is executed, the federal Department of Employment and Immigration is responsible for all costs.

Regardless of the form of parole for departure from Canada, for the purpose section 52(2) of the *Immigration Act*, unless parole is revoked prior to warrant expiry date, the sentence of a prisoner granted parole for deportation is deemed to be completed once the prisoner has left Canada. In the event the prisoner returns to Canada with the prior approval of both parole and immigration officials during the pendency of the sentence, the parolee continues on parole subject to any terms and conditions imposed by the parole authorities.

Prior to the passing of the *Immigration Act*, and a series of amendments to the *Parole Act* during the mid-1970s, some confusion arose as to the stage at which a prisoner could be deported.[196] It was at least

---

expiration of his sentence", the Federal Department of Justice takes the position that an Extradition Order may be executed as soon as a prisoner is eligible for parole, irrespective of whether parole is granted. The Minister has discretion to direct that the order be executed; the Minister will consider, of course, whether or not the parole authorities are prepared to grant parole.

[194] S.C. 1976-77 c. 52 [proclaimed in force April 10, 1978].

[195] Now referred under some sections of the *Immigration Act* as a "Removal Order". See 1976-77, c. 52 [as amended by 1977-78, c. 22, s. 16; 1980-81-82-83, c. 47, s. 23 and Schedule 1, item 5].

[196] For a more detailed discussion of the problems faced by non-Canadians confined in Canadian penal institutions, see I. Kelly, "Immigration, Parole and the Alien Offender" (1977), 3 Queen's L.J. 450.

arguable that a prisoner could not be deported until a period of parole had been successfully completed. However, section 13(3) [now s. 19(3)] of the *Parole Act*[197] was amended to provide that once a prisoner is paroled, his term of imprisonment is deemed under the *Immigration Act* to be completed; thus, a deportation order can be executed and the prisoner deported immediately upon release from close custody. It should be noted, however, that where an appeal against a deportation order is, pending, it is a common practice of parole boards to decline to grant parole until the appeal process is completed, unless a release order has been made by an immigration adjudicator, the Immigration Appeal Board or the courts, pending disposition of an appeal.

Provincial and federal parole boards are quite restrictive in grant-　・ ing full parole releases to non-Canadians to remain in Canada except in cases where a deportable prisoner will not be accepted by another country, and hence must remain in Canada upon expiry of sentence in any event. However, day parole and temporary absence are more available to prisoners in this situation. Section 13(3) [now s. 19(3)] of the *Parole Act* was amended in the 1977 amendments[198] to exclude day paroles from the categories of persons, who, when released by the National Parole Board, become subject to immediate deportation under the *Immigration Act*. At the federal level, day paroles and unescorted temporary absence passes are sometimes granted to alien offenders for purposes of study or work.[199] Because section 21(2) of the *Parole Act*, by referring to section 19 of the Act, deems a person subject to mandatory supervision to be "a paroled inmate on parole," deportation can be effected immediately upon release on mandatory supervision.

Apart from ensuring that a prisoner who leaves Canada voluntarily does not return to Canada during the pendency of the remanet of the sentence, the National Parole Board has, in the past, attempted to have the receiving country exercise "voluntary supervision" over the parolee. Despite the broad powers given to the National Parole Board to impose terms and conditions upon release and to suspend and revoke parole or

---

[197] S.C. 1976-77, c. 53, s. 27. This section was further amended by S.C. 1986, c. 43, s. 8 to confirm that prisoners who surrendered under the *Extradition Act* or the *Fugitive Offenders Act* were in the same position.

[198] S.C. 1976-77, c. 53, s. 28.

[199] Where a day parole or unescorted temporary absence release is granted for employment purposes by the federal authorities, the National Parole Board, *Policy and Procedures Manual* (s. V.E.5.2) specifies that no such release may be effected until the prisoner is in possession of an employment permit from Canada Employment and Immigration. Similar policies are not found in procedural manuals governing work releases on unescorted temporary absence from provincial institutions.

mandatory supervision,[200] failure to comply with terms and conditions of release in another country can be of no legal force or effect in Canada.

(iii) *Forms of Day Parole*

The distinction in law between day and full parole is that the former requires that the prisoner "return to prison from time to time during the duration of the parole or to return to prison after a specified period,"[201] whereas full parole does not require any return to close custody unless "parole is suspended or revoked."[202] While the public perception of day parole is that it is a release to a halfway house rather like T.A.P. release in provincial systems, there are, in fact, many forms of day parole. Despite the fact that most prisoners become eligible for day parole after serving one-sixth of sentence, or 6 months, whichever is greater,[203] it is our experience that the Board is generally loathe to grant day parole release to a halfway house for a period greater than 6 months.[204] Thus, where prisoners are serving longer sentences, the Board has initiated several policy alternatives designed to ease the transition from close custody to full release. While a complete description of the many programs developed across the country would be beyond the scope of this text, and while these programs and policies are frequently modified, some of the more common forms of release prior to full parole eligibility are outlined below.

(A) *Unescorted temporary absence (U.T.A.) prior to day parole.* The prisoner is granted a series of unescorted passes in order to observe his behaviour and performance. Depending on the security level of the institution from which he is released, current Board policy is that such releases will not normally exceed 72 hours per month, excluding travel time. Frequently, these releases are designed in order that a prisoner may attend at a halfway house for assessment purposes.

(B) *Limited day parole.* This is an institutionally based form of parole, where the prisoner is allowed into the community for voluntary or paid work or for socialization. The prisoner usually returns to penitentiary each night or after a few days.

---

[200] *Parole Act*, ss. 13, 16(1)(*e*), 22(1) and (4).

[201] *Parole Act*, s. 2.

[202] *Parole Act*, s. 19(2).

[203] *Parole Regulations*, s. 9(*d*).

[204] The Board's *Policy and Procedures Manual*, s. IX.A.5 indicates that initial grants should not exceed 6 months and that the total duration should not exceed 12 months.

(C) *Day parole to halfway house.* In general, this form of release is intended to be the final release from close custody as part of the transition from incarceration to full parole or release on mandatory supervision. There are two types of halfway houses: a Community Correctional Centre (C.C.C.) is an institution designated as a penitentiary under section 2(1) of the *Penitentiary Act*, while a Community Residential Centre (C.R.C.) is a privately run facility operating under contract with the Correctional Service of Canada,[205] which is not so designated as a penitentiary. A C.C.C. is usually staffed by parole officers who are employees of the Correctional Service of Canada, while direct supervision of prisoners released on U.T.A. or day parole to a C.R.C. is usually conducted by employees of agencies such as the Elizabeth Fry, John Howard or St. Leonard's Societies. Indirect supervision is maintained through regular reporting to a parole officer. Each C.C.C. and C.R.C. facility has its own rules and regulations, both as to conditions of residence and leave privileges. Board policy is that the Director of the residence is authorized to modify these rules in individual cases according to general guidelines. It should also be noted that residence in a C.R.C. or C.C.C. facility does not necessarily require that the individual return each night. Depending upon good behaviour, the prisoner may reasonably expect that as he comes closer to full parole eligibility, he will be permitted to spend more time living away from the residence, the terms of the statute being complied with by regular reporting to a C.C.C. facility or to a parole officer whose office is in a facility designated as a penitentiary.

(D) *Use of private homes.* Since the statutory definition of day parole is sufficiently broad to permit occasional reporting to a penal facility, there is nothing to prohibit the Board from permitting a day parolee to live at home. However, because of adverse publicity surrounding the use of this form of release, the Board is somewhat reluctant to make this form of order except in cases where no C.R.C. or C.C.C. facility is convenient to the day parolee's place of work or study, or where the prisoner is physically or mentally challenged and needs special assistance not available in a halfway house.

(E) *Day parole or U.T.A. prior to mandatory supervision.* As the Board makes increasing use of day parole to provide for gradual and structured release, it is not surprising that orders for release on day

---

205 *Commissioner's Directives*, C.D. 600-1-10-1 (effective October 23, 1984) and C.D. 600-1-10-2 (effective November 30, 1982). See also Correctional Service of Canada, *Case Management Policy and Procedures Manual*, chapters 13 and 14 (the manual is currently under revision).

parole prior to mandatory supervision are made with increasing frequency.[206] These grants of day parole do not generally differ significantly from other types of day parole. However, it should be noted that since eligibility for release on mandatory supervision occurs at 12:01 a.m. on the release date, the Board has developed a practice of granting U.T.A. release on the day previous. In *Re Starr*,[207] the prisoner was released on U.T.A. two days prior to his mandatory supervision release date. While on U.T.A. he committed offences, and the Board purported to revoke his mandatory supervision. Nitikman D.J. held that the Board had acted without jurisdiction as the prisoner was neither on parole nor on mandatory supervision at the time the offences were committed.

The legitimacy of the concept of staged release was challenged in *Tom v. National Parole Board*[208] where a prisoner was serving a life minimum sentence which made him eligible for day parole 3 years prior to his full parole eligibility date. He was advised of Board policy, which stated:

> In any case where the day parole eligibility date is between one and three years prior to the full parole eligibility date, a release program may be initiated subject to the following conditions:
> (a) the first year should be used mainly for temporary absences;
> (b) the second year may be used for special projects, i.e., planned activities for groups of inmates which are designed for specified purposes and are of relatively short duration which can be carried out with the inmate returning to the institution each night, or periodically, or with a group housed in some facility outside of the institution for the duration of the project;
> (c) a more extensive day parole program should only be considered when an inmate is within one (1) year of the full parole eligibility date.[209]

The prisoner stated in his affidavit that he "object(ed) to this policy of staged day parole release," and that he insisted on being considered for day parole upon his eligibility date. Day parole was denied, and this decision was upheld following a re-examination of the decision pursuant to section 22 of the Regulations, the Internal Review Committee (the predecessor of the Appeal Division) stating, *inter alia*, that "Members felt that both you and the Board are faced with restraints and constraints created by the nature of your crime and the time agenda that

---

206 See M. Chitra, "Modern Trends in Parole Granting, 1957-76" (1979), 5 Queen's L.J. 46; *Solicitor-General's Study of Conditional Release—Report of the Working Group*, March 1981, Table A-18.

207 *Starr v. National Parole Bd.*, [1983] 1 F.C. 363 (T.D.). Section 26.3 of the *Penitentiary Act* was not amended in 1986.

208 *Tom v. National Parole Bd.* [summarized in (1983), 10 W.C.B. 293 (Fed. T.D.)].

209 National Parole Board *Policy and Procedures Manual*, s. IX.A.4.

the Board, in its wisdom, perceives societal concerns to impose."[210] It was argued that these statements amounted to an improper fettering of the Board's discretion. After a careful review of the evidence, Nitikman D.J. concluded that "Board policy was but one factor in the decision arrived at . . . [and] the Board and the Review Committee [did not] base their decision on general policy to the exclusion of the merits of the application." Nitikman D.J. found nothing offensive in the Board "considering general policy provided it is used merely as a guideline and not given the force of law,"[211] and cited case law in support of his view.[212] His Lordship went on to say that even if the Board had considered public opinion in arriving at the conclusion that day parole should be denied, this would not be objectionable.

In 1985, in response to perceived public concern about violent offenders being released "early", the Board adopted a policy which generally provided that

> the Board should not consider favourably an application for day parole prior to [full parole eligibility date] if the type of program requested is to a C.C.C. or C.R.C. or would not require nightly return to the institution of which he is a resident . . . [where the prisoner] is serving a definite sentence of two years or more for an offence which involved actual violence or the threat of violence.[213]

Although the policy was not formally continued when the Board's *Policy and Procedures Manual* was revised in January 1988, there can be little doubt that it continues to influence decision-making in cases involving violent offences.

5. RELEASE CONDITIONS

(a) Mandatory Conditions

Section 16(1.1) of the *Parole Act* and section 19.1 of the *Parole Regulations* provide that, unless a variance is sought by the prisoner pursuant to section 16(1.2) of the Act and section 19.2(2) of the Regulations, certain mandatory conditions are deemed to have been imposed in all cases[214] by the Board. Those conditions, as provided in section 19.1

---

[210] *Supra*, note 211.

[211] *Supra*, note 211.

[212] *Re Maple Lodge Farms Ltd. and Canada* (1982), 137 D.L.R. (3d) 558 (S.C.C.), at 561 per McIntyre J.

[213] National Parole Board, *Policy and Procedures Circular*, 1985-2, February 5, 1985.

[214] The usual conditions of day parole are similar, with added requirements concerning residence and a direction that the prisoner return to penitentiary at the end of the day parole period. In addition, the prisoner is required to sign an acknowledgement that he understands that if he does not return, day parole may be terminated or revoked and that he may be charged with being unlawfully at large.

of the Regulations, are that the prisoner must:

(*a*) on release, travel directly to the inmate's place of residence, as noted on the parole or mandatory supervision certificate;
(*b*) report to the parole supervisor immediately on release and thereafter as instructed by the parole supervisor;
(*c*) remain at all times in Canada, within territorial boundaries prescribed by the parole supervisor;
(*d*) obey the law and keep the peace;
(*e*) inform the parole supervisor immediately on arrest or being questioned by the police;
(*f*) report to the police as instructed by the parole supervisor;
(*g*) advise the parole supervisor of . . . [his] . . . address of residence on release and thereafter report immediately
(i) any change in the address of residence,
(ii) any change in the normal occupation, including employment, vocational or educational training and volunteer work,
(iii) any change in the family, domestic or financial situation, and
(iv) any change which may reasonably be expected to affect . . . [his] . . . ability to comply with the terms and conditions of parole or mandatory supervision; and
(*h*) not own, possess or have the control of any weapon, as defined in the *Criminal Code*, except as authorized by the parole supervisor.

Section 19.2(1) of the Regulations directs that at least 15 days prior to the first parole review the Board is required to advise the prisoner of these mandatory conditions,[215] presumably in order that the prisoner may address his mind as to whether he will seek relief from some of them. While the prisoner is entitled to approach the Board for relief even after he has been granted release, it may well be appropriate for the successful conditional release applicant to have a clear understanding of what the decision-maker intends by the wording of these conditions of release, especially when it is recalled that neither the Board's *Policy and Procedures Manual* nor the *Case Management Manual* of the Correctional Service of Canada provides an adequate working definition of such terms as "questioned by the police", "debts", or "weapons". Nor should the prisoner be hesitant to indicate any reservations he may have about the imposition of certain conditions.[216] Since the prisoner must acknowledge in writing that he understands and agrees to the conditions

---

[215] In practice, a form letter is sent to the prisoner upon receipt of his parole application.
[216] In *Sowa v. Canada (Correctional Service)* [summarized in (1986), 16 W.C.B. 302 (Fed. T.D.)] a prisoner released on mandatory supervision sought to prohibit the National Parole Board from restricting his movements to a 25-mile travel radius. Martin J. held that so long as the prisoner was entitled to apply for permission to go outside this radius, the Board was not improperly fettering its discretion by creating a general policy in this respect.

of release on parole or unescorted temporary absence before being released,[217] the appropriate time to raise concern is at the Board hearing.

(b) Special Conditions

Section 16(1)(a) of the *Parole Act* authorizes the Board to impose what are referred to as "special conditions".[218] In *Litwack v. National Parole Board*,[219] the prisoner had been sentenced to penitentiary for a number of fraud-related offences. He was released on parole subject to the following special condition:

> The subject should not be implicated or involved either directly or indirectly in the administration, promotion, purchasing or selling of any enterprises or organizations either for remuneration or non-remuneration purposes.[220]

After a period of time successfully spent on parole, Litwack advised his parole officer that he wished to open a business selling computers to fellow university students, for which he had been granted a line of credit by a government agency. The parole supervisor investigated the parolee's plans and the involvement of other persons who would participate in the proposed operation, and recommended to the Board that the special condition be abolished. In a split decision the Board refused to follow the recommendation and voted to maintain the special condition on the grounds that "it was well justified for reasons of public security." The parolee launched an application for *certiorari* arguing that the Board had "acted unreasonably in failing to revoke restrictive conditions ... which have the effect of making [the Petitioner] virtually unemployable for any of the types of work for which his educational background and experience make him suitable."[221]

Walsh J. ruled that the initial decision to impose the special condition was not unreasonable; even though the prohibition was broadly phrased it did not prohibit the parolee from taking on employment for which he was qualified. Furthermore, the special condition was directed

---

[217] A prisoner about to be released subject to mandatory supervision may refuse to sign the acknowledgment, but he is still bound by the conditions.

[218] "Special conditions" must be distinguished from "special instructions". The latter are interim conditions imposed by a parole officer without Board input. If the parole officer wishes to maintain a special instruction for longer than 60 days, he must seek Board approval, which, if granted, automatically converts the "special instruction" into a "special condition". If no action is taken within 60 days, the "special instruction" lapses.

[219] (1986), 26 C.C.C. (3d) 65 (Fed. T.D.). The case arose at a time when three Board members voted on such cases.

[220] *Ibid.*, at 67.

[221] *Ibid.*

to the reasonable objective of ensuring "that he would not be in a position to defraud anyone during his parole by financial manipulations, as he had done in the past." Walsh J. then proceeded to discuss "certain fundamental principles which evolve in interpreting the Charter in an increasingly liberal fashion". He cited several pre- and post-*Charter* judgments of the Supreme Court of Canada and concluded:

> ... that it is now clear that there is a duty of an administrative tribunal not merely to act fairly but also to act reasonably. Furthermore it is not sufficient to comply merely with procedural fairness but also the substance of the decision must be reasonable on the facts.[222]

He then analyzed the facts and ruled that the decision of the majority of the Board to maintain the condition was "so patently unfair as to require the intervention of the court," because they "still insist on the maintenance of the restrictive condition, without considering that the situation appears to have changed since it was imposed."[223]

In *Bryntwick v. National Parole Board*,[224] it came to the attention of the parole authorities that a parolee had by chance encountered a former criminal accomplice, and had had dinner with him in a public place. The Board advised him that it intended to impose a special condition prohibiting him "from any non fortuitous meetings or communications with people having a criminal record or with whom [sic] you think might have a criminal record," and offered him an opportunity to submit his response. A later letter advised him that the major reason for this proposed condition was "the fact that during your previous parole which was revoked in March, 1982, you recidivated by committing a crime, while in the company of individuals who had a criminal record".[225] The first argument raised by the parolee on a *certiorari* application was that the decision to impose the special condition generally offended section 7 of the *Charter*. In dismissing this argument, Dubé J. commented that "[t]he petitioner has not established any procedural or substantive violation,"[226] and that, in the circumstances of the case, he

---

[222] *Ibid.*, at 73 and 71. Citing *Ref. Re s. 94(2) of the B.C. Motor Vehicle Act* (1986), 23 C.C.C. (3d) 289 (S.C.C.); *Kane v. U.B.C. (Bd. of Governors)* (1980), 31 N.R. 214 (S.C.C.), at 221; *Blanchard v. Control Data Can.*, [1984] 2 S.C.R. 477, at 493-494; *Re Mia and B.C. Medical Services Comm.* (1985), 17 D.L.R. (4th) 385 (S.C.C.), at 411-412, per Lamer J.; *R. v. Weyallon* (1983), 47 A.R. 360 (N.W.T.S.C.).

[223] *Litwack, ibid.*, at 77.

[224] [1987] 2 F.C. 184 (T.D.).

[225] *Ibid.*, at 188.

[226] *Ibid.*, at 194. The prisoner maintained that one of the reasons section 7 was offended was because he had no right of appeal against the imposition of the conditions. Although the prisoner's right to seek a variance of release conditions appears by

could not "find that the board was patently unreasonable in prohibiting the petitioner from meeting with people with a criminal record." A second branch of this argument was that the special condition contravened section 7 in that it was "so imprecise, vague and contradictory as to be incapable of being rationally understood or enforced." After reviewing American case law which had dismissed arguments that non-association clauses were "void for vagueness", Dubé J. held that the impugned clause was "sufficiently clear and precise to be understood and enforced." If the condition were to be interpreted in "any arbitrary or discriminatory" fashion, the parolee "can still look to the Courts for redress".[227] As to arguments based on impermissible interference with his ability to associate and that section 10(1)(a) [now s. 16(1)(a)] of the Act was generally too arbitrary,[228] Dubé J. held that "the type of condition imposed . . . has a rational basis and stands well within reasonable bounds acceptable and accepted in a democratic society",[229] and thus was saved by section 1 of the *Charter.*

The *ratio* of these cases appears to be consistent with cases which have examined various other conditions within a criminal law context. In reviewing probation and bail conditions appellate courts have developed a twofold test: (1) is the condition reasonably related to the probationer's antecedents and to the offence of which he has been found guilty? and (2) is the condition comprehensible and inherently reasonable?[230] Only when a condition—or its interpretation or application—falls below these standards will a court be likely to interfere.

---

section 19.2(2) of the Regulations to be limited to relief from "mandatory terms", it could be argued that section 19.4(2) empowers the Board to grant relief from "any term". Current board policy is that relief from any condition may be sought at any time.

[227] *Ibid.*, at 195 and 198.

[228] It does not appear to have been brought to the court's attention that as part of the 1986 amendments the word "reasonable" has been substituted for "desirable" in section 10(1)(a) [now s. 16(1)(a)].

[229] *Supra*, note 227, at 201.

[230] See the use of the term "reasonable" in sections 515(4)(f) and 737(2)(h) of the *Criminal Code.* See also *R. v. Caja* (1977), 36 C.C.C. (2d) 401 (Ont. C.A.); *R. v. Stennes* (1975), 35 C.R.N.S. 123 (B.C.C.A.); *R. v. Gladstone* (1978), 40 C.C.C. (2d) 42 (B.C. Co. Ct.); *R. v. Doiron* (1972), 9 C.C.C. (2d) 137 (B.C.S.C.); *Arciniega v. Freeman, U.S. Marshall* (1971), 404 U.S. 4; *U.S. v. Toney* 605 F.2d 144 (5th Cir.C.A., 1977). In *In Re Mannino* (1968), 14 Cal.App. 3d 953, it was held that probation conditions which (1) have no relationship to the crime of which the offender was convicted, (2) relate to conduct which is not in itself criminal, and (3) require or forbid conduct which is not reasonably related to future criminality, do not serve the statutory ends of probation and are invalid.

(c) Fines, Compensation and Restitution Orders

Where a fine has been imposed by the sentencing court, coupled with a term of imprisonment in default of payment, and the fine has not been paid at the time of release on parole, the Board may grant parole for a period equal to the custodial period imposed in default of payment, so long as the committal warrant has been executed prior to the parole granting hearing. If the prisoner elects to pay all or part of the fine the warrant expiry date is adjusted accordingly.[231]

There has been some considerable controversy as to whether a federal prisoner can force federal penal officials to receive and execute committal warrants for breaches of provincial statutes or municipal bylaws. In *Durand v. Forget*,[232] the Quebec Superior Court held that *mandamus* could issue to compel the execution of such warrants, but the opposite conclusion was reached by two judges of the Federal Court Trial Division in *Re Bedard and Correctional Service of Canada*[233] and *Dempsey v. Attorney General of Canada*,[234] both of whom considered that while it would be good policy to permit a prisoner to discharge all of his penal obligations at one time, an amendment to section 659(2) [now 731(2)] of the *Code* would be necessary. *Dempsey* was reversed by the Federal Court of Appeal,[235] Hugessen J. holding for the majority that there was nothing in section 659(2) [now s. 731(2)] which limited it to punishments for breaches of federal statutes, nor would such an interpretation offend the division of powers in sections 91 and 92 of the *Constitution Act, 1867*.

If *Dempsey* correctly represents the law, it would appear that section 14 of the *Parole Act* may be used to confer jurisdiction upon the National Parole Board to grant release on any terms so imposed. It remains to be seen, however, whether provincial legislation which purports to make terms of imprisonment imposed in default of payment of fines consecutive both to one another and to any other term of imprisonment which is being served at the time of the execution of the committal warrant, can bind federal authorities in light of sections 717 and 721 of the *Code*.

---

[231] *Criminal Code*, s. 722.
[232] (1980), 24 C.R. (3d) 119 (Que. S.C.).
[233] This result was reached "not without some regret" by Muldoon J. in *Re Bedard and Canada (Correctional Service)*, [1984] 1 F.C. 193 (T.D.). Following this decision, Bedard re-litigated this issue in Quebec Superior Court, which followed *Durand* and issued *mandamus* (November 2, 1983).
[234] (1985), 20 C.C.C. (3d) 363 (Fed. T.D.).
[235] (1986), 25 C.C.C. (3d) 193 (Fed. C.A.).

Where an order for compensation[236] or restitution[237] has been made by the sentencing court, the Board will not generally order compliance with such an order as a condition of release, apparently because it considers that the court possesses sufficient powers to force compliance with its own orders.[238] Nevertheless, brief reference should be made to the case of *Myers*,[239] where the prisoner applied, *inter alia*, for prohibition to prevent the Board from imposing a condition that he make arrangements with the Department of National Revenue for payment of his outstanding income tax liability. While the case was complicated by the fact that the prisoner had absconded to the United States during a temporary absence, and launched his action from that country, Mahoney J. held that because the prisoner had been sentenced for tax evasion, it was "open" to the Board to take into account the efforts Myers had made to settle his outstanding liability to Revenue Canada. While a failure to reach a settlement would not itself be material, the Board could properly look at the reasons for the failure to reach settlement "in so far as they may reasonably be ascribed" to the prisoner.[240]

(d) Probation Orders

The relationship between probation and conditional release has not been entirely clarified by the courts. Since an order of probation may be made as an adjunct to any sentence not exceeding 2 years,[241] even a penitentiary prisoner applying for parole may be subject to a probation order imposed in addition to either a 2-year term of imprisonment or to a reformatory-length sentence being served in penitentiary.[242] While appellate courts have frequently quashed probation orders in such circumstances on the basis that Parliament's intention "was to limit the making of probation orders to situations where ... the totality of all

---

[236] *Criminal Code*, s. 725.

[237] *Criminal Code*, s. 737(2)(*e*).

[238] *Policy and Procedures Manual*, s. V.C.2.3.1.

[239] *Myers v. National Parole Bd.*, [1978] 2 F.C. 696 (T.D.). Affirmed [1982] 2 F.C. 253 (C.A.).

[240] *Ibid.* (T.D.), at 701.

[241] *Criminal Code*, s. 737(1)(*b*).

[242] This could arise either through the operation of section 731 of the *Code*, or where a prisoner has been transferred to a penitentiary pursuant to a federal-provincial agreement, or where the prisoner has received an additional sentence for offences committed while on conditional release and has been returned to penitentiary pursuant to section 25 of the *Parole Act*.

sentences then to be served ... does not exceed ... two years,"[243] the question of the date of commencement of any probation order coupled with a term of imprisonment remains to be finally resolved. In *Constant*,[244] the prisoner had received a sentence of 15 months followed by a period of probation for 1 year "from the date of expiration of his sentence." He was released from close custody as a result of remission (i.e., not on parole) and was charged with being in breach of his probation some 12 months after the date of imposition of the original sentence. Counsel attempted to argue that the accused could not be in breach of his probation because the probation order only came into force 15 months after the original sentencing date. Guy J.A. (Monnin J.A. concurring) held that it was "ludicrous to suggest that there is a period ... when neither the incarceration nor the probation order are in effect."Matas J.A., in concurring reasons, held that the "clearly expressed intent of Parliament" was that the prisoner should become subject to a probation order immediately upon release from close custody. Two judges of the Manitoba Court of Appeal dissented, holding that "anyone outside the court system would assume ... that the [probation] would begin at the end of 15 months from the beginning of his sentence." If this resulted in "a hiatus between the actual incarceration of a citizen and the beginning of a probation order, that is a matter for Parliament to deal with."[245]

Unfortunately a careful reading of the various judgments indicates that the judges in the minority were apparently acting under a misapprehension as to the facts.[246] Counsel for the prisoner argued that "the status of a prisoner released on statutory remission is equivalent to a parolee; he is lawfully at large but still subject to his sentence."[247] It would appear that this may have influenced those judges in the minority to consider that the appellant was "released on parole". This was noted

---

[243] *R. v. Currie* (1982), 65 C.C.C. (2d) 415 (Ont. C.A.) at 416. See also *R. v. Nutter* (1970), 7 C.C.C. (2d) 224 (B.C.C.A.); *R. v. Callaghan* (1972), 9 C.C.C. (2d) 125 (B.C.C.A.); *R. v. Young* (1980), 27 C.R. (3d) 118 (B.C.C.A.); *R. v. Campagne; R. v. Boudreau* (1978), 2 C.R. (3d) S-15 (Ont. C.A.); *R. v. Hennigar* (1983), 58 N.S.R. (2d) 110 (C.A.); *R. v. Hackett* (1987), 30 C.C.C. (3d) 159 (B.C.C.A.); *R. v. Miller* (1988), 36 C.C.C. (3d) 100 (Ont. C.A.).

[244] *R. v. Constant* (1978), 40 C.C.C. (2d) 329 (Man. C.A.). Leave to appeal to S.C.C. denied (1978), 40 C.C.C. (2d) 329 (note).

[245] *Ibid.*, at 332, 333 and 334.

[246] The confusion in this case is compounded by the headnote, which speaks of the appellant breaching the terms of his probation order while "released on mandatory supervision". As noted by Martin J.A. in *Re Dinardo and R.* (1982), 67 C.C.C. (2d) 505 (Ont. C.A.), at 509-510, since this was a reformatory-length sentence, the prisoner could not be released subject to mandatory supervision.

[247] *Supra*, note 244, at 333.

in *Godin*,[248] where a prisoner was charged with breaching his probation at a time when he had been on parole. After reviewing the applicable *Code* provisions and various sections of the Quebec parole statute, Bilodeau J.C.S.P. found that the accused was not on probation and dismissed the charge stating that

> ... parole does not constitute the expiration of the prison sentence but rather a means for it to be carried out under which, for rehabilitation purposes, the inmate is permitted to leave the Detention Centre while still remaining bound by the conditions imposed upon him in order that this means of carrying out the sentence may subsist.
>
> Indeed, the fact that, if the conditions of parole are not respected, such parole can be revoked, constitutes the best evidence that the sentence continues to run and that only its means of execution can be modified.[249]

In sum, where the prisoner is released from a provincial institution as a result of remission accumulated on a reformatory-length sentence, the views of the majority in *Constant* are entirely correct, since the prisoner has completed serving his penal sentence. In those circumstances, it is appropriate that the individual be immediately subject to the probation order. However, if the prisoner is released from close custody by provincial officials on temporary absence or parole, or by the National Parole Board on temporary absence, parole or mandatory supervision, his penal sentence has not been completed, in that he is both subject to control and supervision by parole authorities, may have his release revoked and be returned to close custody. Thus, the period of probation commences only when the prisoner is unconditionally released from close custody.

6. CANCELLATION OF DECISIONS PRIOR TO IMPLEMENTATION

In *Beaumier v. National Parole Board*,[250] the prisoner had been granted day parole, but, because of new information received, the Board changed its mind and cancelled its decision. The prisoner launched *mandamus* proceedings, arguing that the Board had no power to do so. Dubé J. held that the wording of section 6 [now s. 10] of the Act was sufficiently broad to clothe the Board with power to change its own decisions.[251] However, Dubé J. went on to hold that under the statutory

---

248 *R. v. Godin* (Docket no. 01-4113-85, C.S.P. Que., J.C.S.P. Bilodeau, October 18, 1985).
249 *Ibid.*, at 12.
250 [1981] 1 F.C. 454 (T.D.).
251 A similar result was reached by Galligan J. (as he then was) in construing equivalent provincial legislation in *Re McDonald and R.* (1981), 56 C.C.C. (2d) 1 (Ont. H.C.).

framework which existed at that time the prisoner could not claim a right to a rehearing after the negative decision. The prisoner could not invoke the post-suspension provisions contained in the *Parole Regulations* because he had not been released. Furthermore, even conceding that the Board was subject to a duty to act fairly, that principle would not create a right to a rehearing.

The Regulations have now been modified to permit rehearings whenever a cancellation of full parole is recommended or contemplated by the Board. However, the Regulations do purport to allow the Board to cancel a day parole or unescorted temporary absence without hearing. We suggest that this is inconsistent with the ruling of McEachern C.J.S.C. in *Swan v. Attorney General of British Columbia,*[252] and that although the Board may, in certain circumstances, cancel a decision to grant conditional release, a rehearing must be held before such decision may be finally confirmed.[253]

The question of what amounts to "new information" was considered in *Bains v. National Parole Board*[254] where, upon being notified of the prisoner's impending release on day parole, the prosecuting Crown Attorney, senior law enforcement officials, and even the trial judge made negative representations to the Board. The Chairman of the Board directed that the prisoner not be released, pending investigation of the "unusual submissions" made by these various officials. Upon hearing applications for *certiorari* and *mandamus*, Muldoon J. first found that there was almost no new information which had come to the Board's attention since it had made its decision to grant day parole. The various materials merely repeated that which was already known to the Board at the time of the hearing. The only possible new piece of information — comments about the unsavoury background of the prisoner's proposed employer — was irrelevant because at the hearing the prisoner had "offered unreservedly to accept as a strict condition of his day parole the prohibition of his associating with or contacting in any way the said [employer]." Because this was not "new information which [could] be fairly levied against the applicant to his detriment. . . . [the employer's] activities, whether nefarious or not, have no bearing upon the appli-

---

[252] (1983), 35 C.R. (3d) 135 (B.C.S.C.). This case is discussed in detail in Chapters 4 and 8.

[253] While in American law no new hearing is necessary, careful regard must be paid to differing statutory and constitutional frameworks. See *Sexton v. Wise*, 494 F.2d. 1176; *McIntosh v. Woodward*, 514 F.2d 95; *Van Curren v. Ohio Adult and Parole Authority*, 45 Ohio St.2d 298; *Tracy v. Salamack*, 572 F.2d 393 (2nd Cir., 1978); *MacCowan v. Cummings*, 99 Misc. 2d 914 (Sup. Ct. Orleans Co., 1978); *People ex rel. Cunningham v. Met*, 61 A.D. 2d 590 (3rd. Dept., 1978); *Wolff v. McDonnell* 418 U.S. 539.

[254] (1989), 71 C.R. (3d) 343 (Fed. T.D.).

cant's character, temperament or potential for rehabilitation." Thus, "[t]he considerations . . . invoked by the board's chairman [were] extraneous to the board's lawfully-formulated conclusions"; consequently, Muldoon J. granted "certiorari to quash the board's compliance with the chairman's unlawful action, and . . . mandamus requiring the board to implement its decision [to grant day parole]."[255]

7. SUPERVISION WHILE ON CONDITIONAL RELEASE

(a) General

During any period of conditional release, or at the conclusion of unescorted temporary absence passes, reports are submitted to the Board by the supervising parole officer. If the Board decides at the end of a day parole period neither to grant full parole nor to continue day parole, section 16(4) of the *Parole Act* indicates that the Board or designated official may "terminate" day parole. While, as will be discussed in the following chapter, the Board must offer an in-person hearing before making a final decision to terminate day parole prior to the date specified in the original grant of day parole, it would appear that no hearing is mandated where the day parole period expires. In either case, the prisoner is returned to close custody with no loss of remission.

If the parole officer's reports are positive, and the prisoner has, after a period of time on day parole, become eligible for full parole, the Board does not normally schedule a hearing, but conducts the full parole review as a "paper case". This rarely occasions difficulty, although the prisoner might wish to request that a hearing be held. However, where, despite the arrival of the full parole eligibility date, the parole officer recommends (or the Board is inclined to order) that day parole be continued, a hearing should then be held. Although there has been no litigation on this subject, it is our experience that the Board will hold a hearing in these circumstances because of the wording of section 15(1) of the Regulations, which clearly directs that the full parole review "shall be by way of hearing". Thus, unless there have been grounds to cause a suspension of day parole, it would appear that the Board must hold an in-person hearing on or before the full parole eligibility date, and that the prisoner cannot be returned to penitentiary unless the day parole period expires before the arrival of the full parole eligibility date.

If full parole is granted, the prisoner is deemed, by section 19 of the Act, to be serving his term of imprisonment, but, unless and until parole

---

[255] *Ibid.*, at 348 and 349.

is suspended or revoked, he is not liable to be imprisoned and "shall be allowed to go and remain at large according to the terms and conditions of the parole and subject to the provisions of this Act." While initial reporting requirements to both the local police and the parole supervisor are likely to be at least twice per month, Board policy is that, dependent upon performance, the obligation to report may be lessened over time. After 3 years on parole or mandatory supervision every case is considered for "parole reduced", which, if granted, requires the individual only to obey the law, to report once a year, and to notify the parole supervisor of any change of address.[256]

(b) Modification of Release Conditions

When the prisoner released on day or full parole wishes to alter any of the terms and conditions contained in his release certificate, approval by the Board is required, except in emergency situations. Board policy is that at least two members are required to vote on modification or removal of conditions. Conversely, both the Board and the parole supervisor may add further restrictions.[257] While section 16 of the Act specifies that only the Board may establish terms and conditions of release, it would not appear to be an improper delegation of authority to permit the supervising parole officer to add appropriate conditions, especially when it is recalled that section 22 of the Act clearly looks forward to the possibility of a suspension warrant being issued where there is an anticipated breach of conditions of release.

One condition which frequently causes difficulty involves travel outside Canada. Assuming that the prisoner on conditional release can persuade the Board that his reasons for wishing to travel are appropriate, he faces another hurdle in that parole officials may insist that the parolee adduce written proof from immigration officials that he will be permitted entry into the foreign country. While permission can be obtained relatively easily from many jurisdictions, this is not the case where entry is sought into the United States. Convictions for most Canadian offences render the offender inadmissible for entry into that country as "an alien convicted of a crime involving moral turpitude."[258] Narcotics

---

[256] Section 16(1)(*d*) of the Act empowers the Board to grant discharge from parole to any person on full parole other than one serving a life minimum sentence. This power, which is very sparingly exercised, is occasionally used with individuals who have been on "parole reduced" status for a period of time.

[257] See note 222, *supra.* 146, *supra.*

[258] *Immigration and Nationality Act*, 8 U.S.C., s. 212(*a*)(9)(23). The term "moral turpitude" is not defined in the statute, but has evolved out of case law. In general the case law defines it as an act or omission which is *malum in se* and not merely *malum prohibitum.*

offences are not included in the category of crimes involving moral turpitude, but are made a separate excludable category of extreme rigidity. This prohibition may be waived at the discretion of the Attorney General[259] who has delegated this function to District Directors of the U.S. Immigration and Naturalization Service. In most cases, a refusal by the District Director to issue a "waiver of ineligibility" may be appealed to the U.S. Board of Immigration Appeals.[260] If the Applicant is successful at either level, it should be noted that a multiple entry authorization is unlikely to be issued *ab initio*; rather the Canadian parole supervisor will liaise indirectly with the District Director, who usually provides a single entry authorization for each visit.

---

[259] *Immigration and Nationality Act, ibid.*, s. 212(*d*)(3)(B).

[260] In *Matter of Hranka* 16 IN 491 (BIA 1978) the Board determined that a District Director must weigh the following factors: (1) the risk of harm to society if the applicant is admitted; (2) the seriousness of the applicant's prior immigration law or criminal law violation; and (3) the nature of the applicant's reasons for wishing to enter the U.S. for examples of cases involving applicants who have successfully appealed denials by a District Director to the Board of Immigration Appeals, see *Matter of B.* 7 IN Decisions 1 (AG 1956); *De Lucia v. INS*, 370 (F.2d 305) (7 Cir. 1966), cert. denied 386 U.S. 912 (1967); *Tovar v. INS*, 368 (F.2d 1006) (9 Cir. 1966), cert. denied 388 U.S. 915 (1967); *Matter of C.G.*, 8 IN 476 (1959); *Matter of A.*, 11 IN 99 (1965); *Matter of Ray* (unreported BIA 1981, A23 296 068); *Matter of Feder* (unreported BIA 1981, A23 296 414). See also C. Gordon and C. Rosenfeld, *Immigration Law and Procedures*, (Albany, N.Y.: Bender & Co., 1984), s. 1.10e. Of particular interest to Canadians, see S. B. Rawitz, "Criminal Records and Entry to the U.S." 8 Criminal Lawyers' Association Newletter (No. 2), September, 1986.

7

Remission, Mandatory Supervision and Detention

"You mean the monks are trying to get us off the hook with this remission of sins?"

—James Joyce, *The Dead*

"You mean I'm about to be Billed?"
—A prisoner upon learning that his case was being referred for detention under legislation introduced in Parliament as Bill C-67.

1. REMISSION[1]

The concept of remission appears to have been introduced into Canadian law with the enactment of the first *Penitentiary Act* in 1868.[2] That statute established several principles which existed for over a century. First, it extended the concept developed by Captain Alexander Maconachie and his successors that through diligent application to the regime of the penal institution a prisoner serving a definite sentence could earn a number of days of remission during each calendar month. A second principle was that, once earned or credited[3] entitlement to remission could only be taken away following a finding of guilt (either inside or outside the prison) for enumerated offences. Third, remission amounted to an absolute reduction of sentence; when the number of days of remission earned equalled the number of days remaining in the sentence, the prisoner stood to be released from close custody as a free citizen. Finally, although the statutes have been amended from time[4] to time to provide that different amounts of remission could be earned, the

---

[1]   A fuller discussion of the historical development of remission may be found in Chapter 5.

[2]   (31 Vict.), c. 75. Equivalent provisions have been enacted in the various versions of the *Prisons and Reformatories Act* for prisoners in provincial institutions.

[3]   Both systems of granting remission have been tried, sometimes in combination with one another. Since the proclamation in force on July 1, 1978 of amendments to the *Penitentiary Act* contained in S.C. 1977, c. 53, remission must now be earned.

[4]   *Penitentiary Act*, 1883 (46 Vict.), c. 37; 1906 (6 Edw. 7), c. 38; S.C. 1939, c. 6, s. 69; S.C. 1960-61, c. 53, ss. 22-25; S.C. 1968-69, c. 38, ss. 100, 101, 108; S.C. 1976-77, c. 53, ss. 35-44; S.C. 1977-78, c. 22, s. 20.

potential remission of approximately[5] one-third of sentence has existed in Canadian law for many years.

2. MANDATORY SUPERVISION[6]

In provincial systems of imprisonment the original concept of remission-based release as an absolute reduction of sentence still exists; when the prisoner has earned the number of days of remission equivalent to the unexpired balance of the original term of imprisonment, he stands to be released as a free citizen, subject only to other forms of court orders, such as probation or compensation. In these systems of imprisonment, remission may be said to amount to "forgiveness" or "pardon".[7] This was also true of the penitentiary system until 1970. However, the *Ouimet Report* of 1969[8] noted that many of the most difficult prisoners were being released from close custody without any assistance or supervision upon the expiry of approximately two-thirds of their original sentences. The Committee therefore recommended that where a prisoner was released with more than 60 days left to serve on the original sentence, he should be subject to a program of "statutory conditional release". With some modifications this proposal was enacted through a series of amendments to the *Parole* and *Penitentiary Acts* proclaimed in force on August 1, 1970. Under this regime of "mandatory supervision", a person released from a federal penitentiary as a result of accrued remission (where the number of days of remission exceeds 60) remains subject to the control of the parole authorities, just as if he were a prisoner released on parole, until the expiry date of his sentence.[9]

---

5   Due to the way remission is calculated it rarely amounts to exactly one-third of sentence.

6   The historical development of mandatory supervision is discussed more fully in Chapter 5.

7   As noted by Locke J. in *Logan v. William Head Institution (Director)* [summarized (1986), 1 W.C.B. (2d) 307 (B.C. S.C.)], affirmed [summarized (1987), 1 W.C.B. (2d) 441 (B.C.C.A.)], *The Shorter Oxford English Dictionary*, 3d ed. (Oxford: Clarendon Press, 1959), p. 1700, lists the following alternative meanings for the verb remit:

    1. To forgive or pardon (a sin, offence, a person, etc.).

    2. To give up, resign, surrender (a right or possession).

    3. To abstain from exacting (a payment or service of any kind) . . . b. To refrain from inflicting (a punishment) or carrying out (a sentence). . . .

8   Report of the Canadian Committee on Corrections, *Towards Unity: Criminal Justice and Corrections (Ouimet Report)* (Ottawa: Queen's Printer, 1969).

9   A sentence is deemed to expire at midnight of the day preceding the anniversary date of the sentence pronounced by the sentencing judge. This date is called the warrant expiry date (W.E.D.).

Although several cases attempted to challenge the existence of the regime of mandatory supervision on various grounds prior and subsequent to the enactment of the *Canadian Charter of Rights and Freedoms*,[10] these have all met with a singular lack of success. In *Belliveau*,[11] a prisoner moved in the Federal Court Trial Division to challenge the revocation of his mandatory supervision following convictions for drug offences committed while at liberty subject to mandatory supervision. Aided by a law student, and without directly invoking the *Charter* in his pleadings, the prisoner challenged the constitutionality of the legislation. Dubé J. considered four possible arguments based on the *Charter* which he felt might arguably apply to the constitutionality of the regime.

After finding as a fact that "[a]ll the procedural steps called for under the Act and Regulations were taken in due course", and after noting that the prisoner could not "point to any specific act or omission that would be tainted with unfairness" in the revocation proceedings, Dubé J. ruled that no breach of fundamental justice contrary to section 7 could be found. As to section 9 of the *Charter*, the court held that the prisoner had failed to establish any evidence of "unreasonableness, or . . . arbitrariness, or . . . capriciousness of the application of the statute to his own case." While recognizing that totally unfettered discretion might give rise to a suggestion of arbitrariness, "it seems obvious to me that the breaching of a key condition of the mandatory supervision programme by the commission of another crime is good cause for triggering the application of the *Parole Act*."[12] Applying cases such as *Moore*[13] and *Mitchell*,[14] Dubé J. found that the loss of remission conse-

---

10   Being Part I of the *Constitution Act, 1982* [en. by the *Canada Act, 1982* (U.K.), c. 11, s. 1].

11   *R. v. Belliveau* (1984), 13 C.C.C. (3d) 138 (Fed. T.D.). The same result was reached when the prisoner relitigated the issue during the course of *habeas corpus* proceedings in the provincial superior court *Belliveau v. Dorchester Penitentiary (Warden)* (1984), 55 N.B.R. (2d) 82 (C.A.).

12   *Belliveau, ibid.*, at 146 and 147.

13   After her release from the Prison for Women following the decision of Eberle J., *infra*, footnote 26, Moore soon re-offended. Following conviction the Crown launched an application to have her declared to be a dangerous offender. She challenged the constitutionality of the dangerous offender legislation on the basis, *inter alia*, that it offended section 9 of the *Charter*. Ewaschuk J. held that the legislation was consitutional in *Re Moore and R.* (1984), 10 C.C.C. (3d) 306 (Ont. H.C.), (which decision was subsequently expressly approved by the Supreme Court of Canada in *Lyons v. R.* (1988), 37 C.C.C. (3d) 1). However, after imposing the designation and finding that Moore fit the criteria, Ewaschuk J. held that he had a discretion to decline to impose an indeterminate sentence, and exercised that discretion in favour of the prisoner on the facts, a view which was ultimately upheld on appeal in *R. v. Moore* (1985), 16 C.C.C. (3d) 328 (Ont. C.A.).

14   *Re Mitchell and R.* (1984), 6 C.C.C. (3d) 193 (Ont. H.C.).

quent upon revocation "cannot be said to be excessive or disproportionate."[15] Finally, while acknowledging and citing authority to support the proposition that prisoners have consistently expressed their resentment for the regime, he found that mandatory supervision was supportable under section 1 of the *Charter*, in that it could not be said that "the programme has no rational basis, is unreasonable, undemocratic, disproportionate to its objective, offends common sense, or is otherwise unacceptable to a democratic society."[16]

A challenge to mandatory supervision based on section 15 of the *Charter* was attempted in *Dempsey*,[17] where it was argued on behalf of a prisoner recently released from penitentiary subject to mandatory supervision that that regime was constitutionally impermissible, as it did not apply to persons released from provincial institutions by virtue of earned remission. While agreeing with counsel for the intervener Attorney General of Ontario that the reason for the 2-year split in jurisdiction between federal and provincial systems of imprisonment "appears to have been effected on the basis of a pragmatism which is lost in the mists of our country's short history," Muldoon J. reasoned that the history of sentencing, locus of confinement, and conditional release reflected Parliament's intention that offenders be exposed to "an exponentially intensifying continuum of culpability which proceeds from the minor to the grievous." Applying the then applicable "similarly situated" test to the question of equality rights, Muldoon J. found it entirely acceptable that "[t]hose whose depradations are more serious undergo . . . more elaborate supervision during the term to which they are sentenced." Thus, federal and provincial prisoners were not similarly situated because ". . . the standard . . . application of mandatory supervision to the most culpable, the federal inmates, is an equal application of penalty among them which equality does not necessarily demand for the less culpable."[18]

Although the "similarly situated" test has been decisively rejected by the Supreme Court of Canada in *Andrews*,[19] it would seem doubtful whether there would be any point to re-litigating this issue. There are several passages in the judgment of Muldoon J. which suggest that one of the court's reasons for rejecting the various arguments was that the issue simply did not raise a discriminatory practice of sufficient social importance so as to demand the application of section 15. While other pro-

---

[15] *Belliveau, supra*, note 11, at 147.
[16] *Belliveau, supra*, note 11, at 145.
[17] *Dempsey v. R.* (1987), 32 C.C.C. (3d) 461 (Fed. T.D.).
[18] *Ibid.*, at 466 and 476.
[19] *Andrews v. B.C. Law Society*, [1989] 1 S.C.R. 143.

nouncements on equality rights by the Supreme Court of Canada will be necessary before a clear test can be said to have evolved, whether one applies the "pressing and substantial" test espoused by Dickson C.J.C., Wilson and L'Heureux-Dubé JJ., or the "legitimate exercise of the legislative power for the attainment of a desirable social objective" formula of McIntyre and Lamer JJ., or "the importance of the state interest"[20] test suggested by La Forest J., it is doubtful that the differences between federal and provincial prisoners can be characterized as so striking that they would reach a level of constitutional significance. In essence, as noted by Locke J. in *Logan*,[21] by not imposing the mandatory supervision regime on prisoners being released from provincial institutions, provincial legislatures are merely abstaining from enforcing an existing right without cancelling their right to use it in future.

3. RELEASE CONDITIONS

Release subject to mandatory supervision carries the obligation to comply with conditions imposed by the National Parole Board. However, it was not until the 1986 amendments that minimum conditions were specified in legislation. The combined effect of sections 27(1)(*k.1*) and 16(1.1) of the *Parole Act*[22] and section 19.1 of the *Parole Regulations*,[23] is that, subject to any variance which may be granted by the Board under section 16(1.2) of the Act and section 19.2 of the Regulations, the prisoner must, as a minimum:

(*a*) on release, travel directly to . . . [his] . . . place of residence, as noted on the mandatory supervision certificate;
(*b*) report to the parole supervisor immediately on release and thereafter as instructed by the parole supervisor;
(*c*) remain at all times in Canada, within territorial boundaries prescribed by the parole supervisor;
(*d*) obey the law and keep the peace;
(*e*) inform the parole supervisor immediately on arrest or being questioned by the police;
(*f*) report to the police as instructed by the parole supervisor;
(*g*) advise the parole supervisor of . . . [his] . . . address of residence on release and thereafter report immediately
   (i) any change in the address of residence,
   (ii) any change in the normal occupation, including employment, vocational or educational training and volunteer work,
   (iii) any change in the family, domestic or financial situation, and

---

20 *Ibid.*, at 153, 184 and 198.
21 *Supra*, note 7.
22 R.S.C. 1985, c. P-2.
23 SOR/78-428.

    (iv) any change which may reasonably be expected to affect . . . [his]
      . . . ability to comply with the terms and conditions of mandatory
      supervision; and

(*h*) not own, possess or have the control of any weapon, as defined in the
    Criminal Code, except as authorized by the parole supervisor. (*Parole
    Regulations*, s. 19.1)

In addition, the Board is empowered by section 16(1)(*b*) of the *Parole Act*
to impose additional terms and conditions, such as orders restricting
association with named persons or classes of people, abstinence clauses,
or orders that a person take mental health counselling at the direction of
the parole supervisor.[24]

4. "GATING"

Beyond the imposition of conditions of release subject to mandatory supervision, the combined operation of sections 21(1)-(6) and
22(1) of the *Parole Act* is that mandatory supervision may be suspended
and the prisoner returned to close custody pending further investigation
where a Board member or designate is satisfied:

(*a*) that a breach of a term or condition of mandatory supervison has
    occurred, or

(*b*) it is necessary or reasonable to suspend mandatory supervision in order
    to prevent a breach of a condition, or

(*c*) it is necessary or reasonable to suspend mandatory supervision for the
    protection of society. (s. 22(1))

During the summer of 1982, the National Parole Board, responding
to considerable public pressure to limit or abolish mandatory supervision entirely, received a legal opinion that the "protection of society"
clause might be used to extend the Board's jurisdiction by effectively
preventing the release on mandatory supervision of prisoners whom the
Board considered to be particularly dangerous. As the awarding of
remission is a somewhat discretionary act in the hands of penitentiary
officials, and consequently is a matter over which parole officials have
no control, the Board adopted a practice of waiting until the prisoner
was actually released before being met at the penitentiary "gate" with a
warrant suspending his right to be at liberty subject to mandatory
supervision.

The first case[25] to challenge "gating" was *Moore*, where Eberle J.

---

[24] Cases which have considered the reasonableness of conditions are discussed under the
    heading, "Release Conditions", in Chapter 6.

[25] Two of the "gating" cases were decided in favour of the prisoners on the basis that the
    formalties of release had not been complied with. In *Oag (No. 1)* [summarized 9
    W.C.B. 159 (Alta. Q.B.)], the prisoner was removed from the Edmonton Institution on

ruled that since the Board had no role in the granting of remission, it had no discretion to refuse an effective release of the prisoner on mandatory supervision.[26] He further held that the statutory framework indicated Parliament's intention that the Board should have no control over release subject to mandatory supervision. He noted that while the Board was given "exclusive jurisdiction and absolute discretion to grant or refuse to grant parole" under section 6 [now s. 13] of the *Parole Act*, and while sections 10(1)(*e*), 11, 13 [now ss. 16, 17, 19], and 16 to 21 [now ss. 22-25] of the *Parole Act* were made expressly applicable to mandatory supervision, parliamentary intention could be ascertained from the exclusion of [then] section 6 [now s. 13] to a "grant" of mandatory supervision. Similarly, while section 9 [now s. 27] of the *Parole Act* gave the Governor in Council power to make regulations affecting a broad range of releases, the regulations in force at that time contained no power to "grant" mandatory supervision. In essence, Eberle J. held that had Parliament intended to permit gating, it "would and should have said so clearly. . . . [T]he National Parole Board is empowered only to impose such terms and conditions as the Board may deem appropriate for her period of release."[27]

This decision was immediately appealed by the Board to the Ontario Court of Appeal.[28] Speaking for the court, Dubin J.A. extensively reviewed the legislative history of and statutory framework for remission and concluded that, as the Board had no control over the granting of remission, its jurisdiction over the prisoner arose only after release subject to mandatory supervision. Thus, such powers as had been granted to the Board by Parliament to suspend and revoke mandatory

---

his mandatory supervision release date and taken to a nearby police station. While still in handcuffs he was presented with a letter from the Parole Board which indicated that he was being "gated" because his "history of violent behaviour" led the Board to consider that he "represented an undue risk to the community". McDonald J. of the Alberta Court of Queen's Bench held that since the prisoner was never at liberty, the purported suspension of his mandatory supervision was premature. In *Noonan* (Fed. T.D., Rouleau J., February 21, 1983), the prisoner was eligible for release on mandatory supervision. Instead of being released, he was transferred to another penitentiary. Without articulating oral or written reasons, Rouleau J. of the Federal Court, Trial Division, denied an application to quash the suspension warrant. The Federal Court of Appeal unanimously reversed that judgment [1983] 2 F.C. 772, holding that since the formalties of release had not been complied with, the prisoner's right to liberty on mandatory supervision had been illegally suspended.

26 *Re Moore* [summarized (1983), 9 W.C.B. 114 (Ont. H.C.)].

27 *Ibid.*

28 *R. v. Moore* (1983), 33 C.R. (3d) 99 (Ont. C.A.). A similar conclusion was reached by Wright J. of the Saskatchewan Court of Queen's Bench in *R. v. Smith* [summarized (1983), 9 W.C.B. 421].

supervision could be invoked only in response to post-release conduct. Dubin J.A. further stated that he found no ambiguity in the legislation; nevertheless, had he concluded that the statutory provisions were equivocal, he would have construed them in favour of the prisoner.[29]

A few weeks later a majority of the Alberta Court of Appeal arrived at the opposite conclusion.[30] The reasoning of Lieberman J.A. (Stevenson J.A. concurring) commenced from the assumption that the only issue to be determined on appeal was whether ". . . in the exercise of the suspension powers . . . a member of the board [is] entitled to consider only post-release conduct?" Although Lieberman J.A. agreed with the Ontario Court of Appeal that section 16 [now section 22] of the *Parole Act* was not ambiguous, he concluded that the existence of the "protection of society" clause indicated that the Board was not limited to awaiting an actual or apprehended breach, so that "where a prisoner's mental or physical condition had deteriorated but had not manifested itself in any misconduct, on release under mandatory supervision, the Board must surely be able to act." To ignore pre-release history "is not only to redraft the statute but also to offend common sense." . . . "Section 16 . . . clearly embraces questions of intention or condition." In dissent, Moir J.A. noted that "gating" was a new power claimed by the Board. In his view section 16 [now s. 22] of the Act "looks forward" to cover actual breaches of conditions or deteriorating conduct after release. If Parliament had intended "this strange result of permitting appointed bureaucrats to overrule the statutes . . . they ought to have said so."[31]

A majority of the British Columbia Court of Appeal followed the Ontario Court of Appeal, with one important modification. In *Truscott v. Director of Mountain Institution*,[32] Seaton J.A., for the majority, qualified the ruling in *Moore* to conclude that "s. 16 of the Parole Act cannot be invoked by the National Parole Board by reason only of pre-release conduct of the inmate." In a concurring judgment Anderson J.A. acknowledged that amendments to the legislation were required; until that time, however, the Board was limited to considering pre-release history "in the light of post-release conduct in considering whether to

---

29 Dubin J.A. cited with approval a portion of the judgment of Dickson J. (as he then was) in *Marcotte v. Canada (Dep. A.G.)* (1975), 19 C.C.C. (2d) 257 (S.C.C.) at 262, reaffirming the principle that penal statutes must be strictly construed.

30 *Oag v. R.*, (1983), 33 C.R. (3d) 111 (Alta. C.A.) a Crown appeal from a decision of Foisy J. at [1983] 3 W.W.R. 130 (Alta. Q.B.) who followed the rulings in *Moore*.

31 *Ibid.*, at 112, 117-118 and 120.

32 (1983), 33 C.R. (3d) 121 (B.C. C.A.), a Crown appeal from a decision of McKay J. [summarized (1983), B.C.W.L.D. 907]. It should be noted that pending the hearing of the appeal a stay of release was ordered by Craig J.A. in *Re Truscott (No. 2)* [summarized (1983), 9 W.C.B. 413 (B.C. C.A.)].

revoke mandatory supervision." In dissent, Nemetz C.J.B.C. adopted the majority view in *Oag*, stating that he could not "believe that the statute . . . intended that the Parole Board must first await a new victimization before it can exercise its authority to send prisoners to jail".[33]

The Crown appeal to the Supreme Court of Canada in *Moore* and the prisoner appeal in *Oag* were heard jointly by the full court.[34] At the conclusion of oral argument Laskin C.J.C. delivered the unanimous judgment of the court that for the reasons of Dubin J.A., as "extended" by Seaton J.A., the statutory framework then in force could not be interpreted in such a way as to permit gating. Thus, although the Board was authorized to interpret post-release behaviour in light of pre-release history, it could not prevent release from close custody subject to mandatory supervision.

While the gating cases were still before the courts, the government of the day introduced legislation designed to legitimize the practice.[35] Bill S-32 eventually passed the Senate and was introduced (in revised form) before the House of Commons as Bill C-35 in May 1984. It was the government's hope that all-party consensus could be achieved, and that speedy passage of the bill would be forthcoming. However, several members of Extraordinarily, Parliament and some interested Senators expressed their reservations about the proposed amendments, and the Bill died on the order paper when the House prorogued in 1984. Following the election of the new government, Bills C-67 and C-68 were introduced in the Commons in June 1985. After a further round of hearing and amendments proposed by both the government and the opposition, the legislation passed the Commons but was rejected by the Senate. Extraordinarily, Parliament was recalled in the summer of 1986 to pass the Bill in identical form; the Senate chose not to oppose passage, and most of the legislation was proclaimed in force on July 25, 1986.[36]

5. DETENTION

The new legislative scheme provides two routes for referring a prisoner to the Board for consideration for gating (now called deten-

---

[33] *Ibid.*, at 126-127 and 129.

[34] *R. v. Moore; Oag v. R.*, (1983), 33 C.R. (3d) 97 (S.C.C.). Oag later commenced an action for damages for false imprisonment. The Board moved to have the action dismissed on the basis that no action lay in such circumstances. This argument was accepted in the Federal Court Trial Division (*Oag v. R.* (1986), 23 C.C.C. (3d) 20), but was reversed by the Federal Court of Appeal (*Oag v. R.* (1987), 33 C.C.C. (3d) 430). The substantive action is currently pending.

[35] Bill S-32 was introduced in the Senate in early 1983 and was under study by a Senate Committee at the same time the *Moore* and *Oag* cases were before the Supreme Court of Canada.

[36] S.C. 1986, cc. 42 and 43.

tion). The first is that, pursuant to section 21.3 of the amended *Parole Act*,[37] the Commissioner of Corrections is required to cause the Correctional Service of Canada (C.S.C.) to review the case of every prisoner to ascertain:

1. Whether he is serving a sentence for an offence listed in a Schedule appended to the *Parole Act* (generally offences involving death, violence to the person, or weapons).
2. Whether the offence was prosecuted by indictment.
3. Whether, in the opinion of the C.S.C., the offence caused death or serious harm to a victim ("serious harm" being further defined in section 21.2 as meaning "severe physical injury or severe psychological damage").
4. Whether, in the opinion of the C.S.C., there are reasonable grounds to believe that, if released subject to mandatory supervision, the prisoner is likely to commit another offence involving death or serious harm prior to warrant expiry date.

If, in the opinion of the C.S.C., these criteria[38] are met, the case is referred to the Board together with all of the information which C.S.C. considers relevant, at least 6 months prior to the prisoner's scheduled date for release subject to mandatory supervision.[39]

The second route of referral to the Board is designed either for emergency situations where the prisoner's behaviour is perceived to be deteriorating rapidly, or where the C.M.T. come to the view that a prisoner not among the class of those who can be referred is likely to cause "serious harm" if released subject to mandatory supervision. Regardless of whether criteria (1) to (3) above are met, the Commissioner[40] may refer a case to the Board at any time prior to the pre-

---

[37] S.C. 1986, c. 42, s. 5.

[38] Although the legislation lists four criteria, in practice (1) and (2) are usually combined, and C.S.C. referral documents speak only of three criteria. The C.S.C. personnel responsible for examining each case and, if necessary, making the referral, are the prisoner's case management team (C.M.T.). The structure and function of C.M.T.'s are discussed in more detail in Chapters 6 and 12.

[39] In order to reflect the new reality that release subject to mandatory supervision is no longer automatic, section 21.2(1) of the *Parole Act* now uses the term "presumptive release date" (P.R.D.). While this term is correct, it has not yet entered into the prison lexicon, staff, prisoners and Board members still prefer to use the terms "mandatory date" or "M.S.D." We have used the terms interchangeably.

[40] It is unclear from section 21.3(3) whether the Commissioner of Corrections must personally address his mind to each case, rather than delegating this function to lower level officials within C.S.C., as is permitted under section 21.3(2). Since "Commissioner" is defined in section 21.1 as having the same meaning as under the *Penitentiary Act* (R.S.C. 1985, c. P-5) it would seem that section 6 and 9 of that *Act* would permit the

sumptive release date, so long as he is of the opinion that, if released, the prisoner is likely to commit an offence causing death or serious harm prior to warrant expiry date. If the referral is made less than 6 months prior to the scheduled mandatory supervision release date, the Commissioner must specify in writing that he formed his belief on the basis of information which became available in that time period.[41] In all cases, the Commissioner must forward all information which he considers relevant to the Board.

Once the referral has been made, the Board is required by the *Parole Regulations*[42] to hold an in-person hearing with the prisoner within specified time frames, depending on the source and timing of the referral. This has been the subject of recent litigation. While finding on the facts of *Pierce*[43] that the psychologist's report did amount to "new information", Collier J. remarked *in obiter* that had he found that the

---

Commissioner to delegate that function to senior management within the C.S.C. This was adopted by MacKay J. in *Ford v. Canada (Cmmr. of Corrections)* (1990), 54 C.C.C. (3d) 256 (Fed. T.D.). However, the new section 21.4(6) which, in requiring that the consent of the Commissioner be obtained prior to a prisoner being ordered into residence in a penitentiary during his period of mandatory supervision, speaks explicitly of the Commissioner being able to delegate his powers, from which one might be able to infer a parliamentary intention that the Commissioner should personally consider whether he should use his extraordinary powers to refer in emergency situations. In the fiscal year 1987-88 (the first full year after the legislation was proclaimed in force) 34.4 percent of referrals were made by the Commissioner to the Chairman of the National Parole Board while 64.8 percent were made directly by C.S.C. to the Board (National Parole Board, *Detention Program Statistics: Volume 1,* October 1988, unpublished).

41 In *Pierce v. Canada (Cmmr. of Corrections)* (1988), 13 F.T.R. 218 (T.D.), a majority of the prisoner's C.M.T. concluded that there were no grounds for believing that the prisoner would re-offend prior to the warrant expiry date (W.E.D.) The institutional psychologist, who had had several interviews with the prisoner, disagreed with the team. During the course of a later interview with the psychologist, which interview took place less than 6 months before the scheduled release date, the prisoner apparently agreed for the first time "to discuss life events preceeding the present offence". On the basis of information received during this interview the psychologist submitted a report, which the Commissioner later considered in making a referral to the Board. Collier J. held that this was new information within the meaning of section 15.3(3) [now s. 21.3(3)] of the Act, and refused to quash the referral. See also *Re Cunningham and R.* (Ottawa Motions Ct. File no. 241/89, Ont. H.C., Smith J., August 2, 1989) (at the time of going to press this judgment was under appeal to the Ontario Court of Appeal); and *Ford v. Canada (Cmmr. of Corrections), ibid.*

42 SOR/86-817, s. 4.

43 *Supra,* note 41. Although the court made no reference to cases such as *Grabina, Elliott, Collins,* and *Gorog,* it is noteworthy that those cases, which dealt with the effect of procedural defects during the post-suspension process, came to the same conclusion. Those cases are discussed in Chapter 8.

information was not new, any purported referral within 6 months of the presumptive release date would be a nullity. This issue was considered in *Milner*,[44] where no referral was made before the 6-month deadline because of a clerical error. Addy J. held that despite the fact that the various sections of the *Parole Act* and *Parole Regulations* used the word "shall", nevertheless these provisions were "directory" rather than "mandatory", and a failure to observe them did not cause the Board to lose jurisdiction. A related issue arose a few weeks later in *Cleary v. Correctional Service of Canada*,[45] where one of the time frames had not been observed, due to the prisoner's case management team going on strike. In the Trial Division, Jerome A.C.J. held, following *Shubley*,[46] that the statutory provisions were not penal in nature; he then adopted the views of Addy J. in *Milner*. This reasoning was expressly rejected by the Federal Court of Appeal,[47] Iacobucci C.J. holding in oral reasons:

> Whether the legislation is penal or not is irrelevant. What is relevant is that the decision involved is of importance to the Appellant and has serious consequences to him. Moreover, there is little conviction in the "man-datory—directory" dichotomy to answer the question before us. At bottom what we are seeking is legislative intention. According to the *Interpretation Act*, "shall" is to be construed as imperative. But whether failure to comply with a command entails nullity, and if so to what extent, surely depends on the legislative scheme as a whole. . . . In this case, we are of the view that the requirement of fifteen days' notice to the Appellant was clearly intended to allow him a minimum period of time to examine the information that the Board proposed to consider and to meet the case against him. In looking at the notice provision in the context of the *Parole Act* and Regulations, as a whole, and the importance of the subject matter of the hearing before the Parole Board and its consequences to the Appellant, we have no doubt that the time frames in question were intended to be, and are in fact, imperative.

While the court ultimately dismissed the appeal because the prisoner had not been prejudiced by the failure to observe all the time frames, the case stands for the proposition that penal and parole authorities cannot ignore time frames imposed by Parliament.

Subject to information which, in the opinion of the Board, must remain confidential, the Board is obligated to provide all relevant information (or a summary thereof) which it intends to consider during

---

[44] *Milner v. National Parole Bd.*, (File no. T-107-90, Fed. T.D., Addy J., January 22, 1990).

[45] (File no. T-95-90, Fed. T.D., Jerome A.C.J., February 19, 1990).

[46] *Shubley v. R.* (1990), 52 C.C.C. (3d) 481 (S.C.C.). The reasoning in this case has been criticized in A. Manson, "Solitary Confinement, Remission and Prison Discipline" (1990), 75 C.R. (3d) 356.

[47] *Cleary v. (Correctional Service) Canada* (File A-158-90, Fed. C.A., Iacobucci C.J., Hugessen, Desjardins JJ.A., April 3, 1990).

the hearing. This information must be provided in writing[48] at least 15 days prior to the scheduled hearing date.[49] In *Okeynan v. Canada (Prince Albert Penitentiary)*,[50] some of the material disclosed in writing to the prisoner referred to alleged verbal threats and acts of physical violence (both inside and outside the penitentiary) with which the prisoner had never been charged, let alone convicted.[51] In addition to finding that these broad allegations were not sufficiently specific to "give the applicant sufficient details of the allegations to enable him to defend himself,"[52] Strayer J. doubted that they would constitute a "summary" as required by section 17 of the *Parole Regulations*.

In addition to a higher standard of procedural safeguards, the legislative scheme contemplates that detention hearings be different in nature from most other types of hearings. First, section 23(2) of the *Parole Regulations*[53] directs that three members of the Board must vote on each case, as compared with two members for non-lifer cases, thereby emphasizing the seriousness of the process. Again, section 16.2 of the *Parole Regulations* mandates that these hearings are to be voice recorded.[54] Finally, unlike the broad ambiguous phrases contained in

---

[48]   In *Re Hopley* [summarized (1987), 1 W.C.B. (2d) 359-360 (B.C. S.C.)] MacEachern C.J.S.C. directed that a case be remitted back to the Board where the Board had shown the materials on which it intended to rely to the prisoner, but had failed to provide him with copies which he might review at his leisure.

[49]   The *Parole Regulations* permit departures from these time frames when the information only becomes available at the last minute, or where there is an emergency referral.

[50]   (1988), 20 F.T.R. 270 (Fed. T.D.).

[51]   A similar conclusion was reached by Callaghan A.C.J.H.C. within the context of a "15-year review" pursuant to section 672 [now s. 745] of the *Code* in *R. v. Vaillancourt* [summarized (1988), 5 W.C.B. (2d) 183 (Ont. H.C.)].

[52]   See the comments of Reed J. in *H. v. R.* (1985), 17 Admin. L.R. 30 (Fed. T.D.) and the general discussion of confidentiality and disclosure in Chapter 6.

[53]   SOR/86-915, s. 7.

[54]   SOR/86-817, s. 4. Since May 1, 1988 Board policy has been to voice record all hearings. Detention hearings are the only ones which are required by Regulation to be taped. In *Okeynan, supra,* note 50 one of the prisoner's complaints was that he was denied fairness because the voice recording made of the hearing was so unsatisfactory that a complete transcript could not be prepared. Strayer J. held that a failure to make a satisfactory recording would not "automatically nullif[y]" the decision reached by the Board; nevertheless, its absence would be one factor which a judge might take into account in deciding whether a fair hearing had been held. This judgment foreshadowed the judgment of a majority of the Supreme Court of Canada in *Hayes v. R.*, (1989), 48 C.C.C. (3d) 161, where L'Heureux-Dubé J. held that an inability to produce a complete transcript of a trial does not automatically entitle an accused to a new trial; the onus is on the appellant to demonstrate either that there is a serious possibility that there was an error in the transcript, or that the omission deprives him of a ground of appeal in some other way. See also *Desjardins v. National Parole Bd.* [summarized (1989), 8 W.C.B. (2d) 246 (Fed. T.D.)].

section 16(1)(*a*)(i)-(iii) of the Act, section 21.4(5)(*a*)-(*d*) provide notice and direction to the Board as to the matters which it is obligated by statute to consider.

Two cases have questioned whether and to what extent the Board is obligated to examine the basis for the referral. In *Niessen v. National Parole Board*,[55] the prisoner attempted to argue that he had the right to require that members of the case management team be cross-examined at the detention hearing, in order that the Board might determine whether the case should have been referred (presumably because there were differing opinions on the part of the team members). Addy J. held that it would be "manifestly unreasonable" to require the Board to enquire whether the C.S.C. had reasonable grounds to refer the matter to it; "[o]therwise the Board, in every case, would have to conduct what in effect would be two inquiries when the same considerations form the subject matter of both decisions."[56]

In *Bradford v. Correctional Service of Canada*,[57] the case management team contacted a mental health professional who had been involved in treating the child victim both before and after the sexual offence committed upon him by the prisoner. The team requested that the mental health professional provide an opinion as to whether "severe psychological damage" had been caused. In light of the child's previous emotional and adjustment difficulties prior to the offence, the mental health professional reported that he "found it difficult to assess the relationship between the sexual assault on the child and his subsequent behaviourial problems." Despite the equivocal position taken by the mental health professional the C.M.T. concluded that "one does not have to be particularly insightful to realize the impact such an event must have had and is still having on this child", and referred the case to the Board. At the detention hearing, counsel for the prisoner questioned whether there was evidence of "severe psychological harm" as required under sections 21.4 and 21.2(1) of the *Parole Act*. The Board took the position that that issue had already been determined by the fact of the referral, and produced an opinion from Board counsel to the effect that the Board was limited to examining whether the decision to refer "was rational, within the bounds of reason (in other words, is it conceivable that a reasonable person with the same facts could have reached the same conclusion)."[58]

Upon hearing an application to quash the decision to detain, this view of the respective roles of the C.S.C. and the Board was approved by

---

[55] (1988), 19 F.T.R. 297 (Fed. T.D.).
[56] *Ibid.*, at 299.
[57] (1988), 24 F.T.R. 179 (Fed. T.D.).
[58] *Ibid.*, at 186 and 183.

Jerome A.C.J. who held that since the prisoner was allowed an opportunity to address the statutory factors which the Board was required to examine, he could therefore "challenge any characterization of the crime as serious or harm-causing." Because of the various procedural safeguards it was acceptable that the Board's jurisdictional obligations were "limited to ensuring that the C.S.C. members held the appropriate opinions and that those opinions were rationally based."[59] As to an argument developed by analogy from sentencing proceedings to the effect that a tribunal must insist upon strict proof of a fact before it may be acted on,[60] Jerome A.C.J. held that since the detention provisions do not extend a sentence, but only affect the manner of its service, the highest standard of proof was not required.[61]

Once the Board has accepted the referral, has convened the hearing within the appropriate time frames, has given adequate disclosure, and has completed its general review of the case against the general backdrop of the factors mentioned in section 21.4(5)(a)-(d), it must be "satisfied"[63] that the prisoner is likely to commit an offence causing

---

[59] *Ibid.*, at 185 and 184.

[60] *R. v. Sandercock* (1985), 22 C.C.C. (3d) 79 (Alta. C.A.); *R. v. Gardiner* (1982), 68 C.C.C. (2d) 477 (S.C.C.).

[61] Since the release of these decisions, and as the Board and C.S.C. have gained more experience with the detention legislation, in practice more stringent working definitions and standards of proof have been developed. Data for the fiscal year 1987-88 reveal that only 8.3 percent of those potentially referrable for consideration for detention were actually referred. However, among this group, 54.4 percent were ordered detained, 20.0 percent were ordered into residency, 6.4 percent were released subject to "one chance" mandatory supervision, and 13.6 percent were released subject to regular mandatory supervision (National Parole Board, *Detention Program Statistics: Volume 1*, October 1988, unpublished).

[62] Soon after their enactment considerable public attention was focused on the detention provisions when a judge of the British Columbia Supreme Court struck down the entire legislative scheme on the grounds that it did not fulfil the procedural requirements mandated by section 7 of the *Charter* and was not saved by section 1. In *Ross v. Kent Institution (Warden)* (1987), 27 C.R.R. 135 (B.C. S.C.), Meredith J. labelled the Board "little more than a potential Star Chamber" because the disclosure provisions enable "the tribunal to decide guilt or innocence on potentially untested information, perhaps little more than rumour" (at 137). This judgment was quickly reversed on appeal, the British Columbia Court of Appeal holding that the disclosure provisions were adequate, because the prisoner would know at least the gist of any negative allegations and would therefore know the case against him and have a fair opportunity to meet it: see *Re Ross and Kent Institution (Warden)* (1987), 34 C.C.C. (3d) 452. Leave to appeal to S.C.C. refused (1987), 59 C.R. (3d) xxxiv (note) (S.C.C.).

[63] Note the use of this word in contradistinction to section 21.3(2) where C.S.C. need only be "of the opinion" that the various criteria have been met before it may refer to the Board. In *Bradford, supra*, note 57, Jerome A.C.J. cited *Re Henderson and R.* (1982), 60 C.C.C. (2d) 561 (B.C.S.C.) for the proposition that since the Board was the final decision-maker, it was not necessary that C.S.C. be "satisfied" that the criteria were met before it could refer.

death or serious harm.[64] If the Board is so satisfied, it has two options:[65]

1. to direct that the prisoner not be released at the presumptive release date as a result of accumulated earned remission,[66] and that he be detained in penitentiary (subject to annual or Board-initiated reviews discussed below) until warrant expiry date;
2. to direct that the prisoner be released, but that he be required to reside in a community-based residential facility.

If the Board is satisfied that an offence for which the prisoner is serving sentence is one which is on the Schedule, was prosecuted by indictment, and did involve serious harm to the victim, but the Board is not satisfied that, if released, the prisoner is likely to commit another offence involving serious harm prior to warrant expiry date, it is required by section 21.4(4)(*b*) of the *Parole Act* to make a declaration to this effect and to specify its reasons therefore. The reason for this is contained in section 26.1 of the *Penitentiary Act*, which states that if the prisoner's mandatory supervision is subsequently revoked for any reason, he shall both forfeit all remission standing to his credit at the time of

---

64 In a policy directive issued July 24, 1989, C.S.C. case management staff and the Board are reminded that "it is *not* necessary that an offence have a permanent or long-term effect on the victim in order to satisfy the 'serious harm' criterion. For example, if a victim is severely beaten, but recovers completely from the beating, *it is still possible for* that offence to be considered to have caused 'serious harm'." The directive further lists factors which, individually or collectively, should be considered in assessing whether serious harm was caused. These include:
   — the extent of injury to the victim, as assessed or indicated by medical care sought or required;
   — the nature of the offence and the circumstances surrounding it, and in particular whether it involved brutality, excessive force, viciousness, or deviant sexual behavior;
   — the use of a weapon to harm or threaten the victim;
   — whether or not the victim was subjected to prolonged or repeated abuse or terror;
   — any particular vulnerability of the victim, such as being very young, aged, infirm, helpless, or handicapped.

65 According to the Board's Appeal Division, before deciding upon detention the Board must conclude that residency is an inappropriate alternative, and must specify its reasons for so concluding. See *Appeal Division Reports*, Case No. "DET 003", February 20, 1987.

66 For the sake of clarity, section 21.4(8) of the *Parole Act* states that a detained prisoner is not eligible for parole, while section 15.1 of that Act and sections 25(5)–(7) of the *Penitentiary Act* specify that such a prisoner both forfeits existing remission and cannot be released by earning more remission. However, sentence administrators take the view that since an existing sentence may be reduced on appeal, or the Board may be persuaded to change its mind, it is still necessary, however notionally, to credit the prisoner with remission as if he had earned it.

his release subject to mandatory supervision, and shall not be eligible to be credited (for release purposes) with any further remission during the pendency of the sentence.[67] Finally, if the Board is not satisfied that, despite the referral, any of the statutory criteria have been fulfilled, it must direct normal release subject to mandatory supervision, with or without added special conditions.

If the Board elects to order residency during the period of mandatory supervision, section 21.4(4)(*b*) of the *Parole Act* directs that such residence is to be "in a community-based residential facility," which term is defined in section 21.2 (1) as including either a halfway house (government or private), a psychiatric hospital or a penitentiary especially designated pursuant to section 21.6 (2). Under that section, the Governor in Council has designated some multi-level security institutions, most minimum security penitentiaries and government-run halfway houses (called Community Correctional Centres) as community-based residential facilities.[68] However, before a prisoner can be compelled to reside in a penitentiary, section 21.4(6) mandates that the Commissioner of Corrections or designate must consent in writing.[69] It remains to be determined whether a prisoner compelled to reside in a penitentiary can have less access to the community than he would if he were to reside in a halfway house.

If a prisoner is ordered detained, he is entitled by section 21.5 of the *Parole Act* to an annual review of his status.[70] The procedures contained in the legislation specify that these reviews are to be conducted by way of an in-person hearing, with all of the procedural safeguards which existed during the initial detention proceeding. The Board also has the power to review a case of its own motion at any time. Experience to date indicates that "interim" detention orders are frequently made where the prisoner is undergoing (or is about to undergo) a course of treatment which is not scheduled to be completed until after the presumptive release date has been reached. In those cases the Board will, after making the decision to detain, set a review date earlier than 1 year. If the Board elects to revoke

---

[67] This provision is known in prison vocabulary as "one shot" or "one chance M.S." Section 29 of the *Penitentiary Act* also makes these provisions applicable to persons originally ordered detained under section 21.4(4)(*a*) of the *Parole Act* (who might later be released by the Board) and to those ordered into "residency" under section 21.4(4)(*b*) of the Act.

[68] SOR/86-819.

[69] This has, to date, created difficulties in certain parts of the country, where C.S.C. has effectively been able to thwart the intentions of the National Parole Board by refusing to give consent to residence in a facility approved by the latter.

[70] It should be noted that the review must occur 1 year from the date the original detention order was made, not on the anniversary of the presumptive release date.

its previously made order and substitute an order for release, section 21.5(6) details that partial remission is to be re-credited and the prisoner released.

Given the potential consequences of these amendments, it has not been surprising that litigation to challenge the validity of the detention provisions commenced almost immediately. The leading case is *Evans*,[71] where the prisoner had been referred by the Commissioner a few days after the proclamation,[72] and detention was ordered by the Board. The legislation was attacked on the basis that the *Charter* prohibited amendments which affected prisoners already serving penitentiary sentences. Smith J. ruled that even if this were the case, the legislation was saved under section 1 of the *Charter*. This view was sustained on appeal[73] where, after agreeing with the motions court judge that "the enactment cannot be viewed as being either retroactive or retrospective legislation", Robins J.A. examined whether there was any breach of either sections 7 or 9 of the *Charter*. Even though the Crown had conceded that the legislative framework did provide for the deprivation of a liberty interest, the court held that such deprivation did not breach the principle of fundamental justice, as "[t]hese sections do not change the sentence imposed on the inmate by the court that convicted him and, consequently, do not impose an additonal penalty. . . . [T]hey do no more than change the manner or condition under which certain inmates must serve the balance of their sentences." Similarly, the court found that the procedural safeguards indicated that the detention imposed was not arbitrary. The court indicated that "[t]he means chosen by Parliament for the important societal purpose of protecting the public from dangerous inmates are reasonable and demonstrably justified."[74] The same result was reached by the British Columbia Court of Appeal in *Re Ross and Warden of Kent Institution*.[75]

---

[71] *Re Evans and R.* (1987), 30 C.C.C. (3d) 1 (Ont. H.C.).

[72] The legislation contained transitional provisions designed to cover situations arising in the first 6 months following the proclamation.

[73] *Re Evans and R.* (1987), 30 C.C.C. (3d) 313 (Ont. C.A.)

[74] Smith J. had noted that there were procedural defects in the detention process and for that reason alone directed that a new hearing be held. After the dismissal of his appeal to the Court of Appeal, the prisoner invoked his right to a new hearing. Given that his sentence was coming to an end, and not wishing to face the prospect of a complete release without any opportunity for assistance or surveillance, the Board elected to release Evans and ordered him into residency. He committed a sexual assault 4 days after release. Following conviction for that offence, the Crown successfully launched dangerous offender proceedings, and an indeterminate sentence was imposed.

[75] (1987), 34 C.C.C. (3d) 452 (B.C. C.A.).

8

Suspension, Termination and Revocation

To climb a wall and steal apples can be a mere escapade if it's a boy, or a minor offence in a grown man; but in the case of a convict on parole it's a crime—breaking and entering and all the rest of it, not just a case for the magistrate but for trial at the Assizes. And the penalty is not just a few days in gaol, but life imprisonment.

—Victor Hugo, *Les Misérables*

1. THE POWER TO REVOKE WITHOUT HEARING

The usual process of revocation of parole or mandatory supervision[1] is contained in section 22 of the *Parole Act*, which presently provides:

> **22.** (1) A member of the Board or a person designated by the Chairman, when a breach of a term or condition of parole occurs or the Board or person is satisfied that it is necessary or reasonable to do so in order to prevent a breach of any term or condition of parole or to protect society, may, by a warrant in writing signed by the member or designated person,
> (*a*) suspend any parole other than a parole that has been discharged;
> (*b*) authorize the apprehension of a paroled inmate; and
> (*c*) recommit an inmate to custody until the suspension of the inmate's parole is cancelled or the inmate's parole is revoked.
> (2) The Board or a person designated by the Chairman may, by a warrant, transfer an inmate following his recommitment to custody pursuant to paragraph (1)(*c*) to a place where the inmate is to be held in custody until the suspension of his parole is cancelled or his parole is revoked.
> (3) The person by whom a warrant is signed pursuant to subsection (1) or any other person designated by the Chairman for the purpose shall forthwith after the recommitment of the paroled inmate named in the warrant review the case and, within fourteen days after the recommitment or such shorter period as may be directed by the Board, either cancel the suspension or refer the case to the Board.
> (3.1) The Chairman may fix the terms and conditions under which a power may be exercised pursuant to subsection (1), (2) or (3) by any person designated by the Chairman for the purposes of that subsection.

---

[1] Although section 22 speaks only of parole, the same procedures are imported into the regime of mandatory supervision through section 21(2) of the *Parole Act*, R.S.C. 1985, c. P-2.

(4) The Board shall, on the referral to it of the case of a paroled inmate whose parole has been suspended, review the case and cause to be conducted all such inquiries in connection therewith as it considers necessary, and forthwith on completion of such inquiries and its review it shall either cancel the suspension or revoke the parole.

(5) An inmate who is in custody by virtue of this section shall be deemed to be serving his sentence.[2]

In the judgment of the Federal Court of Appeal in *Howarth v. National Parole Board*,[3] Jackett C.J. stated:

> While there are no detailed provisions in the *Parole Act* or in the rules made thereunder concerning the procedure, if any, to be followed by the Parole Board before making an order revoking parole, s. 16 of the Act does lay down steps that, in my view, are conditions precedent to the making of any such order.
>
> . . . .
>
> ... the Parole Board's power to revoke parole can only be exercised in the manner laid down by s. 16 and after all the steps required by that section have been taken.[4]

He added that a failure to comply with the statutory pre-conditions would render a revocation "voidable, at the suit of the paroled inmate".[5] Notwithstanding this reasoning, the National Parole Board continued to act on the basis that section 10(1)(*e*) [now s. 16(1)(*d*) and (*e*)] of the *Parole Act* provided a general power to revoke without implicating the conditions required by section 16 [now s. 22]. Several pre-*Charter* cases[6] considered the implications of these two sections.

In *Ex parte Gorog*,[7] the prisoner had been properly remanded by a magistrate under the procedures in force at that time, but no review of his case occurred within 14 days of his apprehension, as required by section 16(3) [now section 22(3)] of the *Parole Act*. Nevertheless, the

---

2   S.C. 1958, c. 38, s. 12 [as amended by S.C. 1968-69, c. 38, s. 10]. Subsection (1) reenacted S.C. 1976-77, c. 53, s. 29 (proclaimed in force October 15, 1977); re-enacted S.C. 1986, c. 43, s. 12(1) (proclaimed in force July 25, 1986); subsections (2) and (3) reenacted S.C. 1976-77, c. 53, s. 29 (proclaimed in force October 15, 1977); subsection (3.1) enacted S.C. 1986, c. 43, s. 12(2) (proclaimed in force July 25, 1986)] [now R.S.C. 1985, c. P-2, s. 22].

3   (1973), 41 D.L.R. (3d) 309 (Fed. C.A.).

4   *Ibid.*, at 313.

5   *Ibid.*, at 314. Whether the distinction between "void" and "voidable" has any contemporary merit is debatable. Regardless, it is significant that Jackett C.J. recognized that the decision to revoke would be inoperative "as of the time that it was made".

6   Many of these cases are exhaustively discussed in T. Cromwell, "Parole Committals and Habeas Corpus" (1976), 8 Ottawa L. Rev. 560 and "Habeas Corpus and Correctional Law—An Introduction (1976), 3 Queen's L.J. 295.

7   (1974), 21 C.C.C. (2d) 444 (Man. Q.B.).

Board revoked the prisoner's parole 2 days after the expiry of sentence. Solomon J. disagreed with the view of Jackett C.J. in *Howarth*, holding that the 14-day limitation "does not really matter. . . . the limitation provided for in s-s. (3) is for a designated person or officer and not for the Parole Board." Because of the Board's extensive power contained in section 10(1)(*e*) [now s. 16(1)(*d*) and (*e*)] of the Act, whereby it was authorized in its "discretion to revoke the parole of any person who is in custody pursuant to a warrant issued under s. 16 even after the sentence has expired," Solomon J. considered that the Board "has power to deal with all cases whether they have been considered by the designated officer or not."[8]

On appeal of the dismissal of the prisoner's application for *habeas corpus* to the Manitoba Court of Appeal,[9] the majority took a broad view of the powers of the Board. Commenting that the facts were "basically the same" as those which recently had been before that same court in *Mitchell*,[10] Guy J.A. (Monnin J.A. concurring) held that "[o]nce a Court, or two courts, have decided on a sentence . . . the question of parole or probation should not concern the Courts of justice any more. That is strictly a matter for . . . the Parole Board." Citing sections 6, 10 and 23 [now ss. 13, 16 and 28] of the *Parole Act* as they read at that time, His Lordship indicated that "[t]his surely indicates with more than usual clarity the fact that Parliament intended the Parole Board to have power and jurisdiction to parole or not to parole as the particular circumstances seemed to warrant."[11]

A lengthy dissent was delivered by Matas J.A., who distinguished *Mitchell* on the basis that the prisoner's complaint in that case had been that the Board contravened the principles of natural justice by not providing him with adequate notice of the reasons for suspension and revocation. However, in the case at bar, the issue was whether the Board had lost jurisdiction by failing to conduct the review by a designated officer mandated by section 16(3) [now s. 22(3)]. While conceding the discretionary powers contained in sections 6 and 10(1)(*e*) [now ss. 13 and 16(1)(*d*) and (*e*)], Matas J.A. held that such powers "must be exercised in accordance with the Act." To permit the Board to embark on the procedures specified in section 16 and then to proceed in a different way

---

8   *Ibid.*, at 446 and 447.
9   *Ex parte Gorog* (1975), 23 C.C.C. (2d) 225 (Man. C.A.).
10 Although the *Mitchell* judgment of the Supreme Court of Canada was subsequently released and reported, [1976] 2 S.C.R. 570, the judgments of Dewar C.J.Q.B. and the Manitoba Court of Appeal in that case were not reported, but are quoted in the Court of Appeal decision in *Gorog.*
11 *Supra*, note 9, at 227 and 228.

276 / Release From Imprisonment

would render section 16 "nugatory. . . . ss. 6 and 10(1)(*e*) do not override
the clear requirement of s. 16(3) for a review."[12]

Gorog was appealed further to the Supreme Court of Canada. On
March 15, 1976, upon joint motion of the applicant and the respondent
for a consent judgment, the Supreme Court of Canada reversed the
judgment of the Manitoba Court of Appeal.[13] No reasons for judgment
were released.

In the subsequent case of *Grabina*,[14] Goodman J. was faced with a
situation in which there had been a failure to comply with section 16(2)
[now s. 22(2)], as that section read prior to the 1977 amendments. The
prisoner had been apprehended under a parole suspension warrant and
taken to a courthouse in a police car. Since the prisoner had difficulty
walking as a result of a recent operation on his legs, the police officer
attended before a magistrate in the absence of the prisoner, with a copy
of the prisoner's parole identification card. After hearing the officer
testify under oath that he had received the card from the prisoner, the
magistrate signed a committal warrant under section 16(2) [now
s. 22(2)]. In due course, the Board reviewed the case and revoked the
prisoner's parole. Upon hearing an application for *habeas corpus* Goodman J. cited with approval the judgment of Henry J. in *Ex parte
Collins*.[15] In that case parole had been suspended, but the suspension
was cancelled by the designated person under section 16(3) [now
s. 22(3)] of the Act. A few days later, despite the fact that the case had
never been referred by the designated person to the Board under section
16(3) [now s. 22(3)], the Board "overruled" that decision and revoked
the parole. Henry J. held that "the Board, in revoking the applicant's
parole, acted on its own motion and could do so under ss. 6 and 10(1)(*e*).
In so doing, it acted within its jurisdiction and authority and its decision
revoking the parole was validly made."[16]

It may be seen from this, for both Goodman J. and Henry J., that the
Board had the power to revoke a parole of its own motion under section
10(1)(*e*) [now s. 16(1)(*d*) and (*e*)], and was not limited to the revocation
power contained in section 16(4) [now s. 22(4)]. This absolute discretion
to revoke was subject only to two limitations: parole or mandatory
supervision could not be revoked where the prisoner had been discharged upon successful completion of sentence, nor could parole or

---

12   *Supra*, note 9, at 236.
13   (1977), 33 C.C.C. (2d) 207; [1977] 3 W.W.R. 96.
14   *Re Grabina and R.* (1977), 34 C.C.C. (2d) 52 (Ont. H.C.).
15   (1976), 30 C.C.C. (2d) 460 (Ont. H.C.). Affirmed without reasons (1976), 30 C.C.C. (2d)
      460n (Ont. C.A.).
16   *Ibid.*, at 469.

mandatory supervision be revoked where the sentence had expired
(unless on the date of expiry the prisoner was in custody subject to a
warrant issued under section 16 [now s. 22]). On this basis, Goodman J.
was able to distinguish the dissenting judgments of Matas J.A. in *Gorog*
and the judgment of Anderson J. in *Elliott*,[17] since those cases involved
sentences which had expired prior to the revocation of parole. Because
section 10(1)(*e*) [now s. 16(1)(*d*) and (*e*)] allowed the draconian step of
revocation even after the sentence had expired, it was an appropriate
limitation for a court to examine whether the "custody" mentioned in
section 10(1)(*e*) was "lawful custody." In both *Gorog* and *Elliott* the
custody was not lawful because of the failure of the parole authorities to
comply with section 16 [now s. 22]; thus, "the Board would not have
jurisdiction to revoke the parole if the inmate's sentence had expired. . . .
and the eventual results in both of those cases can be justified on that
ground."[18]

Goodman J. was not prepared to leave the aggrieved parolee completely without redress where the procedural requirements specified in
section 16 [now s. 22] had not been followed. Like Jackett C.J. in
Howarth, Goodman J. envisaged "a situation where an inmate would be
held unlawfully in custody and would be entitled to be released upon an
application of *habeas corpus* at any time prior to the actual revocation of
his parole." Since the warrant remanding the prisoner into custody "was
a nullity . . . the applicant was taken into unlawful custody and so
remained until his parole was revoked by the Board". Thus, in response
to the statement of Matas J.A. in *Gorog*, that to read section 10(1)(*e*)
[now s. 16(1)(*d*) and (*e*)] as giving the Board a power independent of the
power to revoke under section 16(4) [now s. 22(4)] would render section
16 "nugatory", Goodman J. indicated that a failure by the person signing
the suspension warrant to carry out the duties imposed by section 16(2)

---

17 *R. v. Elliott* (1976), 34 C.R.N.S. 117 (B.C.S.C.). Anderson J. accepted the dissenting
reasoning of Matas J.A. and held that "[t]he Parole Board and its officers must . . .
carry out the mandatory duties prescribed by Parliament and if they do not . . . they are
acting outside the law and any purported determination made by them is null and
void" (at 122).

18 *Grabina, supra,* note 14, at 61. Goodman J. carefully noted that the consent reversal by
the Supreme Court of Canada of the judgment of the Manitoba Court of Appeal in
Gorog "does not necessarily mean that the Court approved of the reasons given in the
minority opinion" (at 60). The Board may have wished to avoid negative publicity. In
addition to the scathing dissenting remarks of Laskin C.J.C. discussed in Chapters 3
and 5, the Board had been the subject of substantial criticism for its actions in *Mitchell*.
Again, the Board may have considered that the general issue raised by *Gorog* would
soon become moot, since the 1977 amendments (giving credit for "street time") had
been introduced in Parliament by the time the case was before the Supreme Court of
Canada.

or (3) [now s. 22(2) or (3)] would give the prisoner "the right to make his application for a writ of *habeas corpus* immediately upon such breach". For Goodman J. the difference lay between the breach of statutory duties by a Board member or designated official during the suspension process and the plenary powers of the Board itself to revoke. Because of the very broad powers conferred on the Board by Parliament, "failure to comply with the requirements of s. 16 may invalidate the suspension of the parole but does not affect the ultimate decision of the Board with respect to revocation."[19] Thus, we see the genesis of the concept that a subsequent revocation cures defects which may have arisen during the suspension and referral process.

While the requirement that the suspended parolee or person released subject to mandatory supervision be taken before a magistrate was removed in the 1977 amendments,[20] of greater importance was the proclamation of section 20 of the *Parole Regulations*[21] which established the right of a prisoner to an in-person hearing before the Board[22] as part of the section 16 [now s. 22] review process. Inevitably, the question arose as to whether the creation of this "post-suspension hearing" process affected the powers of the National Parole Board to revoke parole or mandatory supervision independent of section 16 [now s. 22] of the Act.

In *Roach v. Director of Kent Institution*,[23] the prisoner had been released on mandatory supervision in late 1981. In April 1982 a suspension warrant was issued, presumably because the prisoner had not reported to his parole officer. Some 2 months later the National Parole Board revoked Roach's mandatory supervision pursuant to section 10(1)(*e*) [now s. 16(1)(*d*) and (*e*)] of the Act (a section which had not been amended in 1977). When he was finally apprehended, the prisoner argued, *inter alia*, that no review of the suspension had taken place within 14 days of the original suspension and, therefore, the Board did not have jurisdiction to revoke mandatory supervision under section 10(1)(*e*) [now s. 16(1)(*d*) and (*e*)]. Craig J.A. (Nemetz C.J.B.C. concur-

---

19 *Grabina, supra*, note 14, at 59 and 61.
20 *Criminal Law Amendment Act*, S.C. 1976-77, c. 53, s. 29.
21 SOR/78-428 [as amended by SOR/81-487; SOR-86-817 authorized by sections 9(1)(*g*), (*i*) and (*k*) [now s. 27(1)(9)(*i*) and (*k*)] of the *Parole Act*, S.C. 1976-77, c. 53, s. 24 (proclaimed in force October 14, 1977)].
22 *Parole Regulations*, s. 23(3). Following the judgments in *O'Brien v. National Parole Bd.* (1984), 43 C.R. (3d) 10 (Fed. T.D.) and *Re Mason and R.* (1983), 7 C.C.C. (3d) 426 (Ont. H.C.), the Regulations were changed to provide that the post-suspension hearing must be before three members of the Board (SOR/84-1123 [proclaimed in force March 7, 1985]). A return to two-member panels was initiated by SOR/86-817, SOR/86-915.
23 (1983), 34 C.R. (3d) 249 (B.C.C.A.).

ring) sketched out the varying views in the cases described above and stated that he agreed with the judgments in *Collins* and *Grabina* to the effect "that strict compliance with the review procedure is not a condition precedent to the board's exercising jurisdiction under section 10(1)(*e*)." Seaton J.A. was somewhat more detailed in his analysis, noting that *Gorog* and *Elliott* were cases involving persons whose sentences had expired at the time parole or mandatory supervision was purportedly revoked. As such, their status was different from that of persons still on parole or subject to mandatory supervision, in that they had "regained the rights that they lost for the period of their sentence." Thus, their paroles could not be revoked under the first branch of section 10(1)(*e*) [now s. 16(1)(*d*) and (*e*)], but only under the second part of that section, which requires compliance with section 16 [now s. 22] as a condition precedent to its operation. However, for persons such as Roach, for whom no question of sentence expiry had arisen, "parole can be revoked at any time, whether proceedings under s. 16 have been properly taken, improperly taken, or not taken at all."[24]

The 1986 amendments to the *Parole Act* entrenched the *ratio* in *Roach*. Section 10(1)(*e*) [now s. 16(1)(*d*) and (*e*)] was separated into two new subsections, which provide that the Board may:

> (*e*) in its discretion, terminate or revoke the parole of any paroled inmate, other than an inmate on day parole, in any case other than that of a paroled inmate to whom discharge from parole has been granted; and
> (*f*) in its discretion, revoke the parole of any person who is in custody pursuant to a warrant issued under section 16, or terminate the parole instead of revoking it as provided for in that section, whether or not the sentence of that person has expired.[25]

A far more sophisticated treatment of these issues was developed by McEachern C.J.S.C. in the post-*Charter* case of *Swan v. Attorney General of British Columbia*[26] where the parolee had "lost contact" with his parole officer. Parole was suspended and revoked in the prisoner's absence. When he was apprehended, the prisoner was informed that he could seek a re-examination of this decision by Board members who had not participated in the original decision, pursuant to section 22 of the Regulations. He was also advised by his parole officer that he could apply for a "post-revocation hearing," a procedure not mandated by statute, which would be granted "only if the board considers such a

---

24 *Ibid.*, at 255 and 251.
25 S.C. 1986, c. 43, s. 6(3) [proclaimed in force July 25, 1986].
26 (1983), 35 C.R. (3d) 135 (B.C.S.C.). The *Swan* case is also discussed in Chapter 4. See also *Kennedy v. National Parole Service* [summarized (1985), 14 W.C.B. 429 (Fed. T.D.)].

hearing will be useful."[27] He elected to invoke the section 22 review procedure, but was unsuccessful in obtaining release. Upon considering an application for *habeas corpus*, McEachern C.J.S.C. commenced his analysis by referring to *Vidlin*,[28] which had interpreted section 13 [now s. 19] of the *Parole Act* as meaning that the issuance of a suspension warrant did not interrupt the running of a sentence where the prisoner was not apprehended. It would therefore be necessary for the National Parole Board to revoke parole or mandatory supervision in order to prevent a sentence from continuing to run while the prisoner remained out of custody. In the case at bar, the real reason the Board had moved to revoke was to prevent the prisoner's sentence from continuing to run while he was still at large. Since "normal" suspension and revocation processes engaged the procedural protections contained in section 16 [now s. 22], McEachern C.J.S.C. commented: "Can the board, having suspended the petitioner's parole, change direction and exercise a general jurisdiction of revocation?" As the sentence had not expired at the time parole was purportedly revoked, he considered himself bound by the *Roach* judgment; consequently, "the parole board had jurisdiction to commence the revocation process under its general power without regard to the absence of a post-suspension review."[29]

However, this did not end the matter. Relying on the familiar statement by the Supreme Court of Canada in *Roncarelli v. Duplessis*,[30] that "absolute power ... without review is unknown to law," McEachern C.J.S.C. regarded himself as duty bound to consider whether the process was marked by "working fair play". He held that revocation should be conceived not as a "single Draconic act of decision, but rather [as] a process which begins with such a decision but also includes whatever other procedures are required by statute *or by the general law* to make revocation complete and effective".[31] The court examined the two processes made available to review the initial revocation decision. Looking at the "offer" of a "post-revocation hearing" (and agreeing that such a hearing "would have been a useful procedure if conducted fairly"), McEachern C.J.S.C. held that

---

27 *Ibid.*, at 139.

28 *Re Vidlin and R.* (1976), 38 C.C.C. (2d) 378 (B.C.S.C.). Provincial penal administrators in Ontario and Quebec are of the view that provincial correctional statutes are sufficiently broadly worded to stop sentences running where a suspension warrant has been issued but the prisoner is not immediately apprehended. British Columbia follows the procedures of the federal authorities. Section 13 [now s. 19] has not been amended in either the 1977 or the 1986 legislation.

29 *Supra*, note 26, at 141 and 143.

30 [1959] S.C.R. 121.

31 *Swan, supra*, note 26, at 143 [emphasis added].

no process which the Board can hold or not hold at its discretion meets the requirements of natural justice, for the simple reason that there can be no confidence in the impartiality of a tribunal . . . that acts, not on principle or in accordance with fixed rules, but only if it thinks the procedure will be useful.[32]

Similarly, while the prisoner had availed himself of the right to a review of the revocation decision pursuant to section 22 of the Regulations, the court expressed skepticism about the quality of factual investigation conducted by the Board's Internal Review Committee, given the "wide discrepancies between the facts alleged by the petitioner and the conclusions of the internal review committee".[33] McEachern C.J.S.C. speculated that, on the facts, the Internal Review Committee (now called the Appeal Division) may have arrived at the wrong conclusion. More important, however, was the denial of any real opportunity to meet the decision-maker, because the maxim that "justice should not only be done, but should manifestly and undoubtedly be seen to be done"[34] had not been followed.

McEachern C.J.S.C. went on to examine three recent developments in Canadian law and concluded that the Board had lost jurisdiction by failing to afford the prisoner a post-revocation hearing as a matter of right. First, he noted a substantial difference in the interests at stake in *Nicholson v. Haldimand-Norfolk Regional Board of Police Commissioners*[35] as compared to the case at bar. Noting that Dickson J. had stated in *Martineau (No. 2)*[36] that the application of the principles of natural justice and fairness will vary according to the circumstances of each case, McEachern C.J.S.C. concluded that while the question of continued employment at issue in *Nicholson* did not require a full-fledged hearing, "this case raises a more serious question about the liberty of a citizen, and that makes a vast difference." He then turned to an examination of sections 7 and 9 of the *Charter*, stating that those provisions "tilt the scales strongly towards the requirements of natural justice rather than just procedural fairness in the post-revocation process." Neither an administrative inquiry under section 22 of the *Parole Regulations* nor a discretionary hearing under the post-revocation hearing process would be sufficient. He concluded that the prisoner's detention would become unlawful "unless there is a proper post-revocation

---

[32] *Swan, supra*, note 26, at 144.

[33] *Swan, supra*, note 26, at 144.

[34] *R. v. Sussex Justices; Ex parte McCarthy*, [1924] 1 K.B. 256, at 259. See also the comments of Thurlow C.J. concerning the utility of section 22 of the Regulations in *Morgan v. National Parole Bd.* (1982), 65 C.C.C. (2d) 216 (Fed. C.A.) at 218-219.

[35] [1979] 1 S.C.R. 311.

[36] [1980] 1 S.C.R. 602.

hearing as of right with natural justice safeguards at least equal to the requirements of the Parole Regulations respecting suspension of parole." Finally, he was prepared to adapt the use of *habeas corpus* to enable the court "to exercise its new constitutional mandate." Instead of simply directing the release of the prisoner, he decided to reserve decision pending the "convening and completing [of] a proper post-revocation hearing".[37]

A similar conclusion on the hearing issue had been reached a few months earlier by Mahoney J. in *Ziatas v. National Parole Board.*[38] In that case the prisoner had been ordered released on day parole on condition that he not associate with members of certain motorcycle gangs. He was observed driving to the halfway house from the penitentiary in company with members of one of the prohibited gangs. Day parole was suspended and the case was referred to the Board under section 16(3) [now s. 22(3)]. The prisoner applied for a post-suspension hearing, but the Board, prior to such hearing, purported to terminate the day parole under section 10(2) [now s. 16(4)] of the *Parole Act*. Mahoney J. quashed the termination decision on the basis that having invoked section 16 [now section 22], the Board could not terminate or revoke day parole without holding the hearing guaranteed by section 16.

While this result is consistent with the thrust of the ruling in *Swan*, it should also be noted that Mahoney J. expressed the opinion *in obiter* that it would have been open to the Board to terminate a day parole without providing the opportunity for a hearing, so long as the Board either initially did not invoke section 16 [now s. 22], or cancelled a suspension warrant issued under section 16 and then exercised its discretion under section 10(2) [now s. 16(4)].[39] It appears that Mahoney J. arrived at this conclusion because section 20 of the *Parole Regulations* referred to the right to a hearing only when a referral had been made to the Board under section 16(3) [now s. 22(3)], while section 10(2) [now s. 16(4)] was an independent source of the Board's power, rather like the general power to revoke under section 10(1)(*e*) [now s. 16(1)(*d*) and (*e*)] confirmed by the British Columbia Court of Appeal in *Roach*. This reasoning is faulty. While most day paroles are, by their very nature, designed to end on a certain date, such as upon completion of a course of work or study,[40] whenever any form of conditional release—unescorted

---

37 *Swan, supra,* note 26, at 146, 147, 147-148.
38 (1983), 70 C.C.C. (2d) 381 (Fed. T.D.).
39 By amending provisions in S.C. 1986, c. 43, s. 6(4), section 10(2) has, with appropriate modifications, become section 10(4) [now s. 16(4)].
40 In *Fisher v. Comm. Nationale des Libérations Conditionnelles* [English text summarized (1986), 15 W.C.B. 469 (Fed. T.D.)], a grant of day parole had been extended on

temporary absence, day or full parole or mandatory supervision—is sought to be ended prematurely on the basis of allegations of wrong-doing on the part of the prisoner, he must be offered the opportunity for an in-person hearing before any final decision is made.

Beyond establishing the right to an in-person hearing in all cases of revocation of parole or mandatory supervision, thereby rendering moot the controversy raised by the various cases considering the impact of *Gorog*, *Swan* should also be seen in stark contrast with the non-interventionist position expressed a decade previously by the respective majorities of the Supreme Court of Canada in *Howarth* and *Mitchell*.[41] As will be demonstrated later in this chapter, *Swan* is consistent with several other post-*Charter* cases. Since *Nicholson* and *Martineau (No. 2)*, many courts appear to have taken heed of Laskin C.J.C.'s warning in *Mitchell* that citizens should not be expected simply to accept the Board's word that it has acted fairly. With the disappearance of the rigid categorization of the functions exercised by a particular tribunal, a more interventionist trend is developing in many courts which have examined parole-related issues. In this regard, it is noteworthy that in *Singh v. Minister of Employment and Immigration*,[42] the Supreme Court's first significant pronouncement on section 7 of the *Charter* (discussed below), three of the judges were prepared to state explicitly that the dissenting views of

---

several occasions, but was eventually not renewed. The prisoner moved for both *certiorari* and *mandamus*. Pinard J. held that "c'est par le pur effet de la loi et non en vertu d'une décision de la Commission Nationale des Libérations Conditionnelles, que le requérant est incarcéré et donc privé de sa liberté depuis le 23 janvier 1985". Thus, because the Board had taken no decision terminating day parole, Pinard J. quoted J.M. Evans, *DeSmith's Judicial Review of Administrative Action*, 4th ed. (London: Stevens & Sons, 1980), at 381 to the effect that "[c]ertiorari will not lie unless something has been done that the Court can quash". As to *mandamus*, Pinard J. noted that the prisoner was not seeking a hearing to determine whether day parole should be continued; rather the application for *mandamus* was sought "ordonnant a l'intimée de remettre le requérant immédiatement en liberté". After noting that case law in the Federal Court clearly established that *habeas corpus* could only be brought in a provincial superior court, Pinard J. concluded that section 7 of the *Charter* did not create a right to a hearing, and distinguished the post-suspension cases of *Morgan, supra*, note 34, *Cadeddu, infra*, note 106, and *Latham, infra*, note 143 on that basis. As previously noted in our discussion of *O'Brien, Staples* and *Singh* in Chapters 4 and 6, we maintain that this is wrong and that a sufficient liberty interest is created by the expectation that day parole will be continued to engage the procedural protections of section 7.

[41] *Howarth v. National Parole Bd.*, [1976] 1 S.C.R. 453; *Mitchell v. R.*, [1976] 2 S.C.R. 570. See *Cardinal v. Kent Institution (Director)* (1986), 23 C.C.C. (3d) 118 (S.C.C.); *Singh v. Min. of Employment & Immigration* (1985), 14 C.R.R. 13. See also the discussion of *Cadeddu* and similar cases *infra*, pp. 303-308.

[42] *Ibid.*

Laskin C.J.C. in *Mitchell* were to be preferred to those of the majority. The judgment in *Swan* should be seen as a significant move in the direction that even though the literal words of the statute may permit a parole board to revoke conditional liberty without invoking section 22, when liberty is at stake courts should be prepared to create procedural safeguards more consistent with evolving notions of justice and fairness.

The 1986 amendments to the *Parole Act* and the accompanying changes in regulations have formalized the result in *Swan*. In addition to adding a power to terminate full parole, section 20.01 of the Regulations now makes it clear that a person whose release was terminated or revoked while he was not in custody may now insist upon a post-revocation hearing.

2. CHALLENGING DEFECTS IN SUSPENSION PROCEDURES

(a) The Power to Issue Suspension Warrants

Section 22(1) of the Act provides that, in addition to members of the National Parole Board, "a person designated by the Chairman" may sign a suspension warrant.[43] This is designed so that local parole officials may act quickly to suspend conditional release without the necessity for intervention by Board members. Typically, the director of the local parole office is designated by the Chairman of the Board to issue and sign such warrants. These designations are published from time to time in the *Canada Gazette*. While the designation made by the Chairman is to the occupant of a certain position, suspension or termination warrants usually do not describe the title of the person issuing the warrant, reciting only that the individual is "a person designated by the Chairman pursuant to the Parole Act". In light of the approval of the doctrine of the "presumption of regularity" by the Supreme Court of Canada in *Sterner*,[44] it is doubtful whether an argument based on the failure of a warrant to describe the issuer's title would be successful. Similarly, it would appear that any possible arguments based on the absence of an express power of delegation have been precluded by amendments to sections 16 and 22 contained in the 1986 amendments.[45]

---

[43] By S.C. 1986, c. 43, s. 6(4) similar powers relating to termination of day parole or unescorted temporary absence are contained in sections 16(3) and (4) of the Act.

[44] *R. v. Sterner*, [1982] 1 S.C.R. 173; see also *Pearce v. Manitoba Penitentiary (Warden)*, [1966] 3 C.C.C. 326 (Man. C.A.). Affirmed [1966] 3 C.C.C. 339n (S.C.C.); *Re Robidoux (No. 2)* (Ont. H.C., Goodman J., August 8, 1978).

[45] S.C. 1986, c. 43, ss. 6(4) and 12(2).

(b) Sufficiency of Reasons for Suspension

The form of suspension warrant typically used by the National Parole Board before the 1977 amendments merely recited that the signing official was authorized to issue the warrant, that the official suspended the prisoner's right to be at liberty on parole or mandatory supervision, and directed a peace officer to arrest the prisoner "and bring him before a magistrate in order that he be dealt with in accordance with law." In *Ex parte Lewis*, Bouck J. held that since the *Parole Act* did not describe the form a suspension warrant should take, "Parliament must have intended that the warrant be in the form prescribed by the common law."[46] Although not all warrants issued at common law were required to state the reasons for issuance on their face, Bouck J. found it significant that most arrest warrants issued at common law "were only executed by a Justice of the Peace after he had examined on oath the party asking for the warrant".[47] Both because parole suspension warrants are not sworn before a Justice of the Peace, and because (prior to the 1977 amendments) the prisoner was not entitled to a hearing at which he would learn of the reasons for arrest, Bouck J. was prepared to hold that the warrant should have stated the reasons for issuance. *Habeas corpus* was therefore granted.

This decision was reversed by the British Columbia Court of Appeal,[48] which held that since the warrant recited that the reason for the arrest was the suspension of the prisoner's parole, that was sufficient. Relying on the judgments of Ritchie J. and Martland J. in *Mitchell* (which had not been released at the time of the judgment of Bouck J.), Farris C.J.B.C. held that since the Board was exercising an administrative function, and was "entitled to make that decision in its absolute discretion," the Board was not required to provide reasons for suspension on any warrant issued by a Board member or designated official.[49]

While neither the 1977 nor the 1986 amendments to the *Parole Act* made reference to the form of warrant to be used when parole or mandatory supervision is suspended, the wording of warrants has been modified. However, while section 22 of the Act refers to the designated official being authorized to issue a warrant when he "is satisfied that it is necessary or reasonable to do so," the usual form of warrant does not contain any recital that the official is so satisfied; rather, suspension warrants now state that the named official "has reasonable and probable

---

[46] (1976), 25 C.C.C. (2d) 124 (B.C.S.C.), at 127.
[47] *Ibid.*, at 128.
[48] *Ex parte Lewis* (1977), 30 C.C.C. (2d) 225 (B.C.C.A.).
[49] *Ibid.*, at 227.

grounds to believe that the said [parolee or person on mandatory supervision] should be apprehended."⁵⁰ Similarly, while section 22 provides that a warrant may be issued "where a breach of a term or condition . . . occurs or . . . in order to prevent a breach of a term or condition of parole [mandatory supervision] or to protect society," a suspension warrant usually does not contain such wording.

These issues were considered by the British Columbia Court of Appeal in two judgments released on the same day. In *Munday*,⁵¹ the prisoner had been released on mandatory supervision, which was then suspended, the warrant being silent as to the grounds for suspension contained in section 16 [now s. 22]. Since no review of the case was conducted within 14 days of execution of the suspension warrant, the suspension was cancelled by the Board. However, before the prisoner was released from custody a new suspension warrant was issued, which referred to the necessity for apprehending the prisoner "in order to prevent a breach of a term or condition" of mandatory supervision. Because the prisoner had never been released prior to the issuing of the second warrant, the judge hearing an application for *habeas corpus* ordered the release of the prisoner on the basis that "there was no rational basis to believe that . . . [the prisoner] . . . should have been apprehended." On appeal Nemetz C.J.B.C. assumed "that the second warrant was issued to cure the careless procedural defects which arose from the issuance of the first warrant." Thus, "the events leading up to the first apprehension could still constitute grounds which could satisfy the designated officer that . . . [the prisoner] . . . should be returned to custody." This view of the suspension process accepts as a curative lever the questionable notion that the designated officer may well be under pressure to make a rapid decision to issue a suspension warrant.Nemetz C.J.B.C. went further to hold that because of the wording of section 16(4) [now s. 22(4)], it was for the Board to decide whether "any rational basis" may have existed for the issuing of the warrant. In his view a judge on a *habeas corpus* application should not look behind a warrant valid on its face "unless it can be shown that it was made in bad faith or contrary to the considerations in s. 16(1)."⁵²

---

⁵⁰ Perhaps it was felt that since Bouck J. had referred with approval to forms of warrants reciting that the person seeking issuance of a warrant for a person's arrest has "reasonable and probable grounds" for so doing, this form of wording should be included in suspension warrants. Prior to the 1986 amendments in section 16(1) [now s. 22(1)] and other sections of the Act made no reference to reasonableness; rather, the designated person could issue a warrant where he considered it "necessary and desirable" [see S.C. 1986, c. 43, ss. 6(1) and (2) and 12(1)].

⁵¹ *Re Munday and R.* (1982), 69 C.C.C. (2d) 436 (B.C.C.A.). A more thorough recitation of the facts may be found in J. Conroy (1982), 3 Canadian Prison Law 435-436.

⁵² *Munday, ibid.*, at 437 and 438.

In its companion judgment, *Hunchak v. National Parole Board*[53] the same court extended this approach. In that case the suspension warrant made no reference to the decision to arrest being necessary for any of the three reasons set out in section 16 [now s. 22]. Nemetz C.J. was prepared to apply the maxim *omnia praesumuntur rite esse acta* to presume that the designated officer was satisfied that grounds for suspension existed, notwithstanding the lack of reference to any of the section 16 [now s. 22] grounds in the warrant. He referred with approval to "the cautionary admonition set out by both Dickson J. and Pigeon J. in *Martineau (No. 2)* in respect of applying the doctrine of fairness in actions of prison authorities." Because a designated officer would be "under the pressure" of making an "on the spot" decision in a situation where "the officer is often under a time constraint," he considered it acceptable for a suspension warrant merely to recite that the officer "has reasonable and probable grounds to believe that the prisoner should be apprehended." In coming to this conclusion the fact that "the prisoner's interests are protected by his right . . . to a post-suspension hearing before the Parole Board . . . [at which] . . . he must be informed of those particulars" appeared to be influential.[54]

While it is acceptable that a warrant need not contain precise details of the allegations which led the designated official to issue a suspension warrant, a warrant which does not contain any reference to reasons for suspension is defective in light of the interpretation of sections 7 and 9 of the *Charter* enunciated in several cases referred to elsewhere in this work. Courts should be prepared to insist that a person deprived of his liberty (however temporarily) by an act of a parole official (who does not have to justify that decision to any individual independent of the parole system) be provided with at least some notice of the reasons for suspension, if only to the extent of ensuring that one or more of the grounds enunciated in section 22 are specified. At the very least the "cautionary admonition" of the Supreme Court of Canada expressed in the prison disciplinary context of *Martineau (No. 2)* merits more detailed definition before its application to the parole suspension context.[55] As noted by Smith D.J. in *Re Dubeau and National Parole Board*

> a parole board, dealing with a case of alleged breach of a parole condition, is not in the same position as is a prison authority dealing with a case of assault by an inmate on a prison guard or official. In the first case the urgency for a quick decision is not so great or apparent as in the second.[56]

53 [Summarized (1982), 8 W.C.B. 146 (B.C.C.A.)].
54 *Ibid.*
55 *Martineau v. Matsqui Institution Disciplinary Bd., supra,* note 36, at 637, per Pigeon J.; at 630-631, per Dickson J.
56 (1981), 54 C.C.C. (2d) 553 (Fed. T.D.), at 564.

(c) The Section 22(3) Review Process

(i) Timing

Section 22(3) of the Act provides that upon recommitment of the prisoner an official designated by the Chairman—in practice a senior local parole officer—is to commence a review "forthwith". Within a maximum of 14 days from the execution of the suspension warrant, the designated person conducting the review is obliged either to cancel the suspension and order that the prisoner be re-released on parole or mandatory supervision, or to refer the case to the Board for its consideration. It should be noted also that this 14-day period can be shortened "as may be directed by the Board."

Even though section 22 addresses itself only to a suspension of parole, since the release of the decision in *Swan*, the section 22(3) procedure is followed when parole has already been revoked. However, since only the Board can revoke a previously granted release, the person conducting the review has no power to overrule the Board and direct that a revocation be cancelled; consequently, all cases of this nature must be referred to the Board. Thus, in that context, the 14-day limitation period is used only as a guide for the designated person conducting the review.

Although section 22 does not formally apply to provincial parole boards, those tribunals have developed policies regarding time frames for the disposition of cases following suspension. For example, in Ontario, the parole supervisor is required to attend on the parolee within 7 days of his apprehension, and to forward a written report to the Vice-Chairman within a further 7 days.

(ii) Sufficiency of the Review

Several cases have considered the adequacy of the review conducted by the designated person under section 22(3). In *Rowling*,[57] mandatory supervision was suspended, but no review of any kind took place before a referral to the Board. By the time an application for *habeas corpus* was argued, no further steps had been taken by the Board. Relying on the statements of Goodman J. in *Grabina*[58] to the effect that a failure to comply with the provisions of section 16 [now s. 22] could give rise to a successful application for *habeas corpus* prior to revoca-

---

[57] *Re Rowling and R.* (1979), 45 C.C.C. (2d) 478 (Ont. H.C.).
[58] *Re Grabina and R.* (1977), 34 C.C.C. (2d) 52 (Ont. H.C.).

tion, Southey J. ordered release of the prisoner. In *Cohen*,[59] the designated person was apparently unable to conduct any review within the 14-day period. Galligan J. held that this was not permitted by section 16(3) [now s. 22(3)] of the Act. Relying on *Rowling*, he held that strict compliance with section 16(3) [now s. 22(3)] was mandatory.

Section 22(3) does not require that the person who signs the suspension warrant be the person who conducts the section 22(3) review. Where staffing commitments permit, the designated person who conducts the review is neither the person who signed the warrant nor the prisoner's acting parole officer, in order that an appearance of neutrality be maintained. Information is gathered from a variety of sources, including the police, the acting parole officer and community contacts, all of which are combined with a review of the prisoner's behaviour while incarcerated or on conditional release. According to Board policy input from the suspended person is also considered to be a desirable, though not an essential step in the decision to refer a case to the Board or to cancel a suspension. To this end, a post-suspension interview is conducted with the prisoner.[60] It is usually only at the stage when the parole officer (who may or may not be the designated person) actually attends at the institution that the prisoner is presented with a written document (called a "Violation Report") which contains an extremely brief (and often incomplete) summary of reasons for suspension. In cases where a new charge has been laid or where there are allegations of a breach of a condition, the reasons for suspension may well have been obvious to the prisoner at the time of the execution of the suspension warrant. However, since section 22 authorizes the issuance of a suspension warrant "to prevent a breach of any term or condition of parole" or "to protect society," the real reasons for suspension may not be clear.

In *Henderson*,[61] a review of the case was conducted by the designated official within the 14-day period. However, this exercise did not include a personal interview with the prisoner, which took place only

---

[59] *Re Cohen and R.* (Weekly Ct. No. 15313/80, Ont. H.C., October 9, 1980). An application for leave to appeal was filed by the Crown with the Ontario Court of Appeal. This appeal was abandoned on June 22, 1981 (Ct. No. 1204/80). A similar conclusion was reached by Hutcheon J. in *Re Smoker* [summarized (1978), 2 W.C.B. 216 (B.C.S.C.)]. In that case, the prisoner was acquitted of escape because the warrant of committal revoking parole was invalid as the designated officer had failed to cancel the suspension or refer the case to the Board within 14 days.

[60] Because of the time constraints imposed by s. 22(3), Board policy is that, wherever possible, this interview should be conducted no later than 10 days following the execution of the warrant (National Parole Board: *Policy and Procedures Manual* s. VI., 6.1). This, however, is not mandated by statute.

[61] *Re Henderson and R.* (1982), 69 C.C.C. (2d) 561 (B.C.S.C.).

after the case had been referred to the Board. It was argued that failure to inform the prisoner of the reasons for suspension of his mandatory supervision and to afford him an opportunity to respond, prior to the referral to the Board, invalidated the review process. While agreeing that "at first blush" the petitioner's argument that the failure to observe the principles of natural justice appeared to have merit, Hinds J. cited with approval the judgment in *Hunchak*, and noted that caution should be exercised by a court in deciding whether to review an "on the spot" decision taken by a designated official. He then noted that the section 16(3) [now s. 22(3)] review "is only an intermediary step in the whole process", which "does not finally determine the status of the inmate". Since section 20 of the Regulations envisages a post-suspension hearing only after a case has been referred to the Board, Hinds J. found it "difficult to comprehend why he should be interviewed prior to the completion of the intermediary step, the review, provided for in section 16(3)." Even though the *Board's Policy and Procedures Manual* indicated that the prisoner under suspension was to be interviewed and "afforded an opportunity to explain his conduct", a procedure which Hinds J. found "laudable, and hopefully . . . followed in most cases," he was not prepared to find that these procedures created any binding legal requirement upon the person conducting the review.[62] A similar conclusion was reached by Macdonell J. in *McNamara v. National Parole Board*, who held that it was not for the court "to review the steps taken or the extent of the evidence investigated or heard by the person designated . . . if the section is otherwise complied with."[63]

The result of the decisions in *Munday, Hunchak, Henderson* and *McNamara* appears to be that since the section 22(3) review process is only an intermediate step in the revocation process, the mere statement by the designated official that he has "reviewed" the case will be sufficient to insulate the review process from judicial scrutiny. This underestimates the real issues at stake during the initial 14 days following the execution of a suspension warrant, especially when one recalls that the Board is not compelled by statute to hold a post-suspension hearing within a certain period of time following referral of a case to it by the designated official. Surely it is not too much to expect that the designated official should be required to afford the person whose right to be at liberty has been suspended, an early opportunity to respond to the allegations which have led to his being in custody. Contemporary notions of elementary fairness and fundamental justice demand that con-

---

62   *Ibid.*, at 565, 566 and 567.
63   (B.C.S.C., Macdonell, J., January 8, 1982).

sideration of the prisoner's version of events be taken into account by the designated official before a decision is made to refer a case to the Board; otherwise, how is the prisoner to know that any serious consideration has been given to the statutorily mandated alternative of cancellation of a suspension by the designated official?

(iii) *Sections 10(b) and 13 of the Charter*

Although the parole officer conducting the post-suspension interview is expected to explain the contents of the Violation Report orally to the prisoner, the timing of such interviews gives the prisoner little opportunity to consider the allegations before being requested to respond to them. This could have grave consequences where the reason for suspension is related to actual or potential court proceedings.[64] Prior to the enactment of the *Charter*, both the Board and C.S.C. had recognized the potential problem of admissions made by prisoners. According to the current C.S.C. *Case Management: Policy and Procedures Manual*, parole officers are expected to warn parolees of the potential danger of any admissions which may be made. Similarly, section 20.1(3)(*b*) of the Regulations indicates that during the course of a Board hearing the assistant may "advise the inmate in respect of any questions put to that inmate by the Board during the hearing".

The post-*Charter* decision in *Carlson*[65] has gone some way toward clarifying the admissibility of statements in a subsequent criminal trial made by a prisoner involved in post-suspension proceedings. In that case, the prisoner's mandatory supervision had been suspended as a result of a charge of manslaughter being laid against him. The prisoner made "several damaging admissions" during the course of a post-suspension hearing. At trial, Crown counsel sought to introduce the evidence of the Board members and the parole officer who had been present at the post-suspension hearing. In giving judgment on a *voir dire*, McKay J. held that the proposed evidence was inadmissible. Even though the "evidence" given at the post-suspension hearing was not under oath and the prisoner could not be said to be "testifying", nevertheless the post-suspension hearing was a "proceeding" within the meaning of section 13 of the *Charter*. Furthermore, because "the consequences of the Board's decision are matters of great significance", the prisoner was "called upon to assert his position." McKay J. therefore ruled that "giving a broad and liberal interpretation to s. 13 of the

---

[64] For pre-*Charter* commentary, see *Re Rain and National Parole Bd.* (1981), 58 C.C.C. (2d) 495 (Fed. T.D.) and *Re Dubeau and National Parole Bd., supra*, note 55.

[65] *R. v. Carlson* (1985), 14 C.R.R. 4 (B.C.S.C.).

Charter, the accused in making his submissions to the Board was in effect testifying as a witness on his own behalf in a proceeding other than the present one and so has the right not to have any incriminating evidence so given used to incriminate him in these proceedings."[66] This is consistent with the view of section 13 of the *Charter* later expressed by Lamer J. (as he then was) in *Dubois*,[67] wherein he concluded:

> the purpose of s. 13 ... is to protect individuals from being indirectly compelled to incriminate themselves to ensure that the Crown will not be able to do indirectly that which s. 11(*c*) prohibits. It guarantees the right not to have a person's testimony used to incriminate him or her in other proceedings.[68]

In that case, a retrial was characterized as "other proceedings" so as to invoke the protection of section 13 to ensure that an accused's earlier testimony not form part of the Crown's case against him. Similarly, statements made at a post-suspension hearing, even one generated by a new criminal charge, should not be available to incriminate the prisoner at a subsequent trial on that charge.

A similar question arises as to whether statements made to a designated officer conducting a review pursuant to section 22(3) should equally be insulated from use by the Crown at a subsequent trial. The suspension and review stages are integral parts of the revocation process. Their object is to determine the propriety of permitting a prisoner to retain his or her conditional liberty. Evidence by an accused at a bail hearing cannot subsequently be used to incriminate him at trial.[69] By the same token, elements of the revocation process which occur prior to the formal hearing before the Board should also be encompassed by the phrase "proceedings" used in section 13. The real issue is whether the making of an incriminating statement by a prisoner during a section 22(3) review qualifies as a "... witness who testifies. ..." As noted in *Carlson*, unlike an interrogation of a suspect by a police officer, the parole officer is required by statute to conduct the review in order to satisfy a major step in the process of revocation. Moreover, co-operation with parole authorities is a condition of the parolee's release. Thus, within the context of the parole process, answers given during the section 22(3) review should be considered as testimony within the meaning of section 13 in order to protect the prisoner against self-incrimination. Applying the reasoning of *Dubois*, section 13 must be interpreted so as not to generate a violation of another *Charter* right—in

---

[66] *Ibid.*, at 6.
[67] *Dubois v. R.*, [1985] 2 S.C.R. 350.
[68] *Ibid.*, at 358.
[69] *R. v. Paonessa* (1982), 66 C.C.C. (2d) 300 (Ont. C.A.).

this case the protection in section 11(*c*) from the compulsion to be a witness against oneself.

Given the obligation on a parolee to co-operate with parole authorities, statements made outside the suspension and revocation process may also be inadmissible in a criminal trial. Several American courts have considered the problem of a parole officer giving testimony concerning admissions made during the course of a supervision interview with a parolee other than as part of parole suspension procedures. Typical of these is *Marrs v. State*[70] where the accused probationer had been questioned by his probation officer about a fire, which the probationer admitted starting. At trial these admissions were ruled admissible, despite the absence of any caution as to the potential consequences of any statement. On appeal, the court quashed the conviction on the basis that the interview with the probation officer amounted to "an official interrogation," such that a "Miranda"[71] warning was required. The court reasoned that probation officers occupy a position of trust and authority which could give rise to the type of psychological pressure that Miranda warnings are designed to mitigate. Further, since probationers are encouraged to treat probation officers as counsellors and confidantes, they might assume that their statements would be treated as confidential.

Before the enactment of section 10(*b*) of the *Charter*, Canadian case law generally accepted that the failure of a person in authority to advise an accused of his right to counsel was only one factor to be considered in determining whether an inculpatory statement would be admissible into evidence in a subsequent court proceeding.[72] However, section 10(*b*) now provides that "everyone has the right on arrest or detention . . . to retain and instruct counsel without delay and to be informed of that right". The scope and impact of section 10(*b*) was examined by the Supreme Court of Canada in *Therens*,[73] which involved a failure by the police to advise a person being detained pending a breathalyzer test of his right to counsel and the consequent question of admissibility of the results of breath samples provided by the accused. Although that case is

---

[70] 452 A. 2d 992 (Md. Spec. App. 1982). See also *State v. Davis*, 67 N.J. 222, 337A. 2d 33 (1975); *State v. Lakas*, 442 P. 2d 11 (1968); *In re Richard T.*, 79 Cal. App. 3d 382, 144 Cal. Rptr. 856 (1978), *per contra*, *Oregon v. Mathiason*, 429 U.S. 492 (1977).

[71] *Miranda v. Arizona*, 384 U.S. 436 (1966).

[72] See *R. v. Letendre* (1975), 25 C.C.C. (2d) 180 (Man. C.A.); *R. v. Settee* (1974), 29 C.R.N.S. 104 (Sask. C.A.); *R. v. Whynott* (1975), 27 C.C.C. (2d) 321 (N.S.C.A.); *R. v. Conkie* (1978), 39 C.C.C. (2d) 408 (Alta. C.A.); *R. v. Chow* (1978), 43 C.C.C. (2d) 215 (B.C.C.A.).

[73] *R. v. Therens*, [1985] 1 S.C.R. 613. This case should be read in conjunction with *Trask v. R.* (1985), 18 C.C.C. (3d) 514 (S.C.C.).

principally important for the court's expanded definition of the term "detained", the various judgments also considered the legal effect of a failure by a person in authority to advise an accused of his right to counsel. The central issue was whether a court was limited by section 24(2) of the *Charter* to admit evidence obtained in breach of a *Charter* right and would in "all the circumstances . . . bring the administration of justice into disrepute," or whether a court could apply a broader exclusionary rule under section 24(1). The trial judge and four of five judges of the Saskatchewan Court of Appeal[74] held that once a breach of *Charter* rights had been established a court was not limited to applying the test in section 24(2), but could use section 24(1) and refuse to admit evidence if it considered such exclusion "to be appropriate and just in the circumstances."

Five separate judgments were delivered by the Supreme Court of Canada in *Therens.* Estey J. (Beetz, Chouinard and Wilson JJ. concurring) held that the question of admissibility of evidence obtained in violation of a *Charter* right "falls to be determined by section 24(2) of the *Charter* and not by reason of subs. (1) of that section". Because there had been a flagrant violation of the right to be informed of the right to counsel "[a]dmitting this evidence under these circumstances would clearly 'bring the administration of justice into disrepute'." While he was not prepared "to expatiate, in these early days of life with the *Charter*, upon the meaning of the expression 'administration of justice' and particularly its outer limits . . .", Estey J. concluded that to do other than reject the evidence in the circumstances of the case "would be to invite police officers to disregard *Charter* rights of the citizen and to do so with an assurance of impunity."[75]

LeDain J. agreed "that section 24(2) was intended to be the sole basis for the exclusion of evidence because of an infringement or a denial of a right to freedom guaranteed by the *Charter.*" Section 24(1) remedies are limited to applications for relief brought under that section, so "to ascribe to the framers of the *Charter* an intention that the courts should address two tests or standards on an application for the exclusion of evidence. . . . would be that s. 24(2) would become a dead letter."[76] LeDain J. went on to consider what test should be applied by a court in determining if, once a breach of *Charter* rights has been established, the admission of evidence so obtained "would bring the administration of justice into disrepute." Expanding upon the views of Lamer J. and Estey

---

[74]   (1983), 5 C.C.C. (3d) 409 (Sask. C.A.).
[75]   *Therens, supra*, note 72, at 621 and 622.
[76]   *Therens, supra*, note 72, at 647 and 647-648.

J. in the pre-*Charter* case of *Rothman*,[77] he concluded that "the two principle considerations in the balancing which must be undertaken are the relative seriousness of the constitutional violation and the relative seriousness of the criminal charge." Although on the facts of the case at bar LeDain J. was prepared to assume good faith on the part of the police, he agreed that "the right to counsel is of such fundamental importance that its denial in a criminal law context must *prima facie* discredit the administration of justice." McIntyre J. agreed generally with LeDain J. but, as a result of the finding of good faith, held conversely that "[t]he exclusion of the evidence in the circumstances of this case would itself go far to bring the administration of justice into disrepute."[78]

Lamer J. discussed whether, as a condition precedent to the application of section 24(2), there must exist more than a temporal relationship between the denial of a *Charter* right and the obtaining of the evidence which is sought to be excluded. On the facts there was undoubtedly a relationship between the denial of the right to counsel and the taking of the breath samples. However, Lamer J. expressly declined to comment "[w]hether s. 10(*b*) extends any further, so as to encompass, for example, the principle of *Miranda* . . . and apply to matters such as interrogation and police lineups".[79] In short concurring reasons Dickson C.J.C. appears to have approved of the "relationship" test enunciated by Lamer J., although it is perhaps noteworthy that he left open the availability of section 24(1) remedies to exclude evidence.

Therens leaves many questions unanswered. However, if section 24(2) is the only avenue through which evidence can be excluded, the relationship between a parole officer or Board member and the prisoner must be carefully explored. Relying on *Marrs*, a Canadian court might be prepared to consider that an inculpatory statement made without the parolee being informed of the right to counsel would "bring the administration of justice into disrepute". Furthermore, trial judges must pay careful attention to such factual matters as whether or not the police (who usually execute suspension warrants) cautioned the prisoner upon initial arrest, whether the prisoner had retained counsel between the time of the execution of the suspension warrant and the post-suspension interview, and the seriousness of the criminal charge.

---

[77] *Rothman v. R.*, [1981] 1 S.C.R. 640. The views of the majority in *Rothman* have now been rejected by a decisive majority of the Supreme Court of Canada in *Hebert v. R.* (June 21, 1990, as yet unreported).

[78] *Therens, supra*, note 73, at 652-653 and 623.

[79] *Therens, supra*, note 73, at 625.

A related issue is the admissibility, at a post-suspension hearing, of statements made by a parolee to a parole officer or other person in authority. American case law indicates that, unless the behaviour of the parole officer is so oppressive as to raise the possibility that any admission could be untrue, statements made during the course of interviews with parole officers are admissible.[80] In the pre-*Charter* case of *Re Rain and National Parole Board*,[81] the major cause for suspension was a new criminal charge. Smith D.J. held that "[t]his being so, his parole officer . . . had not only the right but the duty to question him concerning his conduct." While the prisoner might elect to decline to answer questions relating to the offence during his post-suspension interview, any admissions "made to the supervisor, or someone else . . . would be admissible and would be relevant evidence in deciding whether or not to revoke parole."[82] *Therens* and other post-*Charter* judgments provide some scope for argument that a failure by a parole officer to advise the prisoner (or parolee) of his *Charter* rights may result in the exclusion from consideration by the Board of any statements made or evidence obtained. In the absence of either a valid search warrant or at least a caution as to the parolee's right to consult counsel, can a parole officer search a prisoner, his effects or his residence? Can a parolee be required to submit to planned or random urinalysis testing?[82A] In the absence of a caution can a parole officer conduct an interrogation of the prisoner's whereabouts, associates or activities? What of spontaneous utterances which establish a breach of conditions? These and related questions await interpretation by the courts.

(iv) *Cancellation and Referral*

Once the necessary information has been gathered, a decision to cancel or refer must be made by the designated official. The decision of Landry J. in *MacAllister v. Director of Centre de Réception*[83] is significant in understanding the role of the designated person conducting the section 22(3) review. In that case, upon completing her review within the 14-day period, the designated person cancelled the suspension and directed that the prisoner be released. A Board member familiar with the

---

80 See cases referred to at note 70, *supra*, and *People v. Lipsky*, 102 Misc. 2d 19, 423 N.Y.S. 2d 599 (Monroe Co. Ct. 1979); *People v. Ronald W.*, 24 N.Y. 2d 732, 249 N.E. 2d 882, 302 N.Y.S. 2d 260 (1969).

81 *Supra*, note 64. See also *Re Munday and R.* (1982), 69 C.C.C. (2d) 436 (B.C.C.A.), at 438.

82 *Rain, supra*, note 64, at 502.

82A In the prison context, see *Jackson v. Joyceville Penitentiary (Disciplinary Tribunal)* (1990), 75 C.R. (3d) 174, 55 C.C.C. (3d) 50 (Fed. T.D.).

83 (1984), 40 C.R. (3d) 126 (Que. S.C.).

case disagreed with that decision and issued a new suspension warrant. Subsequently, that Board member conceded that he: "ne possédait aucun élément nouveau et aucun renseignement qui n'étaient déjà en la possession de [la personne désignée] lorsque cette dernière a rendu sa décision."[84] Landry J. noted that the case before him did not challenge the plenary powers of the Board to move directly to revoke a parole, since that issue had been resolved in favour of the Board in *Collins* and *Grabina*.[85] However, an individual Board member did not have the power to overrule a decision taken by a designated person appointed by the Chairman to act under section 16(3) [now s. 22(3)]:

> ... une personne désignée ne peut, en vertu de l'art. 16(1), réviser la décision d'un collègue dûment autorisé et ordonner une suspension pour les mêmes motifs que ceux ayant fait l'objet d'une première adjudication.[86]

If the Board disagreed with a decision to cancel a suspension there were only two alternatives—either it could move directly to revoke parole (as had occurred in *Collins*) or the Chairman could divest the designated person of the power to conduct the review. Landry J. distinguished *Munday* on the basis that the second suspension under consideration in that case:

> ... n'avait pour objet que de corriger des erreurs de procédure affectant le premier mandat. La cour n'avait pas devant elle ... un cas où il apparaisait clairement, suivant les faits, que l'on tentait d'utiliser, comme ici, la seconde suspension comme un moyen de passer outre à une décision prise par une première personne désignée.[87]

While *MacAllister* makes it clear that the decision to cancel or refer is to be taken by the official conducting the review, this decision is usually made after collaboration with other parole officials. Board members are often consulted, particularly where the suspension is based on a breach of a Board-imposed "special condition". There is nothing in the statute or Board policy to preclude submissions being made by, or on behalf of, the prisoner as part of this process. Many parole officials who conduct such reviews are pleased to receive input from counsel or other persons acting on the prisoner's behalf. For example, where the cause of the suspension has been a new criminal charge, it should not be assumed that parole officials either understand or are likely to be aware of the current status of court proceedings. The fact that a court has seen fit to

---

84 *Ibid.*, at 131.
85 *Ex parte Collins* (1976), 30 C.C.C. (2d) 460 (Ont. H.C.); *Re Grabina and R.* (1977), 34 C.C.C. (2d) 52 (Ont. H.C.).
86 *Supra*, note 83, at 134.
87 *Supra*, note 83, at 136-137.

grant judicial interim release, a transcript of proceedings at a bail hearing, affidavit materials, or even counsel's recitation of the contents of discussions with Crown counsel or the investigating officers, are all factors which can be included in the review process.

Where a decision is made to cancel a suspension, it should be noted that release is not necessarily immediate, as penal authorities require that a properly executed document affirming the cancellation decision be delivered to the jail before the prisoner can be released. When additional release conditions are being added to the prisoner's certificate of release on parole or mandatory supervision, the parole officer attends at the institution to conduct a further interview with the prisoner before release is effected. "Special conditions" are imposed by order of the Board, while "special instructions" may be added by the parole supervisor.

Where the case is referred to the Board, a written report or telex message to this effect is sent to the Board's Regional office. No new warrant reflecting the referral is served on the prisoner or lodged with the jail. In three cases consideration has been given as to whether, upon referral, the original suspension warrant is "spent". In a brief endorsement without other reasons, Osler J. ruled in *Re Robidoux*[88] that since, upon referral, the prisoner had been, in the wording of the warrant, "dealt with further pursuant to sections 16 and 20 of the *Parole Act*", the force of the warrant was spent and, in the absence of a new warrant, the prisoner was unlawfully detained. This view was rejected a few months later in *Re Batz*[89] where it was argued that since section 16(1)(*c*) [now s. 22(1)(*c*)] refers to the prisoner being held in custody under a suspension warrant pending cancellation or revocation, there was no authority to detain a prisoner in custody following referral to the Board. O'Driscoll J. held that since only the Board can revoke parole, it was implicit that the original suspension warrant remained in effect pending the decision of the Board.

The same issue arose in a somewhat different way in Re *Roach*[90] where, following referral, the prisoner had not been given 14 days notice of the date set for his post-suspension hearing before the Board, a clear breach of section 20(2)(*b*) of the Regulations. Fawcus J. held that because the Board had purported to deal with the prisoner under sections 16 and 20 [now ss. 22 and 25] of the Act, as specified in the suspension

---

88 (Ont. H.C., Osler J., February 14, 1978).
89 (1978), 4 C.R. (3d) 289 (Ont. H.C.). A similar conclusion was reached by Goodman J. in *Robidoux (No. 2)* (Ont. H.C., August 8, 1978).
90 [Summarized (1981), 7 W.C.B. 352 (B.C.S.C.)]. See also *Osborne v. National Parole Bd.* [summarized 9 W.C.B. (2d) 679 (Fed. T.D.)].

warrant, then at that point the warrant "lapsed". Since the order of revocation was a nullity due to the failure to comply with s. 20 of the Regulations, and since the prisoner was now eligible for release on mandatory supervision, *habeas corpus* was ordered.

The reasoning in *Batz* is to be preferred to the brief endorsement in *Robidoux*; a suspension warrant is not spent upon referral to the Board. However, where a final decision revoking parole is taken, and that decision is illegal due to a procedural defect, the suspension warrant has been spent and the prisoner is unlawfully detained.[91]

3. "OTHERWISE DETAINED" — BAIL HEARINGS AND SUSPENSION WARRANTS

Certificates of conditional release universally contain clauses to the effect that the released person is "to obey the law and keep the peace" and is "to inform the parole supervisor immediately when arrested or being questioned by police." Section 22 does not, however, specify that it is mandatory that a suspension warrant issue when a new charge is laid. Indeed, there are occasions where the parole authorities may be aware of the existence of a new charge, but exercise their discretion not to suspend parole. Nevertheless, since the question of entitlement to a bail hearing when a new charge has been laid and where a suspension warrant has been or is about to be issued has been the subject of considerable litigation, it will be useful to discuss this briefly.

Where a suspension warrant has not yet been issued because the designated official has had no opportunity to consider the matter, it frequently occurs that Crown counsel, acting on the advice of the police, will seek to adjourn the bail hearing for up to 3 days pursuant to section 516 of the *Criminal Code*[92] (or for a longer period with the consent of the accused) to allow time for parole authorities to decide whether a suspension warrant will be issued. Given the broad power of the justice ultimately conducting the bail hearing under section 518(1)(*e*) to "receive and base his decision on evidence considered credible or trustworthy by him in the circumstances of each case," it is often difficult to resist an application for a 3-day remand where the court is advised that consideration is being given to the issuance of a suspension warrant. Although there appears to be no case law directly on point, the judgment in *Ragan*[93] is instructive. In that case, the court had before it no documen-

---

[91] See *Morgan v. Stony Mountain Institution (Director)* (1983), 30 C.R. (3d) 125 (Man. C.A.); *Re Dumoulin and R.* (1984), 6 C.C.C. (3d) 190 (Ont. H.C.).

[92] R.S.C. 1985, c. C-46.

[93] *R. v. Ragan* (1975), 21 C.C.C. (2d) 115 (B.C. Prov. Ct.).

tation or particulars of the offence. The court held that the Crown was entitled to an adjournment under section 457.1 [now s. 516] in order that that material could be obtained from another court where the charge originated, the court clearly anticipating that relevant and credible information would be placed before the justice on the return date.

Prior to the 1985 amendments to the *Criminal Code* there was a question as to the entitlement of a prisoner to a bail hearing when a suspension warrant had been issued and executed, due to the wording of [then] section 457(1), which spoke at that time of a bail hearing being conducted in respect of a person "who is not required to be detained in custody in respect of any other matter." For several years following the proclamation of the *Bail Reform Act*[94] in 1972 Canadian courts were split on this issue.[95] In jurisdictions where justices were of the view that a person "otherwise detained" was not entitled to a bail hearing, the accused whose parole or mandatory supervision had been suspended was placed in a difficult dilemma. Because of the suspension, no bail hearing was conducted. As no bail hearing had been conducted, the accused could not advise the Board (or designated official during the section 16(3) [now s. 22(3)] review stage) of the court's view of judicial interim release. The outcome of a bail hearing may be of considerable significance to the prisoner and the Board, as it is likely to reflect such matters as the seriousness of the offence, the strength of the case against the accused and the assessment by the court of the accused's links with the community.

The question of the right to a bail hearing was resolved in decisions of three appellate courts. In *Adams*,[96] the British Columbia Court of Appeal held that the "otherwise detained" provision did not deprive the justice of jurisdiction to make a bail order. The justice may refuse to make an order until the accused has become not otherwise detained; alternatively, the justice may make a release order which becomes effective upon expiry of the other detention. This view was further refined by the Alberta Court of Appeal in *Re R. and Kennedy; Re R. and Dickson*[97] and by the Ontario Court of Appeal in *Bazouzi*.[98] Both of these courts held that "s. 457(1) merely precludes a justice in those circumstances from releasing an accused without conditions," and did

---

[94] S.C. 1970-71-72, c. 37.

[95] Contrast, for example, *Re Preikschas and Elsenheimer* (1977), 35 C.C.C. (2d) 123 (Alta. T.D.) and *R. v. Albino* (1975), 19 C.R.N.S. 10 (Ont. Co. Ct.) with *R. v. Mallet* (1975), 26 C.C.C. (2d) 457 (Que. S.P.).

[96] *R. v. Adams* (1978), 45 C.C.C. (2d) 459 (B.C.C.A.).

[97] (1983), 1 C.C.C. (3d) 90 (Alta. C.A.).

[98] *Re Bazouzi and R.* (1983), 33 C.R. (3d) 272 (Ont. C.A.).

not affect the jurisdiction of the justice to hold a bail hearing. Any remaining ambiguity was ended when section 457(1) [now s. 515(1)] was amended in December, 1985 to delete the reference to "otherwise detained."[99]

Notwithstanding these decisions and the change in legislation, there may well be circumstances in which it is in the accused parolee's best interests not to launch into a bail hearing at an early stage. Indeed, this was one of the factors which influenced the pre-*Adams* ruling in *Tabish*[100] which held that a justice did not have jurisdiction to hold a bail hearing. In that case, the Crown attempted to force a prisoner serving sentence to proceed with a bail hearing some four months before his release date. Berger J. stated:

> ... while it may not be absurd, it would be unjust for an accused to be required at this stage to answer the Crown's showing. What can he say? He is still in prison. He may not know when he will get out. He may have an application for parole pending. What can he say about his plans? Of what relevance is any evidence regarding his family, his roots in the community, his job prospects and so on? Is he to be expected to ask sureties to come forward? These considerations are premature.[101]

If the accused does not wish to enter into a bail hearing, a practice has developed, in some jurisdictions, of requesting the accused to consent to a detention order being made against him. This is usually justified on the grounds of administrative convenience. It is often encouraged by Crown counsel who will undertake on record that upon a "review" of the detention order (which review would be brought at a time when the accused's other impediments to release have been withdrawn), the Crown will then treat the matter as if the detention order had not been made. Still, there can be no justification for this practice. If the accused is still before the Provincial Court at, or near, the time when he becomes not otherwise detained, he should not be forced to go through the protracted and expensive process of launching a bail review in a higher court. If he is before a superior court of criminal jurisdiction at the time the issue of bail becomes realistic, nothing in Part XVI of the *Code* precludes him from having his initial bail hearing before the appropriate court. Finally, although some of the case law concerning the onus on a bail review brought pursuant to section 520 of the *Code* holds that such a proceeding is a hearing *de novo*,[102] both the practical reality

---

[99] S.C. 1985, c. 19, s. 84(1) [proclaimed in force December 4, 1985].

[100] *R. v. Tabish* (1977), 37 C.C.C. (2d) 363 (B.C.S.C.).

[101] *Ibid.*, at 366-367.

[102] *R. v. Thompson* (1972), 7 C.C.C. (2d) 70 (B.C.S.C.); *Re Powers and R.* (1972), 9 C.C.C. (2d) 533 (Ont. H.C.); *R. v. Sexton* (1976), 33 C.R.N.S. 307 (Nfld. Dist. Ct.).

302 / Release From Imprisonment

and the more recent weight of case law indicates that the accused is required to demonstrate some error in principle in the decision of the justice who imposed the detention order.[103]

The converse problem arose in *Arviv*.[104] While serving a penitentiary sentence the prisoner was charged with other offences, upon which he was refused bail by a justice. After some time he applied to the National Parole Board for a series of unescorted temporary absence passes, which the Board indicated it was prepared to grant if the prisoner were no longer subject to the detention order. Upon hearing an application for a review of the detention order, Borins D.C.J. held that he had no power to make a bail order directing that the prisoner be released, but that he be compelled as a condition of that release to reside at the penitentiary except at such times as he might be permitted to be temporarily absent by order of the Board. To grant an order in these terms would disregard section 457.4(1) [now s. 519(1)], which mandates that a bail order made at a time when a prisoner is otherwise detained can only take effect when "the accused is no longer required to be detained in custody in respect of any other matter".

4. PROCEDURES FOLLOWING REFERRAL

(a) The Right to a Hearing

When a case has been referred to the Board, section 22(4) of the *Parole Act* directs that "[t]he Board shall . . . review the case and cause to be conducted all such inquiries in connection therewith as it considers necessary". This section should be read in conjunction with section 20 of the Regulations[105] which provides that a prisoner may apply for a hearing as part of the review process. However, section 20 purports to limit the classes of prisoners eligible to exercise the right to appear before the Board at a post-suspension hearing. Several cases have directly or inferentially challenged these limitations which specify that the prisoner must be a "federal inmate", a term defined in section 2 of the Regulations as a person "detained in or released on parole from a penitentiary".[106] This represents a legislative attempt to preclude prisoners released on parole from provincial institutions by the National Parole

---

103 *R. v. Horvat* (1972), 9 C.C.C. (2d) 1 (B.C.S.C.); *Hunter v. R.* (1973), 24 C.R.N.S. 197 (Ont. Co. Ct.); *R. v. Lesage* (1975), 25 C.C.C. (2d) 173 (Que. S.P.).
104 *R. v. Arviv* (1988), 38 C.C.C. (3d) 283 (Ont. Dist. Ct.).
105 SOR/70-428; SOR/81-487; SOR/86-817.
106 By section 20(1)(*a*) of the Regulations, the post-suspension hearing processes are also made applicable to persons released on mandatory supervision (SOR/86-817).

Board from the provisions providing a right to a hearing. Similarly, those Regulations dealing with provincial parole boards (contained in Part II of the Regulations) do not contain procedures similar to those contained in section 20, which, by section 3(1) are deemed not to apply to a provincial parole board. Indeed, section 34 specifies that "[n]othing in these Regulations requires a provincial parole board, in considering whether . . . parole should be . . . revoked, to personally interview the inmate".

The lack of opportunity for an in-person hearing as part of the provincial post-suspension process was first challenged in *Cadeddu*.[107] The prisoner had been released on parole by the Ontario Board of Parole, but his parole was suspended following his arrest on new criminal charges. Pursuant to the Regulations under the *Ministry of Correctional Services Act* in force at that time,[108] the prisoner was interviewed by his parole officer who explained the reasons for suspension, cautioned him that any statements he chose to make could be used as evidence, and advised him that he could make submissions to the Ontario Board of Parole on his own behalf or through a lawyer. The Board of Parole held a hearing in the absence of the prisoner and revoked his parole. Upon hearing an application for *habeas corpus*, Potts J. concluded that the statutory framework did not require that the prisoner be offered an in-person hearing as part of the review process. He then considered whether the doctrine of the duty to act fairly, enunciated by the Supreme Court of Canada in *Nicholson*,[109] gave rise to a right to a hearing. The court concluded that, while "*Nicholson* expanded the scope of bodies owing a duty of fairness . . . that decision has . . . [not] . . . enlarged the substance of that duty or altered the authority of . . . [*McCaud, Howarth* and *Mitchell*[110]] . . . as they relate to a right to a hearing."[111] After rejecting fairness as a basis for requiring an in-person hearing, Potts J. then addressed alternative submissions based on sections 7 and 9 of the *Charter*.[112] He stated that, having been granted parole, Cadeddu had "a qualified liberty . . . [interest that] . . . is sufficient to attract the constitutionally mandated protections of s. 7 of the

---

107 *R. v. Cadeddu; R. v. Nunery* (1983), 32 C.R. (3d) 355 (Ont. H.C.).

108 R.S.O. 1980, c. 275.

109 [1979] 1 S.C.R. 311.

110 *Ex parte McCaud*, [1965] 1 C.C.C. 168 (S.C.C.); *Howarth v. National Parole Bd.*, [1976] 1 S.C.R. 453; *Mitchell v. R.*, [1976] 2 S.C.R. 570.

111 *Cadeddu, supra*, note 107, at 366.

112 Potts J. initially rejected the Crown's submission that sections 7 and 9 do not apply when an individual is lawfully detained on the strength of the original warrant of committal.

Charter."[113] Thus, revocation of parole could occur only in accordance with the principles of fundamental justice. He quoted with approval the language of Fauteux C.J.C. in *Duke*, that the "principles of fundamental justice . . . mean, generally, that the tribunal which adjudicates upon his rights must . . . give to him the opportunity to adequately state his case."[114] He concluded that:

> Considering that the rights protected by s. 7 are the most important of all those enumerated in the Charter, that deprivation of those rights has the most severe consequences upon an individual, and that the Charter establishes a constitutionally mandated enclave for protection of rights, into which government intrudes at its peril, I am of the view that the applicant could not be lawfully deprived of his liberty without being given the opportunity for in-person hearing before his parole was revoked.[115]

Although the logic of Potts J. has been criticized[116] on the basis that it is wrong to regard fundamental justice and fairness as distinct and separate procedural standards, the result is clearly correct. *Cadeddu* has been approved in several other cases involving the Ontario and British Columbia Boards of Parole,[117] with the result that provincial authorities have now modified their practices to provide an opportunity for an in-person hearing as part of a decision as to whether parole should be revoked.[118]

In *Ward v. National Parole Board*,[119] a prisoner sentenced to a 3-year term had, under an agreement between the Yukon Territory and the Government of Canada, been housed in and released on parole from a territorial jail; as such he was not considered to be a federal inmate within the meaning of section 2 of the Regulations. Parole release was

---

[113] *Supra*, note 107, at 368.

[114] *Duke v. R.* (1972), 7 C.C.C. (2d) 474 (S.C.C.), at 479.

[115] *Cadeddu, supra*, note 107, at 369.

[116] See A. Manson, Annotation (1983), 32 C.R. (3d) 355; *McInnes v. Onslow Fane*, [1978] 3 All E.R. 211 (Ch.); and *Martineau v. Matsqui Institution Disciplinary Bd.* (1980), 13 C.R. (3d) 1 (S.C.C.), at 35, per Dickson J.

[117] See *Re Nunery* [summarized (1983), 9 W.C.B. 105 (Ont. H.C.)]; *Re Lowe and R.* (1983), 5 C.C.C. (3d) 535 (B.C.S.C.); *Re Dumoulin and R.* (1984), 6 C.C.C. (3d) 190 (Ont. H.C.). It should also be noted that *Cadeddu* was appealed by the Crown to the Ontario Court of Appeal. After oral argument, but before reserved judgment could be delivered, the respondent prisoner was killed by a fellow prisoner. After receiving further submissions as to whether the court should render judgment on the substantive issue, the court held that the appeal had abated (1983), 4 C.C.C. (3d) 112 (Ont. C.A.).

[118] This issue would have been unlikely to arise in Quebec, because by section 32 of the provincial statute (*An Act to promote the parole of inmates*, S.Q. 1978, c. 22), the Quebec Parole Commission is required to see and hear the suspended prisoner and assistant unless the prisoner renounces that right in writing.

[119] [Summarized (1985), 16 W.C.B. 20 (Y.T.S.C.)].

suspended as a result of a new charge being laid. The National Parole Board informed the prisoner that he had no right to a post-suspension hearing and revoked his parole after reviewing "documents provided by the [parole] supervisor." While agreeing with the submission of Crown counsel that there was no statutory right to a hearing, Maddison J. adopted the reasoning in *Cadeddu*, quashed the revocation decision and ordered the release of the prisoner. Following the release of that judgment, the National Parole Board has modified its policies to provide the right to a post-suspension hearing in all cases of federal and provincial prisoners.[120]

The second pre-condition contained in section 20(1)(*b*) before a prisoner can exercise his right to a post-suspension hearing is that the prisoner must be in custody. In light of the conclusion reached in *Swan*[121] (discussed above) this section must now be considered irrelevant. Whether a parolee is in custody at the post-suspension stage or is not apprehended until after a revocation, a hearing which provides the prisoner an opportunity to address allegations is essential.

When section 20 of the Regulations was originally proclaimed, the section stated that parole or mandatory supervision could not be revoked "until a period of fifteen days has elapsed following receipt by the Board of the referral." In *Stevens v. National Parole Board*,[122] the prisoner stood to be re-released as a result of accumulated remission, regardless of whether the Board cancelled the suspension of his mandatory supervision or revoked that release. Since the cause of the suspension was a new charge to which the prisoner had already pleaded guilty, he anticipated that cancellation was unlikely, and asked to be revoked. The Board took the position that since the Regulation was cast in mandatory terms, it was required to wait 15 days before revoking mandatory supervision. In ruling on an application for *mandamus*, Mahoney J. held that the wording of the Regulation was *ultra vires* the regulation-making power contained in section 9(1)(*k*) [now s. 27(1)(*k*)] of the *Parole Act*, because "[a] regulation stipulating that a decision shall not be made within a certain time is not a regulation prescribing the time within which a decision must be made." Furthermore he was also

---

120 This change was announced through National Parole Board, *Policy and Procedures Circular* (1986-5 (July 9, 1986) unpublished. When the 1986 amendments to the *Parole Act* and Regulations were passed and proclaimed in force some 2 weeks later, neither was amended to confirm the right to an in-person hearing. See National Parole Board, *Policy and Procedures Manual*, s. VI.B.1.1.1.

121 *Swan v. B.C. (A.G.)* (1983), 35 C.R. (3d) 135 (B.C.S.C.).

122 [1979] 2 F.C. 279 (T.D.). Being in a position where one is eligible for release regardless of which decision is made by the Board is known in prison jargon as being "a turnaround".

306 / Release From Imprisonment

prepared to find that the Regulation was *ultra vires* the scheme of section 16(4) [now s. 22(4)] of the Act. While 15 days might be a reasonable time for the Board to complete its inquiries, "where less time is required to complete the review and investigation, a regulation requiring that the decision be delayed cannot be given effect over the clear requirement of the Act that it be made forthwith."[123] *Mandamus* was issued directing the Board either to cancel or to revoke if it was able to complete the review prior to the expiry of 15 days from the date of referral. Following this decision, section 20 of the Regulations was amended[124] to provide that the 15 day period can be "waived, in writing, by the inmate."

It is, of course, open to the Board to cancel a suspension prior to the date fixed for a post-suspension hearing, on the basis, for example, of new information which comes to light after the referral has been made. Circumstances such as the disposition of pending criminal charges, confirmation of residential accommodation, or acceptance into a treatment facility might make the Board amenable to a suggestion that a suspension be cancelled without the need for a post-suspension hearing. However, it should be recalled from *Ziatas v. National Parole Board*[125] (discussed above) that the Board is not permitted, without the consent of the prisoner, to substitute a termination decision without completing the post-suspension hearing process following a referral under section 22(3).

The final step which initiates the post-suspension hearing process is the prisoner's application. At the time the parole officer attends to conduct the post-suspension interview, the prisoner is usually presented with a form which simply asks if he wishes to exercise his right to a post-suspension hearing in the event that the case is referred to the Board. If the prisoner initially indicates that he does not want such a hearing, but later changes his mind, this rarely causes difficulty in making arrangements for a hearing, unless in the interim parole has been revoked. However, in *Conroy*[126] the prisoner complained that his parole had been revoked without a hearing. The Board's response was that, despite the fact that the prisoner's counsel had had telephone conversations with

---

Ibid., at 282.
SOR/81-487.
(1983), 70 C.C.C. (2d) 381 (Fed. T.D.).
Re Conroy and R. (1983), 5 C.C.C. (3d) 501 (Ont. H.C.). In *Appeal Division Reports*, Case No. "PROC 016," June 28, 1988, the prisoner had initially expressed his desire for a post-suspension hearing, but had eventually waived his right to a hearing on the basis of a positive recommendation made by his parole supervisor to the Board. The Board did not adopt the recommendation. The Appeal Division ordered a new hearing because "[i]n view of the inmate's earlier interest in a hearing, it is difficult to assess whether or not his subsequent waiver can be considered to be informed."

the parole officer prior to the revocation decision being taken, the prisoner had "declined a hearing". Craig J. held that "[i]f the applicant declined a hearing with full knowledge of his procedural rights and what issues would be decided, then in my opinion he would have no right to complain later."[127] However, he noted:

> Because the applicant was entitled to a hearing he must understand what is to be decided at the hearing; also that he was entitled to assistance, including counsel. There is no evidence before me that he was advised of these matters or that he was aware of them. Also there is no evidence to establish who advised him of the right to a hearing; or whether that person knew what would be decided at the hearing, or that he was aware of the applicant's procedural rights. There is no evidence that the applicant gave any waiver or consent in writing.[128]

Analogizing to medical treatment cases, he held that "to be effective consent must be informed" and that the onus of establishing an informed waiver rests with the Board.

Once the prisoner signs the request and the form has been received by the Board, the combined effect of section 20(1) and (2) of the Regulations is that the Board may not revoke parole without giving the prisoner at least 14 days notice of the date fixed for the post-suspension hearing. Although not reflected in statute, a practice has developed of requesting the prisoner to waive this notice period if the hearing date can be arranged earlier. However, the prisoner is in no way obliged to do so if he feels that he needs more time to prepare. As noted by Thurlow C.J. in *Morgan v. National Parole Board*, "[t]he only conceivable purpose of . . . [s. 20(2)(b)] . . . is to give the inmate an adequate opportunity to prepare to deal with the subject-matter of the hearing."[129] A revocation decision taken at a hearing held less than 14 days from the date the prisoner is given notice is, in the absence of an informed waiver, a nullity.[130]

Section 20(2)(a) of the Regulations directs that the Board is to "commence a hearing as soon as practical following receipt by the Board of the application" for a post-suspension hearing. In *Lennox v. National Parole Board*,[131] the prisoners' cases had been referred and the prisoners had waived the 14-day notice requirement. Although Board members were in attendance a few days later at the institution where the prisoners were located to conduct other post-suspension hearings, the prisoners

---

[127] *Conroy*, ibid., at 511.
[128] *Ibid.*, at 510-511.
[129] (1982), 65 C.C.C. (2d) 216 (Fed. C.A.), at 223.
[130] *Re Roach* [summarized (1981), 7 W.C.B. 352 (B.C.S.C.)].
[131] *Lennox v. National Parole Bd.; National Parole Bd. v. Duncan; Lutz v. National Parole Bd.* (1985), 43 C.R. (3d) 356 (Fed. T.D.).

were not seen. While declining to attempt a compendious definition of the phrase "as soon as practical," Walsh J. held that, in the absence of an explanation from the Board as to why the prisoners were not seen, "it must be concluded that the hearings could have been held ... and by failing to do so the board infringed the mandatory provisions of s. 20(2)(*a*)."[132] Since the Board had thereby lost jurisdiction, the prisoners were ordered released.[133] It should also be noted that Walsh J. expressed the opinion *in obiter* that even if the Board had presented a satisfactory explanation to the court as to why the prisoners had not been seen, he would have been inclined to order that hearings be held at an early date on the basis that "undue delay in connection with such post-suspension hearings is contrary not only to the terms of the regulations but also to natural justice."[134] Thus, even where delay in convening a post-suspension hearing does not result in a loss of jurisdiction, an order for an expedited hearing may be obtained.

(b) Sufficiency of Notice

The issue of notice of matters to be discussed at a post-suspension hearing has occasioned considerable judicial commentary. Litigation has focused on two main subjects — notice requirements and disclosure of information considered by the Board to be confidential. Although these issues tend to overlap in the case law, in this section we restrict our discussion to questions of the sufficiency of notice of the matters to be raised at post-suspension hearings. The reader is referred to Chapter 6 for an analysis of the current state of the law with respect to confidentiality issues.

In *Re Dubeau and National Parole Board*,[135] which can be described as the first post-*Martineau* "fairness" case in the correctional context, the prisoner had been released on parole upon standard terms and conditions, one of which was that he not incur debts by instalment buying without permission from his parole supervisor. The parole officer discovered that the parolee had breached this condition by opening charge accounts at local business establishments. Following a "disciplinary interview" a "special instruction" was added to the parole condi-

---

[132] *Ibid.*, at 361.

[133] Walsh J. was careful to note that the Board was not left entirely without remedy as it could move directly to revoke under section 10(1)(*e*) [now 16(1)(*e*) or (*f*)]. In such circumstances the prisoner would still be entitled to an in-person hearing. See *Swan, supra,* footnote 121.

[134] *Supra*, note 131, at 359.

[135] (1981), 54 C.C.C. (2d) 553 (Fed. T.D.).

tions, which obliged the parolee to seek and obtain permission before obtaining credit. Later that day the parolee was arrested on criminal charges alleged to have occurred after release on parole, but before the addition of the special instruction to his parole certificate. Six days later parole was suspended. Although the reasons for suspension are not specified in the judgment, the Violation Report alleged that the prisoner "had incurred debts without proper permission." The prisoner had not been given any prior notice that he would be questioned about the new criminal charges at the post-suspension hearing. The Board members present at the hearing spent very little time on the allegations of abuse of credit and commenced questioning the prisoner about the new criminal charges. The prisoner "replied that he wanted to call his lawyer and arrange for him to be present."[136] Since the case arose before the proclamation of section 20.1 of the Regulations, the Board members responded that in general lawyers were not permitted at post-suspension hearings and, accordingly, the request for an adjournment to have counsel attend was denied. The prisoner then refused to answer any substantive questions about the new charges; at the conclusion of the hearing parole was revoked. Neither the oral reasons for revocation given at the hearing, nor the written reasons subsequently mailed to the prisoner,[137] referred to the pending charges, but only to "financial irresponsibility . . . indicat[ing] that there has been no basic change in you[r] . . . deceptive behaviour."[138]

While acknowledging "the Board's absolute discretion to revoke or not revoke the applicant's parole," Smith D.J. carefully analyzed the views expressed by various English and Canadian courts and concluded that the modern purpose of *certiorari* "is to see that minor tribunals

---

[136] *Ibid.*, at 556.

[137] Section 21 of the Regulations obliges the Board to notify the prisoner in writing of the reasons for revocation within 15 days after the decision is made. Apart from *Dubeau*, there has been, to date, no Canadian judicial commentary in the correctional context on the quality of the reasoning expressed in such written decisions. In the American context, see *Franklin v. Shields*, 569 F. 2d, at 800-801 (en banc); *U.S. ex rel. Richerson v. Wolff*, 525 F. 2d 797 (CA7 1975), cert. denied, 425 U.S. 914 (1976); *Childs v. U.S. Bd. of Parole*, 167 U.S. App. D.C. 268, 511 F. 2d 1270 (1974); *U.S. ex rel. Johnson v. New York State Bd. of Parole*, 500 F. 2d 925, vacated as moot, 419 U.S. 1015 (1974). The parties to *Franklin v. Shields* did not request that the Parole Board be required to provide a summary of the essential facts: see 569 F. 2d, at 787, 797, and the Fourth Circuit did not address the issue. The Second Circuit in *Johnson* expressly held that the statement of reasons must be supplemented by a summary of the "essential facts upon which the Board's inferences are based" (500 F. 2d, at 934). *Richerson* and *Childs* also indicated that the notice of reasons should include a description of the critical facts. See 525 U.S. 2d, at 804; 511 F. 2d, at 1281-1284, affirming 371 F. Supp. 1246, 1247 (1973).

[138] *Dubeau, supra*, note 135, at 556.

conduct their hearings correctly and fairly." Since there had been no prior notice to the prisoner that he might be questioned about the pending charges and, since "[t]he possibility still exists that the decision of ... [the Board] ... members may have been influenced by their existence," His Lordship held that the Board had not acted fairly and quashed the revocation order.[139]

The Federal Court of Appeal came to a similar conclusion in *Morgan v. National Parole Board.*[140] In that case parole had been suspended, but the only ground for suspension mentioned in the Violation Report delivered to the prisoner was an allegation that he had, without permission, left the halfway house where he was required to reside. Prior to the hearing both attending Board members became aware that the prisoner had been charged with possession of stolen property which had allegedly been found in his room at the halfway house. Without prior notice the Board members raised the subject matter of the charges during the post-suspension hearing. The reasons for revocation referred both to absence from the halfway house without permission and to the arrest of the prisoner in circumstances "highly indicative of involvement in criminal behaviour". The prisoner's initial application for *certiorari* was dismissed by Nitikman J., who held that since post-suspension hearings are designed to be informal, "it is not necessary that everything that will be brought out be detailed before the hearing commences."[141] The issue of fairness was met because "[t]he applicants were fully informed during the hearing why their cases were being reviewed by the Board".[142] On appeal, the judgment of the Trial Division was set aside. Writing for the court, Thurlow C.J. commenced his analysis with the observation that the 14-day notice requirement in the Regulations was designed "to give the inmate an adequate opportunity to prepare to deal with the subject-matter of the hearing." The only matters which the prisoner could prepare himself for were those of which he had been made aware. He concluded:

> it was plainly an occasion, if the procedure was to be fair, for advance notice that the subject would be raised and failing such advance notice for the Board not to sit and wait for the appellant to object but to offer the appellant an adjournment to consider his position with respect to it.[143]

---

139 *Dubeau, supra,* note 135, at 569 and 558. An appeal of this decision was taken to the Federal Court of Appeal, which ruled that the issue was moot (1982), 62 C.C.C. (2d) 191.

140 (1982), 65 C.C.C. (2d) 216 (Fed. C.A.).

141 [1982] 2 F.C. 63 (T.D.), at 75.

142 *Ibid.,* at 74-75.

143 *Supra,* note 140, at 223.

A similar conclusion was reached in *Latham v. Solicitor General of Canada*[144] where Strayer J. quashed a revocation decision because the Board had not notified the prisoner of the "main focus" of its preoccupations. However, in *Greenberg v. National Parole Board* the prisoner claimed that the notice of suspension "was insufficient in that it mentioned some but not all the issues that were raised by the Board at the hearing."[145] Without referring to the judgment in *Morgan*, Pratte J. held that since neither the prisoner nor his counsel "raised any objection or sought an adjournment . . . they must be considered to have impliedly agreed to the discussion of the new issues."[146]

In considering the ramifications of this judgment, it should be noted that Greenberg was represented throughout by counsel, and the case did not concern the delicate issue of questioning about outstanding criminal charges without prior notice, a subject of considerable concern to the judges in the earlier cases. Furthermore, the facts of *Greenberg* disclose that there had been several meetings and exchanges of documents between the prisoner, his counsel and the Board over a period of several months. Indeed, the "fairness" demonstrated by the Board in that case was far in excess of that which can normally be expected. In our opinion, these factors distinguish *Greenberg* and do not restrict the significance of *Morgan, Latham* and *Dubeau* as they relate to notice.

Another issue raised in *Greenberg* was that the prisoner "was never fairly informed of the evidence that was before the Board and which the Board considered relevant to the revocation of the appellant's parole". It appears that during the course of the proceedings the Board received a report indicating that while under suspension the prisoner had been punished by penal authorities for having been found in possession of drugs. The prisoner denied that he had any opportunity to defend himself against these allegations. In the absence of the prisoner and his counsel, the Board interviewed a prison security officer who assured the Board members that the prisoner had received a hearing before being punished. The prisoner was not told of this contradictory evidence. Pratte J. held that "procedural fairness did not require that the appellant be informed of all the evidence that was before the Board. It merely required that he be fully informed of all the facts considered to be relevant that were disclosed by that evidence."[147] Given the impact of a negative credibility finding, there is no excuse for keeping the officer's

---

144 (1984), 39 C.R. (3d) 78 (Fed. T.D.).
145 (1983), 48 N.R. 310 (Fed. C.A.), at 314.
146 *Ibid.*, at 314. A similar conclusion on its facts was reached by Reed J. in *Brook v. National Parole Bd.* [summarized (1984), 12 W.C.B. 108 (Fed. T.D.)].
147 *Greenberg, ibid.*, at 314.

evidence from the prisoner. What appeared black and white to the Board, may have been, in reality, grey.

5. POST-SUSPENSION HEARINGS

(a) Board Members

Sections 36 and 37 of the Regulations[148] mandate that the minimum number of members of a provincial parole board who must vote at a post-suspension hearing is two. In each of the provinces where such boards exist three Board members will usually attend at a post-suspension hearing or vote on the file contents where no hearing has been requested.

Section 23(3) of the Regulations[149] directs that at least two Board members must vote in cases where the National Parole Board has jurisdiction over post-suspension hearings. In *Mason*,[150] the two Board members in attendance at the post-suspension hearing split their votes. Section 23(5) of the Regulations in force at the time authorized the Chairman to assign an additional member to vote. When that procedure was followed, the deciding member voted to revoke mandatory supervision without seeing the prisoner. Ewaschuk J. quashed the Board's decision on the basis that a decision taken by "a faceless and absent bureaucrat who cast his critical vote in some distant unknown place" was "inherently unfair," and violated section 7 of the *Charter*.[151] Current procedure is that in such circumstances a new two-member panel will be convened.[152]

---

[148] SOR/85-236; SOR/86-919.

[149] SOR/85-236; SOR/86-817; SOR/86-919.

[150] *Re Mason and R.* (1984), 7 C.C.C. (3d) 426 (Ont. H.C.).

[151] *Ibid.*, at 429. The case was before the provincial superior court as it involved an application for *habeas corpus* with *certiorari* in aid. Having found that the revocation was invalid, Ewaschuk J. followed *Re Morgan and R.* (1982), 1 C.C.C. (3d) 436 (Man. C.A.) and held that the earlier decision to suspend was no longer valid. However, he declined to order the release of the prisoner, using section 24(1) of the *Charter* to order that a new hearing be held forthwith. For a discussion of the use of this remedy see Chapter 4.

[152] In conformity with this decision the Board is now scrupulously careful to avoid any suggestion of bias or arbitrary behaviour. In *Appeal Division Reports*, Case No. "PROC 012," April 26, 1988, the Appeal Division was confronted with a situation in which a prisoner released on mandatory supervision had disappeared. Following normal procedures, his right to be at liberty had been revoked in his absence. When the prisoner was ultimately arrested, he exercised his right to a post-revocation hearing. One of the attending Board members was one of the members who had previously voted to revoke. On appeal from a decision upholding the revocation, the Appeal Division ordered a new hearing before members who had not been involved in the revocation decision.

(b) Parole Officers and Institutional Personnel

Where a post-suspension hearing is held at a penal facility other than a penitentiary, the prisoner's parole officer will usually attend. When the prisoner is returned to penitentiary, an institutional classification officer and a local representative of the parole service are likely to be present. Since parole officers are required to submit regular detailed progress reports for all persons on conditional release and, since written information, including a "special report" by the parole officer, is forwarded to the Board upon referral of a case by the designated official under s. 22(3) of the Act, the purpose of such persons being in attendance at a post-suspension hearing is not entirely clear. In practice, they seem to play an advisory role—providing an update of information which is not contained in written reports, commenting on the feasibility of proposed release plans, and generally ensuring that Board members are familiar with all facets of the case.[153]

As noted in the discussion of confidentiality issues in Chapter 6, prior to the decisions in *Couperthwaite, Martens* and *Latham*,[154] it was Board practice to allow the presence of parole officers in the hearing room at times when the prisoner was absent. Since these judgments were made the Board has ceased this practice, except where delicate issues of disclosure of confidential information need to be considered. In those rare cases the prisoner is only excluded while the Board hears the confidential information and decides whether and how it is to be shared. There is authority for the position that the Board cannot act on information which it decides not to disclose.[155]

(c) Assistants[156]

In *Latham*, the prisoner had attempted to retain counsel to act as his assistant. He was unable to do so and was assisted by the prison chaplain. One of the arguments advanced by the prisoner, apparently based on American case law, was that section 10(*b*) of the *Charter* imposed an obligation on the Board to provide counsel. Strayer J. found

---

[153] See *Policy and Procedures Manual*, s. VI.B.6.1 and "Administrative Agreement Between the National Parole Board and the Correctional Service of Canada" (revised annually; unpublished).

[154] *Couperthwaite v. National Parole Bd.* (1982), 31 C.R. (3d) 50 (Fed. T.D.); *Martens v. B.C. (A.G.)* (1983), 35 C.R. (3d) 149 (B.C.S.C.); *Latham v. Canada (Solicitor General), supra*, note 143.

[155] See the discussion of confidentiality issues in Chapter 6.

[156] This subject is also discussed in Chapters 6 and 12.

on the facts that the prisoner had not "in any way [been] denied counsel by the board." He then expressed doubt as to whether he had the authority to order the Board, "or appropriate federal or provincial agencies to provide counsel in any future hearing." However, he cautioned that:

> the absence of counsel in a matter of this gravity will be an important factor in assuring the fairness of the process. . . . [If the Board] . . . is not able to demonstrate that it took some initiatives to give the parolee every reasonable opportunity to retain counsel, the integrity of its processes will in my view be vulnerable to attack on the ground of denial of fairness.[157]

In *Re Rain and National Parole Board*, Smith D.J. expanded upon his previous judgment in *Dubeau* and remarked that one of the indicia of unfairness in that case was that "the Parole Board should not have questioned Dubeau about pending criminal charges"[158] without giving him the opportunity to obtain counsel to advise him as to the potential ramifications of making any statement. It is for this reason that section 20.1(3)(*b*) of the Regulations was originally enacted, providing that the assistant may "advise the inmate in respect of any questions put to that inmate by the Board during the hearing." However, in light of the interpretation of section 13 of the *Charter* in *Carlson* and *Dubois*,[159] discussed above, concerns about the admissibility in criminal proceedings of statements made during a post-suspension hearing may no longer be significant. Other issues may, however, arise and no weight should be given to the use of the term "assistant" rather than "counsel".

(d) Types of Decisions

Since the post-suspension hearing is only part of the review process, there are many cases in which the Board will reserve its decision pending, for example, the disposition of criminal charges, confirmation of availability of residential accommodation or other information not available at the time of the hearing, or receipt of an assessment by a mental health professional. As weeks, or even months, may elapse before a final decision is taken, the prisoner, or counsel, is well advised in those circumstances to confirm the oral submissions in written form.

If the decision is to cancel the suspension, the prisoner will not be re-released until the parole officer delivers a "cancellation warrant" to the custodial facility, a process which may take some days. This is done

---

157 *Latham, supra,* note 144, at 92.
158 (1981), 58 C.C.C. (2d) 495 (Fed. T.D.), at 503.
159 *Carlson v. R.* (1985), 14 C.R.R. 4 (B.C.S.C.); *Dubois v. R.*, [1985] 2 S.C.R. 350.

because the Board does not consider a cancellation decision to be final until a telex has been forwarded from the Board's regional office to the local parole office. If additional release conditions form part of the Board's order, the prisoner will not be released until a new release certificate, issued under section 18 of the Act, has been delivered and explained to the prisoner.

Where a decision not to continue a conditional release has been made the Board may make any one of the following orders:

Form of Release	Order	Ramifications
Unescorted Temporary Absence	Termination	Return to penitentiary without loss of remission (*Parole Act*, s. 16(3)).
Day Parole	Termination	Return to penitentiary without loss of remission (*Parole Act*, s. 16(4)).
	Revocation	Return to penitentiary with loss of remission (*Parole Act*, s. 25(2)), subject to partial or full re-credit of remission by Board (*Parole Act*, s. 25(3)).
Full Parole	Termination	Return to penitentiary without loss of remission (*Parole Act*, s. 16(4).
	Revocation	Return to penitentiary with loss of remission (*Parole Act*, s. 25(2)), subject to partial or full re-credit of remission by Board (*Parole Act*, s. 25(3)).
Mandatory Supervision	Termination	Immediate re-release subject to mandatory supervision until W.E.D.
	Revocation	Return to penitentiary with loss of remission (*Parole Act*, s. 25(2)), subject to partial or full re-credit of remission by Board (*Parole Act*, s. 25(3)).

At the time of the post-suspension hearing the Board members will frequently have available a computation of the sentence in the event that they decide to revoke a release. However, such sentence calculations, usually prepared by the Board's own staff rather than by sentence administrators, are often inaccurate. It should not be assumed that prisoners will be able to calculate their own sentences correctly. Prisoners and counsel should seek to obtain accurate information from the

Regional Sentence Administrator of the Correctional Service of Canada.

(e) Re-crediting Remission

The prisoner and assistant should also be prepared to address the question of re-crediting remission as an alternative submission to be made during the course of the post-suspension hearing. Although section 25(3) of the Act requires the Board to address this issue,[160] the Board's *Policy and Procedures Manual* purports to restrict the circumstances under which remission may be re-credited to "exceptional circumstances". This was challenged in *Gregson v. National Parole Board*,[161] where Smith D.J. concluded that while the Board could, as a matter of policy, decide that the power to re-credit remission should be sparingly used, it amounted to an improper fettering of the Board's discretion for it to decide to limit the use of this power only to the circumstances enunciated in a policy directive. Since the release of this judgment, the Board has been more liberal in its use of this power. According to the revised *Policy and Procedures Manual*,[162] the Board is to re-credit remission wherever it "is satisfied that the loss of all remission would be out of proportion to the seriousness of the behavior which led to the revocation."

Prior to the 1986 amendments, neither Part II of the *Parole Regulations* nor any of the provincial statutes or regulations contained any specific reference to the circumstances under which provincial parole boards could consider a re-credit of remission. However, since section 5.1(1) and (2) [now s. 12(1) and (2)] of the *Parole Act* authorized provincial boards "to exercise parole jurisdiction, in accordance with this Act and the regulations," provincial parole authorities were prepared to consider re-crediting remission in rare cases. This has now been confirmed in the new version of section 20(3) of the Act which empowers a

---

[160] One of the present writers commenced a motion to quash that portion of a Board decision relating to the refusal to re-credit remission, combined with a motion for a writ of *mandamus* to reconvene the post-suspension hearing to allow the prisoner to make submissions on this point. The motions were abandoned upon the Board undertaking to hold a new hearing restricted to this issue. The Board has consequently formulated a policy directive reminding Board members of their obligation to canvass this issue at post-suspension hearings. See also *Appeal Division Reports*, Case No. "PROC 018", July 12, 1988.

[161] (1983), 1 C.C.C. (3d) 13 (Fed. T.D.). See also *Gingras v. R.* (Docket no. T-3336-81, Fed. T.D., January 24, 1983).

[162] *Policy and Procedures Manual*, s. VI.G. In practice, revocation is usually reserved for cases in which a new criminal offence has been committed.

provincial parole board to re-credit remission to the same extent as federal authorities.[163]

6. RE-EXAMINATION OF DECISIONS

(a) Negative Decisions

There are two ways in which a revocation (or termination) decision can be reviewed. In *Carde*,[164] mandatory supervision was revoked. The prisoner protested that decision and was granted a new hearing. After the hearing the Board wrote to the penitentiary warden indicating that the Board had changed its decision and had directed that the revocation order be cancelled. The penal authorities refused to release the prisoner because they considered that, having once decided to revoke, the Board was *functus*. Weatherston J. agreed that "it is . . . a general rule that when a subordinate body is empowered to make a decision, once that decision has been made, the body is *functus* in that matter." However, he distinguished cases establishing this principle on the basis that, unlike other tribunals, the Board "is entrusted with exclusive jurisdiction in the entire field of parole of federal prisoners, for the full time of their sentences." Since a revocation order did not deal "with the rights of the parties once and for all time. . . . the National Parole Board must have the implicit power to correct any injustice created by its own act or orders." Thus, the prisoner was ordered released "as if the . . . [original revocation] . . . order . . . had not been made."[165] Since the establishment of a right to a post-revocation hearing arising from *Swan v. Attorney General of British Columbia*,[166] cancellation of revocation decisions has become more frequent.

In *Chester v. National Parole Board*,[167] the Board held a post-suspension hearing at which both alleged breaches of release conditions and re-crediting remission were discussed with the prisoner. Two days later the Board notified the prisoner that his parole had been revoked and that the Board was considering the number of days of remission to be re-credited. A few weeks later the prisoner was notified in writing by Board staff that the Board members had decided to re-credit 852 days of remission. Board staff had erred in interpreting the intention of the attending members. Without any further hearing a letter was sent to the

---

163 S.C. 1986, c. 42, s. 7.
164 *Re Carde and R.* (1977), 34 C.C.C. (2d) 559 (Ont. H.C.).
165 *Ibid.*, at 560, 561, 561-562.
166 (1983), 35 C.R. (3d) 135 (B.C.S.C.).
167 (1989), 48 C.C.C. (3d) 506 (B.C.C.A.).

prisoner informing him that only 305 days of remission were to be re-credited. On the date when he would have been re-released if the larger re-credit had been given the prisoner launched *habeas corpus* proceedings, claiming that the Board was *functus.* The matter came on before McKenzie J., who had previously held in *Dankoski v. Warden of William Head Institution*[168] that, upon discovering a clerical error in the computation of a re-credit of remission after a new release date had been communicated to the prisoner, the Board had no power "to modify the re-credit". McKenzie J. distinguished that decision, holding that so long as the Board was prepared to provide the prisoner with an opportunity to be heard, it had the right to conduct a review of its previous decision.[169]

On appeal, Taggart J.A. noted that while pursuant to the Regulations a prisoner was given the right to demand that the Board reconsider "and review . . . previous decisions due to the passage of time and changed circumstance," no similar powers were given to the Board. After analyzing the statutory powers given to the Board to consider re-crediting remission, the court concluded that "the Parole Board had not [sic] specific, implied or inherent authority" to "reconsider its own concluded, recorded and communicated decision."[170] Had the error been as simple as misspelling a name, or providing a wrong prisoner or record number, the Board could rectify its decision of its own motion, because the substance of the decision would not be changed. However, once a decision (even one erroneously arrived at) had been released, Taggart J.A. cited authority in support of the proposition that an administrative tribunal had no power to modify it unilaterally, unless the statute establishing or regulating the tribunal expressly permitted it to rectify its mistakes.[171]

---

168 [Summarized (1985), 14 W.C.B. 380 (B.C.S.C.)]. Parole was revoked, but the Board elected to re-credit some remission. The letter from the Board to the prisoner confirming this decision specified an incorrect release date. McKenzie J. held that it would be "fundamentally unfair" to permit the Board to regard its decision as a nullity, and ordered the prisoner released. This view was rejected in *Re Hanna* [summarized (1988), 6 W.C.B. (2d) 136 (N.S.T.D.)], the court holding that *Carde* governed the principle that the Board is not *functus.*

169 A similar conclusion was reached by the Nova Scotia Supreme Court in *Re Hanna, ibid.,* where Nathanson J. dismissed an application for *habeas corpus* because the prisoner had had a second hearing before the same Board members who had made the initial erroneous re-credit.

170 *Chester, supra,* note 167, at 514 and 515.

171 *Canada (Employment & Immigration Cmmn.) v. MacDonald Tobacco Inc.* (1981), 121 D.L.R. (3d) 546 (S.C.C.).

(b) The Appeal Division

The second method of reviewing a termination or revocation order made by the National Parole Board in respect of a prisoner released from a penitentiary is provided by section 22 of the Regulations,[172] which currently provides, *inter alia*, that the prisoner may request the Board to re-examine a decision revoking parole or mandatory supervision. Although not mandated by the Regulation, the Board will also permit a prisoner to seek re-examination of a decision terminating unescorted temporary absence, day or full parole, or a decision not to re-credit remission. Indeed, according to current policy, the only decisions which cannot be re-examined are those requiring the votes of Community Board members and denials of day or full parole by exception.[173]

A prisoner may invoke the re-examination procedures as of right if the application is received by the Board within 30 days of the time when the prisoner is notified of the termination or revocation decision. Although the Board is not obliged to consider requests received outside this time period, in practice it does not adhere strictly to the wording of section 22(2) of the Regulation. When the prisoner receives written notice of the revocation decision, a form letter is attached explaining how to commence an application for re-examination.

Re-examination of negative decisions at the federal level is conducted through a specialized "Appeals Division", whose members do not participate in initial decision-making processes.[174] According to section VII.10.1 of the *Policy and Procedures Manual* the Appeals Division may, by majority vote, modify or reverse a decision if it is of the opinion that:

> The decision may have been prejudiced by either a breach of or an improper use of the procedures under the Act, Regulations or policies;
>
> The decision was based on either erroneous or incomplete information;
>
> The information available at the time of the re-examination indicates that the decision was either inequitable or unfair.

---

[172] SOR/78-524; SOR/81-487; SOR/86-817.

[173] *Parole Regulations*, s. 22(1)(*a*); National Parole Board, *Policy and Procedures Manual*, s. VII.5.1. While this policy is ostensibly generous, it has also been used by the Board as a defence to an application for judicial review. In *Pulice v. National Parole Bd.* [summarized 9 W.C.B. (2d) 379 (Fed. C.A.)], the Board persuaded Cullen J. that its policy permitting a review by its Appeal Division precluded relief. The Federal Court of Appeal recognized that, in the very least, an alternative adequate remedy had to be legally enforceable, not a creature of policy.

[174] *Parole Regulations*, s. 22(3). Provincial parole boards do not have formalized review procedures, although decisions can be reviewed on the basis of new information.

The Appeals division is also empowered to direct a new "review" to be conducted by a panel of members who did not take part in the decision being re-examined. Still, the Appeals Division does not have powers parallel to judicial review and ought not to be considered an adequate alternative remedy that precludes judicial review.

(c) Issue Estoppel and Res Judicata

A frequently encountered problem is that conditional release is terminated or revoked as a result of a new charge having been laid. The prisoner is then acquitted of the charge (or the charge is not proceeded with) and seeks re-examination of the Board's original decision. Under the previous re-examination regime the circumstances under which a decision was likely to be changed were very rare. Despite the wording of [then] section 22(3)(*b*) of the Regulations that the Board members re-examining the original decision were to consider "any other relevant information that was not available at the time of [the original] decision," information that the accused parolee had ultimately been acquitted of the charge which resulted in the revocation decision, or that circumstances had changed substantially, tended to have little effect on the outcome of the review.

The judgment of the Federal Court of Appeal in *Morin*[175] has opened the issue as to whether and in what circumstances an acquittal upon a criminal charge may be binding upon parole authorities. The appellant was serving sentence in penitentiary when he was charged with murder arising from the death of another prisoner. Pending his trial he was transferred to a "supermaximal" "Special Handling Unit (S.H.U.)". Although he was acquitted at trial, the penal authorities declined to return him to the regular penal population. The prisoner initially launched *habeas corpus* proceedings to obtain his release from the S.H.U. By coincidence, the application was heard by the same judge who had presided over the murder trial. While concluding that he had no jurisdiction to grant *habeas corpus*, and that the prisoner should seek relief in the Trial Division of the Federal Court,[176] Bergeron J. commented *in obiter* that the reasoning of the penal authorities for continuing to detain the prisoner in the S.H.U. was based on an incorrect and incomplete understanding of the facts. The trial judge "minced no

---

[175] *Re Morin and National S.H.U. Review Committee* (1985), 20 C.C.C. (3d) 123 (Fed. C.A.).

[176] This judgment was ultimately reversed by the Supreme Court of Canada in *Morin v. National S.H.U. Committee* (1986), 23 C.C.C. (3d) 132. See the discussion of this and related cases in Chapter 3.

words in his reaction to the continued supermaximal detention," referring to it as 'untenable'. . . . in total disregard of the rules of natural justice
and fairness."[177]

The case eventually came before the Federal Court of Appeal.
Speaking for a majority of the court MacGuigan J. exhaustively reviewed British, American and Canadian case law and academic commentary on the inter-related concepts of *res judicata*, issue estoppel and
collateral estoppel. He concluded:

> What may usefully be derived from the American experience, I think,
> are two tests of collateral estoppel, *viz.* identity of matter and criminal
> sanctions. In the light of the acceptance of collateral or issue estoppel in
> Canada through the doctrine of *res judicata*, these would seem to be of
> persuasive value as precedents in Canada, despite the absence of a constitu-
> tional charter of rights at the relevant time here.[178]

Applying these tests to the facts of the case at bar, MacGuigan J. found
that since "[t]he very issue which . . . [the Respondent] . . . purported to
decide . . . had already been decided by a jury on the basis of the same
facts. The identity-of-matter test is more than adequately satisfied."
While conceding that there might be circumstances where there might
be "other facts for the decision which had not been available in the
criminal process, or other situations independent entirely of the . . .
murder which could justify the decision to continue Morin's confinement in an SHU," no such materials had been placed before the reviewing court. Thus, "the respondents clearly misdirected themselves as to
the law when they refused to give full effect to the criminal acquittal."[179]

The majority of the court had little difficulty in coming to the
conclusion that the second branch of the test—the existence of criminal
sanctions—had also been satisfied. While "correctional proceedings . . .
fall between the traditional criminal and civil spheres", continued confinement in an S.H.U. was "in character, purpose and effect" a criminal
sanction. This could scarcely be doubted in the circumstances in *Morin*;
however, the question of whether parole revocation proceedings are
criminal sanctions is not free from doubt. In his review of the American
authorities MacGuigan J. held that "[t]he United States cases do not, in
sum, produce a clear result, particularly on the parole or probation
issues in relation to which they have most often arisen."[180] While
contemporary American judgments generally hold that because of the

---

[177] *Supra*, note 175, at 146.
[178] *Supra*, note 175, at 143. The factual underpinnings for the case arose before the
enactment of the *Charter*.
[179] *Supra*, note 175, at 146-147 and 148.
[180] *Supra*, note 175, at 147, 148 and 141.

potential loss of liberty parole and probation revocation proceedings are "criminal in nature, even if not in form," authority also exists in support of the proposition that revocation of parole is remedial rather than punitive, since it seeks to protect the welfare of parolees and the safety of society."[181]

Neither of these issues has as yet been rigorously scrutinized in the Canadian parole context. In *Ng v. National Parole Board*,[182] an application for *habeas corpus* with *certiorari* in aid[183] brought in the provincial superior court, a parolee was charged with drug trafficking offences, as a result of which his parole was suspended and his case referred to the Board. Following a post-suspension hearing parole was revoked because, in the Board's opinion "there was information indicating he was directly or indirectly involved in the commission of a criminal offence." The prisoner was later acquitted at trial, following which he applied for a re-examination of the revocation decision. For reasons not specified in the judgment a post-revocation hearing was convened, the Board indicating that it wished "to hear the applicant's explanations for certain things which took place at his trial and . . . to discuss the matter of $5,000 in cash which they [sic] found hidden in a stereo speaker, and also a set of scales."[184]

Following the hearing the Board upheld the original revocation decision, citing the following reasons:

> The Board has heard your arguments as to why the revocation should be cancelled and has heard your explanations concerning telephone conversations, possession of a set of scales, possession of a large amount of money hidden in your apartment, as well as your continuing relationship with one . . . who pleaded guilty to a charge of conspiracy to traffick in a narcotic which named you as a co-conspirator. The Board is satisfied that you were involved directly or indirectly in criminal activity and are therefore unsuitable to continue with conditional release. On that basis the Board believes the decision of the Board to revoke was proper and will not be interfered with.[185]

---

181 *Standlee v. Rhay*, 555 F.2d 1303 (1975), at 1306.
182 (S.C.O. #997/86, Ont. H.C., June 10, 1986).
183 The Board has on occasion argued that the existence of the re-examination provisions should militate against the application of the remedy of *certiorari* in circumstances where there has been a defect in the section 16(4) review process. This view has been given short shrift by the courts. In *Morgan v. National Parole Bd.* (1982), 65 C.C.C. (2d) 216 (Fed. C.A.), Thurlow C.J. held that re-examination is "no substitute for *certiorari* to quash a decision made without jurisdiction". A similar conclusion was arrived at by McEachern C.J.S.C. in *Swan v. B.C. (A.G.)* (1983), 35 C.R. (3d) 135 (B.C.S.C.), at 140.
184 *Ng, supra*, note 182, at 3.
185 *Supra*, note 182, at 5.

When the case came before the Ontario Court of Appeal,[186] in brief oral reasons the court held that because the Board was not "bound by the technical rules of evidence that govern a criminal trial" it was proper for it

> to take into account the appellant's conduct in the time period under consideration, the evidence of his association with a known trafficker in heroin, and his possession of a large quantity of cash and a set of scales, in deciding whether the appellant had violated his parole or in order to prevent a breach of parole and to protect society, all pursuant to s. 16 [now s. 22] of the *Parole Act*."[187]

However, the Board fell into error when it treated the co-accused's guilty plea as evidence that the parolee was his co-conspirator, in light of the acquittal at trial.[188] Thus, the decision upholding the original revocation order was quashed and a new hearing was ordered before a different panel of the Parole Board.

In *Winters*,[189] mandatory supervision had been suspended as a result of a charge of assault being laid against the prisoner. He was discharged at the preliminary enquiry. He attempted to argue that the discharge precluded the Board from considering his admitted involvement in a scuffle which led to the charge. In a brief judgment, Spencer J. of the British Columbia Supreme Court held that sections 7, 9, or 11(*h*) of the *Charter* were not contravened by the Board relying on the same facts as had been relied upon by the Crown at the preliminary, because of the Board's "exclusive jurisdiction" to decide whether to revoke or continue conditional release.

While these cases may have been correctly decided on their particular facts, further litigation will be necessary to clarify the applicability of the "identity of the subject matter" and the "criminal sanctions" tests in the parole context. A central thread running through the American cases is that collateral estoppel can only be raised "when an issue of ultimate fact has once been determined by a valid and final judgment."[190] Experience demonstrates that it is often difficult, in the

---

186 *Ng v. National Parole Bd.* (Court of Appeal File #392/86, Ont. C.A., November 6, 1986).

187 *Ibid.*, at 2.

188 A further error on the part of the Board was that it "acted on information from statements which it had in its possession and did not make available to the applicant so as to afford him the opportunity to answer them. . . . In short, the Board failed to provide the applicant with relevant information upon which it might judge him." (*Ng, ibid.*, at 2.) See the discussion of disclosure issues in Chapter 6, and *R. v. Savion* (1980), 13 C.R. (3d) 259 (Ont. C.A.).

189 *R. v. Winters* [summarized (1987), 1 W.C.B. (2d) 63 (B.C.S.C.)].

190 *Ashe v. Swanson* (1970), 397 U.S. 436, at 443 per Stewart J.

multifarious fact circumstances which can present themselves in parole suspension cases, to determine what facts were in issue in the other proceedings (usually the criminal trial). For example, where a judgment of acquittal is based on a jury verdict, or where reasons are not delivered by a judge sitting alone, is a parole board to be bound by that finding? As noted by MacGuigan J. in *Morin*,[191] some would support the notion that in order to give meaning to the concept of the presumption of innocence an acquittal can only mean that the trier of fact found the accused to be innocent on all issues, and that the accused should not be in a worse position than before the acquittal.[192] Alternatively, it can be argued that where a verdict of acquittal is based on a general verdict, a parole board should then be required to scrutinize the trial record to determine "whether a rational jury could have grounded its verdict upon an issue other than that which the defendant seeks to foreclose from consideration"?[193] Again, what of cases where information clearly relevant to a parole board is ruled inadmissible at a criminal trial, such as the contents of intercepted communications which, though reflective of guilt, were excluded from evidence because the trial judge rules they were improperly obtained? As well, how should the Board treat the testimony of a child of tender years whose evidence was either not heard by the trier of fact or was not given under oath? In such circumstances can a parole board, acting in fulfilment of its statutory mandate to ensure that continued release "would not constitute an undue risk to society", ignore material which is highly pertinent? Or should a parole board convene some type of hearing to receive the child's "evidence", or to hear the inadmissible wiretap? If so, what extent of cross-examination should be permitted?

While these and related questions await further scrutiny by the courts, the National Parole Board has recently decided[194] to publish reports on major issues identified through the appeal process. In one of the first cases considered,[195] the Appeal Division has formulated its view of the Board's position vis-à-vis revocation of conditional release

---

[191] *Supra*, note 175.
[192] See the subsequent decision of the Supreme Court of Canada in *Grdic v. R.* (1985), 19 C.C.C. (3d) 289, where a majority of the court held that since "an acquittal is the equivalent to a finding of innocence. . . . any issue, the resolution of which had to be in favour of the accused as a prerequisite to the acquittal, is irrevocably deemed to have been found conclusively in favour of the accused" (at 293-294).
[193] *Sealfon v. U.S.*, 332 U.S. 575, at 579.
[194] *Appeal Division Reports*, April, 1989, unpublished, but available upon request from the Appeal Division, National Parole Board or at the Board's Regional offices.
[195] Case No. "PROC 005", June 26, 1987. Care has to be taken to protect individuals' privacy by identifying cases by number only.

when criminal charges are dismissed. While on day parole the prisoner was arrested by police officers in possession of what they considered to be cocaine. At his post-suspension hearing the prisoner did not dispute possession of the drug; rather, he objected only to the allegations as to the quantity seized. However, the charge was withdrawn when a certificate of analysis disclosed that the substance was not cocaine. In upholding a decision to revoke day parole (without re-credit of remission), the Appeal Division held:

> In determining whether or not to revoke parole or day parole and whether or not to recredit remission, the Board considers it has the authority to review all the information available to it. The Board considers that if, in its view, there are reasonable grounds to conclude that a person has become involved directly or indirectly in criminal activity, it has the authority to revoke with or without recredit of remission in order to protect society. This applies whether or not charges have been laid, whether the charges have been stayed or dropped or whether there has been an acquittal. In the instances where the court proceedings have been completed, the Board needs to take into consideration the outcome of those proceedings but is not necessarily bound by it even if the circumstances surrounding the charge or charges are the sole reason for the suspension. In this case, the inmate was arrested at an address occupied by persons active in the drug trade. He was in possession of a substance that was thought to be cocaine and at his post suspension interview he only objected to the quantity that he was claimed to have had. It is thus evident that he was intending to become involved in criminal activity. As a result, the Appeal Division concludes that the decision to revoke the day parole and not to recredit remission was fair, notwithstanding the new information that the substance did not turn out to be cocaine.[196]

While the admission of criminal activity in this case made it easy for the Board (and the Appeal Division) to conclude that the prisoner's behaviour had fallen below that which the Board could reasonably expect, further cases will no doubt raise some of the more difficult issues described above.

(d) Positive Decisions

Two cases have dealt with the question of whether conditional release can be revoked if the Board has previously decided to cancel a suspension either prior, or subsequent, to a post-suspension hearing.[197]

---

[196] *Ibid.*

[197] This is a somewhat different issue than that addressed by Henry J. in *Ex parte Collins* (1976), 30 C.C.C. (2d) 460 (Ont. H.C.). In that case the Board used its power under section 10(1)(*e*) [now s. 16(1) (*d*) and (*e*)] to override a decision to cancel a suspension taken by the designated person conducting the section 16(3) [now s. 22(3)] review. The cases discussed here involve the Board overruling its own previous decisions.

In *Greenberg v. National Parole Board*[198] it was argued that it was a condition precedent to the Board's exercise of its power to revoke that the original suspension remain in place. Without referring to case law on point[199] Pratte J. held that, since section 10(1)(*e*) [now ss. 16(1)(*e*) and (*f*)], and not section 16 [now s. 22], was the source of the Board's revocation powers, "an order of the Board revoking a parole is not void for the sole reason that it was not preceded by a valid suspension." Further, since the Board "exercises a purely administrative function," it was not *functus* when it elected to "reconsider the matter or review its decision."[200] This was carried one stage further by Muldoon J. in *Sango v. National Parole Board*[201] where the prisoner moved to prohibit the Board from convening a post-suspension hearing in light of a previous decision to cancel the suspension. It would appear from the judgment that the suspension had been cancelled following a post-suspension hearing because there were serious questions as to the prisoner's guilt in relation to the criminal charges which had caused the suspension and referral. The prisoner subsequently pleaded guilty to the charges and was sentenced to a further term of imprisonment. The prisoner argued that since he had remained in custody despite the cancellation of the suspension (he had not been granted bail), there was no "*post*-release misbehaviour upon which to base revocation of mandatory supervision." Muldoon J. reasoned that:

> ... surely the respondent Board was scrupulously correct in restoring the applicant's mandatory supervision during the time in which he was merely charged with the offences alleged against him in December, 1982. Due regard for the applicant's constitutional right to be presumed innocent until proven guilty according to law, alone, if nothing else were known of the applicant's behaviour, would dictate prudence. Viewing those pending charges *per se*, the respondent could not know whether the outcome would be an acquittal, a *nolle prosequi*, a finding of guilt, or, as actually occurred, a "guilty" plea. It was only then that, in regard to the pending charges, post-release behaviour upon which revocation might be based was ascertained."[202]

His Lordship then expressly adapted the *ratio* in *Greenberg* to conclude that the Board had neither exceeded nor lacked jurisdiction to convene or continue a post-suspension hearing.

Without accepting that the Board's function can always be characterized as purely administrative except when dealing with re-crediting

---

[198] (1983), 48 N.R. 310 (Fed. C.A.).
[199] See the discussion of cases such as *Collins, Gorog* and *Roach, supra.*
[200] *Supra*, note 198, at 313.
[201] [1984] 1 F.C. 183 (T.D.).
[202] *Ibid.*, at 190.

remission, we maintain that the *Greenberg* and *Sango* cases were correctly decided. The Board is not *functus* if warrant expiry date has not been reached and the original sentence continues to be in existence. So long as the prisoner has a further opportunity to complete the presentation of his case at a hearing (as occurred in *Greenberg,* and as the Board planned to do in *Sango*) in light of changed circumstances, the principles of fairness will not be offended.

9

Temporary Absence Passes

1. ESCORTED TEMPORARY ABSENCES

(a) Provincial Institutions

Section 7(1) of the *Prisons and Reformatories Act*[1] provides legislative jurisdiction for prisoners confined in provincial institutions following conviction for *Criminal Code*[2] offences or other federal statutes to be granted escorted temporary absence (E.T.A.) from close custody by officials "designated by the Lieutenant Governor of the province in which a prisoner is confined." Escorted passes may be granted at any time during the serving of sentence for medical or humanitarian reasons.[3] Institutional directors or senior correctional staff are designated by the responsible Minister to authorize release on temporary absence.[4] In practice, an application for release on escorted temporary absence is made by the prisoner (usually in writing) to the senior correctional officer at the institution where he is serving sentence or awaiting trial.[5]

---

[1] R.S.C. 1985, c. P-20 [formerly R.S.C. 1970, c. P-21, s. 8(1) (as amended by S.C. 1976-77, c. 53 [proclaimed in force July 1, 1978])]. Prisoners serving sentences for offences committed under provincial legislation fall under provincial temporary absence regimes through provincial statutes.

[2] R.S.C. 1985, c. C-46.

[3] *Quaere* whether a remand prisoner may be granted this form of release by institutional officials, as section 8 is clearly limited to sentenced prisoners. While emergency temporary absences are granted from time to time, strictly speaking only a court has jurisdiction to allow release of a remand prisoner.

[4] For example, see *Ministry of Correctional Services Act*, R.S.O. 1980, c. 275, ss. 11 and 27. *Ministry of Correctional Services Regulations*, R.R.O. 1980, Reg. 649, s. 34. It should be noted that section 7(1) of the *Prisons and Reformatories Act* is broad enough to permit the Lieutenant Governor to designate any person to grant escorted passes.

[5] Escorted temporary absences should not be confused with other forms of warrants. A prisoner in transit between institutions is not generally released on temporary absence, since he will not be returning to the original institution; in such cases transfers are usually effected under the authority of the original warrant of committal or under a "warrant of removal" issued under the appropriate provincial statute. Remand prisoners referred for psychiatric assessment are removed from provincial institutions on the strength of the court order made by a Judge or Justice (the form of which is usually endorsed on the committal warrant). Prisoners committed under provincial mental health or communicable disease legislation are taken from confinement pursuant to

Escorted temporary absence passes may also be granted to "penitentiary" prisoners temporarily resident in provincial institutions. Because section 2(1) of the *Penitentiary Act*[6] defines an inmate as "a person, who, having been sentenced or committed to penitentiary, has been received and accepted at a penitentiary . . .", that Act does not apply to prisoners who have not yet actually entered penitentiary. However, as a practical matter, federal inmates in custody in a provincial institution awaiting transfer to a penitentiary should apply to both federal and provincial officials for release on escorted temporary absence. Similarly, prisoners in provincial custody under a warrant of suspension of federal parole or mandatory supervision will require the concurrence of both federal parole officials and provincial correctional personnel before escorted temporary absence may be approved.

Escorted temporary absence passes from provincial correctional institutions for general rehabilitative purposes fall under the same statutory structure as other forms of escorted passes. Longer term passes, whereby a prisoner is released on a regular basis to attend school, maintain employment or engage in volunteer work are, in most provinces, considered under slightly different statutory provisions or regulations. (Since the prisoner is likely to be unescorted while at large from a halfway house or custodial facility, this topic will be considered under the heading "Unescorted Temporary Absences" below.)

(b) Federal Penitentiaries—Non-Lifers

Sections 28 and 30 of the *Penitentiary Act* authorize the Commissioner of Corrections to grant escorted temporary absence for an unlimited period for medical reasons. Institutional directors may grant medical escorted temporary absence passes for up to 15 days; a pass may also be renewed. In addition, the Commissioner's directives[7] made pursuant to section 29(3) of the *Penitentiary Act* provide that in all cases extensions may be authorized in emergency situations. These types of passes are most frequently granted where a prisoner is hospitalized at a public facility. Where a prisoner is sent to a penitentiary medical facility or provincial mental health centre for extended and indefinite periods, a

---

orders made under the relevant provincial statutes. Prisoners found to be insane, mentally ill, mentally deficient, feeble-minded or unfit to stand trial under the relevant provisions of the *Code* are removed from prisons on orders signed by the Lieutenant Governor or designate.

6   R.S.C. 1985, c. P-5 [formerly R.S.C. 1970, c. P-6, s. 2 (as amended S.C. 1976-77, c. 53, s. 35; 1977-78, c. 22, s. 20)].

7   The relevant directives were issued April 16, 1982.

transfer warrant is issued by the institutional director pursuant to section 22 of the *Penitentiary Act.*

The Commissioner of Corrections may grant an escorted absence for up to 15 days for humanitarian or rehabilitative reasons. An institutional director may grant such a pass for up to 5 days; however, current policy is that unless the prisoner has, on a prior occasion during the current sentence, successfully completed either an escorted or unescorted pass, the institutional director is required to consult with the Regional Director General of the Correctional Service of Canada. Escorted releases for humanitarian releases include, but are not limited to, visits to family members who are seriously ill, attendance at funerals, participation in special events such as graduations or religious ceremonies that normally call for family participation, or attendance where hardship is being endured by family and the prisoner's presence would be considered beneficial. Rehabilitative escorted absences include family visits, visits to halfway houses and employers prior to release on parole or mandatory supervision, writing of examinations, attendance at cultural or recreational events within the immediate community, or engaging in community service projects.

Escorted passes for some court appearances are considered as humanitarian releases. In criminal matters where the prisoner is required to appear either as accused or as a witness, no temporary absence application is required. A judge's order, pursuant to section 527 of the *Code*, will be sufficient authority for penitentiary authorities to deliver the prisoner to court.

Section 688(1) of the *Criminal Code* provides that a prisoner appellant who desires to be present at the hearing of an appeal is entitled to appear as a matter of right. Indeed, in *Smith*[8] the Supreme Court of Canada held that in such circumstances an appeal could not be heard in the absence of the appellant.[9] In summary conviction appeals under Part XXVII of the *Code*, section 795 directs that section 688 is incorporated *mutatis mutandis*; therefore, the right to appear in person, where the prisoner is not represented by counsel, is absolute. A prisoner appellant who is represented by counsel is not entitled to appear upon a leave application, on "preliminary or incidental proceedings"[10] or where the appeal is on a ground involving a question of law alone.[11]

---

[8]   *Smith v. R.*, [1965] S.C.R. 568. Proposals currently before Parliament will amend the *Supreme Court Act* (R.S.C. 1985, c. S-26) to limit the rights of prisoner appellants to appear in person before that court. *The Globe and Mail* (26 April 1986) 5.

[9]   Where an appellant has signified, pursuant to provincial appeal rules, that he wishes the appeal to be disposed of in writing, there would appear to be no entitlement to appear at the "hearing" of the appeal.

[10] *Code* s. 688(2).

[11] See *R. v. Elworthy* (1986), 49 B.C.L.R. 188 (B.C.C.A.).

Section 19(3) [formerly s. 16(2)] of the *Penitentiary Act* appears to be somewhat broader than the *Code* provisions. The Commissioner of Corrections or designate may authorize the transfer of the prisoner appellant to a penal facility other than a penitentiary for the purpose of "preparation or presentation of an appeal". In *Walford*,[12] the prisoner sought an order entitling her to remain in British Columbia pending the disposition of her appeal. McFarlane J.A. doubted whether the court had the power to make such an order and noted the existence of the discretionary power given to the Commissioner of Corrections under section 16(2) [now s. 19(3)] of the *Penitentiary Act*. This view was adopted (without reference to *Walford*) by Philp J.A. of the Manitoba Court of Appeal in *Faulkner*;[13] however, in that case Philp J.A. considered that in exercising his authority under section 16(2) [now s. 19(3)] the Commissioner would be subject to a duty of procedural fairness and would be required to receive representations by or on behalf of the prisoner before making his decision.

In non-criminal matters such as appearances before Royal Commissions, Coroner's Inquests, or Commissions of Inquiry under the *Inquiries Act*,[14] where orders or subpoenas have been issued for the attendance of a prisoner, the Commissioner's directives state that he is to be granted an escorted temporary absence, unless, in the opinion of the institutional director, valid reasons exist for non-compliance. In such cases the director is required immediately to seek legal advice. The directives do not directly address other forms of orders or subpoenas; however, under the general rule-making power contained in section 37(3) of the *Penitentiary Act* it can be assumed that similar procedures would be applied, so long as satisfactory arrangements are made in advance for the costs of transporting the prisoner to and from such appearance, and for returning the prisoner to the institution once his attendance is no longer required.

It should also be noted that in most provinces procedures exist in civil cases for the issuance of a writ of *habeas corpus ad testificandum.* For example, Rule 53.06 of the Ontario Rules of Practice provides that an *ex parte* application may be made to the court in which the trial is to be held for an order to produce a prisoner for an examination authorized

---

[12] *R. v. Walford* (1983), 5 C.C.C. (3d) 544 (B.C.C.A.). This was a case in which the prisoner had not actually been received at a penitentiary. Where the prisoner is transferred from a penitentiary to a provincial institution, a transfer warrant rather than a temporary absence permit is used to secure the prisoner's transfer to "provincial" custody.

[13] *R. v. Faulkner*, [summarized (1986), 16 W.C.B. 313 (Man. C.A.)].

[14] R.S.C. 1985, c. I-11.

by the Rules or as a witness at a trial, upon payment of the costs involved.[15] In such cases, the prisoner must be located within the province within which the writ was issued, because a writ of *habeas corpus ad testificandum* issued from one province will not necessarily be acted upon if the prisoner is in a penitentiary in another province.[16] Thus, where no binding court order or subpoena has been issued by a court or other tribunal, the power to grant an escorted temporary absence rests in the institutional director. In considering whether or not to grant such an escorted pass, the director may consider potential security risks, institutional behaviour, the nature of the proposed appearance and financial arrangements.

The issue of a prisoner's right to appear to argue his own application for *habeas corpus* has been considered in the post-*Charter*[17] case of *Olson*.[18] Speaking for the Ontario Court of Appeal, Brooke J.A. noted that at common law there was no right to appear to make an application for a writ of *habeas corpus*; only if the court determined that there was a *prima facie* case would the judge direct that the writ be issued. Because the appellant had raised "serious matters", Brooke J.A. held that the judge hearing the original application should not have decided the sufficiency of the application without affording the prisoner a right to be

---

15 Similarly, for example, Alberta *Rules of Court*, Rule 296; British Columbia *Rules of Court*, Rule 40(37); Nova Scotia *Rules of Practice*, Rule 31.24(6); New Brunswick *Rules of Court*, Rule 55.04.

16 *Commissioner's Directive*, #204, s. 15, issued August 29, 1980. See *McGuire v. McGuire*, [1953] O.R. 328 (C.A.). In *McCann v. R.*, [1975] F.C. 272 (C.A.), Jackett C.J. noted that although Federal Court Rule 334 authorized the court to issue an order for *habeas corpus ad testificandum* to give evidence, the court had no power to direct that the prisoner plaintiffs be present at other stages of the trial. A similar conclusion was reached in *Henry v. Canada (Min. of Justice)* [summarized (1989), 6 W.C.B. (2d) 422 (Fed. T.D.)] where a prisoner attempted to use section 18 of the *Federal Court Act* (R.S.C. 1985, c. F-7) to obtain a writ of *habeas corpus ad testificandum* to enable him to attend at the trial of his application for judicial review. Rouleau J. held not only that such writ could not be issued under section 18, but also that a writ was limited to compelling the appearance of a person as a witness and not as a party. See also *Re Kevork and R.* (1985), 17 C.C.C. (3d) 426 (Fed. T.D.), at 440.

17 *Canadian Charter of Rights and Freedoms* (being Part I of the *Constitution Act, 1982* [en. by the *Canada Act, 1982* (U.K.), c. 11, s. 1]).

18 *R. v. Olson* (1989), 47 C.C.C. (3d) 491 (S.C.C.), upholding (1988), 38 C.C.C. (3d) 534 (Ont. C.A.). The same conclusion was reached in *St-Jacques v. Walsh* [summarized (1988), 5 W.C.B. (2d) 174 (N.B.Q.B.)], where a prisoner having a matter pending in the Federal Court Trial Division brought an application for *habeas corpus* in the New Brunswick Court of Queen's Bench to compel the penal authorities to bring him before the Federal Court to argue his case. Riordon J. stated that he had considered whether to direct that the prisoner be brought before him, but decided not to do so as the material disclosed no evidence of unlawful detention.

heard. However, since all of the material which could have been placed before the Motions Court Judge was now before the Court of Appeal, that court could hear the application. The court then proceeded to dismiss the application as being ultimately without merit. All aspects of this judgment were upheld on further appeal to the Supreme Court of Canada.

(c) Lifers

A prisoner serving life is eligible to apply for E.T.A. release at any point in the sentence.[19] However, section 747(2) of the *Code* mandates that a prisoner serving a life minimum sentence must apply to the National Parole Board for non-medical E.T.A.s. Current Board policy is that applications by lifers for any type of escorted absence must be approved by at least two members of the National Parole Board, regardless of whether the prisoner is incarcerated in a federal or provincial institution. It should also be noted that the institutional director has a veto power, in that he is not, according to Board policy, required to submit the application to the Board if he is not in favour of the proposed release. Finally, Board policy is that the release is not to be approved unless the escort is an employee of the Correctional Service of Canada or a peace officer as defined by section 2 of the *Code*.

2. UNESCORTED TEMPORARY ABSENCES

(a) Provincial Institutions

Section 7(1) [formerly s. 8(1)] of the *Prisons and Reformatories Act* provides that unescorted temporary absence (U.T.A.) may be granted at any point during the serving of sentence for medical, humanitarian or rehabilitative purposes.[20] While section 7(2) provides that in provinces where a provincial parole board has been established the Lieutenant

---

19 The limitation on eligibility for temporary absence contained in section 12 of the *Parole Regulations* (SOR/78-428) does not apply to E.T.A.s, because the definition of temporary absence in section 2 of the Regulations refers only to *unescorted* temporary absences.

20 In *R. v. Fulton* [summarized (1988), 5 W.C.B. (2d) 178 (Sask. Q.B.)], a prisoner had been granted a 15-day release, with instructions to return to pick up another 15-day pass at the end of that period. He did not do so and was charged with being unlawfully at large. The trial judge held that since section 8(1) [now s. 7(1)] spoke only of "a period not exceeding 15 days", there was no authority to grant "back to back temporary absences" and acquitted the accused. This was reversed on appeal, Barclay J. holding that there was no statutory bar to releases which amounted to more than 15 days, so long as no one pass exceeded that period.

Governor may order that no unescorted passes be authorized without the approval of that province's parole board, to date no provincial parole board has become directly involved in initial U.T.A. decision-making. The Ontario Board of Parole has no direct involvement in U.T.A. granting either under the *Ministry of Correctional Services Act* or under applicable Regulations. While the Quebec parole statute similarly excludes any role for the Parole Commission in initial U.T.A. granting, it should be noted that Part II of the Act[21] designates the Parole Commission as exercising appellate jurisdiction where any application for unescorted temporary absence has been denied, or where the prisoner seeks a review of conditions attached to a grant of temporary absence. Section 43 provides that one member of the Parole Commission is to hear such appeals. In British Columbia, the Attorney General is designated as the Minister who may authorize unescorted temporary absences for medical, educational or humanitarian reasons, or to assist in the rehabilitation of the inmate.[22] Thus, the British Columbia Board of Parole has no direct role in unescorted temporary absence granting.[23] In

---

[21] *An Act to Promote the Parole of Inmates*, S.Q. 1978, c. 22. While the Quebec statute provides for in-person hearings at both parole granting and parole revocation hearings, it would appear that a Commission member may decide an appeal against the denial of a U.T.A. without affording the prisoner an opportunity for an in-person hearing.

[22] *Corrections Act*, R.S.B.C. 1979, c. 70. In *R. v. Konkin* [summarized (1979), 3 W.C.B. 343 (B.C. Co. Ct.)] MacEachern Co. Ct. J. held that despite the wording in section 22 of the British Columbia *Correction Act*, which appeared to provide that the appropriate Minister must personally approve a temporary absence for medical purposes in writing, a prisoner detained in pre-trial custody who escaped while being taken to a hospital for medical treatment under escort remained in lawful custody throughout, and therefore could be convicted of escape under the *Code*. Relying on the broad ruling of Dickson J. in *R. v. Harrison* (1976), 28 C.C.C. (2d) 279 (S.C.C.), MacEachern Co. Ct. J. held that "although there is a general rule of construction in law that a person endowed with a discretionary power should exercise it personally, that rule can be displaced by the language, scope or object of a particular administrative scheme."

[23] It should be noted that there is a slight difference in the statutory framework establishing the jurisdiction of the Ontario and British Columbia Boards of Parole. Prior to the enactment of section 5.1 [now s. 12(1) of the *Parole Act* [see S.C. 1976-77, c. 53, s. 22] (proclaimed in force September 1, 1978)] the jurisdiction of these Boards of Parole arose only during the indeterminate or indefinite portions of sentences being served in prisons or reformatories in those provinces. While section 34 of the Ontario *Ministry of Correctional Services Act* grants parole jurisdiction to the Ontario Board of Parole over "any inmate convicted of an offence under any Act of the Legislature, any Act of the Parliament of Canada or against a municipal bylaw", the British Columbia *Correction Act* has divided parole jurisdiction into two parts. Section 25 vests parole jurisdiction in the British Columbia Board of Parole in the case of a prisoner "convicted of an offence against the law of the Province and sentenced . . . to an indeterminate sentence", while section 31 provides that the jurisdiction of the Board of Parole

provinces and territories where no provincial parole board has been established, the National Parole Board similarly has no direct involvement in unescorted temporary absence decisions, as provincial institutions have their own temporary absence programs.

As penal authorities have sought to develop alternatives to the warehousing of prisoners, extensive temporary absence programs have been developed in most provinces. While a detailed review of these programs is beyond the scope of this text,[24] a brief discussion of the Ontario legislation will illustrate the general principles guiding the operation of unescorted temporary absence programs.[25] Section 27 of the *Ministry of Correctional Services Act* provides that the Lieutenant Governor in Council may designate Ministry officials to authorize release on unescorted temporary absence.[26] Pursuant to section 37 of the *Parole Regulations*, each institutional superintendent is required to establish a Temporary Absence Committee to consider any request for unescorted release from a correctional institution involving a period of more than 15 days, or where the prisoner applies to become a resident in a halfway house (called "community resource centre" (C.R.C.)). All applications must be in writing and may be accompanied by other documentation. The Temporary Absence Pass (T.A.P.) committee must consider the application within 15 days of receipt. The prisoner is entitled, as a matter of right, to appear before the committee to make oral representations; the discretion to allow other persons to appear rests in the institutional superintendent. Within 7 days of the completion of its review (not 7 days from the date of the hearing), the committee is

---

"may apply to inmates convicted of offences under an Act of Canada, where that Act or the minister having the administration of that Act so allows." The reason for this minor distinction is probably now only of historic interest. See also *Prisons and Reformatories Act*, s. 13.

[24] In *R. v. Fulton, supra*, note 20, the trial judge had held that an additional reason for acquitting the prisoner was that Saskatchewan's release programs were not "rehabilitative", and thus did not fit within section 8(1) [now s. 7(1)] of the *Prisons and Reformatories Act*. Barclay J. held that release criteria of correctional officials were administrative matters and were therefore not reviewable by the court.

[25] This discussion is limited to consideration of programs for adult offenders. For an overview, see R.G. Fox, "Temporary Absence, Work-Release and Community Based Corrections in Ontario" 4 Aust. and N.Z.J. Crim. 46.

[26] It is noteworthy that a sentencing judge may only recommend or refuse to recommend that a prisoner be considered for temporary absence. It is entirely a matter within the discretion of penal officials whether such relief from imprisonment will be granted. Similarly, a judge cannot preclude a prisoner from applying for temporary absence. In *R. v. Laycock* (1989), 51 C.C.C. (3d) 65 the Ontario Court of Appeal struck down an endorsement on a warrant of committal which purported to deny a prisoner's ability to apply for temporary absence.

required to forward to the superintendent a summary of the prisoner's representations, including any written submissions or documentation, together with the committee's recommendation and its reasons. No time frame is specified for a decision by the superintendent once he has received the committee's report, but he is required to give written notice to the prisoner within 7 days of making that decision. Section 37(6) of the Regulations provides that the superintendent may authorize the release with or without conditions, deny the request, or defer a decision. A denial of an application for temporary absence may be further reviewed, upon receipt of a written application by the prisoner, by the Minister of Correctional Services. It appears that no review is contemplated where a decision has been deferred, which frequently occurs. The materials on review are comprised of the recommendation and reasons of the T.A.P. committee, the superintendent's decision and reasons, and any further written submissions by or on behalf of the prisoner. The Minister is required to make a decision "forthwith"; the Minister's decision is final.

Most C.R.C.s in Ontario are administered by private agencies such as the Salvation Army and John Howard societies. Contractual arrangements are entered into between the Ministry and these agencies. However, halfway houses are not designated as correctional institutions, nor are directors or staff members of such facilities considered to be peace officers under the *Code* or provincial legislation.

In Ontario, U.T.A. release is authorized in writing by the superintendent of the custodial institution from which the prisoner is released. The U.T.A. must be signed by the prisoner prior to release; it typically contains a limitation that he is to obey all rules of the halfway house, and that a breach of any condition of release may cause revocation of the release, institutional charges or further criminal proceedings.[27]

Since a release on temporary absence is considered to be a privilege, section 37(8) of the Regulations provides that where the superintendent of the releasing institution believes on reasonable and probable grounds that a prisoner has breached or attempted to breach a condition of temporary absence, the prisoner may be returned to close custody pending a determination of whether the temporary absence permit should be revoked. Section 30 of the Regulations specifies that within 7 days of the alleged breach, the superintendent is required to notify the prisoner of the substance of the allegation. The prisoner is entitled, upon giving notice within 1 day of learning of the allegations, to an informal in-person hearing ("an interview") with the superintendent, during the

---

[27] *Ministry of Correctional Services Regulations*, s. 35(1).

course of which the prisoner "is entitled to present arguments and explanations to dispute the allegation and to question the person or persons making the allegation as well as any other witnesses to the incident". The superintendent is given a discretion to permit the attendance and participation of any other person. The superintendent is required, within 2 days of the interview, to inform the prisoner of his decision and the reasons for that decision. A review by the Minister of Correctional Services may be requested if the prisoner alleges that the superintendent committed a procedural error or, in certain circumstances, where a forfeiture of previously earned remission or suspension of the right to earn remission is a penalty imposed in addition to revocation of the temporary absence permit.[28] While revocation of a temporary absence permit is, in itself, a serious penalty, it should be kept in mind that other punishments may also be imposed. Section 31 of the Regulations details the additional institutional penalties which may be visited upon a prisoner who has breached a term or condition of temporary absence permit.

Prior to the 1978 revision of the Ontario *Ministry of Correctional Services Act*, the extent of permissible penalties beyond revocation of a temporary absence permit and institutional disciplinary proceedings was canvassed in *Roy*.[29] In that case, the prisoner had been granted permission to be released to a C.R.C. pursuant to section 18(1) of the *Act*. Section 18(2) provided that a prisoner temporarily absent from close custody should comply with any terms and conditions of that pass, and that failure to comply would render the prisoner unlawfully at large and liable to prosecution under section 133(1)(*b*) [now s. 145] of the *Code*. On the last day of his pass the accused was found to be absent from the halfway house without permission (though he was actually arrested inside the C.R.C., a distinction of some importance in light of the judgment in *Seymour*, below), to have consumed alcohol and to have driven a motor vehicle without permission, all of which were breaches of his temporary absence permit. At trial, Clarke Prov. J. found the accused not guilty of the offence, primarily on the basis that to declare a prisoner unlawfully at large under the *Code* for having breached a condition of a provincial statute or regulation represented an attempt to trench upon the criminal law power of Parliament. On appeal by the Crown, the Ontario Court of Appeal took a broad view of the legislative purpose of temporary absence programs.[30] After referring to the enabling provision contained in section 8(1) [now s. 7(1)] of the *Prisons and*

---

28 *Ibid.*, s. 32.
29 *R. v. Roy* (1978), 41 C.C.C. (2d) 65 (Ont. Prov. Ct.).
30 *R. v. Roy* (1978), 45 C.C.C. (2d) 193 (Ont. C.A.).

Reformatories Act,[31] Thorson J.A. held that temporary absence programs were not "self-contained" provisions capable of implementation without "action being taken at the provincial level and by officials of the provincial institutions in question". Thus, section 18(2) did not create a criminal offence; the section did "no more than is necessary to give substance to the scheme of s. 18 taken as a whole." For Thorson J.A. a person who breached a condition of a temporary absence pass was "no longer to be considered as being lawfully at large".[32] The matter was therefore remitted back to the trial judge to determine whether a breach of the *Code* had occurred.

Following the 1977 amendments to the *Prisons and Reformatories Act*, a new version of the *Ministry of Correctional Services Act* was proclaimed in force.[33] Section 18 was repealed and replaced by section 27; the difference between the two sections was that section 27 of the new Act created a new offence and established a penalty provision.[34] In *Seymour*,[35] the prisoner had been released on U.T.A. to a C.R.C., and had breached the conditions of his temporary absence by consuming alcohol. He was charged with being unlawfully at large contrary to section 133(1)(*b*) [now s. 145(1)(*b*)] of the *Code*, despite the existence of the new penalty provision in section 27 of the *Ministry of Correctional Services Act*. Relying on his own judgment in *Copeland*,[36] a case dealing with breach of a condition of a day parole release, Martin J.A. held that only "a wilful breach of a condition which shows an intention by the inmate to withdraw himself from the control, in the sense of custody, of the correctional authorities, renders ... [the prisoner] ... 'at large' within the meaning of s. 133(1)(*b*) of the Code".[37] The appeal by the Crown was therefore dismissed, as no intention to leave the C.R.C. could be found on the facts.

Brief reference should also be made to section 29 of the *Ministry of Correctional Services Regulations* where consideration is being given by

---

[31] R.S.C. 1970, c. P-21, s. 36 [as amended by S.C. 1976-77, c. 53, s. 45].

[32] *Supra*, note 31, at 198.

[33] S.O. 1978, c. 37 [proclaimed in force June 10, 1978] [now R.S.O. 1980, c. 275].

[34] Section 27(2) and (3) provide:

> (2) Every inmate temporarily absent under subsection (1) shall comply with such terms and conditions as are specified and shall return to the correctional institution at the expiration of the period for which he is authorized to be at large.
>
> (3) Every inmate who contravenes subsection (2) without lawful excuse, the proof of which lies upon him, is guilty of an offence and on summary conviction is liable to imprisonment for a term of not more than one year.

[35] *R. v. Seymour* (1980), 52 C.C.C. (2d) 305 (Ont. C.A.).

[36] (1978), 45 C.C.C. (2d) 223 (Ont. C.A.).

[37] *Supra*, note 36, at 312.

penal authorities to the laying of charges either under section 27(3) of the Act or under section 145(1) of the *Code*. In such circumstances the superintendent is directed to consult with the Crown Attorney for the judicial district where the offence has allegedly occurred. The reason for this may be found in section 29(2), which provides that where a prosecution is commenced, all internal disciplinary proceedings are to be discontinued. However, in *Shubley*,[38] the Supreme Court of Canada held that while non-compliance by the Superintendent with section 29 may provide the prisoner with a basis for requesting the Minister to review the decision in accordance with the review procedures contained in section 32 of the Regulations, a breach could not operate to prevent a prosecution in criminal court.

(b) Intermittent Sentences

Provincial legislation does not preclude unescorted temporary absences being granted to prisoners serving intermittent sentences. Indeed, such passes are increasingly granted to permit prisoners to be in the community to perform voluntary activities. In addition, unescorted passes are frequently granted during religious holidays.

Section 21 of the Ontario *Ministry of Correctional Services Regulations* provides that all monies earned for work performed while serving sentence are to be forwarded to the superintendent, who is to hold all such monies in trust pending discharge of the prisoner. The superintendent is authorized to deduct a token sum "as partial reimbursement ... [to the Ministry] ... for the cost of food, lodging and clothing supplied ... by the institution". Pursuant to section 28(1)(*l*) of the Regulations, a failure to pay such a fee constitutes a misconduct for which the prisoner may be disciplined in various ways, including revocation of a temporary absence pass and loss of both remission already earned and the right to earn remission in the future.

A similar scheme appears to exist in most provinces. For example, section 17 of the British Columbia *Correction Act* provides that where a prisoner is released from close custody "to participate in gainful employment for wages", he may be required, either directly or through the employer, to forward all sums earned to the superintendent, who, after making provision for the prisoner's dependents, may deduct both the actual cost of travel expenses and meals and "the cost of his keep at the correctional centre". A failure to comply with such conditions may

---

38 *R. v. Shubley* (1990), 52 C.C.C. (3d) 481 (S.C.C.), affirming (1988), 39 C.C.C. (3d) 481 (Ont. C.A.).

result in internal punishments, including revocation of a temporary absence permit or a potential forfeiture of remission under section 18(3).

Ontario Regulation 515/78[39] went one step further. Purportedly acting under the general authority of section 27(*m*) of the *Ministry of Correctional Services Act*, whereby the Lieutenant Governor was empowered to "make regulations . . . providing for and prescribing fees and charges to recover costs incurred by the Ministry", the Regulation was enacted to provide for fees for room and board for certain persons serving sentences on an intermittent basis. In *Casserley*,[40] the prisoner neglected or refused to pay this fee, nor did he qualify for any of the exemptions provided in the Regulations. As a result, remission was forfeited, and his right to earn further remission was suspended. When he reached that point in his sentence which consisted of the remission which had been forfeited, the prisoner declined to surrender himself into custody, whereupon he was charged with being unlawfully at large. At trial, the accused raised the defence that the Regulation was both *ultra vires* the enabling legislation and the legislative competence of the Province. Belobradic Prov. J. held that the Regulation was not, in pith and substance, concerned with a prisoner's good conduct and discipline while incarcerated, but rather was intended to require a prisoner to pay monies out of earnings made outside the institution. To impose a forfeiture of previously earned remission would ". . . change somewhat the concept of remission. . . . The inmate is deprived of his remission not because of bad conduct while an inmate but because he does not pay moneys out of his earning or savings gained while not in confinement and while on probation. He is put in the position that he might keep his remission not because he earns it but because he pays for it." His Honour therefore held that since the Regulation was designed for "the raising of money . . . [and was not] . . . intended to make correctional facilities more effective", the Regulation was *ultra vires* the legislative competence of Ontario.[41]

Belobradic Prov. J. applied the same logic to hold that the impugned Regulation was also *ultra vires* section 27(*m*) of the *Ministry of Correctional Services Act*. He held that while the Regulation might be applicable to monies earned by a prisoner serving an intermittent sentence on days when that person was actually in custody, nevertheless "to the extent that the Regulation purports to exercise control over moneys he earns out of custody and while on probation," the Regulation was also *ultra vires* the enabling legislation.[42]

---

39 Proclaimed in force July 7, 1978.
40 *R. v. Casserley* (1982), 65 C.C.C. (2d) 439 (Ont. Prov. Ct.).
41 *Ibid.*, at 445 and 447.
42 *Ibid.*, at 448.

In light of the conclusion the trial judge had reached as to the *vires* of the Regulation, there was no need to comment on a further issue raised by counsel. However, he stated that he had "grave doubts about the concept of suspension of eligibility to earn remission"[43] as a penalty which could be imposed in addition to the forfeiture of remission previously earned. Belobradic Prov. J. pointed out that suspension of eligibility to earn remission did not appear to be a penalty authorized under sections 5-7 of the *Prisons and Reformatories Act*. Ontario appears to be the only province which purports to authorize such a penalty upon commission of various types of institutional misconducts.

An appeal by the Crown to the Ontario Court of Appeal in *Casserley* was dismissed.[44] Thorson J.A. delivered the judgment of a unanimous five-person panel, holding that the Regulation was in conflict with section 6 of the *Prisons and Reformatories Act*. Since the regulation was not directed to the prisoner's conduct while incarcerated, but rather "look[ed] to the time when he is out of that place", the use of the Regulation "in this way was to extend the time required to be served by the ... [prisoner] ... in custody beyond the time provided for by Parliament for the expiration of his sentence."[45] However, Thorson J.A. found nothing offensive in law with the concept that fees for room and board could be deducted from a prisoner's earnings from employment while in custody. Thus, it would seem that provincial enactments which impose fees to recover the actual or partial costs of incarceration through establishing a system of compulsory deductions from monies earned while released on temporary absence would be lawful.[46]

---

43 *Ibid.*, at 448.
44 *R. v. Casserley* (1982), 69 C.C.C. (2d) 126 (Ont. C.A.).
45 *Ibid.*, at 133, 134.
46 A frequently encountered issue is whether a prisoner can later claim time spent on T.A.P. as a period when he was unavailable for "insurable employment" within the meaning of section 18 of the *Unemployment Insurance Act, 1971* (S.C. 1970-71-72, c. 48). In *Garland v. Canada (Employment & Immigration Cmmn.)*, [1985] 2 F.C. 508 (C.A.), the prisoner had been released on T.A.P. on "the specific understanding and condition that he reside at his parents' farm ... and work on that farm for the period of this Temporary Absence" (at 511). His T.A.P. certificate reflected that he was not to leave "the immediate designated area". Some time after the completion of his sentence he applied for unemployment insurance benefits. In order to qualify, he was required to have completed a certain number of weeks of "insurable employment". However, section 18(2)(*b*) of the Act provided that if he was "confined in any gaol, penitentiary or other similar institution," his qualifying period could be extended. The Unemployment Insurance Commission rejected his claim for benefits, on the basis that he was not entitled for credit for the time he was physically present on his parents' farm (presumably doing unpaid work). The case eventually came to the Federal Court of Appeal, which, in a split decision, overruled the Commission's decision. Speaking for

(c) Federal Penitentiaries—Definite Sentences

Prior to March 1, 1978, authority to grant unescorted temporary absences from federal penitentiaries to prisoners serving definite sentences was vested in the Commissioner of Penitentiaries[47] and institutional directors.[48] Pursuant to the enactment of section 42 of the *Criminal Law Amendment Act*, sections 26.1 to 26.3 of the *Penitentiary Act* [now ss. 29-31] were proclaimed in force, by which all authority for granting unescorted temporary absences was assigned to the National Parole Board.[49] To complement this legislation, sections 6 and 9(1)(*b*) [now ss. 13 and 27(1)(*b*)] of the *Parole Act* were amended.[50] The combined effect of these provisions is that the Governor in Council is empowered to make regulations "prescribing the portion of the terms of imprisonment that inmates or classes of inmates must serve before temporary absence without escort may be authorized". Section 12 of the *Parole Regulations* contains the various eligibility dates upon and after which a prisoner may apply for unescorted temporary absence. The prisoner must be notified in writing of his eligibility date within 6 months of admission to penitentiary.[51] In the case of a prisoner serving a definite sentence admitted to penitentiary on or after March 1, 1978,[52] eligibility for unescorted temporary absence arises at "one-half the period of time required to be served by the inmate to reach his full parole eligibility date or six months, whichever is the greater".[53] The only exception to these requirements arises where unescorted temporary absence is required to administer emergency medical treatment.[54]

Section 25.2(1) of the *Parole Act*[55] authorizes the National Parole

---

the majority, Heald J. held that "Parliament intended that the class of individuals described in subsection 18(2)(*b*) must necessarily include those prisoners who, while not still remaining in physical confinement, are nevertheless still . . . not yet available for employment" (at 517). Thus, where a prisoner is released on T.A.P. (or parole) to work at non-remunerative employment, he can count such time as if he were still confined. See also *Canada (A.G.) v. Turner*, [1983] 1 F.C. 389 (C.A.).

47 Since re-named Commissioner of Corrections.
48 See *Penitentiary Act*, S.C. 1960-61, c. 53, s. 26.
49 S.C. 1976-77, c. 53, s. 42.
50 S.C. 1976-77, c. 53, s. 24 [proclaimed in force October 15, 1977].
51 *Parole Regulations*, s. 13(*f*).
52 For a discussion of life and indeterminate sentences, see below, heading (d).
53 *Parole Regulations*, s. 12(1)(*b*). A prisoner admitted to penitentiary prior to March 1, 1978 was eligible to apply for unescorted temporary absence at any time during the serving of sentence. However, the practice was not to grant release until 6 months had elapsed since the date of sentencing.
54 *Parole Regulations*, s. 12(2)(*b*).
55 By S.C. 1986, c. 43, s. 14, this power was moved from the *Penitentiary Act* to the *Parole Act*.

Board to grant U.T.A. for an unlimited period for medical reasons and for a period of up to 15 days for humanitarian or rehabilitative reasons. Section 25.2(2) authorizes the Board to delegate the power to grant unescorted temporary absence in the case of an individual prisoner or class of prisoners to the Commissioner of Corrections or to an institutional director. However, this section limits the authority of an institutional director to order release on U.T.A. for a period not in excess of 3 days, except for medical reasons. Thus, even where such delegation has taken place, practical considerations usually require that the Regional Office of the National Parole Board be consulted whenever a lengthier release is under consideration.

At the present time the National Parole Board has delegated authority to grant U.T.A. to institutional directors in cases involving prisoners serving sentences of less than 5 years.[56] Under current policy there are four exceptions to this general rule:

1. where a Crown appeal against sentence is pending;
2. where the prisoner has an outstanding charge for an indictable offence punishable by imprisonment for 2 years or greater;
3. where the National Parole Board has decided to retain its authority over a particular individual (which usually occurs in cases involving prisoners who have breached conditions of previous escorted or unescorted releases or who have been convicted of offences involving violence);
4. where a prisoner is confined in a provincial mental health institution or penitentiary psychiatric facility.

In addition, the National Parole Board[57] has delegated authority to grant U.T.A. to institutional directors in two other cases. The first of these is to permit an institutional director to extend U.T.A. for up to 48 hours due to extenuating circumstances. Again, attendance at funerals of family members or visits to family members who are seriously ill may be authorized by an institutional director without prior approval of the Board in the case of any prisoner serving a penitentiary sentence of less than 5 years; in the case of a non-lifer serving a sentence of 5 years or

---

56 This delegation is considered by the Board to be based on the prisoner's original sentence. According to this interpretation a prisoner whose original term was longer than 5 years and who has been returned to penitentiary with a remanet of less than 5 years must apply to the National Parole Board.

57 The enactment of section 23.2 of the *Penitentiary Act* in 1986 formalized a previous practice whereby the Board delegated the power to wardens to release one day early any prisoners whose release dates arose on a weekend or statutory holiday. This is designed to facilitate release formalities and to enable a prisoner to make reasonable travel arrangements.

more, such U.T.A.s may be authorized by the institutional director so long as the prisoner has successfully completed a previous unescorted temporary absence.[58]

Depending upon the purpose of a U.T.A. application, passes may be granted at various intervals and for prescribed periods. Current policy is that prisoners in minimum security institutions may be granted up to 72 hours unescorted absence per month, while prisoners in medium or maximum security may only apply for up to 48 hours per month. These policies are frequently modified; accurate information should be obtained from Regional Offices of the National Parole Board.

Except in cases of medical emergency, applications for U.T.A. must originate as a written request from the prisoner through institutional personnel. Requests for U.T.A. should be initiated as early as possible in the sentence, as experience demonstrates that at least 3 months may be necessary to allow the bureaucracy to compile documentation. In all non-emergency cases a community assessment must be completed before a decision to grant a first U.T.A. may be considered. Such assessments usually include a police report from the force in the area of destination, an institutional behaviour assessment, general information on the prisoner, a detailed description of the release plan, records of previous conditional releases, reports on immigration status, appellate proceedings and outstanding charges, on-going police investigations, psychological, psychiatric or medical reports, and the views of other persons in the community. After one U.T.A. has been successfully completed, no fresh community assessment is necessary, updating at regular intervals being sufficient. In the event a hearing is held by the Parole Board, an "assistant"[59] may, subject to obtaining a security clearance, attend to make submissions in the presence of the prisoner. Written documentation may also be filed. Where the decision-maker is the institutional director, a formal hearing is not usually held.

An institutional director is not required, except in the circumstances described above, to consult with the National Parole Board prior

---

[58] After one unescorted temporary absence has been successfully completed, the Board usually grants an institutional director written authority to grant subsequent U.T.A. passes for a period of up to 1 year, so long as these conform with general Board policy on frequency and duration. However, unless otherwise specified by the Board, no unescorted temporary absence may be granted within 30 days of a denial of an application for release on parole or U.T.A. As well, unescorted absence for rehabilitative purposes may not be granted to a prisoner on day parole; instead this extra form of leave should be incorporated into the day parole program. Details of these policies may be found in the Board's *Policy and Procedures Manual* (unpublished, but available upon request at the Board's regional offices).

[59] *Parole Regulations*, s. 20.1.

to rendering a decision to grant U.T.A. However, since eligibility for U.T.A. in most cases arises on the same date as eligibility for day parole,[60] considerable consultation usually occurs since unescorted temporary absence is so often linked to other forms of gradual release.

In cases where the National Parole Board retains authority to grant U.T.A., section 23 of the *Parole Regulations* details that the unanimous votes of two members must be cast before U.T.A. may be granted. Section 19 of the Regulations provides that reasons for a negative decision must be delivered in writing to the prisoner. A negative decision may be appealed to the Appeals Division of the National Parole Board.

Standard release conditions include initial reporting to the police force and parole officer in the area of destination, further interviews with local parole officials, remaining within the area of destination, and returning to close custody prior to the expiry of the period of the temporary absence pass. Where a U.T.A. release program has been approved in principle but no implementation date has been established, no release may be effected until the decision-maker has given final approval. In exceptional circumstances an institutional director (who actually issues the necessary documentation) may deny an unescorted absence or series of absences previously authorized by the National Parole Board.

Section 16(3) of the *Parole Act*[61] provides that a member of the National Parole Board or a person designated by the Chairman may terminate an unescorted temporary absence. Pursuant to this authority, by a Memorandum of Agreement between the National Parole Board and the Correctional Service of Canada, the Chairman has delegated authority to terminate unescorted temporary absences to institutional directors and local parole supervisors. Where a breach or apprehended breach of a condition of unescorted temporary absence arises, the issuance of a warrant terminating the temporary absence pass is a necessary precondition to the apprehension of the prisoner. However, if the prisoner is not apprehended during the period authorized for temporary absence, or if the prisoner simply fails to return at the conclusion of the period, the warrant is usually withdrawn. Then, an information that the prisoner is unlawfully at large is laid with the police force closest to the penitentiary and a warrant is issued for the arrest of the prisoner.

Although the bases for termination of an unescorted temporary absence permit are not specified in either sections 13 or 16(3) of the

---

60 *Parole Regulations*, s. 9(*d*). The exceptions are cases involving sentences of less than 2 years or more than 12 years.
61 1986, c. 43, s. 6(4).

Parole Act, the Board takes the position that the same criteria are to be applied in the decision to terminate an unescorted absence as when a parole is suspended under section 16 of the Act. Section 22 provides that a warrant suspending parole may be issued "when a breach of a term or condition . . . occurs or . . . it is necessary or desirable to do so in order to prevent a breach of any term or condition . . . or to protect society".[62] Although there is no case law on point at the federal level, it would appear that the comments of Martin J.A. in *Seymour*,[63] regarding breaches of provincial temporary absence permits would apply equally to a failure to return at the conclusion of an unescorted temporary absence pass or to a breach of other conditions of such passes. However, it should be noted that it is open also to penitentiary authorities to commence internal disciplinary proceedings against a prisoner for breach of a temporary absence permit.[64]

Section 31 of the *Penitentiary Act*[65] states that where a prisoner is given an unescorted absence and a release date (usually a mandatory supervision release date) occurs during that absence, the prisoner is "for the purpose of all entitlements accruing to him on release, be deemed to have been released on the day on which the temporary absence commenced."

In *Re Starr*,[66] the prisoner was granted an unescorted absence 2 days prior to his mandatory supervision release date, which fell on a Sunday. On the Saturday he was arrested and charged with various offences to which he pleaded guilty and was sentenced. The National Parole Board purported to revoke his mandatory supervision. On an application for *certiorari*, Nitikman J. concluded that, since at the time of the commission of the offences the prisoner was not on mandatory supervision, the Board had no power to revoke mandatory supervision. Although section 26.3 of the *Penitentiary Act* is not directly referred to in the judgment, that section affirms that release on mandatory supervision arises as a matter of right upon the mandatory supervision release date. The case stands for the proposition that although the National Parole Board may, under section 16(1)(*b*) of the Act, attach terms and conditions to a

---

62 A more detailed discussion of termination decisions may be found under the discussion of "Suspension and Revocation", above, Chapter 8.

63 (1980), 52 C.C.C. (2d) 305 (Ont. C.A.).

64 For further information on the consequences of a breach of temporary absence see D.P. Cole and J. Willmot, "Some Aspects of the Law Relating to Escapes: Part I — The Calculation of Sentence Following an Escape" (1980), 16 C.R. (3d) 246, and "Part II — Prosecuting and Defending an Escape-Related Offence" (1980), 17 C.R. (3d) 97. On the double-jeopardy aspect see *R. v. Mingo* (1983), 2 C.C.C. (3d) 23 (B.C.S.C.).

65 Formerly section 26.3 [as amended by 1976-77, c. 53, s. 42].

66 [1983] 1 F.C. 363 (T.D.).

release on mandatory supervision, the entitlement to release and the consequent vesting of remission credits on that date, subject to revocation, is absolute.

(d) Lifers and Indeterminate Sentences

U.T.A. eligibility for persons serving life sentences is specified according to the nature of the sentence and the date upon which it was imposed. This arises due to various amendments to the *Criminal Code* during the past two decades. Where a life maximum sentence is imposed eligibility depends on date of sentence. If the prisoner entered the penitentiary prior to March 1, 1978, eligibility arises 6 months later. If the prisoner entered penitentiary after that date, a prisoner serving a life maximum sentence becomes eligible 3 years prior to full parole eligibility date.

Where a life minimum sentence has been imposed, section 747(2) of the *Code* indicates that the prisoner is ineligible for consideration for unescorted temporary absence until he has served "all but three years of his number of years of imprisonment without eligibility for parole". Conversely, since the case of a dangerous offender must be initially considered by the Board 3 years from the date the prisoner was taken into custody (and every 2 years thereafter), a prisoner serving an indeterminate sentence imposed after July 26, 1976 is assured of consideration for unescorted temporary absence at regular intervals under section 695.1 of the *Code*. Cases of prisoners serving indeterminate terms imposed before that date are considered annually. Any type of unescorted temporary absence application for a prisoner sentenced to life as a minimum or serving an indeterminate sentence must be approved by the Board. Section 23 of the *Parole Regulations* provides that four members of the Board must vote on such applications; a majority of votes is necessary to decide the issue. However, it should also be noted that the Chairman of the Board is authorized to direct that more than four Board members shall vote in a particular case.

10

Sentence Calculation and Conditional Release

> While the provisions of the Act appear to be clear as to the circumstances in which they apply, the computations of the terms and duration of imprisonment which they generate are of mind-reeling complexity.[1]

1. INTRODUCTION

The task of calculating a sentence might appear to the uninitiated to be an exercise of mechanical simplicity. Surely, a sentence cast in months and years requires only a calendar and pencil to determine the applicable parole eligibility, presumptive release and warrant expiry dates. Unfortunately, this apparently simple job has, over the past two decades, become highly complex, confused and confusing. The first reason for this lies in the interaction of the principal statutes—the *Parole Act, Penitentiary Act, Prisons and Reformatories Act* and *Criminal Code*[2]—and the desultory fashion by which they have been amended from time to time. Amendments have frequently been effected to achieve particular and isolated objectives. In many instances, however, Parliament has acted with little sense of the impact which would be generated for other elements of the sentencing system.[3] It was not until

---

[1]   *Maxie v. National Parole Bd.* (1985), 47 C.R. (3d) 22 (Fed. T.D.), at 30, per Muldoon J.
[2]   R.S.C. 1985, c. P-2; R.S.C. 1985, c. P-5; R.S.C. 1985, c. P-20; R.S.C. 1985, c. C-46.
[3]   A number of illustrations can be offered. Probably the best example was the amendment of the *Criminal Code*, R.S.C. 1970, c. C-34, by S.C. 1972, c. 13, s. 9 to require the forfeiture of all statutory remission after conviction for escape, while section 22(4) of the *Penitentiary Act*, R.S.C. 1970, c. P-6 required the forfeiture of three-quarters of the prisoner's statutory remission. Ultimately, Reid J. in *Re Clarke and R.* (Ont. H.C., February 7, 1978) held that the latter provision had been repealed by implication. See also the issue raised in *Re Shiminousky and R.* (1981), 64 C.C.C. (2d) 187 (B.C. S.C.) involving the interaction between section 695(5) [now s. 731(5)] of the *Code* and changes in the internal remission regime in determining whether a prisoner serving more than one sentence ought to be confined in a penitentiary because "the aggregate of the unexpired portions of those terms at that time amounts to two years or more. . . ." Esson J., as he then was, held that earned remission already credited should be deducted to determine the unexpired aggregate.

the 1986 amendments that an effort was made to rationalize interacting provisions.

A second reason that sentence calculation has become so complicated has been that all too often sentencing judges are not properly trained or assisted in respect of the technical implications of specific sentencing options. This is compounded by the fact that other judges and sentence administrators may later be called upon to interpret the statutory framework against a backdrop of inconsistent case law. One judge vented his frustration as follows:

> ... it is wholly unacceptable that legislation dealing with such a vital matter as the liberty of the subject should be the platform for litigation in which utterly divergent judicial opinions may be reasonably expressed ... the net effect of such ill-expressed legislation, is a residue of uncertainty, ill will and a sense of dubious justice which must rankle in those least able to cope with such a situation.[4]

Another source of confusion is the bald reality that prisoners can (and all too frequently do) accumulate convictions and their consequences in bizarre circumstances and bewildering combinations which affect the length of terms of imprisonment and the applicable eligibility dates. As a result, penal administrators have adopted a methodology which is cumbersome and complex. This often leads to errors or diverse interpretations. A comprehensive effort has been made in recent years to rectify this situation.[5] However, it is not uncommon to find sentence administrators placing several alternative computations, each with different dates, before a reviewing court.[6]

It is not our goal to provide a complete guide to sentence calculation which will answer all conceivable situations; rather, this chapter attempts to provide a methodology for sentence calculation. It outlines the guiding principles which should assist anyone faced with a calculation problem. We will start with the calculation of a simple sentence and then move to the primary sources of confusion:

• additional sentences and the impact of merger;

• suspension and revocation of conditional release;

• escapes and being unlawfully at large.

---

4   *Re Dean and R.* (1977), 35 C.C.C. (2d) 217 (Ont. H.C.) at 218, per Keith J.
5   For example, in addition to the legislative changes contained in the 1986 amendments to the *Parole Act* and *Penitentiary Act*, Policy and Procedures manuals for federal sentence administrators have recently been developed.
6   A graphic example of this was demonstrated in the case of *Maxie v. National Parole Bd. supra*, note 1, at 45.

2. RELEVANT DATES

The maximum time a prisoner can be compelled to serve in custody is that provided in the sentence pronounced by the trial judge[7] in open court.[8] This is usually translated into a warrant of committal, calendar or certificate of sentence issued by the court in which the prisoner was convicted. These documents provide both the authority to hold the prisoner[9] and the basis from which to calculate the sentence. For sentence calculators there are usually three important dates to determine: parole eligibility date (P.E.D.),[10] presumptive release date (P.R.D.) and warrant expiry date (W.E.D.).

Establishing the P.E.D. is quite simple. The calculator must first ascertain the effective date of the commencement of the earliest of any term imposed (excluding time spent at liberty on appeal bail), and the last day of all terms imposed. The next step is to count the number of days between and including these two dates (excluding any time spent unlawfully at large). Finally, the necessary computation (usually one-third) is done according to the rules specified in the governing legislation.

In the federal system the presumptive release date (P.R.D.) indicates the date upon which a prisoner is eligible to be released subject to mandatory supervision if not previously granted some other form of

---

[7] See the discussion, *infra*, note 28.

[8] This applies even with respect to imprisonment in default of payment of a fine imposed following a criminal conviction (*Code*, s. 718(3). See *R. v. Deeb*; *R. v. Wilson* (1987), 28 C.C.C. (3d) 257 (Ont. Prov. Ct.)). In cases of fine defaults under provincial legislation, any time to be served is usually specified in provincial offences legislation. See *R. v. Hebb* (1989), 47 C.C.C. (3d) 193 (N.S. T.D.).

[9] While local jail authorities require some documentation before they will accept a sentenced prisoner, it frequently transpires that the actual committal warrant will not be delivered to the holding facility until a later date. Practices vary in different jurisdictions. Due to the wording of section 21(3) of the *Penitentiary Act*, a prisoner will not be admitted to penitentiary unless he is accompanied by a committal warrant.

[10] For simplicity's sake, we will deal in this chapter only with the full parole eligibility date (P.E.D.). In Chapter 6, we discussed the various statutes and regulations which stipulate the periods which must be served before a prisoner is eligible for lesser forms of conditional release: full parole, day parole and unescorted temporary absence (U.T.A.). Once a calculation produces an accurate full parole eligibility date, day parole and U.T.A. eligibility dates can be easily determined. It should also be noted that since, by section 13 of the *Parole Regulations* (SOR/78-428), the Board is required to notify federal prisoners of their various eligibility dates, those dates are, in fact, set by the Board rather than by sentence administrators employed by the Correctional Service of Canada (C.S.C.). While in practice the Board usually relies upon data provided to it by C.S.C., differences in interpretation occasionally arise. See, for example, *Re Renard and R.* (1980), 57 C.C.C. (2d) 564 (Que. C.A.).

conditional release by the Board. This form of release is a function of the amount of remission which a prisoner has accumulated. To establish a potential P.R.D. at the beginning of the sentence, it should be assumed that the prisoner will earn the maximum amount of remission available (approximately one-third); that number of days should then be deducted from the last day of the last sentence (W.E.D.). Until the 1986 amendments, the presumptive release date (P.R.D.) was called the mandatory supervision release date (M.S.D.). This phrase, which still appears in contemporary judicial pronouncements, C.S.C. and National Parole Board (N.P.B.) parlance and prison jargon,[11] is somewhat misleading in that it is predicated on the assumption that a prisoner will earn all available remission. However, since, as we have seen in previous chapters, a prisoner may (a) fail to earn remission while serving sentence, (b) lose remission as punishment for a disciplinary offence, (c) lose remission as result of a Board decision to revoke parole or mandatory supervision, or (d) be ordered detained by the board at the conclusion of a 'gating' hearing, at any time during the custodial portion of the sentence, the M.S.D. remains a notional date until it actually arises. The new term introduced in the 1986 legislation—P.R.D.—more accurately reflects the potential date for release subject to mandatory supervision.[12]

While actual release on parole and P.R.D. are affected by the prisoner's behaviour, W.E.D. is fixed from the date the sentence is imposed. Since the introduction of credit for "street time" as part of the 1977 amendments, all that can change as a result of the prisoner's behaviour is the amount of time which the prisoner must serve in custody (assuming that he is not sentenced to any additional terms during the service of the original sentence). In provincial systems, the concept of W.E.D. is only relevant where the prisoner is granted parole, since (as has been shown in Chapters 6 and 7) there is no mandatory supervision in these systems of imprisonment. Where parole is not granted, W.E.D. arises when the prisoner's earned remission and days served equal the length of sentence.

3. CHANGING REMISSION REGIMES

The change in remission regimes has been the source of some difficulty in the past. Before July 1, 1978, a prisoner was automatically

---

[11] Another term which, strictly speaking, is incorrectly used is that a prisoner is released "on" mandatory supervision. In fact, a federal prisoner is released "subject to" mandatory supervision. We have used the terms interchangeably.

[12] In provincial systems, where the regime of mandatory supervision does not exist, P.R.D. is usually referred to as the Satisfaction of Sentence (S.O.S.) date.

granted statutory remission (S.R.) equal to one-quarter of the sentence imposed, immediately upon being sentenced. In addition, 3 additional days of remission per month could be earned depending on performance and conduct.[13] Unlike the current form of earned remission which is subject to forfeiture, old earned remission (O.E.R.) earned before July 1, 1978 could not be lost as a penalty for a disciplinary offence. Moreover, upon revocation of parole or mandatory supervision it was automatically re-credited.[14] Hence, all O.E.R. was, and continues to be,[15] a non-forfeitable credit. As a transitional provision, section 24.2 of the *Penitentiary Act* provided that all prisoners already in the system[16] on July 1, 1978 could earn remission at the rate of 15 days per month like all other prisoners, but only to the point where the aggregate of new earned remission, old earned remission and previously granted statutory remission equalled one-third of the "sentence" being served.[17] Needless to say, section 24.2 generated a number of interpretive issues: how did one determine the "sentence he is then serving" in order to perform the one-third calculation?[18] Did the provisions apply to a prisoner sentenced before July 1, 1978, who was released and subsequently revoked after that date?[19] Most of these transitional issues have long since been resolved. In fact, there are now very few prisoners in the system who are affected by them. Hence, our attention will be directed to the usual case—a prisoner sentenced after July 1, 1978. Nevertheless, careful

---

[13] See *Penitentiary Act*, R.S.C. 1970, c. P-6, s. 24(2) [repealed by S.C. 1976-77, c. 53, s. 41].

[14] This resulted from the combined effect of section 24.1(1) [now s. 26] of the *Penitentiary Act* and section 20(2)(*d*) [now s. 25(2)(*d*)] of the *Parole Act* which provided, upon revocation of parole or mandatory supervision, an automatic re-credit for "any earned remission that stood to his credit upon the coming into force of this subsection", enacted by S.C. 1976-77, c. 53, s. 31. Interestingly, this subsection came into force on October 15, 1977. Therefore, while the issue is now academic, inconsistent timing created two clases of O.E.R., since remission earned after October 15, 1977 but before July 1, 1978 was subject to forfeiture upon revocation, but not by reason of a disciplinary conviction. This is another example of unnecessary complexity injected into the realm of sentence computation.

[15] See *Parole Act*, R.S.C. 1985, c. P-2, s. 25(2)(*d*).

[16] Being in the "system" should refer to all prisoners sentenced to penitentiary or revoked in respect of a parole or mandatory supervision release from penitentiary before July 1, 1978, regardless of the date upon which the prisoner is actually received into penitentiary: see the discussion *supra* at note 14. This view is consistent with the remarks of Cory J. in *Re Van Bree and R.* (1980), 59 C.C.C. (2d) 163 (Ont. H.C.).

[17] Enacted by S.C. 1976-77, c. 53, s. 41, [subsequently repealed by R.S.C. 1985, c. 24 (2nd Supp.), s. 48].

[18] See *Pask and R.* (File no. 7-29900-83, Fed. T.D., Muldoon J., May 23, 1984).

[19] In *Re Lloyd and R.* (Ont. H.C., Linden J., September 15, 1978), it was held that the transitional provision did not apply to limit the earning of future remission in these circumstances.

attention must be paid whenever considering a calculation of a definite sentence commenced prior to the watershed date.

The *Criminal Law Amendment Act, 1977* established the current regime in which any remission credited must be earned (E.R.).[20] It applies to all prisoners sentenced after July 1, 1978. A prisoner can earn up to 15 days remission for each month served[21] which can equal roughly one-third of the sentence imposed. It may seem confusing that the earning of 15 days E.R. during a 30-day month can produce accumulated remission which equates to one-third. The answer may be more easily appreciated when one recognizes that serving 30 days plus earning 15 days E.R. produces a total credit of 45 days.[22]

Another matter of interest to calculators is what happens if a calculation produces a P.E.D. or P.R.D. which arises on a weekend or statutory holiday. In the case of a P.E.D., since the prisoner must

---

[20]   *Penitentiary Act*, R.S.C. 1985, c. P-5, s. 25.

[21]   This statement is accurate as far as the nature of remission credited after July 1, 1978 is concerned. However, there may be some controversy over whether the date of sentencing is the applicable threshold. While the relevant 1977 amendments were proclaimed in force on July 1, 1978 repealing the statutory remission regime, no transitional provisions other than section 24.2 of the *Penitentiary Act* were included to integrate prisoners with statutory remission into the new regime. That provision speaks of an "inmate who has been credited with statutory remission . . .". Previously, section 22(1) of the *Penitentiary Act* provided that statutory remission was credited "upon being received into a penitentiary". Hence, it could be argued that the new regime in its entirety—that is, without resort to the limits provided by section 24.2 and without a credit of statutory remission—applies to all prisoners received in a penitentiary after July 1, 1978. The case of *Re Cunningham and R.* involved a prisoner whose mandatory supervision was revoked prior to July 1, 1978 but was not received into the penitentiary until after that date. The applicant sought *habeas corpus* on the ground that he was entitled to statutory remission on his remanet, the credit of which would result in his release. An order for discharge was issued on consent by Cromarty J. (Ont. H.C.) on August 25, 1978. The Crown did not accept the merits of the applicant's case but, rather, based its consent on equitable grounds due to the inordinate delay experienced in transferring the applicant to the penitentiary. A subsequent case, *Hetherington*, was resolved without litigation and resulted in the decision by the legal advisors to the Solicitor General to credit statutory remission to all prisoners revoked or sentenced prior to July 1, 1978. The underlying rationale was that the qualification dealing with reception in the pre-existing section 22(1) of the *Penitentiary Act* related to the mechanics of crediting but the actual entitlement which existed until repeal arose upon being "sentenced or committed to penitentiary."

[22]   The practice of provincial sentence administrators is to credit all months as if they contained 30 days. Federal sentence administrators compute the credit for each month on a mathematical basis, dependent upon the actual number of days in each month. The amount of E.R. earned during a partial month can be calculated as follows:

$$\frac{\text{x days served}}{[\text{total days in month}]} \times 15 = \text{E.R.}$$

actually serve the requisite number of days, the release will be delaycd until the next working day. Since a release on mandatory supervision is not discretionary (at least where "gating" is not at issue), release cannot be delayed. Prior to the 1986 amendments, it was the practice of the federal authorities to grant an unescorted temporary absence effective the last working day prior to the M.S.D., in order to avoid the necessity of having institutional personnel work overtime to effect the release. In *Starr v. National Parole Board*[23] a prisoner released in this way re-offended during the weekend prior to the actual commencement of his period of mandatory supervision. The Board purported to revoke his right to be at liberty subject to mandatory supervision. Nitikman J. held that the Board had acted without jurisdiction, and quashed the revocation decision. Following this decision, section 20.2(1) [now s. 23.2(1)] of the *Penitentiary Act* was enacted as part of the 1986 amendments.[24] That section provides:

> An inmate, other than a paroled inmate as defined in the *Parole Act*, who is entitled to be released shall be released during the daylight hours of the last working day prior to the ordinary release date of the inmate.

4. THE SIMPLE CALCULATION

The most significant part of any calculation is the collection of all relevant documents and the preparation of an accurate chronology which lists all sentences and other relevant events—conditional releases, suspensions or revocations of conditional release and escapes. To start the process of understanding sentence calculations, we will begin with the simplest example—a single sentence with no intervening or exceptional events. While this example is a matter of simple arithmetic, as we proceed through more complicated examples arising from complex chronologies it can be seen that the methodology employed is an extension of the simple calculation.

Let us assume a prisoner subject to no other sentences is sentenced to 3 years' imprisonment on January 1, 1982. The sentence should first be translated into days in order to integrate leap years[25] and the differences between lengths of various months.[26] This sentence will expire

---

23 [1983] 1 F.C. 363 (T.D.).

24 S.C. 1986, c. 43, s. 21.

25 While these matters are marginal in their impact, much of the mechanics of sentence calculation is devoted to reaching exact dates, taking leap years and short and part months into account.

26 Sentence administrators will forward copies of the actual calculation sheets upon receipt of a direction from the prisoner.

at midnight on December 31, 1984 (1,096 days). The prisoner will be eligible for release on full parole (P.E.D.) on January 1, 1983, after having actually served one-third of the sentence (365 days). The presumptive release date (P.R.D.), assuming that all available remission will be earned, arises at the point when the aggregate of days served and remission earned equals the total sentence. In 1982, the prisoner can earn 180 days E.R. (12 × 15 days per month). The same applies to 1983. Thus, by the end of 1983, the prisoner will have served 730 days and could have earned 360 days remission. The earliest P.R.D. would be January 5, 1984. The calculation would look like this:

January 1, 1982	Sentence of 3 years:	1,096 days
	Less days served to December 31, 1983	−730
	Less E.R. to December 31, 1983	−360
		6 days
	Less days served to January 4, 1984	− 4
	Less E.R. to January 4, 1984	− 2
		0

P.E.D. = January 1, 1983
P.R.D. (M.S.D.) = January 5, 1984
W.E.D. = December 31, 1984

Graphically, the sentence calculation appears as follows:

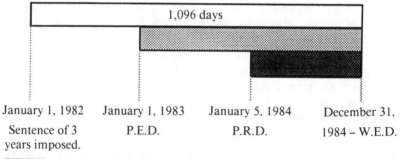

| January 1, 1982 | January 1, 1983 | January 5, 1984 | December 31, |
| Sentence of 3 years imposed. | P.E.D. | P.R.D. | 1984 – W.E.D. |

 Total number of days to be served in custody and on conditional release (1,096 days).

Days to be served on parole assuming that it is granted at P.E.D.

Days to be served on mandatory supervision if the prisoner has not been granted conditional release by the Parole Board. This period reflects the earliest potential mandatory supervision release date. This date would be extended if less than maximum remission is credited.

5. ADDITIONAL SENTENCES

With the exception of conditional release issues, the most common complication to the process of sentence calculation is the addition of new sentences. Often, a prisoner will be accompanied to jail by numerous documents reflecting sentences imposed by different judges, in different jurisdictions on different days. Some sentences may be qualified with the words "concurrent" or "consecutive"; however, it may be unclear to which antecedent sentence or sentences the judge was referring. It is essential that one works from the original documents in order to unearth ambiguities and errors. Although sometimes tedious, a chronological list of all sentences and other relevant events is the necessary starting point. This should reveal which sentences are effectively inconsequential because they are to be served concurrently to an equal or longer sentence. It may also reveal the intentions of sentencing judge. Occasionally, it will even be significant to determine the sequence in which sentences were imposed by a single judge.[27] If the committal documents are unclear, the calculator my be forced to resort to the judge's endorsement on the information or indictment or to obtain a transcript of the sentencing hearing. While obtaining a transcript will accurately establish the real sentence, this will not necessarily resolve the prisoner's problem, since penal authorities consider themselves bound by the wording of the warrant of committal, no matter how inequitable or unintended the result may be. Steps must be taken to obtain a new (or amended) warrant, but this is not always an easy task, nor one that produces a beneficial result.

Cases of discrepancy between the warrant and the pronounced sentence fall into two categories:

1. the sentence was intentionally varied after pronouncement;
2. the warrant, by error or slip, does not accurately reflect the sentence pronounced.

The first category raises the difficult question, often put in terms of *functus officio*, of the power to amend or vary. The second requires rectification, and the question is whether the warrant can be amended administratively, or whether formal judicial intervention, often by way of appeal, is necessary.

For historical reasons, Canadian and British courts have responded differently to the *functus officio* argument. However, both lines of authority reflect a concern both to ensure finality and to maintain a

---

[27] See the analysis of Arnup J.A. in *Re Lauzon and R.* (1981), 58 C.C.C. (2d) 20 (Ont. C.A.), at 27-30.

sentencing process which appears fair and unaffected by extraneous influences. In England, at common law, assize judges adopted the practice of reviewing sentences at the end of their calendar and considered themselves empowered to vary a sentence to correct "slips of the tongue or memory", or if, on reflection, the sentence appeared too severe.[28] It was preferred that any alteration should be expressed in open court.[29] This common law power to vary or rescind was extended to the Crown courts by statute in 1971.[30] Now, the power must be exercised within 28 days,[31] but English courts have consistently held that it ought not to be exercised simply because the original sentence is thought to be inadequate,[32] or because of the prisoner's subsequent conduct.[33]

In Canada, the situation is much less clear. Assuming that the English common law power is available, it would apply only to superior court judges. Moreover, the extent and regularity of criminal court sittings, coupled with the practice of recording proceedings, renders anachronistic any notion of reviewing sentences at the end of the assize

---

[28] See *R. v. Nodjoumi* (1985), 7 Cr.App.R.(S) 183, at 187, per Lawton J.A.
[29] Per Birkett J. in *R. v. Gomer* (1949), 33 Cr.App.R. 91 (C.A.). This caveat was recently repeated in *R. v. Dowling* (1989), 88 Cr.App.R. 88 (C.A.), where a judge, after sentence was imposed, changed it so that it would be served concurrently rather than consecutively to another sentence then being served. Thus, the warrant did not conform with the sentence actually pronouced. Taylor L.J. held:
  . . . if a judge is minded to vary a sentence he has passed or even to clarify a doubt or ambiguity as to the effect of it, he should do so in open court. Only if the matter is finally resoved in open court will all concerned and the public hear the final decision from the judge himself and in his own terms. (At 91).
[30] *Courts Act (U.K.), 1971*, c. 23, s. 11(2), discussed in *R. v. Sodhi* (1978), 66 Cr.App.R. 260.
[31] *Supreme Court Act (U.K.), 1981*, c. 54, s. 47(2).
[32] In *Nodjoumi, supra*, note 28, the prisoner received four concurrent 10-year sentences resulting from an attempt to defraud the Iranian government of 52 million pounds and the kidnapping of three men to avoid discovery of the fraud. Two weeks after the sentences were imposed, the trial judge re-convened the court, heard submissions from counsel, and varied the sentences by making the sentences for false imprisonment consecutive to that for conspiracy to defraud, thereby producing a total sentence of 20 years. The Court of Appeal restored the original sentences, expressing the concern that the appearance of justice required that there be no suspicion that the judge had been influenced extra-judicially. In rejecting the power to vary based on a perception of inadequacy, the court commented that at common law there appeared to be only one example of a variation to increase a sentence, and that occurred in the context of a variation to give effect to the originally expressed sentencing intention: see *R. v. Newsome* (1970), 54 Cr.App.R. 485.
[33] In *R. v. Powell* (1985), 7 Cr.App.R.(S) 247, after being sentenced to 3 months' imprisonment for possession of an offensive weapon, the prisoner began to swear and shout. The sentencing judge withdrew the previous sentence and imposed a new sentence of 6 months. The Court of Appeal considered this variation "plainly wrong".

calendar. In *Smith*,[34] it was held that a magistrate could amend a warrant to correct an error in the formal sentencing while the documents were still in his control, but not after they had been filed in the records of the sessions. *Lee Park*[35] involved a prosecution under the *Opium and Narcotic Drug Act*,[36] which provided for compulsory deportation after sentencing, unless otherwise ordered by the trial judge. Some days after the sentencing, the trial judge purported to order that the prisoner not be deported. The British Columbia Court of Appeal held that the magistrate was *functus* and the order invalid. Subsequent cases have blurred the issue, particularly since they tend to come forward by way of applications for extraordinary relief rather than appeal.[37] An appellate court has the power to vary a sentence, whereas a reviewing judge hearing an application for *certiorari* or *habeas corpus* can only grant or deny relief. The confusion appears to have been caused by the distinction between judicial acts, which relate to the substance of the sentence, and administrative acts, which only record and implement the sentence.

In *Stokes*,[38] McRuer C.J.H.C. remarked on the distinction between trial by magistrate and trial by judge and jury, pointing out that, at that time, only the magistrate was required to sign a formal conviction.[39] Now section 570(5) of the *Code* directs any judge who conducted a trial without a jury to "issue or cause to be issued" a warrant of committal. According to McRuer C.J.H.C., a judge sitting alone without a jury was *functus officio* after imposing sentence and signing the formal committal warrant, whereas after a judge who has presided over a trial with a jury

---

[34] *R. v. Smith* (1911), 19 C.C.C. 253 (N.S. S.C.).
[35] *R. v. Lee Park* (1924), 43 C.C.C. 66 (B.C. C.A.).
[36] S.C. 1911, c. 17.
[37] Clayton Ruby makes this observation in *Sentencing*, (Toronto: Butterworth & Co., 1987) 3d ed. pp. 84-85. In *Re Skied and R.* (1975), 24 C.C.C. (2d) 93 (B.C. S.C.), *habeas corpus* was granted in respect of a prisoner who had been sentenced to 6 months definite and 12 months indeterminate, whose sentence was purportedly amended 5 days later to 12 months' imprisonment, once the sentencing judge learned that the prisoner was above the age for indeterminate sentencing. Munroe J. concluded that the trial judge was *functus* after imposing the first sentence, and that, having served 6 months, the prisoner was entitled to be discharged. In *Re Gallicano*, [1978] 3 W.W.R. 452, the British Columbia Court of Appeal upheld the denial of *certiorari* to a prisoner who had originally been fined $100. After the Crown brought the accused's criminal record to the trial judge's attention, the fine was withdrawn and replaced by a sentence of 30 days' imprisonment. Bull J.A. commented that the trial judge had simply "jumped the gun", and ruled that *certiorari* should not be granted when an appeal was available, even if the sentence was a nullity. While he distinguished *Skied*, where the trial judge was truly *functus*, he also remarked that Munroe J. was wrong in granting relief in the case.
[38] *Ex parte Stokes* (1951), 100 C.C.C. 238 (Ont. H.C.).
[39] *Ibid.*, at 240. See also *R. v. Lalich* [summarized 9 W.C.B. (2d) 93].

pronounces sentence in open court, no administrative process is required to give lawful effect to the sentence. Combined with other judgments which have held that the preparation of a warrant is a purely administrative act,[40] one can conclude that there is no scope for amending the substance of a sentence after it has been pronounced in open court. In substantive terms, a judge is *functus officio* after pronouncing sentence.[41] Relying on a recent and related Supreme Court of Canada judgment,[42] one court concluded:

> In the case before me, after the trial judge imposed the sentences in the first instance, the appellant and her counsel left the courtroom. I conclude that at this point in time the trial judge became *functus officio.* It was at this time that he had "finally disposed of the case". There must be a finality to every trial. If I were to hold that the "re-sentencing" which occurred over one hour after the initial sentencing was valid, it might be argued that the trial judge could have "re-sentenced" the appellant two or three days after the initial sentencing. There is no logic in that.[43]

Situations do arise, however, where the sentence expressed in open court cannot be implemented in the way it was formulated, yet the power to amend is very limited. Supervening statutory requirements have been held to justify alterations. Thus, in *Horsefall,*[44] the Saskatchewan Court of Appeal upheld the legitimacy of an amended warrant which changed a concurrent sentence to a consecutive one in circumstances where the *Code* required it to be served consecutively. A problematic example is the case of sentencing for multiple offences where, by a slip of the tongue or inadvertence, the accurate addition of the terms imposed does not tally with the total term contemplated by the trial judge. Given the universal acceptance of the totality principle for multiple sentencing in Canadian law,[45] it would seem that, if a total term is

---

[40] See, for example, *R. v. Bellefontaine* (1974), 27 C.C.C. (2d) 200 (N.S. Co. Ct.), at 212; *R. v. Fuller* (1968), 5 C.R.N.S. 148 (Man. C.A.); *Re Lynch* (1906), 12 C.C.C. 141 (P.E.I. S.C.).

[41] See *R. v. Hislop,* (Ont. C.A., February 4, 1975), discussed in Ruby, *supra,* note 37, at 85; *Re Skied and R., supra,* note 37, at 94, per Munroe J.; *Re R. and Mroch* (1973), 11 C.C.C. (2d) 528 (Alta. T.D.). See also *R. v. Conley* (1979), 47 C.C.C. (2d) 359 (Alta. C.A.), where the court quashed a declaration of mistrial made after sentence was pronounced on the ground that the judge was *functus.*

[42] *Head v. R.* [1986] 2 S.C.R. 684, at 698, per Lamer J.

[43] *R. v. Kaufman* (Sask. Q.B., Hrabinsky J., April 14, 1989).

[44] *R. v. Horsefall* (1971), 19 C.R.N.S. 79 (Sask. C.A.), dealing with the dismissal of a *certiorari* application in respect of an escape sentence. At that time, the *Code* required it to be served consecutively to the sentence being served at the time of the escape. This requirement has since been removed: see *Code,* section 149, and the discussion of sentence calculation problems arising from escape and related offences, *infra.*

[45] See the discussion of this subject in Chapter 2. See also *R. v. Wagensfeld* [summarized 9 W.C.B. (2d) 236].

expressed in open court, there is power to amend a constituent element to conform with the total term. This power should not be extended to the quantum of the term originally imposed, but only to whether it must be served concurrently or consecutively. It must be remembered that the English common law power of variation did not permit increasing the severity of the sentence originally imposed. Accordingly, if no total term was expressed in open court — a practice that ought not to be encouraged — a trial judge could not amend any of the original sentences so as to increase the totality.

As far as obtaining an amended warrant when an unintended discrepancy is discovered, there ought to be little difficulty. This flows from the fact that the preparation of the warrant is an administrative act. The court which originally issued the warrant should be prepared to issue an amended one to "comply with the sentence imposed by the judge."[46] If there is any dispute as to what sentence was actually imposed, the record ought to prevail over any subsequently prepared warrant.[47] In the modern era of transcribed proceedings, and given the recognized importance of the public expression of the sentence, it seems preferable that a transcript be the controlling document. There may be cases where the intention of the sentencing judge is clear, but there is a question as to whether "any statutory provision or governing authority . . . prevents the judge's intention from being carried out."[48] There will, however, be cases in which a clear intention on the part of the sentencing judge cannot be discerned. The traditional ambiguity rule should apply such that when equally reasonable interpretations are possible the sentence should be interpreted in the way most favourable to the prisoner.[49]

---

[46] Per Anderson J. in *R. v. Craig*, [1977] 3 W.W.R. 1 (B.C. S.C.).

[47] See *R. v. Mitchell*, [1977] 2 All E.R. 168 (C.A.), at 172, where Lawton L.J. held that an endorsement on the record prevailed over the warrant.

[48] Per Arnup J.A. in *Re Lauzon and R., supra*, note 27. As discussed *infra*, the kinds of issues which may interfere with judicial intention usually involve the circumstances in which consecutive sentences can be imposed, the merger of sentences as a result of section 20 of the *Parole Act*, and certain mandatory provisions which have existed from time to time in respect of escapes, the locus of confinement and the revocation or forfeiture of conditional releases.

[49] *Longpré v. R.*, [1978] 2 F.C. 749. However, in *Stashewsky v. William Head Institution (Director)* [summarized (1988), 6 W.C.B. (2d) 265 (B.C. C.A.)], the prisoner had been sentenced to four consecutive terms. The first sentence was ordered to be served "consecutive to any time being served". The other three sentences only referred to "consecutive". The prisoner argued that the sentences for the last three offences should be concurrent to one another. While the Chambers Court Judge had held that there was ambiguity, and applied *Paul v. R.*, (1982), 27 C.R. (3d) 193, the British Columbia Court of Appeal disagreed, holding that had the sentencing judge intended that result, he would have used the word concurrent in reference to the last three convictions.

(a) Concurrent and Consecutive Sentences

Section 721(1) of the *Criminal Code* provides:

> A sentence commences when it is imposed, except where a relevant enactment otherwise provides.

Accordingly, if no qualification is pronounced or required by statute,[50] the sentence commences immediately on the day it is imposed and runs concurrently throughout the period of its validity with any other sentences previously or subsequently imposed affecting the same period of time.[51] A sentencing judge cannot postpone the commencement of a sentence,[52] except in those circumstances when it can be made consecutive to a previously imposed sentence, or in the case of an intermittent sentence.[53] Equally, a judge has no power to "backdate" the commencement of a sentence to a date prior to the date the sentence is imposed.[54] If a judge wishes to give credit for time spent in custody prior to sentence being imposed, section 721(3) of the *Code* indicates that he must reduce the length of the sentence to be served. When a sentence is the subject of an appeal, the power of the appellate court is limited to varying the sentence. Hence, unless the appellate court specifically deals with the commencement of a sentence by ordering that it be served consecutively to another sentence, any reduction or increase in the length of sentence operates from the original commencement date.

If the prisoner remains in custody pending appeal of conviction or sentence, regardless of the disposition of the appeal, all time is credited. However, in *Zitek*,[55] the prisoner had been sentenced to a number of consecutive terms of imprisonment following convictions for several offences. He successfully appealed the first conviction registered. The penal authorities refused to credit him for the time spent in custody pending the conviction appeal, as they considered that since neither section 717 nor section 721 of the *Code* dealt expressly with this fact situation, a consecutive sentence only began on the date the earlier conviction was quashed. Dubin J.A. noted that, were this interpretation to be correct, ironically the prisoner would have been released earlier if

---

[50] For example, see the provisions of the Ontario *Provincial Offences Act*, R.S.O. 1980, c. 400, ss. 64 and 65.

[51] The express use of the word "concurrent" will produce the same result.

[52] Note the precise wording of section 721(1) of the *Code*.

[53] *Code*, s. 737(1)(*c*); *R. v. Downe* (1978), 44 C.C.C. (2d) 468 (P.E.I.S.C. *in banco*); *R. v. Fletcher* (1982), 2 C.C.C. (3d) 221 (Ont. C.A.).

[54] Note the statutory exemptions in the cases of dangerous offenders (*Code*, s. 761.1) and life sentences (*Code*, s. 746).

[55] *Re Zitek and R.* (1987), 30 C.C.C. (3d) 60 (Ont. C.A.).

he had successfully appealed only the sentence for the first offence. As this amounted to a "gross injustice", Dubin J.A. held that once the first conviction and sentence is set aside on appeal, any consecutive sentence would be deemed to have commenced on the day the original sentence was imposed.

If the prisoner obtains bail pending an appeal of either conviction or sentence, section 721(2) provides that time spent lawfully out of custody does not count towards completion of sentence. There are, however, occasions where prisoners are released in error, or are not allowed to surrender into custody due to administrative oversight. In *Stanton*,[56] a prisoner serving sentence was prematurely released through "no fraud or wrongdoing on his part". Linden J. held that in those circumstances time should continue to run. In *Law*,[57] the prisoner had been granted bail pending a conviction appeal on a charge on which he had been sentenced to a term of 2 years. While on bail he committed further offences, for which he was immediately sentenced to terms totalling 7 months. While serving this sentence, he abandoned his conviction appeal. Through inadvertence, this information was never communicated to the penal authorities, who released the prisoner when he had served the requisite portion of the 7-month sentence. Upon discovering their error some months later, the authorities caused the prisoner to be re-arrested, and they refused to credit him for any of the time spent in the community following the erroneous release. The prisoner launched *habeas corpus*. When the case came before the Ontario Court of Appeal it was held that since he knew he had been prematurely released, he could not claim the special circumstances which existed in *Stanton*.

The other element of *Law* relevant for current purposes is that the Supreme Court Judge who had heard the original *habeas corpus* application agreed with the prisoner's position and ordered release. The prisoner remained at liberty until the Court of Appeal reversed the lower court decision. The prisoner again launched an application for *habeas corpus*,[58] claiming that he should be credited for the time spent at liberty between his lawful release on *habeas corpus* and his re-arrest following the allowing of the Crown appeal to the Court of Appeal. Eberle J. held that, absent any statutory authority, the position at common law was that time spent at liberty in these circumstances should not count towards completion of sentence. Nor could the court find any statutory

---

[56] *Re Stanton and R.* (1979), 49 C.C.C. (2d) 177 (Ont. H.C.).

[57] *Re Law and R.* (1981), 63 C.C.C. (2d) 412 (Ont. C.A.).

[58] *Re Law and R. (No. 2)* (1981), 64 C.C.C. (2d) 181 (Ont. H.C.). Affirmed (1982), 65 C.C.C. (2d) 512n (Ont. C.A.).

authority which would afford the prisoner the right to be credited. Eberle J. cited an escape case, *Dozois*,[59] for the proposition that the various statutes allowed credit for time not actually spent in custody only while in transit, in hospital, or while on lawful conditional release.

Several cases have considered whether section 7 of the *Canadian Charter of Rights and Freedoms*[60] allows a court to give credit for time spent out of custody in circumstances other than those which existed in *Stanton*. The leading case to date is *Lawrence*,[61] where a prisoner who had been granted bail pending the outcome of an application for leave to appeal to the Supreme Court of Canada had been informed that he had not been granted leave. He attempted to surrender into custody on several occasions, but the penal authorities, erroneously believing that they could not accept him until a new committal warrant had been issued, refused to admit him. By the time the authorities were prepared to admit him, he had already spent more time awaiting surrender than he would have spent in custody had he been allowed to surrender. Noting the strain on the accused and his family, Steele J. held that "to return the accused to jail now would constitute a departure from the basic principles that underlie our understanding of fair play and would be a violation of the fundamental tenets of the justice system."[62] In these circumstances, "administrative hindrance" caused a breach of section 7, and a section 24(1) order was issued quashing the committal.[63]

The power of a sentencing judge to order sentences to be served consecutively is found in section 717(4) of the *Code*. That section provides in part:

> (4) Where an accused
> (*a*) is convicted *while under sentence for an offence*, and a term of imprisonment ... is imposed,
>
> . . . .
>
> (*c*) is convicted of more offences than one before the *same court at the same sittings*, and
>
> . . . .
>
> (ii) terms of imprisonment for the respective offences are imposed

59 *Re Dozois and R.* (1981), 61 C.C.C. (2d) 171 (Ont. C.A.).
60 Being Part I of the *Constitution Act, 1982* [enacted by the *Canada Act, 1982* (U.K.), c. 11, s. 1].
61 *R. v. Lawrence* (1989), 47 C.C.C. (3d) 462 (Nfld. T.D.).
62 *Ibid.*, at 463 (headnote).
63 See also *Re Lachance and R.* (1985), 22 C.C.C. (3d) 119 (Que. S.C.); *Foley v. Court of General Sessions of the Peace*, (1989), 66 C.R. (3d) 91 (Que. S.C.).

. . . .

the court that convicts the accused may direct that the terms of imprisonment shall be served one after the other. [Emphasis added.]

The key phrases— "while under sentence for an offence" and "before the same court at the same sittings"—were comprehensively analyzed by the Supreme Court of Canada in *Paul*.[64] The appellant had pleaded guilty to a number of charges before the same judge, on three different days. The trial judge imposed a series of concurrent and consecutive sentences in respect of the convictions. On appeal, the prisoner argued that, while he was convicted by the same court, the convictions arose at different sittings. Therefore, section 645(4)(*c*) [now s. 717(4)(*c*)] could not apply and, since he was not "under sentence" when convicted, section 645(4)(*a*) [now s. 717(4)(*a*)] was also not applicable. Accordingly, he contended that the sentencing judge had no power to order that the sentences in respect of convictions entered on the second and third occasions be served consecutively to the sentences for convictions registered on the first occasion.

Lamer J., writing for a unanimous court, embarked upon a comprehensive historical and teleological analysis of the power to sentence consecutively. After examining the development of the common law and the English and Canadian statutory predecessors to section 645 [now s. 717], he found that codification in Canada precluded any arguments based on a residual common law. In his view, the premise for consecutive sentencing was the concern that offences be punished individually and proportionally to the seriousness of the offence without resort to increasingly higher concurrent sentences simply to provide an increased total term for multiple offences.[65] To appreciate the scope of sections 645(4)(*a*) and (*c*) [now ss. 717(4)(*a*) and (*c*)] he traced their origins to the common law as described by the House of Lords in *R. v. Wilkes*[66] and the English Draft Code of 1879. Two governing principles flow from *Wilkes*:

1. punishments should not be postponed until the future; and
2. when more than one offence is involved, punishment should be "neither longer nor shorter, wider or narrower, than that specific offence deserves".[67]

The power to impose consecutive sentences derives from the sec-

---

[64] *Paul v. R.* (1982), 27 C.R. (3d) 193 (S.C.C.).

[65] *Ibid.*, at 205.

[66] (1770), 98 E.R. 327.

[67] *Supra*, note 64, at 211, quoting from *Wilkes*.

ond principle outlined in *Wilkes*. The House of Lords held that being subject to a sentence of imprisonment was not a ban to an additional sentence "by tacking one imprisonment to the other". This was amplified so as to apply regardless of whether the "judgment" for the different offences occurred at the same time. Lamer J. concluded that "judgment" referred to the imposition of sentence and not to the time of conviction. The origin of both the phrase "before the same court at the same sitting" and the reference to the time of conviction, was attributed to the Draft Code of 1879. Lamer J. explained that the phrase was intended merely to apply to sentences imposed by the same judge or panel of judges. This preserved the common law, which provided that a sentence could be made consecutive to a sentence previously or simultaneously imposed. The Draft Code, however, refined the common law as it related to sentences imposed by different judges by requiring that the subsequent sentence could only be served consecutively to a previous sentence if it had already been imposed at the time of the subsequent *conviction*. Lamer J. suggested that the Commissioners' concern must have been to ensure that sentences not be wrongly or unwittingly aggravated by two judges taking into account multiple convictions so as to increase the individual sentences they both imposed. Clearly, the mischief of double aggravation is only a danger when different judges are involved. In essentially the same form, the provisions of the Draft Code were adopted into Canadian law in 1886,[68] as follows:

> ... Parliament, when enacting that section in the statute in 1886, and later on in the Code, intended to enact the common law to the extent and with the limitation intended by the commissioners in the English Draft Code.[69]

Of course, the difficulty in *Paul* arose from the recognition that "same sittings" could not mean what it did at the time of *Wilkes* and the Draft Code, given the growth of the criminal courts, most of which sit continuously and have no terms or sessions as existed in the 18th and 19th Centuries. Notwithstanding concern about the contemporary validity of the policy considerations which generated the change to the common law, Lamer J. concluded that section 645(4)(*a*) [now s. 717(4)(*a*)] applied only to sentences imposed by different judges, while section 645(4)(*c*) [now s. 717(4)(*c*)] referred to sentences imposed by the same judge regardless of the timing of the conviction. Thus, section 717(4)(*c*) empowers a judge to order that a sentence be served consecutively to any

---

68   *An Act Respecting Punishments, Pardons and the Commutation of Sentences*, R.S.C. 1886, c. 181, s. 27.
69   *Wilkes, supra*, note 64, at 227, per Lamer J.

sentence still extant or simultaneously imposed. In situations where different judges are involved, section 717(4)(*a*) permits consecutive sentences if the previous sentence existed at the time of conviction. Therefore, in *Paul* the limitation found in section 645(4)(*a*) [now s. 717(4)(*a*)] did not apply to the appellant's case and the appeal was dismissed.

But how does one deal with the questions of remission, parole eligibility and sentence calculation when applied to cumulative sentences, both consecutive and concurrent? The answer lies in the "merging" provisions of the *Parole Act.*

(b) The "Merger" Provisions of the Parole Act

Prior to the enactment of the *Criminal Law Amendment Act, 1968-69*,[70] the service of terms of imprisonment did not involve any concept of merger. Sentences were treated as discrete units of time. This situation generated substantial confusion with respect to parole and remission. As demonstrated in the case of *Re McCaud*[71] statutory remission entitlements accrued individually for each sentence, each sentence produced its own independent parole eligibility date, and the consequences of parole revocation when a prisoner was released on parole in respect of a number of sentences were different, depending on the various expiry dates. In an effort to respond to these problems, and to "abrogate"[72] the decision in *McCaud*, the 1968-69 statute established the concept of merger. Essentially, its purpose was to combine all sentences of imprisonment which a prisoner was serving, whether concurrently or consecutively, to create one total term of imprisonment to which the parole, mandatory supervision and remission regimes could apply. As described by Muldoon J. in *Pask*:

> [The merger provision] of the *Parole Act* . . . provides the manner in which sentences of concurrent imprisonment and consecutive imprisonment are to be rationalized. It enacts that the terms of imprisonment to which the inmate or other convicted person has been sentenced shall, for all purposes of this Act . . . and the *Penitentiary Act*, among others, be deemed to constitute one sentence consisting of a term of imprisonment commencing on the earliest day on which any of those sentences of imprisonment commences and ending on the expiration of the last to expire of such terms

---

70 S.C. 1968-69, c. 38.

71 (1969), 7 C.R.N.S. 222 (Ont. S.C.). This case is known as the second in the "McCaud trilogy". In light of Mr. McCaud's contributions to Canadian prison law, it is perhaps worth noting that as of July 1990, he still "owes" Canadian penal authorities 189 days, less remission.

72 *Re Dean and R.* (1977), 35 C.C.C. (2d) 217 (Ont. C.A.), at 223-224.

of imprisonment. [The merger provision] then deals with the composition of a deemed sentence, and necessarily so, because it must deem various concurrent and consecutive terms of imprisonment to have been imposed under one sentence even although they were in reality imposed by different sentences possibly pronounced at different times and in different places.[73]

The original version[74] of the merger provisions was contained in section 14 of the *Parole Act*. That section read:

> **14.** (1) Where, either before, on or after the 25th day of March 1970,
>> (*a*) a person is sentenced to two or more terms of imprisonment, or
>> (*b*) an inmate who is in confinement is sentenced to an additional term or terms of imprisonment,
>
> the terms of imprisonment to which he has been sentenced, including in a case described in paragraph (*b*) any term or terms that resulted in his being in confinement, shall, for all purposes of this Act, the *Penitentiary Act* and the *Prisons and Reformatories Act*, be deemed to constitute one sentence consisting of a term of imprisonment commencing on the earliest day on which any of those sentences of imprisonment commences and ending on the expiration of the last to expire of such terms of imprisonment.
>
> (2) This section does not affect the time at which any sentences that are deemed by subsection (1) to constitute one sentence commence pursuant to subsection 649 (1) of the *Criminal Code*.[75]

Although this section has been modified on several occasions since it was first introduced, the principle remains the same. A useful example demonstrating the principles involved in the application of the merger provisions to a sentence calculation is the case of *Ismond*,[76] where the prisoner was serving a 3-year term imposed on October 4, 1973. As a result of accumulated statutory and earned remission, he was entitled to be released on mandatory supervision on October 23, 1975, and to remain subject to that regime until his warrant expiry date of October 3, 1976. However, on February 17, 1975, he received a sentence of 18 months "to run concurrently with any other sentence being served". By application of the merger provision, Bouck J. concluded that:

(a) the two terms of imprisonment constituted "one sentence";
(b) the "one sentence" began on the date the first sentence was imposed (October 4, 1973);
(c) the "one sentence" expired on the latest expiry date of the two terms of imprisonment.[77]

---

73   *Pask v. R.* (File no. T-29900-83, Fed. T.D., Muldoon J., May 23, 1984).
74   For an account of the early history of this provision and its proclamation, see *Ex parte Beaucage* (1977), 31 C.C.C. (2d) 219 (Ont. C.A.) at 222-227, per Kelly J.A.
75   R.S.C. 1970 (1st supp.), c. 31, s. 1 [as amended by S.C. 1977-78, c. 22, s. 19].
76   *R. v. Ismond*, [1976] 3 W.W.R. 677 (B.C. S.C.).
77   *Ibid.*, at 680.

In order to determine the effect of the second sentence, the calculator should first convert the original sentence of 3 years into days (October 4, 1973 to October 3, 1976 = 1096 days). Next, the calculator determines the number of days remaining in that sentence on the date the second sentence was imposed (February 17, 1975 to October 3, 1976 = 595 days). Finally, the 18-month sentence should similarly be converted into days (February 17, 1975 to August 16, 1976 = 547 days). Since at the point the second sentence was imposed the prisoner had remaining in the original sentence more days to serve (595 days) than the number of days contained in the second sentence (547 days), the second sentence was entirely "subsumed"[78] by the "remanet"[79] of the original sentence. As a result, the prisoner's remission credits applied to the merged sentence such that he ought to have been released on the original release date, regardless of the second sentence. Bouck J. therefore granted *habeas corpus.*[80]

While this case explains the application of the merger provisions, the following example demonstrates how the situation changes when a second sentence, although directed to be served concurrently, expires at a date *later* than the expiry date of the original sentence.[81] Assume the same basic facts as *Ismond*, but make the further assumption that on February 17, 1975 a concurrent sentence of 2 years was imposed. To ascertain both P.E.D. and P.R.D., it is first necessary to determine the length of the merged term. As shown in the previous example, it commenced on the date the first sentence was imposed (October 4, 1973) and extended to the expiry date of the last term (February 17, 1975 + 2 years = February 16, 1977). This produces a merged term commencing on October 4, 1973, and running until February 16, 1977, a total of 1,232 days. Since P.E.D. arises at one-third of term, that date is determined by dividing the total merged term by 3 ($\frac{1}{3}$ of 1,232 = 410$\frac{2}{3}$ rounded up to 411 days), and by then adding that number of days to the commencement date of the earliest sentence (October 4, 1973 + 411 days = November 19, 1974). Under the remission regime in force at that time, the potential

---

[78] This term appears in the judgment. It has now entered the parlance of sentence administration.

[79] Section 2 of the *Regualtions* defines "remanet" as "the portion of the term of imprisonment that remains, at any time, to be served by that inmate".

[80] Bouck J. was asked to consider the interpretation of the sentences at a point where the prisoner was well past P.E.D.; therefore, the case makes no reference to that calculation. Since this becomes more relevant in the examples which follow, it should be noted that P.E.D. is calculated on the basis of one-third of the total merged term ($\frac{1}{3}$ of 1096 = 365$\frac{1}{3}$, rounded up to 366 days). October 4, 1973 + 366 days = October 5, 1974.

[81] This type of sentence is referred to in sentence administration jargon as "concurrent, not subsumed".

M.S.D. (since July 25, 1986, properly called P.R.D.), assuming that no remission was lost and all remission was earned, could be calculated as follows:

	1,232 days
Less S.R. (¹/₄)	−308
Days to serve (1,232 − 308)	924
Less days served to December 31, 1973 (including O.E.R. at 3 days per month)	−97
	827
Less days served to December 31, 1975 (including O.E.R. at 3 days per month)	−802
	25
Less days served to January 22, 1976 (including O.E.R. at 3 days per month)	−25
	0

Thus, the prisoner would stand to be released subject to mandatory supervision on January 22, 1976. He would have been subject to mandatory supervision until his W.E.D. of February 16, 1977.

This calculation of M.S.D. involved the remission regime which was abolished by the 1977 amendments. The current regime provides that a prisoner can earn up to 15 days remission for each month actually served in custody.[82] The same example can be transposed into the present system by assuming sentences imposed on October 3, 1983 and February 17, 1985. The calculator, commencing with a merged term of 1,232 days, should ignore S.R. and accumulate E.R. at 15 days rather than 3 days per month, as follows:

	1,232 days
Less days served to October 31, 1983 (including 14 days E.R.)	−43
Less days served to December 31, 1983 (including 30 days E.R.)	−91
	1,098
Less days served to December 31, 1985 (including 360 days E.R.)	−1,091[83]
Less days served to January 4, 1986 (including 2 days E.R.)	−6
	1

Using this regime, the P.R.D. was January 5, 1986,[84] at which time,

---

[82] A prisoner released on day parole can continue to earn remission at the same rate, because section 19(1) of the *Parole Act* provides that a day parolee "shall be deemed to be continuing to serve his term of imprisonment in the place of confinement from which he was released on that parole".

[83] 1984 was a leap year.

[84] The fact that the P.R.D. under this regime is January 5, 1986 illustrates why the

assuming that all remission was earned and none was lost,[85] the prisoner would stand to be released and to be subject to mandatory supervision until his warrant expiry date of February 16, 1987.

A further situation to be considered is the imposition of a consecutive sentence. Essentially, this is an easier calculation because it does not involve any question of subsumption, but merely requires adding the new term onto that previously imposed. Again, building on the basic facts of *Ismond*, assume that on February 17, 1975 a sentence of 2 years consecutive was imposed. Strictly speaking, this term would not commence until the expiry of the previously imposed 3-year term. However, from the perspective of determining P.E.D. and P.R.D., the prisoner would be deemed by the merging provisions to be serving a merged sentence of 5 years (1,826 days) which commenced on October 4, 1973. The W.E.D. would be October 3, 1978. P.E.D. would be calculated by dividing the total number of days by 3 ($\frac{1}{3}$ of 1,826 = 608 $\frac{2}{3}$ rounded up to 609 days) and adding that number to the commencement date of the term (October 4, 1973 + 609 days = June 4, 1976[86]). Modifying the dates of imposition of the sentences by 10 years to bring them within the current remission regime (as was done in the previous example), P.R.D. would be calculated as follows:

	1,826 days
Less days served to October 31, 1983 (including 14 days E.R.)	−42
Less days served to December 31, 1983 (including 30 days E.R.)	−91
	1,693

---

previous remission regime was characterized as providing remission totalling "almost" one-third of sentence (M.S.D. = January 22, 1986). The current regime is much closer to the one-third figure; it also provides a marginally greater remission potential. Another feature of the new regime, albeit minor, is that remission is rounded up so that one-half day counts as a day to produce the P.R.D.

[85] If the sentences were such that the prisoner had not been released from custody prior to the proclamation of the "gating" legislation on July 25, 1986, the prisoner's P.R.D. might be affected by the possible application of that legislation.

[86] This example demonstrates graphically why, as discussed in Chapter 6, the Board is very hesitant to grant parole release while there are outstanding charges. As we have already seen, P.E.D. on the original 3-year term was October 4, 1974. Had the prisoner been granted parole at that time, he would have been on parole release at the time the additional sentence was imposed on February 17, 1975. If the charge resulting in that sentence had been outstanding at the time parole was granted, the Board would have been powerless to suspend or revoke that release, because the prisoner would not have breached a term or condition of release. The Board would be placed in the odd situation that its previous parole grant would have been "rendered inoperative" by the imposition of the additional sentence. Of course, where the offence leading to the additional sentence is committed while on parole release, the Board may intervene, as discussed *infra*.

Less days served to December 31, 1986 (including 540 days E.R.)	−1,636
	57
Less days served to January 31, 1987 (including 15 days E.R.)	−46
Less days served to February 6, 1987 (including 3 days E.R.)	−9
	2

Thus, assuming that all remission was earned, no remission was lost, and that the prisoner was not "gated", he would then stand to be released on the P.R.D. of February 7, 1987, and would have been subject to mandatory supervision until W.E.D. on October 3, 1988.[87]

While the original merger enactment was intended to alleviate problems and remove confusions,[88] in its technicality it generated an array of new problems probably unforeseen by the drafters, particularly with respect to the interaction of the merger provisions and various versions of the *Criminal Code* dealing with escape sentences.[89] Some of these issues were of general applicability and some of a more anomalous nature.[90] Many of these have been rationalized by the 1986 amendment to the Act, which now provides:

> **20.** (1) Where, either before, on or after the coming into force of this section, a person sentenced to a term of imprisonment that has not expired is sentenced to an additional term of imprisonment, the terms of imprisonment to which the person has been sentenced shall, for all purposes of the *Criminal Code*, the *Penitentiary Act*, the *Prisons and Reformatories Act* and this Act, except subsections (1.1) and (1.2), be deemed to constitute one sentence consisting of a term of imprisonment commencing on the earliest day on which any of the sentences of imprisonment commences and ending on the expiration of the last to expire of those terms of imprisonment.[91]

---

87 These examples are relatively simple, as we have intentionally avoided any complicating factors which can often unpredictably arise. The principal complication arises when a conditional release is combined with a new sentence. As well calculations are exacerbated by escapes and disappearances. These are discussed in the next sections.

88 The apparent remedial purposes of merger were discussed in R. Price, "*Doing Justice to Corrections? Prisoners, Parolees, and the Canadian Courts*" (1977), 3 Queen's L.J. 214, at 257. He refers to two pre-existing problems: (1) separate parole for separate sentences, as in *Ex parte Dodge*, [1972] 1 O.R. 753 (H.C.); and (2) separate sentences served individually in sequence as in *Re McCaud* (1969), 7 C.R.N.S. 222 (Ont. H.C.), such that it was difficult to determine what sentence a prisoner was serving at a given time. Thus, it appears that the intention behind merger was simply to create a single aggregate term upon which remission, parole eligibility, and revocation (or forfeiture) consequences would operate.

89 See, for example, *Re Clarke and R.* (Ont. H.C., Reid J., February 7, 1978).

90 *Re Lauzon and R.* (1981), 58 C.C.C. (2d) 20 (Ont. C.A.).

91 S.C. 1984-85-86, c. 68, s. 10.

This new provision will be considered in more detail in the following sections.

6. CONDITIONAL RELEASE

When a prisoner is conditionally released from close custody, he or she remains under supervision and subject to conditions until warrant expiry date. During that period, the Parole Board has the power to revoke the release and return the prisoner to custody (see Chapter 8). Upon a revocation of parole, day parole or mandatory supervision, the remanet of the prisoner's sentence must be re-calculated to take into account the days served on conditional release and the remission consequences. The simple case may be complicated by the addition of new sentences invoking the operation of section 20. Another problem arises from disappearance while on release; all too frequently, the relevant statutes offer little guidance as to their application to complex fact situations.

Due to a series of statutory amendments, different formulae are applied depending upon the date of commencement of the original sentence and the date of release and revocation. There is a considerable body of case law dealing with sentence calculation and forfeiture of conditional release, indeterminate sentences, statutory remission credits and pre-1977 revocations.[92] Many of the issues canvassed in those decisions are rarely encountered now and are usually only of historical interest. Within the history, however, there are two significant dates to note. The statutory remission (S.R.) regime was repealed as of July 1, 1978; hence, as discussed in section 3, above, prisoners sentenced or revoked after that date did not receive the benefit of a statutorily allocated amount of remission. More importantly, before October 15, 1977 prisoners received no credit towards their sentence for days served on conditional release. Since the 1977 amendments, as of October 15, 1977, prisoners receive credit for time at liberty (commonly known as "street time").[93] Thus, since the 1977 amendments, in most cases of release and revocation, the original expiry date is unaffected. Although in cases of long sentences which commenced before July 1, 1978, it is

---

[92] See Price, *supra*, note 88, at 221-237.

[93] While this change applies to all revocations, strangely, it takes into account only those days spent unsuspended on release after that date. Accordingly, a prisoner released on parole on October 1, 1972, suspended on October 17, 1977 and subsequently revoked, would receive credit for only 2 days. The period October 1, 1972, to October 14, 1977 (1,740 days) would have to be re-served. Thus, the warrant expiry date would be extended by that period.

occasionally necessary to integrate the old remission situation into a calculation, this is becoming rarer as time passes. Accordingly, the following discussion is restricted to the post-1977 era.

(a) Revocation: The Simple Case

Upon release on parole or mandatory supervision, the period between the date of release and the warrant expiry date is known as the "remanet". If it passes uneventfully, the warrant expires and no further power can be exercised over the prisoner by reason of the previously imposed sentence.[94] However, if conditional is suspended, terminated, or revoked, the prisoner may be arrested and incarcerated on the strength of a warrant issued by the parole authorities. Upon re-confinement and revocation,[95] the period of time to be served before again becoming eligible for release is determined, in the simple case, by operation of section 25 of the *Parole Act*. By simple case, we mean a revocation without an additional sentence. Section 25(2) provides:

> ... where any parole is revoked, the paroled inmate shall, whether the inmate was sentenced or granted parole before or after the coming into force of this subsection, *serve the portion of the term of imprisonment that remained unexpired at the time parole was granted, including any statutory and earned remission, less*
>
> (*a*) any time spent on parole after October 14, 1977.
> (*b*) any time during which the inmate's parole was suspended and the inmate was in custody;
> (*c*) any remission earned after October 14, 1977 and applicable to a period during which the inmate's parole was suspended and the inmate was in custody; and
> (*d*) any earned remission that stood to the credit of the inmate on October 15, 1977. [Emphasis added.]

---

94 Note the difference between section 16(1)(*e*) and (*f*) of the *Parole Act*. The question of the National Parole Board's power to revoke conditional release after W.E.D. is discussed in Chapter 8.

95 If a *suspension* warrant is executed, but the suspension is later cancelled by the designated parole official or by the Board (see Chapter 8), there are no remission consequences. Upon delivery of the cancellation warrant to the jail, the prisoner is released and is credited for the time spent in custody as if he had been at liberty on conditional release. If conditional release is *terminated* the prisoner does not lose remission; he is doubly credited for the time spend in custody pending the decision to terminate. Not only is the prisoner credited towards W.E.D. for time spent in custody on a day-for-day basis, as if he had been at liberty on conditional release, but he is also allowed to earn remission for those days spent in custody. Only if conditional release is *revoked* is there any deemed loss of remission.

This section—and more specifically the phrase "portion of the term which remained unexpired at the time parole was granted"—appears to create an uncomplicated calculus of debits and credits. All remission accumulated as of the date of release[96] is automatically lost as a direct consequence of the revocation unless, pursuant to section 25(3) of the Act, the Board exercises its discretion to re-credit remission. Note that the prisoner receives credit for all days spent lawfully on release before suspension, days spent in custody after suspension, any remission earned between suspension and revocation,[97] and, in rare cases, old earned remission (O.E.R.) earned prior to October 15, 1977.

For the purpose of the mathematical calculation of new release dates, the remanet can be treated analogously to a new sentence. Although conceptually attractive, a remanet is not a new sentence originating from the date of revocation. Rather, it is a period of time that, subject to the additional credits provided by section 25(2) of the *Parole Act*, continues to be part of the original sentence.[98] The rejection of the "new sentence" argument explains why, as a matter of law, P.E.D. does not change following revocation.[99] Further, the original warrant expiry date continues to apply unless additional sentences have been imposed or there has been a period of disappearance while on release, as discussed below.

The following example illustrates the operation of section 25(2):

---

[96] This includes remission earned while on day parole.

[97] In *Harris v. R.* (File no. T-936-86, Fed. T.D., June 13, 1986), it was held that the wording of section 20(2)(*c*) [now s. 25(2)(*c*)] of the Act was sufficiently broad so as to entitle a prisoner who had had previous suspensions cancelled, to claim remission earned during those suspensions if his parole was ultimately revoked. This was summarily reversed by the Federal Court of Appeal [summarized (1988), 6 W.C.B. (2d) 289].

[98] The "new sentence" argument arose in the past decade in two contexts. In *Re VanBree and R.* (1980), 59 C.C.C. (2d) 163 (Ont. H.C.), it was argued that pre-July 1, 1978 statutory remission reduced the size of the remanet such that, once taken into account, it ceased to play a role for the purposes of section 24.2 of the *Penitentiary Act*, the transitional provision which placed a cap on the prisoner's ability to earn remission. This argument was rejected. As well, in the line of escape cases commencing with *Clarke, supra*, note 89, the "new sentence" argument was used to produce a new statutory remission, credit on the unexpired portion as set out in section 137 [now s. 149] of the *Code* at the time. Ultimately, however, the courts concluded that the remanet in the escape context was not a new sentence. *McIntyre v. R.* (1982), 70 C.C.C. (2d) 542 (Fed. C.A.).

[99] As discussed in Chapter 8, the Board has decided as a matter of general policy that conditional release will not usually be favourably considered until at least 6 months have elasped from the date of revocation.

January 1, 1985	Sentence of 3 years	<u>1,095</u> days
January 1, 1986	Release on full parole	
February 1, 1986	Parole suspended, warrant executed	
March 1, 1986	Parole revoked, no re-credit of remission	
	Less days served to January 1, 1986	−365
	Less days on street to February 1, 1986	−31
	Less days served in custody on suspension	−28
	Remanet (as of March 1, 1986)	<u>671</u> days

To calculate the prisoner's new P.R.D., one would then work forward, crediting any remission earned while in custody on suspension, and assuming that the prisoner earned 15 days of remission for each month served:

Less E.R. on suspension	−15
Less days served to December 31, 1986, including 150 days E.R.	−455
Less days served to April 30, 1987, including 60 days E.R.	−180
Less days to May 13, 1987 including 7 days E.R.	<u>−20</u> 1

In essence, this treats the problem as a simple sentence of 671 days commencing on March 1, 1986, subject to the additional credit for remission earned while in custody between suspension and revocation. However, to perform the calculation properly, the mathematical exercise outlined here must be undertaken. Thus, if the prisoner then earned every day of available remission and did not lose any as a result of internal disciplinary sanctions, he would be entitled to release on mandatory supervision on the new P.R.D. of May 14, 1987.[100] The prisoner's W.E.D. would remain at December 31, 1988.

(b) Revocation and Additional Sentences

Before the 1977 amendments, a conviction for an indictable offence punishable by more than 2 years imprisonment resulted in the auto-

---

[100] This simple calculation of a new presumptive release date assumes that all remission standing to the credit of the prisoner at the date of release was lost upon revocation by virtue of section 25(2) of the Act. As discussed earlier, section 25(3) of the Act empowers the Board to re-credit some or all of the lost remission.

matic "forfeiture" of parole or mandatory supervision.[101] The Act required that the new sentence be served consecutively to the remanet. While the automatic "forfeiture" provision has been repealed, a new conviction may be sufficient reason for revocation. In fact, a substantial number of revocations arise by reason of, or at least are accompanied by, new convictions in the imposition of additional sentences.[102] In the discretion of a sentencing judge, a new sentence can be ordered to be served concurrently or consecutively to the remanet of a pre-existing sentence.[103] The following will help to illustrate the combined effect of sections 20 and 25(2) of the *Parole Act* and additional sentences:

January 1, 1985	Sentence of 3 years	1,095 days
January 1, 1986	Release on full parole	
February 1, 1986	Parole suspended, warrant executed,[104] facing new charge	

---

[101] R.S.C. 1970, c. P-2, s. 21 [repealed by S.C. 1976-77, c. 53, s. 32].

[102] For example, the National Parole Board's *Briefing Book for Members of the Standing Committee on Justice and Solicitor General* (Vol. III, pp. 561-565) published in 1987, noted that, from 1977-78 to 1981-82, 12.1 percent of full parole cases and 19 percent of mandatory supervision cases were revoked by reason of new convictions. During that period, 7,855 prisoners were released on full parole and 12,816 prisoners were released on mandatory supervision.

[103] One must always keep in mind that sentence administrators may also add their own gloss in interpreting judicial intention. An example of this arose in *Re Carriere and R.* (Toronto Motions Court File no. 1747/89, Ont. H.C., August 22, 1989), where a prisoner had been released subject to mandatory supervision. Some 2 months later his right to be at liberty was suspended as a result of new charges being laid. He was subsequently sentenced to "6 months Gaol" on one count of possession of property obtained by crime and to "6 months consecutive Gaol" on one count of unlawful possession of a credit card. Mandatory supervision was then revoked, leaving the prisoner with a 83-day remanet on the original term. The sentence administrator interpreted these sentences as totalling 12 months consecutive and purported to apply section 20(1.1) and (1.4) of the *Parole Act*. Counsel for the prisoner took the position that the sentences for the new offences should be interpreted as 12 months concurrent, since (a) in the absence of a judicial declaration to the contrary, the first sentence was clearly concurrent to the remanet of the previous sentence, and (b) in the absence of a further judicial pronouncement that the sentence was "consecutive to any other sentence being served"—the second sentence was consecutive only to the first sentence. In those circumstances section 20(1) of the *Parole Act* applied, with the result that the 83-day remanet was subsumed into the concurrent 12-month sentence. The prisoner's view was adopted by Philp J.

[104] It frequently transpires that a parolee may be in custody as a result of a new charge being laid, but that the parole suspension warrant is not executed for some days. Despite the opening words of section 25(2), it is the current practice of sentence administration to give credit for all time spent in custody, regardless of the date of execution of the suspension warrant.

March 1, 1986	Parole revoked, no re-credit of remission	
March 31, 1986	Convicted and sentenced to 3 years concurrent	

Pursuant to section 721(1) of the *Code* the additional sentence commences when imposed and will expire on March 30, 1989. Accordingly, as we have already seen, pursuant to section 20(1) of the *Parole Act*, the prisoner is deemed to be serving a merged term commencing on January 1, 1985 and expiring on March 30, 1989, a total of 1,550 days. The calculation would be:

January 1, 1985	Merged term	1,550 days
	Less days served to December 31, 1985	−365
	Less days served on street to February 1, 1986	−31
	Less days served in custody on suspension	−28
	Days to serve from March 1, 1986	1126
	Less E.R. on suspension	−15
	Less days served to December 1, 1986 including 150 days E.R.	−456
	Less days served to December 31, 1987 including 180 days E.R.	−545
	Less days served to February 29, 1988 including 30 days E.R.	−90
	Days to serve	20
	Less days served to March 13, 1988 including 7 days E.R.	−20
		0[105]

The same presumptive release date—March 13, 1988—could have been reached by starting on March 1, 1986, the date of revocation, and then merging (*i.e.*, adding) the remanet with the new sentence. Of course, it is necessary to remember the remission credit earned while on suspension. The lengthier approach going back to January 1, 1985 responds accurately to the actual effect of section 20; while cumbersome, it permits the

---

[105] Note that the parole eligibility date, calculated on the basis of a merged sentence of 1,550 days commencing January 1, 1985, becomes May 31, 1986, only 2 months after the imposition of the new sentence.

calculator to pick up any errors which may have occurred along the way.[106]

Using the same basic example, assume the sentence imposed on March 31, 1986 was 3 years' imprisonment to be served *consecutively* to the sentence being served. In this situation, there is a merged term of 6 years commencing on January 1, 1985, a total of 2,191 days. The calculation would be:

January 1, 1985	Merged sentence of 6 years	2,191 days
	Less days served in custody, on the street, or in custody on suspension to March 1, 1986	−424
	Days to serve as of March 1, 1986	1,767
	Less E.R. on suspension	−15
	Less days served to December 31, 1986 including 150 days E.R.	−456
	Less days served to December 31, 1987 including 180 days E.R.	−545
	Less days served to December 31, 1988 including 180 days E.R.	−546
	Less days served to April 30, 1989 including 90 days E.R.	−180
	Days to serve	25
	Less days served to May 17, 1989 including 8 days E.R.	−25
		0[107]

The P.E.D. becomes January 1, 1987, calculated on the basis of a

---

[106] When one receives a calculation from a sentence administrator, it often commences on the revocation date with a stipulated remanet. The lengthy approach illustrated above will check the accuracy of the remanet. It is important to remember, however, that revocation results in lost remission. This is subject to any re-credit pursuant to section 25(3) of the Act and remission earned while on suspension, which is preserved by section 25(2). Accordingly, when using the long method the calculator must be careful not to give remission in respect of the period between sentence and revocation, except for re-credits or remission earned while on suspension.

[107] As a brief check on the calculation, total the remission which the prisoner is eligible to earn (593 days) and add it to the P.R.D. The result should be the warrant expiry date: 593 days from May 17, 1989 brings us exactly to December 31, 1990.

merged sentence of 6 years commencing January 1, 1985. The new P.R.D. is May 17, 1989, and the W.E.D. is December 31, 1990.[108]

The combination of conditional release and an additional sentence has, in the past, produced some anomalous results. One major problem appears to have been resolved by the 1986 amendments to section 20.[109] Previously, the merger provision contained in the predecessor section 14 applied only when (*a*) a person is sentenced to two or more terms of imprisonment, or (*b*) an inmate who is in confinement is sentenced to an additional term or terms of imprisonment. In *Booth*,[110] two prisoners on mandatory supervision were jointly accused of committing a new offence. While their right to be at liberty on mandatory supervision was suspended for a time, the Board chose not to revoke them, and directed that the suspensions be cancelled. Nevertheless, the prisoners remained in custody as a result of their failure to satisfy a justice that they should be granted judicial interim release. They were then convicted of the offences which had triggered the suspensions, and received new concurrent sentences of imprisonment. The Board then decided to revoke mandatory supervision. The prisoners launched *habeas corpus* proceedings, arguing that their new concurrent sentences must merge with the sentences from which they had been released on mandatory supervision, as they were in custody at the time of sentencing. This would have resulted in the application of their remission credits to the merged sentence, which would, in effect, erase the new custodial sentence, much the same as occurred in *Ismond*. The Ontario Court of Appeal noted a distinction between the cases. By interpreting section 14(1)(*a*) as relating only to cases where multiple sentences were imposed simultaneously, and by limiting the application of section 14(1)(*b*) to encompassing only those prisoners who were already serving a sentence *in confinement* as a result of a suspension or revocation of conditional release when the additional term was imposed, the court concluded that section 14 did not apply. The court reasoned that, if section 14(1)(*a*) was intended to apply to anyone subject to an unexpired sentence, whether in confinement or not, then section 14(1)(*b*) would be superfluous. Accordingly, even though the prisoners remained *in custody* throughout, and were only revoked subsequent to the imposition of the new sentences, they could not use the merger provision to their benefit, since when sen-

---

108 In the case of a simple revocation, the warrant expiry date will only change from what it would otherwise be if there is a gap during which the prisoner is suspended but not in custody.

109 See S.C. 1986, c. 43, s. 10 [proclaimed in force July 25, 1986].

110 *R. v. Booth* (Ont. C.A., September 17, 1979).

tenced they were not *in confinement* within the meaning of the *Parole Act.*

This issue no longer arises since section 14(1), in its current form in section 20, does not now have an "in confinement" requirement. Merger normally applies to all sentences regardless of whether the prisoner is serving the earlier sentence in custody or on release. However, to prevent the frustration of sentencing judges' intentions, parole or mandatory supervision is now deemed to be "interrupted" in certain circumstances, and is not resumed until the new sentence has been served. This mechanism is discussed in the following section.

(c) The "Interruption" Provisions of the Parole Act[111]

Occasions arise when a released prisoner receives a new custodial sentence but the Board chooses not to terminate or revoke the release. One example of this arises where the Board views[112] the new sentence as both unrelated and insignificant in comparison to the prisoner's general progress on release and the extent of the potential consequences of revocation and recommitment. For example, a short sentence for a driving offence may not compel revocation when the prisoner's original incarceration arose from illegal conduct which appears to have been overcome. Another example occurs when a prisoner is convicted and sentenced in respect of an offence which took place before the release,[113] or even before the incarceration. In either example, revocation could not be affected since it must be based on post-release conduct or breaches of conditions.[114] But how do these new sentences affect the period of release and its calculation when there is no revocation and, as discussed above, no merger?

Prior to the 1986 amendment, in the absence of revocation, a new concurrent sentence imposed on a parolee not under suspension was treated by the penal authorities as a separate sentence which had no impact on a remanet.[115] However, where a sentence was ordered to be

---

[111] The combined interaction of the various sections of the *Parole Act* make it clear that interruption also applies to a prisoner released on day parole.

[112] It is not always the case that the parole supervisor is necessarily aware of brief incarceration. A common example arises where a person on conditional release may be arrested for non-payment of warrants issued under provincial offences legislation, and is held until the warrants have been paid off or satisfied by serving the specified period of time.

[113] See *Re Dinardo and R.* (1982), 67 C.C.C. (2d) 505 (Ont. C.A.), discussed *infra.*

[114] See *R. v. Moore; Oag v. R.* (1983), 33 C.R. (3d) 97 (S.C.C.).

[115] B. Mann, *A National Parole Board Handbook for Judges and Crown Attorneys* (Ottawa: Ministry of Supply and Services Canada, 1983), p. 55. This Handbook has now been re-issued under the title, *A Guide to the Parole Act and Regulations* (1988).

served consecutively, penal authorities became concerned about clarifying the commencement date of the new custodial term. It seemed absurd that a prisoner should complete parole and then return to custody to serve a consecutive sentence.[116] The legislative response, at least for prisoners released on mandatory supervision, was to introduce the concept of interruption.[117] Section 15(4) [now s. 21(5)] provided:

> Where an inmate subject to mandatory supervision commits an additional offence for which a consecutive sentence of imprisonment is imposed and mandatory supervision is not revoked, the period of mandatory supervision is interrupted and is not resumed until the later sentence has been served.

By restricting its applicability to mandatory supervision, Parliament accepted the view that supervision on the street was a useful, if not essential, aspect of release. Moreover, by excluding parole, Parliament recognized that while pre-release conduct could not justify revocation of mandatory supervision, such conduct could justify a refusal to grant one of the discretionary forms of release.[118] Unfortunately, Parliament did not adequately address the practical implications of the enactment. First, in respect of prisoners on conditional release, sentencing judges do not necessarily agree about, or always understand, the impact of the conditional release situation on sentencing (see Chapter 2). Hence, whether a sentence is ordered to be served concurrently or consecutively is often more a function of fortuity or general practice than a real assessment of the intended relationship between the sentence being imposed and the release background. Again, while section 15(4) [now s. 21(5)] permitted the correctional authorities to give some effect to consecutive sentences by way of interruption,[119] and thus avoided the

---

[116] In our view, in the absence of a revocation, the simple and correct answer would have been to treat the consecutive endorsement as surplusage, since there was no subsisting custodial term to which it could be added. This approach has been used in similar circumstances (see *Re Zitek and R.* (1987), 30 C.C.C. (3d) 60 (Ont. C.A.).

[117] S.C. 1976-77, c. 53, s. 28(1).

[118] While the set of factors to be considered are not listed in the *Parole Act* or *Regulations* (except for the reference in section 21.4(4.1) to "gating" proceedings), most American parole statutes stipulate relevant items which include, understandably, conduct in custody and pre-incarceration history: see Appendix to *Greenholtz v. Inmates of Nebraska Penal Complex* (1979), 91 S.Ct. 2100.

[119] While section 15(4) was in effect, the phrase "Burns ruling" appeared commonly in the jargon of the trade with respect to the issue of conditional release, revocation and new sentences. While it was an interesting and highly relevant concept, it was not a judicial pronouncement; rather the "Burns ruling" was an interpretive opinion offered by one of the counsel to the National Parole Board which was accepted by the Board and by C.S.C. It applied to a sub-set of additional sentence cases. It arose when a prisoner, having been released on parole or mandatory supervision, was returned to custody on

discomfort which flowed from ignoring a judicial direction, it only achieved this end in respect of mandatory supervision. Moreover, section 15(4) did not address how, in practical terms, interruption would take place: was the term of supervision resumed after release from custody or upon warrant expiry?

Many of these questions have been resolved by the recent amendments[120] which integrate the concept of interruption with the merger provision in section 20. This seems to be a sensible approach since, as is apparent from *Booth*, interruption really is the "flipside" of merger. The *Parole Act* now provides:

> **20.** (1.1) Where an inmate whose parole has not been terminated or revoked is sentenced to a consecutive term of imprisonment, the sentence the inmate was serving on parole is interrupted and is not resumed until the later sentence has expired or until the parole of the inmate has been terminated or revoked.
>
> (1.2) Where an inmate referred to in subsection (1.1) is sentenced to an additional term of imprisonment while the sentence being served on parole is interrupted,
>> (*a*) if the additional term is concurrent with the later sentence, the later sentence and the additional term shall, for all purposes of the *Criminal Code*, the *Penitentiary Act*, the *Prisons and Reformatories Act* and this Act, be deemed to constitute one sentence consisting of a term of imprisonment commencing on the day on which the later sentence commences and ending on the expiration of the last to expire of the terms of imprisonment; and
>> (*b*) if the additional term is consecutive to the later sentence,

---

suspension and subsequently received a new sentence. A prisoner on suspension was "in confinement" within the meaning of section 14(1)(*b*) as it previously existed; hence, merger would apply. According to the ruling, if the new sentence—whether consecutive or concurrent—affected the sentence calculation such that the prisoner was no longer eligible for release on parole or mandatory supervision, the Board could not revoke the release. The rationale was that, since a referral to the Board required it, pursuant to section 22(4) to revoke or cancel the suspension, if the new sentence precluded returning the prisoner to the street, then the Board could not embark on the question of revocation since the alternative choice was not available. Accordingly, since no revocation could occur, the prisoner forfeited no remission pursuant to section 25(2), and was simply returned to custody to serve the merged sentence consisting of the remanet as of the date of suspension and the new sentence. While the "Burns ruling" saved remission for many prisoners, its applicability seems to have been deliberately precluded by the 1986 amendments. Section 16(2) of the Act now empowers the Board to exercise its general power of revocation regardless of the impact of any new sentence of imprisonment:
> **16.**(2) The authority conferred on the Board by paragraphs 16(1)(*d*) and (*e*) may be exercised notwithstanding any new term of imprisonment to which the inmate becomes subject after the release of the inmate on parole.

[120] Section 15(4) was replaced by S.C. 1986, c. 43, s. 11(2).

(i) in the case of an inmate who has been granted, with respect to the later sentence, parole that is not revoked or terminated, the rule set out in subsection (1.1) applies, and

(ii) in any other case, the rule set out in paragraph (*a*) applies.

(1.3) Where an additional term referred to in subsection (1.2) is concurrent with or consecutive to the sentence interrupted pursuant to subsection (1.1), the additional term shall be deemed only to be concurrent with or consecutive to the later sentence only.

(1.4) Where a parole of an inmate referred to in subsection (1.1) is terminated or revoked, the inmate shall serve the total of

(*a*) the unexpired portion of any sentence being served on parole; and

(*b*) the unexpired portion of any later sentence.

(1.5) The unexpired portion of a sentence referred to in paragraph (1.4)(*a*) shall, where the parole has been revoked, be calculated in accordance with subsection 25(2).

(1.6) For the purpose of this section "later sentence" means

(*a*) the consecutive term referred to in subsection (1.1); or

(*b*) the sentence determined in accordance with subsection (1.2).[121]

While the new enactment does not apply to concurrent sentences, it provides a common response to new consecutive sentences, regardless of whether the unrevoked prisoner is on parole or mandatory supervision. As well, section 20(1.1) makes it clear that the term of release does not become operative again until the new consecutive sentences expire.[122] The combination of the new subsections accommodate the

---

[121] S.C. 1986, c. 43, s. 10; R.S.C. 1985, c. 35 (2nd Supp.), s. 9.

[122] This seems to mean warrant expiry rather than custodial release. The provinces have not established mandatory supervision regimes and, therefore, release from a provincial institution by reason of earned remission is not followed by supervision until warrant expiry. Section 731(2) of the *Code* provides that when a person who has been sentenced to imprisonment in a penitentiary receives, "before the expiration of that sentence", another sentence of imprisonment for a term of less than 2 years, the subsequent term shall be served in a penitentiary as well. In *Dinardo, supra*, note 113, the Ontario Court of Appeal was faced with a prisoner who had been released on mandatory supervision and then convicted of an offence committed before his release. Accordingly, the new conviction was not an appropriate ground for revocation and the prisoner's mandatory supervision remained unrevoked. He was sentenced to a term of 18 months' imprisonment and transferred to a penitentiary to serve that term. The court agreed that, by reason of section 659(2) [now s. 731(2)], the new sentence should be served in a penitentiary even though it was less than 2 years. Martin J.A. interpreted "expiration" in section 659(2) as referring to the warrant expiry date rather than to the expiration of the custodial part of the prisoner's original sentence. The *Dinardo* decision suggests that any interrupting sentences, no matter how brief, should also be served in a penitentiary. Transfers to the penitentiary for short interrupting sentences will likely be cumbersome and even counter-productive. On the other hand, if the prisoner remains in a provincial institution to serve the interrupting sentence, then release by reason of earned remission will not be followed by supervision and the

concepts of both merger and interruption. While the interruption of the term of release occurs upon imposition of a consecutive "later sentence", the interruption ceases if there is a subsequent revocation or termination. At that point, the new sentence and the remanet would merge. As well, anticipating the situation where further sentences are imposed during the period of interruption, sections 20(1.2) and (1.3) provide for the merger of additional sentences with the "later sentence", which earlier had triggered the interruption, thereby extending the period of interruption. The new amendments even attempt to anticipate the problems which can arise when a prisoner has had his release interrupted by reason of a "later sentence" and then is granted parole in respect of that "later sentence". If the prisoner receives an additional sentence, but the Board chooses not to revoke or terminate the new release, the additional sentence triggers a new interruption.[123]

Legislation that introduces complex mechanisms like merger and interruption invariably leads to controversy when it is applied to unusual circumstances. In these situations, resort to basic principles of statutory interpretation, the general framework of sentence calculation and the ambiguity principle ought to provide answers to unforeseen problems. However, this is not always the case. One issue which has produced recent litigation involved the complicated circumstances of a

---

interrupted mandatory supervision will not recommence until the expiry of the warrant for the new sentence. This gap, during which no conditions would apply and revocation could not be effected, is inconsistent with the purposes underlying the regime of mandatory supervision and the mechanism of interruption. *Dinardo* represents the rare case where the new conviction and sentence related to pre-release conduct and, hence, could not be a ground for revocation. The more common situation giving rise to interruption will be a person receiving a new sentence which, because of the nature of the offence or the shortness of the sentence, the Board does not consider warrants revocation. Thus, it is reasonable to assume that Parliament contemplated that new sentences which result in interruption will likely be shorter terms of imprisonment. The ruling in *Dinardo* provides the means by which the interrupting sentences will be served in a penitentiary and, thus, avoids the gap that would follow if the sentence was served in a provincial institution. However, notwithstanding *Dinardo*, one must be circumspect about the extent to which Parliament fully understood the implications of interruption, since gaps in supervision will necessarily arise in respect of any new sentence of 4 months or less. This results from the fact that section 21(2) of the *Parole Act* makes mandatory supervision applicable to any release by reason of remission where "the term of the remission exceeds sixty days". Any sentence of 4 months or less will not produce more than 60 days' remission. Hence, upon release from custody in respect of the new interrupting sentence, the prisioner will not be subject to conditions or amenable to revocation for a period equal to the amount of remission earned, since the original term of mandatory supervision does not "kick back in" until the expiry of the warrant for the new interrupting sentence.

123 See section 20(1.2)(*b*)(i).

release, and a new consecutive sentence, followed by another concurrent sentence and then a revocation of the original release. For ease of explanation, we will use original term, second sentence and third sentence to refer to the interrupted term, the consecutive "later sentence" and the concurrent "additional sentence" respectively. Up to the point of the ultimate revocation, sections 20(1.2)(*a*) and (1.3) would operate to postpone the resumption of the original remanet until the merged new sentences had expired. This would ignore the trial judge's direction that the third sentence be served concurrently to all sentences because of the explicit deeming provision in section 20(1.3). Upon revocation, however, no interruption takes place and the calculation is determined by section 20(1.4) which provides that the prisoner serve the aggregate of the original remanet and the second sentence. Full effect could be given to the sentencing judge's direction by commencing the third sentence upon its imposition so that it runs concurrently to this aggregate. However, the C.S.C. has taken the position that the third sentence can only be concurrent to the second sentence, both of which will be followed by the remanet. This operates to the prisoner's detriment if the third sentence extends beyond the second sentence. The rationale for this approach apparently is that, at the time of imposition of the third sentence, the prisoner was serving only the second sentence pursuant to section 20(1.1). This curious position is reminiscent of the pre-merger era when sentences were served as individual units.[124] One would have thought it would have been rejected by reference to the general merger provision in section 20(1)[125] combined with the fact that it countermands the trial judge's direction to the prisoner's detriment. At the very least, the governing statutory provisions are ambiguous and should be interpreted in the prisoner's favour.[126] The C.S.C. position has been upheld in one case now on appeal to the Ontario Court of Appeal.[127] In the Federal Court case of *Fontaine*,[128] Jerome A.C.J. held that section 20(1.3) indicated a parliamentary intention that the *Parole Act* could override judicial sentencing discretion.

While Parliament has accommodated both merger and interruption into the current release regime, there is a significant distinction between the two which should be kept in mind when calculating sentences. The opening words of section 20(1), the merger provision, are:

---

[124] See, for example, *Re McCaud* (1969), 7 C.R.N.S. 222 (Ont. S.C.).

[125] See *Re Dean and R.* (1977), 35 C.C.C. (2d) 217 (Ont. C.A.).

[126] See *Re Carriere and R., supra*, note 103, for the application of the ambiguity principle in related circumstances.

[127] See *Re Brant and R.* (Ont. H.C., Chadwick J., May 29, 1990).

[128] *Fontaine v. C.S.C.* (Fed. T.D., Jerome A.C.J., August 21, 1990).

Where either before, on or after, the coming into force of this section, . . .

This preface suggests that all calculations for the purposes of determining release dates or remission credits should be effected pursuant to the current merger provision regardless of when the sentences were imposed. The interruption provisions contained in sections 20(1.1) to (1.6) are not prefaced with the same phrase. They only apply in cases of additional sentences imposed after July 25, 1986. This is consistent with the notion that the length of a sentence, as compared to the manner in which it must be served, should not be varied retroactively.

Within the jigsaw puzzle of sentence calculation, merger and interruption appear to be carefully crafted pieces which reflect appreciation of the practical effects which these mechanisms produce. However, we maintain that it is still important to ask whether the concept of interruption is consistent with both the reality and the conceptual basis of release from imprisonment. By extending the mechanism of interruption to parole, Parliament has redressed the apparent inconsistency that was created by the previous section 15(4). However, in doing so it has cast doubt on what is the real rationale for interruption. Because parole is usually denied where the Board has concerns about post-release conduct that may result in prosecution, the interruption provision should only apply in cases where the new sentence arises while the prisoner is released on parole, but the new sentence is considered insignificant or unrelated.[129] One can assume that, to fit into the categories which will not compel revocation, the conduct cannot be serious and, hence, the sentence will be short. If so, what is the point of extending the release period? This question is particularly interesting when one recognizes that short sentences will produce the "gap" problem discussed above.

The answer must lie either in a rehabilitative concern or simply a positive response. Many critics of the mandatory supervision regime argue that its central feature is surveillance and not supervision; that it is intrinsically punitive and not rehabilitative or facilitative. These arguments suggest that interruption represents simply another punitive response to prisoners in order to extend the period of control. Regardless of the rationale for interruption, little is gained by the mechanism and the new complexities which it will doubtless generate are not worth the exercise. Furthermore, coherence is not achieved by requiring prisoners to return to the penitentiary to serve short sentences. The penitentiary milieu is so far removed from the reality of the community that one

---

[129] For exampie, where the parolee is prosecuted for offences arising prior to incarceration for the offence(s) on which he has been paroled. See the discussion of *Dinardo, supra,* note 122.

cannot seriously argue that a mechanism which necessarily requires a return to penitentiary has anything to do either with rehabilitation or reintegration. Interruption is yet another example of an uncoordinated and unintegrated approach to sentencing, imprisonment and release.

(d) Disappearance While on Release

Section 19(1) of the *Parole Act* states that "the term of imprisonment of a paroled inmate, shall, while the parole remains unrevoked, be deemed to continue in force until the expiration thereof according to law". By virtue of section 21(2), this provision applies equally to persons released on mandatory supervision. In conceptual terms, section 19(1) appears to enshrine the notion that conditional release is an alternative mode of serving a term of imprisonment—that is, unless a revocation is effected, the term of imprisonment is deemed to continue until W.E.D. is reached. Practical problems arise when persons on conditional release disappear or simply cannot be located by parole authorities. The usual practice has been to suspend release and to issue a suspension warrant authorizing the apprehension of the individual and a return to close custody pending an investigation of the circumstances.[130] However, section 19(1) refers to revocation and not suspension. Hence, at least arguably, the sentence would continue to run.

In *Vidlin,*[131] a suspension warrant was issued because the prisoner had failed to report to his police officer. He was not apprehended until after the date upon which his sentence was scheduled to expire. On an application for *habeas corpus,* Anderson J. held that the issuance of a suspension warrant did not prevent the sentence from running during the period of suspension. Accordingly, the sentence expired prior to the execution of the warrant and there existed no power to pursue the suspension process towards revocation. As a result of this ruling, the federal parole authorities developed the practice of requesting the Board to exercise its general power to revoke under section 10(1)(*e*) [now s.16 (1)(*d*)] prior to the warrant expiry date once a suspension warrant has been outstanding for more than 60 days.[132]

Although the prisoner was released in *Vidlin,* the ruling raises questions about the calculation of sentences when suspension warrants are issued but not immediately executed. Upon revocation, section

---

[130] See the discussion of *Swan v. B.C. (A.G.)* (1983), 35 C.R. (3d) 135 (B.C. S.C.) in Chapter 8.

[131] *Re Vidlin and R.* (1976), 38 C.C.C. (2d) 378 (B.C. S.C.). It is noteworthy that no effort was made to legislate away the holding in this case in the 1986 amendments.

[132] See the comments of McEachern J. in *Swan, supra,* note 130.

25(2)(*b*) provides credit for days in custody after suspension. This appears to be inconsistent with the rationale of *Vidlin* that a sentence continues to run after suspension. In *Re Bishop*,[133] a prisoner who had disappeared challenged a calculation of his remanet which did not credit him with the time between suspension and his apprehension on the suspension warrant. Hinds J. distinguished *Vidlin* by characterizing the point in issue in that case as involving "the determination of whether an inmate's parole could be validly revoked after the expiry of the scheduled term of imprisonment."[134] The prisoner in *Bishop*, on the other hand, had been validly revoked and was seeking credits towards his remanet, which conformed with the notion of a sentence that continued during the suspension period. To reconcile sections 13(1) and 20(2) [now ss.19(1) and 25(2)], Hinds J. relied upon two day parole cases, *Ex parte Davidson*[135] and *Re Zong and Commissioner of Penitentiaries*,[136] relating to earlier versions of the *Parole Act* which provided for automatic forfeiture. In *Zong*, Le Dain J. concluded that:

> . . . section 13 must be construed to mean that provided the inmate's parole is not revoked or forfeited he is deemed to be serving his term of imprisonment while he is on parole, but upon revocation or forfeiture he loses the benefit of this provision and is required by the terms of ss. 20 or 21 as the case may be, to serve the portion of his term of imprisonment that remained unexpired at the time his parole was granted. . . . this is the only way that effect can be given to both provisions.[137]

Hinds J. reasoned that since section 13(2) [now s. 19(2)] describes the effect of parole while it is neither revoked nor suspended, and section 13(1) [now s. 19(1)] describes the effect of parole while it is unrevoked, these sections are irrelevant when parole has both been suspended and revoked. Thus, only section 20 [now s. 25] applies to determine the calculation of the remanet on revocation. As a result, the credit for "time spent on parole" provided by section 25(2)(*a*) refers only to the pre-suspension period before the authority to be at large was withdrawn. The only credits which relate to the suspension period are those contained in section 20(2)(*b*) and (*c*) [now s. 25(2)(*b*) and (*c*)] which apply to prisoners on parole or mandatory supervision, have been suspended and are *in custody*.

The decision in *Bishop* was approved a few months later in an oral judgment of the British Columbia Court of Appeal in *Scott*.[138] This

---

[133] [Summarized (1984), 11 W.C.B. 266 (B.C. S.C.)].

[134] *Ibid.*

[135] (1975), 22 C.C.C. (2d) 122 (B.C. C.A.).

[136] (1975), 22 C.C.C. (2d) 553 (Fed. T.D.). Affirmed (1976), 29 C.C.C. (2d) 114 (Fed. C.A.).

[137] *Ibid.*, at (Fed. C.A.), at 120-121.

[138] The prisoner raised the same issue as part of two separate in-person appeals. *R. v. Scott* [summarized (1984), 12 W.C.B. 114 (B.C. C.A.), and (1984), 12 W.C.B. 500 (B.C. C.A.)].

appears to entrench the somewhat anomalous distinction between a parolee who evades capture until after the expiry of his period of parole or mandatory supervision and a parolee who is apprehended prior to his warrant expiry date. The former cannot be revoked, unless the Board resorts to its general power prior to expiry, while the latter can be revoked and receives no credit for the time on suspension before apprehension. Thus, the prisoner's warrant expiry date is extended by the number of days between the issuance of the suspension warrant and his apprehension.

While it may seem attractive to deny credit to a parolee who has disappeared, the effect of *Vidlin* is to benefit the person who manages to avoid apprehension until after warrant expiry. The practice of revoking after 60 days permits the Board to retain power over the parolee regardless of apprehension, but provides no incentive for him to return to the fold. The consequences of this practice have been somewhat ameliorated by the decision in *Swan*, requiring a post-revocation hearing. Thus, there exists some opportunity to offer an explanation which might result in a reversal of the decision to revoke.

Before leaving the issue of disappearance, two further questions need to be raised. First, not all parolees who have been apprehended on suspension warrants will be revoked. These people will not be affected by the gap between suspension and apprehension by reason of section 19(1) and the decision in *Vidlin*. What happens, however, if by reason of subsequent events the person is suspended again and ultimately revoked? The ruling in *Bishop* would suggest that a strict application of section 25(2) would operate to deny credit for this earlier period, even though it is unrelated to the current revocation process. Secondly, there are numerous prisoners who are subject to suspension warrants but who are apprehended as a result of another process. The suspension warrant is unexecuted, but the time, if the parolee is subsequently revoked, qualifies as time in custody while suspended. Both sections 25(2)(*b*) and (*c*) refer to "time during which the inmate's parole was suspended *and* the inmate was in custody". Neither provision requires explicitly that the custody be linked to the suspension. Hence, credit should be allowed both by reason of a strict reading of the statute and to avoid the potential for abuse which would arise from a deliberate failure to execute a suspension warrant. Despite the ruling in *Kent v. Director of Stony Mountain*,[139] it is the current practice of sentence administrators to allow credit for any time spent in custody.

---

[139] (Man. Q.B., June 10, 1982).

7. ESCAPE AND RELATED OFFENCES

The special treatment afforded by the *Code* and other penal statutes to the offences commonly known as escapes,[140] has confounded lawyers, sentence administrators, sentencing judges and appellate courts. While much of the source of controversy was removed by the *Criminal Law Amendment Act, 1977*, its legacy remains. One still sees a few calculations which antedate its enactment and involve pre-1977 escapes. As well, the arcane rulings which were generated by the pre-1977 confusion have spawned other rulings which occasionally have contemporary impact. For the most part, however, escape sentences can now be treated like other sentences, and the following discussion is purposefully brief. Its historical content will probably interest only a select few. It does, however, dramatize the failure of legislators to appreciate fully the systemic effect of enactments to address particular situations which inevitably collide with other provisions dealing with other situations.

(a) Pre-October 15, 1977

During this period, section 22(4) of the *Penitentiary Act* provided for the forfeiture of three-quarters of the statutory remission standing to a prisoner's credit at the time of an escape upon conviction for the escape. As of July 15, 1972,[141] the *Criminal Code* provided:

> **137.** (1) Except where otherwise provided by the *Parole Act*, a person who escapes while undergoing imprisonment *shall, after undergoing any punishment to which he is sentenced for that escape, serve the portion of the term of imprisonment that he was serving, including statutory remission but not including earned remission,* at the time of his escape that he had not then served minus any time that he spent in custody between the date on which he was apprehended after his escape and the date on which he was sentenced for that escape. [Emphasis added.]

On its face, this enactment appeared to deal with all the components of the service of escape sentences: consecutive, remanet, remission and credit for pre-sentence custody. The phrase "serve the portion of the term of imprisonment that he was serving, including statutory remission but not including earned remission" was borrowed from the *Parole Act* and had been interpreted in that context as providing for the

---

[140] The offences delineated in the relevant portion of section 149 of the *Code* comprise escaping from lawful custody and being unlawfully at large. Prior to December 4, 1985, these offences were prosecuted purely by indictment; by virtue of S.C. 1974-785-76, c. 93, s. 7(1), prosecutions for these offences are now Crown elections.

[141] R.S.C. 1970, c. C-34 [as amended by S.C. 1972, c. 13, s. 9].

forfeiture of *all* statutory remission standing to the prisoner's credit at the time of the escape.[142] Thus, section 137(1) [now s. 149(1)] of the *Code* was plainly and directly inconsistent with section 22(4) of the *Penitentiary Act*, as it read at the time.

In *Clarke*,[143] Reid J. held that the enactment of section 137(1) [now s. 149(1)] repealed by implication section 22(4) of the *Penitentiary Act*.[144] At first glance, this would appear to have a detrimental effect on the prisoner's sentence, since it required the forfeiture of all statutory remission rather than just three-quarters. However, Reid J. took the calculation exercise a step further by holding that section 137 created a new term of imprisonment consisting of the merger of the remanet of the previous sentence plus the escape sentence, which required a new credit of statutory remission. Section 22(1) of the *Penitentiary Act*, as it read at the time, provided a statutory remission credit of one-fourth of sentence to every person "sentenced or committed to the penitentiary for a fixed term". Accordingly, escapes prior to July 15, 1972 resulted in the loss of three-fourth of a prisoner's statutory remission. In both cases, however, prisoners derived a benefit due to the subsequent credit of statutory remission on the new term. The extent of this benefit depended upon the length of the original sentence and the point during that sentence at which the escape occurred. The benefit decreased as one moved farther into the sentence since a shorter remanet produced a smaller credit on the new escape term.[145]

(b) The Criminal Law Amendment Act, 1976-77

The major impact of *Clarke* was the notion that the escape provision created a new term. This was significant because a new term attracted another grant of statutory remission. Whether this concept should have been extended to forfeitures and revocations under the provisions of the *Parole Act* as they had previously stood became academic, due to the repeal of the statutory remission regime as of July 1,

---

[142] *Howley v. Canada (Deputy A.G.)* (1977), 30 C.C.C. (2d) 106 (S.C.C.).

[143] *Re Clarke and R.* (Ont. H.C., Reid J., February 7, 1978).

[144] A penal statute has the effect of repealing by implication an earlier penal statute if both provisions affix different punishments to the same offence: see P. St. J. Langan, *Maxwell's Interpretation of Statutes*, 12th ed. (London: Sweet & Maxwell, 1969), at 195; *Mitchell v. Brown* (1858), 1 E. & E. 267; *Henderson v. Sherborne* (1837), 150 E.R. 743.

[145] Algebraically, it could be shown that the new calculation format was always beneficial to the prisoner, although this benefit, compared to the previous format, diminished to zero if the escape occurred on the prisoner's release date.

1978. As well, section 137 of the *Code* was amended and re-shaped,[146] making no reference to remission or to the components of an escape sentence, and permitting a trial judge to choose between a concurrent and consecutive sentence.

The concept of the "new term" developed in *Clarke* came back to the detriment of prisoners in determining the maximum remission a prisoner could earn during the transition between the old remission regime and the current one. Section 24.2 of the *Penitentiary Act* put a cap on accumulated remission (whether statutory or earned) at one-third of the "sentence he is then serving". It was suggested by institutional authorities that, in cases of escape sentences, the single sentence which generated the one-third limit began on the date the escape sentence was imposed since it created a new sentence.[147] This position was rejected by the Federal Court of Appeal in *MacIntyre*.[148] Both concurring judgments rejected the "new term" concept and, by application of then section 14(1) of the *Parole Act*, deemed the single sentence to commence on the date of the original sentence, prior to the escape.[149]

(c) Current Calculations

Much of the above history has little practical application to current calculations since there are now very few prisoners in the system whose sentences begin before 1977. However, another aspect of the decision in *MacIntyre* raised an issue which has led to considerable litigation. In that case, between the date of the escape and the date of imposition of the sentence for the escape, the prisoner received another sentence of 9 years for offences committed while unlawfully at large. Notwithstanding the express statutory reference to section 14 [now s. 20] of the *Parole Act* in the escape sentencing provisions in the *Code*, the question arose as to how an intervening sentence could be integrated with the requirements

---

[146] S.C. 1976-77, c. 53, s. 6.
[147] This was the necessary implication of *Re Sowa and R.* (1979), 50 C.C.C. (2d) 513 (Sask. C.A.). Perhaps because this case was argued personally by the prisoner, the judgment makes no mention of section 24.2 of the *Penitentiary Act; cf. MacIntyre, infra,* note 148.
[148] *Re MacIntyre and R.* (1982), 70 C.C.C. (2d) 542 (Fed. C.A.), reversing (1981), 64 C.C.C. (2d) 360 (Fed. T.D.).
[149] In *Pask v. R.* (File no. T-29900-83, Fed. T.D., Muldoon J., May 23, 1984), the same reasoning was applied to pre-1977 forfeitures of parole, such that the limit on remission that could be earned under the new regime was calculated on the basis of a single sentence which antedated the forfeiture. This permitted prisoners who had been forfeited or revoked before October 15, 1977 to re-earn much of the statutory remission lost as a result of the forfeiture or revocation.

of section 137 [now s. 149] of the *Code*. Since the 1977 amendments to the *Code*, escape sentencing is determined by an amended provision:

> **149.** (1) A person convicted for an escape committed while undergoing imprisonment shall be sentenced to serve the term of imprisonment to which he is sentenced for the escape *either concurrently with the portion of the term of imprisonment that he was serving at the time of his escape that he had not served or*, if the court, judge, justice or provincial court judge by whom he is sentenced for the escape so orders, *consecutively* . . . .[150] [Emphasis added.]

Thus, the sentencing judge seems to be empowered to treat escape sentences like those applicable to other offenses. A careful reading of this power to sentence concurrently or consecutively, however, indicates that it relates only to the unexpired portion of the original sentence. Section 149(1) does not speak to the question of an intervening sentence.

In a consent judgment in *Sinobert*,[151] the legal advisors to the federal Solicitor General accepted the position advanced by the prisoner, namely that an escape sentence could not be made consecutive to an intervening sentence, but only to the portion of the original sentence still remaining to be served at the time of escape. Because this had the effect of reducing the total sentence (by effectively making the punishment for the escape concurrent with the punishment for offences committed while unlawfully at large), it was not surprising that prisoners began to launch applications for *habeas corpus*.[152] *Sinobert* was quickly followed in several judgments.[153]

---

[150] R.S.C. 1985, c. 27 (1st Supp.), s. 20. Although section 133(1) [now s. 145(1)] of the *Code* was modified from an indictable offence to a Crown election offence, no attempt was made to amend the substantive provision contained in section 137 [now s. 149].

[151] (Ont. H.C., September 3, 1982).

[152] It is important to note the position of the federal authorities following *Sinobert*. Sentence administrators were instructed to conduct audits of all sentences and to advise prisoners potentially affected by the ruling to seek legal advice. At the same time, however, C.S.C. took the position that since the actual committal warrants in each case were valid on their face until effectively quashed by an order for *habeas corpus*, it would not unilaterally re-compute sentences of all affected prisoners. In other words, while C.S.C. would advise prisoners of their potential right to a reduction of sentence, and would usually instruct counsel for the Attorney General of Canada not to oppose (but not to consent to) an order for *habeas corpus*, prisoners would still have to litigate their way out of jail. This led to a large number of consent *habeas corpus* judgments. An attempt to reduce the volume of litigation by launching a class action was dismissed by the Federal Court in *Deane v. C.S.C.* (1986), 2 F.T.R. 239 (T.D.), the court holding that it had no power to order the defendant to re-compute all sentences.

[153] *R. v. Naugle* (1985), 68 N.S.R. (2d) 99 (T.D.); Bernier v. R. (No. 500-10-000034-858, Que. C.A., May 16, 1986); *R. v. Bush* (Ont. C.A., June 10, 1987); *Re Frankum and R.* (1986), 29 C.C.C. (3d) 477 (B.C. C.A.).

It was equally not surprising that because prisoners were "immunized from punishment for their escapes"[154] provincial Attorneys General, who in our constitutional structure have more responsibility for the punitive aspect of sentencing principles than their federal counterparts, began to seek ways to avoid the thrust of the *Sinobert* line of cases. In *Gould*,[155] counsel for the Attorney General of Ontario sought and was granted an extension of time to appeal both the escape sentence and the intervening sentence for an offence committed while unlawfully at large. Accordingly, the court was able to vary both sentences so as not only to conform with the provisions of section 137 [now s. 149] of the *Code*, but also to give effect to what appeared to be the sentencing judge's intention.[156]

In a trilogy of cases recently argued together[157] Crown counsel persuaded a majority of the Ontario Court of Appeal that even in the absence of an appeal against the fitness of the sentences imposed for the

---

[154] The phrase is from *Frankum, ibid.*

[155] *R. v. Gould* (Ont. C.A., June 11, 1985), reversing *R. v. Gould* (Ont. H.C., February 19, 1985).

[156] *Gould* may have been complicated by the fact that it would appear that trial counsel inadvertently misled the judge who sentenced the prisoner both for the escape and for the offence committed while unlawfully at large. In the later case of *Bush* (Ont. C.A., June 10, 1987), the appellant had escaped while he was both serving a sentence and awaiting the continuation of a trial on a robbery charge. He was re-arrested and subsequently sentenced to 11 years for the armed robbery. A month later, he was convicted of escaping lawful custody and sentenced to 18 months "consecutive to time serving". The phrase "time serving" would necessarily mean both the sentence being served at the time of the escape and the intervening 11 years sentence. The appellant argued that, in order to conform with section 137 [now s. 149] the escape sentence could not be consecutive to the robbery sentence as the judge who had sentenced the prisoner for the escape (who was not the same judge who sentenced the prisoner for the robbery) was only empowered to make it concurrent or consecutive to the remanet of the original sentence. In response, the Crown argued that "this would be an absurd conclusion because the result is that escpaees in these situations would be immunized from punishment". The court concluded that the appellant was correct, particularly after considering the French version of section 137 [now s. 149]. It allowed the appeal in order that the 18-month sentence for escaping lawful custody be served consecutively to the remanet of the original sentence.

[157] *R. v. Easton; R. v. Young; R. v. Phillips;* (Ont. C.A., July 17, 1989). *Easton* and *Young* were Crown appeals from the decisions of a Motions Court judge quashing sentences imposed for escape which purported to sentence the prisoners to terms "consecutive to any time now being served". *Phillips* was an appeal by the prisoner from the dismissal of a Motions Court judge of his application for an order directing that a sentence imposed for escape was illegal "because it was made consecutive not to the time being served at the time of the escape but rather to a sentence imposed after the escape". As this book goes to press, leave is currently being sought to appeal these decisions to the Supreme Court of Canada.

offences committed while unlawfully at large and the sentence imposed for the escape (as was the case in *Gould*), it had the power to reverse the sequence of sentences in order to achieve the intention of the sentencing judges. The majority held that even though the Motions Court judges had not been asked to adjudicate upon the sentences imposed for the offences committed while the prisoners were unlawfully at large, nevertheless those sentences "formed part of the proceedings" before those judges. Accordingly, the Motions Court judges (and therefore the Court of Appeal) had the power to deal with those sentences by virtue of the closing words of section 777 of the *Code*, which section in essence provides that a judge or court hearing an application for *certiorari* may "deal with the proceedings in the manner that the court or judge considers proper".

Galligan J.A. dissented, holding that since only the legality of the sentences imposed for the escapes were before the Motions Court judges, neither they nor the Court of Appeal had the jurisdiction to deal with the sentences for the other offences. Even though the remedial powers conferred by section 777 "are broad in their terms", Galligan J.A. was "unable to read [them] as authorizing the use of the remedial powers to vary sentences the legal validity of which are not called into question in the proceeding then before the court." In the absence of a Crown appeal to the Court of Appeal against the fitness of all of the sentences, the Court of Appeal "had no power to reverse the sequence of the sentences."[158]

The dissent is compelling. At issue in a *habeas corpus* proceeding is the legality of the sentence. If successful, the usual order is a discharge from custody or order that the prisoner be moved to a regime where confinement would be lawful.[159] Unlike an appellate court, the judge hearing the application has no power to vary the sentence, even to give effect to the sentencing judge's intention.

It is only through an appreciation of the erratic history of the *Code* provision that one can understand its current structure.[160] It remains important that counsel be sensitive to the intricacies of the current provision, both to enable appropriate submissions to be made in the

---

[158] *Easton; Young; Phillips, ibid.*

[159] See the discussion of *habeas corpus* in Chapter 3. The only qualification to this statement of remedial scope is section 775 of the *Criminal Code* which has no bearing on issues of this sort: see A. Manson, *Bail and Habeas Corpus* (Law Society of Upper Canada: Criminal Law Developments, 1985).

[160] In *Frankum, supra,* note 153, at 479, Lambert J.A. noted *in obiter* that "[i]t may well be that legislative consideration, or reconsideration, of the relationship between s. 137 of the *Criminal Code* and s. 14 of the *Parole Act* will be the only way to resolve the many anamalous situations that were illustrated, during argument, by example".

course of sentencing for an escape-related offence, but also in respect to advising prisoners of possible appeals or sentence calculation problems arising from erroneous interpretations of the various provisions.

8. CAUTIONS ABOUT CALCULATIONS

As stated at the outset, the most important step in completing a calculation is the preparation of the chronology of events which corresponds to the warrants and facts of each prisoner's case. The foregoing discussion makes it apparent that there are a number of events which should immediately attract the calculator's attention:

1. Consecutive sentences.
2. Conditional release and subsequent revocations.
3. Periods of suspension and any remission earned while in custody on suspension.
4. Periods of suspension, followed by revocation, when the prisoner was not in custody.
5. Escape sentences which need to be related to the *Code* provision applicable at the time of the sentence.
6. Any remission earned before October 15, 1977.

We would be remiss if we did not leave this subject without one further comment. In talking to prisoners, lawyers and penal administrators who have had the experience of attempting to translate several warrants into eligibility and release dates in whose accuracy all may have a reasonable degree of confidence, one often hears "computers" offered as a solution. Technology, however, cannot cure the problems of poor drafting and conflicting consequences which all too often plague sentence calculations. Given the interaction between sentencing powers, locus of confinement, merger, interruption, remission and conditional release, it is almost inevitable that changes intended to effect one result will produce unexpected effects elsewhere in the system. For too many years these effects have been inconsistent, anomalous and irreconcilable. This is the result of almost three decades of tinkering. Regardless of one's view of imprisonment and conditional release and their various justifications, there can be no excuse for a legal infrastructure which generates uncertainty and confusion on the part of those most intimately affected by it.

Many of the recent amendments contained in the 1986 amendments[161] reflect the admirable intention of removing inconsistencies;

---

[161] It is noteworthy that it took almost 9 years to pilot these "housekeeping" amendments through the Canadian parliamentary system. Even more significant was that the only reason they were enacted in 1986 was that they were "piggybacked" onto the "gating" legislation.

however, the task is only partly finished. At this stage of statutory "adhesion" it may be impossible to make fundamental changes. It is time to isolate all statutory provisions which impact on sentences and sentence calculation in order to replace them with a coherent system which would be simple, clear, capable of effecting judicial intention, and productive of like results in like situations. In our view, legislative drafters, legislators, sentence administrators, and the judges ultimately called upon to interpret these provisions should all commence their projects by reminding themselves of Dickson J's. over-riding concern expressed in *Marcotte v. Deputy Attorney General of Canada*:

> It is unnecessary to emphasize the importance of clarity and certainty when freedom is at stake. No authority is needed for the proposition that if real ambiguities are found, or doubts of substance arise, in the construction and application of a statute affecting the liberty of a subject, then that statute should be applied in such a manner as to favour the person against whom it is sought to be enforced. If one is to be incarcerated, one should at least know that some Act of Parliament requires it in express terms, and not, at most, by implication.[162]

9. ETHICAL ISSUES

It is not uncommon that a prisoner will seek an opinion on the accuracy of a calculation and that the lawyer will discover that an error has been made in the prisoner's favour. The various Professional Rules of Conduct indicate that there is no obligation on a lawyer to bring this to the attention of institutional authorities. However, the client should be advised that an audit may take place or that some subsequent event may attract a re-calculation which brings to light the earlier error. In discussions or correspondence with institutional authorities, the lawyer should be careful not to mislead either by offering an inaccurate factual account or calculation which, according to law, he or she knows to be wrong. This caveat is not simply a righteous-sounding reiteration of the advocate's duty. The prison and parole contexts are, unfortunately, pervaded by mutual mistrust. Credibility is a valuable commodity which can easily be eradicated.

---

[162] (1974), 19 C.C.C. (2d) 257 (S.C.C.), at 262.

11

Pardons and
the Royal Prerogative of Mercy

The law concerning punishment is a categorical imperative and woe to him who rummages around in the winding paths of a theory of happiness looking for some advantage to be gained by releasing the criminal from punishment. . . .[1]

1. HISTORY

The oldest form of relief from the imposition of a punishment or sentence is the exercise of some form of pardoning power. Examples can be traced back to the ancient kingdoms of Israel and Greece.[2] In England, the Royal Prerogative of Mercy as an instrument exercised by or in the name of the Crown has its roots in the Anglo-Saxon period. Initially, the power to pardon was virtually the sovereign's monopoly.[3] However, before Henry III came of age, pardons were granted on the authority of his regent, sometimes with the advice of the King's council. These pardons took the form of letters patent issued under the King's seal or, occasionally, the seal of the regent himself.[4] This practice evolved such that while the King was away on campaign, the pardoning power was usually delegated to the Chancellor who issued pardons in the King's name.[5]

Pardons were considered to be an aspect of the general power of a sovereign to determine appropriate punishment. Later, as statutes were enacted prescribing specific penalties for offences, the power to grant pardons became the King's residual role in the process of punishment. For example, during the reigns of Athelstan and Edmund, early statutes

---

[1]   I. Kant, *The Metaphysical Elements of Justice* (New York: Bobbs-Merrill, 1965), p. 100.

[2]   See S. Rubin, *The Law of Criminal Correction*, 2d ed. (St. Paul: West Publishing, 1973) pp. 657-658. The original chapter in the first edition was written by H. Weihofen.

[3]   It could also be exercised by the Lords of the Palatinates of Chester and Durham: see N. Hurand, *The King's Pardon for Homicide Before A.D. 1307* (Oxford: Clarendon Press, 1960), pp. 214-215.

[4]   *Ibid.*

[5]   *Ibid.*, pp. 219-221.

stipulating punishment were qualified by the phrase "unless the King was willing to pardon him".[6]

The power to pardon has been described by the author of *Kenny's Outlines of Criminal Law* as a residual aspect of the criminal law:

> It has often been maintained that a perfect code would remove all necessity for a power of pardon. . . . But long experience has shown that human foresight is incompetent to frame and human language to express a faultless scheme of legislation. The power of pardon therefore is one which is indispensible to the side administration of penal justice.[7]

Before 1307, pardons were used principally to excuse homicides in cases of mischance, involuntary killing and defence of life and property.[8] As well, the grant of a pardon was the only way for an infant or mentally disabled person to escape the death penalty for murder.[9] While these were the primary functions of pardons in medieval times, abuses of the power were common, as were complaints of favouritism, elitism and financial gain.[10] Notwithstanding examples of manipulation, it is clear that the antecedent rationale of the pardoning power lay in notions of justice and mercy. As the criminal law began to recognize concepts of excuse, justification and incapacity, the traditional role of the pardon diminished substantially. In the early years, however, its primary use was to prevent the death penalty in situations where it seemed harsh, unjust or inappropriate to the circumstances of the offence or the offender.[11]

The role of the pardon developed a further dimension when it became used as an aid to prosecutions. In order to obtain evidence of crimes, pardons were promised to accomplices who were prepared to give testimony which led to the conviction of their confederates. In the 17th and 18th Centuries, there were 14 statutes in England which provided free pardons for those whose evidence resulted in the conviction of one or more accomplices.[12] These were pardons granted in

---

6   See VI Athelstan, c. 1 and II Edmund, c. 6, referred to in Hurand, *supra*, note 3, p. 1.
7   J.W.C. Turner, *Kenny's Outlines of Criminal Law*, 19th ed. (Cambridge: Cambridge University Press: 1966), p. 635, para. 784.
8   See Hurand, *supra*, note 3, p. viii.
9   *Ibid.*
10 *Ibid.*, p. vii: Edward I obtained recruits by promising pardons. See also K. Moore, *Pardons: Justice, Mercy and the Public Interest* (New York: Oxford University Press, 1989); C.H. Rolph, *The Queen's Pardon* (London: Cassell Ltd., 1978), pp. 18-21.
11 *Ibid.*, p. 224. See also Rubin, supra, note 2, pp. 657-660.
12 See L. Radzinowicz, *History of English Criminal Law, Vol. 2* (London: Stevens & Sons, 1956), pp. 40-42. Prior to this time, persons indicted for felonies could confess before plea and accuse another in order to obtain a pardon. This practice was called "approvement" and only applied in capital cases: see 4 Blackstone's Commentaries 330.

advance of conviction, and often in advance of prosecution. They can best be characterized as a form of immunity given in exchange for testimony. In most cases, the statutory offer was available to any person not in custody who secured the conviction of at least two accomplices.[13]

With respect to Canada, the first Governors General were entrusted by the monarch to exercise personal discretion over pardons.[14] However, as a result of the controversy over the pardon granted to Ambrose Lepine,[15] new Letters Patent and Instructions were issued to the Governor General in 1878.[16] In capital cases, the Instructions required the Governor General to receive the advice of the Privy Council. In other cases, the advice of at least one minister was required.[17] In 1892,

---

[13]   *Radzinowicz, Ibid.*

[14]   With respect to convictions arising from statutes of a provincial legislature the Lieutenant Governor of the province has the power to grant a pardon: *Canada (A.G.) v. Ontario (A.G.)*, [1890] O.R. 222. Affirmed (1894), 23 S.C.R. 458.

[15]   In this case, it appears that the Governor General acted alone due to the controversy that existed within the Cabinet. Ambrose Lepine was a Métis leader involved with Riel in what is commonly called the Red River rebellion. As adjutant general in the provisional government, he presided over the court martial which resulted in the death of Thomas Scott. In 1873, he was tried as an accomplice to the murder of Scott. Although convicted and sentenced to hang, the sentence was commuted to 2 years' imprisonment plus forfeiture of his civil rights. The latter penalty was ultimately removed. For an account of this case, see T. Foran, *The Trial of Ambrose Lepine at Winnipeg for the Wilful Murder of Thomas Scott* (Montreal: Lovell, 1874).

[16]   These instructions were re-issued in much the same form in Letters Patent granted in 1931 and 1947. The 1947 version, which is currently operative, reads:

> And We do further authorize and empower Our Governor General, as he shall see occasion, in Our name and on Our behalf, when any crime or offence against the laws of Canada has been committed for which the offender may be tried thereunder, to grant a pardon to any accomplice, in such crime or offence, who shall be given such information as shall lead to the conviction of the principal offender, or of any one of such offenders if more than one; and further to grant to any offender convicted of any such crime or offence in any Court, or before any Judge, Justice or Magistrate, administering the laws of Canada, a pardon, either free or subject to lawful conditions, or any respite of the execution of the sentence of any such offender, for such period as to Our Governor General may seem fit and to remit any fines, penalties, or forfeitures which may become due and payable to Us and We do hereby direct and enjoin that Our Governor General shall not pardon or reprieve any such offender without first receiving in capital cases the advice of Our Privy Council for Canada and, in other cases, advice of one, at least, of his Ministers.

It is interesting that the primary use, as signified by the order of the elements in the instructions, refers to pardons for accomplices who give evidence, a statutory form of pardon which no longer exists. It continues, however, to be recognized as a ground for a conditional pardon: see the discussion, *infra*, at pp. 408-409.

[17]   This process is discussed in *Re Royal Prerogative of Mercy Upon Deportation Proceedings*, [1933] 2 D.L.R. 348 (S.C.C.), at 361-362.

the first *Criminal Code* contained a provision which empowered the Governor in Council to grant "a free pardon or a conditional pardon to any person who has been convicted of an offence".[18] This power, distinct from the pardoning power which resides in the Crown, extends to the remission of pecuniary penalties but not to remission of sentences of imprisonment. With respect to the statutory manifestation of the pardoning power currently found in sections 749 and 750 of the *Code*, it is expressly stated that its enactment does not limit the availability or exercise of the Royal Prerogative of Mercy.[19]

2. MODES OF EXERCISE

There are two basic forms of pardon: free and conditional. These are not to be confused with the statutory "pardons" granted pursuant to the *Criminal Records Act*.[20] There are, as well, other manifestations of the exercise of the Royal Prerogative of Mercy, particularly remission of sentence[21] and amnesty.

The nature of a free pardon was considered in *Hay v. Justices of the Tower Division of London*.[22] Hay had received a free pardon under "Her Majesty's Sign-Manual" in respect of a sentence of 7 years penal servitude for a felony. He wished to obtain a licence to sell spirits but the statute regulating such licences provided that "every person convicted of a felony" was disqualified. Baron Pollack described a free pardon as a "purging of the offence" which went beyond a mere discharge from

---

[18] See sections 966, 967 and 970 of the 1892 *Code* adopted from R.S.C. 1886, c. 181, ss. 38-42; also see S.C. 1902, c. 26, ss. 1-2.

[19] See *Criminal Code*, R.S.C. 1985, c. C-46, s. 751.

[20] R.S.C. 1985, c. C-47. These "pardons" are granted on the pre-conditions that the convicted person has served whatever sentence was imposed and waited a prescribed time thereafter. The focus of the inquiry is on the person's conduct *after* conviction. They do not reflect an aspect of the historical pardoning power grounded in notions of mercy and justice. The investigation is carried out by the Clemency and Pardons Division of the National Parole Board and the procedure is described in the Board's *Policy and Procedures Manual* (Revised January, 1988), section X, at 1-10. The Manual (at 1) explains the purpose of this form of relief as:

> an attempt to remove formally the stigma that often restricts or adversely affects an individual's peace of mind, social endeavour or career. It indicates that the applicant has successfully re-integrated into society.

[21] This should not be confused with earned remission, a discretionary grant of credits towards a sentence awarded by penal administrators pursuant to section 25 of the *Penitentiary Act*, R.S.C. 1985, c. P-5, and s. 6 of the *Prisons and Reformatories Act*, R.S.C. 1985, c. P-20.

[22] (1890), 24 Q.B.D. 561.

punishment.[23] Quoting from Hawkins, *Pleas of the Crown*, he commented that a pardon "does so far clear the party from the infamy and all other consequences of his crime, that he may not only have an action for a scandal in calling him traitor or felon after the time of the pardon but may also be a good witness . . .".[24] In other words, the free pardon placed the individual in the position of someone who had never been convicted.[25] It was a response to an issue of justice and operated to negate the existence of the original conviction. Thus, Hay was entitled to obtain a licence.

The *Policy and Procedures Manual* of the National Parole Board indicates that "a free pardon is given only when the innocence of the convicted person is established".[26] This would seem to suggest that, if a free pardon signifies innocence, then it should only be granted when innocence has been proven. However, the ruling in *Hay* did not necessarily go this far. Moreover, this jump in reasoning ignores the burden on the state to prove guilt beyond a reasonable doubt in order to secure a conviction. A.T.H. Smith, in his comprehensive examination of the exercise of the Royal Prerogative in England,[27] has discussed the controversy over the meaning of a free pardon. He refers to the *Thomas* case[28] in New Zealand where the High Court was faced with the question of whether a Royal Commission investigating police malpractice could hear evidence tending to show Thomas' guilt after he had received a free

---

[23] *Ibid.*, at 564.

[24] *Ibid.*

[25] While Pollack remarked that there had been a distinction between a pardon under the Sign-Manual and one under the Great Seal, he noted that 7 & 8 George IV, c. 28, s. 13 provided that "such pardon is equivalent to a pardon under the Great Seal". A similar provision was included in the Canadian *Criminal Code* of 1892, section 1076(2) and is now encompassed by section 749(2) of the 1985 *Code*. The distinction, while only of historical interest now, was that a pardon issued under "sign-manual" alone (the Sovereign's signature) was not a complete irrevocable pardon: see 4 Blackstone's Commentaries.

[26] See *National Parole Board Policy and Procedures Manual, supra*, note 20, at 13.

[27] A.T.H. Smith, "The Prerogative of Mercy, The Power of Pardon and Criminal Justice" [1983] *Public Law* 398.

[28] *Re Royal Commission on Thomas Case*, [1980] 1 N.Z.L.R. 602. Arthur Thomas had been granted a free pardon in 1979 in respect of a conviction 6 years earlier for the murder of David and Jeanette Crewe. The pre-amble to the pardon contained the following:

And whereas it has been made to appear from a report to the Prime Minister . . . that there is real doubt whether it can properly be contended that the case against Arthur Allan Thomas was proved beyond reasonable doubt.

A Royal Commission was established in 1980 to inquire into the circumstances of the investigation and prosecution. An excellent feature film, "Beyond Reasonable Doubt" (Satori Entertainment Corporation, 1983), has been made about this distrubing case.

pardon. The court concluded that the effect of the pardon was not absolute vindication but rather a declaration that the person was wrongly convicted.[29] This conclusion, however, was directly related to the specific terms of Thomas' pardon.[30] Accordingly, it may have been the specific circumstances rather than the appellation "free pardon" which influenced the court's view of the effect of the pardon. The Home Office in England has gone even further in refining the ruling in *Hay* by characterizing a free pardon as simply producing the result that "a conviction is to be disregarded so that, as far as is possible, the person is relieved of all penalties and other consequences of the conviction".[31] Consequently, Smith concludes "that it is not possible to generalize about the legal effects of a free pardon".[32]

The nature of a conditional pardon is equally nebulous. Blackstone explained a conditional pardon in the following terms:

> ... the king may extend his mercy upon what terms he pleases; and may annex to his bounty a condition, either precedent or subsequent, on the performance whereof the validity of the pardon will depend: and this by the common law.[33]

Rubin, in his treatise on the *Law of Criminal Correction*, described a conditional pardon as "the forerunner of parole" which has "sometimes been used as a substitute for a parole system".[34] In essence, it represents a substitution of one form of sentence for another. The prisoner is free of the consequences of the original punishment so long as he abides by the conditions imposed. Thus, it is distinct from a remission of sentence. The *Policy and Procedures Manual* provides that a conditional pardon which basically cancels a sentence in whole or in part may be granted where there is "satisfactory indication of rehabilitation and evidence of hardship out of proportion to the nature of the offence".[35]

---

[29] *Ibid.*, at 620-621.
[30] *Ibid.*, at 620. The court says:
> In the *terms of the pardon* Thomas is to be considered to have been wrongly convicted and he cannot be charged again with the murder of either Harvey or Jeanette Crewe.
[31] See Smith, *supra*, note 27, at 419. This view would appear to be simply a restatement of the section from Halsbury's Laws of England, 4th ed., Vol. 8, para. 952.
[32] Smith, *ibid.*, at 419.
[33] 4 Blackstone's Commentaries 394.
[34] S. Rubin, *The Law of Criminal Correction*, 2d ed. (St. Paul: West Publishing, 1973), p. 582.
[35] *Supra*, note 20, at X-13. An interesting contemporary use of the power to grant conditional pardons was through the mechanism of the "Inquiry into Habitual Criminals in Canada" (the Leggatt Commission). "Habitual Criminal" legislation was introduced in the *Code* in 1947, and was amended from time to time until 1977, when it

In *Reddekopp*,[36] the prisoner had been serving a sentence of life imprisonment and had received a pardon as a result of representations to the Solicitor General based on his deteriorating medical condition exacerbated by his confinement in penitentiary. After his release, his subsequent conduct gave rise to an attempt to revoke his conditional pardon. While there was some argument as to whether the pardon was, in fact, conditional or free, it appears from the judgment that Henry J. accepted the characterization of the pardon as a conditional one. When the purported revocation was challenged by way of *habeas corpus*, Henry J. ruled, first, that the prisoner could be admitted to bail pending the hearing of the application.[37] Secondly, he held that the onus was on the Crown to show that the conditions had been breached such that the Governor in Council was justified in terminating the pardon. Upon hearing the evidence, the prisoner was ultimately released.

A remission of sentence is similar in origin to a conditional pardon in that it flows from a conclusion that the sentence appears unduly harsh

---

was abolished and replaced by "Dangerous Offender" legislation (S.C. 1976-77, c. 53), following a finding by the Ouimet Committee that "the bitch" had been applied to "persistent offenders who, while constituting a serious social nuisance are not dangerous". In 1983, Professor Michael Jackson published a research study entitled *Sentences That Never End: The Report of the Habitual Criminal Study*, examining the status of 18 offenders who remained incarcerated under the legislation following the repeal of the habitual offender provisions. The Leggatt Commission was appointed by the Minister of Justice and the Solicitor General to:

(*a*) inquire into and review the cases of the 93 persons still having the status of Habitual Criminal under the terms of legislation repealed by Parliament in 1977, with a view to determining which Habitual Criminals no longer present a danger to the personal safety of others having regard for the criteria and philosophy set out in Part XXI of the Code;

(*b* make recommendations in each case to the Minister of Justice and the Solicitor General of Canada, as to whether or not the Habitual Criminal should be granted relief from continued preventive detention; and

(*c*) identify and recommend to the Minister of Justice and the Solicitor General of Canada, the most appropriate and expeditious mechanism for granting relief in the appropriate cases.

After holding public hearings in each case, recommendations were made to the Minister of Justice and the Solicitor General. Because so many of the persons subject to the legislation had experienced considerable difficulties in adjusting to street life, actual releases were effected through the use of the conditional pardon in that the offenders were released subject to parole conditions and supervision. If their behaviour was acceptable for a period of time, they were then granted full release from Habitual Criminal status. For some who had successfully been released in the past, full pardons were recommended and granted.

[36] *Re Reddekopp and R.* (1983), 33 C.R. (3d) 389 (Ont. H.C.)

[37] *Ibid.*, at 392. Henry J. added that the onus was on the Crown to show cause why the applicant ought not to be granted bail.

or inappropriate. However, unlike a conditional pardon, it operates to end the sentence. In *Hay*, the concurring judgment of Hawkins J. distinguished between a free pardon and remission of sentence and indicated that the latter were often granted in response to contrition or cooperation.[38] The National Parole Board's Manual describes remission as "the erasure of whole or part of the sentence imposed by the court because some illegality or undue hardship is created by that sentence".[39] The Manual adds that the usual reasons for considering remission are "pure compassion on the existence of inequality." For example, in the famous case of *Dudley*,[40] which involved the conviction of two sailors lost at sea who killed and consumed a 17-year-old crew member apparently in order to survive. While the necessity argument did not prevail,[41] the ultimate conviction was surrounded with controversy and led to intense debate over the inappropriateness of the death sentence.[42] The distinction between a free pardon and remission or commutation of sentence was clearly on the mind of Sir William Harcourt, the Home Secretary. In a letter to his son he discussed the option of a free pardon and commented that, to do so would "pronounce it an innocent act and deserving of no punishment."[43] Instead, the sentence was commuted to 6 month's imprisonment.[44]

Another form of exercise of the Royal Prerogative of Mercy is the granting of amnesties. These are usually short periods of remission granted to all prisoners in recognition of some event. In Canada, amnesties have been granted as a result of the Silver Jubilee of King George V,[45] the visit of King George VI and Queen Elizabeth in 1939, the Coronation of Queen Elizabeth II in 1953, and the Royal Visits in 1957 and 1959.[46]

---

[38] *Supra*, note 22, at 567.

[39] *Supra*, note 20, at 14.

[40] *R. v. Dudley*, (1884), 14 Q.B.D. 273 (C.C.R.).

[41] *Ibid.*, at 288, per Lord Coleridge, during which he observed "if in any case the law appears to be too severe on individuals, to leave it to the Sovereign to exercise that prerogative of mercy which the Constitution has intrusted [*sic*] to the hands fittest to dispense it."

[42] See the discussion of the pardon debate in A.W. Brian Simpson, *Cannibalism in the Common Law* (Chicago: University of Chicago Press, 1984), pp. 242-247.

[43] *Ibid.*, pp. 246-247.

[44] *Ibid.*, p. 247.

[45] See *Jacob v. Seguin*, [1936] 2 D.L.R. 21 (Que. S.C.).

[46] It was the amnesties in respect of the Royal Visits of 1957 and 1959 which gave rise to the sentence calculation issue in *Re McCaud*, [1970] 1 C.C.C. 293 (Ont. H.C.) and the subsequent enactment of section 14 [now s. 20] of the *Parole Act*, discussed in Chapters 4 and 9.

3. PREMISES FOR EXERCISING MERCY

Due to the infrequence of its exercise[47] and the absence of careful reasoning explaining the conceptual premises for its exercise, there is considerable controversy about the proper scope of inquiry and the relevant grounds for the exercise of the Royal Prerogative of Mercy. Smith writes:

> Much confusion arises because of the failure to distinguish between the various conceptually different uses to which the prerogative of mercy is put.[48]

As discussed in the historical account of the Royal Prerogative of Mercy, it was used initially to ameliorate the harshness of the developing criminal law. In particular, it was the tool by which the sovereign was able to avoid capital punishment in cases which, by reason of incapacity or excuse, a mandatory death penalty was considered an inappropriate response to the actual responsibility of the prisoner. As substantive criminal law developed to embrace concepts of incapacity and excuse, this role for the Royal Prerogative was substantially reduced. However, the excessive nature of a punishment when viewed in light of the prisoner's conduct in particular circumstances has continued to be an accepted basis on which to exercise the Royal Prerogative. Smith points out that commutation of the death sentence for murder "was usually an exercise of mercy in this sense rather than legal justice".[49] Harshness as a ground for a pardon, usually a conditional one, encompasses the circumstances of an ill or elderly prisoner for whom continuation of a term of imprisonment will be extraordinarily difficult.[50]

A further use of the Royal Prerogative, again amply grounded in its history, is as a response to the fallibility of the judicial process. In fact, the long debate in England during the 19th Century about the need for an appellate court revolved around the adequacy of the Royal Prerogative and its ability to respond to the grievances of those who claimed they were wrongly convicted.[51] Smith described this use of the pardoning

---

[47] Since 1980, only 9 prisoners have been granted pardons in Canada: see "Canada's Oldest Woman Prisoner Wins Royal Pardon", *The Kingston Whig-Standard* (30 June 1990) 3.

[48] *Supra*, note 27, p. 398.

[49] *Supra*, note 27, at p. 398-399.

[50] See the case of *Reddekop, supra*, note 36 and the pardon granted to Annette Proulx who was released at age 75, having served 11 years of a first-degree murder term (*supra*, note 47).

[51] See L. Radzinowicz and R. Hood, *A History of English Criminal Law, Vol. 5* (London: Stevens & Sons, 1986), pp. 762-767. The authors quote an 1870 address in Parliament by Lord Penzance who said: "Justice should be done in the name of justice, not in the name of mercy. Mercy begins where justice ends; and this is a system of eking out imperfect justice by irregular mercy."

power as "an acknowledgement that the judicial process is fallible, and that the rules of procedure and evidence do not always give rise to a correct decision about guilt or innocence ...".[52] A recent and tragic illustration is the posthumous pardon granted to Timothy Evans in 1966 for a murder he did not commit.[53] The New Zealand case of *Thomas* is an example of a pardon granted in response to a public appeal and subsequent inquiry which suggested that police officers had planted incriminating evidence in order to obtain a conviction.[54]

The third category of circumstances which might generate the use of the Royal Prerogative finds its source in the 17th and 18th Century statutes whereby pardons were exchanged for evidence against accomplices.[55] These can be described as situations where the public interest can better be served by relieving the prisoner from the full penalty imposed by law. The purpose may be inconsistent with the notion of a free pardon but can fit within the ambit of both conditional pardons or remission of sentence. Smith uses recent spy swaps as an example of this form of the pardoning power.[56]

In Canada, this form of the pardoning power was used extensively in the 1930's to deport aliens who had been convicted of criminal offences and sentenced to terms of imprisonment. Ultimately, this practice gave rise to the question of whether a prisoner could refuse a pardon granted either conditionally or unconditionally.[57] Relying on American authority, the Supreme Court of Canada characterized the grant of a pardon as "the determination of the ultimate authority that the public welfare will be better served by inflicting less than what the judgment fixed".[58] Refusing to draw an analogy between a pardon and a private gift which might require acceptance, the court held that a prisoner was not free to refuse the pardon. Given that this conclusion flowed from an inquiry into the nature of the pardoning power as part of the

---

52 *Supra*, note 27, p. 399.
53 For accounts of the Evans/Christie case, see Ludovic Kennedy, *10 Rillington Place* (London: Victor Gollancz, 1961); Eddowes, *The Man on Your Conscience* (London: Cassell and Co., 1951).
54 *Supra*, note 28.
55 See L. Radzinowicz, *History of English Criminal Law, Vol. 2* (London: Stevens & Sons, 1956).
56 A.T.H. Smith, "The Prerogative of Mercy, The Power of Pardon and Criminal Justice" (1982), Public Law 398. See p. 399 and footnote 7 in which Smith speaks of the release of Mr. and Mrs. Kroger after being sentenced to 20 years imprisonment for spying. The home secretary did not use the word "pardon" but described his position as "a recommendation to ... for remission of the remainder of the sentence."
57 See *Re Royal Prerogative of Mercy Upon Deportation Proceedings*, [1933] 2 D.L.R. 348 (S.C.C.).
58 *Ibid.*, at 352, relying on the judgment of Holmes J. in *Biddle v. Parovich* (1927), 274 U.S. 480.

constitutional scheme, it seems that it would apply to all modes of exercising the power with the exception of the statutory pardoning power now found in sections 749 and 750 of the *Code.*

4. SECTION 690 AND MERCY

In 1923, the predecessor of the current section 690 was enacted creating a statutory role for the Minister of Justice in respect of applications for mercy.[59] The provision currently reads:

> **690.** The Minister of Justice may, upon an application for mercy of the Crown by or on behalf of a person who has been convicted in proceedings by indictment or who has been sentenced to preventive detention under Part XXI,
>
> (*a*) direct, by order in writing, a new trial or, in the case of a person under sentence or preventive detention, a new hearing, before any court that he thinks proper, if after inquiry he is satisfied that in the circumstances a new trial or hearing, as the case may be, should be directed;
>
> (*b*) refer the matter at any time to the court of appeal for hearing and determination by that court as if it were an appeal by the convicted person or the person under sentence of preventive detention, as the case may be; or
>
> (*c*) refer to the court of appeal at any time, for its opinion, any question upon which he desires the assistance of that court, and the court shall furnish its opinion accordingly.[60]

It is not uncommon for prisoners who have exhausted all statutory routes of appeal to seek the intervention of the Minister of Justice. The past few decades reveal a small number of cases which have been returned either to a trial court or to an appellate court. This often arises when there is reason to believe that the convicted person was the wrong person.[61] The most well-known example is the case of Donald Marshall.[62] Another famous case, Steven Truscott, was also returned to

[59] (13 & 14 Geo. 5), c. 41, s. 9 (repealed and replaced s. 1022 of the *Criminal Code*, R.S.C. 1906, c. 146).
[60] R.S.C. 1985, c. C-46, s. 690.
[61] See, for example, *R. v. McNamara*, [1964] 3 C.C.C. 32 (Ont. C.A.).
[62] On June 16, 1982, the Honourable Jean Chrétien, Minister of Justice, announced in the House of Commons that the Marshall case had been referred to the Nova Scotia Supreme Court for a determination pursuant to section 617(*b*) [now s. 690(*h*)] of the *Code*: see Commons Debates, 1st Sess., 32nd Parl., Vol. XVI, at 18, 520. Subsequently, the Nova Scotia Supreme Court, Appeal Division confirmed that he ought not to have been convicted but added that "any miscarriage of justice was more apparent than real"—a strange remark in respect of someone who had served 11 years in penitentiary for a murder he did not commit: see M. Harris, *Justice Denied: The Law Versus Donald Marshall* (Toronto: Macmillan 1986). On October 28, 1986, the Government

court[63] but not through the operation of section 690. The consideration by the Supreme Court of Canada[64] was the result of a reference by Order-In-Council issued pursuant to section 55 of the *Supreme Court Act*.[65] There have also been examples of section 617 [now s. 690] being used in respect of the fitness of sentences imposed in light of new psychiatric evidence[66] and whether, in light of psychiatric evidence not adduced at trial, a prisoner was insane within the meaning of section 16 of the *Criminal Code*.[67] In these kinds of cases, the reference resulted in each being treated as if it was a new appeal, albeit in light of new and fresh evidence. Other references have sought the opinion of the court on specific legal or evidentiary issues such as, for example, whether new evidence indicated that an accused was incompetent at the time of his trial to instruct counsel[68] and whether new evidence would be admissible at a new trial in light of concerns about its probative value and its nature as, potentially, hearsay.[69]

Prior to the enactment of section 690 and its predecessors, it seems clear that legal and evidentiary issues could be the appropriate subjects for consideration on an application for the Royal Prerogative of Mercy. The question naturally arises as to whether the enactment of section 690 in any way abrogates or limits the Royal Prerogative such that the only avenue for a claim of a default in justice, as compared to a claim for mercy, must be to the Minister of Justice pursuant to section 690.

Whether a statute can limit the royal prerogative to pardon was raised in the case of *Ex parte Armitage*.[70] Wurtele J. concluded:

---

of Nova Scotia established a Royal Commission to examine the case. It has spawned much controversy and considerable litigation particularly with respect to the Commission's ability to inquire into Nova Scotia cabinet discussions: see *Re R. and Royal Commission into the Donald Marshall Jr. Prosecution* (1988), 42 C.C.C. (3d) 129 (N.S. T.D.). Reversed (1988), 44 C.C.C. (3d) 330 (N.S.C.A.). See also the Commissioners' Report, *Royal Commission on the Donald Marshall, Jr. Prosecution* (Province of Nova Scotia, 1989), Vol. 1, Findings and Recommendations, pp. 113-127.

63 For an examination of this case see Trent, *Who Killed Lynn Harper* (Montreal: Optimum Publishing, 1979); I. LeBourdais, *The Trial of Steven Truscott* (Montreal: McClelland & Stewart, 1966).

64 [1967] S.C.R. 309.

65 P.C. 1966/760, issued April 26, 1966, which formed the question:

Had an appeal by Steven Murray Truscott been made to the Supreme Court of Canada . . . what disposition would the Court have made of such an Appeal on a consideration of the existing Record and such further evidence as the Court, in its discretion, may receive and consider.

Eight judges would have dismissed the appeal (Hall J. dissented).

66 *R. v. Roberts* (1962), 39 C.R. 1 (Ont. C.A.).

67 *Reference Re R. Gorecki (No. 2)* (1976), 32 C.C.C. (2d) 135 (Ont. C.A.).

68 *Reference Re R. Gorecki (No. 1)* (1976), 32 C.C.C. (2d) 129 (Ont. C.A.).

69 *Re Latta* (1976), 30 C.C.C. (2d) 208 (Alta. C.A.).

70 (1902), 5 C.C.C. 345 (Que. K.B.).

It is a provision of our general public law that the royal prerogatives are not affected nor curtailed in any way by any enactment in a statute, unless they are expressly mentioned or referred to.

. . . .

But although a royal prerogative cannot be affected or curtailed by the enactment of a statute, without express words to that effect, it may be enlarged and extended by a statute which does so in general terms.[71]

There is, however, the later authority of the judgments from the House of Lords in *Attorney-General v. De Keyser's Royal Hotel, Ltd.*,[72] which addressed whether a prerogative power may be limited by implication from a statute dealing with the same or related subject matter. The case dealt with the Crown's prerogative to occupy premises during wartime. A statute was passed empowering the Crown to billet soldiers, a power "which it might theretofore have done by virtue of its prerogative". The issue raised was the impact of the statutory power on the pre-existing prerogative power. Lord Sumner, speaking for himself, concluded:

There is no object in dealing by statute with the same subject-matter as is already dealt with by the prerogative, unless it be either to limit or at least to vary its exercise, or to provide an additional mode of attaining the same object.[73]

This judgment, in combination with those of the other Lords, would indicate that a prerogative power can be limited by implication. However, one must note Lord Sumner's reference to the alternative purpose of providing "an additional mode of attaining the same object."

It would seem that this was Parliament's intention in establishing section 690. The original enactment which empowered the Minister of Justice to intervene in cases of applications for mercy contained the following clause:

(*a*) if he entertains a doubt whether such person ought to have been convicted, may, after such inquiry as he thinks proper, instead of advising His Majesty to remit or to commute the sentence, direct by an order in writing a new trial at such time and before such court as the Minister of Justice thinks proper; or

. . . .

(*c*) at any time, if the Minister of Justice desires the assistance of the court of appeal on any point arising in the case with a view to the determination of the petition, he may refer that point to the court of appeal for its opinion

---

71   *Ibid.*, at 351-352.
72   [1920] A.C. 608.
73   *Ibid.*, at 561.

thereon, and that court shall consider the point so referred and furnish the Minister of Justice its opinion thereon accordingly.[74]

The power to refer the matter back to court for a new trial or to seek an appellate court's opinion was an alternative to advising "His Majesty to remit or to commute the sentence". Thus, the provision can be viewed as empowering the Minister to seek the assistance of the judicial system in responding to legal or evidentiary issues. This was not a substitute for the Minister's ability to recommend a pardon but rather was an alternative or adjunct to it. In this way, the provision can be characterized, in Lord Sumner's words, as "an additional mode of attaining the same object". Accordingly, there is no merit to the argument that the enactment of section 690 and its predecessors abrogated the Royal Prerogative by restricting it only to cases of mercy and directing questions of justice to the Minister of Justice.[75]

5. REVIEWABILITY

Until the enactment of the *Canadian Charter of Rights and Freedoms*,[76] most courts agreed that the exercise of a Royal Prerogative power was not reviewable except to the extent of inquiring into the scope of the power and whether the act in question exceeded that scope. Probably the single example of judicial support for examining the exercise of a prerogative power was the judgment of Lord Denning M.R. in *Laker Airways v. Department of Trade*[77] where he said:

> Seeing that the prerogative is a discretionary power to be exercised for the public good, it follows that its exercise can be examined by the courts just as any other discretionary power which is vested in the executive. . . . when discretionary powers are entrusted to the executive by statute, the courts can examine the exercise of those powers to see that they are used properly, and not improperly or mistakenly. By "mistakenly" I mean under the influence of a misdirection in fact or in law. Likewise it seems to me that when discretionary powers are entrusted to the executive by the prerogative—in pursuance of the treaty-making power—the courts can examine the exercise of them so as to see that they are not used improperly or mistakenly.[78]

---

[74] See, *supra*, note 59.

[75] It should be remembered that while the practice has developed that all applications for the exercise of the Royal Prerogative of Mercy are directed to the Solicitor General for his advice to the Governor General, the Letters Patent which confirm the power speak only of the advice of "one, at least, of his Ministers": see, *supra*, note 16.

[76] Being Part I of the *Constitution Act, 1982* [enacted by the *Canada Act, 1982* (U.K.), c. 11, s. 1].

[77] [1977] 1 Q.B. 643 (C.A.).

[78] *Ibid.*, at 705-706.

This view of the scope of reviewability extends to a consideration of the underlying premises for a decision, both factual and legal.[79]

More recently, the House of Lords considered the issue of reviewability when a Minister ordered, on the grounds of protecting the security of military and official communications, that headquarters staff could no longer be represented by a national union.[80] The order had been issued without any consultation with staff or the union. Ordinarily, a failure to consult would be considered unfair. Here, it was argued that national security, and particularly the concern to avoid disruption by reason of a labour dispute, required that the issue be left to the executive. The question of the reviewability of the exercise of a Royal Prerogative power was raised as a preliminary hurdle. Lord Scarman held that reviewability should not be determined by reference to the source of the power exercised but rather by a consideration of the subject matter.[81] He equated the review of prerogative powers with the review of the exercise of statutory powers and ruled that "the royal prerogative has always been regarded as part of the common law."[82] Hence the fact that the Order in Council was made pursuant to a Royal Prerogative was irrelevant to the question of review.[83]

Section 32(1)(*a*) of the *Charter* places prerogative powers on a different constitutional plane:

32. (1) This Charter applies
(*a*) to the Parliament and government of Canada in respect of all matters within the authority of Parliament including all matters relating to the Yukon Territory and Northwest Territories; ...

Section 52 of the *Constitution Act* makes it clear that its provisions, including the *Charter*, are the supreme law of the land. In the case of

---

[79] This suggests a scope for review broader than review based simply on abuse of discretion and authority as, for example, in *Roncarelli v. Duplessis*, [1959] S.C.R. 121, where Rand J. stated:
... that an administration according to law is to be superseded by action dictated by and according to the arbitrary likes, dislikes and irrelevant purposes of public officers acting beyond their duty, would signalize the beginning of disintegration of the rule of law as a fundamental postulate of our constitutional structure. (At 142.)

[80] *Council of Civil Servants v. Minister For the Civil Service*, [1984] 3 W.L.R. 1174 (H.L.).
[81] *Ibid.*, at 1193.
[82] *Ibid.*
[83] Lord Diplock and Lord Roskill agreed with Lord Scarman's focus on subject matter rather than source. Interestingly, Diplock J. considered the specific subjects of prerogative powers which would be reviewable and included pardons: *ibid.*, at 1195. Conversely, Lord Roskill excluded the Royal Prerogative of Mercy from his list of reviewable subjects: *ibid.*, at 1203.

Operation Dismantle Inc. v. R.,[84] Dickson C.J.C., speaking for the majority, held:

> I agree with Madame Justice Wilson that cabinet decisions fall under s. 32(1)(*a*) of the *Charter* and are therefore reviewable in the courts and subject to judicial scrutiny for compatibility with the Constitution. I have no doubt that the executive branch of the Canadian government is duty bound to act in accordance with the dictates of the *Charter*. Specifically, the cabinet has a duty to act in a manner consistent with the right to life, liberty and security of the person and the right not to be deprived thereof except in accordance with the principles of fundamental justice.[85]

Subsequently, in *Schmidt*, an extradition case, LaForest J. confirmed the views expressed in *Operation Dismantle* regarding the relationship between executive acts and the constraints on power entrenched in the *Charter*.[86] Also, the Federal Court of Appeal has held specifically that an application to the Minister of Justice under section 617 [now s. 690] was reviewable to ensure that the process proceeded fairly and in accordance with the principles of fundamental justice.[87]

Within the context of a section 690 application or an application for the exercise of the Royal Prerogative of Mercy, it is unclear exactly what procedural elements are required in order to constitute a "fairly conducted inquiry". At the very least, the responsible member of the Executive must be prepared to consider with an open mind all material submitted by a prisoner and also to ignore all extraneous material unrelated to the issues posed by the application. In some cases, it may even be arguable that a full and fair inquiry must include a personal opportunity to present his situation at least in front of a representative of the decision-maker. With respect to applications for the Royal Prerogative which are ultimately determined by the advice emanating from the Solicitor General, the Clemency Division of the National Parole Board has been delegated the function of preparing the case and submitting a recommendation.[88] There have been situations where representatives of the Clemency Division have conducted personal interviews with the prisoner, particularly when issues of inequity or hardship are raised by the petition. Given the facility with which National Parole Board members attend at penal institutions, a personal interview should

---

[84] [1985] 1 S.C.R. 441.
[85] *Ibid.*, at 455.
[86] *Canada v. Schmidt*, [1987] 1 S.C.R. 500, at 521.
[87] *Wilson v. Min. of Justice* (1985), 20 C.C.C. (3d) 206 (Fed. C.A.), relying on *Operation Dismantle Inc.*, *supra*, note 84.
[88] *Parole Act*, s. 22(2).

be a minimum requirement except in the most obviously unacceptable applications.[89]

6. CONCLUSION

Within our constitutional structure, the adjudication of guilt or innocence is the responsibility of the judiciary and the pardoning power is clearly residual and extraordinary. Nonetheless, it exists in recognition of the fallibility of legal institutions and continues to be an aspect of the administration of justice. While its exercise cannot be compared to a judicial process, it is essential that it be carried out carefully, fairly and solely with regard to those factors which shed light on blameworthiness in legal terms and the equity of the punishment in human terms. Simply because the power resides in the executive is no excuse for precluding accountability to the applicant and to the public. As well, any reluctance to re-assess old facts must be measured against the importance of the liberty interest at stake and the recognition that the system is fallible. Surely this is the principal lesson of the Donald Marshall case.

---

[89] The Board's manual simply says that the Board should specify "the nature of the investigations required;" there is no process prescribed beyond indicating that two Board members vote on the recommendation: see note 20, at X-16.

12

Parole Board Advocacy

Stand up with your Thief, you're on his parole. . . .

—Bob Dylan

1. THE FIRST INTERVIEW

The purpose of this chapter is to provide practitioners with a brief introduction to the major features of preparation for and attendance at parole board hearings. More detailed information on specific issues is contained in other chapters of this book. The reader is cautioned that policies and procedures are subject to continuous modification.

While any conscientious practitioner must commence representation of a client with a thorough initial interview, it is particularly important in the parole context that solicitor and client develop a clear understanding both of what the client seeks and what is feasible. The lawyer should keep in mind throughout that since the relationship between a prisoner and institutional officials is one of captive and captor, the penal environment is almost inevitably characterized by an atmosphere of hostility and mistrust. For example, while most prisoners are made eligible by statute for day parole at one-sixth of term, Parole Board policy for some years has been that for those serving sentence for crimes involving violence to the person, release on any form of community-based day parole is unlikely to be granted until at least one-third of term has been served. If, as frequently occurs, parole and penal personnel informally indicate to a prisoner that despite excellent institutional behaviour and a carefully thought-out release plan at the one-sixth point, they will nevertheless not support him until the "mandated" amount of time has been served, resentment can easily arise. Similarly, having been brought to prison only after extensive procedural protections have been exhausted, a prisoner can easily become frustrated when he is told that the release decision-maker will be invited to make a decision about his freedom based perhaps on rumour and unsubstantiated hearsay, for example that he has been "muscling" unnamed prisoners, or that he is a "known drug user/trafficker". The lawyer is often a prisoner's only independent source of information and advice about the parole system. Accordingly, there is a particular obligation in this environment to ensure that advice is only provided following a detailed examination of all of the facts and circumstances of a particular case. In our experience it is all too often the case that the lawyer inadvertently contributes to institutional tension by telling the client what the client may wish to hear, rather than providing an accurate and dispassionate analysis of the actual situation.

Once lawyer and client have some understanding of what the client wants and can reasonably expect at that stage in the sentence, the lawyer should ensure that he obtains a series of written directions authorizing the release of materials. The form of the release is not important, although it is usually advisable to include the client's "F.P.S." number (the identification system used by the R.C.M.P. fingerprint service upon first arrest for an indictable offence, usually consisting of six numbers followed by a letter). At a very minimum these should be addressed to the trial lawyer, the institutional sentence administrator, the National (or provincial) Parole Board, and any mental health professionals who have treated the prisoner. Similarly, a copy of the most recent parole application should be obtained from the client; if no application has been completed, counsel should request that the institutional parole officer attend to ensure that an application—usually a very simple one page form—is taken and forwarded to the appropriate authorities. Since in our experience bureaucratic inertia is the greatest impediment to timely parole decision-making, it is important even at this early stage for the lawyer to ascertain the status of the parole application (or post-suspension proceedings), in order to ensure that appropriate input is made. For example, one of the reasons that a parole application should be filed 4 to 6 months in advance of the prisoner's eligibility date is in order to allow time for community assessments to be completed; if the lawyer is aware of sources of community support, he may be able to expedite the process by having those persons contact the parole officer assigned to conduct the assessment. Conversely, if a hearing date has already been established which does not fit the lawyer's calendar, early notification that the prisoner wishes an adjournment of the hearing to secure the services of counsel may save busy Board members and case management teams considerable time and labour.

During the first interview counsel should introduce the penitentiary prisoner to the concept of the case management team (C.M.T.). In addition to the prisoner himself, other members include the institutional case management officer (informally known as the prisoner's "C.O."), a parole officer from the local parole office (P.O.), and, in institutions operating under a living unit system, a living unit development officer (informally known as an "L.U." or "L.U.D.O.").[1] As well

---

[1] At the provincial level less formal structures exist.

as generating institutional performance reports and summaries of information for release decision-makers, these officials are expected to work closely with the prisoner during the course of serving sentence.

Counsel should strongly advise the client to co-operate fully with his case management team (or equivalent provincial authorities). The client should understand that because the Parole Board will likely see him for less than 1 hour, the Board members are likely to rely heavily on the views and recommendations of the case management team.[2] Because the composition of case management teams frequently changes during the service of sentence, prisoners should be encouraged to create and maintain a written record of the contents of important meetings with the team; copies of correspondence should be forwarded to counsel.

2. SOURCES OF INFORMATION

It is difficult to formulate any hard and fast rule as to whether counsel should contact institutional or community members of the C.M.T. Some will welcome input, particularly where the prisoner may have unrealistic expectations of the parole process. On the other hand, some members of case management teams consistently reject any approach by counsel. This seems to stem in part from a concern that they may somehow be held accountable for any statements which they may make during the course of any discussions, particularly if the lawyer appears aggressive or demanding. At the same time it should not be forgotten that control over information represents a considerable source of power which some institutional and parole personnel seem unwilling to relinquish. A lawyer should not be surprised to be informed that a team member will share nothing beyond the final report which is sent to the Parole Board immediately before a hearing date.

One source of information which is often overlooked is an application by, or on behalf of, the prisoner under the *Privacy Act* (or equivalent provincial legislation). At least in cases involving prisoners who have served more than 3 years we recommend that applications be made at least to those registers which contain "institutional" and "community case management" files, "parole board" files, and two specialized files currently called "discipline and dissociation" and "psychology."[3] If psychiatric reports are not in either the Parole Board or psychology files,

---

[2] The "concurrence rate" between what the team recommends and what the National Parole Board decides consistently averages approximately 85%.

[3] The names and identification numbers of the various databanks containing these files are changed from time to time.

they may be contained in a separate register called "health care." In certain cases, an application for access under the legislation may be the only way to obtain necessary materials. For example, while the case management team are compelled, according to C.S.C./Board policy, to release to counsel a copy of their final report to the Board, historical documentation, which may be necessary to understand the position currently being taken by the team, will not be released unless a formal application is made under the Act. Counsel are cautioned that it may take several months to obtain even partial access to the material due to the extensive vetting process which must occur in order to satisfy the various exemptions permitted under the legislation.[4]

Since access to the Parole Board file should reveal the names of previous decision-makers, a related issue which counsel should consider is whether contact with Board members prior to a hearing is desirable. To those trained in a litigation system which dictates that contact with a decision-maker is usually inappropriate and sometimes improper, it may come as a surprise that many Board members are content (and sometimes eager) to discuss cases in which they participate. Full-time Board members in particular are likely to have had many formal and informal contacts with long-term prisoners; in our experience they will sometimes be prepared to discuss a case, so long as it is understood that any such discussions bind neither themselves nor the Board. A common example of this arises where, in a previous decision, the attending Board members have, in their written comments, indicated that the prisoner should undertake an institutional course of study or treatment before favourable consideration will be given for conditional release. Where this course becomes available in a facility outside the institution, contact with those Board members (or the senior regional Board member) may be appropriate to determine whether it is worth developing a proposal for the new program prior to the next hearing. However, it should also be kept in mind that Board members do not usually review files until a few days before a scheduled hearing date; consequently, there may be little point to pre-hearing contact. In such circumstances, we recommend that a written inquiry is more likely to be of assistance than a telephone call. If counsel is hesitant to initiate contact, or a Board member declines to communicate informally, formal liaison mechan-

---

4   Counsel should also be aware that material supposedly in one file is often missing from that file, but may be found in another seemingly unrelated file. Conversely, numerous copies of irrelevant or superfluous materials may be repeated *ad nauseam* in every file to which one can gain access. Data collection and retention methods all too frequently seem capricious or random.

isms exist between the Board and the Correctional Service of Canada (C.S.C.) through the case management team.

As counsel becomes familiar with the history of a case, all written documentation should be carefully reviewed with the client. Counsel should clarify with the client who should retain documents prepared or received. This may be particularly relevant in post-suspension cases where the prisoner's ability to maintain the privacy of materials in overcrowded local jails or detention centres may be extremely limited. At the same time counsel should keep in mind that as studies consistently reveal that functional illiteracy among prisoners is inordinately high, it should not be assumed that clients fully comprehend written documentation placed before them.

3. PAROLE BOARD PROCEDURES

Since May 1, 1988, all National Parole Board hearings are audiotaped (provincial Parole Boards still rely on extensive, but occasionally incorrect, notes taken by attending Board members). Since there is no other form of record of the proceedings, counsel should request a copy of all tapes from previous hearings from the Board's regional office. "Prisoners' copies" of the tapes are currently made available without cost within approximately 1 week of receipt of the request. For decisions taken prior to May 1, 1988, counsel should request from the Board copies of the "Board Members Comment Sheets".

An application for conditional release should itself generate a series of reports. If the client indicates in his application that he proposes to reside at a certain address and be employed with a firm, the community assessment is designed to confirm residence and employment. In this regard, it is important to understand two factors. First, recognizing the difficulty of securing a position while still incarcerated, the Board will not usually discriminate against a person who has been unable to arrange employment; however, the Board will expect that the prisoner demonstrate that a serious effort has been made, such as contacting agencies which specialize in assisting ex-offenders or applying to educational facilities. Second, while case management teams often resist the effort required to process alternative applications, it is entirely appropriate to approach the Board with more than one release plan.

The community assessment forms part of the "Progress Summary" which the case management team is required to produce for the Board prior to the hearing. In post-suspension cases, the operative document is called a "Special Report". These documents are expected to summarize what is known of the offence, to review the offender's institutional history (including reports from security, line, recreation and employment staff), to report on the attitude of the police force in the proposed destination (if the supervising force in the area of destination is not the force which investigated the original offence, reports from both will be requested), and to outline known details of performance on previous conditional releases (including bail and probation). Although policy varies from time to time, counsel should be aware that in virtually any case involving wilfully causing death or serious physical or psychological harm, the Board will not give serious consideration to a proposal for release without internal and external assessments by psychologists and/or psychiatrists. Where treatment is suggested and is available within correctional facilities (however belatedly), release will not be granted until such treatment program has been completed and a positive report obtained. If treatment is available outside the institution, counsel should be prepared to develop and present a release program which includes a treatment component.

4. DISCUSSING THE OFFENCE

One issue which often causes particular difficulty for the lawyer preparing for a Parole Board hearing is that of the client's attitude to the facts underlying the offence. Where the sentence imposed is more than 5 years, current Board Policy is that every effort will be made to secure at least a transcript of the judge's reasons for sentence, the theory being that such transcript will contain an accurate description of the facts. Absent reasons for sentence or a full trial transcript, the Board will write to the sentencing judge requesting a letter detailing a summary of the facts from his trial notes, much like a trial judge's report to the Court of Appeal under section 682 of the *Code*. If neither of these is available during the preparation of the Progress Summary, the C.M.T. will rely on a statement of facts provided either by Crown counsel or by the investigating police force.[5] While practices vary considerably across the country, counsel should be aware that very often the police information forwarded to the C.M.T. or the Board is comprised of the initial synopsis prepared at the time of arrest for purposes of a judicial interim release hearing. This may be considerably different from the actual facts found by the trier of fact. While some members of case management teams are grateful for input from counsel, in our experience there is little point in attempting to persuade these officials to present a more balanced version of the facts, as most feel that this is a matter which should be dealt

---

[5] Counsel can often expedite the process by obtaining a copy of the Crown brief or synopsis from trial or appellate counsel.

with by the Parole Board at the hearing. Thus, counsel should be in a position by the time of the hearing to refute any exaggerated factual assertions which may be contained in such reports.

Even if the information forwarded by the court or the police is entirely comprehensive and accurate, the client will often seek to minimize or deny his culpability in order to attempt to present well before the Parole Board. While Board policy is that a claim of innocence will not rule out favourable consideration for conditional release, nevertheless counsel should place considerable priority on ensuring that the client is aware that much of the hearing will involve a detailed discussion of the circumstances of the offence. Since the Board views its statutory mandate as obligating it to measure the progress of the offender since the time of sentencing, and sees as part of that function the need to probe the offender's understanding and internalization of his culpability, counsel should thoroughly prepare the client for such questioning. Similarly, if the client has any previous adult record of any kind, he should be ready to answer questions about the circumstances of these offences. Finally, although section 13 of the *Canadian Charter of Rights and Freedoms*[6] probably insulates the client from subsequent questioning about outstanding charges, counsel should be aware and prepare the client for possible questioning in this area.

All of these various written materials are then summarized by the case management team[7] under the heading "Appraisal and Recommendation". Following a series of homicides committed by persons on various forms of conditional release in 1987 and 1988, new policies were instituted, according to which case management teams are required to address themselves under this heading principally to the issue of risk to the community to which the offender seeks release. The final recommendation is expected to be specific.[8] The Progress Summary will be shared with the prisoner,[9] and a copy will be forwarded to counsel upon request. Since this document is probably the most important piece of evidence before the Board, it is critical that counsel review it with the client in considerable detail, and that both be prepared to deal with it at the hearing.

One of the other new policies instituted in 1988 is that the Progress Summary contains statistical information on the likelihood of re-

---

[6]   Being Part I of the *Constitution Act, 1982* [enacted by the *Canada Act (U.K.)*, c. 11, s. 1].

[7]   The document is usually written by the C.M.O.C.

[8]   Where team members differ in their views, they are expected to include these differences of opinion and the reasons therefor.

[9]   Because of security concerns, the prisoner may not be allowed to retain a copy of the Progress Summary.

cidivism for similar offenders in similar circumstances. The prisoner's total score is derived from such factors as number of convictions, age at first offence, and highest formal educational level achieved. This unusual and unreliable information has been characterized as "an attempt . . . to import the science of statistical analysis in order to dress up what, in the last true analysis, amounts only to would-be clairvoyance."[10]

5. PRE-HEARING CONSIDERATIONS

It often transpires that a case management team recommends that a prisoner waive his right to a hearing until some future event has transpired, such as completion of an assessment or treatment program. If there are any outstanding Crown appeals, charges or unexecuted committal warrants, the reality of Board practice is that decision-making is likely to be deferred until such matters have been disposed of, on the basis that any increase in sentence could affect the parole eligibility date, and render any release "inoperative" (see Chapter 6). If the prisoner insists on proceeding, it is our experience that not only is the recommendation likely to be negative, but also the prisoner may well be described in the Progress Summary as "resistant to authority" or "lacking common sense." Prisoners quite naturally (and perhaps justifiably) feel that unless they waive their right to a hearing, a negative recommendation on their files is likely to jeopardize future chances for parole. While each case must be carefully analysed, we are generally of the view that the opportunity for a first hearing (usually at one-sixth of term) should not be waived, even though there may be little realistic hope of release at that stage. Although many members of case management teams are very experienced, they are not necessarily accurate predictors of what the Board will do. Consequently, a prisoner is usually well-advised to go to a Board hearing, in order to hear from the decision-makers what they will expect him to accomplish before favourable consideration will be given to conditional release rather than rely on the views of the C.M.T. as to what the Board might do. Indeed, "one-sixth review" is rapidly becoming an occasion for the case management team as well as the prisoner to seek some clarification of expectations from the Board.

Another type of hearing which should not generally be waived is that involving first eligibility for release for a lifer or "high profile" offender. Such hearings are often critical because they involve the Board considering in principle whether, in terms of the offence and institutional conduct (in the broadest sense), the prisoner is fit for release, as

---

[10]   *Bains v. National Parole Bd.* (1989), 71 C.R. (3d) 343 (Fed. T.D.), per Muldoon J.

distinct from evaluating the merits of a particular release plan. In such cases, despite what may be written in the formal Progress Summary, the case management team will often adopt a neutral position, leaving it up to the Board to decide whether the prisoner is ready for (or the community is prepared to accept) some form of conditional release. Counsel should encourage clients in such circumstances to seek very limited release, such as a series of monthly unescorted temporary absence passes designed to de-sensitize the community, rather than to press forward with more ambitious plans which are likely to have little hope of success at earliest eligibility.

Counsel should take a different view of post-suspension hearings. Where the basis for the suspension is an allegation of a return to criminal activity, and there appear to be defences to the charge, there seems to be little point in proceeding with a hearing until after the charge has been tried or withdrawn. Otherwise the client faces the risk that the Board will decide the case on the basis of the "official" information available to it at the time it is asked to take the decision. Since all the Board usually has available to it is the initial incriminating synopsis prepared by the police upon arrest for the assistance of Crown counsel at a judicial interim release hearing, the Board will generally tend to favour this over any explanation which may be provided by the prisoner. If the decision is to terminate or revoke, the prisoner may later invoke the internal appeal procedure; however, this tends to be a somewhat cumbersome and sometimes fruitless endeavour. Adjournments *sine die* may be easily arranged by a telephone call or fax message to the Board's regional office.

Whatever the form of hearing, written submissions and material in support of an application are of considerable assistance in ensuring that the client's case is clearly understood by the Board. Counsel should keep in mind that few Board members are legally trained; consequently, they are likely to appreciate, particularly in commercial cases, a clear and concise explanation of the circumstances of the offence. At the same time, in preparing for a hearing counsel should be aware that given the "absolute discretion" granted to the Board by section 13 of the *Parole Act*,[11] as has been demonstrated in Chapter 8, Board members do not usually regard themselves as bound by the rules respecting the admissibility of evidence or the need for proof beyond a reasonable doubt. Thus, counsel should be ready to address controversies which may have been resolved in the prisoner's favour at trial, such as evidence from improperly intercepted private communications or the evidence of

---

[11]   R.S.C. 1985, c. P-2.

unsworn witnesses. Finally, as the various parole statutes (and inter-pretative case law) contemplate that rumour and hearsay can play a role in the parole process, counsel will not serve the client well by adopting an adversarial stance which posits that such matters are *ab initio* inad-missible; rather, counsel should be prepared to demonstrate that such sources are unreliable and should carry little weight.

During the pre-hearing phase many friends and families of pris-oners may wish to be of assistance. Although Board members claim that they are not influenced by large numbers of supportive letters, there can be little doubt that an indication of community support is likely to be of assistance in obtaining conditional release. Thus, we recommend that separate letters be written by each person who is prepared to offer support. Although these should be addressed to the Board, they need not be sent individually to the Board's regional office; counsel can collect them from the writers and forward a package of materials to the Re-gional Director approximately 1 week prior to the scheduled hearing date (letters and other materials received after that time may be filed at hearing). The letters should detail who the writer is, how long and in what context they have known the parole applicant, their reaction to the offender following the commission of the offence, whether the writer has kept in contact with the offender (particularly if he has visited the prisoner since incarceration), the writer's estimation of how the prisoner is likely to respond to conditional release, and what practical or emo-tional support the writer is prepared to offer if release is ordered. The letters need not be typed, nor do they need to be grammatically perfect; the fact that people write is often more important than the content. At the same time counsel should not be concerned if support letters are not available. In our experience the Board is sensitive to the fact that many prisoners either have limited community resources available, or that they have deliberately concealed their whereabouts from friends, family or associates.

Perhaps the most important area in which counsel can be of assist-ance to a client is in reviewing the differences between court and Parole Board proceedings. Above all, the client must be made to understand that the process he is about to undergo is inquisitorial; thus, while the client's oral participation at trial may have been limited to entering a plea, he must understand that he will be required to answer questions about matters which he may find emotionally very difficult, that the questioning may range far beyond the immediate circumstances of the offence, and that if he refuses to answer the Board is likely to draw a negative inference. Similarly, answers which are perceived by the at-tending members to be incomplete or evasive are likely to indicate to the Board that the prisoner has not fully accepted responsibility for his criminal activity, and thus is more likely to re-offend if granted conditional release.

While counsel should therefore emphasize not only that the client must speak but also that he must be frank and open, counsel should at the same time reassure the client that Parole Board hearings are deliberately designed to be very informal in order that the parole applicant not feel intimidated. While facilities vary considerably across the country, there are several common elements which serve to emphasize the informal nature of the proceeding. First, apart from the tape-recording device (which most clients find completely unobtrusive after the first few minutes), there is little sense that one is speaking "for the record". Thus, the participants in the process are encouraged to use everyday language (interpreters will be provided at government expense upon sufficient notice being given), a matter which is of considerable reassurance to prisoners who are worried about their ability to express themselves. This air of informality is further emphasized by the fact that the Board members usually open the hearing by introducing themselves and shaking hands with the applicant. All participants sit around the same table; in our experience hearings are more akin to discussions rather than formal presentations. While Board members' questioning is often intense, it is rarely offensive and seldom abusive.

6. THE HEARING

In preparation for the hearing all attending Board members will have read at least the Progress Summary, reports from mental health professionals (if not summarized in other documents), and any submissions or support letters filed by, or on behalf of, the prisoner. When the files for forthcoming hearings are distributed a few days in advance by Board staff, current practice is that one member will be randomly assigned to "lead" on a case. Among other responsibilities, the "leader" is expected to read the entire Board file.

We strongly recommend that, just as in litigation, counsel attempt to discover as much as possible about "the predilections of individual members."[12] There may well be strategic benefits in deciding whether to proceed. The Board's workload is sufficiently heavy that it is usually quite easy to adjourn a hearing in the hope that the composition of the Board may change on a later occasion.

---

[12] R.R. Price, "Bringing the Rule of Law to Corrections" (1974), (No. 3), 16 Can. J. Crim. and Corr. 209, at 218.

Although the governing Regulation specifies that only one "assistant" may attend on behalf of a conditional release applicant, a practice has developed in many parts of the country that, so long as it is understood that the non-lawyer says very little, the Board will, upon receiving a request in advance, permit more than one person to attend. If the institution is aware that he plans to attend, a lawyer or articling student who can produce proof of professional status does not need security clearance;[13] non-lawyers must provide their full name and date of birth to the case management team 15 days before the scheduled hearing date. Counsel is well-advised to have an employer, family member or interested institutional official attend wherever possible. Not only does that person's presence emphasize continued community support, but also, the Board may, as part of its assessment of the prisoner's fitness for release, gently probe the dynamics of the relationship between the prisoner and his supporter.[14]

In order to represent the client effectively, counsel must understand that the use of the term "assistant" in section 20.1 of the *Parole Regulations*[15] is not merely to indicate that persons other than lawyers may attend at Board hearings. Although counsel is present as an advocate, since the hearing is inquisitorial there is no one against whom counsel can act as an adversary. Indeed, counsel should recall throughout that as far as the Board is concerned, the only occasion on which he may speak, as outlined in the Regulation, is at the end of the hearing when he is given an opportunity to address the Board on behalf of the client. Furthermore, while the Board usually permits counsel to interject during the course of a hearing, aggressive tactics are frequently unlikely to advance the client's cause. The Rules of Professional Conduct of most provincial law societies mandate that counsel treat administrative tribunals "with courtesy and respect". While counsel must be prepared to

---

13 Although the Board is generally prepared to make efforts to accommodate counsel's schedule, every effort should be made to be at the institution at the scheduled time. Further, advance communication of anticipated delay is essential. In *Appeal Division Reports* Case No. "PROC 013," May 27, 1988, the assistant had advised that he could not attend until a certain time, and had been assured by the case management team that this would not present a problem. When the assistant arrived, he discovered that the Board had proceeded more expeditiously with other cases than had been anticipated. The panel members (who had to travel a long distance to another institution for the following day) had offered the prisoner the option of proceeding without his assistant, or adjourning the case for approximately 1 month. Because specific arrangements had been made, the Appeal Division directed that a new hearing be held.

14 The supporter will not likely be subjected to detailed questioning, most Board members being of the view that they may only ask pointed questions of the actual parole applicant.

15 SOR/81-318.

place firmly on record his objection to what he believes are substantive, procedural or evidentiary errors, it is appropriate for counsel during the Board's questioning to seek permission to make a statement or to draw the Board's attention to a piece of written material.

The first stage of a parole hearing is that the "leader" reviews a checklist of procedural safeguards to ensure, *inter alia*, that the prisoner is aware of the purpose of the hearing, and that he has received disclosure of the written materials to be relied upon. As it occasionally transpires that the Board has, in its file, materials to which the team has not had access, or to which it has not referred in the Progress Summary, it is useful for counsel to interject at this point to detail what reports have been received, or of which he and the client are aware. The next phase is that the institutional and community members of the case management team are asked by the "leader" to summarize the case. In post-suspension cases held in local detention centres, usually only the supervising parole officer attends. Unless there is new information not already included in the Progress Summary, the oral presentation by the case management team usually only highlights the contents of that report. However, it sometimes transpires that there is confidential information which the team possesses, and which it wishes to share with the Board. As discussed in Chapter 6, if the Board is not already aware of the information, it must decide whether the information is relevant to its decision-making function. If so, the Board must then go on to consider whether the "gist" or the complete details of the information can be shared with the prisoner. To accomplish this the Board will ask the prisoner and assistant to leave the room while the matter is discussed with the team. Aware of the fundamental injustice in making decisions about freedom on the basis of undisclosed information, the Board is moving ever closer to a policy of full disclosure. In our experience, there is little which is not ultimately disclosed. Often the case management team simply prefers that the Board make the final decision about whether matters should be shared, rather than taking that responsibility upon itself.

A current problem to which counsel should be attuned is that of attitudes of the victim, the victim's family and the community at large. The Board now places considerable emphasis on attempting to obtain "victim impact statements" or similar information as part of the post-trial information-gathering process. Counsel should not hesitate to remind the Board that while evidence as to the effects of the crime on the victim is subject to cross-examination if it is sought to be introduced as part of the sentencing process, there is no opportunity to do so in the parole context. This may be particularly significant in detention cases, where one of the statutory criteria which the Board must consider is whether there is evidence of "severe physical or psychological harm"; the Board should be reminded to resist any temptation to assume the harm from the very nature of the offence. Secondly, counsel should not be particularly concerned if police comments as to the parole applicant's suitability for release are highly negative in tone; Board members are well aware that, as part of the ongoing opposition of many police forces to the concept of parole for persons convicted of violent offences, many such reports voice police objections "on behalf of the victim/community" to conditional release. In our experience, Board members tend to treat such reports as an anodyne. Finally, although the Board will meet with victims or persons in the community opposed to release, and will advise them of scheduled hearing dates, under current practice they will not be allowed to attend unless the prisoner and Board members consent. Subject to confidential matters (such as continuing threats) being raised, disclosure will be made to the parole applicant of the expressed objections to his release.

Once the team members have presented the case the "leader" will commence thorough and probing questioning of the prisoner. As the Board's jurisdiction to grant release commences from the offence, much of the hearing is likely to be occupied in discussing the facts and circumstances of the crime, the criminal record and pre-incarceration lifestyle of the applicant. Above all, the prisoner is expected to demonstrate in some significant way that he has gained some insight into the circumstances which led to the offence. After these subjects have been reviewed in considerable detail, the leading Board member will usually question the prisoner about his performance and behaviour while incarcerated, particularly his participation in any kind of treatment programs. The client should be advised that experienced Board members are likely to have a detailed knowledge of the content of these programs, and sometimes with the personnel who administer them. For example, if the prisoner has enlisted in Alcoholics Anonymous, he may be asked to detail the major recommended steps towards an alcohol-free lifestyle, and to name the officials responsible for administering the program in the institution. While there is no guarantee that frankness will lead to success, deceit will inevitably result in failure, if discovered. Finally, the leading board member will discuss the release plan in some detail. Although the other Board member is entitled to intervene at any point, typically he does not do so, deferring questions until the "leader" has finished.

In the context of a post-suspension hearing, it is important to keep in mind that the questioning frequently ranges far beyond the specific incident which has precipitated the suspension. For example, although a single occurrence may have led to suspension and referral, the prisoner and assistant should be aware and fully prepared to deal with that issue in the context of previous behaviour while incarcerated or on conditional release. The following subjects are usually addressed:

- Behaviour while on conditional release prior to the incident triggering the suspension and referral.
- The prisoner's relationship with the parole officer.
- Employment or educational endeavours.
- The extent of, and commitment to, participation in mental health, alcohol or drug treatment programs.
- Behavioural patterns while in a halfway house.
- Community support and/or reaction to suspension or release.
- Plans for future release if the suspension is cancelled.

While the Board will consider legal defences or mitigating circumstances where a new charge has been laid, in the post-suspension hearing context Board members do not regard themselves as constrained by the formal rules of the criminal law respecting the admissibility of evidence, the presumption of innocence, or the necessity for proof beyond a reasonable doubt.[16] The Board is usually more interested in examining whether, in all of the circumstances, there is an indication of criminal activity or behaviour which the Board considers to fall below the standards acceptable for a person subject to conditional release.[17] At the same time it should not be assumed that a plea or finding of guilt will automatically result in a decision to terminate or revoke conditional release. Each case is discussed and determined upon its particular facts. For example, the Board may be satisfied that the period of time already spent in custody, combined with the penalty imposed by the court, are sufficient deterrents to the individual parolee.

In considering in advance what submissions might be made, counsel should commence with the statute. Unfortunately, phrases such as "whether the inmate has derived the maximum benefit from imprisonment", or "whether reform and rehabilitation would be furthered by a grant of parole", or "whether the risk to society would be undue", are so broad as to be almost devoid of substantive meaning. Nevertheless, since these are the statutory criteria which the Board is expected to consider, counsel's submissions must at least implicitly address them.

---

[16] See the discussion of the judgment of the Federal Court of Appeal in *Morin v. National Special Handling Unit Review Committee* (1985), 46 C.R. (3d) 238 and related cases in Chapter 8.

[17] Automatic "forfeiture" of conditional release upon conviction for an indictable offence, which used to be contained in section 17 of the *Parole Act* (R.S.C. 1970, c. P-2) was repealed, effective October 15, 1977, by S.C. 1976-77, c. 53, s. 30.

Because Board members are usually well-prepared for hearings, and because counsel's submissions usually follow directly on from the questioning of the prisoner, counsel should not generally be lengthy (as a useful guide, counsel might do well to keep in mind that the original version of the governing Regulation spoke of the right to sum up for a period of not longer than 10 minutes). As with other litigation, the most effective submissions are likely to be those which address, in a realistic manner, the issues focussed on during questioning by the decision-maker. In the parole context it is usually fairly easy to address the substantive issues; most Board members make it a practice to be explicit in their enunciation of their concerns. It is considered good practice for counsel to ask directly whether the Board wishes to hear submissions on a particular point. It is useful for counsel to differentiate between the types of hearings involved. Unlike the parole granting stage, in detention and post-suspension cases counsel may play a slightly different role since the Board is involved in deciding whether to deprive a person of a qualified right to liberty.

Once submissions are completed the Board typically asks whether any participant has anything to add arising from the discussion. If so, counsel is given a brief right of reply. All parties other than the Board members then retire from the hearing room to await the decision and reasons. After a few minutes all are invited to return, whereupon the "leader" will announce the decision and reasons which he will have written on the "Board Members Comment Sheet", a copy of which should be photocopied and given to counsel immediately following the hearing. As these comments will later be typed and formally placed on the prisoner's parole file within 15 days of the decision,[18] it is sometimes useful for counsel to initiate a discussion of any wording which may seem ambiguous. This is frequently the case in regard to non-standard conditions of release. If the parties are not clear in their intent, it may later be difficult to recreate the atmosphere of the hearing, particularly for parole supervisors who were not present. Similarly, where the prisoner will continue to be involved with the case management team, it may well be of assistance to both that the Board members describe in some detail what they expect should occur prior to the next hearing or decision.

The Board has one additional statutory obligation in post-suspension cases where a decision is taken to revoke conditional release. Section 25(3) of the *Parole Act* requires the Board to consider whether or not to re-credit any remission. While a more detailed discussion of the

---

[18]   This is required by section 21 of the Regulations.

factors which the Board must consider may be found in Chapter 8, counsel are reminded that they should be prepared to address this issue as an alternative during the course of his submissions.

7. POST-HEARING REMEDIES

If a client is disappointed with a Board decision, he is likely to raise immediately the possibility of invoking internal or judicial review. Unfortunately, the illusion that an internal or external appeal will be successful often impedes the prisoner from focussing in on the Board's concerns. Counsel should be very cautious about offering advice until he has reviewed his notes, listened to the audio-tape and read the formal comments and reasons for decision. Furthermore, it is worth reminding the prisoner that any judicial review or appeal of the decision is likely only to result in a new hearing. Although one of the powers of the Appeal Division of the National Parole Board (provincial boards have less formal review procedures) is that it may substitute the decision that, in its opinion, should have been made, experience demonstrates that the Appeal Division is loathe to interfere, except in the most obvious cases, with the decision of those who had the opportunity of observing the demeanour of the prisoner.

8. "PAPER CASES"

One final area of interest to counsel involves non-panel reviews (often referred to as "paper cases"), where a decision is scheduled to be taken without a hearing. Frequent examples of this are unescorted temporary absence decisions for religious holidays, decisions about full parole where the prisoner is successfully completing a community-based day parole, decisions respecting modification of release conditions, or internal appeals to the Appeal Division. In all of these examples, counsel should first determine whether, by statute or policy, the client has a right to a hearing, and whether that right should be waived. At the very least counsel should advise the client not to waive the right to a hearing until there has been an opportunity to scrutinize the latest Progress Summary prepared by institutional or parole personnel for the Board. If it is not supportive of the prisoner or parolee (or, as occasionally transpires, it does not reflect what the prisoner wishes to apply for), counsel should consider whether to advise the client to insist on the right to a hearing. Again, where there seem to be communication difficulties between the prisoner and his team or parole supervisor, it may be useful for counsel to request, through the Regional Director or Senior Board Member, that the Board convene a hearing to review and clarify the contentious issues. If there is no right to a hearing and the Board declines to direct one, counsel should be prepared in appropriate cases to make detailed written submissions to the Board, all of which will be carefully reviewed by randomly selected Board members. The form of the submissions is not important, so long as they are concise and relevant.

13

Conclusion: Re-Shaping Early Release

... History, as one of the human sciences, has a discrete but important role to play in combating carceral power and the coercive structures of thought that underpin it. ... It can help to pierce through the rhetoric that carelessly presents the further consolidation of carceral power as reform. As much as anything else, it is this suffocating vision of the past that legitimizes the abuses of the present and seeks to adjust us to the cruelties of the future.[1]

1. INTEGRATION AS A SYSTEMIC GOAL

Imprisonment involves an exercise of power by the State in response to an allegation, finding or perception that an individual has breached or threatened the order of the community. It may be defined as the coercive separation of individuals from the community for custodial or punitive purposes. The custodial objective can be elusive. Within the criminal process, it encompasses pre-trial custody, confinement to assess fitness for trial and the dispositions resulting from findings of unfitness or not guilty by reason of insanity. In many of these cases, the custodial objective becomes blurred by assertions of therapeutic interests.[2] Hence, the criteria for release from confinement are often vague and unrelated to the conduct which generated the process. Because our focus is on the parole process and its related mechanisms, we have restricted our attention to imprisonment as a function of punitive goals.

The sentencing process is the vehicle through which punishment is imposed after a finding of criminal responsibility. It is an integral element of the criminal process. It determines and inflicts sanctions in the name of the community and imprisonment is its bluntest instrument. In Canada, a vast system of penitentiaries, prisons and other facilities have evolved to implement sentences of imprisonment. They range from the "super maximum" security setting of Special Handling

---

[1] M. Ignatieff, *A Just Measure of Pain: The Penitentiary in The Industrial Revolution 1750-1850* (New York: Pantheon, 1978), p. 220.

[2] See, for example, the justification accepted by the Ontario Court of Appeal for indefinite confinement after a finding of "not guilty by reason of insanity" in *R. v. Swain* (1986), 50 C.R. (3d) 97 (Ont. C.A.), currently on reserve in the Supreme Court of Canada.

Units to the open environment of community-based "correctional" facilities.

Beyond providing information and analysis of the law and practice surrounding conditional release from imprisonment, the thesis of this book is that there needs to be much better integration of the constituent elements which impose and administer punishment. The instruments by which our community responds to those found guilty of criminal conduct, need to be harmonized within a framework of common objectives and coherent principles. The rules of criminal responsibility cannot be divorced from the consequences of a finding of guilt. After conviction, the processes of sentencing, imprisonment and release must also play coherent and integrated roles. An inquiry into the theories of criminal responsibility, the nature of imprisonment and even a careful analysis of the sentencing function are beyond the scope of this book. That task would be especially difficult given the growing skepticism that the criminal justice system as a whole lacks a unifying conception of its societal function. Yet the principles of criminal responsibility, sentencing and imprisonment are all inextricably bound up within an examination of the utility, efficacy and integrity of a release mechanism. It is our goal, through an explication of release from imprisonment in Canada, to advance the debate over whether, and how, mechanisms of release should be re-designed to ensure that the elements of the criminal process act and speak consistently with clarity, fairness and common purpose.

2. THE NATURE OF IMPRISONMENT IN CANADA

With the building of the first penitentiary at Kingston in 1835, Canada joined the United States, Britain and various European countries in looking to a controlled structure as the primary instrument of penal policy.[3] As in England,[4] growing disaffection with capital punish-

---

[3]   Classically, it has been asserted that the birth of the penitentiary in the late 18th and early 19th Centuries was a logical response to the reduction in the number of capital crimes combined with the loss of opportunities to transport convicts. More recently, a number of critiques have characterized the development of the penitentiary as an element of the social, political and economic contexts of the times: see D. Rothman, *The Discovery of the Asylum* (Boston: Little, Brown & Co., 1971); M. Foucault, *Discipline and Punish* (New York: Pantheon, 1978); M. Ignatieff, *supra*, note 1; D. Melossi and M. Pararino, *The Prison and the Factory: The Origins of the Penitentiary System* (Totowa, N.J.: Barnes & Nobel Books, 1981).

[4]   See L. Radzinowicz, *A History of English Criminal Law, Vol. 1* (London: Stevens & Sons, 1948), pp. 151-164. The author points out that in 1805, of 4,605 persons committed for trial, only 2,783 were convicted. Of these, 350 were sentenced to death, but only 68 were executed (p. 166).

ment as the mandatory response following conviction for numerous crimes had led to an obvious divergence between what the law required and how it was implemented.[5] By 1833, hanging had been formally removed as the penalty for petty offences in Upper Canada.[6] The provinces of Canada had some experience with a variety of sanctions based on public humiliation, including the pillory and the barbaric practice of branding, but these had fallen into disuse by the 1830's.[7] Banishment continued to be provided by statute, but, while commonly used, was considered inefficacious.[8]

Transportation to penal colonies in Bermuda, New South Wales and Van Dieman's Land (Tasmania) was available until 1853, and was used, sometimes in substitution upon commutation of a sentence of death, and commonly in response to political prisoners and to deserters from British garrisons.[9] Local gaols existed in each of the districts of Upper Canada, established by the District Board of Magistrates and supervised by the Sheriff of each district.[10] Under-funded and ill-conceived, the local gaols were lamentably inadequate. Beattie has described them as "places of detention where prisoners were herded together indiscriminately to await trial or the execution of their sentence."[11] While the incidence of crime was not particularly high, the stresses of industrialization and increased immigration combined with American and British influences to produce public concern about the community's ability to address the potential for disorder.

In 1831, the legislature of Upper Canada appointed a committee to consider the efficacy of building a penitentiary. The committee's Report

---

[5] See *Report of a Select Committee on the Expediency of Erecting a Penitentiary*, Journal of the House of Assembly of Upper Canada (1831), Appendix, p. 211, reprinted in Beattie, *infra*, note 6, pp. 80-86.

[6] See Statutes of Upper Canada 1833 (3 Wm. 4), c. 4. Also see J.M. Beattie, *Attitudes Towards Crime and Punishment in Upper Canada, 1830-1850: A Documentary Study* (Toronto: Centre of Criminology, 1977), p. 10. This development arrived earlier in Nova Scotia, New Brunswick and Prince Edward Island: see Statutes of Nova Scotia, 1758 (32 Geo. 2), c. 13; Statutes of New Brunswick, 1789 (29 Geo. 3), c. 7; Statutes of P.E.I., 1793 (33 Geo. 3), c. 1. By 1841, capital offences in the new united Provinces of Canada had been reduced to treason, rape, carnal knowledge with a girl under ten, and sodomy: see Provincial Statutes of Canada, 1841 (4 & 5 Vict.), c. 27, ss. 2, 15, 16, and 17.

[7] J.A. Edmison, "Some Aspects of 19th Century Canadian Prisons" in W.T. McGrath, Ed., *Crime and Its Treatment in Canada*, 2d ed. (Toronto: MacMillan, 1976) pp. 350-351.

[8] *Ibid.*, pp. 351-352, and *Report of a Select Committee, supra*, note 5.

[9] See Edmiston, *supra*, note 7, and the discussion of transportation in Chapter 5.

[10] See R. Splane, *Social Welfare in Ontario, 1791-1893: A Study of Public Welfare Administration* (Toronto: University of Toronto Press, 1965) p. 120; Beattie, *supra*, note 6, pp. 13-14.

[11] Beattie, *supra*, note 6, p. 13.

criticized the manner in which fines, banishment and corporal punishment were imposed and characterized imprisonment in the local gaols as "inexpedient and pernicious in the extreme".[12] Endorsing the idea of a penitentiary in Upper Canada, the Report concluded:

> A penitentiary, as its name imports, should be a place to lead a man to repent of his sins and amend his life, and if it has that affect, so much the better, as the cause of religion gains by it, but it is quite enough for the purposes of the public if the punishment is so terrible that the threat of a repetition of it deters him from crime, or his description of it, others. It should therefore be a place which by every means not cruel and not affecting the health of the offender shall be rendered so irksome and so terrible that during his afterlife he may dread as a repetition of the punishment, and, if possible, that he should prefer death to such a contingency.[13]

After some debate, two commissioners, H.C. Thompson and John Macaulay, were appointed to devise a plan for the establishment of a penitentiary in Upper Canada.

During this period there was an active international debate about the nature of, and appropriate design for, penal institutions, much of which focussed around the need for solitary confinement and the need for surveillance. Jeremy Bentham's "Panopticon", characterized by the maintenance of discipline through constant surveillance throughout all times of the day and all periods of incarceration, influenced both the physical and conceptual structuring of the prisons in France[14] and England.[15] Foucault speaks of the "Geneva model", in which prisoners were segregated into different areas and groups consisting of those who needed to prove themselves, those who were being punished, and those who were entitled to reward.[16] Reform movements in the United States produced the "Auburn" and "Pennsylvania" models.[17] At the Auburn State prison, the "congregate system" was imposed, in which prisoners were confined to their cells separately, but were brought together during

---

12 See *Report of a Select Committee, supra,* note 5.
13 *Ibid.,* reproduced in Beattie, p. 82. See also the *Report of the Chief Justice and Judges to the Lieutenant Governor on the Subject of the Local Gaols,* Journal of the House of Assembly (2nd Sess., 12th Parl.), Appendix, in which prisoners were described as "in a state of suffering from the want of what we regard as the very necessaries of life."
14 See Foucault, *supra,* note 3, pp. 249-251.
15 See Ignatieff, *supra,* note 1, p. 113. Bentham's technique of management based on a factory model and economic incentives was rejected, because, in Ignatieff's view, it was "out of sympathy with the reformer's conception of imprisonment as a religious penance."
16 See Foucault, *supra,* note 3, pp. 245-246, describing a prisoner's progress through four distinct phases: (1) intimidation through confinement; (2) work in isolation;' (3) moralization by lectures; and (4) working in common with others.
17 See the discussion in M. Jackson, *Prisoners of Isolation: Solitary Confinement in Canada* (Toronto: University of Toronto Press, 1983), pp. 16-22.

the working day for organized labour. In Pennsylvania, imprisonment in the Cherry Hill Penitentiary was premised on a regime of strict separation through 24-hour solitary confinement and individual work assignments carried out in isolation.

While these various models produced different physical structures, they all contained common ingredients: labour, discipline and an emphasis on moral reformation. This should be no surprise given the influence generated by John Howard's *The State of the Prisons*, published in 1777. Howard's vision of the penitentiary included a regime of established rhythms, repetition of activity, prayer, confinement in cells and constant inspection.[18]

The Commissioners visited American institutions at Auburn, Sing-Sing, Blackwell's Island, and the Penitentiary of Connecticut, but were prevented by a cholera epidemic from actually visiting the State Penitentiary at Philadelphia.[19] The Commissioners commented that both the Pennsylvania and Auburn models were built "on the grand principle of solitary confinement". Ultimately, they favoured the "congregate" system which they had observed at Auburn, considering it a "beautiful example of what may be done by proper discipline, in a prison well constructed."[20] Both from their report and their correspondence with the Deputy Keeper at Auburn, the Commissioners expressed their positive impressions of the regime of silence and non-communication imposed at that institution, where even prisoners working together did not know each others' names.[21]

The first *Penitentiary Act*,[22] and ultimately the building of the penitentiary at Kingston in 1835, resulted from the Commissioners' Report. The preamble to the 1834 statute reads:

> If many offenders convicted of crime were ordered to solitary imprisonment, accompanied by well-regulated labour and religious instruction, it might be the means under providence, not only of deterring others from the Commission of like crimes, but also of reforming the individuals, and inuring them to the habits of industry.

Disciplinary rules were adopted which clearly reflected commitment to the mechanisms of obedience, submission, diligence and silence.[23]

---

[18] See Ignatieff, *supra*, note 3, p. 53, Foucault, *supra*, note 31, p. 149, and the *Penitentiary Act* of 1779.

[19] See *Report of the Commissioners*, Journal of the House of Assembly (1832-33), Appendix, reprinted in Beattie, *supra*, note 6, pp. 86-92.

[20] *Ibid.*, in Beattie, p. 91.

[21] *Ibid.*, in Beattie, pp. 89-90 and 93-96.

[22] 1834 (4 William 4), c. 37.

[23] It is of more than picaresque interest to note that prisoners ". . . must not exchange

Clearly, the beginning of the Canadian Penitentiary system was well-grounded in a concern for moral reformation and productive labour through discipline.

In preparing his report[24] to the House of Assembly on prisons and penitentiaries in 1836, Charles Duncombe visited prisons in New York, Maine, Massachusetts, Connecticut, Pennsylvania, Maryland, Ohio, and Kentucky. After commenting on the productivity and cost-efficiency of prison labour, he decried the use of flogging and other fear-producing mechanisms, but still maintained the importance of moral reformation as a focus for penitentiary confinement. He commented that:

> The energies of the law and the suppression of crime, are most potent and availing when directed with a constant reference to the moral faculties of our nature. . . .[25]

His criticisms of American prisons were not conceptual, but rather concentrated on the American failure to maintain the "system of prison discipline . . . with the same intelligent and disinterested zeal with which it was begun there. . . ."

By the end of the 19th Century, five penitentiaries had been built in what are, to this day, the five correctional regions.[26] James Moylan, the Inspector of Penitentiaries, advocated the increased use of separation of prisoners to keep the "habitual and hardened criminals from the neophytes" and to provide newcomers "with the solitude necessary to reflect their weakness and future reformation."[27] In 1914, it was reported that prisoners in Canadian penitentiaries spent more time alone in their cells than in any prison on the continent.[28] A Royal Commission noted:

> Solitary imprisonment, labour and religious instructions, have been the only agencies employed for the reclamation of the unfortunates. The first of these three has always been a prominent feature of discipline.[29]

---

looks, wink, laugh, nod, or just speak to each other, nor shall they make use of any signs, except as such are necessary as to explain their wants. . . ."; see M. Jackson, *supra*, note 17, pp. 27-28.

24 Reprinted in Beattie, *supra*, note 6, pp. 107-112. The report was delivered on March 28, 1836: see Minutes of House of Assembly, 2nd Sess., 12th Parliament (6 Wm. 4). Duncombe was a very energetic member of the House who was often assigned special tasks. He left the county after the 1837 rebellion.

25 *Ibid.* pp. 108-109.

26 In addition to the Kingston Penitentiary in Ontario, prisoners were confined to St. Vincent de Paul Penitentiary in Quebec, Dorchester Penitentiary in New Brunswick, the Manitoba Penitentiary, and the British Columbia Penitentiary.

27 *Report of the Minister of Justice as to Penitentiaries in Canada for the Year Ended, June 30, 1889* (Ottawa: Queen's Printer), reproducing the 14th Annual Report of the Inspector of Penitentiaries, 53 Victoria, Sessional Papers (No. 10), at xii.

28 *Report of the Royal Commission on Penitentiaries* (King's Printer, 1914), at 6.

29 *Ibid.*

In 1936, Mr. Justice Archambault and two others were appointed as a commission to "enquire into and report upon the penal system of Canada".[30] Reporting in 1938, the chapter on prison discipline commenced with the following statement of its objective:

> Discipline should never be confused with punishment. It is a system of training, with the object of inculcating obedience to rules and respect to their authority, and its intended effect is orderly conduct.[31]

The description of the disciplinary regime which followed in the *Archambault Report* cannot be distinguished from the regime which existed in 1835, either in respect of offences, punishments, or procedure.

By the late 1980's, the face of the Canadian penitentiary system has changed dramatically over the 150 years of its development. We now have a large number of institutions, spread across five regions from the Atlantic to the Pacific, reflecting a multi-tiered classification system.[32] Institutions are classified by security rating as either minimum, medium, or maximum. As well, we have two Special Handling Units or super maximum institutions. In some regions, specific institutions have been designated for protective custody prisoners. Aside from the classification of prisoners, the contemporary penitentiary system employs, particularly in its newer facilities, high-technology physical and perimeter security. From the programming perspective, in varying degrees, there are some professional services and some vocational opportunities. Particularly in the modern facilities, the internal environment of confinement has been substantially ameliorated with respect to opportunities for recreation, visits with one's family and library.

Notwithstanding all of these changes, it is our view that the model of the penitentiary currently operating in Canada is the same model which operated in 1835. It is premised on the disciplinary regime and the dichotomy between power and powerlessness which discipline necessarily generates. Regardless of whether one subscribes to the moral/religious or the labour market objective as the 19th Century rationale for the disciplinary regime,[33] it is clear that discipline was intended to be the

---

[30] See *Report of the Royal Commission To Investigate the Penal System of Canada* (*Archambault Report*) (Ottawa: King's Printer, 1938), at v. The other two members of the Commission were R.W. Craig, a Winnipeg lawyer, and Henry Anderson, a Toronto journalist.

[31] *Ibid.*

[32] The multi-tiered classification system applies only to institutions for men, since currently the only penitentiary for women is the Prison for Women in Kingston, Ontario.

[33] See the discussion of these historical views in Chapter 2.

instrument of other ends. Now, discipline has become its own self-evident and self-justifying rationale.

Of course, in the formal sense, prison discipline has changed significantly, due in part to the judicially imposed obligation of fairness and the constitutionally entrenched imperative of fundamental justice. These developments apply most directly to the formal disciplinary process and, to some extent, to subsidiary acts of discipline such as transfers to higher security. However, they have not changed the essential characteristic of the disciplinary regime in terms of its power dynamic and transformative objective. Power and powerlessness continue to be the dominating features of Canadian penitentiaries. Like water in a pipe, the power of the disciplinary regime flows until it reaches an open valve. While fairness and fundamental justice regulate the valve of the formal disciplinary process, the assertion of power simply flows to other aspects of penitentiary life: visits, searches, correspondence, and anything else which continues to be characterized as a privilege within the absolute discretion of the penitentiary authorities. As a result, the structural and organizational changes described above can only be characterized as cosmetic. The Canadian penitentiary remains essentially the same.

This conclusion about the static nature of penitentiary imprisonment cannot be ignored. We cannot hide from it by investing all of our energies in re-constructing a Criminal Code or in reforming the structure of sentencing.

3. SENTENCING REFORM IN THE 1980's

In its 1987 report, the Canadian Sentencing Commission recognized that the nature of sentencing has remained essentially unchanged:

> A review of the numerous reports which have been written on various aspects of the penal system provides overwhelming support for the impression that the history of punishment in Canada—and particularly the history of incarceration—is simply a series of perfunctory changes.[34]

Following the lead of the Law Reform Commission, the Sentencing Commission accepted the principle of restraint as the guiding theme for sentencing reform. Focussing on the breadth of discretion which characterizes our current sentencing regime, the Commission translated concerns about disparity, uncertainty and unpredictability into a proposed guidelines scheme for sentencing. This adoption of "just deserts" as the

---

[34] *Report of the Canadian Sentencing Commission, Sentencing Reform: A Canadian Approach* (Ottawa: Queen's Printer, 1987) pp. 21-22.

dominant rationale for sentencing accords with the popular trend in American sentencing reform.[35] Uniformity, at least in respect of approach, is achieved by ranking offences and classifying factors in terms of blameworthiness. Proportionality is the unifying concept, rekindling memories of Cesare Beccarea's "perfect syllogism." While there can be no excuse for condoning and maintaining disparity based on race, class and gender, it is not clear and incontrovertible that the imposition of an artificial uniformity on an unequal world really serves to alleviate disparity in more than a superficial way.

A number of American jurisdictions have moved to a structured sentencing model.[36] The more recent trend towards structured regimes has been attributed to the pragmatic expedients of correctional management and over-crowding, not the substantive issues of proportionality and certainty.[37] The Canadian Sentencing Commission appears to have been particularly impressed by the presumptive guidelines regime developed in Minnesota, although it chose not to replicate it in all respects.[38]

This is not the appropriate place to examine the Commission's recommendations in detail. However, because the Commission includes the abolition of parole as part of its package, a brief summary of the general scheme is necessary before we express our concerns about this particular recommendation. The principle elements of the proposed regime are the use of presumptive dispositions for all offences, followed by the application of pre-determined ranges in each case where a custodial disposition is chosen. The presumptive disposition allocated to each offence indicates how the sentencing judge should respond to the initial question of whether a custodial or non-custodial alternative is appropriate. The three factors which determine this choice are the

---

[35] See the work of A. Von Hirsch, commencing with his book *Doing Justice: The Choice of Punishments* (New York: Hill and Wang, 1976). See also the special edition on "Sentencing" (1990) 32 Can. J. Crim. 381-502, containing numerous articles by Von Hirsch and others, commenting on the proposals of the Canadian Sentencing Commission.

[36] The Report refers to 17 U.S. states which have some form of structured model (p. 286). By 1988, new guideline schemes had been approved in Louisiana, Oregon, Tennessee and the District of Columbia, and a federal guidelines model began in 1987: see K. Knapp, "Structured Sentencing: Building an Experience" (1988), 72 Judicature 46, at 46-48.

[37] Knapp, *ibid.*, at 48.

[38] See *Report, supra*, note 34, at 296-299. A study prepared for the Commission by A. Vining, *Issues Relating to Sentencing Guidelines: An Evaluation of U.S. Experiences and Their Relevance for Canada* (Supply & Services Canada, 1988), relied heavily on the reports of the Minnesota Sentencing Commission and accounts by its staff members (see notes 7-10).

nature of the offence, the seriousness of the act itself within the category of the offence and the offender's previous record. In accordance with the principle of restraint, these factors are sequentially pre-allocated in an effort to ensure that less serious matters do not inappropriately produce custodial dispositions.

The four presumptive dispositions are: (1) IN, (2) OUT, (3) QUALIFIED IN, and (4) QUALIFIED OUT. The first two indicate an assessment that the nature of the offence should pre-determine the answer to the custodial issue.[39] The qualified presumptions would apply to those offences which do not inherently point in one direction or the other but, rather, encompass a broader spectrum of conduct require-ment assessment of seriousness in each case. This involves a considera-tion of the particular act and whether the offender has previously been convicted of a relevant offence. Thus, the QUALIFIED OUT presump-tion means that a non-custodial disposition is mandated unless the offence committed is serious within its own category *and* the offender has a relevant record.[40] Conversely, QUALIFIED IN means that the offender should be incarcerated *unless* the offence is not serious *and* the offender has no relevant previous record.[41] Although the sentencing judge can depart from the presumptive disposition if "explicit reasons" are provided, this part of the scheme should encourage the use of non-custodial alternatives in many situations where currently short sen-tences of imprisonment are usually imposed.

The major focus of our interest is the situation where the threshold choice leads to imprisonment. In these cases, the Commission recom-mends the development[42] and application of a national set of sentencing guidelines which would determine the usual range of sentence for a given offence. The guidelines would permit some flexibility within each

---

[39] For example, the Commission recommends an OUT presumption for assault, theft of a credit card, causing a distrubance, possession of a narcotic, etc. IN presumptions would apply to escape, forcible confinement, impaired driving causing bodily harm, making counterfeit money, manslaughter, sexual assault with a weapon, etc. See Appendix E to the *Report, supra*, note 34, for a complete list.

[40] Examples of proposes QUALIFIED OUT dispositions are pointing a firearm, public mischief, infanticide, impaired driving, uttering threates, mischief to property, theft over $1,000 etc.: See Appendix E to the *Report, supra*, note 34, for a complete list.

[41] Examples of proposed QUALIFIED IN dispositions are sexual assault, break and enter a dwelling house, promoting race hatred, assault causing bodily harm, etc.: See Appendix E to the *Report, supra*, note 34, for a complete list.

[42] This would be effected and periodically reviewed by a permanent sentencing commis-sion consisting of at least seven members, the majority of whom would be judges: see Chapter 14 of the Report. Proposed guidelines would be tabled in Parliament and would come into effect 90 days later unless a specified number of M.P.'s brought forward a negative resolution: see *Report, supra*, note 34, pp. 305-309.

range; a sentencing judge could depart from the range, up or down, in response to a "non-exhaustive" list of mitigating and aggravating factors.[43] Of course, departure must be accompanied by explanatory reasons and would be subject to appellate review.

Three other elements are relevant to our consideration of the new regime advocated by the Commission. First, the Commission recognizes the anachronism of the current structure of maximum penalties[44] and recommends a review of all offences. The new structure would reserve life imprisonment as the mandatory penalty for murder and high treason,[45] but would rank all other offences in terms of "relative seriousness" and then allocate maximum penalties between 6 months and 12 years.[46] While the stipulated ceiling is 12 years, the possibility of longer sentences is maintained in cases of multiple sentencing or the "enhanced" sentence which we will examine later. Secondly, the Commission recommends the maintenance of remission-based release such that a prisoner could earn credits for "good behaviour" up to a maximum of one-quarter of the judicially-imposed sentence.[47] Thirdly, the Commission recommends the abolition of parole except in cases of life imprisonment.[48]

While the Commission's proposed reform package contains a number of valuable elements and reflects an important contribution to the sentencing debate, we do not accept the utility of, or justification for, the abolition of parole recommendation. In conceptual terms, the Commission argues that the exercise of parole denigrates the "meaning of a sentence" and is inconsistent with a guidelines scheme premised on just deserts. The concern appears to emanate, in some degree, from the perception, both by judges[49] and the public,[50] that parole operates idiosyncratically and inconsistently to produce early release in unwarranted

---

[43] A sentencing judge can look to other factors beyond the articulated list to justify departure: see *Report, supra*, note 34, pp. 320-321. Recognizing that some individual factors relate to race and gender or the social and vocational context produced historically by these factors, the Commission observes that they should never be used to increase a sentence but may be invoked in mitigation: see *Report, supra*, note 34, pp. 322-323.

[44] See *Report, supra*, note 34, pp. 195-196.

[45] See *Report, supra*, note 34, pp. 261-263.

[46] The new structure would permit maxima of 6 months, 1 year, 3 years, 6 years, 9 years, and 12 years: see *Report, supra*, note 34, pp. 201-203.

[47] See Report, *supra*, note 34, pp. 246-248. This recommendation is premised on the dubious proposition that remission is an important tool of prison administration in maintaining discipline.

[48] See *Report, supra*, note 34, pp. 237-244, and Recommendation 10.1 specifically.

[49] See *Report, supra*, note 34, p. 56.

[50] See *Report, supra*, note 34, p. 92.

cases. The Commission offers three reasons for recommending the abolition of parole:

1. parole conflicts with the principle of proportionality;
2. parole introduces uncertainty into the sentencing process; and
3. parole transfers decision-making power from judges.[51]

An organized system of conditional release has existed in Canada for over 90 years. As shown in Chapter 5, since the 1920's critics of the Remission Service and National Parole Board have been neither infrequent nor shy. Throughout, there have been significant misperceptions about parole, usually generated by inaccurate or incomplete media reporting of sensational cases. It is not our role or our intention to defend the process of early release as it has existed since 1959;[52] throughout this book we have been sharply critical of many aspects of legislation, practices and policies. Our disagreement with the Sentencing Commission about early release flows from two propositions. First, we maintain that a structured process of early release can be integrated into the sentence process in a consistent, coherent and fair way. Secondly, so long as the nature of imprisonment remains cast in its 19th Century form and long custodial sentences continue to be common in Canada, we believe that early release is an essential safeguard to blunt the debilitating impact of imprisonment.

Whether early release diminishes the "meaning" of a sentence is a function of one's understanding of the "meaning" of the judicially-announced sentence as it relates to the entire sentencing process. We agree with the Commission that "the meaning of a sentence must be clear to all involved in the sentencing process."[53] There can be no excuse for confusion or disparate impressions. Historically, misunderstanding has been caused by the various bases upon which sentences can be justified and a failure to express clearly the reasons for a particular sentence. As the Commission correctly points out,[54] the formal structure of sentencing and the degree of public misunderstanding contribute to confusion. As well, the common rhetoric of deterrence, rehabilitation, punishment and denunciation is inadequate to inform anyone—the offender, the victim, the public, penal administrators, or parole deci-

---

[51] See *Report, supra*, note 34, pp. 244-245.
[52] The National Parole Board was established in 1959: see *Parole Act*, S.C. 1958, c. 38.
[53] See *Report, supra*, note 34, p. 244. One commonly hears journalists reporting a prosecution with reference to the maximum penalty provided by the *Criminal Code*, (R.S.C. 1985, c. C-46) even though there is little chance that such sentence will be imposed.
[54] See *Report, supra*, note 34, pp. 87-98.

sion-makers—how they ought to interpret the sentence. The Commission holds the view that the only relevant message is the "real time" which a prisoner will serve. Accordingly, viewed in those terms, the prospect of early release after one-third of a sentence or day parole after one-sixth necessarily denigrates from the initial pronouncement. This, however, is not the only perspective. In our opinion, different messages ought to be conveyed to different audiences. But each must be communicated clearly.

Sentences must be understood as containing two components. The first is the minimum custodial term, which is a function of applying the relevant parole eligibility rule to the sentence pronounced. The second aspect is the maximum custodial term (or, more appropriately the maximum period of State control), as determined by the sentence pronounced. The denunciatory aspect of punishment is provided by the recognition that a minimum period will be served. Deterrence is satisfied by communicating that offences akin to the one committed can produce incarceration for the stipulated maximum period. The amount of time actually served will be determined by the early release process and will depend on individual circumstances.

Blameworthiness is reflected by the recognition that imprisonment for some period is required. This assessment can encompass the nature of the offence and the relative seriousness of the particular act, including a consideration of the offender's previous record for related offences. If properly understood, the judicial function provides the legal authority for confinement and supervision until the sentence is completed and expresses to the community the relative sanction for the conduct in question. Individual circumstances are not submerged into a process of superficial uniformity[55] but, rather, become the dominant factors in determining release. Sentencing and release should be integrated within a coherent regime, yet kept distinct so long as the role of each can be clearly articulated and mutually understood.[56] (Later, we offer a conceptualized model for early release which, in our view, maintains the integrity of the judicially-pronounced sentence without uncertainty and unfairness.)

---

[55] As discussed in Chapter 2, see *R. v. Sandercock* (1986), 22 C.C.C. (3d) 79 (Alta. C.A.), a product of the Alberta "starting point" regime in which previous good character is negated as a mitigating factor by subsuming it into the description of the archetypical category.

[56] The Commission's concern about the Parole Board acting as a "sentence equalizer" is misleading: see *Report, supra,* note 34, pp. 240-241. Manslaughter sentences are a dubious source of comparison given the variety of situations, conduct and victims involved. A more critical analysis is required beyond simply comparing average time served.

Our major concern about the proposed abolition of parole is in relation to the operation of the Commission's guideline scheme as the source of sentences of imprisonment. In our opinion, the scheme recommended by the Commission will continue to generate large numbers of sentences of imprisonment, including long sentences, without providing an adequate opportunity for review to respond to changing circumstances and ameliorate the rigours of long-term confinement. First, there is the inherent danger of a guideline's models that, to promote consistency and reduce disparity, they encourage sentencers to aim for a median. Thus, while a jurisdiction may experience a reduction at the high end, it may also experience an increase at the lower end.[57] Secondly, the commission proposes that 47 offences have a maximum of 9 or 12 years' imprisonment with presumptive custodial dispositions and a further 18 offences with 6-year maxima and presumptive custodial dispositions. This must be appreciated in light of the proposal for "enhanced" sentences where, in cases of serious personal injury of a brutal nature or a pattern of serious repetitive behaviour, the sentence can exceed the maximum by 50 percent without any opportunity to earn remission credits.[58]

Clearly, the scheme as proposed will continue our history of long sentences of imprisonment, yet there will be no opportunity for review and early release. The enhanced sentence is intended to replace the current dangerous offender regime. In this context it is important to note that one of the factors which persuaded the Supreme Court of Canada to reject a constitutional challenge to the dangerous offender provisions was the availability of parole review and the potential for conditional release.[59]

Thirdly, the Commission has failed to deal adequately with the problem of multiple sentencing. Criminal lawyers and sentencing judges recognize the frequency of this issue, whether it arises in the context of sentencing for various offences or sentencing a person already serving a term of imprisonment. The current practice is explained in terms of the "totality principle"[60] which is a vague and often unhelpful expression of the concern that the cumulative impact of individual sentences not be

---

[57] Interestingly, evaluations of American guideline models reveal a general increase in the severity of sentencing: see M. Tonry, "Structuring Sentencing" (1988), 10 *Crime & Justice, A Review of Research* 267. *Cf.* A. Von Hirsch, The Politics of "Just Deserts" (1990), 32 Can. J. Crim. 397, at 400-402.

[58] See *Report, supra*, note 34, pp. 213-217.

[59] See *R. v. Lyons*, [1987] 2 S.C.R. 309.

[60] See C. Ruby, *Sentencing*, 3d ed. (Toronto: Butterworth's, 1988), pp. 38-41. See also the discussion of the totality principle in Chapter 2.

excessive or debilitating. The Commission suggests that it has a new response, the "total sentence."[61] This proposal would require a judge to indicate the appropriate sentence for each offence, but then to impose the appropriate total sentence, which could not exceed the lesser of "the sum of the maxima provided for each offence or the maximum provided for the most serious offence enhanced by one-third." Beyond defining the maximum total sentence, the Commission offers no explanation of how an appropriate total sentence should be determined, except to refer back to the current application of the totality principle. Moreover, the response of the "total sentence" is recommended only in respect of sentences imposed at one hearing. Other situations of multiple sentencing which commonly occur would continue to be determined by the judicial choice of concurrent or consecutive sentences.[62]

This simplistic response to multiple sentencing presents a gaping potential for the continuation of long, merged terms of imprisonment. This is especially clear when one appreciates that the Commission's research shows that the majority of judges and prosecutors do not, in general, support presumptive guidelines.[63] This does not mean that participants will attempt to subvert the scheme if implemented. However, given the broad sentencing discretion left in place by the multiple sentencing problem, the possibility of deviation and the availability of enhanced sentences, we ought to be concerned about how judges who have been sentencing for years will respond to guidelines which do not conform with their experience.

Shortly after the release of the Sentencing Commission's Report in 1987, the House of Commons Standing Committee on Justice and Solicitor General began an inquiry into sentencing and conditional release which resulted in its 1988 report entitled *Taking Responsibility*.[64] The Committee's review began during the tail-end of the renewed debate on capital punishment and shortly after a night supervisor at a half-way house was murdered by a prisoner on day parole.[65] After a series of public and in camera hearings and the reception of hundreds of briefs, the Committee offered a number of recommendations, the most significant of which, for our purposes, was the retention

---

[61] See *Report of the Canadian Sentencing Commission, Sentencing Reform: A Canadian Approach* (Ottawa: 1987), pp. 223-224.

[62] See *Report, ibid.*, p. 226.

[63] *Ibid.*, Minority Report of Commissioner Pateras, p. 340.

[64] *Report of the Standing Committee on Justice and Solicitor General on its Review of Sentencing and Conditional Release*, David Daubney, Chairman, Minutes of Proceeding and Evidence, 2nd Sess., 33rd Parliament, 1986-87-88, Issue No. 65, August 16-17, 1988, hereinafter referred to as the *Daubney Report*.

[65] See *Daubney Report, ibid.*, p. 1, referring to the murder of Celia Ruygrok.

of parole.[66] With respect to the processes of conditional early release, it recommended better sharing of information,[67] open hearings[68] and the statutory entrenchment of decision-making criteria.[69]

The Committee also recommended changes in eligibility rules, such that prisoners would only become eligible for day parole 6 months before full parole eligibility;[70] persons convicted of violent offences would not be eligible for full parole until one-half of the sentence of imprisonment had been served.[71] Prisoners would no longer earn remission; if they failed to obtain early release from the Parole Board they would be entitled to release (subject to the detention power) for a period of 12 months or one-third of the sentence, whichever would be shorter.[72] Accordingly, the recommended successor to the current regime of mandatory supervision would dramatically reduce the period of conditional release for people serving sentences greater than 3 years. Other aspects of the *Report*, too numerous to discuss here, deal with the internal operations of parole decision-making and parole supervision. With respect to the sentencing process, the Committee did not support the introduction of presumptive or mandatory guidelines.[73]

As the 1980's closed, the context of the debate over sentencing, imprisonment and release had expanded to include new participants, new data and new directions. The bookshelves of lawyers, bureaucrats, observers and academics began to sag under the weight of official reports, each dealing with discrete aspects of the criminal justice process. Soon the final report of the Correctional Law Review project will be added to the mass of research and analysis.[74] The material generated

---

[66]   See Recommendation 45, *Daubney, Report, Ibid.*, pp. 185-188.

[67]   *Ibid.*, Recommendation 40 spoke to the obligation of the criminal process to provide the Correctional Service of Canada with relevant information about the offender and the offence, while Recommendation 44 addressed some of the concerns expressed at the Inquest into the death of Celia Ruygrok that information about a released prisoner be "communicated to all persons who will have dealings with the offender in the community residential centre staff, and community resource persons": see pp. 171-172, and 178-184.

[68]   Recommendation 41, subject to concerns about "privacy or security": see *Daubney Report, ibid.*, pp. 172-173.

[69]   Recommendation 46: see *Daubney Report, ibid.*, pp. 188-191.

[70]   Recommendation 49: see *Daubney Report, ibid.*, pp. 192-193.

[71]   Recommendation 47: see *Daubney Report, ibid.*, pp. 190-191. Violent offences were defined as those offences which currently render a prisoner eligible for "detention" under section 21.3 or 21.4 of the *Parole Act* (R.S.C. 1985, c. P-2), as set out in the Schedule: see Chapter 7.

[72]   Recommendation 53: see *Daubney Report, Ibid.*, pp. 195-196.

[73]   See *Daubney Report, ibid.*, pp. 60-65.

[74]   See Solicitor General Canada, *A Framework for the Correctional Law Review*, Working Paper No. 2, June 1986.

by these agencies has often been thoughtful and creative, but sometimes has been pedestrian, knee-jerk and regressive. It is all too easy to be swayed by the occurrence of tragedy and brutality. It is too easy to forget that our community's reactive resort to imprisonment takes its own destructive toll. The human spirit is neither invulnerable nor indefatigable.

We have attempted to argue that a practicable, purposive and humane criminal justice system requires the integration of all its elements within a coherent and consistent framework. The process of reform also requires an integrated approach. After an experience of more than 150 years with penitentiary imprisonment, the impact of its daily rigours and internal structures can no longer be ignored. Similarly, we cannot ignore the fact that despite the enactment of increasingly repressive parole legislation since 1959,[75] neither the perception nor the reality of a safer community has been improved.

4. RE-SHAPING EARLY RELEASE

So long as Canada's criminal justice process continues to incarcerate large numbers of men and women for long periods of time, we believe that an early release mechanism is an essential concomitant of the sentencing process. If re-integration into the community is a real objective of the criminal process, the intervening stages of imprisonment and release cannot continue to treat individuals as human grist for the disciplinary mill. Life in the modern community is too complex and demanding; success requires self-direction and self-esteem, the very aspects of personality which the disciplinary process seeks to diminish in exchange for malleability and conformity. A fair opportunity for early release is necessary to ameliorate the inevitable consequences of imprisonment for those who present no significant risk to the community.

Thus, we advocate a model which both attempts to promote the concept of restraint and seeks to promote a safer community.[76] The following scheme reflects those elements which we consider essential for an equitable and effective early release mechanism. The model is premised on presumptive release for the majority who present no signifi-

---

[75] See the discussion of the evolution of mandatory supervision and detention in Chapters 5 and 7.

[76] An earlier version of this model was prepared for, and included the report of, the Canadian Bar Association's Special Committee on Release and Imprisonment (C.B.A., August 1988). The authors acknowledge valuable advice provided by their Committee colleagues: John Conroy (Chair), Chester Cunningham, Michael Jackson, Alison MacPhail and Roger Tassé.

cant risk, and continued confinement for those who can properly be classed as representing a danger to the community. While far from ideal, we believe a reformed system must contain the following integrated elements:

(a) A Clear, Statutorily Entrenched Mandate

The mandate of the release process and its relationship to the sentencing process must be clearly articulated and well understood by all participants in the criminal justice system. There can be no excuse for the degree of confusion and mutual misunderstanding that currently exists. Moreover, the release agency's mandate must be entrenched in statutory form, to provide guidance and to reflect a commitment to re-integration. The agency's mandate should be:

1. to review and monitor sentences of imprisonment in order to authorize conditional release when further confinement cannot be justified; and
2. to monitor and assist the re-integration of persons released from imprisonment during the period of control imposed by the sentencing judge.

(b) Eligibility Periods Should be Denunciatory and Short

For each sentence of imprisonment, Parliament should define a release ineligibility period or portion chosen to express the denunciatory aspect of sentencing. This period should bear a relation to the actual harm or offence to the community caused by the prisoner's conduct. If imprisonment is the appropriate form of punishment (a sentencing choice which, by statute should not be allowed to be made without first considering and publicly rejecting available alternatives) the ineligibility period should ensure a minimum of incarceration commensurate with the community's legitimate concern to denounce harmful and illegal conduct. The traditional concerns of individual deterrence or incapacitation to reduce risk to the community are issues which relate not to the offence but to the offender; they are addressed by the early release review process.

Assuming that the question of general deterrence continues to be a valid aspect of sentencing, it is answered by the sentence itself which conveys to the community the amount of State control which may be imposed for a similar offence. This scheme maintains the functional integrity of both sentencing judges and the early release agency, addresses the historical objectives of the sentencing process, and permits the early re-integration of prisoners who present no significant risk. It is this last factor, combined with our proposals to ensure an effective and open release process, that persuades us that the eligibility portion should be short.

In some jurisdictions, trial judges are empowered to impose or alter the conditional release ineligibility period. In our view, this function should be performed by Parliament. Because the period of parole ineligibility satisfies the denunciatory aspect of sentencing, this decision should be made in general terms by a body accountable to the community for which it speaks. The judicial discretion to impose a sentence of imprisonment (subject to appeal by the prisoner or the Crown) plays an appropriate role in addressing the denunciatory aspect by setting the term to which the fractional ineligibility period will apply. An aggravated offence compels a longer sentence, but permitting an increase of parole ineligibility presents a continuation of the disparities which the Sentencing Commission has condemned.

The current scheme, based generally on one-third of the sentence, should be retained simply because it seems to work.[77] Certainly, there is no magic in the fraction. Any alteration should be downward, since an effective early release mechanism should operate only to ensure the continued confinement of prisoners who present risk. Moreover, individual acts of violence and brutality are encompassed by the length of the term imposed by the sentencing judge against the backdrop of maxima laid down by Parliament and rules developed by appellate courts. Notwithstanding a sense of frustration and impotence in the face of media accounts of violent crime, little is achieved and much may be lost by permitting vengeful motives to dominate the criminal justice debate.

(c) Presumptive Release

Subject to the qualifications below, all prisoners should be *entitled* to conditional release after serving the relevant eligibility period. We acknowledge that there will be some people who ought to be confined for

---

[77] While public and formal complaints have often been registered against this fraction, it appears never to have been debated in Parliament nor in Committee. According to the personal recollections of former Board Chairs Frank Miller and William Outerbridge, the one-third rule was originally developed as a matter of policy by the Remission Branch of the Department of Justice (the predecessor to the National Parole Board) during the 1920's, as representing that portion of the sentence which generally balanced denunciation against the inevitably brutalizing effect of imprisonment. When the National Parole Board was formed in 1959, it adopted the one-third fraction as a matter of internal policy.

longer periods by reason of the risk which they present. The presumption, however, favours release. Accordingly, the burden of justifying further confinement (even up to the maximum period of control established by the sentence) should rest on the State. Thus, presumptive release will be denied only:

1. when correctional authorities can demonstrate to the releasing authority that further incarceration is justified by showing a likelihood that, if released, the prisoner will cause serious physical harm, death or severe psychological harm to others; or
2. in exceptional cases, as defined below, where the prisoner cannot satisfy the releasing agency that further incarceration is unjustifiable in that conditional release presents no undue risk of serious harm to others.

An exceptional case is one which involves a conviction for a crime of violence where the trial (or appellate) judge, in open court, after notice to the convicted person, has characterized the offence as exceptional by reason of brutality or the infliction of psychological terror resulting in serious physical harm or debilitating psychological injury. These elements must be found to have accompanied the offence.

Essentially, by imposing the label of "exceptional", the trial (or appellate) judge can deny presumptive release to the convicted person by shifting the onus of the release decision onto the prisoner. Thus, the label should only be imposed after the convicted person has had an opportunity to challenge the proof of the triggering elements, and to adduce evidence which may satisfy the trial (or appellate) judge that the occurrence was situational, out of character or not likely to be repeated.

(d) Presumptive Day Parole Release

In stipulating an appropriate parole ineligibility period, Parliament should also provide for day parole eligibility. Subject to the qualifications above, some form of conditional release should be a presumed entitlement, whether in the form of day release from a halfway house, or as a series of passes as the precursor to day parole.

While the current scheme is often characterized as permitting day parole or unescorted temporary absences after one-sixth of a federal sentence, this is inaccurate. Subject to the rarely used power to grant parole by exception, no conditional release can be authorized until 6 months have been served. For sentences between 2 years and 12 years in length, the prisoner must serve one-sixth of the sentence to qualify for conditional release. For longer sentences, there is no eligibility for any form of conditional release until 2 years prior to full parole eligibility, (or 3 years in the case of life minimum sentences for murder).

We acknowledge that there is no magic in any particular fraction or period. However, a regime of presumptive release, including the availability of some form of conditional release prior to full parole, raises certain prerequisites which suggest that the current eligibility scheme ought to be retained. First, there must be a minimum period of confinement within which to assess the prisoner. Secondly, the period between the first stage of early release and ultimate release on parole must be long enough (for prisoners serving a long sentence) to accommodate a gradual transition where warranted, but also short enough so as not to encumber someone who does not need the structure of day parole.

There are two essential concomitants of presumptive day parole release:

1. The Correctional Service of Canada must be organized to ensure that, unless it intends to show cause why a prisoner represents a significant risk of harm as discussed above, the prisoner will have moved to a minimum security setting by the time of day parole eligibility. A prisoner's classification or placement should never be a bar to presumptive day parole release.
2. Both in respect to unescorted passes and day parole, adequate resources in the community must be provided to accommodate the numbers and needs of released prisoners. The current attitude that long-term community-based day parole is counter-productive[78] is a function of the limitations of the present regime which, in some cases, compels greater burdens on an individual than are necessary.

(e) Release Conditions

As demonstrated in Chapter 6, release conditions can only be imposed if they are reasonable and are directly related to the re-integration of the prisoner and the diminution of risk of harm to others. Restraint should be the operative principle and minimum intrusion the guiding premise. The imposition of conditions involves an inquiry into the substantive nature of the proposed condition and the degree of impact on the liberty of the prisoner. The releasing agency must be prepared to justify any condition as reasonable, directly connected to the diminution of risk, and must represent a minimum impairment of liberty.

---

[78] See *Tom v. National Parole Bd.* [summarized (1983), 10 W.C.B. 293 (Fed. T.D.)], discussed in Chapter 6.

(f) Recommitment

Persons on conditional release should be subject to recommitment. However, recommitment should not be a punitive tool. It should be seen as the mechanism to return a prisoner to custody to avoid harm (or a substantial risk of harm) to others. The entire re-integrative process, including the potential for recommitment, must be viewed functionally in relation to the background and individual objectives of the prisoner.

Recommitment to custody should occur only when a person's conduct represents a failed attempt at re-integration, or presents a substantial risk of failure. As in the current system, a breach of conditions, even a new criminal charge, should not necessarily result in recommitment, which, in turn, should not be simply an instrument for extending the penitentiary's disciplinary regime into the community. Any breach, misconduct or other unusual conduct must be viewed in the light of the particular prisoner's plans, opportunities and objectives; it should only lead to recommitment if it represents reasonably perceived failure or risk of failure. In essence, the decision to recommit involves balancing the individual's prospects for re-integration with the concern to protect community members from harm.

After recommitment, a prisoner should be eligible for another conditional release. However, he would bear the burden of persuading the releasing agency that further confinement is not justified in that:

1. conditional release is a timely step towards successful re-integration; and
2. release presents no likelihood of harm to others.

Clearly, some time will elapse between recommitment and subsequent release because, at the very least, realistic new plans must be developed; however, there should be no formal minimum period of confinement after recommitment.

(g) Criteria for Decision-making

Both with respect to release and potential recommitment, the releasing authority must develop and promulgate substantive criteria for decision-making. While administrative guidelines which prescribe the kinds of information and assessments needed by the decision making process may be helpful, these should not be confused with substantive criteria which delineate the bases upon which decisions can be made. An adjudicative process which can result in decisions having substantial impact on a person's liberty can only operate fairly if it is essential that criteria for negative decisions are clearly articulated and statutorily entrenched.

(h) Open Hearings

As a general rule, hearings should be open to the public. A releasing agency must make its decisions fairly and openly to ensure confidence in its processes. Public accountability is the best safeguard against arbitrary, ill-prepared and inconsistent decision-making. In the past, the sensationalized reporting of a small number of cases has generated misunderstanding and scepticism about parole. An open process should provide a better-informed climate for observation and criticism.

As with the judicial process, there will be some cases where privacy concerns should be given paramountcy over openness. These may relate to the prisoner, the prisoner's family, sources of information or a victim. As well, there will be situations where the reporting of details of a release plan will significantly decrease the likelihood of successful re-integration. The releasing agency must have the power to control its own process, including the ability, in an appropriate case, to exclude persons from a hearing. In respect of the media, this power should extend to restricting the publication of names or details, with an accompanying enforcement mechanism for breaches. While decision-makers must be prepared to account to the community for their decision, the context within which discretion is exercised must be tailored to the objectives of the power and the real interest of the participants. The importance of privacy, and in some cases even anonymity, cannot be dismissed entirely unless openness is achieved at too high a cost.

(i) Fair Hearings

In all cases where conditional release (or the continuation of conditional release) is in issue, hearings must be conducted according to appropriate standards of fairness and fundamental justice, including adequate notice of issues in controversy, full disclosure of material in the hands of the decision-maker, and representation by counsel. As well, hearings must be scheduled in a timely fashion. Administrative delay can easily subvert justice.

With respect to disclosure of confidential information, the rule of the day should be sufficient disclosure of the substance and detail of adverse allegations to enable a fair opportunity to respond. Only in the following circumstances can discloure be denied:

1. The decision-maker has considered the affect of disclosure on the source of the information or a third party and concluded that disclosure will place that person in danger.
2. The decision-maker has considered the impact of non-disclosure on the prisoner's opportunity to respond.
3. The decision-maker has taken all the available steps to confirm the validity and accuracy of the information.
4. The decision-maker has considered techniques for disclosing the gist of the information but has concluded that no satisfactory disclosure can be made without endangering the source or third party.[79]

Non-disclosure will be a rare case. Given the liberty interest of the prisoner which is at stake, the decision-maker should be compelled to seek judicial authorization for non-disclosure. This will produce consistency and will inject some level of external scrutiny to ensure that the prisoner not be compelled to accept an institutional conclusion on faith.

(j) Publication of Decisions

To ensure consistency and predictability, and to enhance a prisoner's opportunity to prepare a case for consideration by the releasing agency, the agency's decisions should be published. This will also serve to enhance public and media appreciation of the agency's function. As well, it will assist the agency in developing a "jurisprudence" of decision-making over time. Published decisions need sufficient detail to make them useful to others, but need not identify a case in a way which will prejudice a successful release. Ordinarily, reasons should include a description of the offence, the length of and justification for the sentence, the release decision and the reasons upon which it is based.

(k) End of Remission-based Release

As part of the adoption of the presumptive release model proposed above, remission can only be characterized as a superfluous, coercive tool. It is not necessary for internal disciplinary control. The earning of remission is not related to the substantive criteria for release. Remission-based release should not be maintained within a framework where release is determined by a combination of presumptive eligibility, as determined by the sentence, and the residual issue of risk is delegated to the release decision-maker.

---

[79] The rationale for these proposed rules is discussed in Chapter 6.

Currently, the forfeiture of remission is a potential penalty for disciplinary offences. There is a real concern that the elimination of remission will result in an increased use of dissociation as a sanction. The abolition of earned remission must be accompanied by a statutory mechanism dealing with the imposition of disciplinary penalties which ensures that penitentiary disciplinary tribunals do not resort to an increased use of dissociation as an alternative. It is only within the context of a presumptive release model that we advocate the abolition of remission.

(l) Resources

The releasing agency must have access to, and control over, adequate resources to ensure that prisoners have a fair opportunity to meet the substantive criteria for release. This includes the need for adequate psychiatric and psychological treatment and assessment services, so that, in cases where risk is an issue, timely and impartial data can be placed before the releasing agency. Moreover, the facilitation of success while on conditional release often requires the provision of assistance in the form of counselling or access to relevant vocational, life skills or substance abuse programs. It is essential that adequate resources be available to ensure that prisoners can obtain these forms of assistance.

5. CONCLUSION

This model is not offered as a panacea for the defects in our methods of imposing punishments on offenders. It is simply a small step towards a system of criminal justice that operates fairly and openly. It is intended as an intermediate step in a process of reform that we hope will include a re-examination of the utility of large-scale, long-term imprisonment. Sadly, it is predicated on the assumption that, at least in the short run, imprisonment will continue to be our community's response to problems which lie deep and hidden within its social structure. Incarceration serves the processes of self-deception and self-interest which seek to ignore entrenched issues of economic disparity, class and race.

APPENDIX I

PAROLE ACT
R.S.C. 1985, c. P-2

An Act to provide for the conditional liberation of persons undergoing sentences of imprisonment

SHORT TITLE

1. This Act may be cited as the *Parole Act.* R.S., c. P-2, s. 1.

Short title

INTERPRETATION

2. In this Act,

Definitions

"Board" means that the National Parole Board established by section 3;

"Board"
«*Commission*»

"day parole" means parole the terms and conditions of which require the inmate to whom it is granted to return to prison from time to time during the duration of the parole or to return to prison after a specified period;

"day parole"
«*semi-liberté*»

"inmate" means a person who is under a sentence of imprisonment imposed pursuant to an Act of Parliament or imposed for criminal contempt of court, but does not include

"inmate"
«*détenu*»

(*a*) a child within the meaning of the *Juvenile Delinquents Act*, chapter J-3 of the Revised Statutes of Canada, 1970, as it read immediately prior to April 2, 1984, who is under sentence of imprisonment for an offence known as a delinquency under that Act.
(*b*) a young person within the meaning of the *Young Offenders Act* who has been committed to custody under that Act, or
(*c*) a person in custody soley by reason of a sentence of imprisonment that has been ordered to be served intermittently pursuant to section 737 of the *Criminal Code*;

[repealed, R.S. 1985, c. 35 (2nd Supp.), s. 1.]

"magistrate"
«*magistrat*»

"parole" means authority granted under this Act to an inmate to be at large during the inmate's term of imprisonment and includes day parole;

"parole"
«*libération . . .*»

"parole supervisor" «*surveillant . . .*»

"parole supervisor" means a person charged with the guidance and supervision of a paroled inmate or of an inmate who is subject to mandatory supervision;

"paroled inmate" «*libéré . . .*»

"paroled inmate" means a person to whom parole has been granted;

"provincial parole board" «*commission provinciale*»

"provincial parole board" means, in relation to any province, a parole board appointed pursuant to section 12 and includes

(*a*) the Board of Parole that Ontario may appoint pursuant to subsection 12(1) of the *Prisons and Reformatories Act*, if that board has been appointed to act as a parole board under this Act, and

(*b*) the Board of Parole that British Columbia may appoint pursuant to subsection 13(1) of the *Prisons and Reformatories Act*, if that board has been appointed to act as a parole board under this Act. R.S., c. P-2, s. 2; 1976-77, c. 53, 17; 1980-81-82-83, c. 110, s. 77.

ESTABLISHMENT OF THE NATIONAL PAROLE BOARD

Board established

3. (1) There is hereby established a board, to be known as the National Parole Board, consisting of not more than thirty-six members to be appointed by the Governor in Council to hold office during good behaviour for a period not exceeding ten years. R.S. 1985, c. 34 (2nd Supp.), s. 1.

Chairman and Vice-Chairman

(2) The Governor in Council shall designate one of the members of the Board to be its Chairman and one to be its Vice-Chairman.

Executive committee

(3) There shall be an executive committee of the Board, consisting of not more than ten members appointed by the Governor in Council on the recommendation of the Solicitor General of Canada, whose duties and powers may be prescribed by the regulations. R.S., c. P-2, s. 3; 1976-77, c. 53, s. 18.

Temporary substitute members

4. (1) In the event that a member of the Board is absent or unable to act, the Governor in Council may appoint a temporary substitute member to act in the place of that member.

Powers and duties

(2) A temporary member appointed pursuant to subsection (1) has all the powers and duties of a member appointed pursuant to subsection 3(1), subject to any limitation in that respect that the Chairman may direct.

Temporary members

(3) The Governor in Council may appoint, to hold office during good behaviour, temporary members to act as members of the Board for a period not exceeding three years as the Governor in Council considers necessary to eliminate any accumulation of matters pending before the Board. R.S. 1985, c. 34 (2nd Supp.), s. 2.

Voting

5. (1) Each member of the executive committee of the Board has one vote in respect of each matter referred to it as prescribed by regulation and if the number of votes in respect of any matter is equally divided, the chairman has an additional vote.

(2) Where regulations are made pursuant to paragraph 27(1)(*f*), the Board shall not grant a parole unless the conditions prescribed by those regulations are complied with. R.S. 1985, c. 35 (2nd Supp.), s. 2.

Minimum number of votes

6. The Board may, with the approval of the Governor in Council, make rules for the conduct of its proceedings, including the fixing of a quorum for any meeting or hearing, and the performance of its duties and functions under this Act or any other Act of Parliament. R.S., c. P-2, s. 3; 1976-77, c. 53, s. 18.

Rules of procedure

7. (1) The head office of the Board shall be at Ottawa, but meetings of the Board may be held at such places as the Board determines.

Head office

(2) The Board shall have an official seal, R.S., c. P-2, s. 3.

Seal

8. (1) Notwithstanding section 3, the Solicitor General of Canada may, on the recommendation of the Chairman of the Board, designate representatives of the police forces in any region of Canada, of the provincial government thereof and of the municipal or other local authorities therein or members of local professional, trade of community associations to constitute a regional panel for that region.

Regional panels

(2) When reviewing, with or without a hearing, for the purposes of granting parole or an unescorted temporary absence, the case of an inmate sentenced to life imprisonment as a minimum punishment, an inmate in respect of whom a sentence of death has been commuted to life imprisonment or an inmate sentenced to detention in a penitentiary for an indeterminate period, the Chairman of the Board of the member of the Board designated by the Chairman shall select two persons to act as additional members of the Board from the regional panel constituted for the region that, in the opinion of the Chairman or the member, is the most appropriate.

Additional members

(3) A person selected pursuant to subsection (2) to act as an additional member of the Board has, subject to the regulations, the same powers and duties including the right to vote as the other members of the Board at the hearing or the review without hearing for which the person was selected. R.S. 1985, c. 35 (2nd Supp.), s. 3.

Effect

9. (1) The Chairman may establish divisions of the Board, each consisting of two or more members of the Board, and may direct any of those divisions to carry out such times and places as are specified by the Chairman, such of the duties and functions of the Board specified by the Chairman as are authorized by rules made by the Board under section 6 to be carried out by a division of the Board.

Divisions of the Board

(2) A division of the Board established pursuant to subsection (1) may, in carrying out the duties and functions specified by the Chair-

Powers of divisions of the Board

man, exercise all of the powers conferred on the Board by this Act or any other Act of Parliament.

Acts of division of the Board

(3) For the purposes of this Act, any act or thing done by a division of the Board in accordance with a direction by the Chairman made pursuant to subsection (1) shall be deemed to be an act or thing done by the Board.

Review by designated members

(4) Subject to any regulations made pursuant to paragraph 27(1)(*f*), the Chairman may, at any time before parole is granted, direct that a review of a case shall be conducted by a number of members of the Board designated by the Chairman. R.S., c. P-2, s. 5; 1976-77, c. 53, s. 21.

Remuneration

10. (1) Each member of the Board shall be paid such remuneration for his services as is fixed by the Governor in Council, and is entitled to be paid resonable travel and living expenses incurred while absent from his ordinary place of residence in the course of his duties.

Member of Public Service

(2) Where a member of the Board is, at the time of his appointment, an employee in the Public Service, the member shall be given leave of absence, without pay, by his department and be paid as a member of the Board.

Expenses of additional member

(3) A person selected pursuant to subsection 8(2) to act as an additional member of the Board is entitled to be paid such honorarium as may be prescribed by regulations made pursuant to paragraph 27(1)(*n*) for each day that that person is so acting and reasonable travel and living expenses incurred while absent from his ordinary place of residence in the course of his duties.

Superannuation

(4) The members and staff of the Board shall be deemed to be employed in the Public Service for the purpose of the *Public Service Superannuation Act*. R.S., c. P-2, ss. 4, 26; 1976-77, c. 53, ss. 18, 19.

Chief executive officer

11. (1) The Chairman of the Board is its chief executive officer and has supervision over and direction of the work and the staff of the Board.

Staff

(2) The officers, clerks and employees necessary for the proper, conduct of the business of the Board shall be appointed in accordance with the *Public Service Employment Act*. R.S., c. P-2, s. 4.

PROVINCIAL PAROLE BOARDS

Provincial boards

12. (1) The lieutenant governor in council of a province may appoint a Board of Parole for that province to exercise parole jurisdiction, in accordance with this Act and the regulations, in respect of inmates detained in a provincial institution, other than inmates sentenced to life imprisonment as a minimum punishment, inmates in respect of whom sentences of death have been commuted to life imprisonment or inmates sentenced to detention in a penitentiary for an indeterminate period.

(2) A provincial parole board for Ontario or British Columbia may, in addition to its other duties, exercise the same jurisdiction as a provincial parole board appointed pursuant to subsection (1).

Ontario and British Columbia

(3) Where an inmate who has been granted parole by a provincial parole board moves to another province, the provincial parole board of that other province may, with the consent of the board that granted the parole, exercise jurisdiction over that inmate.

Inmate moving to another province

(4) An inmate who is paroled by a provincial parole board and who moves to a province in which no such board has been appointed falls under the jurisdiction of the National Parole Board thereafter until the inmate again moves into a province for which a provincial parole board has been appointed whereupon subsection (3) again applies to the inmate. 1976-77, c. 53, s. 22.

Idem

POWERS AND DUTIES OF BOARD

13. Subject to this Act, the *Penitentiary Act* and the *Prisons and Reformatories Act*, the Board has exclusive jurisdiction and absolute discretion to grant or refuse to grant parole or a temporary absence without escort and to terminate or revoke parole or to revoke release subject to mandatory supervision. R.S. 1985, c. 35 (2nd Supp.), s. 4.

Jurisdiction of the Board

14. (1) Where a person is

Additional jurisdiction

(*a*) sentenced to a term of imprisonment in respect of which the Board has exclusive jurisdiction to grant, refuse to grant or revoke parole, and
(*b*) at the time of the sentence or at any time during the term of imprisonment, sentenced to a term of imprisonment imposed under an enactment of a provincial legislature that is to be served either concurrently with or immediately after the expiration of the term of imprisonment in respect of which the Board has exclusive jurisdiction,
the Board has, subject to this Act, exclusive jurisdiction and absolute discretion to grant, refuse to grant or revoke parole in relation to both of those terms of imprisonment.

(2) Subsection (1) shall come into force in respect of any of the Provinces of Ontario, Quebec, Nova Scotia, New Brunswick, Prince Edward Island and Newfoundland or in respect of the Yukon Territory or the Northwest Territories on a day to be fixed by proclamation made after the passing of an Act by the legislature of the province named in the proclamation authorizing the Board to exercise the additional jurisdiction described in subsection (1). R.S., c. P-2, s. 7.

Coming into force

15. (1) Subject to subsection (2), the Board shall review the case of every inmate sentenced to imprisonment in or transferred to a penitentiary for two years or more and shall do so at the times prescribed by the regulations but not later than the day on which an inmate has served the portion of the term of imprisonment, as prescribed by the regulations, that must be served before day parole may be granted.

Review of cases

Exception

(2) The Board is not required to review, pursuant to subsection (1), the case of an inmate who advises the Board in writing that the inmate does not wish to be granted parole by the Board, and who has not, in writing, revoked that advice.

Where sentences less than two years

(3) The Board shall, at times prescribed by the regulations, review such cases of inmates serving a sentence of imprisonment of less than two years as are prescribed by the regulations, on application made by or on behalf of the inmate.

Decisions

(4) On completing the first review of the case of an inmate as required by subsecton (1), the Board shall decide

(*a*) in all cases, whether to grant or refuse day parole; and

(*b*) in repsect of such classes of inmates as are prescribed by the regulations, whether to grant or refuse parole, other than day parole, or to defer that decision.

Idem

(5) On reviewing the case of an inmate as required by subsection (3), the Board shall decide whether to grant or refuse the parole applied for by or on behalf of the inmate and for which the inmate is eligible at the time of the review. R.S. 1985, c. 34 (2nd Supp.), s. 3.

Powers of Board

16. (1) The Board may

(*a*) grant parole to an inmate, subject to any terms or conditions it considers reasonable, if the Board considers that

(i) in the case of a grant of parole other than day parole, the inmate has derived the maximum benefit from imprisonment,

(ii) the reform and rehabilitation of the inmate will be aided by the grant of parole, and

(iii) the release of the inmate on parole would not constitute an undue risk to society;

(*b*) impose any terms and conditions that it considers reasonable in respect of an inmate who is subject to mandatory supervision;

(*c*) grant discharge from parole to any paroled inmate, except an inmate on day parole or a paroled inmate who was sentenced to death or to imprisonment for life as a minimum punishment;

(*d*) in its direction, terminate or revoke the parole of any paroled inmate, other than an inmate on day parole, in any case other than that of a paroled inmate to whom discharge from parole has been granted; and

(*e*) in its discretion revoke the parole of any person who is in custody pursuant to a warrant issued under section 22, or terminate the parole instead of revoking it as provided for in that section, whether or not the sentence of that person has expired.

Mandatory conditions of parole and mandatory supervision

(1.1) Subject to subsection (1.2), the Board is deemed to have imposed such mandatory terms and conditions as may be prescribed by the regulations for the purposes of this subsection in respect of an inmate released on parole or subject to mandatory supervisions.

(1.2) On an application made in accordance with the regulations to the Board by or on behalf of an inmate released on parole or subject to mandatory supervision, the Board may, in accordance with the regulations, relieve the inmate of compliance with, or vary in respect of the inmate, any term or condition referred to in subsection (1.1).

Application for relief from mandatory conditions

(1.3) Where an inmate is released on parole or subject to mandatory supervision, the inmate shall comply with any instructions given by the parole supervisor in respect of any term or condition of parole or mandatory supervision in order to prevent a breach of any such term or condition or to protect society.

Compliance with instructions

(2) The authority conferred on the Board by paragraphs 16(1)(*d*) and (*e*) may be exercised notwithstanding any new term of imprisonment to which the inmate becomes subject after the release of the inmate on parole.

Subsequent term of imprisonment

(3) The Board or any person designated by the Chairman may terminate a temporary absence without escort granted to an inmate pursuant to section 25.2 or 25.3 and cause to be issued a warrant, in writing, authorizing the apprehension of the inmate and the recommitment of the inmate to custody as provided in this Act.

Termination of unescorted temporary absence

(4) The Board may terminate the parole of any paroled inmate and cause to be issued a warrant, in writing, authorizing the apprehension of the inmate and the recommitment of the inmate to custody as provided in this Act.

Termination of parole

(5) The Chairman may fix terms and conditions under which a power may be exercised pursuant to subsection (3) by any person designated by the Chairman for the purposes of that subsection. R.S. 1985, c. 34 (2nd Supp.), s. 4; c. 35 (2nd Supp.), s. 5(1)-(4)

Exercise of delegated powers

17. Subject to such regulations as the Governor in Council may make in that behalf, the Board is not required, in considering whether parole should be granted or revoked, to personally interview the inmate or any person on behalf of the inmate. R.S., c. P-2, s. 11; 1976-77, c. 53, s. 26.

Personal interview

18. (1) Where the Board grants parole to an inmate, or an inmate is released from imprisonment, subject to mandatory supervision, the Board shall issue a parole certificate or mandatory supervision certificate under the seal of the Board and in a form prescribed by it and cause the certificate to be delivered to the inmate, who shall sign the certificate, and the Board shall cause a copy of the certificate to be delivered to the inmate's parole supervisor.

Parole and mandatory supervision certificates

(2) Where an inmate refuses to sign a certificate mentioned in subsection (1), the inmate shall nevertheless be subject to the conditions of the relese. R.S. 1985, c. 35 (2nd Supp.), s. 6.

Refusal to sign certificate

Effect of parole **19.** (1) The term of imprisonment of a paroled inmate shall, while the parole remains unrevoked, be deemed to continue in force until the expiration thereof according to law, and, in the case of day parole, the paroled inmate shall be deemed to be continuing to serve his term of imprisonment in the place of confinement from which he was released on that parole.

Idem (2) Until a parole is suspended or revoked, or a day parole is terminated, or except in accordance with the terms and conditions of a day parole, the inmate is not liable to be imprisoned by reason of his sentence and shall be allowed to go and remain at at large according to the terms and conditions of the parole and subject to the provisions of this Act.

Term deemed completed (3) Notwithstanding subsection (1), for the purposes of subsection 50(2) of the *Immigration Act,* section 24 of the *Extradition Act* and section 17 of the *Fugitive Offenders Act,* the term of imprisonment of a paroled inmate, other than an inmate on day parole, shall, while the parole is not terminated or revoked, be deemed to be completed. R.S. 1985, c. 35 (2nd Supp.), s. 7.

Term to include period of remission **19.1** Where

(*a*) authority is granted to an inmate under this Act to be at large during the term of imprisonment of the inmate, or
(*b*) a person who is at large by reason of statutory or earned remission is subject to mandatory supervision under this Act,
the term of imprisonment of the inmate or person, for all purposes of the Act, includes any period of statutory remission and any period of earned remission standing to the credit of the inmate or person when released. R.S. 1985, c. 35 (2nd Supp.), s. 8.

Consecutive and concurrent sentences **20.** (1) Where, either before, on or after the coming into force of this section, a person sentenced to a term of imprisonment that has not expired is sentenced to an additional term of imprisonment, the terms of imprisonment to which the person has been sentenced shall, for all purposes of the *Criminal Code,* the *Penitentiary Act,* the *Prisons and Reformatories Act* and this Act, except subsections (1.1) and (1.2), be deemed to consitute one sentence consisting of a term of imprisonment commencing on the earliest day on which any of the sentences of imprisonment commences and ending on the expiration of the last to expire of those terms of imprisonment.

Interruption (1.1) Where an inmate whose parole has not been terminated or revoked is sentenced to a consecutive term of imprisonment, the sentence the inmate was serving on parole is interrupted and is not resumed until the later sentence has expired or until the parole of the inmate has been terminated or revoked.

Additional terms (1.2) Where an inmate referred to in subsection (1.1) is sentenced to an additional term of imprisonment while the sentence being served on parole is interrupted, (*a*) if the additional term is concurrent with the later sentence, the later sentence and the additional term shall, for all purposes of the *Criminal Code,* the *Penitentiary Act,* the *Prisons and Reformatories Act* and this Act, be deemed to constitute one sentence consisting of a term of imprisonment commencing on the day on which the later sentence commences and ending on the expiration of the last to expire of the terms of the imprisonment; and

(*b*) if the additional term is consecutive to the later sentence,

    (i) in the case of an inmate who has been granted, with respect to the later sentence, parole that is not revoked or terminated, the rule set out in subsection (1.1) applies, and

    (ii) in any other case, the rule set out in paragraph (*a*) applies.

(1.3) Where an additional term referred to in subsection (1.2) is concurrent with or consecutive to the sentence interrupted pursuant to subsection (1.1), the additional term shall be deemed to be concurrent with or consecutive to the later sentence only. *[Concurrent and consecutive terms]*

(1.4) Where a parole of an inmate referred to in subsection (1.1) is terminated or revoked, the inmate shall serve the total of *[Revocation or termination]*

(*a*) the unexpired portion of any sentence being served on a parole; and

(*b*) the unexpired portion of any later sentence.

(1.5) The unexpired portion of a sentence referred to in paragraph (1.4)(*a*) shall, where the parole has been revoked, be calculated in accordance with subsection 25(2). *[Calculation of sentence]*

(1.6) For the purpose of this section, "later sentence" means *[Definition of "later sentence"]*

(*a*) the consecutive term referred to in subsection (1.1); or

(*b*) the sentence determined in accordance with subsection (1.2).

(2) This section does not affect the time at which any sentences that are deemed by subsection (1) to constitute one sentence commence pursuant to subsection 721(1) of the *Criminal Code,* R.S., c. P-2, s. 14; R.S., c. 31 (1st Supp.), s. 1; 1977-78, c. 22, s. 19; R.S. 1985, c. 35 (2nd Supp.), s. 9. *[Interpretation]*

21. (1) Where an inmate is released from imprisonment prior to the expiration of his sentence according to law soley as a result of remission, including earned remission, and the term of the remission exceeds sixty days, the inmate shall, notwithstanding any other Act, be subject to mandatory supervision commencing on the inmate's release and continuing for the duration of the remission. *[Mandatory supervision]*

(2) Paragraphs 16(1)(*d*) and (*e*), subsection 16(2), sections 17 and 19, subsections 20(1) and (1.1) to (1.6) and sections 22 to 25 apply to an inmate who is subject to mandatory supervisions as though the inmate were a paroled inmate on parole and as though the terms and condi- *[Effect of mandatory supervison]*

tions of the mandatory supervision were terms and conditions of the parole.

Inmate may choose to remain

(3) Notwithstanding subsection (1), an inmate who is eligible for release subject to mandatory supervision may choose to remain in the institution to complete his sentence, but such a choice is not binding on an inmate who subsequently chooses to be released on mandatory supervision.

Subsequent choice to be released

(4) An inmate's subsequent choice to be released on mandatory supervision shall be respected as soon as is reasonably possible, but the inmate shall not require to be released other than during the daylight hours of a normal work week.

(5) [Repealed R.S. 1985, c. 35 (2nd Supp.), s. 10(2).]

Application

(6) This section applies in respspect of persons who were sentenced to imprisonment in or transferred to any class of penitentiary on and after August 1, 1970, R.S., c. P-2, s. 15; 1976-77, c. 53, s. 28. R.S. 1985, c. 35 (2nd Supp.), s. 10(1).

Effect of remission

21.1 Remission is credited, in accordance with the *Penitentiary Act* and the *Prisons and Reformatories Act,* against the sentence being served by an inmate and entitles the inmate to be released from imprisonment prior to the expiration of the sentence according to law unless the Board directs pursuant to paragraph 21.4(4)(*a*) that the inmate shall not be so released. R.S. 1985, c. 34 (2nd Supp.), s. 5.

Definitions

21.2 (1) In this section and sections 21.3 to 21.6,

"Commissioner"
«commissaire»

"Commissioner" has the same meaning as in the *Penitentiary Act;*

"community-based residential facility"
«établissement . . .»

"community-based residential facility" means a place offering accommodation or treatment

(*a*) to paroled inmates and other persons, or
(*b*) exclusively to paroled inmates and inmates who are subject to mandatory supervision.
and includes a psychiatric hospital of facility and a penitentiary designated pursuant to subsection 21.6(2);

"inmate"
«détenu»

"inmate" means a person sentenced to imprisonment in or transferred to any class of penitentiary before or after the coming into force of this section;

"presumptive release date"
«date . . .»

"presumptive release date" means, in respect of an inmate, the earliest day on which the inmate may be entitled to be released from imprisonment;

"serious harm"
«tort considérable»

"serious harm" means severe physical injury or severe psychological damage;

"Service" has the same meaning as in the *Penitentiary Act.*

"Service"
«*Service*»

(2) For the purposes of section 21 to 21.6, a reference to the expiration of a sentence of an inmate according to law shall be read as a reference to the day on which the sentence expires, without taking into consideration any remission standing to the credit of the inmate. R.S. 1985, c. 34 (2nd Supp.), s. 5.

Reference to expiration of sentence according to law

21.3 (1) The Commissioner shall cause the case of an inmate to be reviewed by the Service, before the presumptive release date of the inmate, where the inmate is serving a term of imprisonment that includes a sentence imposed in respect of an offence mentioned in the schedule that had been prosecuted by indictment.

Case management review by Service

(2) Where the Service, after reviewing the case of an inmate pursuant to subsection (1), is of the opinion that

Referral of case by Service to Board

(*a*) the inmate is serving a term of imprisonment that includes a sentence imposed in respect of an offence mentioned in the schedule that had been prosecuted by indictment,

(*b*) the commission of the offence caused the death of or serious harm to another person, and

(*c*) there are reasonable grounds to believe that the inmate is likely to commit, prior to the expiration according to law, of the sentence the inmate is then serving, an offence causing the death of or serious harm to another person,

the Service shall, not later than six months before the presumptive release date of the inmate, refer the case to the Board together with all information that, in the opinion of the Service, is relevant to the case.

(3) Where the Commissioner believes on reasonable grounds that an inmate who is serving a sentence imposed in respect of any offence, whether or not that offence is mentioned in the schedule or caused the death of or serious harm to another person, is likely, prior to the expiration according to law of the sentence the inmate is then serving, to commit an offence causing the death of or serious harm to another person, the Commissioner shall refer the case to the Chairman of the Board, together with all information in the possession of the Service that, in the opinion of the Commissioner, is relevant to the case, as soon as practicable after the belief is formed, but not later than six months before the presumptive release date of the inmate unless

Case referral by Commissioner to Chairman of Board

(*a*) the Commissioner formed the belief on the basis of
(i) behaviour by the inmate that occurred within those six months, or
(ii) information obtained within those six months; or
(*b*) any of the sentences included in the term of imprisonment the inmate is then serving has been reduced or a conviction in respect of any such sentence has been quashed on appeal.

(4) The Service shall, on the request of the Board, take all reasonable steps to provide the Board with any additional information that is relevant to a case referred pursuant to subsection (2) or (3).

Board's request for information

Cases referred to Chairman dealt with expeditiously

(5) Where the case of an inmate is referred to the Chairman of the Board pursuant to subsection (3) during the six months immediately preceding the the presumptive release date of the inmate, the Board shall,

(*a*) if the case if referred to the Chairman more than four weeks prior to the presumptive release date, hold a hearing pursuant to subsection 21.4(2) before the presumptive release date;

(*b*) if the case is referred to the Chairman within the four weeks immediately preceding the presumptive release date but more than three days prior thereto, and

(i) a hearing may be held pursuant to subsection 21.4(2) before the presumptive release date, hold that hearing before that date, or

(ii) a hearing may not be held pursuant to subsection 21.4(2) before the presumptive release date, hold an interim hearing before that date; or

(*c*) if the case if referred to the Chairman within the three days immediatley preceding the presumptive release date, hold an interim hearing within the three days after the day on which the case is referred.

Interim hearing

(6) An interim hearing pursuant to subparagraph (5)(*b*)(ii) or paragraph (5)(*c*) shall be held in the manner prescribed by the regulations.

Decision after interim hearing

(7) On completion of an interim hearing held pursuant to subparagraph (5)(*b*)(ii) or paragraph (5)(*c*), where the Board is of the opinion that, on the basis of all the information provided to the Chairman of the Board pursuant to subsection (3) or to the Board pursuant to subsection (4), a sufficient case is made out to hold a hearing pursuant to subsection 21.4(2), the Board shall hold the hearing as soon as practicable but not later than four weeks after the case is referred to the Chairman of the Board pursuant to subsection (3). R.S. 1985, c. 34 (2nd Supp.), s. 5.

Review by Board

21.4 (1) The Board shall, at the time and in the manner prescribed by the regulations, review the case of every inmate referred to it by the Service pursuant to subsection 21.3(2) or referred to the Chairman of the Board pursuant to subsection 21.3(3).

Hearing to be held

(2) Notwithstanding section 17, in reviewing a case pursuant to subsection (1), the Board shall

(*a*) cause to be conducted all such inquiries in connection therewith as it considers necessary; and

(*b*) subject to subsections 21.3(6) and (7), hold a hearing at the time and in the manner prescribed by the regulations.

Confinement pending hearing

(3) Where the case of an inmate is referred to the Chairman of the Board during the six months immediately preceding the presumptive release date of the inmate, the inmate is not entitled to be released from imprisonment prior to the rendering of the decision of the Board in connection therewith.

(4) On completion of the hearing and review of the case of an inmate pursuant to this section, where the Board is satisfied that the inmate is likely to commit, prior to the expiration according to law of the sentence the inmate is then serving, an offence causing the death of or serious harm to another person, the Board may, by order,

(*a*) direct that the inmate shall not be released from imprisonment prior to the expiration according to law of the sentence the inmate is serving at the time the order is made, or

(*b*) impose, subject to subsection (6), as one of the conditions of the release subject to mandatory supervision of the inmate, residence in a community-based residential facility,

and, where the Board is not so satisfied, the Board shall make an order declaring whether, at the time the case was referred to the Board, the inmate was serving a term of imprisonment that included a sentence imposed in respect of an offence mentioned in the schedule that had been prosecuted by indictment and whether, in its opinion, the commission of the offence caused the death of or serious harm to another person.

(5) For the purpose of determining the order to be made in respect of an inmate pursuant to subsection (4), the Board shall take into consideration any factor that is relevant to the case of the inmate and, without limiting the generality of the foregoing.

(*a*) a pattern of persistent violent behaviour established on the basis of any evidence and, in particular,

(i) the number of offences committed by the inmate causing physical or psychological harm,

(ii) the seriousness of the offence for which the sentence imposed is then being served,

(iii) reliable information demonstrating that the inmate has had difficulties controlling violent impulses to the point of endangering the safety of any other person,

(iv) the use of weapons in the commission of any offence by the inmate,

(v) explicit threats of violence,

(vi) behaviour of a brutal nature associated with the commission of any offence by the inmate, and

(vii) a substantial degree of indifference on the part of the inmate as to the reasonably foreseeable consequences, to other persons, of the behaviour of the inmate;

(*b*) psychiatric or psychological evidence that the physical or mental illness or disorder of the inmate is of such a nature that the inmate is likely to commit, prior to the expiration according to law of the sentence the inmate is then serving, an offence causing the death of or serious harm to another person;

(*c*) reliable information the existence of which compels reaching the conclusion that the inmate is planning to commit, prior to the expiration according to law of the sentence the inmate is then serving, an offence causing the death of or serious harm to another person, and

(*d*) the availability of supervision programs that would offer adequate protection to the public from risk the inmate might otherwise present until the expiration according to the law of the sentence the inmate is then serving.

Consent of Commissioner

(6) The Commissioner or a person designated by the Commissioner must consent, in writing, to the residence in a penitentiary of an inmate in respect of whom an order is made pursuant to paragraph (4) (*b*).

Decision and reasons of Board given to inmate

(7) The Board shall, after completing its review of the case of an inmate pursuant to this section, cause to be given to the inmate a copy of its decision and, where applicable, a copy of an order made pursuant to paragraph (4)(*a*) or (*b*) and of any other conditions imposed on the inmate, together with the reasons for the decision of the Board.

(*a*) where the case was referred to the Board not later than six months before the presumptive release date of the inmate, at least two months before that presumptive release date; or
(*b*) where the case was referred to the Board during the six months immediately preceding the presumptive relese date of the inmate, as soon as practicable after the completion of the review.

Ineligibility for parole

(8) An inmate who is in custody pursuant to an order made under paragrapgh (4)(*a*) is not eligible for parole. R.S. 1985, c. 34 (2nd Supp.), s. 5.

Yearly reviews

21.5 (1) The Board shall review the case of every inmate who is subject to an order made pursuant to paragraph 21.4(*a*) forthwith after the expiration of one year following the day on which the order was made and every year thereafter during which the inmate is subject to the order.

Confirmation, revocation or variance of order for detention

(2) The Board may, on the completion of a yearly review of the case of an inmate pursuant to subsection (1), confirm or revoke the order made pursuant to paragraph 21.4(4)(*a*) in respect of the inmate or substitute therefor an order pursuant to paragraph 21.4(4)(*b*).

Applicable provisions

(3) Subsections 21.4(2), (5) and (6) apply, with such modifications as the circumstances require, in respect of a yearly review pursuant to subsection (1).

Idem

(4) Subsection 21.4(7) applies, with such modifications as the circumstances require, in respect of a yearly review pursuant to subsection (1) as if it were a case to which paragraph 21.4(7)(*b*) would apply.

Power to revoke detention order

(5) The Board may, at any time, revoke an order made pursuant to paragraph 21.4(4)(*a*) or substitute therefor an order made pursuant to paragraph 21.4(4)(*b*).

Deemed recredit of remission for release

(6) Where an order made pursuant to paragraph 21.4(4)(*a*) is revoked or an order made pursuant to paragraph 21.4(4)(*b*) is substituted by the Board pursuant to this section, the remission of that

portion of the sentence the inmate is serving at the time of the revocation or substitution that

(*a*) was forfeited pursuant to subsection 25(6) of the *Penitentiary Act*, and

(b) entitles the inmate to be released subject to mandatory supervision until the expiration of the sentence according to law

shall be deemed to be recredited by the Board. R.S. 1985, c. 34 (2nd Supp.), s. 5.

21.6 (1) The Governor in Council may make regulations   Regulations

(*a*) prescribing the time when and the manner in which a review of the case of an inmate pursuant to section 21.4 or 21.5 and the hearing pursuant to subparagraph 21.3(5)(*b*)(ii), paragraph 21.3(5)(*c*) or subsection 21.4(2) is to take place;

(b) prescribing the minimum number of members of the Board who must be present during and vote in respect of a hearing held pursuant to subparagraph 21.3(5)(*b*)(ii) or paragraph 21.3(5)(*c*) or vote in respect of a case reviewed pursuant to section 21.4 or 21.5 and the minimun number of affirmative votes required in the making of a decision pursuant to subsection 21.3(7) or section 21.4 or 21.5;

(c) prescribing the information, and the form thereof, to be supplied or made available to an inmate or any other person by the Board before the commencement of or during hearing held pursuant to subparagraph 21.3(5)(*b*)(ii), paragraph 21.3(5)(*c*) or subsection 21.4(2) and the time within which such information is to be supplied;

(d) prescribing the information or classes thereof that may be withheld from an inmate or other person before the commencement of or during a hearing held pursuant to subparagraph 21.3(5)(*b*)(ii), paragraph 21.3(5)(*c*) or subsection 21.4(2) and the circumstances in which the Board may withhold such information;

(e) prescribing that an inmate is entitled to assistance at a hearing held by the Board pursuant to subparagraph 21.3(5)(*b*)(ii), paragraph 21.3(5)(*c*) or subsection 21.4(2) and the kind and extent of such assistance, and the persons or class of persons who may provide such assistance;

(f) prescribing the type of record to be kept by the Board of the hearing held pursuant to subparagraph 21.3(5)(*b*)(ii), paragraph 21.3(5)(*c*) or subsection 21.4(2) or any other proceedings held in respect of a review of the case of an inmate pursuant to section 21.4 or 21.5; and

(*g*) prescribing the time when and the manner in which an inmate may apply to the Board for a re-examination of the decision made in respect of the review of the case of the inmate pursuant to section 21.4 or 21.5, the manner in which the re-examination will be conducted and the time when and the manner in which the inmate will be informed of the decision rendered in connection therewith.

(2) The Governor in Council may, by order,   Designation

(*a*) designate any penitentiary within the meaning of the *Penitentiary Act* for the purpose of the definition "community-based residential facility" in section 21.1; and

(*b*) amend the schedule by adding thereto or deleting therefrom an offence under any Act of Parliament. R.S. 1985, c. 34 (2nd Supp.), s. 5.

Suspension of parole and apprehension of paroled inmate

22. (1) A member of the Board or a person designated by the Chairman, when a breach of a term or condition of parole occurs of the Board or person is satisfied that it is necessary or reasonable to do so in order to prevent breach of any term or condition of parole or to protect society, may, by a warrant in writing signed by the member or designated person,

(*a*) suspend any parole other than a parole that has been discharged;

(*b*) authorize the apprehension of a paroled inmate; and

(*c*) recommit an inmate to custody until the suspension of the inmate's parole is cancelled or the inmate's parole is revoked.

Place of recommitment

(2) The Board of a person designated by the Chairman may, by a warrant, transfer an inmate following his recommitment to custody pursuant to paragraph (1)(*c*) to a place where the inmate is to be held in custody until the suspension of his parole is cancelled or his parole is revoked.

Review of suspension

(3) The person by whom a warrant is signed pursuant to subsection (1) or any other person designated by the Chairman for the purpose shall forthwith after the recommitment of the paroled inmate named in the warrant review the case and, within fourteen days after the recommitment or such shorter period as may be directed by the Board, either cancel the suspension or refer the case to the Board.

Exercise of delegated powers

(3.1) The Chairman may fix the terms and conditions under which a power may be exercised pursuant to subsection (1), (2) or (3) by a person designated by the Chairman for the purposes of that subsection.

Idem

(4) The Board shall, on the referral to it of the case of a paroled inmate whose parole has been suspended, review the case and cause to be conducted all such inquiries in connection therewith as it considers necessary, and forthwith on completion of such inquiries and its review it shall either cancel the suspension or revoke the parole.

Effect of suspension

(5) An inmate who is in custody by virtue of this section shall be deemed to be serving his sentence. R.S., c. P-2, s. 16; 1976-77, c, 53, s. 29; R.S. 1985, c. 35 (2nd Supp.), s. 11(1), (2).

PROCEDURE ON TERMINATION OR REVOCATION OF PAROLE

Apprehension

23. Notwithstanding section 19, when any parole is terminated or revoked, the Board or any person designated by the Chairman may, be a warrant in writing, authorize the apprehension of the paroled inmate to custody as provided in this Act, and, until the recommitment, the paroled inmate is deemed not to be continuing to serve the term of imprisonment. R.S. 1985, c. 35 (2nd Supp.), s. 12.

24. (1) A warrant issued under subsection 16(2) or section 22 or 23 shall be executed by any peace officer to whom it is given in any part of Canada and has the same force and effect in all parts of Canada as if it had been originally issued or subsequently endorsed by a provincial court judge or other lawful authority having jurisdiction in the place where it is executed.

Warrants for apprehension

(2) Where a peace officer believes on reasonable grounds that a warrant issued under subsection 16(2) or section 22 or 23 is in force in respect of an inmate, the peace officer may arrest and remand the inmate in custody.

Power of arrest without warrant

(3) Where an inmate is arrested pursuant to subsection (2) and remanded in custody, the peace officer making the arrest shall cause the inmate to be brought before a person designated by the Chairman of the Board.

Inmate to be brought before designated person

(*a*) where the person is available within a period of twenty-four hours after the inmate is arrested, without unreasonable delay and in any event within that period; and
(*b*) where that person is not available within the period referred to in paragraph (*a*), as soon as possible.

(4) Where an inmate is brought pursuant to subsection (3) before a person designated by the Chairman of the Board, that person

Release or remand of inmate

(*a*) if that person is not satisfied that there are reasonable grounds to believe that the inmate in repsect of whom the warrant referred to in subsection (2) was issued, shall release the inmate; or
(*b*) if that person is satisfied that there are reasonable grounds to believe that the inmate is the inmate in respect of whom the warrant referred to in subsection (2) was issued, any remand the inmate in custody to await execution of the warrant, but it no warrant for the inmate's arrest is executed within a period of six days after the time the inmate is remanded to such custody, the person in whose custody the inmate then is shall release the inmate. R.S. 1985, c. 34 (2nd Supp.), s. 6.

25. (1) On revocation of an inmate's parole, the inmate shall be recommitted to the place of confinement from which he was allowed to go and remain at large at the time parole was granted or to the corresponding place of confinement for the territorial division within which the inmate was apprehended.

Place of recommittal

(2) Subject to subsection (3) and section 26.1 of the *Penitentiary Act*, where any parole is revoked, the paroled inmate shall, whether the inmate was sentenced or granted parole before or after the coming into force of this subsection, serve the portion of the term of imprisonment

Effect of revocation of parole

that remained unexpired at the time parole was granted, including any statutory and earned remission, less

(*a*) any time spent on parole after October 14, 1977;

(*b*) any time during which the inmate's parole was suspended and the inmate was in custody;

(*c*) any remission earned after October 14, 1977 and applicable to a period during which the inmate's parole was suspended and the inmate was in custody; and

(*d*) any earned remission that stood to the credit of the inmate on October 25, 1977.

Recrediting remission

(3) Subject to the regulations and subsection 25(7) and section 26.1 of the *Pententiary Act*, the Board or a provincial parole board may recredit the whole or any part of the statutory and earned remission that

(*a*) stood to the credit of an inmate at the time parole was granted; and

(*b*) in the case of a revocation of day parole, the inmate earned while on that day parole. R.S. 1985, c. 34 (2nd Supp.), s. 7(1), (2).

Board may cancel or vary order

25.1 The Board may on application therefor and subject to the regulations, cancel or vary the unexpired portion of a prohibition order made under subsection 259(1) or (2) of the *Criminal Code* at any time after

(*a*) in the case of a prohibition for life, ten years following the commencement thereof; or

(*b*) in the case of a prohibition for a period exceeding five years but less than life, five years following the commencement thereof. R.S. 1985, c. 27 (1st Supp.), s. 201.

TEMPORARY ABSENCE WITHOUT ESCORT

Definition of "Inmate"

25.1 In section 25.2 and 25.3, "inmate" means an inmate within the meaning of the *Penitentiary Act*. R.S. 1985, c. 35 (2nd Supp.), s. 13.

Unescorted temporary absence

25.2 (1) Subject to the regulations, where, in the opinion of the Board, it is necessary or desirable that an inmate should be absent, without escort, for medical or humanitarian reasons or to assist in the rehabilitation of the inmate, the absence may be authorized by the Board for an unlimited period for medical reasons and for a period not exceeding fifteen days for humanitarian reasons or to assist in the rehabilitation of the inmate.

Board may delegate

(2) The Board may, if it has determined that an inmate or a class of inmates is one for whom or which temporary absence without escort is appropriate, delegate its authority under subsection (1) in respect of that inmate or class of inmates to

(*a*) the Commissioner, within the meaning of the *Penitentiary Act*, or

(*b*) the member in charge of a pentitentiary in respect of a period of absence not exceeding fifteen days for medical reasons and in

respect of a period of absence not exceeding three days for humanitarian reasons or to assist in the rehabilitation of the inmate,
subject to any conditions it deems advisable and for such period as it
sees fit. R.S. 1985, c. 35 (2nd Supp.) s. 13.

25.3 (1) Where, pursuant to an agreement made under subsection
22(1) of the *Penitentiary Act*, and inmate has been admitted to a
provincially operated mental hospital or to any other provincially
operated institution in which the liberty of the patients is normally
subject to restrictions, the officer in charge of the provincial institution
may permit temporary absences from that institution without escort
when the officer is delegated that authority by the Board.

Where inmate transferred to provincial institution

(2) For the purposes of subsection (1), the Board may, if it has
determined that an inmate or a class of inmates is one for whom or
which temporary absence without excort is appropriate, delegate its
authority to grant temporary absences without escort to that inmate or
class of inmates to the officer in charge of the provincial institution
referred to in subsection (1) subject to any conditions it deems advisable and for such period as it sees fit. R.S. 1985, c. 35 (2nd Supp.), s. 13.

Delegation of authority

ADDITIONAL JURISDICTION

26. The Board shall, when so directed by the Solicitor General of
Canada, make any investigation or inquiry desired by the Solicitor
General in connection with any request made to the Solicitor General
for the exercise of the royal prerogative of mercy. R.S., c. P-2, s. 22;
1972, c. 13, s. 74; 1974-75-76, c. 93, s. 101.

Clemency

REGULATIONS

27. (1) The Governor in Council may make regulations

Regulations

(*a*) prescribing the times when the Board must review cases of
inmates and the manner of reviewing those cases and prescribing
when the review must be by way of a hearing before the Board;
(*b*) prescribing the portion of the terms of imprisonment that inmates or classes of inmates must serve before temporary absence
without escort may be authorized pursuant to section 29 or 30 of the
penitentiary Act or parole may be granted;
(*c*) prescribing the portion of the terms of imprisonment that inmates must serve before day parole may be granted;
(*d*) [Repealed, R.S. 1985, c. 35 (2nd Supp.), s. 14(2).]
(*e*) prescribing the class of cases of inmates serving a sentence of
imprisonment of less than two years that must be reviewed by the
Board on application:
(*f*) prescribing the minimun number of members of the Board who
must vote on a review of a case of an inmate or on a hearing of a
parole application by an inmate, and prescribing the minimum
number of affirmative votes required in any such review or hearing
to grant a parole;
(*f.*1) prescribing the circumstances in which a member of the Board
may or must withdraw from voting in a case;

(*g*) prescribing the circumstances in which an inmate is entitled to a hearing on any review on his case for parole;

(*h*) prescribing the information that must be supplied or made available to an inmate or any other person by the Board before or during any review, with or without a hearing, with respect to any parole, temporary absence without escort or release subject to mandatory supervision of that inmate, the form of the information and the circumstances in which and the time within which it must be so supplied or made available;

(*h*.1) prescribing the information or classes thereof that may be withheld from an inmate or other person before or during a review, with or without a hearing, with respect to the parole, temporary absence without escort or release subject to mandatory supervision of that inmate, and prescribing the circumstances in which the Board may withhold that information;

(*i*) prescribing the circumstances in which an inmate is to be entitled to assistance at a hearing before the Board, the kind and extent of the assistance and the persons or class of persons who may provide the assistance;

(*j*) prescribing the circumstances in which the Board must provide the inmate with its reasons for any decision made by the Board with respect to the parole, temporary absence without escort or release subject to mandatory supervision of the inmate and the form in which the reasons must be provided;

(*k*) prescribing the time within which the Board must conduct a hearing and render a decision after referral to it of a case pursuant to subsection 22(3);

(*k*.1) respecting, for the purposes of subsection 16(1.1), mandatory terms and conditions in respect of an inmate released on parole or subject to mandatory supervision;

(*k*.2) providing for the manner of applying, pursuant to subsection 16(1.2), for relief from or variance of a mandatory term or condition prescribed pursuant to paragraph (*k*.1) and the manner in which the Board makes a decision with respect to the application;

(*l*) prescribing the circumstances in which the Board mut re-examine a decision to deny parole, other than day parole, or to revoke parole or mandatory supervision;

(*m*) prescribing the terms and conditions under which the Board may recredit to an inmate the remission of any part thereof, that the inmate is required to serve as a result of the revocation of the inmate's parole;

(*n*) prescribing the honorarium to be paid to persons selected to act as additional members of the Board pursuant to subsection 8(2);

(*n*.1) prescribing special circumstances in which an inmate is eligible for parole, notwithstanding that the inmate would not, by virtue of this Act and the regulations, otherwise be eligible for parole; and

(*o*) providing for such other matters as are necessary to carry out the provisions of this Act or to facilitate the carrying out of the functions of the Board.

Special or general

(2) A regulation made under subsection (1) may be made to apply

(*a*) generally or to a specified area or region of Canada in which a provincial parole board is being established; or

(*b*) to a certain class or classes of inmates.

(3) Subject to subsection (4), when a provincial parole board has been appointed in a province, the lieutenant governor in council of the province may, in respect of that provincial parole board and the inmates under its jurisdiction, make regulations in like manner and to like purposes as the Governor in Council may make regulations respecting the National Parol Board and inmates under its jurisdiction.

Provincial powers

(4) A regulation made under subsection (3) that is inconsistent with a provision of this Act or a regulation made under subsection (1) is void to the extent of that inconsistency R.S., c. P-2, s. 9; 1976-77, c. 53, s. 24; R.S. 1985, c. 34 (2nd Supp.), s. 8; c. 35, s. 14(1)-(6);

Saving

PROCEDURE AND EVIDENCE

28. Any order, warrant or decision made or issued under this Act is not subject to appeal or review to or by any court or other authority R.S., c. P-2. s. 23.

Order, etc., final

29. Any order, warrant, decision or certificate purporting to be sealed with the seal of the Board or to be signed by a person purporting to be a member of the Board or to have been designated by the Chairman to suspend parole or to authorize the apprenhension of an inmate whose parole has been revoked is admissible in evidence in any proceedings in any court and is evidence of the statements contained therein without proof of the ease of the Board or of the signature or offical character of the person appearing to have signed it. R.S., c. P-2, s. 24; 1976-77, c. 53, s. 33.

Evidence

SCHEDULE
(Sections 21.3 and 21.4)

1. An offence under any of the following provisions of the *Criminal Code*;

(*a*) paragraph 81(2)(*a*) (causing injury with intent);
(*b*) section 85 (use of firearm during commission of offence);
(*c*) subsection 86(1) (pointing a firearm);
(*d*) section 144 (prison breach),
(*e*) section 236 (manslaughter);
(*f*) section 239 (attempt to commit murder);
(*g*) section 244 (causing bodily harm with intent);
(*h*) section 246 (overcoming resistance to commission of offence);
(*i*) section 266 (assault);
(*j*) section 267 (assault with a weapon or causing bodily harm);
(*k*) section 268 (aggravated assault);
(*l*) section 269 (unlawfully causing bodily harm);
(*m*) section 270 (assaulting a peace officer);
(*n*) section 271 (sexual assault);

(*o*)   section 272 (sexual assault with a weapon, threats to a third party or causing bodiliy harm);
(*p*)   section 273 (aggravated sexual assault);
(*q*)   section 279 (kidnapping);
(*r*)   section 344 (robbery);
(*s*)   section 433 (arson);
(*t*)   section 434 (setting fire to other substance);
(*u*)   section 436 (setting fire by negligence); and
(*v*)   paragraph 465(1)(*a*) (conspiracy to commit murder).

2. An offence under any of the following sections of the *Criminal Code*, chapter C-34 of the Revised Statutes of Canada, 1970, as they read immediately before January 4, 1983:

(*a*)   section 144 (rape);
(*b*)   section 145 (attempt to commit rape);
(*c*)   section 149 (indecent assault on female);
(*d*)   section 156 (indecent assault on male);
(*e*)   section 245 (common assault); and
(*f*)   section 246 (assault with intent). R.S. 1875, c. 34 (2nd Supp.), s. 9.

APPENDIX II

FORMS

1. Certiorari — Federal Court Trial Division

IN THE FEDERAL COURT OF CANADA

[TRIAL DIVISION]

BETWEEN:

(*Name of Prisoner*)

Applicant

—and—

(*Name of Agency*)

Respondent

NOTICE OF MOTION

TAKE NOTICE that a motion will be made to the Court on bahalf of
_____ at _____ on _____, the _____ day of
_____, 19__, at 10:30 o'clock in the forenoon or so soon thereafter as counsel
can be heard:

(*Specify order or orders requested.*)

The said application is made upon the following grounds:

(*Specify with particularity the grounds of error alleged.*)

AND TAKE NOTICE that if you wish to oppose this motion you must file an
Appearance on or before the date upon which the motion is returnable.

AND TAKE NOTICE that in default of filing an Appearance you are not entitled to
file any material on the motion.

DATED AT _____, THIS _____ DAY OF _____, 19___.

_____
Counsel for the Applicant.

TO: Federal Department of Justice
AND TO: The Registrar

2. Habeas Corpus — Alberta

IN THE COURT OF QUEEN'S BENCH OF ALBERTA

JUDICIAL DISTRICT OF _____

IN THE MATTER OF _____, INCARCERATED PURSUANT TO A WARRANT OF COMMITTAL DATED THE _____ DAY OF _____, AND PRESENTLY IN THE CUSTODY OF THE WARDEN OF _____ INSTITUTION AT _____, ALBERTA;

AND IN THE MATTER OF AN APPLICATION FOR AN ORDER IN THE NATURE OF *HABEAS CORPUS AD SUBJICIENDUM*, WITH *CERTIORARI* IN AID THEREOF AND FOR AN ORDER PURSUANT TO SECTION 24(1) OF THE *CANADIAN CHARTER OF RIGHTS AND FREEDOMS* GRANTING SUCH REMEDY AS MAY BE APPROPRIATE AND JUST;

BETWEEN:

HER MAJESTY THE QUEEN

Respondent

—and—

(Name of Prisoner)

Applicant

NOTICE OF MOTION

TAKE NOTICE that an application will be made before the presiding Judge of this Honourable Court at _____, Alberta on _____ the _____ day of _____ 19___, at the hour of 2:00 o'clock in the afternoon or so soon thereafter as the motion may be heard, whereupon you are to show cause why an Order in the nature of *Habeas Corpus Ad Subjiciendum* should not issue to the Warden of _____ Institution at _____, Alberta, directing him to have before a Justice of the Court of Queen's Bench of Alberta the said _____, a prisoner detained in his custody, that the Court may cause to be done thereupon what of right and according to law the Court shall see fit to be done, and for an Order in the nature of *Certiorari* in aid thereof to remove into this Honourable Court the Warrant of Committal made on the _____ day of _____, by Mr. Justice _____, the evidence taken at the hearing and all things touching the matter, to bring up the said Warrant of Committal to be quashed in so far as it provides that the Applicant shall be detained;

AND FURTHER, application will be made for an Order pursuant to section 24(1) of the *Canadian Charter of Rights and Freedoms* declaring the Applicant's detention under the aforesaid Warrant of Committal an infringement of the Applicant's constitutional rights or granting such other remedy as the Court considers appropriate and just in the circumstances;

ALL OF WHICH ORDERS ARE SOUGHT ON THE FOLLOWING GROUNDS:

(Specify with particularity the grounds of error alleged.)

AND FURTHER TAKE NOTICE that in support of such application will be read the Affidavit of _____, sworn the _____ day of _____ 19___, the warrant of Committal dated the _____ of _____ 19___, and such further and other material as Counsel may advise and this Honourable Court may permit.

DATED at _____, Alberta this _____ day of _____ 19___.

_____
Counsel on behalf of the Applicant.

TO: Clerk of the Court
    of Queen's Bench

TO: Agents for the Attorney
    General of Alberta

TO: The Warden of _____

TO: Department of Justice
    Agents for the Attorney
    General of Canada

3. Habeas Corpus — British Columbia

IN THE SUPREME COURT OF BRITISH COLUMBIA

BETWEEN:

(Name of Prisoner)

Petitioner

AND:

HER MAJESTY THE QUEEN

Respondent

PETITION FOR AN ORDER FOR RELIEF IN THE NATURE
OF HABEAS CORPUS WITH CERTIORARI IN AID

TO THE RESPONDENTS:

TAKE NOTICE that the petitioner hereby applies to this Honourable Court for an order for relief in the nature of habeas corpus ad subjiciendum with certiorari in aid pursuant to ss. 482(3)(c) and 774 of the *Criminal Code*, R.S.C. 1985, c. C-46, the *Criminal Rules, 1977*, and Rules 10 and 63 of the *Rules of Court*, that the petitioner be released from custody forthwith.

AND FURTHER TAKE NOTICE that on the hearing of this petition will be read the affidavit of ————————————————— and such other materials as counsel deems advisable and this Honourable Court permits.

IF YOU WISH TO BE HEARD AT THE HEARING OF THIS PETITION OR WISH TO BE NOTIFIED OF ANY FURTHER PROCEEDINGS, YOU MUST GIVE NOTICE of your intention by filing a form entitled "Appearance" in the above Registry of this court within the time for Appearance endorsed hereon and YOU MUST ALSO DELIVER a copy of the "Appearance" to the Petitioner's address for delivery, which is set out in this petition.

YOU OR YOUR SOLICITOR may file the "Appearance". You may obtain a form of "Appearance" at the Registry.

THE ADDRESS OF THE REGISTRY IS:

The address for delivery of documents is the address of the Petitioner's solicitor:

AND FURTHER TAKE NOTICE that the ground on which this application is based is as follows:

(*Specify with particularity the grounds of error alleged.*)

DATED at ——————, this —————— day of —————— 19—.

————————————————
Counsel for the Petitioner

4. Habeas Corpus — Manitoba

IN THE QUEEN'S BENCH, WINNIPEG

IN THE MATTER OF: An application for a Writ of Habeas Corpus ad subjiciendum with certiorari in aid thereof.

AND

IN THE MATTER OF: The Criminal Code of Canada

BETWEEN:

(*Name of Prisoner*)

Applicant

—and—

THE WARDEN OF _____ INSTITUTION,

Respondent

TO: The Warden of _____ Institution
AND TO: The Deputy Attorney General of Canada
AND TO: The Department of Justice of Manitoba

ORIGINATING NOTICE OF MOTION

TAKE NOTICE that an application will be made on behalf of _____, the Applicant herein, before the Presiding Motions Court Judge at the Law Courts Building, Broadway and Kennedy Street, in the City of Winnipeg, on _____ day the _____ day of _____ 19__, at the hour of 10:00 o'clock in the forenoon, or so soon thereafter as the motion may be heard, whereupon you are to show cause why a writ of Habeas Corpus should not issue to the Warden of _____ Institution, Correctional Service of Canada, directing him to have before a Judge of the Court of Queen's Bench, the body of the said _____, a prisoner detained in the custody, that the Court may cause to be done thereupon that which of right and according to law the Court shall see fit to be done and for a writ of certiorari in aid thereof if required, on the following grounds:

(*Specify with particularity the grounds of error alleged.*)

AND FURTHER TAKE NOTICE that in support of such application will be read the Affidavit of the said _____, the exhibits therein referred to, and such further and other material as counsel may advise and this Honourable Court permit.

DATED at _____, Manitoba this _____ day of _____, 19__.

_____

Solicitor for the Applicant

5. Habeas Corpus — Ontario

ONTARIO COURT (GENERAL DIVISION)

BETWEEN:

REGINA

Respondent

—and—

(*Name of Prisoner*)

Applicant

NOTICE OF APPLICATION

TO THE RESPONDENT

A LEGAL PROCEEDING HAS BEEN COMMENCED by the Applicant. The nature of the application appears on the following page.

THIS APPLICATION will come on for hearing before a Judge of the Ontario Court (General Division) on _____ day the _____ day of _____, 19___, at 10:00 o'clock in the forenoon or so soon thereafter as the matter may be heard, at Osgoode Hall, 130 Queen Street West, Toronto, Ontario.

IF YOU WISH TO OPPOSE THIS APPLICATION, you or an Ontario lawyer acting for you must forthwith prepare a Notice of Appearance in Form 38C prescribed by the Rules of Civil procedure, serve it on the Applicant's lawyer, and file it, with proof of service, in this court office, and you or your lawyer must appear at the Hearing.

IF YOU WISH TO PRESENT AFFIDAVIT OR OTHER DOCUMENTARY EVIDENCE TO THIS COURT OR WISH TO EXAMINE OR CROSS-EXAMINE WITNESSES ON THIS APPLICATION, you or your lawyer must, in addition to serving your Notice of Appearance, serve a copy of the evidence on the Applicant's lawyer, and file it, with proof of service, in the court office where the Application is to be heard as soon as possible, but no later than 2:00PM on the day before the hearing.

IF YOU FAIL TO APPEAR AT THE HEARING, JUDGEMENT MAY BE GIVEN IN YOUR ABSENCE AND WITHOUT FURTHER NOTICE TO YOU.

Date: Issued by: _____

Local Registrar, S.C.O.
145 Queen Street West
Toronto, Ontario

APPLICATION

1. The Applicant makes Application for:

A Writ of Habeas Corpus ad Subjiciendum with Certiorari in aid and will move that you show cause why the Writ should not be to the Superintendent of the _____ Institution directing him to have before a Judge of the Ontario Court (General Division) the body of the prisoner, _____, so that the court may determine the sufficiency of his detention and cause to be done what of right and according to law the court shall see fit to be done.

2. The grounds for the Application are:

(Specify with particularity the grounds of error alleged.)

3. The following documentary evidence will be used at the hearing of the Application:
   (a) The Affidavit of the Applicant sworn the _____ day of _____, 19___; and,

   (b) Such further or other material as counsel may advise and this Honourable Court may permit.

   Dated at _____ this _____ day of _____, 19___.

   _____
   Applicant's Counsel

TO: The Attorney General of Ontario
720 Bay Street
Toronto, Ontario

AND TO: The Warden
_____ Institution

AND TO: The Federal Department of Justice

6. Habeas Corpus — Nova Scotia

IN THE SUPREME COURT OF NOVA SCOTIA

[TRIAL DIVISION]

IN THE MATTER OF THE APPLICATION OF _____ AN INMATE OF THE _____ INSTITUTION, A FEDERAL PENITENTIARY IN _____, NOVA SCOTIA, FOR A WRIT OF *HABEAS CORPUS AD SUBJICIENDUM* WITH *CERTIORARI* IN AID

—and—

IN THE MATTER OF THE LIBERTY OF THE *SUBJECT ACT* R.S.N.S. 1967, c. 164

—and—

IN THE MATTER OF SECTION 10(a) OF THE *CANADIAN CHARTER OF RIGHTS AND FREEDOMS*

ORIGINATING NOTICE

(APPLICATION INTER PARTIES)

TAKE NOTICE that an application will be made on behalf of _____, the applicant herein, before the presiding judge in the Supreme Court Chambers at the Law Courts, 1815 Upper Water Street, Halifax, Nova Scotia, on the _____ day of _____ A.D., 19___, at the hour of ___ o'clock in the fore noon or so soon thereafter as the application may be heard, whereupon you are to show cause why an order in the nature of *habeas corpus ad subjiciendum* should not issue to the warden of _____ Institution in the Town of _____, County of _____, Province of Nova Scotia, directing to have before a judge of the Supreme Court of Nova Scotia the body of the said _____ a prisoner detained in his custody together with the cause of his detention, to the end that the court may determine the sufficiency thereof and cause to be done what of right and according to law the court shall see fit to be done, and for an order in the nature of *certiorari* in aid thereof, on the following grounds:

(*Specify with particularity the grounds of error alleged.*)

AND FURTHER TAKE NOTICE that in support of the application will be read the affidavit of _____, the exhibits therein referred to which are attached to this application, and such further and other material as counsel may advise and this honourable court allow.

DATED AT HALIFAX, Nova Scotia, this _____ day of _____, A.D., 19___.

_____
Solicitor for the Applicant

TO: Warden, _____ Institution
AND TO: Attorney General of Nova Scotia
AND TO: National Parole Board
           1222 Main Street
           Fourth Floor
           Moncton, N.B.

7. Habeas Corpus — Quebec

PROVINCE OF QUEBEC,
DISTRICT OF _____,
NO:

SUPERIOR COURT
(Criminal Jurisdiction)

(*Name of Prisoner*)

Applicant,

vs

_____

Respondent,

APPLICATION FOR THE ISSUANCE OF A WRIT OF HABEAS CORPUS AND A WRIT OF MANDAMUS IN AID—APPLICATION FOR A REMEDY IN VIRTUE OF SECTION 24(1) OF THE *CANADIAN CHARTER OF RIGHTS AND FREEDOMS*, and *CONSTITUTION ACT 1982.*

TO ANY ONE OF THE HONOURABLE JUDGES OF THE SUPERIOR COURT, CRIMINAL JURISDICTION SITTING IN AND FOR THE DISTRICT OF _____, YOUR APPLICANT RESPECTFULLY SUBMITS:

(*Provide brief statement of facts and issues in consecutively numbered paragraphs.*)

WHEREFORE, your Applicant respectfully requests that this Honourable Court,

ISSUE A WRIT OF HABEAS CORPUS ORDERING RESPONDENT _____ TO BRING YOUR APPLICANT BEFORE THIS HONOURABLE COURT AND TO SHOW THE CAUSE OF HIS DETENTION;

AND BY FINAL JUDGMENT TO INTERVENE HEREIN BY

— Ordering Respondent to _____;

— Order the release of your Applicant from custody;

— Such other remedy as this Honourable Court considers appropriate and just in the circumstances in virtue of section 24(1) of the *Canadian Charter of Rights and Freedoms.*

The whole respectfully submitted

_____
Attorney for Applicant

8. Habeas Corpus — Saskatchewan

SASKATCHEWAN

APPLICATION FOR WRIT OF HABEAS CORPUS

IN THE MATTER OF (*name of person detained*), of ＿＿＿＿＿＿ Saskatchewan;
(*If applicable add* :
"AND IN THE MATTER OF" *name of statute or regulation and section thereof.*)

NOTICE OF MOTION FOR HABEAS CORPUS AD SUBJICIENDUM

TAKE NOTICE THAT an application will be made to a judge in chambers, at the Court House, ＿＿＿＿＿ (*address in full*) ＿＿＿＿＿, Saskatchewan on the ＿＿＿＿＿ day of ＿＿＿＿＿, 19＿, at ＿＿＿＿＿ o'clock in the ＿＿＿＿＿ noon, or so soon thereafter as counsel can be heard, by ＿＿＿＿＿ (*where applicable add* : on behalf of ＿＿＿＿＿), for a Writ of *Habeas Corpus ad subjiciendum*, directed to ＿＿＿＿＿, and to all officers of ＿＿＿＿＿ having the body of＿＿＿＿＿ in their charge or detained in their custody by whatever name he may be called to have the body of the said ＿＿＿＿＿ before a judge in chambers at the Court House, ＿＿＿＿＿ (*address in full*) ＿＿＿＿＿, Saskatchewan forthwith, that this Honourable Court may then and there examine and determine the validity of such detention.

AND FURTHER TAKE NOTICE that on the hearing of this Motion will be read the following, all filed:
1.
2. *etc.*
Dated, *etc.*

(*Signature*)

To: ＿＿＿＿＿,

or other person having custody of the said ＿＿＿＿＿＿＿＿＿＿＿.

WRIT OF HABEAS CORPUS AD SUBJICIENDUM

ELIZABETH THE SECOND
To: ＿＿＿＿＿,
or other person having the custody of ＿＿＿＿＿＿＿＿＿.

GREETING:

WE COMMAND YOU that you have in our Court of Queen's Bench for Saskatchewan at the Court House at ＿＿＿＿＿ (*address in full*) ＿＿＿＿＿ before a judge of the court (*or*, The Honourable ＿＿＿＿＿) on the ＿＿＿＿＿ day of ＿＿＿＿＿ 19＿, at ＿＿＿＿＿ o'clock in the ＿＿＿＿＿ noon, (*or*, immediately) the body of＿＿＿＿＿ being taken and detained under your custody as is said, together with this writ or a copy thereof and that you then and there make return to this writ setting forth the day and cause of his being taken and detained, by whatsoever name he may be called therein, that our Court may then and there examine and determine the validity of such detention.

AND TAKE NOTICE that in default hereof the Court may at the said time and place, or as soon thereafter as counsel may be heard, be moved to commit to prison you or any person who shall be in contempt in not obeying this writ.

This writ was issued by order of Mr. (*or* Madam) Justice _____
Dated, *etc.*

Local Registrar.

(*Set forth address information of party at whose instance the writ was issued.*)

ORDER OF DISCHARGE IN APPLICATION FOR HABEAS CORPUS

Before _____ the _____ day _____
in Chambers. of _____, 19__

ORDER OF DISCHARGE

On the application of _____ (*where applicable add*: on behalf of _____) and on hearing counsel for the applicant (*or*, the appellant), and on hearing counsel on behalf of the Attorney General (*or* respondent, *or as the case may be*), and on hearing read (*here set forth the material used on the application*) all filed, it is ordered:

1. That _____ is hereby discharged forthwith out of the custody of _____.

(*Where applicable, as where an order is made under the Criminal Code, add*:

2. That no civil proceeding shall be taken against _____ or against any officer who acted under the conviction, order or other proceeding or under any warrant issued to enforce it.)

Local Registrar.

ORDER OF HABEAS CORPUS AD SUBJICIENDUM

Before _____ the _____ day _____
in Chambers. of _____, 19__

ORDER OF HABEAS CORPUS AD SUBJICIENDUM

IT IS HEREBY ORDERED that _____ (*where applicable add*: and all other officers of _____ having the custody of _____) have in Her Majesty's Court of Queen's Bench for Saskatchewan at the Court House at (*address in full*), Saskatchewan before a judge of the couirt (*or*, The Honourable _____) on the _____ day of _____, 19__ at _____ o'clock in the _____ noon, (*or*, immediately) the body of _____ being taken and detained under the custody of the said _____, as is said, together with this order or a copy thereof, and that the said _____ then and there make return to this order setting forth the day and cause of his being taken and detained, by whatsoever name he may be called therein, that this Court may then and there examine and determine the validity of such detention.

AND IT IS FURTHER ORDERED that in default hereof the applicant shall have leave at the said time and place, or as soon thereafter as counsel for the applicant may be heard, to apply to commit to prison you or any person who shall be in contempt in not obeying this order.

Issued by order of Mr. (*or* Madam) Justice ————————————————————.
Dated, *etc.*

Local Registrar.

(*Where order was issued ex parte, set forth address information of party at whose instance the order was issued.*)

APPENDIX III

TABLE OF ELIGIBILITY REVIEW DATES*

Length of Sentence	Time to be Served Before Review		
	Temporary Absence	Day Parole	Full Parole
0 to 2 years less a day	N/A	½ time before PED(1)	⅓ of sentence
2 to 5 years	If entered penitentiary before March 1/78, 6 months after entrance; on or after March 1/78, 6 months after sentencing or ½ time before PED, whichever is longer	For 2 to 12 year sentences, 6 mos. or ½ time to PED, whichever is longer (2)	⅓ of sentence or 7 years, whichever is less except if violent conduct and a sentence of 5 or more years is involved, then it is ½ of sentence of 7 years, whichever is less (see Parole Act and Regulations)
5 to 10 years			
10 years or more excluding life sentences		For sentences of 12 years or more, 2 years before PED	
Life as a maximum punishment (for crimes other than 1st or 2nd degree murder)	If entered penitentiary before March 1/78, 6 months after entrance; on or after March 1/78, 3 years before PED	5 years	7 years

NOTE: 1) PED refers to full parole eligibility date. It is calculated from sentencing date except for lifers and those serving indeterminate sentences where it is calculated from date of arrest.

2) In most cases, because most federal inmates are serving terms ranging from 2 to 12 years, review for day parole will occur at ⅙th of the sentence.

3) In the case of life sentences, time spent while on bail or unlawfully at large does not count as time served prior to a parole eligibility review date.

* As of September 1, 1990. Proposals announced by the Minister of Justice and Solicitor General in the summer of 1990 will, if passed by Parliament, modify some of these review dates.

Length of Sentence	Time to be Served Before Review		
	Temporary Absence	Day Parole	Full Parole
Preventive detention (as a habitual or dangerous sexual offender)	1 year	1 year	1 year
Detention for an indeterminate period (since Oct. 15/77 as a dangerous offender)	3 years	3 years	3 years
Life for murder before Jan. 4/68	3 years after entered penitentiary	3 years before PED	7 years
Life for murder Jan. 4/68 to Jan. 1/74			10 years
Life: death commuted before Jan. 1/74			
Life for murder, Jan. 1/74 to July 26/75	3 years before PED	3 years before PED	10-20 years: Judicial Review possible at 15 years
Life: death commuted Jan. 1/74 to July 25/76			
Life: death not commuted July 26/76			25 years: Judicial Review possible at 15 years
Life for 1st degree murder on or after July 26/76			
Life for 2nd degree murder on or after July 26/76			10-25 years: Judicial Review possible at 15 years

Index